Praise for John Eliot Gardiner's BACH

"It is hard to imagine what the English maestro John Eliot Gardiner . . . might do to surpass *Bach* in its commitment, scope and comprehensiveness. . . . [He] has done a masterly, monumental job of taking the measure of Bach the man and the musician."
—*The New York Times*

"It is Gardiner's experience as a conductor that informs so much of this book. Not only does he explain the harmonic, contrapuntal and polyphonic underpinnings of Bach's music. . . . [He] also comments on these scores from practical experience, having spent countless hours working out instrumental balances and sonorities, textures and dynamics, in concert halls and churches alike."
—*The Washington Post*

"Monumental. . . . What Gardiner offers is an intimate knowledge of the choral music . . . and a powerful sense of its cultural context, structural evolution and doctrinal intent. . . . His 'portrait' reads like a pilgrim's progress, in which a privileged man-of-the-modern-world is transformed by Bach's musical revelation."
—*Financial Times*

"Learned, amiable. . . . [Gardiner's] depth of knowledge permeates his writing."
—*The New York Times Book Review*

"Very rewarding. . . . This book is not a biography in the conventional sense . . . but an attempt to uncover the man through his music. . . . [Gardiner] discovers a wealth of hitherto unseen invention and ingenuity."
—*The Economist*

"It never happens often enough, but now and then, a subject gets the book it deserves. So it is with John Eliot Gardiner's *Bach*."
—*The Daily Beast*

"An erudite work resting on prodigious research and experience and deep affection and admiration."
—*Kirkus Reviews*

"An inspiring book. . . . Superb, timely, thought-provoking, authoritative and extremely useful and readable. . . . It should find its way onto any serious music-lovers' shelves. From there it must often and regularly be taken off and read." —Classical.Net

"Mr. Gardiner writes in the refreshing voice of a man who has studied and performed Bach's music for decades. . . . Bach's music is one of mankind's greatest achievements, and his genius touches upon matters eternal and profound. His choral music is less well known than it should be—especially the cantatas, which Gardiner lauds as 'gripping musical works of exceptional worth.' Spurred by *Bach: Music in the Castle of Heaven*, many listeners will discover them for the first time." —*The Wall Street Journal*

"Typical John Eliot to combine so much erudition with even more passion and enthusiasm. It made me want to rush and listen to all the pieces whether familiar or unfamiliar. A treasure chest."
—Simon Rattle, principal conductor of the Berlin Philharmonic

"*Bach* is a unique portrait of one of the greatest musical geniuses of all time by one of the greatest musical geniuses of our own age. John Eliot Gardiner uses his extraordinary immersion in Bach's music to illuminate Bach the man more brilliantly than in any previous work, and has created his own deeply moving work of art." —Amanda Foreman, author of *A World on Fire*

"A superb achievement, scholarly, lively, controversial and judicious. Like all great biographies of creative artists, it builds a bridge from the past to the present and brings the work to new life." —Ian Bostridge

"A tremendous feat of narrative. . . . [Gardiner] tells this long and richly involved story in a way that makes everything clear, and sets the life and the music in a historical perspective where every detail is relevant and every comment illuminating. Simply as a biography this is splendid, but the fact that it comes with such a wealth of musical understanding and experience makes it invaluable. I learned an enormous amount, and I know I'll return to it again and again." —Philip Pullman

John Eliot Gardiner

BACH

John Eliot Gardiner is one of the world's leading conductors, not only of Baroque music but across the whole repertoire. He founded the Monteverdi Choir and Orchestra, the Orchestre de l'Opéra de Lyon, the English Baroque Soloists, and the Orchestre Révolutionnaire et Romantique. He has conducted most of the world's great orchestras and in many of the leading opera houses. He lives and farms in Dorset, England.

BACH

BACH

Music in the Castle of Heaven

JOHN ELIOT GARDINER

Vintage Books
A Division of Random House LLC
New York

FIRST VINTAGE BOOKS EDITION, MARCH 2015

Originally published in Great Britain as *Music in the Castle of Heaven* by Allen Lane, an imprint of Penguin Books, London, and subsequently in the United States in hardcover by Alfred A. Knopf, a division of Random House LLC, New York, in 2013.

The Library of Congress has cataloged the Knopf publication as follows:
Gardiner, John Eliot.
Bach : music in the castle of heaven / by John Eliot Gardiner. —
First American edition.
pages ; cm
1. Bach, Johann Sebastian, 1685–1750.
2. Composers—Germany—Biography. I. Title.
ML410.BIG34 2013 780.92—dc23 [B] 2013030398

Vintage Trade Paperback ISBN: 978-1-4000-3143-6
eBook ISBN: 978-0-385-35198-0

Printed in the United States of America
10 9 8 7 6 5 4 3 2 1

To fellow travellers through Bach's landscape

Contents

List of Illustrations

Endpapers: *Matthew Passion*, fair copy in Bach's hand, Nos. 23–4 (see pp. 397–8) (Staatsbibliothek zu Berlin – PK, Musikabteilung mit Mendelssohn-Archiv)

FIRST INSET

1. Georgenkirche, Eisenach (photo: Constantin Beyer)

2a & b. *Neues vollständiges Eisenachisches Gesangbuch*, 1673 (courtesy of the Bachhaus Eisenach / Neuen Bachgesellschaft)

3a. 'The Whole World in a Cloverleaf' (courtesy of the Bachhaus Eisenach / Neuen Bachgesellschaft)

3b. 'Buno's Dragon' (Universitätsbibliothek Halle: AB 51 21/ K.22)

4. Heinrich Schütz (Leipzig, Universitätsbibliothek / bpk / Staatsbibliothek zu Berlin – Musikabteilung mit Mendelssohn-Archiv)

5a & b. Organ tablature transcriptions (Klassik Stiftung Weimar, Herzogin Anna Amalia Bibliothek, Fol 49/11 [3, 2]. Photos: Olaf Mokansky)

6. *Concordia Cantata*, title page (bpk / Staatsbibliothek zu Berlin – Musikabteilung mit Mendelssohn-Archiv)

7a & b. The Dukes of Saxe-Weimar (Klassik Stiftung Weimar, Museen KGr/04542, KGr1982/00171)

7c. Wilhelmsburg, Weimar, *c.* 1730 (Klassik Stiftung Weimar, Museen KHz/01388. Photo: Sigrid Geske)

8. Himmelsburg (interior), *c.* 1660 (Klassik Stiftung Weimar, Museen G 1230. Photo: Roland Dreßler)

SECOND INSET

9. Thomasschule and Thomaskirche, 1723 (Stadtgeschichtliches Museum Leipzig, 2808 a)

10. Thomasschule and Thomaskirche, 1749 (Stadtgeschichtliches Museum Leipzig, 2708 e)

11. Six Leipzig burgomasters: Abraham Christoph Platz, Gottfried Lange, Adrian Steger, Christian Ludwig Stieglitz, Jacob Born, Gottfried Wilhelm Küstner (Stadtgeschichtliches Museum Leipzig, Porträt A 1a, A 42, A 76c, A 39, A 48b, A 50a)

12–13. Calov Bible: title page and annotation (courtesy of Concordia Seminary Library, St Louis, Missouri. All rights reserved.)

14. The Lutheran Liturgical Year (courtesy of James Thrift)

15. Bach's First Leipzig Cantata Cycle, 1723/4 (courtesy of James Thrift)

16. Bach's Second Leipzig Cantata Cycle, 1724/5 (courtesy of James Thrift)

THIRD INSET

17. Christian Romstet, 'The Tree of Life' (courtesy of the Bachhaus Eisenach / Neuen Bachgesellschaft)

18. Haussmann, Portrait of Bach, 1746 (Stadtgeschichtliches Museum Leipzig, XX11/48)

19. Haussmann, Portrait of Bach, 1748 (courtesy of William H. Scheide, Princeton, New Jersey)

20. Viola d'amore, with inset of the opening phrase of 'Erwäge' (photo courtesy of Catherine Rimer)

21. Oboe da caccia (photo: Robert Workman)

22. Violoncello piccolo by A. & H. Amati, Cremona, *c.* 1600. On loan to the Royal Academy of Music Museum from the Amaryllis Fleming Foundation (photo: Simon Way. Image reproduced by kind permission of the Trustees of the Amaryllis Fleming Foundation and the Royal Academy of Music, London)

TEXT ILLUSTRATIONS

Copper engraving of the sun – considered the embodiment of goodness and perfection – with Bach at its centre and surrounded by other German composers as its 'rays', designed by the English organist Augustus Frederick Christopher Kollmann and published in the Allgemeine musicalische Zeitung, *Vol. I (1799). Haydn is said 'not to have taken it amiss, nor that he was placed next to Handel and Graun, still less that he found it wrong that Joh. Seb. Bach was at the centre of the sun and hence the man from whom all true musical wisdom proceeded'.*

Acknowledgements

I owe an immense debt to three amazing women: to Tif Loehnis, my niece, goddaughter and former literary agent, who gave me the encouragement and belief to get started; to Debbie Rigg, my long-suffering PA, friend and ally, who typed innumerable drafts of the manuscript and witnessed my pitifully slow coming to terms with a computer; and above all to my wife Isabella, who cherished and nurtured a husband daft enough to embark on writing a first book in his sixties and, who when asked, often came up with a formulation that was clearer than my own. They would all know that, although I had chosen to write about Bach, I am equally (though differently) drawn to the three 'B's – Beethoven, Berlioz and Brahms – and could have mustered equivalent fervour for writing about Monteverdi, Schütz or Rameau. But Bach is utterly central to my life as a musician, and, as Haydn is said to have remarked when shown this copper engraving by A. F. C. Kollmann (1799), Bach was indeed 'the centre of the sun and hence the man from whom all musical wisdom proceeded' (see illustration).

I owe special thanks to John Butt for acting as an inspirational 'tutor'; to the path-finding brilliance of Laurence Dreyfus; to Nicolas Robertson, whose gimlet eye has saved me from further gaffes (and whose own book on Bach must surely follow); to Robert Quinney for his astute criticism; to the generous support of Peter Wollny and Michael Maul of the Bach-Archiv, Leipzig; and to the expertise of David Burnett, who answered my litany of *cris de cœur* with friendly forbearance. I would like to thank all three of my daughters – Francesca (for sharing with me a writer's woes), Josie (a brilliant line editor) and Bryony (a saviour when gremlins threatened to make whoopee in my laptop) – for putting up with a frequently distracted parent.

Last but not least, I would like to thank Donna Poppy for her exemplary and tactful copyediting and Jeremy Hall for running to earth the illustrations and without whose eagle eye and attention to detail the design and look of the book would have been compromised. My thanks to all of the above, plus the many friends and distinguished colleagues (listed below) who read and commented on sections of the book and who encouraged me to find my voice as a writer, to be true to it and to resist the insidious pressures to conform:

Sir David Attenborough
Manuel Bärwald
Reinhold Baumstark
Tim Blanning
Michael Boswell
Robert Bringhurst
Neil Brough
Gilles Cantagrel
Rebecca Carter
Sebastiano Cossia Castiglioni
Eric Chafe
Kati Debretzeni
John Drury
Iain Fenlon
Christian Führer
Hans Walter Gabler
Andreas Glöckner
Bridget Heal
the late Eric Hobsbawm
Colin Howard
Emma Jennings
Jane Kemp
Ortrun Landmann
Robin Leaver
Robert Levin
Fiona Maddocks
Robert Marshall
Gudrun Meier
Howard Moody
Michael Niesemann
John Julius Norwich
Philip Pullman
Richard Pyman
Jane Rasch
Catherine Rimer
Stephen Rose
William and Judith Scheide
Richard Seal
Ulrich Siegele
George Steiner
Richard Stokes
Andrew Talle
Raymond Tallis
Ruth Tatlow
James Thrift
Teri Noel Towe
David Watkin
Peter Watson
Henrietta Wayne
Geoffrey Webber
Peter Williams
Christoph Wolff
Hugh Wood
David Yearsley

My thanks also go to the Master and Fellows of Peterhouse, Cambridge; the librarians of the UCL, of the Rowe Music Library in King's College,

Cambridge, of the Music Department of the Cambridge University Library and of Oxford's Bodleian Library; the staff of the Bach-Archiv, Leipzig; the BBC TV team who worked with me on a documentary entitled *Bach: A Passionate Life* (2013); and to Stuart Proffitt as commissioning editor and to the Penguin team of Richard Duguid, Rebecca Lee, Stephen Ryan and David Cradduck for their professional and friendly input during the final stages of preparation. Thanks also go to *Granta* magazine, who commissioned a small part of the material used in this book in *Granta 76: Music*, in 2001.

For providing illustrations gratis, my thanks go to the following individuals and institutions:

Mark Audus; Bach-Archiv Leipzig; Bachhaus Eisenach/Neuen Bachgesellschaft; Breitkopf & Härtel; Concordia Seminary Library, St Louis, Missouri; Catherine Rimer; William H. Scheide/Scheide Library, University of Princeton; Sibley Music Library, Eastman School of Music, University of Rochester; Sotheby's London; Stadtarchiv Mühlhausen; James Thrift.

A Note on the Text

For the sake of brevity the Sundays in the liturgical year will be abbreviated as follows: Tr + 1 (the first Sunday after Trinity); Epiphany + 4 (the fourth Sunday after Epiphany).

The author's recordings of Bach are available on Soli Deo Gloria (www.monteverdiproductions.co.uk) and Deutsche Grammophon (www.deutschegrammophon.com).

Complete texts and translations of the cantatas are available on www.bach-cantatas.com and in *Johann Sebastian Bach: The Complete Church and Secular Cantatas*, Richard Stokes (trs.) (Long Barn Books, 1999).

Monetary units:

1 pf. (pfennig)
1 gr. (groschen) = 12 pf.
1 fl. (florin or gulden) = 21 gr.
1 tlr (thaler) = 24 gr. (or 1 fl. + 3 gr.)
1 dukat = 72 gr. (or 3 tlr).

Abbreviations

BD	*Bach-Dokumente*, Vols. I–III
BJb	*Bach-Jahrbuch*
BWV	*Bach-Werke-Verzeichnis*, Bach's work-list
JAMS	*Journal of the American Musicological Society*
JRBI	*Journal of the Riemenschneider Bach Institute*
JRMA	*Journal of the Royal Musical Association*
KB	*Kritische Berichte* (critical commentary to the NBA)
LW	*Luther's Works*: American edition (55 vols.), St Louis, 1955–86
MQ	*Musical Quarterly*
NBA	*Neue Bach-Ausgabe*
NBR	*New Bach Reader*
SDG	Soli Deo Gloria, Bach's habitual dedication of his music to God's glory (also the record label of Monteverdi Productions)
WA	*Luthers Werke*: *Kritische Gesamtausgabe* (65 vols.), Weimar, 1883–93
WA BR	*Luthers Werke*: *Kritische Gesamtausgabe. Briefwechsel* (18 vols.), Weimar, 1930–85
WA TR	*Luthers Werke*: *Kritische Gesamtausgabe. Tischreden* (6 vols.), Weimar, 1912–21

N
■ Places J.S. Bach lived and worked
Eisenach 1685–1695
Ohrdruf 1695–1700
Lüneburg 1700–1702
Weimar 1703
Arnstadt 1703–1707
Mühlhausen 1707–1708
Weimar 1708–1717
Cöthen 1717–1723
Leipzig 1723–1750
□ Places Bach visited
○ Places for reference
0
50 miles
0
50 km
Lübeck
Hamburg
Lüneburg
R. Elbe
BRANDENBURG
R. Oder
Berlin
R. Wesser
Hannover
Magdeburg
Zerbst
Cöthen
Göttingen
Sangerhausen
Halle
R. Elbe
Cassel
Mühlhausen
Leipzig
Naumburg
Weissenfels
SAXONY
Weimar
Zeitz
Dresden
Eisenach
Erfurt
Jena
Gera
Altenburg
Ronneburg
Ohrdruf
Arnstadt
THURINGIA
Gehren
Schleitz
Carlsbad

Bach's field of activity in Northern and Central Germany.

Preface

Bach the musician is an unfathomable genius; Bach the man is all too obviously flawed, disappointingly ordinary and in many ways still invisible to us. In fact we seem to know less about his private life than about that of any other major composer of the last 400 years. Unlike, say, Monteverdi, Bach left behind no intimate family correspondence, and very little beyond the anecdotal has come down to us that can help in painting a more human portrait or to allow a glimpse of him – as son, lover, husband or father. Perhaps there was a fundamental reluctance in him to pull back the curtain and reveal himself; unlike most of his contemporaries, he turned down the opportunity to submit a written account of his life and career when the opportunity arose. The limited, heavily edited version that we have inherited is one he himself spun and handed down to his children. It is not surprising some have concluded that Bach the man is something of a bore.

The idea that a more interesting personality lies behind this apparent disjunction between the man and his music has exercised his biographers from the very beginning, with inconclusive results. In any case, do we really *need* to know about the man in order to appreciate and understand his music? Some would say not. Not many people, however, are content to follow Albert Einstein's summary advice: 'This is what I have to say about Bach's life's work: listen, play, love, revere – and keep your trap shut.'[1] On the contrary, in most of us there is an innate curiosity to put a face to the man behind the music that holds us so tightly in its grip. We yearn to know what kind of a person was capable of composing music so complex that it leaves us completely mystified, then at other moments so irresistibly rhythmic that we want to get up and dance to it, and then at others still so full of poignant emotion that we are moved to the very core of our being. Bach's sheer stature as a composer is baffling and in many respects out of scale with all normal human achievement, so we tend to deify him or to elevate him to the superhuman. Few can resist the temptation to touch the hem of the garment of a genius – and, as musicians, we want to shout about it from the rooftops.

Yet, as can be seen from the Chronology (p. 559), there are pitifully few incontrovertible facts to support such an idealised view of Bach the man. In adding to them, it seems we must content ourselves with a handful of mostly dull and clumsy letters as the sole indications of his patterns of thought and of his feelings as an individual and as a family man. Much of his writing is pedestrian and opaque, consisting of detailed reports on the workings of church organs and worthy testimonials for his pupils. Then comes an endless stream of complaints to municipal authorities on his working conditions and gripes about his pay. There are also fretful self-justifications and sycophantic dedications to royal personages, always apparently with an eye to the main chance. We sense entrenched attitudes but seldom a beating heart. Even sparring polemical exchanges were conducted at second hand through an intermediary. There is no proof of his having compared notes with his peers, although we may infer that he did do this from time to time (see p. 63), and little to enlighten us about his approach to composition, his attitude to work or to life in general.* His usual answer (as reported by his first biographer, Johann Nikolaus Forkel) to those who asked him how he had contrived to master the art of music to such a high degree was blunt and unilluminating: 'I was obliged to be industrious; whoever is equally industrious will succeed equally well.'[2]

Faced with this paucity of materials, his biographers from Forkel (1802), Carl Hermann Bitter (1865) and Philipp Spitta (1873) onwards have been driven back to the *Nekrolog*, the obituary hastily written in 1754 by his second son C. P. E. Bach and his pupil Johann Friedrich Agricola, to the testimony of his other sons, pupils and contemporaries, and to the web of anecdotes, some of which he himself could well have embroidered. Even with these, the picture which emerges is for the most part formal and two-dimensional: that of a musician who insists he was self-taught, of a man discharging his responsibilities with aloof recti-

* In a speech to mark the bicentenary of Bach's death Paul Hindemith referred to Bach's 'clam-like reticence toward his work' – so different to that of Beethoven or Wagner, whose attitude towards many of their creations we know. As Hindemith rightly said, 'Having this statue constantly before our eyes [that banal figure of a man in a frock coat, with a wig he never takes off] has impaired our view of the true stature of Bach, both of the man and of his work' (Hindemith, *J. S. Bach. Ein verpflichtendes Erbe – Festrede am 12 September 1950 auf dem Bachfest in Hamburg* (trs. as *J. S. Bach: Heritage and Obligation*, 1952)).

tude, and of someone totally immersed in the making of music. Once in a while, when his eyes lifted from the page, we get flashes of anger – a cameo of an artist driven to distraction by the narrow-mindedness and stupidity of his employers and forced to live, in his own words, 'amid almost continual vexation, envy and persecution'.[3] This has opened the floodgates to conjecture – ingenious attempts made by successive biographers to straddle the chasm-like gaps in the sources from which they have squeezed every last drop, and to supplement them with speculation and inference. This is the point where mythology takes hold – of Bach as exemplary Teuton, as a working-class hero-craftsman, as the Fifth Evangelist, or as an intellectual of the calibre of Isaac Newton. We seem to be battling not just with the nineteenth-century bias towards hagiolatry but with peculiarly resistant twentieth-century strains of politically inflected ideology.

A nagging suspicion grows that many writers, overawed and dazzled by Bach, still tacitly assume a direct correlation between his immense genius and his stature as a person. At best this can make them unusually tolerant of his faults, which are there for all to see: a certain tetchiness, contrariness and self-importance, timidity in meeting intellectual challenges, and a fawning attitude towards royal personages and to authority in general that mixes suspicion with gain-seeking. But why should it be assumed that great music emanates from a great human being? Music may inspire and uplift us, but it does not have to be the manifestation of an inspiring (as opposed to an inspired) individual. In some cases there *may* be such a correspondence, but we are not obliged to presume that it is so. It is very possible that 'the teller may be so much slighter or less attractive than the tale.'[4] The very fact that Bach's music was conceived and organised with the brilliance of a great mind does not directly give us any clues as to his personality. Indeed, knowledge of the one can lead to a misplaced knowingness about the other. At least with him there is not the slightest risk, as with so many of the great Romantics (Byron, Berlioz, Heine spring to mind), that we might discover almost too much about him or, as in the case of Richard Wagner, be led to an uncomfortable correlation between the creative and the pathological.

I see no need for us to stand Bach in a flattering light or to avert our eyes from possible movement in the shadows. Some recent biographies try to put a brave face on his personality and interpret everything in a rosy way, one belied by the surviving sources. To do so is to underestimate the psychological toll that a lifetime, not so much of tireless application, as of bowing and scraping to his intellectual inferiors, could have had on his state of mind and well-being. Any God-like image that we superimpose on Bach blinds us to his artistic struggles, and from that point on we cease to see him as a musical craftsman par excellence. Just as we are so accustomed to seeing Brahms as a fat old man with a beard, forgetting that he was once young and dashing – 'a young eagle from the north' as Schumann described him after their first meeting – so we tend to see Bach as a bewigged, jowly old German Capellmeister and attach that image to his music, in the face of all the youthful exuberance and unparalleled vitality that his music so often conveys. Suppose instead we start to view him as an unlikely rebel: 'someone who undermined widely acclaimed principles and closely guarded assumptions [about music]'. This, Laurence Dreyfus suggests, 'can only be good, since it allows us to take those inchoate feelings of awe which many of us feel upon hearing Bach's works and transform them into a vision of the composer's courage and daring, thus letting us experience the music anew . . . Bach and his subversive activities might provide the key to his achievement, which, like all great art, is attuned to the most subtle manipulations and recasting of human experience.'[5] Dreyfus's refreshing and persuasive corrective to the old hagiolatry is in perfect accord with the line of inquiry I will pursue in the central chapters of this book.

That is just one side of the coin. For, despite all the recent flood of scholarly writing on individual aspects of Bach's music and the heated controversy over how it was once performed and by whom, Bach as *Mensch* continues to elude us. Sifting through the same old piles of biographical sand for the umpteenth time, it is easy to assume that by now we have exhausted their potential to yield up fresh nuggets of information. I do not believe this to be the case. In 2000 the American Bach scholar Robert L. Marshall, sensing that a comprehensive reinterpretation of Bach's life and works was long overdue, claimed that he and his fellow scholars were 'avoiding this challenge and we knew it'. He was certain that 'the surviving documents, as recalcitrant as they are, can be made to shed more light on Bach the man than may first appear'.[6] Marshall has since been vindicated by the brilliant, indefatigable sleuths working in the Bach-Archiv in Leipzig, even if the exciting new evidence uncovered by them has so far only been partially assimilated. As its research director, Peter Wollny, described it to me, the process is 'like picking up the odd shard of marble from the foot of a statue: you don't really know whether it is part of an arm, an elbow or a kneecap, but it is still Bach's and you need to alter your speculative image of his completed statuary from the new evidence'. Might there, then, be more priceless nuggets still lurking somewhere in the archives? With the opening up of libraries in countries of the former Eastern Bloc and the avalanche of sources suddenly available to scholars via online digital access, the chances of their discovery are higher now than at any time in the last fifty years.*

There is also the possibility that, by focusing on the familiar sources and desperately trying to add to them, all the time we have been looking in one direction, while missing evidence of the most revealing sort that is right under our noses: the evidence of the music itself. It is the anchor to which we can return again and again, and the principal means of validating or refuting any conclusion about its author. Self-evidently, the more closely you scrutinise the music from the outside as a listener, and the more deeply you get to know it from the inside as a performer, the better are your chances of uncovering the wonders it has to offer – and not only that, but of gaining insight into the man who created it in the first place. At its most monumental and imposing – say, in *The Art of Fugue* or the ten canons of the *Musical Offering* – we come up against membranes so impenetrable as to thwart even the most persistent search for the face of its creator. Bach's keyboard works maintain a tension – born of restraint and obedience to self-set conventions – between form (which we might describe variously as cool, severe, unbending, narrow or complex) and content (passionate or intense) more palpably and obviously than does his texted music.† Many of us can only marvel and

* For example, the Bach-Archiv in Leipzig (in cooperation with the *Staatsbibliothek zu Berlin*, the computing centre of Leipzig University, and other partners, and funded by the *Deutsche Forschungsgemeinschaft*) is working on a project named *Bach Digital* aimed 'at digitising every existing Bach autograph in the world and thus to make the culturally most valuable pool of Bach sources available to a wider circle of users'.

† But, as Robert Quinney has pointed out to me, keyboard instruments were Bach's bread and butter, and the music for organ and clavier can give us a particular insight into the workings of his mind. As with all expert improvisers, Bach's brain and fingers were connected with a febrile instantaneousness (working together literally *extempore*); we can readily believe that the keyboard music retains a charge of this 'real-time' creation, unmediated by the painful compositional process to which so many other composers have been subject – Bach's habit of revising music notwithstanding. And text is never far from his organ music, whether that of the chorales on which the preludes elaborate, or in the uncanny speech-like profile of many of his fugue subjects.

retreat, surrendering to seams of thought that run more profoundly and more immutably in their dispassionate spirituality than in almost any other kind of music.

The moment words are involved the attention is deflected away from form and towards meaning and interpretation. Part of my aim in this book is to show how clearly Bach's approach in his cantatas, motets, oratorios, Masses and Passions reveals his mind at work, his temperamental preferences (including, where it applies, the very act of choosing one text over another) as well as his wide-ranging philosophical outlook. Bach's cantatas are of course not literally diary entries, as though he were straightforwardly penning a personal narrative. Entwined in the music and situated behind these pieces' formal outer shell are the features of this intensely private, multifaceted human being – devout at one moment, rebellious the next, deeply reflective and serious for the most part, but lightened by flashes of humour and empathy. Bach's voice can sometimes be heard in the music and, even more importantly, in the way traces of his own performance are woven into it. These are the tones of someone attuned to the cycles of nature and the changing seasons, sensitive to the raw physicality of life, but buoyed up by the prospect of a better afterlife spent in the company of angels and angelic musicians. It is this that has prompted the book's subtitle, describing both the physical reality – the 'Himmelsburg' in Weimar was Bach's workplace for nine formative years – and providing a metaphor for the seat of divinely inspired music (see pp. 182, 299–300, 458 and 553–4). The music gives us shafts of insight into the harrowing experiences he must have suffered as an orphan, as a lone teenager, and as a grieving husband and father. They show us his fierce dislike of hypocrisy and his impatience with falsification of any sort; but they also reveal the profound sympathy he felt towards those who grieve or suffer in one way or another, or who struggle with their consciences or their beliefs. His music exemplifies this, and it is in part what gives it its authenticity and colossal force. But most of all we hear his joy and sense of delight in celebrating the wonders of the universe and the mysteries of existence – as well as in the thrill of his own creative athleticism. You have only to listen to a single Christmas cantata to experience festive elation and jubilation in music on an unprecedented scale, one beyond the reach of any other composer.

* * *

The purpose of this book is *rencontrer l'homme en sa création.*[7] Its aim is therefore very different from that of a traditional biography: to give the reader a real sense of what the act of music-making would have been like for Bach, inhabiting the same experiences, the same sensations. By this I am not proposing a direct correlation between works and personality – more that the musical side is able to refract a broad range of life experiences (many of which may not in essence be so very different from ours), something which is set at an angle to the habitual connection between life and works. Bach's personality was developed and honed as a direct consequence of his musical thought. The patterns of his actual behaviour were secondary to this, and in some cases can be interpreted as the result of an imbalance between his life as a musician and his everyday domestic life. By looking at the twin processes of composing and performing Bach's music, we can put the human likeness of the composer himself into relief – an impression that can only be strengthened by the experience of re-creating and re-performing it now.

I seek to convey what it is like to approach Bach from the position of a performer and conductor standing in front of a vocal and instrumental ensemble, just as he himself habitually did. Naturally I am aware that this is treacherous ground, and that any 'evidence' drawn from it can easily be dismissed as subjective and invalid – just 'an updated version of the romantic view of music as autobiography', one that claims 'an impossible authority' for its speculations.[8] It is of course tempting to believe that one can understand a composer's aims while under the influence of the emotion the music evokes, although this may not be the case at all.* But that does not mean that subjectivity per se is inimical to more objective truth or undermines its conclusions. Ultimately all truths are subjective to one degree or another, except perhaps those of

* Peter Williams, one of the most perspicacious of Bach's recent biographers, warns 'The exquisite world of imagination opened up by any powerful music is itself problematic, for it tempts listeners to put into words the feelings it arouses in them and so to visualise a composer's priorities and even personality. There must be few people who have played, sung, listened to or written about Bach's music who do not feel they have a special understanding of him, a private connection, unique to themselves, but ultimately coming from their idea of what music is and does. This might be quite different from the composer's' (Peter Williams, *The Life of Bach* (2004), p. 1). He is of course quite right.

mathematics. In the past Bach scholarship has suffered from the distancing, or in some cases the removal, of the subject (the author) from the object (the composer) of the study. But once an author's subjectivity is virtually expunged or remains unacknowledged, it follows that facets of Bach's personality are closed off to investigation. In the introductory chapter I explain the background to, and nature of, my own particular subjectivity. This may be forgiven, I hope, should others, as a result, be encouraged to analyse their own subjective responses to the composer and to consider the extent to which those responses have given rise to the conception that we have of him.

Writing this book over several years has meant searching for ways in which scholarship and performance can cooperate and be made to coalesce fruitfully. It has entailed delving into the evidence that could shed new light on Bach's background, piecing together the biographical fragments, re-examining the impact of his orphancy and the circumstances of his schooling, scrutinising the music and keeping a weather-eye out for those instances in performance when his personality seems to rise through the fabric of his notation. Despite the huge debt I owe to the experts and scholars who have guided me and perhaps averted me from disaster, what is presented here is very much one person's vision. I have set out to provide a straightforward structure (though not always articulated in strictly chronological order): fourteen different approaches, fourteen spokes of a wheel, all connected to a central hub – Bach as man and musician. Each spoke, though it bears a relation to its neighbours and opposites, is there to guide the reader from one point to another within its specific topic. Each of these 'constellations' (Walter Benjamin's description of much the same thing) explores a different facet of his character and each proposes a fresh vantage point from which to view the man and his music.

In counterpoint to this I have introduced a series of footnotes in the spirit of the biographer Richard Holmes: 'as a sort of down-stage voice, reflecting on the action as it develops, and suggesting lines of exploration through some of the biographical and critical issues raised'.[9] Nevertheless I am not trying to be comprehensive – far from it. If you are looking for analyses of the monumental works for clavier and organ or for individual solo instruments this is not the place to find them: they could never be treated in depth alongside the vocal music and would need a separate volume to themselves.* My focus is on the music I know best – the music that is linked to words. I hope to show that, because of their connection with words and texts, there are things said in the cantatas, motets, Passions and Masses that are unsurpassed in Bach's output, things which up to this point no one had ever tried or dared to say, or been able to say, with sounds. I find that the practical familiarity this brings opens the door to fresh views on why and how particular works evolved as they did, on how they are sewn together and on what they seem to tell us about the man who composed them. For me the excitement of rehearsing and performing these works – in effect living inside them over a concentrated span – has lit a fire which has burnt with increasing heat ever since I first encountered them. It is this rich, sonorous world and the delight I take in it, both as a conductor and lifelong student of Bach, that I most want to convey.

As a listener, critic or scholar you normally have a margin of time in which to measure and reflect on your response to Bach's music. Analysis of musical structure has its uses, but it gets you only part of the way: it identifies the mechanical bits, and describes the component engineering, but it doesn't tell you what it is that makes the motor purr and hum. As with many composers, but particularly in Bach's case, it turns out to be much easier to trace the craftsman-like procedures he used to elaborate and transform musical material than to define or penetrate to the core of his initial inventive formulations. Whereas over the past century musical analysis has brought us far in comprehending Bach's craftsmanship, the techniques we habitually use to analyse music when it is joined to verbal expression are of little use. We need a different tool-kit.

Performance, on the other hand, removes the last possibility of sitting on the fence: you are obliged to commit to a view and an interpretation of a work in order to present it with full belief and conviction. I try to convey what it feels like to be in the middle of it – connected to the motor and dance rhythms of the music, caught up in the sequential harmony and the intricate contrapuntal web of sounds, their spatial relations, the kaleidoscopic colour-changes of voices and instruments (singly and severally as well as in their collisions). This is perhaps the sort of task that

* However, the literature here is extensive, led by Laurence Dreyfus, *Bach and the Patterns of Invention* (1996), David Schulenberg, *The Keyboard Music of J. S. Bach* (1992) and Peter Williams, *The Organ Music of J. S. Bach* (second edition, 2003).

astronauts would have faced in describing the moon if we hadn't actually seen their images on our screens back on earth; or that confronts those who, having taken hallucinogenic drugs, emerge from a dream world with (what I imagine to be) weird sensations whirring around inside them, struggling to convey what it felt like to be in a parallel dimension under their influence.

Imagine, instead, what it feels like to stand chest-deep in the ocean, waiting to snorkel. What you see are the sparse physical features visible to the naked eye: the shore, the horizon, the surface of the sea, maybe a boat or two, and perhaps the bleached outline of fish or coral just below, but not much else. Then you don your mask and lower yourself into the water. Immediately you enter a separate, magical world of myriad tints and vibrant colours, the subtle movement of passing shoals, the waving of sea anemones and coral – a vivid but wholly different reality. To me this is akin to the experience and shock of performing Bach's music – the way it exposes to you its brilliant colour spectrum, its sharpness of contour, its harmonic depth, and the essential fluidity of its movement and underlying rhythm. Above water there is dull quotidian noise; below the surface is the magical world of Bach's musical sounds. But even once the performance is over and the music has melted back into the silence from which it began, we are still left with the transporting impact of the experience, which lingers in the memory. Strong, too, is the sense of a mirror being held up to the man who created this music in the first place – one that vividly reflects his complex and rugged personality, his urge to communicate and share his view of the world with his listeners, and his unique capacity for bringing boundless invention, intelligence, wit and humanity to the process of composition.

Emphatically, Bach the man was not a bore.

I

Under the Cantor's Gaze

In the autumn of 1936 a thirty-year-old music teacher from Bad Warmbrunn in Lower Silesia suddenly appeared in a Dorset village with two items in his luggage: a guitar and a portrait in oils of Bach. Like old Veit Bach, the founder of the clan, escaping from Eastern Europe as a religious refugee almost four centuries earlier, Walter Jenke had left Germany just as Jews were being banned from holding professional posts. He settled and found work in North Dorset, married an English girl and, with war imminent, looked for a safe home for his painting. His great-grandfather had purchased a portrait of Bach in a curiosity shop sometime in the 1820s for next to nothing. Doubtless he did not know at the time that this was – and still is – by far the most important Bach portrait in existence. Had Jenke left it with his mother in Bad Warmbrunn, it would almost certainly not have survived the bombardment or the evacuation of Germans from Silesia in the face of the advancing Red Army.*

I grew up under the Cantor's gaze. The celebrated Haussmann portrait of Bach[1] had been given to my parents for safekeeping for the duration of the war, and it took pride of place on the first-floor landing of the old mill in Dorset where I was born. Every night on my way to bed I tried to avoid its forbidding stare. I was doubly fortunate as a child in that

* This is the slightly later and much better preserved of Elias Gottlob Haussmann's two Bach portraits (1746 and 1748, see Plates 18 and 19) showing the bewigged composer holding a copy of his six-part canon BWV 1076 (see Chapter 14, p. 546). Since 1950 it has been in the William H. Scheide Library in Princeton, New Jersey.

I grew up on a farm and into a music-minded family where it was considered perfectly normal to sing – on a tractor or horseback (my father), at table (the whole family sang grace at mealtimes) or at weekend gatherings, outlets for my parents' love of vocal music. All through the war years they and a few local friends convened every Sunday morning to sing William Byrd's *Mass for Four Voices*. As children my brother, sister and I grew up getting to know a grand miscellany of unaccompanied choral music – from Josquin to Palestrina, Tallis to Purcell, Monteverdi to Schütz, and, eventually, Bach. Compared to the earlier polyphony, Bach's motets, we found, were a lot more difficult technically – those long, long phrases with nowhere to breathe – but I remember loving the interplay of voices, with so much going on at once, and that pulsating rhythm underneath keeping everything afloat. By the time I was twelve I knew the treble parts of most of Bach's six motets more or less by heart. They became part of the primary matter in my head (along with folksongs, ribald poems in Dorset dialect and heaven knows what else, stored in my memory) and have never left me.

Then, during my teens, I came to know some of his instrumental music: the Brandenburg Concertos, the violin sonatas and concertos (with which, as a distinctly average fiddle-player, I often struggled – and usually lost – between the ages of nine and eighteen, at which stage I switched to the viola), some of the keyboard pieces and several cantata arias for alto, of which my mother was very fond. Even now I cannot hear arias such as 'Gelobet sei der Herr, mein Gott' ('The Lord be praised') or 'Von der Welt verlang ich nichts' ('I ask nothing of the world') without a lump in my throat, remembering her voice floating across the courtyard from the mill-room. But my early apprenticeship in Bach, the nurturing of a lifelong engagement with his music and a longing to understand the stern Cantor at the top of the stairs, I owe to four remarkable teachers – three women and one man – who helped to determine the kind of musician I was to become.

The man was Wilfred Brown, the great English tenor, who visited my school when I was fourteen, singing both the Evangelist and the tenor arias in a performance of Bach's *John Passion*. I was so captivated that, unpardonable in a principal second violin, at one point I stopped playing altogether and just gawped. As an interpreter of Bach's Evangelist, Bill Brown was nonpareil. His singing was characterised by an extraordinary subtlety of inflection and word-painting, and by a pathos that was inseparable from his own Quaker beliefs and the humility they brought, something I recognised from my mother's Quaker upbringing. Later on he offered to give me singing lessons from the time I was sixteen until I was twenty-two, sometimes travelling to Cambridge to do so and always refusing a fee.

Imogen Holst, daughter of Gustav and amanuensis to Benjamin Britten, was a regular visitor to my parents' home and sometimes led their choral weekends and gave singing lessons to me and my sister. She, I suppose more than any other musician I had encountered at that early stage, stressed the importance of dance in Baroque music. This was so clearly visible in her own interpretation and her way of conducting Bach that someone once filmed her just from the waist downwards while conducting the *B minor Mass*. To this day, thanks to Imo, I feel that the worst interpretative sin (committed with painful regularity even now) is to *plod* in Bach; denying or resisting the rhythmical elasticity and buoyancy of his music ensures that its spirit shoots out of the door. In speaking touchingly of her father, she stressed the indispensability of music, that it was a part of life that 'can't be done without'.

Letting Bach dance was one lesson well learnt; the other was how to make him 'sing'. This sounds so obvious and so much easier than it is in practice. Not all of Bach's melodies are singer-friendly or melodious in the way that, say, Purcell's or Schubert's are. Often angular, the phrase-lengths uncomfortably long, peppered with little curlicue flourishes and ornaments, they require a lot of purpose, underpinned by iron breath-control, before they can truly sing. And that applies not just to the vocal lines, but to the instrumental ones as well. This I learnt from my violin teacher, Sybil Eaton, a pupil of the celebrated Greek violinist and musicologist Minos Dounias. Sybil certainly 'sang' when she played the fiddle, but, through her inspirational teaching and sheer love of Bach, she was also able to help her pupils to take melodic wing, whether we were playing concertos, solo partitas or obbligato parts to arias from the Passions or the cantatas.

The person who crystallised all these ideas for me was Nadia Boulanger, justly recognised as the most celebrated teacher of composition in the twentieth century. When she accepted me as a student in Paris in 1967, she had just turned eighty and was partially blind, but with all her other faculties in tip-top order. Her way of teaching harmony was founded on Bach's chorales, which she regarded as models of how to establish a beautiful polyphony – with each voice being accorded equal importance while still playing a different role in the four-way conversation, now advancing, now retreating: contrapuntally conceived harmony, in other words. She insisted that the freedom to express yourself in music, whether as a composer, conductor or performer, demanded obedience to certain laws and the possession of unassailable technical skills. One of her favourite sayings was 'Talent [by which I think she meant technique] without genius is not worth much; but genius without talent is worth nothing whatsoever.'

Confined for two years to an unvarying diet of harmony and counterpoint exercises and *solfège* (the particularly nasty but effective French system of ear-training), I metaphorically kicked and scratched like a cornered animal. On at least one occasion, from sheer frustration, Hindemith's *Elementary Training for Musicians* ended up in the gutter – thrown out of the window of my bed-sit in the 4th arrondissement. But I owe her a colossal debt. She had a way of challenging every preconception as well as a knack of exposing one's shortcomings, technical or otherwise, quite mercilessly. She saw something in me that I did not even see in myself. It was only after I had left the *boulangerie* that I realised that what had seemed like torture at the time was actually an act of kindness, equipping me to avoid certain professional embarrassments in the future. And, despite her severity, she was extraordinarily generous, even bequeathing to me her unique collection of transcriptions of Renaissance and Baroque music (from Monteverdi to Rameau), including scores and parts of her favourite Bach cantatas, all meticulously annotated – some of my most treasured possessions.*

How was I to translate this painfully acquired theory and ear-training into actual sound when standing in front of a choir and orchestra? Luckily by this stage (1967–8), while I was a student in Paris and Fontainebleau, from time to time I had access to an 'instrument' in London – the Monteverdi Choir. It had all started back in 1964 when I was in my third year at Cambridge. My tutor, the social anthropologist Edmund Leach, authorised me to take a year off from the History tripos to sieve through the possible directions my life might take and, crucially, to find out whether I really had it in me to become a full-time musician.

* These, along with many other scores and parts transcribed by Nadia Boulanger and left to me in her will, are now on permanent loan to the Royal Academy of Music in London.

Ostensibly I was there to read Classical Arabic and medieval Spanish; in practice the task I set myself was to perform Monteverdi's 1610 *Vespers*, a work that, although I had first heard it as a child, was still very little known and had never before been performed in Cambridge. Despite the dual handicap of my relative inexperience as a conductor and my little formal musical training up to that point, I had set my heart on conducting one of the most challenging works in the choral repertoire. I spent the best part of that year studying the original part-books on microfilm and, with the encouragement of the Professor of Music, Thurston Dart, preparing a new performing edition. I also ended up doing everything involved in planning a public performance in King's College Chapel – from assembling and training the choir and orchestra, to having the tickets printed and putting out the chairs.

Vibrant colour contrasts and passionate declamation seemed to me to be the hallmark of this music. The test for me was whether I could draw any of that from a group of student singers trained in a totally different tradition. To that extent the Monteverdi Choir started life as an anti-choir – in reaction to the well-mannered euphony and blend which characterised the celebrated chapel choir at King's in my day, whose mantra was 'Never louder than lovely'. Their style was summed up for me by a performance, at Boris Ord's memorial service, of *Jesu, meine Freude* – that most extended and interpretatively challenging of Bach's motets – sung in English with effete and lip-wiping prissiness: 'Jesu . . .' (pronounced *Jeez-ewe*), followed by a huge comma and expressive intake of breath, '. . . priceless treasure' (pronounced *trez-ewer*). I seethed. How had the wonderfully exultant music that I had known since I was a child come to be treated in such a precious, etiolated way? Was this not like adding a layer of face powder and a few beauty spots to the dour old Cantor's portrait?

My first attempt at performing Monteverdi's masterpiece took place in March 1964 with some of the same performers. It fell a long way short of the ideals I had set for it, yet people who heard it were encouraging, even enthusiastic. For me it was not just a test of skill, but the epiphany I had been searching for. The decision was made: better to follow an overwhelming passion, even one that would need years of study and practice and with absolutely no guarantee of success, than to pursue safer career paths for which I might already have had the rudimentary technical qualifications. I was encouraged to persist in my rebellion against the vestiges of Victorian performance and to find a more permanent footing for the Monteverdi Choir. My starting-point, then as now, was to bring passion and expressivity to the vocal music of the Baroque, and, as appropriate, to the nationality, period and personality of the composer. In a typical programme, such as we gave in the Cambridge Festival in 1965, devoted to music by Monteverdi, Schütz and Purcell, we set out to enable listeners to hear the idiosyncratic approach of each master sung in the original language, to follow each composer as he experimented with music based on recitation over a figured bass line and revelled in the new expressive range it offered. It was heady stuff, and our efforts were doubtless crude and exaggerated; but at least they did not sound half-baked or indistinguishable from Anglican pieties during a wet November Evensong.

I was desperately short of working models. Nadia Boulanger no longer conducted. Nor did Thurston Dart, from whose Sherlock Holmes–like approach to musicology I had learnt a great deal in the postgraduate year that I studied with him after he moved to King's College, London. I did, however, have the luck to observe the distinguished keyboard virtuoso and conductor George Malcolm. George knew how to draw dazzling performances of a most un-English ardour from his choir at Westminster Cathedral, and, amazingly, he took the trouble to travel up to Cambridge to hear my first *Vespers* performance. Here was a true master and, I felt, a kindred spirit, whose approbation and encouragement at that stage made all the difference to me, although he had virtually given up choral conducting.

Then, at a friend's invitation, I went to hear Karl Richter conduct his Munich Bach Choir in 1967. Richter was acclaimed as the foremost exponent of Bach's choral music at the time, but even his muscular LP recordings of cantatas hadn't prepared me for the oppressive volume and sheer aggression of the motet *Singet dem Herrn* as delivered by seventy lusty Bavarians from the gallery of the Markuskirche. This was a world apart from the mincing 'holy, holy' approach of King's or the Bach Choir in London in their annual Good Friday *Matthew Passion* outing at the Royal Festival Hall, but hardly more inspiriting. Nor did Richter's thunderous approach to the *Goldberg Variations* next day on a souped-up Neupert harpsichord, given in the Musikhochschule (Hitler's former residence), do much to restore my faith. Here, as in most of the live performances or recordings that I had access to, Bach came over as grim, sombre, po-faced, lacking in spirit, humour and humanity. Where was the festive joy and zest of this dance-impregnated music? A few years later I heard a performance of the *John Passion* under Benjamin Britten, a very fine conductor who combed out the separate strands of Bach's elaborate counterpoint before my ears, revealing the work's drama from the inside. Yet, even so, to me it sounded fatally 'English'. I felt a similar disappointment when I first heard Mozart played in Salzburg and Vienna in 1958: the elegant surface of the playing seemed to overlay and disguise the turbulent emotional inner life of the music.

My own start was hardly promising. In the hot summer of 1967, when most of Nadia Boulanger's composition class decamped from Paris to the Palais de Fontainebleau to be joined by the *crème de la crème* of the Juilliard and Curtis schools of music, she decided that it was time for me to conduct something under her scrutiny. She set me the challenge of Bach's *Bleib bei uns*, that touching Easter cantata (BWV 6) which tells the story of the two disciples encountering their risen Lord on the road to Emmaus. The American Conservatory at Fontainebleau was not like Cambridge University, with its considerable reserves of choral scholars and eager student singers. Apart from one talented mezzo, there were absolutely no singers at all – just a bunch of recalcitrant 'peenists' (as they habitually referred to themselves). These I had to recruit, cajole and transform into a four-part ensemble capable of passing muster in Bach's magical eventide opening chorus, in order to establish my credentials as a conductor to my teacher. Until that point Mademoiselle, as everyone called her, had never heard or seen me conduct, though she seized on every occasion to remind me that my harmony and counterpoint exercises were 'a *tragédie* without name'. If you have ever heard a group of American pianists (who could all, no doubt, toss off a Chopin étude or Liszt prélude at the drop of a hat) trying to sing in four parts in German, you will know what I, and they, suffered. The 'orchestra' consisted solely of my fellow student and countryman Stephen Hicks, playing on an out-of-tune organ (he had first introduced himself to me in Mademoiselle's class as 'Stephen 'icks, best organist in West Molesey'). As well as conducting this motley ensemble I also had to sing the tenor recitative and play the viola obbligato in the alto aria, while Stephen manfully filled in all the rest on the organ. Came the day and the Jeu de Paume was packed with sweltering students. A few very elderly ladies in black sat in the front row, with my Venerable Teacher in the middle. The performance began, and the VT instantly fell sound asleep. In fact I doubt whether she heard a single note of it, which, all things considered, was perhaps just as well.

Grateful as I was, life at the *boulangerie* was suffocating, and I hankered for the opportunity to apply all this rigorous theory and discipline to some hands-on conducting experience in the real world of professional music. To the disgust of Mademoiselle, who expected that, like many of her American pupils, I would remain with her to study Théodore Dubois's *Traité d'harmonie* for at least another five years, I applied for the job of apprentice conductor to the BBC Northern Orchestra in Manchester. This was a highly accomplished, somewhat hard-bitten orchestra who made it abundantly clear how fortunate you were as a fledgling conductor to be standing in front of them: you could expect no favours and would either sink or swim. My main practical assignment was to conduct a different concert overture at the start of each programme. If the piece lasted, say, twelve minutes, I would be allocated a maximum of nine minutes in which to rehearse it before the live broadcast. The trick with a wonderful sight-reading orchestra like this was to know what to prioritise, when to intervene and what to leave to chance and the extra spurt of adrenalin and focus that came when the red light went on. It was a valuable training ground and taught me the rudiments of how to make best use of costly rehearsal time.

Back in London things were on the move with the Monteverdi Choir. By extending our repertoire forwards chronologically and geographically northwards from the Venetian composers (the Gabrielis and Monteverdi) to the Germans (Schütz and Buxtehude) and to the English Restoration composers (Blow, Humfrey and Purcell), we were heading inexorably towards a confrontation with those twin colossi, Handel and Bach. Over the next ten years (1968–78) I was fortunate in being able to recruit a top-notch modern chamber band to work alongside the choir – the Monteverdi Orchestra – comprising some of the very best freelance chamber musicians on the London scene. These players showed me extraordinary trust through their willingness to experiment, undertaking not just travels to the wilder shores of the Baroque by means of oratorios and operas which were then virtually unknown, but also stylistic explorations involving the use of outward-curved Baroque bows, *notes inégales*, mordents, inverted mordents, *coulés* and ornamental twiddles of all sorts.

Then suddenly we hit a brick wall. The fault was neither theirs nor mine, but that of the instruments we were using – the same as everyone else had been using for the past hundred and fifty years. However stylishly we played them, there was no disguising that they had been designed or adapted with a totally different sonority in mind, one closely associated with a late-nineteenth- and early-twentieth-century (and therefore anachronistic) style of expression. With their wire or metal-covered strings they were simply too powerful – and yet to scale things down and hold back was the very opposite of what this music, with its burgeoning, expressive range, calls for. To unlock the codes in the musical language of these Baroque masters, to close the gap between their world and ours, and to release the wellspring of their creative fantasy meant cultivating a radically different sonority. There was only one thing for it: to re-group using original (or replica) Baroque instruments. It was like learning a totally new language, or taking up a new instrument but with practically no one to teach you how to play it. It is hard to convey what ructions, disappointments and excitements this entailed. Some felt it to be a terrible betrayal; to others, including most of the singers in the Monteverdi Choir, it was an inexplicably backward step. But a few brave souls took the plunge with me: they bought, begged or borrowed Baroque instruments, and we became the English Baroque Soloists.

That was in 1978. More intrepid pioneers had got there ahead of us of course. It might have felt so at the time, but mine was not a lone voice. Among my Cambridge contemporaries were both Christopher Hogwood – later recognised as one of the most influential proponents of the historically informed early-music movement – and the charismatic 'Pied Piper', David Munrow, who, in a career lasting barely ten years, did more than anyone else to popularise early music in Britain. Along with Trevor Pinnock, the distinguished harpsichordist, they too had formed their own period-instrument bands – the English Concert (1972) and the Academy of Ancient Music (1973). Actually the real Amundsens were the Dutch, Austrians and Flemish – explorers such as Gustav Leonhardt, Nikolaus Harnoncourt and the Kuijken brothers, all of whom had already been experimenting with period instruments for several years before that. Then in their wake came a trickle of British freelance musicians, who are among the most flexible and pragmatic in the world: they saw the opportunities and soon acquired the taste.

Taste, but as yet not much technique – a failing seized upon by some of the conventional old-timers, particularly in the symphony orchestras, who began to sense the slight breeze of a challenge to their monopoly and now, rather gratifyingly for them, found an easy target to criticise. But people were quick to realise there really is a difference in performance between those who are committed to re-making music and inhabiting it afresh, and those bent on just dispatching it with efficiency and technical skill. Initially, as with all breakaway movements, its pioneer leaders – many of them self-taught – were prone to overstate their case and to leave dangling in the air the misleading thought that by getting the instruments right you got to the 'truth' of the music. Again the problem was one of models, or rather the lack of them. It was a heady time, the air abuzz with controversy and passionate self-defence. No one knew for certain how these old instruments were really meant to sound. Never before had practising musicians needed to become so erudite. But two performers can assiduously read the same eighteenth-century violin tutor or treatise and still come to alarmingly divergent conclusions in the interpretation of it. It just goes to show that research into performance practice is quite distinct from performance itself, and, as Richard Taruskin was quick to point out, sound scholarship does not necessarily result in good music-making.* Inevitably there was much imitation and much refutation: one person's audacious experiment could easily be rubbished by some and received as Gospel by others. Mannerism ruled the day, with sickly swells and bulges galore, particularly among the string players. (I was often reminded of Mademoiselle's quizzical inquiry of one pupil prone to exaggerated phrasing: 'Why do you make your music in hammocks, my dear?')

For the greater part of those few years I found the whole experience

* At a time when a fashion for the virtues of 'under-interpretation' was beginning to take hold in England among certain early-music practitioners, Taruskin was also one of the first to question what he called the 'naive assumption that re-creating all the external conditions that obtained in the original performance of a piece will thus re-create the composer's inner experience of the piece and allow him to "speak for himself", that is, unimpeded by that base intruder, the performer's subjectivity'. He also identified a danger in an over-reverential attitude to the concept of *Werktreue* ('truth to the work'), one that inflicts 'a truly stifling regimen by radically hardening and patrolling what had formerly been a fluid, easily crossed boundary between the performing and composing roles' (Richard Taruskin, *Text and Act* (1995), pp. 93, 10). More recently John Butt has given a brilliant disquisition on the two worlds of performance and scholarship in *Playing with History: The Historical Approach to Musical Performance* (2002).

nerve-racking. I mourned the easy technical fluency and surefootedness of my disbanded Monteverdi Orchestra and its open-minded players. I was dismayed by the technical fallibility of these new 'old' instruments, which were turning out to be treacherous to master for all concerned. Squawks and squeaks were endemic, and the sound of snapping hygroscopic gut E strings filled the air. Conducting them suddenly felt like driving an old banger with dodgy brakes and steering. But slowly the instruments began to yield up their secrets to the players and to guide us all to pathways of fresh expressive gestures and sounds. Some observers were inclined to fetishise these instruments, as though they alone led to the holy grail of 'authentic performance' and were its sole guarantors. But, while I delighted in the new expressive potential and palette of colours, I could never forget that we were using them not as an end in itself but as a means – to get closer to the transparent sound world of Baroque composers, and (in the overused analogy beloved of music critics) to remove the layers of dirt and varnish that had accreted over time.

At any rate, it was with this raw and untried ensemble that I accepted my first invitation to perform at the Ansbach Bach Festival in 1979, then considered to be the Mecca, or Bayreuth, of Bach performance in Europe. It had been Karl Richter's launchpad in southern Germany, and now its platform was being offered to a relatively untried Englishman and his group. Our approach was seen to be radically 'different' and provoked controversy. Since the nineteenth century, Bach had been revered in Germany as the Fifth Evangelist, his church music corralled in the support of modern evangelical Lutheranism. Listening to us, the conservative defenders of a largely fictitious and self-aggrandising Bach performance tradition found the 'old' instruments foreign to their tastes – which was only to be expected, and a reaction that we became used to over the next twenty years. Perhaps what surprised them more, however, was the concentrated care we gave to the pronunciation and projection of the text – the declamation of the German words directed towards bringing out the rhetoric and drama – and what some listeners identified as a sense of occasion in our performances. It felt good to contribute in a positive way towards demystifying Bach's image in the land of his birth. We were immediately invited to return to the Bachwoche Ansbach for five concerts in 1981 and subsequently to record all the major Bach choral works for Germany's top label, Deutsche Grammophon.

At about the same time we embarked on an ambitious ten-year

assignment based on annual visits to the Göttingen Festival, of which I had been appointed artistic director. This was to revive the dramatic oratorios and operas of Handel, whose music, even more than that of Bach, had undergone an astonishing process of bowdlerisation over the years – even a partial appropriation by the Nazis in the 1930s as a vehicle for patriotic propaganda – and was now in urgent need of reappraisal. Here, too, we encountered mild scepticism at first, but soon found that German attitudes towards Handel were less entrenched than those in England, his adopted country (and than they were towards Bach). Gradually we were greeted with a more open-minded response – a mixture of astonishment and patriotic pride – to our interpretation of this magnificent, partially known repertoire. Alongside these European concert appearances, our recordings of a whole range of works – some old war-horses like *Messiah* and the *Christmas Oratorio*, but also forgotten masterpieces like Rameau's *Les Boréades* and Leclair's *Scylla et Glaucus* – found favour with audiences and started to win international recognition.

* * *

Though increasingly busy as a guest conductor in opera houses and with symphony orchestras, I found myself coming back to my home base with fresh enthusiasm: the English Baroque Soloists provided a living laboratory in which to test new theories, to exchange views and approaches, and were now showing a willingness to strike out on new paths away from what were becoming the sapping orthodoxies of period-instrument style. Suddenly you could hear the music leap from the confines of its encasement. The moment these old instruments were let loose on music that had once been the exclusive preserve of the scaled-down modern symphony orchestra, what for years had seemed 'ye olde' and remote now sounded new-minted. It felt fine to ruffle a few feathers if it meant we could discover and share insights into the music we all cared about so much.

From the 1980s onwards our repertoire was constantly expanding. The bicentenary of the outbreak of the French Revolution was the moment when the Orchestre révolutionnaire et romantique was born, using many of the same players as the English Baroque Soloists, but playing turn-of-the-century instruments. Together we moved forwards – from Haydn, Mozart and Beethoven to Weber, Berlioz, Schubert, Mendelssohn, Schumann and Brahms, even to Verdi, Debussy and Stravinsky. It was an enthralling process of re-discovery, giving the lie to the hoary old notion of a single, inexorable developing tradition within Western classical music, and to an enervating mid-twentieth-century tendency to iron out crucial temperamental and stylistic differences between composers by playing everything on the same 'instrument': the standard modern symphony orchestra. Our aim was always to strip away layers of accreted performance practice to reveal each of these composers – and each significant work of each composer – in their individual plumage, testing the ability of this 'old' music to survive in our time. The quest was (and is) to locate the sharp and vivid colours at its core and to re-discover that *élan vital* in the music that appeals to us *now.* Surprisingly often, centuries-old music turns out to feel more modern than whole swathes of music from the last hundred years.

But time and again I found myself drawn back to the music of Bach as to a lodestone. Just as I had discovered earlier how valuable it was to come to grips with Monteverdi in order to understand the way music and words could be fruitfully combined in all forms of dramatic music, so I now came to realise that to make headway as a conductor I would first need to study and to learn to perform the music of Bach, for it forms the very bedrock of what we loosely refer to as classical music. Without an understanding of *him* I would forever be groping in the dark when interpreting Haydn, Mozart, Beethoven and their Romantic successors, very few of whom managed to resist his influence. Although I had been mulling over it for years, it was not until the autumn of 1987 that I found the opportunity (and the courage) to conduct the *Matthew Passion* for the first time. It was in East Berlin, and in the audience were GDR soldiers weeping quite openly. Perhaps on that side of the border this most universal of music had become fossilised in some prescribed – and largely spurious – local tradition. By approaching it afresh, free of ritualised clichés, we were unwittingly opening the floodgates for an emotional response to it.

But it was not all one-way traffic: two years earlier members of the Leipzig Radio Chorus appeared at a rehearsal of Handel's *Israel in Egypt* that I was preparing with the Monteverdi Choir in the western gallery of Leipzig's Thomaskirche. This led to an impromptu performance of Bach's motet *Singet dem Herrn* sung by both choirs, making a lasting impression on all the participants. Then, in 1987, there was a tour of the *B minor Mass* in Japan, memorable for the concentrated response of a largely Buddhist and Shinto audience.

But increasingly I felt there was something incomplete in my understanding of how Bach the man connected to his unfathomable music. Even after living with the main choral masterpieces for so long, there were vital pieces of the jigsaw still missing. If I had been an accomplished keyboard player I might have found what I was looking for in the vast and endlessly fascinating repertoire that includes the *Goldberg Variations* and the *Well-Tempered Clavier*. But, as a choral man and someone who has always responded to words, I felt the key for me must lie in the nearly 200 church cantatas to have survived; I was certain that they contained individual buried truffles, although as yet I had unearthed only a few of them. To get an idea of the cantatas' importance in the estimation of Bach's sons and pupils, one has only to look at the list of his unpublished works in his obituary: they chose to place 'No. 1: Five Full Annual Cycles of Church Pieces for All the Sundays and Feast-Days' almost in banner headlines at the head of his work-list. This led me to question why Bach had lavished so much time and care on them, and why, in an initial two-year spurt of frenzied creativity, he composed well over a hundred in Leipzig, doggedly refusing to share the punishing weekly burden of composition with others. Given that they were written in Dickens-like weekly instalments, one wanted to know just how consistent they were in terms of overall quality: if, as Theodor Adorno claimed, 'Bach was the first to crystallize the idea of the rationally constituted work',[2] do the cantatas qualify? Are they genuinely significant? Can they escape their original literary and liturgical origins and limitations and bridge the gap between his culture and ours? This set me off wondering what might be the most effective way of performing them now – how to release them from the dead hand of nineteenth- and early-twentieth-century Lutheran evangelism on the one hand, and the secular piety of typical concert-hall fare on the other.

I find it difficult to pinpoint exactly when the idea of the Bach Cantata Pilgrimage first arose. What had started out as an intuition born of a lifelong fascination with Bach only gradually acquired shape and substance before growing into a coherent practical endeavour.* It seemed that no one had previously attempted to perform them within a single calendar year in their exact original liturgical positions. In 2000 we would be

* The trigger may have been a chance reading in a record magazine of an announcement that I was due to record all 200 of them for Deutsche Grammophon. As at the time I was recording about one cantata CD per year, I calculated that with three cantatas per CD, at that rate I would need to reach the grand old age of 120 before the job was done.

celebrating the birth of the founder of one of the world's great religions and the 250th anniversary of Bach's death. What more appropriate way to do so than via the work of its greatest musical advocate, with performances of all the cantatas concentrated within a single year? Bach's Lutheran faith is encapsulated in this extraordinary music. It carries a universal message of hope that can touch anybody regardless of culture, religious denomination or musical knowledge. It springs from the depths of the human psyche and not from some topical or local creed.

Perhaps, too, there were insights to be gained by replicating the rhythms of Bach's own practice. We set about constructing a journey that he himself theoretically could have made (though of course in actual fact he travelled far less than, for example, Handel). It would need to begin in Thuringia and Saxony, where he spent his working life, and encompass those places and churches where we know that he sang, played and performed, and then fan out north, west and east, following the dissemination of the Reformation and retracing the old trade routes of the merchant adventurers and the Hanseatic League. Out of this choice came the idea to perform only in churches of exceptional architectural beauty, often in venues lying well off the beaten concert track, and to take the music to communities showing a particular enthusiasm for Bach's music, with whom we could connect by inviting them to sing in the closing chorales of the cantatas. By visiting some of Europe's most ancient places of worship – like the abbey of Iona off the west coast of Scotland, or Santiago de Compostela in northern Spain, or the once-pagan temple that became Santa Maria sopra Minerva in Rome – the journey could be construed as a musical pilgrimage.

And so, eventually, the Bach Cantata Pilgrimage was born. Though originating in earlier concert tours with the Monteverdi Choir, and informed by the same mindset, the BCP was on a different scale from anything we – or perhaps any other musical organisation – had previously undertaken. In its scope and in the way it was realised it broke all conventional rules of concert-tour organisation. It was an epic endeavour, fraught with logistical problems and beset from the start by financial constraints, yet one that seemed to resonate within the imaginations of the participants more and more as the year wore on. None of us had ever undertaken a year-long journey or a musical enterprise confined to a single composer before. It was an entirely new experience to have all one's thoughts and efforts directed towards its implementation and guided by its onward momentum. Following Bach's seasonal and cyclical arrangement of cantatas for an entire year provided us with a graphic musical image of the revolving wheel of time to which we are all bound. Here, at last, was one way of solving the enigma of how this music brimming over with vigour and fantasy could have emerged from beneath the wig of that impassive-looking cantor, whose portrait had dominated my view of him as a man ever since I was a child.

Since the completion of the BCP my approach to conducting Bach's more celebrated choral works – his two Passions, the *Christmas Oratorio* and the *B minor Mass* – has been affected by that deep immersion in the cantatas. From the moment one sees these great works as belonging to the same world as the cantatas, as emanations from the same inventive mind, they no longer feel quite so intimidating, and begin to reveal more of their creator's character. By working through my own reactions to them and development as a musician, my engagement with Bach has deepened – an attachment that has run in parallel with the independent research I have carried out in preparation for this book. Over the past twenty years I have been absorbing the riveting material that has become newly available since the opening out of archives in the former GDR, and using these rich findings to delve into the origins and the historical context for the coming into being of Bach's music.

One of the underlying premises of the BCP was a feeling I found I shared with several other musicians: that our need to study, listen to and grapple with Bach's music is perhaps greater today than at any time in the past. Many of us also hoped that by emphasising this particular manifestation of our common cultural heritage, it would raise the spirits of those who came to hear us, no matter whether they were listening to it, or whether we were playing it, for the first, second or twenty-second time.

Milan Kundera once described the intrinsic elusiveness of the present moment:

> There would seem to be nothing more obvious, more tangible and palpable than the present moment. And yet it eludes us completely. All the sadness of life lies in that fact. In the course of a single second, our senses of sight, of hearing, of smell, register (knowingly or not) a swarm of events and a parade of sensations and ideas passes through our head. Each instant represents a little universe, irrevocably forgotten in the next instant.[3]

The miracle of music is that it allows us to step aside momentarily from Kundera's temporal evanescence. A musical work such as a Bach cantata is manifestly a journey from a beginning, through a middle, and to an end, and yet at that end the light it casts in the memory on all that has gone before creates the feeling that we are constantly in a state of arrival – leading to a sense of being aware of, and thus valuing, our own consciousness, both now and in what went before. And, if we accept that one part of the human psyche searches for a spiritual outlet (and, indeed, a spiritual input), then however materialistic our society may have become, however agnostic the *Zeitgeist*, for those who have the ears to hear it, the confident and overwhelmingly affirmative music of Bach can go a long way towards meeting this need. For Bach is of the very front rank of composers since 1700 whose entire work was geared, one way or another, towards the spiritual and the metaphysical – celebrating life, but also befriending and exorcising death. He saw both the essence and practice of music as religious, and understood that the more perfectly a composition is realised, both conceptually and through performance, the more God is immanent in the music. 'NB', he wrote in the margin of his copy of Abraham Calov's Bible commentary: 'Where there is devotional music, God with his grace is always present.'[4] (See Plate 13.) This strikes me as a tenet that many of us as musicians automatically hold and aspire to whenever we meet to play music, regardless of whatever 'God' we happen to believe in.

So, at a time when the churches have long since lost their drawing power in the West, our choice to perform the cantatas of Bach in churches merely underscored the once-living context of this music. The course of the Bach Cantata Pilgrimage is a story for another place and another time; but we were to ask ourselves several times in the course of that year whether Bach's original purpose (and perhaps also its effect), besides meeting an urgent need for inspiration and solace, was to jolt his first listeners out of their complacency and to spotlight meretricious aspects of their lives and conduct. Bach, the supreme artisan, disdained by some of Leipzig's intelligentsia for his lack of university training, and conscious of his place in his family's history, honed his skills to the point where his craftsmanship, his imaginative gift and his human empathy were in perfect balance. The rest was up to God.

2

Germany on the Brink of Enlightenment

Without language we would have no reason, without reason no religion, and without these three essential aspects of our nature, neither mind nor bond of society.

– Johann Georg Hamann[1]

The 'Germany' in which Bach was born in 1685 was a peculiar political jigsaw – a multitude of independent duchies, principalities and imperial 'free' cities. If you were to turn the individual pieces over blank-side up you would probably have no difficulty in fitting them back together again, so random were the sizes of the separate *Länder*, so quirky their geographical shapes. The Holy Roman Empire, itself territorially and structurally subdivided, had shrunk during the past century to a mere shadow of its former self. In Auerbach's Tavern in Leipzig the song went up:

> The Holy Roman Empire, we all love it so;
> But how it holds together, that we do not know.[2]

The German jurist and political philosopher Samuel von Pufendorf observed wryly in 1667 that, being neither a 'regular kingdom' nor a republic, 'we are therefore left with calling a [political] body "German" that conforms to no rule and resembles a monster.'[3] Did Bach ever even think of himself, first and foremost, as a German, as opposed to a Thuringian or a Saxon? He was born in Eisenach, in the heart of the Thuringian Forest, the youngest son of the town piper, and his dialect was probably strong enough to make him seem a foreigner to his exact contemporary Georg Friederich Händel, born only forty miles away in a former corner of Saxony that had recently become part of Prussia.

Neither of these future musical giants, therefore, was likely to have been concerned or terrorised by Pufendorf's monster.

At the time of their birth, the Electorate of Saxony was still the dominant force in northern Germany, thanks to its wealth and to its Elector's position as the leader of the Protestant body, the *Corpus Evangelicorum.** But when Friedrich Wilhelm (1620–88) acceded as Elector of Brandenburg and Duke of Prussia in 1640, dynastic power began to shift inexorably from the imperial Habsburgs in Austria and Bohemia to the Hohenzollerns further north – and was solidified the moment his son Friedrich III overruled the advice of his closest counsellors and crowned himself King Frederick I of Prussia in 1701. Meanwhile, despite its obvious absurdities and disparate nature, the Empire survived, thanks to the skill with which the Habsburgs managed to blur the division between state and civil society, drawing the several layers of the German-speaking world into the political process.

Immediately bound to the Emperor were the 'Imperial Knights' – the heads of around 350 noble landowning families who exercised administrative responsibility for about 1,500 estates covering almost 5,000 square miles. More powerful still – and considerably less biddable – were the landed and urban elites right across the Empire who had won a say for themselves through representation in the legislative body, the *Reichstag*. Pufendorf commented 'the Estates of Germany ... have a considerable share of the sovereignty over their subjects ... a main obstacle to the Emperor making himself absolute.' A double layer of institutions thus restricted the Emperor's untrammelled sovereignty – the Reichstag itself, which from 1663 on was in permanent session in Regensburg, and the 300 or so *Reichsstände*, those constituent principalities with a direct or indirect vote in the Reichstag. Their most powerful constitutional weapon was the electoral pact known as the *Wahlkapitulation*, which a Prince-Elector swore to abide by prior to his coronation and was obliged to sign as a condition of his election.

Forming a second layer of authority within each Reichsstand were

* Formally organised in 1653 to provide the civil administration and security of German Protestants, its presidency stayed permanently attached to Saxony even after August the Strong converted to Catholicism in order to win election as King of Poland in 1697. With the advantage of hindsight we can see August's decision as a terrible mistake, but to many contemporaries the addition of Poland's quantity to Saxony's quality seemed to confirm the latter's status as the chief rival to the Habsburgs.

the *Landstände*,* each with its own local legislative body known as the *Landschaft*, noted for its elaborate protocols. Pufendorf concluded, 'Though it is certain that Germany within itself is so potent, that it might be formidable to all its neighbours if its strength was well united and rightly employed; nevertheless this strong body also has its infirmities which weaken its strength and slacken its vigour, its irregular constitution of government being one of the chief causes of its distemper.' One of its 'infirmities' was caused by the fact that most of the Landschaft proceedings between the several factions and lobbies were conducted in writing – an administrative hindrance. In electoral Saxony, it was precisely this 'irregular constitution' – and the continual tension between those loyal to the Elector (the ruling or Absolutist Party) on one side, and those nobles and urban middle-class burghers who had formed an uneasy alliance to curb his power (the Estates Party) on the other – that was a constant factor all through Bach's working life in Leipzig.

Imperial power was weakened still further by the fifty or so 'free' cities, or *Reichstädte*, the richest of them (which included Hamburg and Frankfurt am Main) forming self-governing enclaves brooking no outside interference and with total control over their own trade. In his early twenties Bach was to work as a municipal musician in one of these 'free' cities (Mühlhausen) and to visit several others. Parallel to this, a complex imperial system of legal regulations had accreted over the centuries, throttling, if not altogether paralysing, the channels of trade and physical communication (barges on the Rhine, for instance, were required to pay frontier tolls on average every six miles). From the administration and interaction of these principalities, the German bureaucratic mentality was born, and with it the defining protocols and stultifying niceties of rank that were a constant in Bach's life and a bone of contention in his disputes with employers.†

* * *

* For example, the Electorate of Bavaria was a Reichsstand, but within its boundaries there were Landstände, representing the church and the nobility. The mix varied from one Reichsstand to another: in some the church was not represented, in others the nobles were not.

† Coincidentally, in the year of Bach's birth, Louis XIV revoked the Edict of Nantes (1598) and with it the limited degree of toleration accorded to French Protestants. Suddenly there was a flood of Huguenot refugees spreading north to Holland and England but also east across the Rhine. In welcoming around 14,000 of them to settle in his territories, the Elector Frederick William of Brandenburg set a trend for further waves of immigration by refugees of conscience – from Bohemia and Austria as well as from France – a *Peuplierungspolitik*

Suppose we were able to travel back in time to this curious patchwork that constituted Germany at the time Bach was born. What would be the things to strike us most forcefully: evidence of vigorous urban renewal, signs of a predominantly rural society beginning to mend, or the still-visible scars of war? The Thirty Years War had been the longest, bloodiest and most destructive to be fought on German soil and retained that reputation until the late twentieth century. The Silesian poet Andreas Gryphius (1616–64) witnessed it all at first hand and wrote of the pointlessness of human existence. One of his sonnets, 'Menschliches Elende' ('Human Misery'), from his *Kirchhofs-Gedanken* (*Cemetery Thoughts*) of 1656, begins:

> What then is man? A house of grim pain,
> A ball of false hopes, a madness of this time,
> A theatre of bitter fear filled with keen sorrow,
> A soon melting snow, a burnt-out candle.*

Now, almost forty years since the Peace of Westphalia (1648) had brought it to a close, the war's horrors were still present in everyone's memory.

The nearest we have to a contemporary war diary, full of atrocity and lurid details, are two novels by Hans Jakob Christoffel von Grimmelshausen – *Der abenteuerliche Simplicissimus* (1669) and *Trutz Simplex* (1670), the latter a 'detailed and miraculous account of the life of the arch-swindler and renegade Courage'. Based on his first-hand experiences as a stable boy in the Imperial Army and later as a regimental clerk, they provide a catalogue of wanton murder, rape and cannibalism. But, even allowing for the degree of fictitious reportage that stoked the persistent pathos-laden portrayal of the war by nineteenth- and early-twentieth-century German historians, the general impression is still a bleak one: with countless villages and hamlets flattened by the invading armies, Germany's medieval towns pillaged and burnt beyond recognition, whole regions depopulated by military action, families

---

which was soon to have an impact both in repopulating rural areas decimated by plague and in augmenting the skilled labour force of the towns, so providing Prussia and the other Länder which followed its lead with a significant economic edge over the old Empire.

* *Was sind wir Menschen doch? Ein Wohnhaus grimmer Schmerzen,*
Ein Ball des falschen Glücks, ein Irrlicht dieser Zeit,
Ein Schauplatz herber Angst, besetzt mit scharfem Leid,
Ein bald verschmelzter Schnee und abgebrannte Kerzen.

decimated and the survivors' lives turned upside down. Inevitably the countryside suffered more than most towns, because that was where the battles were fought, Thuringia being one of the worst affected areas. Wherever Wallenstein or the invading Danes and Swedes trod – particularly along the older trade routes that linked the main commercial towns – the process of economic recovery was painfully slow.

Wave after wave of plague followed in the wake of war: weakened by hunger, victims' bodies provided easy prey for the pathogens spread by the armies. Plague was responsible for a higher death toll than the conflict itself. Roughly one third of Saxony's population, and half of Thuringia's, had been wiped out. But we should be wary: these demographic losses – whether due to slaughter, malnutrition or disease – may have been exaggerated in the surviving sources.[4] Local officials had an interest in massaging the figures upwards, hoping thereby to qualify for tax relief or an increased share of government restoration funds. Take the case of a major commercial centre like Leipzig. During the war years it had suffered three epidemics – in 1626, 1636 and 1643 – and still continued with its biennial trade fairs. Yet, more than thirty years after the ending of the war and well on the way towards recovery, the city was sent reeling again by a fresh outbreak in 1680, which, according to the diary kept by Rektor Jakob Thomasius, took away 2,200 souls in five months – far more than the sum of all the previous epidemics and more than 10 per cent of the entire citizenry.*

From our twenty-first-century perspective it is easy to exaggerate and over-dramatise the effects of the Thirty Years War on Germany as a whole – if only because the impact of this prolonged conflict was so varied and localised. In the past, German historians were inclined to blame the war for the economic malaise, whereas it can now been seen to be part of a longer trend of overall decline and shifting patterns of commerce which had begun years before. The lucrative trade with Italy, once plied by great entrepreneurs such as the Fuggers of Augsburg, was now reduced to a trickle.† Europe's demographic centre of gravity was

* Yet, for a short time, when famine and sickness blighted the Saxon countryside during the 1630s, it seems the population of Leipzig actually increased by as much as a third (see Geoffrey Parker (ed.), *The Thirty Years' War* (second edition, 1997), p. 189).

† Recent climatic changes had made the Alpine passes more arduous; yet German travellers were still drawn to Italy like moths to a light – not so much to trade as to admire Italian art of the past and music very much of the present.

moving northwards, and in parallel motion its commercial future was heading to the Hanseatic ports along the Atlantic seaboard. Trade and manufacture were generally slower to rally than the population, with recovery more rapid in the towns, more gradual in the countryside. It needs little imagination to envisage the vast amounts of grain and beef required to feed successive marauding armies living like locusts off the land. The rural community survived gnawing hunger, living, like Grimmelshausen's 'strange vagabond', on buckwheat, beechnuts, acorns, frogs, snails and whatever vegetables could be salvaged.[5] Now things were getting back to normal; but it would be another ninety years before the enlightened despot Frederick the Great recognised that 'agriculture comes first among human activities. Without it there would be no merchants, no courtiers, no kings, no poets and no philosophers. The only true form of wealth is that produced by the soil.'[6]*

All the while a solution lay at hand to the problem of battle-proof food supplies: the common potato. Originating in the Andes (somewhere in modern-day Peru or Bolivia) and known in Europe since the late 1500s, where it was thought to have aphrodisiac properties, it was inexplicably slow to catch on. As every gardener knows, the potato is a miracle tuber – easy to plant, fast growing, susceptible to blight, yet capable under the right conditions of producing spectacular yields – five times that of any other European crop and ten times that of wheat (slightly less for rye), which more than compensates for its lower calorific value. Crucially important, an army could camp all summer on a potato field without damaging the autumn crop. Antoine-Augustin Parmentier discovered the potato for France as a prisoner of the Prussians during the Seven Years War, but it was not until the 1770s that it was grown extensively as a field-crop in Germany. Even then the burghers of Kolberg complained to Frederick the Great that 'the things have neither smell nor taste, not even the dogs will eat them, so what are they to us?' But eventually Kartoffel-mania took hold; so that when, for example, Mr and Mrs Henry Mayhew spent a year in Thuringia (1864), they found that in Bach's birthplace

* Farmers have always known this, as well as being the first to acknowledge – and to complain – that the growing of crops is a hazardous enterprise bedevilled by the usual vagaries of weather and common rights of grazing. For everyone else its centrality to existence was taken completely for granted – that is ignored, in 1685 and for ever after.

> the quantity of potatoes consumed by the people of Eisenach is really incredible, and hence the reason for the universal manure-storing throughout the city. Half an acre of potato land yields upon the average 36–40 sacks of 100 and odd pounds each, or between 3,600 and 4,000 pounds' weight, and this is what each Eisenach family requires every year for the consumption of their pigs and themselves. In fact, many of the modern Saxons know no other food – living even harder than the poorest Irish do in our country; the members of the family eating no less than 2,000 pounds' weight of potatoes in the course of the year, which is at the rate of more than 5 pounds a day.[7]

Almost certainly, potatoes never formed a significant part of Bach's staple diet, but, while he manifestly never suffered from malnutrition, successive generations of his ancestors did – and we can only lament that they had no access to the common spud.

* * *

At the time of Bach's birth, one geophysical feature predominated: the forest.* The Thüringerwald simply *was* the rural landscape, extending to the very margins of villages and settlements (those that had not simply vanished during the war), and even to sizeable towns such as Eisenach, which had a current population of around 6,000 inhabitants. More serious even than the wartime damage to the standing timber and the biodiversity of the understorey was the loss of practical silvicultural know-how – the care and replenishment of forests. To make matters worse, princely landowners had started to take an interest in the way their forests were managed, the huntsman eclipsing the trained forester (just as today the pheasant and the gamekeeper have more sway than

* Arriving there from Wessex in southern England in the eighth century, St Boniface came across a Thuringian tribe worshipping a Norse deity in the form of a huge oak tree. Legend has it that he removed his shirt, grabbed hold of an axe, and without a word hacked down the six-foot-wide wooden god. Thereupon Boniface stood on the trunk and challenged the tribal chieftains: 'Now, how stands your mighty god? My God is stronger than he!' The crowd's reaction was mixed, but the first conversions had begun. It was slow progress and it took until the twelfth century for the Cistercians to cement the process. The monks also knew intuitively that soils in which timber trees flourished so impressively were also well suited to the growing of domestic crops, so beginning a process of self-sufficiency which eventually led to the characteristic mosaic of arable fields and woodland in Thuringia we recognise today.

the genuine woodman). Since the ending of the war, all across German lands forests were being felled at unsustainable rates without efforts to tend, restore or replant them, though the preponderant beech stands of the Thüringerwald seem to have escaped the greedy felling for naval timber that took place elsewhere, beech being an unsatisfactory timber for ship building. By 1700 the Saxon mining industry centred on the Erzgebirge (Ore Mountains) had consumed great swathes of forest and the livelihoods of thousands were threatened due to an acute scarcity of timber. When it is not worked regularly, woodland tends to disappear; the idea of sustainability emerges only in times of crisis and scarcity. It was an idea that found its champion in Hans Carl von Carlowitz (1645–1714), a tax accountant and mining administrator from Freiberg in middle Saxony; he was the first to give a clear formulation of the concept of sustainability in forestry: how to foster natural regeneration, collect seeds from seed trees, prepare the soil for planting on bare ground, care for seedlings and saplings, and maintain the varied and subtle ecosystem (not that he called it that) of the coppice cycle.[8] Difficult as it is to measure Carlowitz's influence – the extent to which aristocratic landowners followed his recommendations, and at what pace – there are signs of a slow, painful process of recovery in forest management in Bach's lifetime.[9]

* * *

Es spukt hier! – 'It's spooky here!' This seems to have been a common reaction to the war-scarred landscape of central Germany for several generations after the signing of the Peace of Westphalia: the emptiness of the primeval forest with its undertones of demonic power unleashed by the long war. One could argue that it persisted at least until the dawn of the Romantic era, coming to a head in the central scene of Weber's great opera *Der Freischütz* (1821) – the *furchtbare Waldschlucht* ('The fearsome Wolf's Glen'), a legendary abyss in the depths of the *Urwald*, where lurks everything vile, horrifying and evil.[10] The idea obtained that lasting damage had been perpetrated not just on the physical features of the landscape, but also on the collective psyche – as though local populations beginning to rebuild their lives had been forced to come to terms with a subtle impairment to their spiritual environment, as well as with the destruction of their houses and holdings. This is of course impossible to describe precisely, being a product of a complex interaction between physical location and what goes on in the minds and the subconscious of local inhabitants, each with his or her own private baggage of beliefs, rituals and superstitions.* Our modern compartmentalised ways of thinking, looking and hearing can shut us off from observing these inner workings of the past. But a cognitive exploration or scanning of these mental 'fields' – one which aims to identify features of past consciousness left in the landscape alongside the physical scars – could help us towards a deeper understanding of the cultural and psychological world into which Bach was born. As it is, there is enough circumstantial evidence to suggest that the German heartlands remained in a state of trauma long after the invading armies had retreated from the bloody religious wars, and that an intensely rural area like Thuringia, rich in the archaeology of its landscape – sacred sites, rivers, forests and hills – retreated into a kind of self-imposed provinciality; sealed against the outside world and far removed from the literary and scientific movement we now call the 'Age of Enlightenment', it seemed to be awaiting both economic and spiritual renewal.

Symbolically it was a ducal forester, Johann Georg Koch, who, as one of Bach's two godfathers, stood next to the baptismal font to witness his baptism. As a young lad Bach had only to step outside the family home in the Fleischgasse and pick his way through the crowds, the pigs, the poultry and the cattle, before he found himself in the dense woodland that encircled the Wartburg, the hilltop castle overlooking the town. Sylvan myths and pagan rituals (such as the fertility festival Sommergewinn, usually celebrated on the third Saturday before Easter) could not easily be suppressed; to the Thuringians, the forest, home to presiding tribal divinities, retained the magic aura of the wilderness, and was a source of 'natural' meteorological phenomena – like the violent electrical storms, of which Luther was apparently terrified, convinced that they came from the Devil. So they said prayers in church, roared

* According to Peter H. Wilson, 'The war nonetheless left people traumatized. Though patchy, there is evidence of what today would be called post-traumatic stress disorder' (*Europe's Tragedy* (2009), p. 849) and of a parallel emphasis on penance and piety in the Lutheran apocalyptical response to the war (see Thomas Kaufmann, *Dreißigjähriger Krieg und westfälischer Friede. Kirchengeschichtliche Studien zur lutherischen Konfessionskultur* (1998), pp. 34–6, 76, 101, 106).

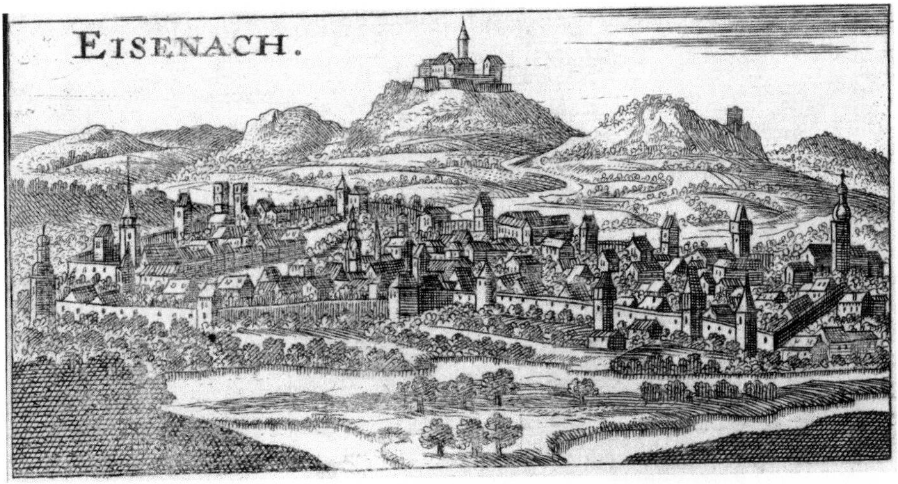

A seventeenth-century engraving of Eisenach, with the Wartburg in the distance.

out their hymns, rang the church bells to ward off hurricanes and tempests, and in wartime took to the woods for refuge.

Even with a powerful layer of Protestant theology added to the inhabitants' lives, the forest remained both mysterious and threatening, as can be seen in the paintings by Luther's friend Lucas Cranach, in the woodcuts by Albrecht Dürer, emphasising its engulfing luxuriance, and in the landscape paintings of Albrecht Altdorfer. Music was there to give strength as well as to placate the tutelary sylvan gods. It is surely no accident that in a land of much communal music-making, so many folksongs rich in woodland themes should have survived. The power of song here was perhaps not quite that of the Australian Aboriginals – the principal means by which they marked out their territory and organised their social life – but it did not lag far behind, the thinnest of membranes separating song, creation-myth, landscape and boundaries. One can picture the day on which the fifteen-year-old Bach first set off on foot out of his Thuringian homeland with his companion Georg Erdmann, the boys singing to keep up their spirits on their 200-mile tramp northwards along rutted cart tracks to Lüneburg.

For the budding choristers, song was both their passport and their meal ticket.*

***

Vestiges of this superstitious consciousness prevalent in Thuringia at the time of Bach's birth coexisted with a vigorous renewal of Lutheranism and, in its wake, religious music. Several of the secular folksongs that Luther had enjoyed as a university student in Erfurt and accompanied on his lute had gradually forced their way into his church, but with new respectable texts: the colourful imagery and bawdy suggestiveness of the originals, together with their substrata of pagan myth and folk-memory, had been sublimated in the sturdy vernacular hymns that Bach sang as a boy and knew by heart. Luther had been determined to make religious experience vivid to his fellow Germans through language that was colloquial, lucid and rhythmic, capable at times of rising to emotional heights with sudden urgent phrases, but also of reinforcing shared identities and absorbing the full mythology of a collective past. He had been concerned that, in participating in liturgical music, people's hearts and minds should be in harmony with what they were expressing through their mouths: 'We must take care . . . lest the people sing only with their lips, like sounding pipes or harps (I Corinthians 14:7), and

* One wonders whether in Bach's day the word *Laub* ('leaves') still retained its sixteenth-century connotation of tabernacle or holy sanctuary as well as of foliage (see Simon Schama, *Landscape and Memory* (1995), p. 585, n. 61). It is possible that Thuringian trees were no more to him than simply the fixtures and fittings on the stage-set of his childhood – undeniably there, unremarkable and almost unnoticed, but I doubt it. At all events, my instinct is that, besides any residual religious associations the forest may still have retained, Bach could have learnt lessons about his human limitations and presumptions by observing trees and woods whose lives and timeframes do not conform to tidy human models. Maybe he even learnt the importance of wildness to the human spirit – as an antidote to the rigour and disciplined structure of his Lutheran education. When recounting her travels up the Amazon and witnessing the destruction of the rainforest by the logging companies, the author Jay Griffiths howls, 'if you take people out of their land, you take them out of their meaning, out of their language's roots. When wild lands are lost, so is metaphor, allusion and the poetry that arises in the interplay of mind and nature' (*Wild* (2007), pp. 25–7). We cannot of course tell whether Bach was aware of, let alone inspired by, 'the long cyclical rhythms' by which the forest renewed itself, and of the tension between those concerned with its survival and those who had a stake in its open areas for grazing (the commoners, in other words). Richard Mabey tells us that an acre of old woodland containing, say, thirty 300-year-old beeches can be renewed by just ten new seedlings reaching adulthood every hundred years (*Beechcombings* (2008), p. 84).

without understanding,' he wrote.[11] He himself contributed new German texts to sixteen out of the twenty-four hymns printed for the first time in 1524. One of the most stirring of them – 'Ein' feste Burg ist unser Gott' ('A mighty fortress is our God') – has music *and* words by Luther, voicing in an irresistible way the conviction and solidity he had found in God's protection during his own private struggles with Satan. Singing these chorales and psalms in the vernacular, both in church and at home, became the hallmark of Lutheran Protestants such as the Bach family, united in fervent companionship – rather as the collective chant does on the terraces of football stadiums today. According to the philosopher Johann Gottfried Herder (1744–1803), the chorales retained the moral effectiveness (he called it a 'treasury of life') that German folk-poetry and folksong had once possessed but by his day had lost.*

A century after his death, traces of Luther's influence were everywhere to be found in Thuringia, not least in its musical life (see Chapter 5). Even the smallest parish church could soon boast its own pipe organ, often with a specially decorated casement and framed by a curved choir gallery from where local craftsmen and farm workers, standing in a group, could sing during the service.† Though these foundations were strong, and though the newly forged links between music, language and the preaching of God's Word were firmly lodged in the minds of Thuringians, the entire process was severely undermined by the spiralling violence of the Thirty Years War. Fear of death was matched by fear of life itself, which had become tainted through the sustained distress of warfare, malnutrition and disease. With average life expectancy falling

* Herder deplored what he saw as the separation of words and music – the moment the poet begins to write 'slowly; in order to be read', art may be the winner, but there is a loss of magic, of 'miraculous power' (Herder's *Sämmtliche Werke*, Bernhard Suphan (ed.) (1877–1913), Vol. 8, pp. 412, 390). He spoke of linguistic petrifaction, and of how, in Isaiah Berlin's words, 'writing is incapable of that living process of constant adaptation and change, of the constant expression of the unanalysable and unseizable flow of actual experience, which language, if it is to communicate fully, must possess. Language alone makes experience possible, but it also freezes it' (Isaiah Berlin, *Three Critics of the Enlightenment* (2000), p. 194). It will be a pervasive theme of this book to show how Bach's texted music possesses exactly this 'living process' and the constant and essential expression of the 'flow of actual experience', which, according to Herder, language on its own lacks and petrifies.

† They still do. Before our cantata concert in Eisenach on Easter Day 2000, the pastor of the Georgenkirche invited me, and members of my choir and orchestra, to lead the singing in the Hauptgottesdienst. In the middle of the Mass we were suddenly joined in the organ gallery by a group of local farmers who sang a short litany in Thuringian dialect and departed.

to thirty, never had the words from the burial service *Mitten wir im Leben sind* ('In the midst of life we are in death') held such poignancy. Indoctrinated by the message from the pulpits that the war was the scourge of God to punish a sinful people, many of the survivors felt that God had indeed deserted them.[12] Old images of the late-medieval Totentanz – those lurid paintings of naked women in the grip of leering and cavorting skeletons that appeared on the walls of many German churches (at least those that had been left un-whitewashed by the Reformation, such as Bernt Notke's in Lübeck's Marienkirche, which Bach visited as a twenty-year-old) – acquired a new eerie relevance. Much of the music to emerge from the war years (including that of Bach's immediate ancestors) now gave a similar topical emphasis to the vanity of human existence. And, while domestic and parochial music-making may have survived furtively, the more sophisticated and innovative ensemble-based music of the towns and ducal courts suffered badly. Typical of German church musicians of the time, Johann Vierdanck (organist in Stralsund, on the Baltic coast) bemoaned the fact that as a result of the war 'nothing but weeping and wailing is to be heard' in thousands of places instead of the usual sacred music.[13]

The clearest evidence of this malaise comes from the foremost German musician of his day, Heinrich Schütz (1585–1672), who, after two spells of study in Venice, first as a pupil of Giovanni Gabrieli, later conferring with Claudio Monteverdi, spent his thirty-third to sixty-third years in the eye of the war's storm as Capellmeister to the Dresden Court. (See Plate 4.) His letters convey a picture of widespread depredation and demoralisation, but also the immense courage required to keep alive one's personal faith – or any artistic outlet for it – in such straitened circumstances. Nonetheless he managed under these stressful conditions to compose music of a persuasive and consoling profundity. Schütz took it as a personal affront that for some years the Dresden Court, which he loyally served, had reneged on its obligations to the musicians on its payroll. With their salaries now frozen, Schütz paid them 300 thalers out of his own pocket, realised from his own 'securities, paintings and silver'. The case of Georg Kaiser, his favourite bass, caused him particular anguish. Writing to the Elector in person in May 1652, Schütz reported that Kaiser was living 'like a sow in a pigsty, with no bedding, lying on straw; from poverty he has recently pawned his coat and his jacket and now paces about his house like a beast in the forest ... on no account must he be let go ... another like him cannot be found'. Schütz's sense of outrage at this indignity built to a climax: 'I find it neither praiseworthy nor Christian that in a land so highly esteemed, less than twenty musicians cannot or will not be supported, and I live in a most sublime hope that your Electoral Highness will have a change of heart.'[14]

Further west in Thuringia, a similar lot might so easily have befallen the Bach family, and it was uncertain whether they would survive in their chosen profession into the new century. Here the status of craftsmen – and that included musicians – remained precarious. Heavily reliant on the guild system of patronage, they existed from hand to mouth, dependent, like Schütz, on the whims of their employers, easily disrupted by budgetary cuts and subject to illicit undercutting by freelance *bierfiedler* ('beer fiddlers'). As skilled professionals they found themselves obliged to maintain an uneasy balance between working at court and for the municipality. Each activity commanded its own system of fees. Eisenach, as the seat since 1672 of an independent duchy, was perhaps more fortunate than many Thuringian towns in having Duke Johann Georg (1665–98), a keen patron of the arts. One moment Bach's own father, Ambrosius, might have to appear dressed in livery to play for the Duke as part of his private orchestra, the next he might be found trumpeting 'tower pieces' outside on the balcony of the town hall, or playing 'church pieces' inside to adorn the liturgy. It would take a generation before the benefits of this artistic patronage began to percolate through to all levels of the town's society.

It has been suggested that Thuringia was developing into 'an economically and culturally vigorous region' so soon after the ending of the war, because it was placed at an 'important intersection of east–west and north–south Continental trade routes which made the area particularly susceptible to foreign influences ... [where] as almost nowhere else to such an extent, the manifold European trends met and merged, generating a unique climate'.[15] There is, alas, little evidence for this. On the contrary, most of the townspeople, despite the ducal patronage, found themselves in 1700 'in so bad a situation that many of them had no daily bread to consume at home but were too ashamed to go to the alms-houses, especially the many widows'.[16] The days when Eisenach had benefited from a flourishing internal trade route, linking Frankfurt, Erfurt and Leipzig and thence to the Baltic ports, were long since past, while the brief period of its cultural flowering still lay a little way in the future, in the period when Telemann made an impact on the music at court as its Capellmeister (1709–12). All through Bach's childhood, Eisenach was sealed in a provincial time warp.

* * *

To locate the most active centres of German music-making in the years leading up to Bach's birth one needs to look not at Thuringia but to the Hanseatic and Baltic ports where commerce had been quickest to revive, or to the musically active courts of Gottorf and Wolfenbüttel in northern Germany. It was there, paradoxically, that the vogue for Italian music was strongest. The influence of Catholic Church music, first via the Venetian composers Monteverdi and Grandi, and later through the Roman Giacomo Carissimi, acted as a blood transfusion to the music of the Lutheran Church. It inspired a whole generation of exceptionally talented composers, all born around the middle years of the seventeenth century, of whom Buxtehude was just the most famous. The names Bruhns, Förtsch, Meder, Theile, Geist, Österreich and Schürmann are little known today (even less than those of the previous generation, Förster, Weckmann, Bernhard, Krieger, Rosenmüller and Tunder), yet all of them had studied in Italy, met Italian musicians in employment in northern Europe, or encountered Italian music by means of the manuscript anthologies that circulated within the musical fraternity. Only a tiny fraction of their output exists in print today, but it is enough to whet one's appetite for hearing more of it performed.* These composers gave a new creative impetus to the process of grafting Italian styles of church music on to the native rootstock, fusing the vigour of vernacular declamation with the colour and passion of Italian sonorities. Given the bitter feeling between Catholic and Protestant, and the traces which remained of a deep-seated Germanic fear of the corruptive forces of Italian culture – going all the way back via the Renaissance humanist Conrad Celtis to Tacitus – this is remarkable.† But it is typical of the

* Their music has come down to us thanks to tireless copyists like Gustav Düben and Georg Österreich, and is discussed by Geoffrey Webber, whose stimulating *North German Church Music in the Age of Buxtehude* (1996) first inspired me to dig a little deeper into untapped treasure and to explore examples of it in the Berlin Staatsbibliothek.

† Tacitus' successor and advocate Conrad Celtis (1459–1508) beat the German drum in revolt against Italian culture: 'To such an extent are we corrupted by Italian sensuality and by fierce cruelty in extracting filthy lucre,' he maintained, 'that it would have been far more holy and reverent for us to practice that rude and rustic life of old, living within the bounds

inquisitive yet easy-going pragmatism of creative musicians in all ages that they should wish to source and acquire new techniques regardless of their provenance. In this way three successive generations of German composers, beginning with Schütz, came to acknowledge Italy as *die Mutter der edlen Musik* ('The mother of noble music') – both church and theatre music. Such an exchange of ideas across political and administrative frontiers, and across religious divisions, suggests a parallel with what George Steiner calls the '*communitas* of the sciences ... the ideal of a commonwealth of positive, beneficial truths, transcending the bloody, infantile conflicts of religious, dynastic and ethnic hatreds ... As Kepler reportedly said, amid the massacres of religious wars, the laws of elliptical motion belong to no man or principality.'[17] The same could be said of music.

More remarkable still was the way these composers somehow managed to skirt around the ideological tensions that had built up between the two competing strands of Lutheranism – Orthodoxy and Pietism, the latter emerging strongly as a movement of renewed spirituality within the Lutheran Church in the wake of the Thirty Years War. Their music displayed enough rhetorical vigour to win the approval of the Orthodox clergy, while their setting of devotional texts managed to find favour with some Pietists. At a superficial level the Pietists could be seen as 'anti-musical' in so far as they disapproved of concerted music in church as a matter of principle – of anything except for the plainest of congregational hymn-singing and a rather bland, sentimental type of 'spiritual song', and, even then, they debated hotly whether to restrict hymns to singers who shared the emotional tenor of the text, or even to

of self-control, than to have imported the paraphernalia of sensuality and greed which are never sated, and to have adopted foreign customs' (quoted in Schama, op. cit., p. 93). Bach's life is sandwiched between that of Celtis and that of another fervent custodian of German folk-memory, Johann Gottfried Herder. Herder argued 'for a culture organically rooted in the topography, customs, and communities of the local native tradition ... folklore, ballads, fairy tales, and popular poetry' (op. cit., pp. 102–3). Springing from a clan of musicians, Bach would instinctively have shared Herder's notion of what it is to belong to a family, a sect, a place, a period, a style, and of the role of music in cementing all of these: 'Their songs are the archives of their people, the treasury of their science and religion ... a picture of their domestic life in joy and in sorrow, by bridal bed and graveside ... Here everyone portrays himself and appears as he is' (translation in Burton Feldman and Robert D. Richardson (eds.), *The Rise of Modern Mythology 1680–1860* (2000), pp. 229–30).

abolish the use of Christian songs in open assemblies.* Gottfried Vockerodt, headmaster of a school in Gotha, encapsulated their position. Claiming that the first Christians knew only music that honoured God, he insisted that it should inspire devotion and be performed from the heart, not for worldly pleasure or ostentation. Pointing to the example of several dissipated Roman emperors (Nero, Claudius and Caligula), he warned that 'the misuse of music . . . is a most dangerous reef, along which many a young soul, as if called by Sirens . . . falls into dissoluteness and ungodliness.'[18] This was part of a pamphlet war between him and Johann Beer, a prolific novelist who was also concertmaster and librarian at the Weissenfels Court. Poking fun in his *Ursus murmurat* (*The Bear Growls*) and *Ursus vulpinatur* (*The Bear Turned Fox*) at Vockerodt's arguments, Beer insisted on the validity of music-making as a purely secular activity and as a suitable recreation for princes, arguing that musicians should be judged not on their behaviour or religious beliefs but purely on their musical achievements.[19]

Whenever their influence was in the ascendant, the Pietist clergy generally saw off any newfangled experiments that gave a prominent role to instruments in embellishing liturgical music. In their eyes this distracted the congregation from becoming more deeply involved and from focusing on God's Word. They were intensely loyal to the emotional core of Lutheranism, which, after all, issued from the psychological crisis of one profoundly neurotic monk who found peace in the surrender of his problem to Christ (the 'lion of Judah' who 'ends his victorious fight' over all the enemies of full humanity), enabling him to recover his own humanity. This psychological and emotional core to Lutheranism was what distinguished it from Calvinism, which from its inception was

* This was the conclusion of Johann Anastasius Freylinghausen (1670–1739) in introducing his *Geistreiches Gesangbuch* of 1704, while at the same time admitting the power of song to move sinners. The preface of a Pietist hymnal of 1733 gives specific instructions for its readers and singers to experience the emotions depicted by inspired hymnists so that 'he seizes all of the Psalms' powers and motions in himself and begins to sing as if the songs are not strange to him, but rather as if he had composed them himself, as his own prayer produced with the deeper sensations of his heart' (Wolfgang Schmitt, 'Die pietistische Kritik der "Künste": Untersuchung über die Entstehung einer neuen Kunstauffassung im 18. Jahrhundert', Diss. Köln (1958), p. 54). It was an issue that concerned the Orthodox clergy as much as the Pietists: outward conformity in worship and its music must be considered insufficient if it is not underpinned by an inner spirituality on the part of all worshippers.

systematic and intellectual (its founder being a lawyer), and the Pietists stayed with the old lambent naivety of the Luther of his conversion, convinced as they were that Orthodoxy had lost touch with the needs of ordinary Lutherans. One might expect them to have favoured English Puritan literature, yet ironically their emphasis on meditative forms of worship made them the natural allies of the very sort of Latin mystical poetry that was being revived by their arch-enemies, the Jesuits, in the Counter-Reformation countries of the south – authors such as St Bernard of Clairvaux and Thomas à Kempis, as well as the erotically saturated Song of Songs from the Old Testament. By this route composers such as Buxtehude or Bruhns managed to legitimise their powerfully expressive settings of sacred texts – introduced by the back door, as it were.

It took considerable ingenuity to placate the emphatic Pietist commitment to sober spiritual edification, all the while composing to an Orthodox agenda – one that saw concerted music as an indispensable part of worship, vigorously defending Article V of the Augsburg Confession (1530), which stated that faith comes through the preaching of the Gospel and the administration of the sacraments, and not through some independent inspiration of the Holy Spirit.[20]* A musical cauldron had been heated in the most unpromising and frigid of climates. It would be misleading to present the musical achievements of these composers as merely the necessary prelude to those of Bach – as part of

* Although Pietists were vociferous in their condemnation of the kind of luxury and ostentation characteristic of Baroque culture in general, and of a blurring of the boundaries between the secular and the religious, which they held to be incompatible with true Christianity, they themselves were not beyond reproach. They were perceived as subversive and dangerously egalitarian, and an official investigation by the Leipzig authorities in 1689–90 pointed to irregularities in their conventical gatherings (known as *collegia pietatis*) where free discussion of scriptural interpretation took place beyond the control of the clergy, breaking standard social divisions and allegedly accompanied by sexual impropriety. For example, Elisabeth Karig accused a medical student, Christian Gaulicke, of telling her and another woman that 'if she wanted to be enlightened, she should undress as if she were going to bed, and tried to explain this to her from the Bible' (Tanya Kevorkian, *Baroque Piety: Religion, Society, and Music in Leipzig 1650–1750* (2007), p. 164). Others complained that the Pietists inspired or partook of sexual orgies – slander, no doubt, but a consequence of the emotional incontinence of the 'born again', like members of many subsequent renewal movements. In this respect the German Pietists were different from the English Puritans with whom they seem otherwise to have shared so much. They were forced to go underground in Leipzig soon after 1690.

a teleological 'advance' – but they certainly form the backcloth to his arrival on the musical stage of northern Germany.

* * *

Meanwhile this new lease of religious life in Germany clashed so noisily with the simultaneous birth and rapid progress of modern science, one suspects that they were permanently at cross-purposes – a little like Galileo and his adversaries. In his *Dialogues on the Two Chief Systems of the World*, Galileo insists on *how* things happen, while his opponent Simplicius counters with a ready-made theory as to *why* things occur. Galileo's supreme achievement was, of course, to elaborate and build on Copernicus's discovery that the sun was the centre of the universe and the earth and planets rotated around it. From the moment when the seven cardinals who made up the Inquisition tribunal examining Galileo in 1633 stated unequivocally that 'the proposition that the sun is the centre of the world and immovable from its place is absurd, philosophically false, and formally heretical because it is expressly contrary to Holy Scriptures', the Catholic Church confirmed itself as a reactionary bastion against scientific investigation. Protestants, too, railed against Copernicus, leading Erasmus to comment that the sciences fell into ruin wherever Lutheranism prevailed. But this is not entirely fair, seeing that the Protestant world, despite its divisions, allowed natural philosophy a degree of room to manoeuvre denied to it by the Catholic Church. A generation after Galileo, Isaac Newton could still firmly believe as an Anglican that his discoveries 'pointed to the operations of God', while both Gottfried Leibniz (1646–1716) and his pupil Christian Wolff (1679–1754) gave a valuable boost to Orthodox Lutheranism by seeking to convince Germany's princes and intellectuals that the mechanistic laws of the new science were compatible with the 'moral necessity' of a God who consciously and eternally chooses the maximum degree of perfection.

Among the most teasing questions that arise the moment one tries to establish a cultural and intellectual context for Bach's appearance on the musical scene of Europe is the extent to which he, or any of his peers, was aware of the scientific revolution of the seventeenth century.* Yet, in

* If Bach had been taught at school that man was not the centre of the universe and that the earth rotated around the sun, would his acceptance of the main tenets of Lutheranism, which later fuelled his prodigious output of church music, have received a nasty blow?

Bach's case, a capacity for dealing with abstractions and for eliciting from them clear-cut demonstrative trains of reasoning was to provide the springboard for his imaginative thought as a composer.* Isaac Newton was born the year after Galileo died (1642), exactly one hundred years after Copernicus had published his *De revolutionibus*. From these foundations a coherent scheme of scientific thought emerged, one formulated by mathematicians for use by mathematicians, with Isaac Newton as its spearhead. In his *Philosophiae naturalis principia mathematica* (1687) Newton showed how his principle of universal gravitation accounted for the motions of heavenly bodies and of falling bodies on earth: every piece of matter attracts every other piece with a force proportional to the product of their masses and inversely proportional to the square of the distance between them. He prepared the way for a mechanisation of heaven and earth, for, although God might still have His place in a post-Newtonian universe, it was only as the original creator of the mechanism that then operated to a simple natural law requiring no continuous application of force. Initially Newton's ideas were accepted only by an intellectual elite, and it took at least a generation before they acquired sufficient currency for Alexander Pope to be able to write the following epitaph intended for Newton's tombstone in Westminster Abbey:

> Nature and Nature's laws lay hid in night;
> God said, Let Newton be! and all was light.

In such a mechanistic view of the universe there was no legitimate place for superstition; yet belief in witchcraft and magic (manifestly) persisted in Europe all through the Middle Ages, beyond the Reformation and throughout the seventeenth century. There is a certain irony here in that Newton and his contemporary Robert Boyle, besides their empirical scientific work, which undermined the very foundations of witchcraft and all other forms of magic, were also themselves alchemists. Newton wrote two million words on theology and alchemy, and took a

* As we shall see, later in life he certainly shared with Galileo an attachment to 'irreducible and stubborn facts', with Spinoza (as proposed by John Butt in Chapter 5 of *The Cambridge Companion to Bach* (1997)) the belief that 'the more we understand singular things, the more we understand God' (*Ethics*, Part V, 24) and with Leibniz the idea that 'the means of obtaining as much variety as possible, but with the greatest possible order . . . is the means of obtaining as much perfection as possible' (*Monadology*, paras. 57–8).

keen interest in astrology. Boyle challenged traditional chemistry in *Sceptical Chymist; or, Chymico-Physical Doubts and Paradoxes* in 1661 but also practised alchemy and could never abandon his belief in miracles. Despite the dissemination of empirical knowledge, witches were still being accused, tortured and executed in parts of Germany well into the eighteenth century. In and around Leipzig there were ten documented trials for witchcraft between 1650 and 1750.[21] Bach himself could have witnessed the cases brought in 1730 against two women by a Leipzig physician on charges of quackery and the practice of magic. This shows how superstition and 'enlightenment' continued to coexist even in a university town, and how slowly a heliocentric and mechanistic view of the universe impinged on ordinary citizens, on Saxon society as a whole and, as we are about to see, on the teaching in schools.

* * *

If it were possible to peer into the classrooms of a typical Latin School in Thuringia at the turn of the seventeenth to eighteenth century and to eavesdrop on the way lessons were taught, what would we notice? Our eye might first be drawn to ten pictures pinned to the walls – of fantastical animals including a dragon, a griffin and a Cerberus, each creature standing allegorically for a different millennium or century and arranged alphabetically. This was not school artwork, but part of an ingenious method recently developed by the Lüneburg theologian and pedagogue Johannes Buno (1617–97) to jog pupils' memory through a simultaneous interconnection between animals, letters, numbers, and specific historical figures or epochs. (See Plate 3b.) Then we could not fail to be struck by the sheer amount of music in class. In his famous poem entitled 'Frau Musica', Luther had personified music and singing as a lady who 'gives God more joy and mirth / than all the pleasures of the earth'.[22] More valuable even than 'the precious nightingale', Music was created by God to be His true songstress and mistress, one who tirelessly offers Him thanks:

> For she sings and dances day and night
> Never tiring [of singing] His praise.

Singing became the main element in musical tuition within the Lutheran school system of the day. Morning school began at 6 a.m. in summer and at 7 a.m. in midwinter, and started with the collective

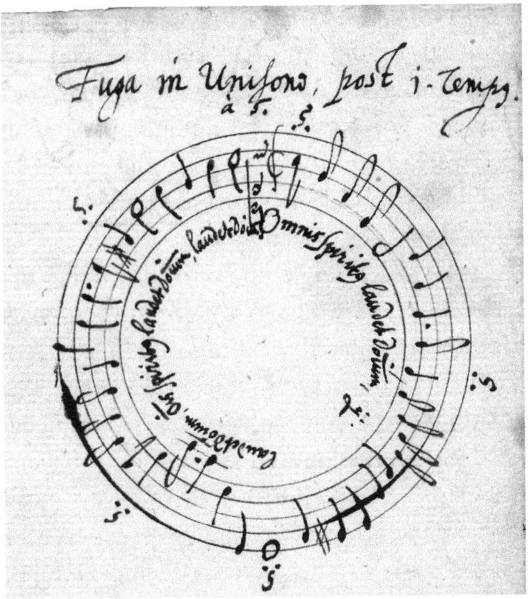

Five-part circular canon by Johann Hermann Schein (1586–1630) of the kind used to train schoolchildren to sing polyphony.

chanting of the *Katechismuslied*, its six basic tenets apportioned to each of the six weekdays, set to music by sixteenth-century composers such as Vulpius, Calvisius, Gesius and, later, by J. H. Schein, who was cantor of the Thomaskirche in Leipzig. Group singing practice was scheduled to take place five times a week in the first hour after the midday meal (presumably on the advice of German physicians, who believed that singing aided digestion).[23] The local cantor was seen primarily as a schoolteacher.* 'What is music?' he might challenge the assembled pupils. 'A science of singing' was the answer they were expected to chorus in reply.[24]

As Luther said, 'A schoolmaster must be able to sing; otherwise I won't acknowledge him.'[25] Besides the cantor, other members of a Latin

* This responsibility was laid down as early as 1528 in a church ordinance by Luther's disciple Johann Bugenhagen: 'It is your particular duty that you teach singing to all children, old and young, learned or less so, to sing together in German and in Latin, moreover also figural music not only as is customary, but also in future in an artistic manner, so that the children learn to understand the voices, the clefs, and whatever else belongs to such music, so that they learn to sing dependably, purely in tune, etc., etc.' (Georg Schünemann, *Geschichte der Deutschen Schulmusik* (1928), p. 83).

School staff were often expected to be proficient in music. In an updated version of the medieval trivium, music in Lutheran schools was considered an adjunct to the study of grammar, logic and rhetoric, while singing was valued as a proven way of helping pupils to commit things to memory.[26] They were taught the practical rudiments of music – rules for clefs, rests and intervals, sight-reading and part-singing – mostly by singing in canon. The beauty of canon-singing lay in its simplicity of means. All it took was just a single line of music, either distributed to the class or sung by the teacher. The first voice or group began, then, at a given point, the second entered with the same melody, and so on – enough to reveal independence of voice lines and, through their combination, the ability to create polyphony. A fully fledged piece of harmony, formed by the layering and spacing out of melodic entries, emerged miraculously – neatly illustrating the way music could be regarded, as one seventeenth-century theorist proposed, as 'a Godly act . . . its song and sound . . . a heart-bell, which penetrates every little vein of the heart and its Affects (be a man a very Stoic or an immovable trunk)'.[27] It was also a vivid aural replica of the Pythagorean harmony of the spheres and of man's place within the universe.

Theology, too, seemed to permeate every lesson and every subject. Luther's close collaborator Philipp Melanchthon had defined the basic curriculum back in 1522, warning, 'If theology is not the beginning, the middle and the end of life, we cease being men – we return to the animal state.'[28] Everything therefore had to be directed towards 'the practice of God-fearing' (*die Übung der Gottesfurcht*) and memorising the official articles of the Lutheran Church, the so-called *Formula of Concord*. These had to be recited again and again until they were perfectly remembered. Luther continually emphasised the need for the physical and the spiritual to be joined together. In his *Table Talk* (of which Bach later had at least one copy) he said, 'Music is a conspicuous gift of God and next [in importance] to theology. I would not want to give up my slight knowledge of music for a great consideration. And youth should be taught this art; for it makes fine, skilful people.' So, instead of abolishing Latin Schools like the one he himself had attended in Eisenach between the ages of fourteen and eighteen, he and Melanchthon went on to reconstitute them, placing music at the very centre of the curriculum. Luther reasoned that if children were taught the new music in school – *his* music (and that of his

Six-part retrograde cruciform canon by Adam Gumpelzhaimer (1559–1625), from the Compendium musicae latino-germanicum *(1625).*

colleague Johann Walter*), set to *his* words – they would be able to lead the congregations in the new hymnody and sing polyphonic settings of these melodies in alternation with the congregational unison. How widely successful he was in this is hard to establish.

Sixteen hour-long lessons were assigned each week to the study of around 200 closely printed pages of Hutter's *Compendium locorum theologicorum* (1610), said to encapsulate the essence of Lutheran theology. Thirty-four articles defining key doctrinal points were presented in a question-and-answer format that needed to be studied and recited by rote. The articles were calibrated in order of difficulty – beginning with the Scriptures as the source of truth, through Christ and the Trinity, Providence, Original Sin, predestination, freewill, justification, good works, the nature of the sacraments, and finally the conceptions of the Last Judgement and eternal life. Once again music was used to help memorise these crucial tenets of theology and so-called facts of the world: if you sang them and repeated them enough, they were sure to stick in the memory. It is also striking how closely their arrangement mirrored the construction of the Lutheran liturgical year. (See Chapter 9 and Plate 14.) Bach's fluent way of connecting to them, and the underlying seasonal rhythms in his cantatas, may well have been implanted from the moment, aged ten, that he began to learn Hutter's *Compendium* by heart in the Klosterschule at Ohrdruf.

With music and theology together accounting for almost half the curriculum and taught by the same master, we would not be surprised to find the three 'R's relegated to third place, with physics, Latin, Greek and history limping behind and making up the rest. Laid out according to the precepts of Andreas Reyher, rector of the Gymnasium in nearby Gotha, this became Bach's syllabus in Ohrdruf. According to Reyher, only eight textbooks were ever needed,† while his recommended texts for reading exercises were the fourth book of Moses and Chapter 11 of St Matthew's Gospel. From these Reyher claimed, 'a boy can learn all

* Johann Walter's *Chorgesangbuch* of 1524 was compiled to combine these educational and liturgical targets – songs, Luther explained in his preface, that were 'arranged in four to five parts to give to the young who should at all costs be trained in music and other fine arts . . . Nor am I of the opinion that the Gospel should destroy and blight all the arts, as some of the pseudo-religious claim. But I would like to see all the arts, especially music, used in the service of Him who gave and made them' (LW, Vol. 53, p. 316; WA, Vol. 35, pp. 474–5).

† These comprised the German ABC, a reading primer, the Catechism, Catechism-primer, the Gospels, the Psalter, a German songbook and a sum book.

his letters'. Selective Classical authors were taught alongside the basic skills of reading and writing, logic and rhetoric, all presented from the same theological perspective, reflecting what has been called Luther's 'passionately anti-rational position'[29] Even numeracy was taught in connection with the Bible, by means of Caspar Heunisch's *Hauptschlüssel über die hohe Offenbarung S. Johannis* (*The Main Key to the Revelation of St John*, of which Bach later owned a copy). In practice it does not seem as though the instruction of arithmetic had progressed much beyond the basic ability to count, add, subtract and calculate simple fractions during the previous two hundred years. In so far as the natural sciences in their most primitive form featured at all within this syllabus, they were taught from a selective Lutheran perspective adhering to a post-Aristotelian model. Writers such as Pythagoras, Euclid, Galen, Ptolemy and Boethius were still considered to speak authoritatively on cosmology, physics and mathematics, even though their once-stable foundations of scientific knowledge had recently been demolished.

Even history was taught from the same partial and parochial Lutheran point of view. Here the recommended textbook was the *Historia universalis* (1672) of the same Johannes Buno whose illustrated sequence of mythological creatures we noticed on the classroom walls earlier.[30] Buno took extraordinary liberties in selecting just those bits of the Classical past that could most easily be made to fit into his providential view of history, and ignoring all the rest. Conveniently for him, James Ussher (Anglican Archbishop of Armagh and Primate of All Ireland between 1625 and 1656) had recently established beyond doubt, through a complicated correlation of Middle Eastern histories and Holy Writ, that the Creation occurred on the evening preceding Sunday, 23 October 4004 BC.[31] Adam lived till he was 930 years old. 'Nothing happened', Buno states categorically, in either the sixth or the tenth century. And *Historia nihil repraesentat quod Christianus* ('History is nothing but the demonstration of Christian truth'). So, naturally enough, Church history predominates: the saints – Augustine, Basil, Gregory and Ambrose – are praised for their 'glorious writings', while the sinners – the Manichaeans, the Montanists, the Pelagians and the Arians – are pilloried for their 'errors' as heretics, along with the prophet Muhammad and a succession of errant popes. The figure of Louis XIV just manages an appearance before Buno winds up his quick trot through history in 1672.

It is easy to ridicule Buno's approach, vivid and attractive as it was in creating a pictorial narrative in pupil's minds, and weaving together sacred and secular history in a single quilt.* His naivety was of the sort that Descartes no doubt had in mind when he concluded that the study of history, like travel, while harmless enough as a form of entertainment – one composed of 'memorable events' which might conceivably 'elevate the mind' or 'help to form the judgement' – was hardly an occupation for anyone seriously concerned with increasing knowledge.[32] In Buno's hotchpotch of fables, travellers' tales and facts, cherry-picked and adjusted to the credulity of his readers, Descartes would have found no trace of a coherent methodology. Faced with this sort of genial tosh, intended of course to underpin the basic institutions of society in general and of the Lutheran Church in particular, there were no clear-cut rules or premises from which valid conclusions could be deduced, no material amenable to reasonable standards of proof.

In addition to Buno, the little ancient history that was taught in the Latin Schools of the day came in the shape of Flavius Josephus (AD *c.* 37–95), whose writings on Hebrew history and theology were seized upon by the Protestant clergy as supporting evidence to account for the fall of the Temple of Jerusalem as predicted by Jesus. A short list of Classical authors, chosen not for their quality as literature but for their mastery of Latin grammar and syntax, was headed by Cicero – his letters *De officiis* and *De inventione* and his anti-Catiline orations – texts perfectly judged to sharpen the dialectic wits of future defenders of the faith. The list also included works by Horace, Terence and Virgil, as well as Curtius Rufus' gripping life of Alexander the Great – complete with mouth-watering tales of heroic bravery, exotic oriental customs and

* One of the more original features of Buno's *Historia* was his way of selecting ten mnemotechnical illustrations to be absorbed in patterns influenced by late-medieval memory tracts, and all devised to enhance retention. Buno graphically subdivided world history into the four biblical millennia before Christ's birth and the seventeen centuries after that. As we have seen, these folio-sized illustrations mounted on canvas were for display on classroom walls, each subdivided into ten smaller frames that need to be read in a zigzag pattern for the first five frames, and in an inverted Z-pattern for the second group. Each of the seventeen centuries after Christ's birth is awarded a separate illustration. Buno's technique went on being used in German schools well into the 1720s, anticipating the 'pedagogical realism' of the late eighteenth century. (See Plate 3b.) As another contemporary saw it, historians, though they declare their intention to follow the path of truth rigorously, are often prone to 'afflict the world of learning with false annals, which ought rather to be buried in eternal night' (J. B. Mencken, *De charlataneria eruditorum* (1715)).

romantic attachments. The New Testament, not surprisingly, was used as the chief textbook for the learning of Greek.

Despite such occasional yarns and the various musical diversions, overall one senses an unremitting joylessness emanating from this syllabus. In the classrooms of the more unimaginative and pedantic schoolmasters, it may have amounted to little more than drudgery. Elsewhere, in schools where teachers had come under the influence of the Moravian reformer Jan Amos Comenius (1592–1670), shafts of sunlight were theoretically able to penetrate. The Klosterschule in Ohrdruf (previously a monastic school) to which Bach moved from Eisenach after his parents' death and attended for four and a half years, is alleged to have been just such a place, famous in the district for having adopted Comenius's curricular reforms. His method stressed the importance of cultivating a favourable environment for learning, of encouraging pleasure as well as moral instruction through study, and of helping pupils to learn progressively from concrete examples, stage by stage – from a knowledge of things (including songs and pictures) rather than through words alone. This was a contemporary restatement of St Augustine's contention that 'to enjoy is to cleave fast in the love of a thing for its own sake'. Beyond that, Comenius advocated teaching in the vernacular, his Latin primer, for instance, providing simultaneous training in German and Latin, with the texts arranged in parallel columns.[33] So, instead of splitting up the disciplines, he deliberately searched for points of contact between them and tried to bring all branches of knowledge into one consistent scheme of *sapientia universalis*.

Like so many laudable endeavours by successive educationalists over the centuries, there was a chasm here between aspiration and reality. Even with a partial application of Comenius's reforms, there is every reason to doubt whether conditions within the Eisenach and Ohrdruf classrooms were as conducive to acquiring *sapientia universalis*, let alone 'enlightenment', as many of Bach's biographers would have us believe. It all depends on what sources you read.* Christoph Wolff, for

* The traditional, idyllic portrait of Bach's first school years relies heavily on two rose-tinted sources: Paullinus's *Annales Isenacenses* (1698) and Johann von Bergenelsen's *Das im Jahr 1708 – lebende und schwebende Eisenach*. Bergenelsen ends his glowing account of the Lateinschule by extolling the harmonious rapport he claims to have noticed between teachers and their model pupils: 'So it seems that all the Christian well-educated pupils have a healthy outlook and go about with a bright aura. When one goes into a classroom one notices all the pupils sitting together, rich and poor, boys and girls. All have their own

instance, claims that such was the 'excellent leadership and high reputation' of Eisenach's Latin School that it 'attracted students from a wide region',[34] and Martin Petzoldt resolutely insists on the 'essential stability and quality of the school' in Bach's time there, 'guaranteed' by the amicable triumvirate of *Rektor* (i.e., headmaster), *Ephorus* (i.e., school inspector) and *Kantor*.[35] However, research begun in the 1930s in the town archives by Hermann Helmbold, and in the 1990s by Rainer Kaiser, paints a very different picture, suggesting that the Eisenach boys of the time were typical ruffians: rowdy, subversive, thuggish, beer- and wine-loving, girl-chasing, known for breaking windows and brandishing their daggers to impress.[36] The problem was not new. Back in 1678 Georg von Kirchberg reported an overall 'slackness and contempt for good discipline' to the Eisenach Consistory.[37] More disquieting were rumours of a 'brutalisation of the boys' linked to evidence that many parents kept their children at home – not because they were sick but for fear of what went on in or outside school. This forced the consistory to issue a rule making it compulsory for all children over the age of five to attend any one of the eight German (primary) schools before moving on to the Latin School. Offending parents henceforth faced a stiff fine or even imprisonment. Bach's frequent absences from the Latin School in Eisenach – 96 days absent in his first year, 59 in his second and 103 in his third – are traditionally attributed to his mother's illness, to his unofficial apprenticeship to his father, requiring him to help with a plethora of activities – from restringing fiddles and polishing brass instruments to watching and helping his father copy out his cousin's compositions – and to his attending the frequent family musical assemblies which must have seemed almost like a convocation of guild members. This is not altogether convincing, and there could be alternative, more disquieting explanations.

By 1688 – three years after Bach's birth – prevalent conditions in the Latin School had reached a nadir, the consistory claiming that the school had fallen 'into an altogether great decline'.[38] Another five years passed before they got round to appointing the deputy head, Christian Zeidler, as a substitute for the ailing headmaster, Heinrich Borstelmann, and to

primer in front of them, and while one spells out his ABC, another is learning his capital letters, the third reads aloud, the fourth prays, the fifth makes a pretty speech, the sixth recites his catechism, and all are watched over by a schoolmaster.' It reads like a piece of modern free school propaganda.

drawing up a memorandum with his recommendations for improving this situation. This was the very year in which Bach enrolled in the *quinta*. One of Zeidler's main concerns seems to have been the turmoil prevailing in the separate classrooms, caused, first, by an overall shortage of books; by the simultaneous use of different grammars and lexicons as textbooks; and, finally, by serious overcrowding. This became so acute that by Bach's second year there were 339 boys enrolled in the school (without, apparently, any form of playground in which to let off steam). In church the boys were crammed together up in the choir loft or sat on correctional benches (*Schwitzbäncken*). They contributed so much to the general hubbub that parishioners complained they were distracted from attending to the sermon. Zeidler came up with a number of practical but fairly unimaginative remedies, including a system whereby each teacher took direct responsibility for his class both in school and at church. Pupils were encouraged to sing along in the chorales from their hymnals. The younger children in the *quinta* were allowed to leave after the set Gospel and Epistle readings. He advocated the enlargement of the choir loft – though this had to be deferred for several years. Looking for a 'suitable recreation' to keep the boys occupied, in 1693, against the rector's advice, he even wrote the text for a school nativity play intended as an edifying piece of music-theatre ('eine erbauliche *Comoedia*').[39] Regrettably the music for this play – perhaps by Cantor Dedekind or the organist Johann Christoph Bach – has not survived, and we will never know whether young Sebastian Bach was inside church taking part, or outside with his mates creating mayhem.

* * *

Of one thing we can be quite certain: there is no hint of a spirit of empirical scientific inquiry in Bach's curriculum and no notion of what Copernicus, Kepler and Galileo had propounded or achieved. Where Lutheran teachers may have been prepared to give up the flat-earth implications of the Scriptures and to adopt the spherical system of Ptolemy in its place, it is doubtful whether many were yet aware of Kepler's study of the orbits of the planets (1609), which in turn had led to Newton's law of gravity (1687), or ready to abandon the idea of a rigid, rotating firmament. Newton formalised Galileo's discoveries in his first law of motion: 'every body continues in its state of rest or of uniform motion in a straight line except in so far as it may be compelled by force to change that state.' This contained the repudiation of a belief that had blocked the progress of physics for the past 2,000 years and continued to do so in the Latin School system throughout Bach's school years.

Clearly, the philosophical debates of the late seventeenth century, which turned on the question of whether the universe consisted of observable phenomena governed by eternal mathematical principles, were utterly remote from the teaching methods current in the schools Bach attended. The extremes of abstract thought and what Jonathan Israel has called that 'vast turbulence in every sphere of knowledge and belief which shook European civilisation to its foundations' seem to have left large parts of Germany in a state of comatose indifference.* It is hard to find any evidence to support the case that a 'Crisis of the European Conscience' (the title of a book by the French historian of ideas Paul Hazard, written in 1935) made any sort of impact on what was taught in the German classrooms of the 1690s, or indeed what was taught for the next fifty or sixty years. In the upper echelons of German academic life the expulsion of the Professor of Philosophy, Christian Wolff, from the University of Halle in November 1723 – accused by his colleague Joachim Lange of teaching a doctrine of the 'absolute necessity of things', akin to Spinozism, and later by Johann Franz Buddeus of trying as a mathematician 'to explain everything in a mechanistic way' – marked a watershed of a significant kind, because 'virtually the whole of German academe now slid into bitter wrangling and acrimony'.[40] But even then, in the 1720s and 1730s, the chances were that unless you had been to university, you would have been blissfully untouched by Galileo, Newton or Leibniz, and completely unaware of the attack on Cartesian reductionism by the brilliant Neapolitan professor of rhetoric Giambattista Vico (1668–1744), whose fame began to spread only during the Counter-Enlightenment of the 1820s.

By and large the fizz and turmoil of seventeenth- and eighteenth-century philosophical discourse were situated somewhere high in the intellectual stratosphere, far too remote to make an impact on the lives

* Tim Blanning suggests a comparison here with the comment made by Edmund Burke on the British radicals who welcomed the French Revolution at the end of the century: 'half a dozen grasshoppers under a fern make the field ring with their importunate chink, whilst thousands of great cattle, reposed beneath the shadow of the British oak, chew the cud and are silent' (*The Pursuit of Glory: Europe 1648–1815* (2007), p. 475).

and attitudes of ordinary German citizens. This is not to claim that Bach, as a provincial Thuringian, could not have developed a powerful, far-seeing intellect; on the contrary, as many have claimed, his music points to a degree of sophistication of thought not dissimilar to that of any of the leading mathematicians or philosophers of the day. The point here is that the quasi-scientific thoroughness with which he later constructed his music cannot have been imbued in him as a schoolboy by anything approaching a Rationalist or an Enlightened education. Nevertheless herein may lie something that could conceivably help to explain the exceptionally advanced perception of proportion that he later manifested in his compositions: the very fact that numeracy was not taught as a separate discipline in Bach's school years may have freed him to make the sort of spontaneous interconnections which so easily disappear from a child's instinctive feel for numbers once it is taught in isolation. Vico recognised this when he wrote: 'This faculty is mother wit, the creative power through which man is capable of recognising likenesses and making them himself. We see it in children, in whom nature is more integral and less corrupted by convictions and prejudices, that the first faculty to emerge is that of seeing similarities.'[41] God, Bach may have thought, worked with and through numbers, and he may have concluded, quite instinctively, that music followed the natural manifestations of mathematical law – a perfect example of His creative power. It was one of the great avatars of the Enlightenment, Gottfried Leibniz, who famously said, 'Music is the hidden arithmetical exercise of a mind unconscious that it is calculating.'[42]*

The purpose here has not been to mock the ignorance of German society, nor the backwardness of the Latin School system, so much as to emphasise that Christianity – in its revisionist Lutheran Orthodox form – still occupied centre-stage in the school curriculum and, as a result, informed and influenced the patterns of thought of the overwhelming majority of German citizens. As Tim Blanning has argued, the eighteenth century has as much claim to be called the Age of Religion as

* Writing to the composer Ludwig Senfl, Luther had claimed 'the prophets did not make use of any art except music: when setting forth their theology they did it not as geometry, not as arithmetic, not as astronomy, but as music, so that they held theology and music most tightly connected, and proclaimed truth through psalms and songs.' There was nothing, of course, to have prevented Bach from reconciling this view of music as 'sounding theology' with the alternative concept of it as 'sounding number', as formulated by Leibniz.

the Age of Reason. All the churches – Catholic, Calvinist and Lutheran (both Orthodox and Pietist) – were flourishing, with public and private discourse both dominated by religion (substantially more so in the first half of the century than in the second). And it was in this respect that music had a vital role to play, though often in an atmosphere of mistrust, discord and only partial effectiveness. It would take more than a musician of genius to buck that trend.

3
The Bach Gene

Thus even in the Bach family a robust mediocrity held sway. Only a few of them achieved anything out of the ordinary . . . The unusual concentration of musical talent within an area so narrowly enclosed (in family as well as geographically), with Johann Sebastian as a culminating point in an ever-increasing and then suddenly ebbing flood of talent, remains a unique phenomenon.

– Christoph Wolff[1]

In Italy, there were the Scarlattis, in France, the Couperins, in Bohemia, the Bendas. But in Thuringia – the provincial heart of Germany – was to be found the most extensive network of practising musicians in the history of Western music: the Bachs. Such a coincidence of parallel musical dynasties across late-seventeenth-century Europe is odd; and maybe it is no more than that – a coincidence. No literary or artistic lineages lasting more than a couple of generations are recorded for the same period, for example. Somehow one would need to trace the lineal descent of artisans in related trades or crafts to gauge whether the endemic political instability and precariousness of existence might account for the somewhat covert, guild-like passing on of craft-master skills from father to son in the wake of the Thirty Years War. Until well into the eighteenth century this was the initial conduit of learning for most musicians within these dynasties, conscious of pursuing an honourable family trade and increasingly aspiring to respectability as 'artists'. Employment and survival were what counted here in the first place. If this meant uprooting, as in the case of the Bohemian linen-weaver Jan

Jiří Benda, and moving lock, stock and barrel to Potsdam in 1742 with his wife and musically gifted children, so be it. Two of his composer violinist sons, Franz and Johann (Jan Jiří junior), already held positions in the court orchestra of Frederick the Great and were well on the way to careers of distinction. Now two more, Georg and Josef, were to enrol, while the youngest, Anna Franziska, was training as a Kammersängerin. In due course the Benda boys were all to make names for themselves: Franz and, to a lesser extent, Jan Jiří as violinist, teacher and composer, Georg as Capellmeister and composer of German melodramas. With twelve of the next generation entering the music profession, the Bendas were to outlast the Bachs and become the longest dynasty of professional musicians on record. After moving to Brazil during the middle years of the twentieth century they survived into the present century.

The Scarlattis achieved notoriety as well as fame, but lasted for a couple of generations only. Pietro Scarlatti, a Sicilian who died *c.* 1678, identified five of his eight children as having musical ability. Speculatively, and no doubt to avoid the famine and political convulsions prevalent in Palermo, he sent two of his sons to study in Naples. In 1672 the twelve-year-old Alessandro, along with his two sisters, Melchiorra and Anna Maria, were sent to Rome. Both girls trained and had some success as opera singers, but their various liaisons and indiscretions – a secret marriage to a priest, affairs with court officials – caused embarrassment to the family and doors to open for their brilliantly gifted younger brother. Soon obliged to leave behind the rich pickings of wealthy patrons in Rome, Alessandro and his sisters headed for Naples, where, as mistress to the viceroy's secretary, Melchiorra clinched her brother's appointment as *maestro di cappella* in 1684. As soon as the viceroy heard of the affair, he dismissed his secretary and two other officials who had been involved with what he called these *puttane commedianti.* Alessandro's forty years of fame as a prolific composer of operas, serenatas, oratorios and cantatas were spent shuttling to and fro between Naples and Rome (with shorter, less productive forays to Florence and Venice), trying to satisfy a variety of aristocratic patrons to shield himself from financial ruin and constant worries about his ten children. Of the three who became musicians, it was Domenico, the youngest and exact contemporary of Bach, who showed the most talent. Alessandro referred to him as 'an eagle whose wings were grown; he must not remain idle in the nest, and I must not hinder his flight'. But interfere he did with the over-solicitous traits of a Sicilian patriarch, to the point that Domenico, aged thirty-two, was forced to resort to the law to secure his independence. To escape this paternal suffocation he resigned his positions in Rome, forsook opera, fled first to Lisbon and then to Madrid. The break, while brutal, was cathartic: free now to experiment in what he modestly called 'an ingenious jesting with art', he set about creating that corpus of more than 500 dazzling one-movement keyboard sonatas that has held its place in the repertory ever since. Standing well outside the contemporary Baroque concepts of sequential and consecutive expansion, the sonatas were also beyond the reach of parental criticism.

Active in and around Paris and Versailles as organists, harpsichordists, composers and teachers for more than two centuries (*c.* 1640 to *c.* 1860), it was the Couperins who, in their own distinctive Gallic fashion, were the most successful and, in career terms, the most exemplary of these Baroque dynasties. Their rise to eminence and fame began with the rapid transition from peasant labourers to farmer-proprietors in the parish of Chaumes, a day's journey south-east of Paris. The chance patronage of a local dignitary facilitated the initial move of Louis Couperin in 1653 to a stable position as organist at St Gervais in Paris, a job that carried with it guaranteed rent-free accommodation and the right for successive family members to inherit the position and occupy the lodgings – a prerequisite seldom replicated in the case of the Bach family in Thuringia. This was the springboard for the next generation, beginning with François Couperin (known as *le grand*), and they rose to various prestigious positions in the royal chapel and at court, obtained the valuable royal privilege of printing and selling music,* and even accepted Louis XIV's offer of ennoblement, an honour which was put in the way of those who were respectably employed and able to pay for the privilege (an early instance of cash for peerages). The Couperins made opportune marriages to worldly-wise spouses with legal or business pedigrees as well as conspicuous musical talent. At least six of the female members of the family achieved public recognition, holding positions in Paris or at court such as *ordinaire de la musique de la chambre du roi pour le*

* This was in extreme contrast to Bach's struggles to get his music into print. Bach's admiration for Couperin's music is well attested, though the letters they are said to have exchanged were used as jam-pot covers later on, or so the story goes.

clavecin. They were able to form a kind of family corporation in the century before the French Revolution, one ensuring that the multiple functions of organ-playing, keyboard lessons and singing in concerts at church were covered by its different members.*

Surely the same could be said of the clan-like Bachs? The opening line of the *Nekrolog* reads 'Johann Sebastian Bach belongs to a family which seems to have received a love and aptitude for music as a gift of Nature *to all its members in common*' (my italics). If this were true, why is every single one of the fifty-three 'musical Bachs' listed by Johann Sebastian in the genealogical notes he compiled in 1735 a male? Mothers, wives and daughters are nowhere to be found, despite the fact that his mother Maria Elisabeth Lämmerhirt came from a well-to-do family in Erfurt with marital connections to at least three composers; that both his first and second wives were trained singers; and that there were musical daughters among his progeny included in his claim that his children 'are all born *musici*'. (Lutheran Germany was evidently more prone to male chauvinism than even the France of the *ancien régime*, although Louis XIV's establishment of a boarding school for girls in 1684 at the prompting of Madame de Maintenon marked a significant change in the social attitude to women.) While they selected female partners with well-attested musical pedigrees (what in farming circles is known as 'breeding up'), the Bachs were unwilling to countenance anything beyond biological and domestic roles for their womenfolk. Regardless of any musical chromosomes passed by the various Bach wives on to their offspring, and leaving aside the support, encouragement, burden-sharing and even inspiration that they may have given to their husbands, the degree of egalitarian, cooperative job-sharing characteristic of Armand-Louis Couperin would have been unthinkable within the Bach family.

The truth is that any endeavour to reconstruct the origins and development of the Bach dynasty cannot wholly escape this male bias and selectivity, one that was shared and solidified by Sebastian himself, who,

* Almost the last of the line, Gervais-François (1759–1826), 'in one of the most bizarre scenes of the Republican aberration (6 November 1799) . . . found himself playing dinner music on the greatest organ in Paris, at Saint-Sulpice, while Napoleon and a nervous Directory, which was to be overthrown three days later by its guest of honour, consumed an immense banquet in the nave below, watched over by a statue of Victory (herself about to be overthrown) whose temple the church had become' (David Fuller in *New Grove*, Vol. 4, p. 873). Somehow one cannot picture any of the Bachs, even at the nadir of their fortunes, undertaking an equivalent gig.

at the age of fifty, had the idea of preparing and annotating the first draft of the *Ursprung der musicalisch-Bachischen Familie* (*Origin of the Musical Bach Family*). Corrected and added to by Emanuel and Johann Lorenz Bach in the 1770s, this document is still the best source we have of his family's history, itself the product of (male) family lore and hearsay evidence, as well as snippets of chronicled fact, and the main reason why in the history books the Bachs continue to eclipse all other musical dynasties.[2] Successive scholars have tried to find more reliable source material but with limited success. As a result, it seems impossible to sidestep the sense of inexorable progress over six generations in 200 years, set out in an almost apostolic succession that culminates with the emergence of J. S. Bach and his sons, then drops off into a steep decline with the generation of his grandchildren. Up to that point each male member of the Bach clan was virtually preordained to become a trained musician, with the church (or in some cases the court) and the municipality as the main sphere of his activity. Council minutes for Erfurt in 1716 refer to the 'local privileged band of town musicians or so-called Bachs'.[3] From the outset the family set a premium on craftsmanship and self-reliance. Inevitably, there was a distinctly religious aspect and purpose to the way they made music.

* * *

The single most important book of Sebastian Bach's musical upbringing was a hymnal – the *Neues vollständiges Eisenachisches Gesangbuch* (*The New Complete Eisenach Songbook*), compiled by Johann Günther Rörer in 1673. Between the ages of four and ten Bach must have sung from it every single day in church or in school. Within the thousand pages of this fascinating compendium are to be found several of the chorale tunes that would resurface in Bach's church cantatas. His earliest experiences of music were thus indivisible from its role in acts of worship: these hymns that he sang and heard – either *a cappella*, with organ or concerted with instruments as sanctioned by Luther – reflected the changing seasons and fitted tidily into the liturgical celebrations of the turning year. Twelve copper-engraved illustrations added by Johann David Herlicius to the hymnal served to reinforce these connections between music and Scripture and to evoke the physical landscape of Bach's childhood. The town of Eisenach features on the title page; and a biblical superscription shows King Solomon kneeling at the altar while 'all the Levites who were singers, namely Asaph, Heman and

Jeduthun and their sons and brothers . . . stood to the east of the altar with cymbals, psalteries and harps, and next to them 120 priests who blew trumpets' (II Chronicles 5:12). (See Plates 2a and b.) Did anyone point out to him the similarity to his own extended family of versatile musicians participating in liturgical music-making? This was the very bedrock of Bach's understanding of his future role as a church musician. Here, too, were the seeds of that preoccupation later in life with family trees and musical archives – his pride in the Bach genealogy and that 'thirst for legitimacy of foundation, for empowering ancestry' which, George Steiner tells us, inspires so much German thought and politics.[4]*

In celebrating his fiftieth year as a jubilee year, Sebastian Bach was following a biblical injunction (Leviticus 25:10–13) and cementing the parallels between his own family and those of the divinely ordained Levite musicians who served under David and Solomon led by Asaph as royal Capellmeister. Patriarchal values were traditionally held by the Bachs to be essential to their survival. This is the way the authors of the *Nekrolog* referred to the family's respect for roots and locality: 'It would be something to wonder at that such fine men should be so little known outside their fatherland if one did not bear in mind that these honourable Thuringians were so content with their fatherland and their standing that they would not venture far from it at all, even to go after their fortune.'[5] We will find that this turns out to be an important point of difference between Sebastian Bach and his peer group (particularly Handel), who tended to measure status and success in terms of foreign travel leading to fruitful employment in a prestigious city or a royal court. In contrast, Bach's pronounced sense of his roots and the idea of belonging to a distinct group (made up both of family and of broader cultural elements) linked by 'some impalpable common gestalt'[6] appears to anticipate the theories of Herder by some forty years.

It is in the light of this connection that the choice in the *Ursprung* of Veit (or Vitus) Bach as the family patriarch acquires its special significance. It is not as though this miller-baker from Wechmar (patron saint

* Perhaps, as John Butt suggests, German composers in particular felt insecure in not having a long, secure cultural hinterland in the way that France and many other countries had (after all, Germany only became a country around 1870). There is a sense that they were always seeking to ground themselves, as it were, in an Old Testament past. In this respect Bach made a convincing Old Testament figure before the 'New Testament' of Beethoven.

St Vitus) was the sole candidate, the only one to show musical talent; nor was he anything approaching the earliest of the identifiable Bachs. Parish records reveal a prolific colony of Bachs spread across Thuringia, beginning with a Günther Bache mentioned in 1372, many with the popular Christian name Johannes, or its diminutives Hans and Johann, and popping up frequently throughout the fifteenth and sixteenth centuries. Were they disqualified from the honour of being the first of the apostolic line because they were mostly peasants or miners? And exactly which Veit are we talking about? Vitus was the patron saint of Wechmar in an area where several of the family branches were concentrated. There was one Veit Bach documented in 1519 as living near by in Presswitz; a second (1535–1610) left Thuringia for Frankfurt (Oder) and, later, Berlin; a third was born in Oberkatz in 1579; a fourth married Margareta Volstein in 1600, the same year another Vitus Bach departed for Mellrichstadt; while a sixth (profession unknown and for a long time assumed to be the original Veit Bach of the *Ursprung*) died in Wechmar in 1619. But none of these quite fitted the bill as the man described in the *Ursprung*:

> Veit Bach, a white-bread baker in Hungary, was compelled to escape from Hungary in the sixteenth century because of his Lutheran faith. Hence, after converting his property into cash, as far as this could be done, he moved to Germany, and finding adequate security for his Lutheran religion in Thuringia, settled at Wechmar near Gotha, and continued his trade there. What gave him most delight was his little cithrinchen* which he used to take with him to work and play while the mill was grinding [his flour]. A pretty noise the pair of them must have made! However, it taught him to keep time, and that is apparently how music first came into our family.[7]

This Veit stands out first (like Albrecht Dürer's father) as a religious refugee during the violent Counter-Reformation backlash that led to the expulsion of Lutherans and Anabaptists from the Holy Roman Empire in the mid sixteenth century. Secondly, he decides to move to Thuringia – Bach country par excellence – even if (as seems likely) he came from

* A *cithrinchen* was a form of cittern: bell-shaped with four ranks of metal strings and played with a quill plectrum. As a miller and baker Veit Bach's fondness for the instrument is mirrored by its popularity in England, where it was traditionally played by cobblers, tailors and barbers.

there in the first place and was merely repatriating himself and his immediate family as a *Herkomling*. Thirdly, though not yet a full-time professional, Veit's passion for music is there for all to see. Taken together, these were compelling reasons for Sebastian Bach to nominate his great-great-grandfather as founder of the dynasty and as the exemplary family patriarch.

After Veit come three Johanns, all familiarised as Hans. The eldest, possibly Veit's brother or cousin, is recorded as a city guardian in Wechmar in 1561; another, perhaps a nephew, starts as a carpenter and moves on to Würtemberg as a *Spielmann* (a minstrel-fiddler) and court jester of a certain respectability (judging by his two rather impressive portraits, one an etching, the other a copperplate engraving); while the third – Veit's son – trains as a baker but is drawn to music, and he too becomes a Spielmann. The first of the Bachs to receive a basic grounding in music, he moves off the bottom rung of the professional ladder: as *Stadtpfeifer* (town piper, or a city wait) he is much in demand to deputise for town musicians all over Thuringia, before being obliged to take charge of his father's mill for the last seven years of his life. This Hans and Veit's other son – Lips, a carpet-maker – both appear as householders on the Wechmar register in 1577, after the death of their father. The first Bach to graduate to full-time musician is Caspar (born *c.* 1578), probably a nephew of Veit. As one of a trio of full-time town pipers, he lives as a *Türmer*, or 'castle-pigeon', first in Gotha and then, two years after the Thirty Years War broke out, in Arnstadt, ready to 'strike the hours, look out day and night for riders and carriages, watch closely all roads on which more than two riders were approaching, and also report whenever he observed a fire nearby or in the distance'.[8] Said to be the oldest town in Thuringia, Arnstadt was where the Bach family were most active for the next eighty years.

Next comes the first generation to experience genuine hardship as a result of the war. Caspar's musically gifted son, Caspar junior, is sent to study abroad by Count Schwarzburg of Arnstadt, and then disappears from the records. Of his four brothers, three are full-time musicians and the fourth blind. They all die in the 1630s. Now comes a rallying point, a period in which all three of Veit's grandsons – Johann, Christoph and Heinrich – manage to survive the trauma of the war years. Each goes on to found a significant dynastic branch. By mid century all of them have become full-time professional musicians, surviving on miserly salaries:

Heinrich as organist, Johann and Christoph as heads of local town bands. In terms of the family history this is a critical generation, one that shows grit, frugality and adaptability when it comes to soaking up pressures of war, plague and near-starvation. Exceptionally determined, finding ingenious ways to collect fees due to them from private citizens to supplement their meagre salaries, they vary in their success at stifling the urge to complain. Even the long-suffering Heinrich is driven to point out to Count Schwarzburg (three years after his appointment as organist) that so far he has not received any remuneration for a whole year, having to 'beg for it almost with tears'.[9] Only after thirty-one years of service in Arnstadt does it occur to him to ask for his yearly entitlement to grain. One is reminded of the *cri de cœur* of an earlier composer, Michael Praetorius: 'it is regrettable how very small are the salaries paid even in some illustrious cities to their masterly organists. These men can make but a wretched living and sometimes even curse their noble art and wish they had learnt how to be a cowherd or some humble artisan instead of an organist.'[10] In fact this generation of Bachs does both: as smallholders they grow their own subsistence crops (though no potatoes as yet, as we saw in Chapter 2, p. 23), and as artisans they learn the skills to make the musical instruments that they play. Their choice of spouses is canny, Heinrich and Johann both marrying daughters of the town piper from Suhl. Heinrich's six children and all three of Johann's sons live to maturity, but it is not clear whether any of Christoph's survive other than the 'triple team of Bach brothers – George, Johann Christoph and Ambrosius', all versatile musicians.

The family had now come through the most difficult times imaginable. Music to them was never a side issue – they clung to it for survival.* United in their commitment to music as a vocation, now was the time to consolidate their position – by versatility and tenacity. A more variegated pattern, in terms both of character and temperament and of career trajectory, begins to emerge with this fourth generation, all born towards the end of the war, in the 1640s. Of these, Johann's three sons fared the worst. All three were town musicians in Erfurt, the eldest and youngest

* Their modern counterparts are The Blue Notes – in the way they fought apartheid in South Africa with their highly individual and searing style of jazz. I remember coming across what Moholo said and writing it down: 'When people are oppressed, they sing. You see it all over the world and through history. They may be sad, but they sing. It's like squeezing a lemon – the juice comes out.'

falling victims to the plague in 1682, while the middle son, Johann Aegidius, versatile like his father Johann, hung on to positions as organist and as a member of the town band. He survived until 1716, aged seventy-one. Consolidation, then, for the status-hungry Bachs but as yet no expansion in an area where there were probably more organists per square mile than anywhere else in Europe.

Christoph's three sons survived the war but struggled to stay afloat, their lifespan similar to that of their father (who died aged forty-eight when they were in their teens). Georg supported himself initially as a schoolteacher before becoming a cantor – a significant step up the social ladder – in faraway Franconia. The identical twins, Ambrosius and Christoph, were only sixteen when both their parents died. A pathetic letter to Count Schwarzburg with a request to allow them and their handicapped sister to draw their father's salary for the current quarter is the starting-point for a portrait of the twin brothers. Though granted, it was not enough to keep them in Arnstadt. Taken in by their uncle in Erfurt, the boys enrolled in the town band in which their father had once played. Even though they were so close and so alike (family legend insisted that their wives could not tell them apart), their paths soon diverged – Christoph gravitating back to Arnstadt (principally, it seems, as a violinist at court and as a town musician), Ambrosius moving on to Eisenach as head of the town-piper band and court trumpeter.

Christoph junior's situation in Arnstadt was anything but stable: first, his annual salary, even less than his father's, amounted to just thirty gulden plus a certain amount of grain and firewood. Then he got himself betrothed to the 'wrong' girl, and had to plead to the higher court of the consistory in Weimar before he was able to extricate himself. His name is also associated with the first documented case of anti-Bach feeling. The elderly town musician Heinrich Gräser began a bitter campaign against Christoph, piqued beyond endurance by what he saw as the Count's favouritism towards him and the extended Bach family whenever music was required at special functions. He resented the Count's habit of summoning other Bachs from Erfurt when there were perfectly capable musicians on hand in Arnstadt. Gräser's attacks gradually turned nastier and more personal, targeting Christoph's arrogance, his habit of 'guzzling tobacco', and his flashy and superficial fiddle-playing (like 'swatting at flies'), at which point all the Arnstadt Bachs closed ranks with their Erfurt cousins, demanding that Gräser be made to make a public apology. In the end the old Count dismissed both Gräser and Christoph Bach in 1681, but the latter was reinstated a year later by the Count's son, while Gräser was left empty-handed.[11] This went to the heart of the resentment struggling musicians in the region felt towards the nepotism of the Bachs. An Erfurt citizen by the name of Tobias Sebelisky was once threatened with a five-thaler fine if he hired any musician to play at his daughter's wedding who was not a member of the town band, as 'no others but the Bachs . . . were privileged to perform'.[12]

The twins needed tact and skill in handling people. But, looking at the oil painting of Ambrosius, that is not the first quality that strikes one. Dressed in some kind of loose oriental cloak, he gazes out of his portrait like a prosperous brass-player – fat-chinned, full-nosed, lazy-eyed, stubborn and evidently fond of drink. But, as so often in the Bach family, there are two sides to the coin of his personality. Ambrosius seems to have had the knack of identifying friends when and where they mattered most, one being Duke Johann Georg I of Eisenach, who made him an affiliated member of his court Capelle in 1671. He also saw to it that the town councillors who had appointed him *Hausmann* (head town piper) in October 1671 granted him and his family full citizenship

Portrait of Johann Ambrosius Bach (1645–95) by Johann David Herlicius, commissioned by the Eisenach Court as a mark of his high standing.

once he had found the means to buy his own house in April 1674. Evidently they were dazzled not by his creative flair (he was not known to be a composer) but by his virtuosity as a performer, and had come to rely on him as a resourceful musician. 'He shows such outstanding qualifications in his profession,' they noted, 'that he can perform both *vocaliter* and *instrumentaliter* in church and in honourable gatherings in a manner we cannot remember ever to have witnessed in this place before.'[13] They were also impressed by his modesty – the way he 'conducted himself in a quiet and Christian way agreeable to everybody'. This is one trait he did not pass on to his youngest son.

Once again there is no escaping the male exclusivity in matters of family lore and social interaction. No more than a year after being appointed to the Erfurt *compagnie* of musicians in 1667, Ambrosius Bach had married Elisabeth Lämmerhirt, the daughter of an Erfurt municipal councillor. To the disappointment of early-twentieth-century biographers searching for a potent admixture of plebeian and patrician blood in Sebastian Bach's immediate ancestry to account for his startling gifts, the Lämmerhirts were *arrivistes*, newly prosperous furriers in Erfurt – though originally they stemmed from the same Thuringian peasant stock as the Bachs, with whom their fortunes were now intertwined. Like them they were migrants during the religious wars of the sixteenth century, in their case to Silesia, returning to Erfurt at the outset of the Thirty Years War. Elisabeth's older half-sister Hedwig had married Johann Bach (Sebastian's paternal great-uncle and the first composer of note in the family), and her brother Tobias and his wife were in due course to leave significant legacies to their nephew Sebastian. Yet, for all their marital and godparental ties to the Bachs and other professional musicians, the Lämmerhirts had previously sired no musicians themselves, save for one: the celebrated composer and theorist Johann Gottfried Walther (1684–1748), who shared a maternal grandfather with Sebastian and was later to become a close colleague when they were both employed in Weimar.*

From the time that he moved to Eisenach, Ambrosius proved to be conspicuously clever at living within his means – a yearly payment of forty florins plus free lodging for the first three years of his stay there. Yet, over twenty-four years there, he and his wife succeeded not only in

* David Yearsley points to 'the degree of cooperation, even friendly competition, that existed between the two men', cultivating 'almost in tandem' chorale preludes, canons and the 'esoterica of learned counterpoint' (*Bach and the Meanings of Counterpoint* (2002), pp. 47–8).

cramming their household with eight of their own offspring, her mother, his slow-witted sister and, for a couple of years, an eleven-year-old second cousin, but also in feeding two apprentices and two journeyman assistants. That Ambrosius was no easy touch is clear from the petition he wrote to the Eisenach Council in 1684, the year before his youngest son Sebastian was born, in which he listed his various hardships. It seems that he had ingratiated himself with his employers too well, for when, after thirteen years' unblemished service, he asked permission to move back to Erfurt, he was turned down flat. (Given Erfurt's extreme susceptibility to plague, this was perhaps just as well.) An improvement in his situation at the Eisenach Court began with the return of Daniel Eberlin to take charge of the princely bands, and an annulment of a cut in his courtly salary. Added to this was his satisfaction as a father in seeing his eldest son Johann Christoph safely posted off to Erfurt to study with the famous teacher Johann Pachelbel (1653–1706) and later of guiding (or at least witnessing) the first musical steps of his youngest son, Johann Sebastian.

Ambrosius's musical versatility, his single-minded attachment to his craft and his pursuit of regimens of technical self-improvement seem to have been typical of the post-war generation of Bach brothers and cousins, united by a fierce clannish loyalty and a determination to protect their privileged right to trade as professional musicians wherever they saw fit. Their creative gifts are displayed in the *Alt-Bachisches Archiv*, a collection of vocal music by several members of the family (not always clearly differentiated or attributed).* Providing us with a priceless treasury of music composed by, and circulating within, the family in the latter half of

* Over the generations various family members seem to have had a hand in copying, revising and adding to this remarkable collection, which was considered lost for fifty years after the ending of the Second World War, until it resurfaced in the Ukraine State Archives in Kiev. Subsequent scholarship suggests that it was initially assembled not as a Bach family document but by the Arnstadt cantor Ernst Dietrich Heindorff for use there, and that from him it went first to the Arnstadt organist Johann Ernst Bach and only on his death in 1739 did much of it pass on to Sebastian (see Peter Wollny, 'Alte Bach-Funde', BJb (1998), pp. 137–48). This does not rule out the possibility that he was already familiar – perhaps even from an early age – with many of its contents, in particular the works of his father's cousins Michael and Christoph, which together form a high proportion of the collection. Ultimately it was thanks to Sebastian, his reverence for the music of his ancestors, and his role in revising, copying and performing several of these works during his Leipzig years and then passing them on to his second son Emanuel that we have this precious evidence of the music of his forebears that, apart from anything else, permits us to gauge the stylistic provenance of his own music.

the seventeenth century, it also opens tantalising windows on the social life of the Bachs. For example, it includes a cantata by the elder brother, Georg, written for the three of them when Christoph and Ambrosius visited him in Schweinfurt in 1689 to celebrate his forty-sixth birthday. The title page portrays not simply the *concordia* that existed between the three brothers but its attributes: *florens* ('flourishing'), in the form of a three-leaf clover; *firma* ('firm'), shown as a padlock binding three chains; and *suavis* ('sweet'), illustrated by a triangle with three jingling rings attached. In a process not unlike Euclid's superimposition of triangles, the triple symbolism is carried through systematically even into the way the music is composed. (See Plate 6.) Scored for three voices (two tenors and bass) and three violas da gamba, the cantata has three themes that are ingeniously developed, each subject entering three times and so on – its almost wearisome consistency and thoroughness ultimately detracting from the inventiveness of an otherwise charming piece.

In marked contrast to Ambrosius and his two brothers, none of them principally a composer, were their first cousins, Michael (1648–94), Christoph (1642–1703) and Günther (1653–83). All three boys had been trained by their father, Heinrich, himself 'a good composer and of lively disposition', according to C. P. E. Bach. While Günther, the youngest, 'was a good musician and a skilful builder of various newly-invented musical instruments', the two elder sons were to emerge as composers of distinction. Michael was considered to be *ein habiler Componist* (an 'able' or 'handy' composer) by his future son-in-law, Sebastian – a judgement borne out by the concerted motets and dialogues preserved in the *Alt-Bachisches Archiv.* They show him to have had a solid technical command, a natural facility and a characteristic Italianate fluency and euphony; those of his organ chorales that can be identified in the Neumeister Collection bear a similarity to ones by Sebastian (BWV 1090–120). Yet for sheer quality and individuality the vocal compositions of Christoph Bach leap out from the *Archiv* as being of a totally different order.*

* There must have been so much more of Johann Christoph's music – including music known to J. S. Bach – that over the years has succumbed to the ravages of time, fire and neglect than the handful of works we have today. These include two strophic funerary 'arias', both set for four voices, both deceptive in their apparent simplicity, both wonderful examples of 'hidden' art in which subliminal complexities of metre and harmony are brought into play. One lives in hope that the brilliant musicological sleuths currently working in the Leipzig Bach-Archiv will soon lay their hands on previously undiscovered treasures.

It is the sense of vision his music displays that is so impressive, and his ability to match vivid verbal imagery with the kinds of arresting sonorities that few other composers of the time dared to explore. It comes as no surprise, then, to find Sebastian singling out Christoph for special mention: he was *ein profonder Componist* ('a profound composer'). To this Emanuel appended the claim, 'This is the great and expressive composer.'[14] With these compositions garnered from the *Alt-Bachisches Archiv* we have at last something with which to measure the creative achievements of these first three generations of Bachs and a benchmark against which we can assess the emergence of Sebastian as a creative artist. As the main scholar of the *Alt-Bachisches Archiv* concludes, 'they meant more to [him] than merely family keepsakes – they clearly helped him to establish his own historical and artistic position. He measured his skill against them.'[15]

* * *

Having reached indubitably the most brilliant and fêted composer in the family thus far, one is tempted to seize gleefully on the impact his music might have made upon Sebastian at the expense of all other plausible influences. A distinguished line of biographers beginning with Forkel and Spitta have used Bach's lineage to infer that first and foremost he was the product of his ancestry; but the issue is so much more complex than this. Born to the most musically dominant family in the region and into a society where music permeated so many aspects of life – at home, in school, in rituals of play and worship – Bach offers a prima facie case for nature and nurture being in propitious accord; so much is obvious. Yet, inconveniently for his biographers, Sebastian, the acknowledged musical genius of the family, did not carry the DNA of the more creative family line and of Christoph in particular (though his first two sons, Wilhelm Friedemann and Carl Philipp Emanuel, did, their mother being the daughter of Johann Michael Bach). The evidence we have for the emergence of Sebastian's creative talent is so slender, while the uncertainties and details of his development and its timing are so numerous. We cannot even be sure of the exact role that his parents played in his earliest musical experiences – whether, for example, the very first musical sounds that registered with him were of his mother singing to him, or the degree to which his father – or the great organist-composer Christoph – moulded his earliest musical education.

Ultimately the responsibility for a child's musical education lay with the local cantor. It was his job to select the best voices, to teach boys to sing and to prepare them for the Sunday services of the town's three main churches. In the three towns where Bach acquired the rudiments of his musical education – Eisenach, Ohrdruf, and Lüneburg – he encountered four cantors. The first was Andreas Christian Dedekind, who was also his form master in the *quarta* of the Latin School in Eisenach. Sebastian would have had to pass an audition before Dedekind to become a member of the *chorus symphoniacus* (founded in 1629 in order 'to foster finer musical instruction of the Latin School pupils').[16] The choir statutes of Eisenach's Georgenkirche demanded that pupils should not only 'understand clefs, time signatures and rests' but should be able to sing at sight 'a fugue, motet and concerto'. Then, in Ohrdruf, his cantor was the infamous bully Johann Heinrich Arnold (see Chapter 6) and later Elias Herda, who as a former chorister himself could have facilitated Bach's move to Lüneburg in 1700, where the cantor was August Braun, about whom next to nothing is known. As a member of Braun's *Mettenchor* (Matins Choir), an elite chamber choir of fifteen voices, he would have been expected to sing fluently in canon and to be able to read at sight polyphonic motets of the Renaissance as well as the more complex music by recent and modern composers.* But no sooner had Bach arrived there, aged fifteen, than 'his uncommonly fine soprano voice' split in two: 'He kept this quite new species of voice for eight days, during which he could neither speak nor sing except in octaves' – before having to admit defeat (at quite an age by the norms of the day).[17] All the vocal training he had acquired to this point – breath

* The *Eisenacher Kantorenbuch*, compiled around 1535 by Wolfgang Zeuner and containing the core repertoire of the *chorus symphoniacus* in Bach's time, comprised Latin motets by composers such as Josquin, Obrecht, de la Rue, Rener, Galliculus, Johann Walter, Stölzer, Isaak, Senfl, Finck, Rein and Musa. The choir library in Lüneburg, on the other hand, at the time of Bach's arrival in 1700 was rated as one of the most comprehensive assemblages of contemporary church music in northern Germany. Compiled by successive cantors of the Michaeliskirche, eager to seek out the newest and best of church music circulating in manuscript all over Germany and from south of the Alps and to snap up any modern music from the moment it appeared in print, the library comprised over 1,100 pieces by seventy-five different composers (and several other anonymous ones), ranging from older-style polyphonic motets, to concerted psalm and canticle settings, to Latin hymns, biblical dialogues, or *scenas*, and the most up-to-date arias and *Stücke* – prototypes of the future church cantata. All this was lost to posterity when the library went up in flames (see *Rekonstruktion der Chorbibliothek von St Michaelis zu Lüneburg*, Friedrich Jekutsch (ed.) (2000), p. 200).

control and the agility needed for rapid passagework and trills and the many demands of part-singing – was of inestimable value the moment he himself, aged eighteen, was put in charge of his first choir and began composing figural music.

Yet many pieces in the musical jigsaw of Bach's early training are still missing. It is often assumed that, in addition to his singing in church, Bach, like Luther, was a *Currender*, a member of those street-busking choirs in Eisenach, Ohrdruf and Lüneburg which collected charitable money; but exactly what he sang, where he sang and with whom he sang – these are questions for which we have no definite answers. Bach himself would have us believe that he was to all intents and purposes self-taught. That, too, was the line maintained within the family and in the *Nekrolog*'s reference to his mastery 'learned chiefly by the observation of the works of the most famous and proficient composers of his day and by the fruits of his own reflection upon them'.[18] So that in identifying three individuals who might have figured prominently in shaping his overall musical development, we are fighting an element of official denial: Johann Christoph of Eisenach (no mention of any formal teaching role here); Johann Christoph, his eldest brother (his instruction being 'designed for an organist and nothing more');[19] and that other organist-composer, Georg Böhm (where the words 'his teacher' are crossed out by C. P. E. Bach, perhaps recalling a paternal rebuke).[20] Scholars have of course been on the trail of all three for some time, particularly that of Böhm, the easiest to identify as a credible teacher and a composer with palpable stylistic affinities to Bach. So far attempts to establish an exact teaching role for either of the two Johann Christoph Bachs have proved rather more elusive – the elder cousin because he inhabited a different aesthetic milieu, the brother because of his alleged heavy-handedness *in loco parentis*. We need to re-examine them in sequence.

* * *

One suspects that if his surname had been anything but Bach, or if the world had never heard of Johann Sebastian, the fame of Johann Christoph of Eisenach would be secure today and that we would value his music entirely on its own terms. Christoph stood out from the pattern of a family of musicians in which 'a robust mediocrity held sway'.[21] There can be little doubt that he was the most exciting and innovative musician in the musical landscape of Sebastian's early childhood and the one most likely to have been reponsible for the boy's first impressions of organ music. Forkel tells us that 'he is said never to have played on the organ in fewer than five real parts',[22] which must have been magical to a musical child of eight or nine.* A fascination for the mechanics and inner workings of church organs originated during the hours the two could have spent together, we might speculate, with Christoph trying to coax life out of the old three-manual organ of the Georgenkirche while his young cousin looked on.

Ever since the mid 1660s, after he had moved from Arnstadt to the town of Eisenach to play and care for the organ of its main church and to play harpsichord at the Duke's newly established court, Christoph Bach had had more than his fair share of financial set-backs and health concerns. Unlike the more prosperous Ambrosius Bachs, Christoph and his family were constantly obliged to change rented lodgings, some of them plague-contaminated, as the town refused to provide a house for its long-serving organist. After twenty years as town organist he started to look for a way out of Eisenach – and almost found one in 1686, after a promising audition for the same post in Schweinfurt, only to be pipped to the post by a successful colleague from Eisenach (galling enough) and thwarted by the Duke's refusal to let him go because of his debts. Thereafter his social situation gradually deteriorated, and he ended his thirty-eight years in Eisenach disillusioned and impoverished. The most poignant of his letters, written in October 1694, was addressed to the Duke in person: 'Here in my wretched, pitiable situation, my house is filled with so many invalids it looks like a field hospital. God has laid this heavy cross upon me and I am unable to obtain the necessary food and medicines for my sick wife and children. My severe penury has so exhausted and drained me I have not got a penny left. And so I am compelled in my wretched state to seek mercy in the arms of my saviour ... and beg from your most gracious hands that I, a miserable servant, may

* This is the testimony of Emanuel Bach, who must have got it from his father (BD III, No. 666/ NBR, p. 298). As Richard Campbell writes, 'the adding of parts [layers of melody] to an existing line, to build up texture and define the contours of harmony, is the basis of the polyphonic tradition in Western music, and ideally the "whole" thus created should be greater than the sum of the parts themselves – not only the logic and beauty of the individual lines but the relationships between them have to be heard and considered. The ability to *improvise* in five real parts, if that is what Emanuel Bach meant by "play", is a very rare skill indeed, only to be acquired with immense diligence' (liner notes to SDG 715).

be given some corn for my poor wife and children, and whatever else your Highness might be pleased to confer on me.'

From the barrage of complaints to a tight-fisted, uncooperative town council, which called him a *querulant und halsstarriges Subjekt* ('a querulous and stubborn fellow'), the abiding impression we get of Christoph Bach is of a feisty, combative individual, cantankerous and insecure, father to an overcrowded household, prone to constant domestic upheavals, sickness and incipient penury. But his letters may also be read as the calculated strategy of a proud musician prepared to enter the fray and stand up for himself (and in this respect, he is very like what we know of Monteverdi).They show that he was willing to work the system to his best advantage, and that he was neither shy of giving his employers detailed practical recommendations on how to redress his wrongs, nor of playing them off against each other. His complaints about his miserable domestic circumstances need to be balanced against the evidence of his unselfish tenacity in campaigning over many years for a fine new organ for the Georgenkirche (and obtaining it posthumously), the trouble he took to draw up extensive technical specifications for it, and not least his ensuring that the organ-builder, G. C. Stertzing, was paid a deposit, enough for him and his workers to feed themselves while occupied in building it. Christoph was presumably the chief motor behind the organ-fund appeal that eventually reached a figure of over 3,000 thalers, far exceeding the actual costs. The overall impression we have is of an utterly devoted single-minded professional musician, wedded to his chosen instrument and to the craft of composition. In his embattled state a strong sense of self-worth could easily lead to feelings of being persecuted and, like his young cousin Sebastian in times to come, to incomprehension at the doltish attitude of the philistine authorities and their failure to provide rewards commensurate with his expertise and his artistic standing.

Once we put aside the letters of complaint, manipulative or otherwise, and turn to his music, we gain a more nuanced and rounded picture – of a man of many moods. Part of his distinctive expressive armoury as a composer of vocal music is the skill he shows in replicating lifelike mood-swings within a single work, rejecting beauty in favour of emotional truth. Time and again we find him drawing on every available element – a gradual build-up of voices or instruments, abrupt switches of tessitura, harmony and rhythmic activity – to vary the momentum, to lead to, and recede from, climaxes in a persuasive and organic way. The music reveals a passionate temperament: a man capable of high spirits, mellowness as well as misanthropy, and many subtler intermediate gradations. While it is true that the majority of his chosen texts are all of a piece with his letters, mostly in the language of the day, *überschwemmt mit Sorgen* ('flooded with worries'), his music goes a long way beyond merely matching phrases such as 'I am overcome with wretchedness', 'my body is pathetic and suffering', 'my days are gone like a shadow' and 'I wither like a weed, and my sinews are crushed into shards'. Christoph finds room for drama as well as pathos. He can also counter these variations on the theme of woe with sober reflections such as *ob's oft geht hart, im Rosengart' kann man nicht allzeit sitzen* (in essence, 'The going is often tough, but life is not just a bed of roses'). Indeed, his life may have been one of toil and misery (*mein Leid ist aus, es ist vollbracht*/'my suffering is at an end; it is finished'), but it is also one 'which has given me so much goodness' and which leads to a future paradise. Here is a man evidently struggling to keep his faith burning and his hopes alive, when despair must have seemed the easier, indeed the inescapable, option.

In this respect he reminds me strongly of Heinrich Schütz. The moment you begin to study and fall under the spell of Christoph's solo arias and laments[23] you cannot fail to notice how they are couched in a highly sophisticated declamatory style, with the characteristic speech-rhythmic inflections that Schütz pioneered two generations earlier, but here controlled less austerely and within a still bolder harmonic framework. Beyond this Christoph exhibits a sureness of design in the balancing contrasts he achieves in motet and aria form, between sections in triple and common time (another Schützian trait), homophony with polyphony. Indeed, unequivocally Schützian features are plentiful and audible in Christoph's music and substantiated by a link, albeit at one remove – the lessons he took in his youth from Jonas de Fletin, who had studied with Schütz in Dresden.* At the deeply affecting conclusion of his five-voiced motet, *Fürchte dich nicht*, he reverses the convention

* Jonas de Fletin was town and court cantor in Arnstadt from 1644 to 1665, while Johann Christoph's father, Heinrich Bach, was the successor as main organist in Arnstadt to another musician with a close link to Schütz, Christoph Klemsee, who had studied alongside Schütz in Venice as a pupil of Giovanni Gabrieli (see Hans-Joachim Schulze, *Studien zur Bach-Überlieferung im 18. Jahrhundert* (1984), p. 180).

of assigning the voice of God to a single voice (or to twin voices, as in Schütz's *Resurrection Oratorio* of 1623): Isaiah's comforting message takes the form of a solo quartet addressed to the (as yet silent) penitent, apparently on the verge of expiry.* This concludes with the words *du bist mein* set to the most intricate polyphony. When the soprano finally enters with *O Jesu, du mein Hilf* (from a funeral hymn by Johann Rist), there is a momentary intertwining of the two common words *du* and *mein* – as though a halting contact has just been made from one world to the next. This can be heart-stopping in performance, especially if the sound of the soprano reaches the listener at some remove (say, from a church's distant gallery), as though she is already set on her final journey.

Is Christoph, then, one of the very few credible conduits between that earlier master, Heinrich Schütz, and Sebastian, his own first-cousin-once-removed? German musicologists, intent on establishing a German artistic succession from one master to the other, have for generations struggled to 'prove' this influence – of Schütz on J. S. Bach. The problem is that the music tells a different story: one combs through Bach's music without finding hard evidence that he truly knew, let alone directly emulated, Schütz, and the features of Christoph's music that seem to resurface in that of Sebastian's are by and large not of the Schützian sort. On the other hand there could be more tenuous, metaphysical links between the three: like Schütz before him and Sebastian after, Christoph seems to have been drawn to moral puzzles and the hundreds of ways in which good contends with evil. All three composers, it seems, were willing to probe the darker recesses of the human mind and to proffer solace by means of their music. Perhaps composers of their stature were perplexed (exasperated even, in the case of both Bachs) by the need to explain something so simple and obvious to listeners who refused to see the truth staring them in the face. Indeed, that could be one definition of the role of the composer of the time: to explain the self-evident and, through music, to release

* It is an exact reversal of the procedure he uses in the dialogue *Herr, wende dich und sei mir gnädig*, where the interventions of the solo bass as *Vox Dei* (accompanied by violin and viol consort) become gradually more expansive, creating the illusion that the grace of God sought by the four penitent upper voices is distant to start with, but becomes ever-more present in the course of the utterance. This might have lodged in Bach's memory when years later he took a similar approach to his cousin in BWV 67, *Halt im Gedächtnis Jesum Christ*: at his fourth attempt to allay the disciples' fears, the bass representing the risen Christ is accompanied by peaceful strings and winds (see Chapter 9, p. 313).

the turbulent emotions that rack people's lives even (or especially) when they try to suppress or deny them. With all three composers we come across instances of the way their contrasting personalities seep through the cracks of their music, humanising them more vividly than the pathos of indignant or pleading letter-writing ever could.

There is one major exception to such self-revealing music: Christoph Bach's twenty-two-part setting of words from the Apocalypse, *Es erhub sich ein Streit* (*There arose a dispute in heaven*). Creating a magnificent tableau in sound, Christoph portrays the great eschatological battle in which the archangel Michael and his angelic squadrons fought the dragon and snuffed out a mutiny led by Lucifer and the forces of darkness. Emanuel told Forkel how 'my late father once performed it in church in Leipzig, and everyone was astonished by its effect.'[24] But did Sebastian first hear it – or even sing in it – as a boy? Since one of his own St Michael's Day cantatas begins with these same words describing the war of the worlds, we can make a rare direct comparison of music by the two leading Bachs, both immense in conception and sustained bravura, yet providing very different experiences for the listener. Expanding on to a larger canvas the vivid drama-infused treatments of isolated biblical incidents he might have gleaned from Schütz, Christoph Bach finds superbly graphic musical analogies to the events he is chronicling, without, as Emanuel later commented, 'any detriment to the purest harmony'. Within the family, Christoph was revered for being 'strong in the expression of words and in the invention of beautiful ideas'[25] – and here is the reason why. The halo of beatific string sounds of the *sinfonia* soothes the listener up to the moment when two solo basses appear and sing: are these dispatches from the front line or war reporters furtively recording their commentaries in the build-up to battle? Their antiphonal exchanges become steadily rougher, and they start to roar like a couple of meths-drinking tramps. Then almost imperceptibly the drumming begins. One by one four field trumpeters bugle out their alarm calls and the voices start to pile up, while the circling angels size up the dragon and plan their attack. Soon a space opens up between the two five-voiced choirs – two hostile armies at the ready in battle formation – and a column of sound, six octaves tall, has been built up. Far above the fray the archangel Michael, as chief trumpeter, blasts his battle orders in a high *clarino* register. Up to this point there have been sixty bars seemingly stuck on the common chord of C major – not the least brilliant sign of Christoph making fertile use of limited means (his fanfares being constrained by the series of whole tones playable on his natural trumpets). With the pressure of expectation for a clear victor (or at least for something to change) building to a climax, the harmony swerves abruptly to B♭ with the word *verführet* ('tempt'): the effect is to give banner headlines to the cunning 'deception' of the Devil.

The victory celebrations that follow are wholly absent when we turn to Sebastian's portrayal of the same scene in his Leipzig cantata of 1726 (BWV 19). Here it is the singers who strike out as the main combatants. Like a wind that has blown up into a gale in just a few seconds, they lead the doubling instruments (strings and three oboes) into battle with a ferocious confrontational swagger and impel the trumpets to follow in their wake. It is only when they pause for the first time in thirty-seven bars that the instruments really hit their stride (in a four-bar *Nachspiel*). But that turns out to be merely the A section of an immense *da capo* structure such as someone of Christoph's generation could never have used. The B section starts out with the advantage now tilted in favour of the 'raging serpent, the infernal dragon', manifested in seventeen bars of 'furious vengeance' dominated by the choir. Then, while the singers catch their breath, the orchestra advances the story. The swinging rhythm of the tell-tale *hemiola* reveals this to be the turning-point in the battle. Back comes the choir, now on its own and in block harmony, to announce Michael's victory, while the continuo rumbles on. But the piece does not end there. For the next twenty-five bars Bach shakes his kaleidoscope to give us a gleeful account of the final moments of the battle – the repulse of Satan's last attack by Michael's inner guard and a lurid portrayal of Satan's cruelty (a slow, screeching, chromatic descent in the sopranos) – before the whole battle is relived again from the beginning. One senses that Bach was spurred on by his cousin's audacity and fired up by his sense of drama. He was also stimulated by the availability of a virtuosic group of trumpeters, the municipal Stadtpfeifer of Leipzig under their 'Capo' Gottfried Reiche – just as Berlioz was a century or so later by the newly available military *cornets à pistons* in his *Symphonie fantastique* and by the saxhorns to emerge from Adolphe Sax's workshop when composing his epic opera *Les Troyens*. Bach uses his high brass in strongly contrasting ways: at one extreme, in the opening chorus, thrusting upon the listener the scale and significance of these apocalyptic encounters; at the other, in the tender E minor aria for tenor

('Bleibt, ihr Engel'), evoking the ever-watchful protection afforded by the guardian angels as they wheel around in the stratosphere.

Operating in the dying years of the seventeenth century – that 'warlike, various and tragical age'[26] – Christoph was more of a miniaturist than Sebastian. But even allowing for the obvious generational differences of style, one is struck by basic similarities of outlook and temperament between the two Bachs: by their characteristic predilection for life/death juxtapositions, together with that subtle blend of intense subjectivity and polyphonic distance – a form of objectivity that is one of the hallmarks of Sebastian's style. We do not know exactly when Sebastian first became aware of Christoph's music, but it is possible that he was infected at an early age by his cousin's burning desire to *communicate* through music. Christoph might have shown him how, even on a small scale, it can be a receptacle in which to pour all of life's anguishes, one's faith and one's passion (a theme to which we shall return in Chapter 5) and act as a proto-Romantic vehicle for self-expression. At moments when one is most aware of the insufficiency of language as a medium for conveying the ineffable, both these Bachs can astonish, each in his own way, with music that reveals intimations of heightened awareness.

In marked contrast to the extraordinary depth of expression and the recurrent emphasis on hardship that Christoph's music evinces comes a surprisingly light-hearted side. At over six hundred bars and lasting over twenty minutes, his nuptial dialogue *Meine Freundin, du bist schön* (*My beloved, thou art fair*) is his most substantial single work, one that provides a window on to the Bach family at play, revealing their mutual interdependence and interaction. Composed for the marriage feast of his namesake and first cousin, the twin brother of Ambrosius, in Ohrdruf in 1679, it comes down to us in a set of parts copied mainly by Ambrosius himself. Attached to these, also in Ambrosius's hand, is a lengthy commentary on the piece ('Beschreibung dieses Stückes'), comical in its flamboyance and strained in the way he tries to relate the biblical text to the circumstances of this bridal couple. It amounts to an imaginary *mise en scène* (complete with bullet points and references). Christoph-the-bridegroom was marrying, at the age of thirty-four (unusually late for a Bach), a girl he had been courting for some while. The delay was due to his difficulties in extricating himself from an earlier liaison and an alleged pledge of marriage (see above, p. 60). Here would be one reason for the furtive tone to the opening exchanges between bridegroom (bass) and bride (soprano), their planned garden assignation, the emphasis on secrecy and, not least, the clever choice of selected verses from the Song of Songs. Christoph-the-composer's evocative music suggests a far steamier series of encounters than Ambrosius's rather prim, but perhaps ironic, account would suggest. In an extended chaconne a series of delicately adumbrated variations of foreplay gives way to a gradual build-up of flagrant sexual tension. The carousing becomes ever more explicit – in the fast, ornamented turns that Christoph requires his singers to negotiate in their intoxicated state, in the gurgling sextuplet divisions of the solo violin and the repeated, drone-bass, open-string unisons of the string-players – by which stage, judging by the hockets and hiccups written into their vocal lines, both bride and groom are now decidedly the worse for wear. Here the music is far more than just picturesque: Christoph achieves subtle variations of word-setting, of interplay between the singers and the players, and an inexorable escalation of Rabelaisian debauchery.

It was a custom for the Bachs to hold annual get-togethers in one of the Thuringian towns. Once assembled they always began by singing a chorale. 'From this pious commencement they proceeded to drolleries which often made a very great contrast with it,' Forkel relates.[27] The rowdier things got, it seems, the greater the opportunity for extemporary jam singing, with all the brothers, organists, cantors and town musicians competing in the spicing up of popular songs which they transformed as quodlibets with plenty of satirical and sexual innuendo. Sebastian himself left us just two – one as the final variation of his *Goldberg Variations* (BWV 988), in which he combines the tunes of 'Ich bin so lang nicht bei dir g'west' ('It's been an age since I last saw you') and 'Kraut und Rüben haben mich vertrieben' ('Cabbage and turnips have driven me away'), and the fragment of a wedding quodlibet (BWV 524) composed about the time of his own first marriage (1707), which begins with the word *Steiß* ('arse').

One would of course love to know Sebastian's reactions when he first came across Christoph's nuptial cantata, before adding a new title page of his own to the score – 'Tempore Nuptiarum. Dialogus è Cantic: a 4 Voci Concert . . . di J. C. Bach'. Was the work revived at family weddings (such as that of his eldest brother, Johann Christoph, in 1694), and did he himself perform it? Though we have burlesques by Sebastian in the form of the *Coffee* and *Peasant* cantatas (BWV 211 and 212), and a number of wedding cantatas, as far as we can tell he himself never composed an extended nuptial dialogue quite like this in which the citations from the Song of Songs are treated more or less literally, topically or in the manner of a poetic conceit.

As we shall see when discussing his cantatas and Passions, his settings of texts from that book's transparently erotic imagery are invariably allegorical, corralled into the service of the church. They belong to a tradition that goes back to Origen (third century AD), which saw the church accept the male and female lovers as symbols, respectively, of Jesus and the individual Christian soul. So the *sponsa* with her rapturous swooning represents the soul in its urgent craving for mystical union with Christ. The soprano/bass duet ('Mein Freund ist mein / und ich bin sein') from BWV 140, *Wachet auf, ruft uns die Stimme*, is merely the best known of several of Bach's cantatas that treat this theme of the bridegroom (Jesus) eager to receive his bride (the Christian *anima*) in mystic union as part of a musical tradition that goes back to Palestrina and Clemens and thence to Monteverdi, Grandi and Schütz.* His own first attempted *ciacona*, to a different *ostinato* bass, comes in the finale to what may have been his very first church cantata, BWV 150, *Nach dir, Herr, verlanget mich*. Though commissioned by the mayor of Mühlhausen, it could have been composed while he was still in Arnstadt (see Chapter 6, p. 177fn) – birthplace of Christoph (to whom, as we shall shortly see, Sebastian may well have owed his first professional appointment). Perhaps it was a veiled tribute to the most remarkable of all his kinsmen, whose music, as he came to know it, provided Bach with templates of how to balance polyphony and harmony, how to structure musical paragraphs and how to reach a judicious accommodation between words and music and their competing priorities. It looks

* Referring to the many examples of this in Bach's music, the theologian John Drury reflects 'if one is to think of a central thing about being human, it is the need for a response from some other – a person, or it could be a work of art or music – and the fulfilling joy of getting one. It applies at home and at work, needs urgently to be there when we are born and when we are dying, and really everywhere and always: you take on another (all that other, not just the nice bits), and that other takes on you (all of you). Religion, not least the Christian religion, is deeply aware of this. Sacrifice, so central to the Gospel texts of Bach's Passions, is such a mutual exchange: pitched beyond morals into the realm of "amazing grace" and its unclenched exchanges. Protestants like Bach found it in those texts – and indeed the whole New Testament is saturated in it. This longed for reciprocity (it has an erotic ache to it) seems to be what makes life worth living' (private correspondence, Apr. 2013).

like a perfect example of nature and nurture conspiring to coalesce in the fruitful germination of such an immense talent. But this still lies some way into the future.

* * *

Now we return briefly to the image we had earlier of Johann Christoph Bach struggling to repair the old Georgenkirche organ in the company of Sebastian, his young cousin, still small enough 'to crawl behind the organ's façade and observe what was happening inside; here he would have seen metal and wooden pipes, wind chests, trackers, bellows, and other components of a large-scale mechanical instrument whose complexity was unsurpassed by any other machine in the seventeenth century'.[28] (This is pure conjecture; but at least it gives a plausible explanation of the origins of his 'life-long fascination with [the] design and technology' of what Nicholas Brady called the 'wondrous machine' of his age.) Suddenly the west door of the church is thrown open and somebody shouts out the terrible news that Sebastian's mother has just died. 'There is always one moment in childhood when the door opens and lets the future in,' according to Graham Greene in *The Power and the Glory*, and for Bach it was in his ninth year. Tragedy had struck. Within a matter of months he lost first his mother and then his father. The family home was broken up. No trace of it exists today, and the *Bachhaus* in Eisenach visited by countless pilgrims is a fake, though since 2000 it has been transformed into an impressive museum.* He, together with his thirteen-year-old brother Jacob, was sent away to live in the house of Johann Christoph – not his cousin the organist, but his elder brother of the same name whom he barely knew – in Ohrdruf, thirty miles to the south-east. This was an existential moment. Whatever his previous patterns of instinctive or unthinking childhood behaviour – and, as we shall see, we cannot be certain whether he was temperamentally more inclined at this stage to studious application or to high spirits and a free-range boisterousness – he had been brutally rocked back on to his heels. It was a triple bereavement. 'Behind the complicated details of the world stand the

* Ambrosius's house was on the site of the present Lutherstrasse 35 and occupied about 1,500 square feet of living space for between five and eight family members, two to three journeymen, presumably two adults and two younger apprentices and at least one maid (Ulrich Siegele, '"I had to be industrious . . .": Thoughts about the Relationship between Bach's Social and Musical Character', JRBI, Vol. 22, No. 2 (1991), p. 8).

simplicities: God is good, the grown-up man or woman knows the answer to every question, there is such a thing as truth, and justice is as measured and faultless as a clock.'[29] Henceforth Bach's view of the world would be more circumspect and guarded.

* * *

Ohrdruf in 1695 was a comatose provincial town with 2,500 inhabitants and a bad public-health record. It had no permanent court, no Stadtpfeiferei, and nothing to match the quotidian hive of activity that marked out the parental home in Eisenach as the hub of a comprehensive music-providing business. Bach's eldest brother had been organist of the Michaeliskirche since he was nineteen, and seems to have decided early on not to overexert himself. Feeling on his own admission 'a better love towards music than to study',[30] he did his best to escape the non-musical responsibilities expected of a town organist. The relationship between the two brothers – fourteen years apart – was perhaps strained from the outset. They had never before lived under the same roof, and, if Sebastian had been given a say in his own future, one imagines that he might have preferred to stay in Eisenach, apprenticed to the older Johann Christoph, a familiar and more charismatic role model.* The first time the brothers met face to face may even have been at the elder brother's wedding in Ohrdruf in October 1694 – one of those legendary gatherings of the Bach clan that even the great Johann Pachelbel (with whom the bridegroom had studied for three years) attended. Barely a year after getting married, Johann Christoph and his wife Johanna were expecting their first child. Neither had anticipated responsibility for housing, feeding and teaching this pair of younger brothers. Yet the custom of the day was that the eldest would house them as apprentice-pupils until they reached the age of fifteen. While Johann Jacob eased the domestic burden by returning to Eisenach the following year as an apprentice to his father's successor, Sebastian would later repay this debt to his elder brother by a reciprocal tuition of two of his teenage sons. At all events, at some time

* It is unlikely, however, that this was a realistic alternative, intriguing as it may at first appear. For a start, Johann Christoph Bach of Eisenach had an extensive family of his own and a far from stable domestic situation: he was obliged to move his family from one rented apartment to another, as we have seen. One wonders at what point in Johann Sebastian's life he saw parallels between his own situation and that of his elder cousin – particularly as regards those draining battles over turf with recalcitrant town council officials and the need constantly to plead one's cause on behalf of one's profession.

after the ten-year-old began his keyboard studies with his eldest brother, there is assumed to have been some friction between the two, the precocity and enviable technical fluency of Sebastian irking his brother – together with all those other irritating personality traits that can act like sandpaper between siblings when forced into an awkward teacher-pupil relationship. Well before his four and a half years in Ohrdruf were up (so goes the story, one first told by Forkel), Sebastian thirsted for technical as well as creative stimulus beyond what his brother could offer him.

Some biographers have detected a certain heavy-handed authoritarianism in Christoph – conscious that *in loco parentis* he needed to do his best with this gifted sibling – lurking at the back of the celebrated anecdote first reported in the *Nekrolog*. This is of the young Bach's clandestine copying by moonlight of keyboard pieces by Froberger, Kerll and Pachelbel, of his being apprehended and scolded, and of his painstaking efforts being confiscated by a peevish elder brother 'without mercy'. It smacks of legend – of a story heavily embroidered in the remembering and rehearsing of it. Ask most people what they recall of an incident in their childhood and they will, as likely or not, come up with a version subtly tweaked and dramatised by constant re-telling – especially, as seems likely with Bach, if he wanted his children to know and understand how he had heroically overcome all obstacles set in his path.* It is as though, aged thirteen, he had already grasped that the fastest route to musical proficiency would come by copying out and studying examples of all the best music he could lay his hands on, with or without permission.† The route to prowess for a Baroque composer was not by poetic musing or by waiting for inspiration to strike, but by hard work. As Johann Mattheson put it, 'Invention requires fire and spirit, the arrangement of it order and proportion; its working out cold

* Timothy Garton Ash on the subject of how 'personal memory is such a slippery customer' quotes one of Nietzsche's epigrams: '"I did that," says my memory. "I can't have done that," says my pride and remains adamant. In the end – memory gives way.' Garton Ash continues: 'The temptation is always to pick and choose your past, just as it is for nations: to remember Shakespeare and Churchill but forget Northern Ireland. But we must take it all, or leave it all, and I must say "I"' (*The File* (1997), p. 37).

† This was standard post-Renaissance practice in which the learning of rules (*Preceptum*), studying and analysing the examples of recognised masters (*Exemplum*) and imitating their work (*Imitatio*) lay at the heart of pedagogy. In 1606 Joachim Burmeister (*Musica poetica*, p. 74) devoted a whole chapter to the study of *Imitatio*, which he described as 'the striving and endeavour dexterously to reflect upon, emulate and construct a musical composition through the analysis of artful example'.

blood and calculated reflection.'[31] Bach himself is said to have reasoned in later life, 'that which I have achieved by industry and practice, anyone else with tolerable natural gift and ability can also achieve.'[32] We can of course take it at face value and accept that this was genuinely how Bach remembered the incident and wished his children to know about how he conquered resistance and persisted. Then it would fit into part of the wider process of his grieving for his parents: the energetic absorption in the secret copying (lasting six months) which may have been his defence against mourning, the shock not just of being disciplined by his brother (although his parents would surely have done the same for his act of 'innocent deceit' as well as being concerned about damage to his eyesight and lack of sleep) and of being deprived of the fruits of his labour, but of being scolded and with no one to speak up for him.* In this romanticised scenario Bach learnt the need for secretiveness and to be utterly self-reliant from then on. But why should we assume that his brother was not complicit in strengthening this desire to master everything there was to know about music?

We saw at the outset that in Bach's case so much biographical research consists in sifting for shards of evidence at the foot of an incomplete statue. A breakthrough came in 2005 with the discovery in Weimar of four music fascicles improbably catalogued under theological manuscripts and, as such, providentially preserved in the vaults of a library that had been heavily damaged by fire the previous year.[33] Two of these were transcriptions – in what was rapidly confirmed as Bach's teenage handwriting – of works by Dietrich Buxtehude and Johann Adam Reincken in German organ tablature. (See Plates 5a and b.) Written on just one damaged piece of paper, the Buxtehude chorale fantasia *Nun freut euch, lieben Christen gmein* seems to have been copied by Bach while he was still under his brother's tutelage in Ohrdruf.[34] This gives a completely new twist to the 'Moonlight' incident. It demolishes the traditional interpretation: that Christoph gave his industrious brother music to study but jealously withheld access to the more chal-

* Christopher Hitchens, when interviewing the writer Philip Pullman ('Oxford's Rebel Angel' in *Vanity Fair*, Oct. 2002), points out that Pullman's experiences 'as part orphan and part stepchild were not wasted on him'. He quotes Pullman: 'When you are a child your feelings are magnified, because you haven't any experience with which to compare them . . . So the smallest hint of injustice prompts you to think – which is itself unfair – that "my real father wouldn't have treated me like that."'

lenging works in his collection. The fresh evidence of this Buxtehude transcription points to an authorised ('Daylight') copying under Christoph's scrupulous supervision in which Sebastian's handwriting even looks similar to examples of his elder brother's hand. Given that the process of transcription in tablature was only the first stage before studying how to play the work, it also points to the likelihood that under his brother's tutelage he had acquired virtuoso keyboard skills to a much higher standard than what he had led his sons to believe in later life.* Besides the impressive technical strides he had made while in Ohrdruf, he demonstrated in this transcription his determination to master – again with his brother's help – one of the most complex and ambitious pieces of the contemporary north German organ literature: a work for cognoscenti, not for inclusion as part of the standard liturgy. We are now obliged to reconsider the role of Christoph Bach in the musical development of his much younger brother. Suddenly the esteem in which he was held locally as *optimus artifex* – 'a very artistic man' – takes on a completely different air.

* * *

After just over four years living with his brother, whose custodial responsibilities had now been fulfilled, Bach's abrupt departure from Ohrdruf mid-term was officially recorded as *ob defectum hospitiorum Luneburgum concessit*. Scholars have argued over the precise meaning of this phrase,[35] but in essence it indicates the withdrawal of the free board granted him and others by well-to-do citizens of the town. Hitherto the costs of his food and lodging had been underwritten by a trust set up in 1622 by the Count of Obergleichen (the last of his line) intended as an incentive to keep the best local boys at the school and so to qualify for places at Jena University; but we do not know why Bach's name is not at the foot of the pleading letter of protest (signed by fifteen pupils, including his friend and travelling companion Georg Erdmann) sent in February 1699 to the new absentee Graf von Hohenlohe

* In the *Nekrolog*, Emanuel paid tribute to his uncle's 'guidance' in laying 'the foundations for his [father's] playing of the clavier'; yet several years later he played down the quality of instruction provided, reporting to Forkel, as we saw earlier, that it 'may well have been designed for an organist and nothing more'. It is symptomatic of the difficulties the Bach sons had in squaring the evidence with their father's accounts of his early life.

complaining that the fund had run dry.* Bach's exit from Ohrdruf had less to do with the withdrawal of his stipend, or the increasingly cramped living quarters in his brother's house due to his expanding family, or the worsening economic situation due to the billeting of troops in the town, and more to do with his having made other plans.[36] He was now nearly aged fifteen, already well qualified academically and more or less at the top of his class. Faced with the choice of either bailing out of school altogether or of leaving 'home' and continuing his higher education elsewhere, Sebastian seems to have made up his mind to follow the example of Elias Herda, his cantor in Ohrdruf, and apply for a choral scholarship in northern Germany. For candidates applying to the Michaelisschule in Lüneburg, there were two prerequisites: (1) they must be children of poor people with no other means at their disposal; (2) they must have good voices so as to be of use singing in the choir and at church.[37] Bach qualified on both counts. As we know from the *Nekrolog*, at this age he had an 'uncommonly fine soprano voice'. The traditional narrative links Bach's move to Lüneburg, with Herda's supposed help, to the pipeline of Thuringian boy trebles supplying the Mettenchor at the Michaelisschule, and then comes to a full stop, or rather a question mark, at the point where Bach's voice breaks. But it now appears that the procedures for accepting choral scholars at the Michaelisschule were far more complicated and tedious than previously assumed – the issuing of a passport and the other travel formalities alone occupying several months and ultimately controlled more by the ducal chancery in Celle than by the authorities at the Michaelisschule.[38]

The Ohrdruf school register makes an intriguing distinction, stating that, whereas Georg Erdmann simply left (*abiit*), Bach 'took himself off' (*Luneburgum concessit*) a week before his fifteenth birthday. Leaving Ohrdruf in the throes of some kind of epidemic, the two boys set off on foot on their 200-mile journey northwards. There are raindrops on the manuscript of Bach's Buxtehude transcription that indicate it may have travelled in his rucksack. Arriving in Lüneburg in time for the busy

* In effect they were threatening to leave the school unless the funds were reinstated to help the best ten pupils with their lodging allowance. It was not forthcoming, and seven out of fifteen signatories in the *prima* left the school within a twelvemonth, several recorded as *ob defectum hospitiorum* – a phrase intended no doubt by the rector to shame the Count into reconsidering his decision (see Michael Maul, '*Ob defectum hospitiorum*: Bachs Weggang aus Ohrdruf' in *Symposium: Die Musikerfamilie Bach in der Stadtkultur des 17. und 18. Jahrhunderts* (Belfast, July 2007)).

Holy Week and Easter services of 1700, they threaded their way through to the former Benedictine monastery on the western wall and the fourteenth-century abbatial Michaeliskirche. They promptly enrolled at the Latin Grammar School at the start of the school year. Already by the Saturday before Palm Sunday in 1700, both boys were singing in the Mettenchor of the Michaelisschule. Proof of Bach's presence in the school in Lüneburg is confined to just two receipts relating to the distribution of proceeds from busking (*Mettengeld*) in 1700 – in other words for just a couple of semesters.[39] It has been assumed that he stayed on at least until 1702 in the *prima*, but there is no solid evidence for this, nor once his voice had broken that he was able to maintain his choral bursary. That does not rule out the possibility that, like Cantor Braun before him, he may have been offered the position of *Regalist* or *Positivschläger* (a keyboard role sometimes assigned to former trebles at that time) and switched to accompanying the choral performances and retaining his right to free tuition and board at the Michaelisschule, though not to lodging.

Given the degree of cooperation and cordial relations that existed between Sebastian and his eldest brother in later life, it is quite plausible that the idea that the youngest sibling should leave Ohrdruf for Lüneburg at the age of fifteen was part of a plan hatched by them a year or even two years earlier. The choral scholarship was a temporary measure – a sideshow. The main target was the celebrated organ virtuoso and composer Georg Böhm, Thuringian by birth* and currently organist of the Johanneskirche on the other side of town. By this stage Sebastian might already have set his sights on becoming a virtuoso organist, having shown that he was willing to work hard to realise that ambition while under his brother's tutelage. During his adolescence Christoph had studied with Johann Pachelbel and brought back to the family base his knowledge of the middle German organ school together with manuscript examples of the repertoire – so there would have been no

* There was also a family connection: Christoph's father-in-law, Bernhard Vonhoff, a town councillor in Ohrdruf, had attended both the Gymnasium in Gotha and Jena University with Böhm. It is quite likely that as a student in Goldbach and Gotha, Böhm had taken lessons from members of the Bach family; if so, by accepting Sebastian as his pupil, he would have been returning a favour. Christoph had studied with Pachelbel in Erfurt at the same time as Johann Christoph Graf, who journeyed north in 1694 'so that he could learn something in the ways of composition from Herr Böhm in Lüneburg' (J. G. Walther, *Musicalisches Lexicon* (1732), p. 288).

point in paying again for the same repertoire that Christoph, or more likely Ambrosius, had already purchased. If, at the same age, Sebastian were to move to Lüneburg and study with Georg Böhm, the family could eventually acquire a fresh and valuable repertoire and mastery of the techniques of the influential northern German school of organ composition.

With the discovery in 2005 of the oldest known manuscripts in Bach's handwriting, the earliest dating from when he was thirteen (referred to above), the cloud of doubt that has hovered over his teenage years and the fog of mythology that has gathered around the anecdotes surrounding his time in Ohrdruf and Lüneburg begin to lift. It now seems fairly likely that, from the moment that his voice broke, Bach went to live in Georg Böhm's house as his pupil and possibly as his amanuensis. The second transcription in tablature ends with a Latin inscription in Böhm's hand – *Il Fine â Dom. Georg: Böhme descriptum ao. 1700 Lunaburgi* (see Plate 5b) (though some might quibble that this in itself proves neither tutelage nor domicile). Certainly Bach was copying music from Böhm's library on Dutch paper exclusively reserved for the master and his handwriting had at this stage become very similar to that of Böhm. Here is enough to contradict the enigmatic crossing out of the crucial word – 'his [Lüneburg] *teacher* Böhm' – by Emanuel in his letter to Forkel (to which we already referred) as a sign of the second son's loyalty to his father in insisting that he never had an official teacher and owed everything to his own strict regimen of autodidactism.

On the basis of the new evidence it is now likely that at fifteen Sebastian Bach could play the most difficult organ literature of the day and that in Böhm he had a powerful advocate, one who was well able to introduce him to his Hamburg teacher, Reincken (see Plate 5b).* Reincken's playing was characterised by its flamboyance, its dramatic power, and by those abrupt and wild flights of fantasy that distinguished the northern artistic lineage from the style of Pachelbel and the Thu-

* This is borne out by the presence in his library of Reincken's *An Wasserflüssen Babylon* from which Bach made his copy – the only surviving contemporary source today. By the end of Bach's first year at Lüneburg, his first cousin Johann Ernst, who had been at school with him in Ohrdruf, apparently 'visited Hamburg for half a year at great expense, in order to improve his understanding of the organ'. Did the two make the rounds of the seventeen magnificent new Schnitger instruments in the Hamburg area? If he had still been tied to the Mettenchor and its heavy roster of services, his time to do so would have been severely restricted.

ringian organ schooling Bach had received from his elder brother. Reincken's influence spilt over into Bach's own earliest pieces, in which stern essays in fugal writing alternate with fantasy-full improvisatory episodes and a peppering of dissonance almost as extreme as in the vocal music of Monteverdi and his German imitators. From the *Nekrolog* we hear how twenty years later Bach himself returned to play the organ in the Catherinenkirche for two hours at a stretch in the presence of Reincken, 'who at that time was nearly a hundred years old' and who 'listened to him with particular pleasure'.[40] Bach chose 'at the request of those present' to improvise on none other than the old master's chorale variations on *An Wasserflüssen Babylon* – 'at great length (for almost half an hour) and in different ways' that no doubt included allusions to, and interpolations from, Reincken's work. For this he was shown 'much courtesy' by the old composer. To have been told 'I thought that this art was dead, but I see that in you it still lives'[41] must have moved Bach deeply.

But of the two, it was Böhm who was ultimately the more influential teacher and composer. His fine *Geistreicher Lieder* ('songs full of wit or conceit') were published in the year Bach began his studies, and many of his chorale settings re-surface in the anthologies that Sebastian and his eldest brother were soon to collate. We can readily believe that Bach 'loved and studied Böhm's work', as C. P. E. Bach wrote to Forkel, pieces such as the ornate and emotionally charged chorale variations on *Vater unser im Himmelreich*.[42] Here, under Böhm's guidance, he was exposed for the first time to the 'French taste' in music of which Böhm was an expert and which was to play such a fertile role in his musical universe. Later on, Bach's style of organ-playing was characterised by its idiosyncratic approach to registration ('in his own way', wrote Emanuel, 'astounding other organists'), derived perhaps from the French timbre-conscious approach to combining organ stops that Böhm may have taught him. Böhm's influence can be heard in Bach's later organ chorales, BWV 718, 1102 and 1114, and in a more tangible form if we can believe that the chorale partitas BWV 766, 767, 768 and 770 'were probably worked out in Lüneburg under Böhm's watchful eye'.[43] No doubt it was also thanks to Böhm that Bach experienced a French-style orchestra at first hand whenever the Capelle of the Duke of Celle visited Lüneburg. Long after his departure from Böhm's house, the two men remained in close contact.

* * *

The end of his formal schooling was a pivotal moment for Bach. He did not have the parental support or the money to move on to university or even to continue his lessons with Böhm. So far he had taken the bold step of leaving home for two years of intensive study. Now, aged seventeen, came the crucial choices: to take the fashionable (risky but usually lucrative) course of applying to join the Hamburg opera company, using it, as Handel did, as a springboard to fame abroad and greater breadth of experience; or to commit to a career for which he was now expertly trained – as an organist and church musician. Here Böhm was perfectly placed to give counsel, having worked regularly as a continuo player in the Hamburg opera orchestra until 1698 and part time since then. When asked by Forkel what took his father from Lüneburg to Weimar (in 1702), Emanuel replied simply, *Nescio* – 'I do not know.'[44] We, on the other hand, know that in July 1702 Bach applied successfully for the organist's job in Sangerhausen, only for the church authorities to be overruled in November by the Duke of Weissenfels, who favoured another, more experienced candidate. By Christmas or shortly afterwards he was in Weimar and listed as a lackey (payments due to 'Dem *Laquey* Baachen' are recorded) to the junior duke, Johann Ernst. This was hardly the position he was hoping for and he needed further guidance.* Bach himself later described his position as that of *HoffMusicus* (court musician) and more grandly still as *Fürstlich Sächsischer HoffOrganiste zu Weimar* (court organist to the Saxon Prince in Weimar).[45] The best source of advice would have been back where he started, in Eisenach, in the person of his father's cousin Johann Christoph, who had just turned sixty and was now the unofficial head of the Bach clan. We do not know for sure whether Bach returned to his Thuringian roots, but there were strong grounds for doing so.

News would have reached him that Christoph, after years of struggling to provide for his ailing wife and seven children, was now in very poor health. After the excitement of his formative training in Lüneburg and the organ visits to Hamburg, Sebastian would surely have been

* It seems that it was Johann Effler, the elderly court organist in Weimar, a former colleague of Bach's father and with close professional ties to the family stretching over thirty years, who negotiated the opening at Weimar for Sebastian after the Sangerhausen débâcle, allowing him to deputise for him now and again in the short time he spent there. He may also have put in a good word for him when the Arnstadt job (see below) loomed into view and facilitated his return to Weimar in 1708 (see Wollny, op. cit.).

bursting to display his new skills, his powers of improvisation and perhaps even a few compositions he might have been bold enough to show to such 'a profound composer'.[46]* It would not have been surprising for him to have consulted Christoph over his career prospects here in the family heartland, and to make sure that his candidature for any future opening did not conflict with the aspirations of his siblings or cousins (he had attended school in Eisenach with the two youngest of Christoph's sons) or indeed with those of any of the more senior members of the family. Re-encountering this former urchin, now almost a grown man, Christoph would have taken immediate pride and pleasure in his dazzling talents and been happy to advise.

No one was more qualified to evaluate Sebastian's skills than Christoph Bach or better placed to plan with him how to secure a position. Conveniently, Christoph's brother-in-law, the Arnstadt burgomaster Martin Feldhaus, was responsible for supervising the work of J. F. Wender in building a new organ at the Neukirche in Arnstadt, one which would soon need professional assessment. Having witnessed Sebastian's virtuosic skills as a performer, and then his technical skill in appraising the incomplete Stertzing organ in Eisenach (and how it stood comparison with the magnificent Schnitger instruments he had recently heard and possibly played in northern Germany), Christoph would have been perfectly confident about recommending Sebastian for both Arnstadt jobs – as 'assessor' of the Wender organ, and, since the post had fallen vacant, as organist of the Neukirche. Besides Sebastian, there were probably ten other Bachs qualified to fill such a vacancy, four of them Christoph's own sons, with Sebastian's own brother and former organ-teacher, Christoph of Ohrdruf, probably the strongest and most

* Bach would also have been keen to see and hear for himself how the realisation of his cousin's great dream was progressing: the construction of a grand, new, fifty-eight stop, four-manual organ with pedals for the Georgenkirche. Bach had known its builder, G. C. Stertzing, from childhood, probably from the moment he was big enough to crawl in and out of the chests of pipes while Stertzing and Christoph Bach together struggled to repair the old instrument, dating from 1576. Later, living under his brother's roof, in Ohrdruf, he could easily have made visits to Stertzing's workshop. Now at seventeen he was himself proficient and expert enough to assess Stertzing's work on the new instrument that Christoph claimed, more in hope than reality, 'more and more reaches the state of completion'. It was not completed for another four years, by which time Christoph was dead.

experienced candidate of all.* Sebastian had good cause, then, to travel on from Eisenach to Ohrdruf during the summer of 1702. His eldest brother would likely have made it immediately clear that he was well settled in Ohrdruf and would not stand in Sebastian's way should he be offered the chance to assess the brand-new instrument at the Neukirche or to become its full-time organist.† Sebastian would also have been able to hand over to his brother valuable keyboard manuscripts that included eleven works by his teacher Georg Böhm, together with some by his predecessor, Christian Flor, and a group of pieces by leading French composers of the day – all as a way of discharging the obligations he owed to his brother for his earlier training and for Christoph's acquiescence in the move to Lüneburg. This was just the first of many future exchanges of manuscript material for two new anthologies of contemporary music on which the brothers were to collaborate over the next few years.[47]

Meanwhile the way was clear for Sebastian to accept the invitation of Martin Feldhaus, the part-time mayor of Arnstadt, to examine and assess the new church organ. One day in June 1703 a private coach drew up at the castle gates in Weimar to transport the Duke's lackey twenty-five miles south-west to Arnstadt. Feldhaus had taken a gamble in hiring his wife's eighteen-year-old cousin to judge whether the 800 florins voted by the town fund for the building of a new organ was good value for money. In the last resort, however, any right of approval of a musical post in Arnstadt lay with the local count, Anthon Günther II of Schwarzburg. He had consistently asked for a Bach, so he should have one – the best available, coming with the highest plaudits and at a very

* Arnstadt was a town with which Christoph had strong links ever since he deputised for a year (1690) for his ailing great-uncle Heinrich. His godfather was Christoph Herthum, who was Heinrich Bach's successor as court and town organist, and who would have a leading say in the new appointment. Herthum also had a vested interest, seeing that his own son-in-law, Andreas Börner, was currently playing for the services at the Neukirche and thus had a legitimate prior claim. An already complicated situation received another twist in that Herthum was related by marriage to the Bachs (his wife, Maria Catharina, was sister to Christoph of Eisenach).

† Over the years Sebastian's eldest brother seems to have feathered his nest very comfortably at Ohrdruf, his career decisions made in the firm expectation of his wife's inheritance. Already in 1696 he had felt confident enough to turn down the interest shown by the main church of nearby Gotha for him to replace his former teacher Pachelbel. Eleven years later, thanks to his wife, he became the householder of 'Haus und Hof' in the *Langgassen* quarter of the town, which had six meadows and seven acres attached to it.

reasonable cost. On his arrival Bach immediately set to work, and for the next couple of days he was called upon to draw on all his technical know-how: measuring the wind-pressure and the thickness of the pipes (checking for example whether Wender had taken the usual short-cut of substituting lead for tin in the out-of-sight pipes); assessing the voicing of the reeds and especially the three big sixteen-foot stops, the quality of the touch and the rebound of the keys. We learn from Emanuel that the first thing his father would habitually do in trying out an organ was to see whether it had 'good lungs': 'To find out, he would draw out every speaking stop, and play in the fullest and richest possible texture. At this the organ builders would often grow quite pale with fright.'[48] Eventually he expressed his satisfaction with the new instrument and a fortnight later, now back in Weimar, Bach received his full examiner's fee and expenses – paid out of the town's tax on beer – followed by confirmation of an offer of the organist's post at the Neukirche: a contract was drawn up on 9 August and signed by the Count. It is not clear how Bach managed to extricate himself from Duke Johann Ernst's employ in Weimar, but on 14 August he gave his acceptance to the Arnstadt Consistory and entered upon his duties at the Neukirche in Arnstadt.

* * *

Earlier in that year, just after his eighteenth birthday, the family lost in quick succession, first Maria Elisabeth, the wife of Christoph of Eisenach, and a fortnight later the great Christoph himself. And so this most central figure of the pre-Sebastian Bachs never lived to see his cherished organ project completed, nor did he witness the spectacular creative development of his young cousin – not even the precarious first steps of a career that he may well have helped to nurture and guide. With his death, it was Sebastian Bach who had now demonstrated beyond all cavil that he had the musical gifts to be taken seriously within this most musical family (the Arnstadt appointment was, in a way, proof of it). Thus far he had shown not just a strong natural ability but also a singleness of purpose that enabled him to deal with adversity. There is a popular belief that talent is based on an inborn ability which makes it certain that its possessor will excel; but the story of Bach's youth indicates just how much the nurturing of his talent depended on chance as well as on planning. Without the inspirational presence of the elder Christoph, Sebastian's musical upbringing could well have lacked that essential initial spark and turned out far more humdrum. Had he not been apprenticed to his elder brother on the death of his parents, his keyboard ability could have lain dormant for a number of years and he might not have been technically advanced or confident enough to move away from his homeland and apply for tuition from the third of his mentors, Georg Böhm. Without Böhm, entrée to the rich cosmopolitan musical life of Hamburg with its new opera house and its many fine church organs might have proved a lot more difficult. Without the opportunity to observe the great organ-builder Arp Schnitger at close quarters and to hear Böhm's teacher Johann Adam Reincken play these fine organs, there might have been no consolidation of his talents and no qualification at such a young age to be considered seriously for the Arnstadt post. These are just the first in a series of plausible connections to be made between the established events of Bach's life, the verifiable circumstances of his childhood and schooling, the works he studied and imitated, and the music he himself would soon begin to compose. Having been made to rely on his inner resources for much of his adolescence as a result of being orphaned, yet driven forwards by a palpable ambition to shine and a voracious musical curiosity, at eighteen Johann Sebastian Bach was ready to stand comparison with his peers – that cluster of composer-musicians of exceptional talent born in, or just before, 1685.

4
The Class of '85

Unus homo est quod vult, fit quod lubet, agit quod placet.

Man alone is whatever he chooses to be. He becomes whatever he desires to become, and does what pleases him.

– Giambattista Vico, *Le orazioni inaugurali*, No. 3, Naples, 1700*

Three musicians of immense future distinction turned eighteen in 1703 – Domenico Scarlatti, Johann Sebastian Bach and the one who later styled himself George Frideric Handel. Born just two years before them was the Frenchman Jean-Philippe Rameau, while the two eldest in this class of six (and the most celebrated in their day), Johann Mattheson and Georg Philipp Telemann, were born in 1681. From our later vantage point what strikes us is the decisive influence at least four of them had – and still have – on the subsequent standard performing repertoire that led to Haydn, Mozart and beyond, and to the first three being accorded posthumous and enduring canonical status in the course of the nineteenth century. That, of course, is not the way others saw them at this time; rather, they appeared as fledgling musicians just emerging into the glare of public scrutiny in varied plumage and in different states of preparedness. While it is not hard to discern a genetic predisposition towards music in the cases of Scarlatti and Bach (as we discussed in

* Professor of Rhetoric at the Royal University of Naples, Vico also maintained that the first means of human expression was singing – a startling anthropological claim, later to gain endorsement, with relevance to the founding fathers of opera and their belief that music could bring historic or allegorical characters to life through its convincing powers of expression (*Scienza nuova* (1725), I.2.lix).

Chapter 3), for the others it entailed conscious choice, even when there were clear signs of early aptitude – as with Mattheson – or manifest talent pitted against paternal resolve – in the case of Telemann and, to a lesser extent, with Handel and Rameau. But, in any case, aged eighteen, it was not primarily as 'composers' that they announced themselves to the world. At this point we are still a century away from the Romantic cliché of the composer as an isolated creative genius fighting his inner demons in a lonely attic.

The Class of '85 were essentially craftsmen and versatile, all-round musicians. They were also brilliant virtuoso performers. Bach, Handel and Scarlatti were on the verge of being recognised as the leading keyboard exponents of their day, with Rameau not far behind. Armed with these qualities of flair, versatility, craftsmanship and keyboard expertise, they had every reason to feel confident in entering the music profession. The division between composers and theorists was nothing like as rigid then as it later became, and the membrane separating composer and performer was non-existent. What marked out the Class of '85 from previous generations was almost as much the exceptional potential they demonstrated as the fresh opportunities opening up ahead of them: theirs was the first generation of musicians able to see clear water between themselves and the fading spectre of continuous warfare and devastation – the malaise which through most of the previous century had blighted the struggles of their parents' and grandparents' generations to earn a secure living through music. Now, forty years later, in a less precarious environment, Pastor Sebastian Kirchmajer noted that 'most people love and learn gladly only those arts which adorn and fill the purse, or which otherwise bear profit.'[1]

Which, then, of these six musicians were tipped by the pundits of compositional form in 1703 to be the front-runners destined for fame and future glory? The clear favourite was Telemann. Having shown promising early 'form', at twenty-two he was already well into his stride. Son of a university-educated deacon in Magdeburg (who died before Telemann reached the age of four), partially self-taught as a musician,*

* Remarkably, in his three autobiographies Telemann mentions no teachers other than the cantor in Magdeburg, though he was evidently encouraged to teach himself by headmasters in Zellerfeld and Hildesheim. How he came to model his style on that of Steffani, Rosenmüller and Caldara, no one has so far been able to explain, beyond the fact that 'modelling' was an ingrained feature of educational method at the time.

Engraving by G. Lichtensteger of Georg Philipp Telemann (1681–1767), the most prolific of Bach's peers, revered at the time as the leading German composer of the first half of the eighteenth century.

he claimed to have composed his first opera when he was only twelve. In 1701, having deliberately left all but one of his music materials (instruments and compositions) at home, he went to Leipzig with the firm intention – so he tells us – of studying law at its Pauliner College. Stumbling across the lone composition, his roommate soon let it slip that in their midst was a musician of extraordinary proficiency. In rapid succession we find Telemann performing his setting of Psalm 6 the following Sunday at the Thomaskirche; commissioned by the mayor of Leipzig to compose a new church cantata every fortnight for performance there – much to the annoyance of its cantor, Johann Kuhnau; founding the *collegium musicum* – an accomplished semi-professional orchestra which 'often assembled up to forty students' at a time (he clearly had a knack of drawing talented student musicians into his orbit and holding their attention); appointed to the post of first organist and director of music at the Neukirche; and finally nominated, aged twenty-one, as music director of Leipzig's citizens' opera house. Within three years he would have at least four operas to his name. No wonder that in his vexation Kuhnau tried to discredit him as a mere 'opera musician'.*

Much further south, experts of form would have fancied the prospects and rich talent of the Neapolitan thoroughbred, Domenico Scarlatti. He certainly had pedigree: having trained and then worked alongside his father, the distinguished composer Alessandro, he had been appointed organist and composer to the royal chapel in Naples before he had turned sixteen; at eighteen he had just returned to his post in Naples after four months in Florence and was busy composing his first two operas. But, according to Alessandro, neither Naples nor Rome was good enough for his son. Soon he was dispatched to Venice, still the epicentre of opera production, as it had been for a hundred years. With the wisdom of hindsight and in view of Domenico's subsequent reputation – as a composer not of operas but of brilliant and quirky keyboard sonatas – his father's vow not to pinion his young 'eagle' of a son assumes a poignant and prophetic aspect.

Jean-Philippe Rameau started as the rank outsider. His academic results were said to be deplorable despite his quick-wittedness; but the seeds of a late-germinating attraction to opera may have been sown at this stage by his Jesuit teachers' strange initiatives in didactic music-theatre that formed a part of their teaching curriculum. With his mind set on becoming a musician, parental hopes of seeing him enter the law were dashed from the moment his organist father consented to his leaving Dijon at the age of eighteen to study music in Italy. After studying for a few months in Milan, he drifted off to join a troupe of itinerant artistes 'as first fiddle', and we know nothing about the extent or quality of his Italian musical training – only that in later life he regretted that it had been so brief. On his return to France he served for a while as organist at Avignon Cathedral and then, from 1703, more permanently at Clermont-Ferrand, where he was already at work on his *Premier Livre de pièces de clavecin*, published in 1706. Later acknowledged as the leading savant of the science of contemporary music, Rameau, at the age of fifty, would emerge as one of the most distinctive musical voices

* Beneath the surface of this rivalry were the seeds of a dispute over the role of university students and other supernumeraries taking part in the musical liturgy of the Leipzig churches, plugging the gaps left by the undermanned professionals and the Thomaner as part of a complex barter system which spelt future trouble for Kuhnau's successor, J. S. Bach (see Chapter 8).

of the late Baroque, becoming the greatest exponent of *tragédie lyrique* and *opéra-ballet* in the history of French opera, though few at this stage could have predicted it.

Johann Mattheson, son of a prosperous Hamburg tax collector, was a child prodigy. From the age of six he received private music tuition, studying the keyboard, a variety of instruments and composition. He was singing treble in various city churches in his own compositions and to his own organ accompaniment at the age of nine, before he could even reach the pedals. Hamburg's Theater am Gänsemarkt had been launched as a commercial enterprise in 1678 as the first public opera house to open outside Italy. At fifteen Mattheson was treading its boards, taking many of the female leads. At sixteen he had graduated to tenor roles and had begun composing operas. At eighteen he took the title role in his own *Die Plejades, oder das Sieben-Gestirne*. By his own rarely modest testimony, Mattheson was now the *Haupt person* – the main man – of the Hamburg Opera, to which he stayed attached until he was twenty-three, since it gave him 'the best possible opportunity' as regards composition – far beyond what traditional conservatories might have taught him.[2] The goal of composers, he claimed in 1700, should be to write music to generate 'especially intense, serious, long-lasting and extremely profound emotions', although, on the evidence of his own *Der edelmüthige Porsenna* (1702), he fell a long way short of his ambition.* Mattheson was perhaps too clever for his own good; nonetheless the smart money was on this sophisticated and broadly educated polymath. Later on he wrote about music from the vantage point of practical experience, not only as an observer but also as a trained professional. He considered opera houses essential to civic pride, a necessity, like having efficient banks: 'The latter provide for general security, the former for education and refreshment . . . where the best banks are, so too are the best opera houses,' he maintained.[3]

Handel's start in music was almost as promising. His elderly father – surgeon and *valet de chambre* to the Duke of Saxe-Weissenfels in the city

* It used to be thought that Mattheson's music was destroyed in the bombing raids in Hamburg during the Second World War, and that in any case his operas were likely to have been a pale shadow of those by Reinhard Keiser – works that were given sometimes in the vernacular, some in Italian, and others in a curious hybrid made up of German recitative and Italian arias. However, a revival in Boston during 2005 of Mattheson's *Boris Goudenow* (1710), recovered along with others of his operas from Moscow and St Petersburg, seems to have made a marginally more positive impression of his gifts as an opera composer.

Mezzotint of Johann Mattheson (1681–1764), singer, composer, pundit and music theorist, after a portrait by Johann Salomon Wahl.

of Halle, which had been badly affected by the Thirty Years War and recently annexed to Prussia – allegedly opposed his son's joining a profession which he regarded as 'a sort of peddler's calling: cheap huckstering when all else failed'. But this most likely belongs to the same category of childhood anecdotes told to family and pupils that we have already encountered with Bach – serving to bolster an image of a disadvantaged childhood and of youthful resolve to pursue a chosen career regardless of obstacles – a recurring theme in musicians' autobiographies of the time and in the novels of Wolfgang Caspar Printz (in particular his *Musicus vexatus . . . Cotala*, 1690). Handel's musical education in Halle was actually fortunate in a number of ways. As his teacher for keyboard and in composition he was lucky to find Friedrich Wilhelm Zachow, the progressive organist of the Marienkirche and director of the local *chorus musicus*. Zachow's expert private tuition was complemented by an exposure to the richly imaginative German and Latin church music of Halle's vice-Capellmeister, Johann Philipp Krieger, to the music Handel compiled during his Italian travels (sold to the Marienkirche before he moved on to

Weissenfels),* and to the dramatic works that gave Handel his first impressions of German court opera. Access to contemporary Italian music in a variety of genres both for church and for opera, just before the Pietist clergy placed a total embargo on Latin-texted church music in Halle, may have instilled in the young Handel an urge to follow Krieger's footsteps across the Alps and experience it at its source.

This more cosmopolitan and worldly view probably gave Handel the edge at this stage over Bach, who was his exact contemporary, in spite of their sharing many elements of basic musical education as well as a Luther-impregnated outlook on life. In 1702, at the age of seventeen, he had already matriculated at Halle University, where he 'must have been aware of the strongly progressive trend in philosophical sciences at the university' as represented by Christian Thomasius and later (after Handel had left) by Christian Wolff, turning Halle into 'one of the centres of the German Enlightenment'[4] – at a time when Bach did not have the equivalent financial means to extend his formal education beyond his school years in Lüneburg. In the spring of the following year, perhaps counselled by his new friend Telemann, such were his musical ambitions 'goading him beyond the narrow confines of Halle, with its petty feuds and commercial smugness', that Handel packed his bags and set off for Hamburg 'on his own bottom, and chiefly with a view to improvement', as his first biographer, John Mainwaring, put it.[5] Luckily for him, soon after his arrival he fell in with Mattheson (four years his senior), who claimed to have acted as his worldly-wise guide to this city of adventure. 'Handel came to Hamburg in the summer of 1703 rich only in ability and good intentions,' Mattheson characteristically wrote later. 'I was almost the first with whom he made acquaintance. I took him round to all the choirs and organs here, and introduced him to operas and concerts.'[6] In August they travelled together to Lübeck – full of camaraderie and bravado, and trying to outsmart each other composing 'numerous double fugues in the carriage' – ostensibly to audition for Buxtehude's post as organist of the Marienkirche. But there was a snag: marriage to the outgoing organist's mature daughter was apparently part of the deal, and they both shied away, neither feeling 'the smallest

* Krieger (1649–1725) had studied in Venice with Johann Rosenmüller for a couple of years in the 1670s. He went on to compose eighteen operas to German texts and over 2,000 church cantatas, of which only seventy-six are extant, but enough to provide a measure of his influence on the young Handel.

inclination' in that department. Twice already Handel had been given the chance to become a German church musician as Bach was, and twice he had turned away from it, sensing – and no doubt urged in this by Mattheson – the stronger lure of the magical world of opera.

The opening of the Theater am Gänsemarkt in Hamburg in the late 1670s acted as a magnet to ambitious north German musicians. Here was the basis for a future career – risky, but with high rewards. Mattheson, Handel and Telemann all found themselves drawn to Hamburg and its opera house at various stages, and, in the case of the first two, it was where they would serve their theatrical apprenticeship under Reinhard Keiser. A brilliant and prolific composer, Keiser seems to have cut a restless and somewhat dissolute figure, greatly admired by his peers – Scheibe, Mattheson and Hasse. His importance in Charles Burney's eyes was that he displayed 'all the vigour of a fertile invention and correctness of study and expression'. Bach certainly came to know his music and may have taken a lead from Keiser in his dramatic use of arioso in his Passion music. As for Handel at this stage, we have only Mattheson's less than reliable testimony that, on his arrival in Hamburg in 1703, 'he composed long, very long arias, and really interminable cantatas, which had neither the right kind of skill nor of taste, though complete in harmony, but the lofty schooling of opera soon trimmed him into other fashions.'[7] Despite its precarious debt-ridden state, its frequent changes of management and its vulnerability to periodic civil unrest, the Hamburg Opera stood as a beacon for opportunity and employment to a budding musician. Constant sniping from an ever-watchful clergy (or 'biblical police', as they were occasionally referred to) meant that religious themes were sometimes offered by way of appeasement. Although a peculiar eclecticism prevailed, with recitative in German often linking bravura arias sung in Italian, it offered the chance to learn and to become immersed in the latest Italian and French idioms. According to Mattheson – he can only have been thinking of Hamburg – a civic opera house was a 'musical university', a laboratory in which to experiment as both performer and composer.*

* Elsewhere Mattheson expressed his belief in the intrinsic worth of opera: 'A good opera-theatre is nothing less than an academy of the fine arts – architecture, perspective, painting, machinery, dancing, acting, ethics, history, poetry and especially music – where all together are at once conjoined and continually experimented with anew for the pleasure and edification of distinguished and intelligent audiences. However, without such a well-planned

The differing approaches of this Class of '85 to the world of opera give us an inkling as to the range of their interests, orientations and ambitions. In autobiographical submissions of the time it was considered *de rigueur* to emphasise diligence in seeking out opera houses on one's travels. So Telemann feels we should know that he travelled as a youngster all the way to Brunswick and Berlin just to experience opera at first hand, but gained access 'concealed by friends, since admission was granted to few outsiders'. Opera hung around his throat 'like a thunderstorm', he tells us. Now, at twenty-one, he himself is already in charge of an opera-theatre in Leipzig. Handel, with Mattheson at his side, strides boldly into Hamburg's Theater am Gänsemarkt and gets himself hired on the spot as a violinist in Reinhard Keiser's orchestra. Domenico Scarlatti, meanwhile, is doing just the opposite: trying to sidle out of parental reach and the fixed plan to propel him into the world of opera. Rameau – who will prove in the long term to be the most original opera composer of the five – has perhaps not yet given the matter a moment's thought.*

Though the Class of '85 were born into a variety of musical cultures, opera provided them with a common aesthetic or institutional framework. The exception is Bach. As we saw earlier, he had every reason to be drawn to Hamburg at this time. His motives in making several trips from Lüneburg were essentially no different from those of any young provincial organist, like Johann Conrad Rosenbusch, for example, going to Hamburg around this time – 'to become skilful in the future through keeping the company of other famous artists, and, where possible, to seek out his luck'. Bach's prowess as a keyboard player may, as Forkel put it, have inclined him 'to try to do, to see, and to hear everything which, according to the ideas he then entertained, could contribute to his improvement'.[8] But there is no evidence to suggest that he confined his visits to its churches, deliberately shunning the theatre as home to

nursery like opera . . . the best as well as the worst music must finally become spoilt and become extinct. Indeed even in the church it will no longer have an enduring place. The downfall of opera causes the downfall of the very essence of music.' Almost as an afterthought Mattheson added, 'Operas are the academies of music, as concerts are its grammar schools, but in the church is found its true calling, and in heaven its eternal place, yes, so to speak, its place and voice' (*Die neueste Untersuchung der Singspiele* (1744), pp.103–4).

* It would be reasonable to assume that they all shared an acceptance of the sustaining utility of the passions, or 'affections', in 'strengthening and prolonging thoughts in the soul . . . which otherwise might easily be erased from it' (Descartes, *Les Passions de l'âme* (1649)).

'the twisted serpent of opera';* nor that the very opportunities that Handel was soon to seek within its walls, Bach passed over 'with indifference.'[9] Just because the writers of his obituary do not mention the Hamburg opera or any contact with its leading light, Reinhard Keiser, does not mean that Bach 'at the time had no particular interest in opera'.[10] We saw earlier that his Lüneburg teacher, Georg Böhm, who played harpsichord continuo there in the summer season,† had the entrée to Reinhard Keiser and the Gänsemarkt personnel, as well as to Johann Adam Reincken, the doyen of north German organists, at St Catherine's. Reincken himself was a co-instigator of the opera house and a director of its governing board. Either of these men could easily have accompanied Bach, given him letters of introduction to attend Keiser's theatre or even arranged for him to participate in any of the twelve operas Keiser composed for Hamburg between 1700 and 1702. We can surmise that his natural musical curiosity drew Bach as a listener into its orbit, even if, once in, what early biographers identified as an innate shyness held him back from the networking needed for success in a pressurised world whose purpose was to satisfy 'the vanity of [its] individual executants'.[11]

There is, however, the possibility that Bach dipped his toe in these

* This was the description given to it (*die krumme Operen Schlange*) by Joachim Gerstenbüttel, an ultra-conservative and musical director of Hamburg's five major churches (see F. Krummacher, *Die Choralbearbeitung in der protestanischer Figuralmusik zwischen Praetorius und Bach* (1978), p. 199). Operas, according to Bach's future colleague in Leipzig, Johann Christoph Gottsched, 'pour out their poison through lascivious verse, soft tones, and indecent movements of the operatic heroes and their "goddesses"' (Philip Marshall Mitchell, *Johann Christoph Gottsched (1700–1766): Harbinger of German Classicism* (1995), p. 37). It is a recurrent theme in Bach historiography. Spitta refers to opera as 'a foreign growth on German soil, rich in foliage but barren in fruit'. He writes disparagingly of 'these gaudy and uninspiring phantasmagoria' and contrasts opera composers with 'a number of vigorous and highly endowed artists, who would have laughed to scorn existence itself if they had been desired to fritter their talents for nothing better than the trivial amusement of a heartless crowd' (*The Life of Bach*, Clara Bell and J. A. Fuller Maitland (trs.) (1899 edn.), Vol. 1, p. 467). Assumption of the same high moral ground persists in more recent treatments, including that of Malcolm Boyd in attributing Thuringia's (and, by implication, Bach's) 'resistance to opera' to its 'strong Lutheran tradition' (M. Boyd, *Bach* (1983), p. 27). From that it is a short step to the recurrent warnings by German historians that German culture should remain untainted by foreign influence.

† The name 'Behm' appears from Easter 1694 to Shrove Tuesday 1695 in the debt register of the opera's leaseholder Jakob Kremberg (W. Schulze, *Die Quellen der Hamburger Oper 1678–1738* (1938), p. 158). This was some three years before Böhm was appointed organist of the Johanniskirche in Lüneburg in Aug. 1698.

theatrical waters and recoiled – not from any kind of Lutheran prudery but simply because the music he heard there left him cold. While he might have admired and learnt from Keiser's use of orchestral colour and rhetorical word-painting,* just as likely the short-breathed structure, the deficiencies in coherent tonal planning, the failure to sustain the musical argument, and the fudges and compromises to which opera is prone were likely to disenchant a musician of Bach's seriousness of purpose.† As a result he chose to distance himself from a line of development that most composers of his generation seemed hell-bent on pursuing. The very particular training Bach had received to this point, with its concentrated Lutheran emphasis, meant that there was always a cleft separating his outlook, preoccupations and expectations from those of his peers, one that in time would open into a vast chasm as each stuck doggedly to his respective path.

So the bookmakers of 1703, noting an absence of declared operatic ambition, would automatically have expected Bach to be a back marker. Career prospects were less glittering without the social advancement that rubbing shoulders with those who patronised opera normally brought. But that does not imply that Bach was insulated from, or unaware of, the 'stuff' of opera in the state into which it had by then evolved, let alone reluctant in future to make use of such techniques

* Indeed, according to Mattheson, Keiser was the first – along with himself, naturally – to adopt 'the oratorical and rational manner in fitting music to words'. C. P. E. Bach later on considered that in 'the beauty, novelty, expression, and mind-pleasing qualities of his melody' Keiser was a match for Handel, and he placed Keiser on a shortlist of ten composers whom his father in his last years 'esteemed highly' (NBR, pp. 400, 403).

† And who would not be put off and unnerved if your first taste of opera was the blood-curdling story of two locally famous Hamburg pirates? This was Keiser's double-decker opera *Störtebecker und Jödge Michaels* given on consecutive evenings in 1701. Two more of Keiser's double-deckers, one based on the story of Ulysses, the other on the legend of Orpheus, and *Der Sieg der fruchtbaren Pomona*, followed in 1702, as well as Mattheson's interminably dull *Der edelmüthige Porsenna*. Keiser's offerings for 1703 included a Roman costume drama centring on the sex-versus-*raisons d'état* dilemma of the Emperor Claudius in which Italian-texted arias were incorporated for the first time in a Hamburg opera. There was also a biblical drama featuring the 'wisdom triumphing over life' of Solomon, in which eight of the arias were by G. C. Schürmann. Taken together, these 'operas' were probably typical of the current heterogeneous mixture of styles and languages given as part of a single evening's theatrical entertainment. It is revealing that Keiser, as head of one of the first commercial opera-theatres to depend primarily on public support to remain solvent, admitted that he felt obliged to open its doors to hillbilly and low-life characters coming on stage – though never, he says defensively, giving in to *den mauvais goût des Parterre* (*Avertissement* to his opera *La fedeltà coronata* (1706)).

within his own work whenever it suited his purposes. Friedrich Blume's half-century-old conclusions are still valid today: 'there remains the possibility that the youthful Bach may have absorbed influences here [at the Hamburg opera] that did not bear fruit until later in his life, an assumption that is all the more likely since from 1714 on Bach reveals himself in his cantatas as a dramatist of high rank, and also since he could scarcely have had any other opportunity between 1702 and 1714 to become familiar with the operatic world. In his cantatas it can be seen on many a page that this world was not foreign to him. Where else could he have gotten to know it if not from his Lüneburg period and from his trips to Hamburg?'[12] We shall see shortly that Bach was to seize on a mutant type of opera that was to serve his purpose when composing the more dramatic of his church cantatas and Passions.

The rest of his peer group no doubt shared the underlying assumption, later voiced by Burney, that opera was now the dominant artistic form and Italian-style opera its only true and pure cultivar. Any composer of stature and with an interest in theatre will sooner or later therefore write an opera.* From this many music historians have concluded that opera in its first hundred years gradually got 'better'. On the contrary, in the course of the seventeenth century, bleached of narrative coherence and with its initial energetic feeling for contrasts diminished, it actually faded. The immediate background to the emergence of the Class of '85 is the feverishly creative development of a parallel alternative organism, one that we should not equate with opera, although it has many features in common with it. Four representatives of seventeenth-century musical genius, Monteverdi, Schütz, Charpentier and Purcell – each in a different country, each blessed with a vivid theatrical imagination, acute responsiveness to language and exceptional musical

* This is connected to what Curtis Price refers to as 'the dubious evolutionary history of seventeenth- and eighteenth-century English music drama' and the questionable 'assumption that opera in the Italian style is the apex of music-drama and that those hybrids which mix song and speech are necessarily inferior' (*Henry Purcell and the London Stage* (1984), pp. 357, 3). Gary Tomlinson has done his best to warn against the tendency of musicologists to endorse 'universalizing views of operatic history'. He, in contrast, perceives its 'shifting, shimmering metaphysics' and suggests that 'The effects of operatic singing constitute one subspecies within a huge family of human experiences brought about by heightened utterance ... Though we habitually conceive it as a unitary progress, operatic history might rather be rethought as a set of diverse manifestations, differing at fundamental levels of cultural formation, of the older, deeper and broader impulse to voice an ordering of the world that includes invisible terrains' (*Metaphysical Song* (1999), pp. 157, 5, 4, 5).

inventiveness – sought to control its flow and to find new outlets for it. The results of their work in giving dramatic life to poetic texts are to be found not only in the mainstream but in variant forms and tributaries: in oratorios, biblical dialogues and *histoires sacrées*, as well as in different kinds of secular music composed in 'theatre style' that was not necessarily intended for the operatic stage. So that when we say that opera was 'in the air' *circa* 1700, therefore, we can point to two broad manifestations: on the one hand, Italian-style opera as it had by then evolved, heading towards a Metastasian ideal of drama that depicted moral forces, with a poetic style adjusted to the vocal lines; on the other, instances of dramatic music in which a probing exploration of music's capacity to encompass and to express powerful human emotions had already led to compositions of striking originality.* For a variety of reasons the latter did not require – or, in some cases, actively rejected – scenic representation in a conventional theatrical mould. The '85ers were the first generation in a position to confront these two poles and to choose or seek a synthesis between them. The way we define opera *circa* 1700 may help us to throw light not just on the choices facing Bach and his brilliant peer group at the outset of their careers, but on the cultural milieu which demarcates the changing role of music in early-eighteenth-century society.

* * *

The path to that definition begins at some point in the second half of the sixteenth century with the emergence of an identifiable 'spirit of music-drama' – one, but only one, manifestation leading to what is commonly classified as opera. Convenient as it is to date the inception of the genre from 1600, and to narrow it down to 'court opera', it is salutary to remember that its pioneers never referred to their works as 'opera' at any stage, nor even as *drammi per musica*. Wholly caught up in exploring erudite techniques of what they called 'speaking in melody', they were not primarily concerned with consistency of musical means in expressing dramatic action. Indeed, that they could not come up with a single

* This is not to imply that the Italian poet Pietro Metastasio (1698–1782) was indifferent to depicting human passion in his opera librettos. He saw them as 'the necessary winds by which one navigates through the sea of life', agreeing with Descartes (*Les Passions de l'âme*) that all the passions are 'good in themselves' and that 'we have nothing to avoid but their evil use or excesses.'

name for the new genre suggests a fair degree of uncertainty, or at least ambiguity, as to what it really was they were inventing or reinventing. We in turn should be wary about projecting on to their experimental works our latter-day notions of what might typically constitute opera – preposterous, expensive, and prone to diva tantrums and self-indulgence. It was not as if the Florentine Camerata were suddenly able to deliver 'opera' from the primordial soup: it needed an exceptional musician – a composer of genius – to make sense of this rich but sometimes crude miscellany of stylistic initiatives and to bind them together with a convincing dramatic thread. At the turn of the century there was not enough purely musical interest to hold the listener's attention, nor sufficient invention to supply and shape the sung line to its text. Giulio Caccini blew his big opportunity in *Il rapimento di Cefalo* in 1600 by boring his Florentine audience with long stretches of unvaried recitative. No one had yet hit upon a coherent musical idiom that could ensure musical continuity and clear structural paragraphing.

Claudio Monteverdi, amazingly, provided all of these missing elements in his very first through-composed work for the stage, *L'Orfeo*, given at the Mantuan Court in 1607. He recognised that the hitherto unexploited potential of what the Florentines called the 'new music' was to allow the singer's voice to fly free above an instrumental bass line, giving it just the right degree of harmonic support and ballast. Melodic shapes and rhythmic patterns no longer needed to be tethered by the guy-ropes of rigid polyphonic structure. Before *L'Orfeo* no one had grasped this potential freedom to manoeuvre or used it to plot expressive rises and falls for singers that encouraged spontaneous spurts of movement: to rush, drag or clash against the metrical beat and regular strummings of the plucked continuo instruments. It was with *L'Orfeo* that Monteverdi made the decisive creative leap – from a pastoral play, intended to be sung and not spoken throughout, to a musical-drama with emotions generated and intensified by music. Not only was speech treated dramatically, but the drama of sung speech now also approached the condition of music. By stealing the clothes of the Florentine Camerata, Monteverdi showed up the inadequacy of the original wearers. The radicalism of *L'Orfeo* may not be fully recognised by audiences even today. In an age when the emotional life of human beings was becoming a topic of the utmost fascination – with philosophers and playwrights trying to define the role of passions in human destiny, and with painters as varied as Velázquez, Caravaggio and Rembrandt all intent on portraying the inner life of men and women – Monteverdi stood head and shoulders above contemporary musicians in the consistent way he explored and developed musical themes of 'imitation' and 'representation'. We now refer to *L'Orfeo* as an opera and think of it as the beginning of the genre; but that is because we are looking at it backwards via the perspective of Wagner or Verdi. To Monteverdi it was a *favola in musica*, a fable in music: the surprise for the contemporary listener was that 'all the actors are to *sing* their parts', as Carlo Magno wrote in 1607, revealing that he did not know quite how to describe the new style of *recitar cantando*.[13] Indeed, Monteverdi was mapping out a new musical terrain with a fresh vision of music capable of pursuing a life of its own, one that would dominate composition for the next century and have an indirect but decisive bearing on Bach's development.

* * *

Some unconscious inkling of the way the senses vary and clash in their receptivity to visual, aural and tactile stimuli may have been at the root of the anxiety that churchmen on both sides of the denominational divide in 1600 felt about religion borrowing the clothes of secular theatre. They bridled at the infiltration of 'operatic' techniques within their walls and liturgy. Contemporary musicians found ways, as musicians invariably do, to skirt around these rigid functional categories and, magpie-fashion, to pick and steal just what attracted them, maintaining only the thinnest formal veneer for the sake of propriety, while choosing the frame, design and modes of expression. They selected, first, the appropriate affective response and then the musical shapes to describe it – and not the other way round. Monteverdi and Schütz might have reasoned that their audiences, whether in church or in the theatre, were similarly susceptible to the persuasive power of music to enhance and vivify narrative. When it came to story-telling, the Bible was a proven repository, rich enough to match any of the ancient secular myths or historical accounts of the past. From the moment that the listener accepts the inherently ludicrous notion that characters, whether biblical or historical, are in the habit of *singing*, rather than of speaking, their thoughts, there is, in a sense, little to choose between, say, a Cleopatra mourning the loss of Caesar's love or a Mary Magdalene grieving at the sepulchre: both are 'operatic' characters with whom the listener can identify. It is not the physical space or auditorium, or the presence or absence of sets and costumes, which decides what does, or does not, truly qualify as 'operatic': the common denominator is music linked to a poetic text as a means for the transmission and expression of human emotion in a hundred different ways that can reach the listener's heart.*

The least troubled in this regard were the Venetians. Even in the early spasms of economic decline and embattled by the Ottoman Turks, Venice was still the fulcrum of the arts in Italy. Proud of their mythical Republican image and cussed opposition, both political and theological, to Rome, Venetian citizens valued their basilica as a shrine in which state ceremonial music and an adroit deployment of choral groups – in antiphony, *en échelon* or in echo permutations – coexisted with the most rapt, intimate meditations in sound now stealing the voluptuous vocabulary of early opera. When Monteverdi put these styles side by side in his great *Vespro della Beata Vergine* (1610), he made the richest and most highly patterned mosaic in music hitherto composed – a veritable *opera sacra* in performance – demonstrating just how likely was the failure of any insistence by the Counter-Reformation on the formal separation of sacred and secular in terms of dramatic representation. It is significant that the first monodic sung dramas performed in Florence coincided in 1600 with the first surviving play set entirely to music: Emilio de' Cavalieri's sacred *La rappresentazione di anima, e di corpo* (*Illustrations of Body and Soul*), performed in the Oratorio del Crocifisso, Rome, in the presence of high-ranking clerics and nobles. If any of these amounted to 'opera' – albeit the first hesitant experiments in that direction, whether sacred or secular, we should resist the idea of a smooth teleological progress towards Mozart and beyond. For opera did not emerge organically as did other new musical forms such as the concerto or the symphony. What appeared in the years around 1600 was a tangled skein of disorderly threads. To achieve a future coherent identity these needed to be woven tightly enough to pass through the eye of a needle. That simply did not happen in any consistent way for

* The German theologian Gottfried Ephraim Scheibel (1696–1759) maintained that the musical sounds 'that give me pleasure in an opera can also do the same in church, except that it has a different object . . . if our church music today were a little more theatrical it would be more beneficial than the stilted compositions that are ordinarily used in churches' (*Zufällige Gedancken von der Kirchenmusic* (1721); see *Bach's Changing World* (2006) pp. 236–8). This was by no means a universally accepted view.

several generations. It is therefore more instructive to treat music-drama (not to be confused with 'opera') as what Richard Dawkins calls a 'replicator', an organism that mutates through successive generations, sometimes with enough success to perpetuate the line and, at others, falling away as expendable and non-regenerative. This might help to explain the many false starts, spluttering initiatives, parallel genres and unpredictable re-appearances, often in improbable contexts, over the next hundred years. The seventeenth century is rich in the emergence of such experimental operatic offshoots, many of which burgeoned into the cultural habitat of our Class of '85.

* * *

For its first half-century, then, music-drama coexisted in church and the milieu of secular courts. One of the early criticisms of sung drama, including of Monteverdi, was its inherent lack of naturalness – something he, for one, was determined to rectify, convinced that where spoken theatre might fail, music could bring the stiff figures of heroic tragedy to life. All through his career Monteverdi was devoted to moving the passions of his listeners, convinced that only by means of music could words be cuffed and bullied into prising open the door to the deepest realms of feeling. He was supreme in judging how and when to increase the emotional heat and to enhance the intensity of discourse by varied musical techniques. By the time Venice opened its doors to public opera in 1637, Monteverdi had ensured that the old world of the madrigal, in which he had served his apprenticeship, and the new world of opera had grown steadily closer. A comment of the time was that the 'general public' had learnt 'to appreciate anything and everything represented in music' – in other words, 'why people sing' even in the throes of passion.[14] Where previously court audiences could learn to accept divinities, demigods or fictitious Arcadian personages* – or even biblical figures – breaking into song, now to a mercantile Venetian audience there was

* The epic, whether drawn from mythology or ancient history, was an outlet for the expression of controversial ideas or reflections on contemporary life. Simon Towneley Worsthorne identified it as 'an early subterfuge; even Tasso's *Aminta* [set by Monteverdi for the Parma festivities of 1628] clothed in pastoral guise members of the court of Mantua [just as in Monteverdi's *Il ballo delle ingrate* performed there in 1608 with its poignant topical references to the flinty scorn of the court ladies towards their suitors]. The mind was quick to catch an allusion; symbols and images were readily understood and appreciated, a whole world lay readily at hand' (*Venetian Opera in the Seventeenth Century* (1954), pp. 151–2).

nothing incongruous about a pair of real lovers expressing their desire and pain of parting in song. This is what Monteverdi does with exemplary skill in the first scene for the two main lovers in *L'incoronazione di Poppea* (Act I, Scene iii). At this point not only had he totally mastered the Florentine ideal of *recitar cantando*, but he had learnt to vary the mixture by the strategic placement of little arias or duets in music that was responsive in its rhythmic suppleness to every single word. Remarkably he showed how the fluidity and seeming fragility of stretches of music-drama could be maintained at a time of increasing standardisation of form.

In this he was vastly influential. Take as an example the descending tetrachord which, through Monteverdi's treatment of it, becomes from then on a comprehensive musical symbol for expressing grief, sorrow and regret.* Cavalli employs it to poignant effect for Cassandra in his *Didone*, as does Purcell in an even more famous lament sung by his Queen of Carthage. In due course Bach will use it for the opening chorus of his Weimar cantata BWV 12, *Weinen, Klagen, Sorgen, Zagen*, which in time will grow into the Crucifixus of the *B minor Mass*. Giovanni Rigatti, a singer and junior colleague of Monteverdi at St Mark's, takes it as the basis of a psalm-setting, *Nisi Dominus*, and even puts a gloss on Monteverdi's rubric about varying the tempo to suit the mood and *affetto* of the words.† But Monteverdi also knew when a song was called for – and there is no shortage of them in his final opera, *L'incoronazione di Poppea* – some catchy, almost like folksongs, some rhythmic canzonettas or ariette (a Venetian speciality that persisted right up to the time that Handel wrote his *Agrippina* there in 1708), and some more sensuous as in the Nero/Poppea love scenes. Therein lay a danger – of a formal separation between recitative and arias. As long as there was the masterly control of a Monteverdi – and to some extent that goes also for his successors Cavalli and Cesti, and for Domenico Mazzocchi in Rome – to bring pressure on the librettist to vary the poetic metre and ensure gradations in discourse through a fluid transi-

* Two of the better known instances can be found in his *Lamento della ninfa* and the final Poppea/Nero duet (if it is indeed by him). See the article on 'The Descending Tetrachord: An Emblem of Lament' by Ellen Rosand (MQ, Vol. 65 (1979), pp. 346–59).

† 'The opening of this work should be grave, with alterations of tempo in appropriate places as I have indicated in the singers' and players' parts, so that the text is matched by as much feeling as possible' (Rigatti, *Messa e salmi* (1640)).

tion from expressive sung speech to song and back again, it could be averted. But even Monteverdi's protégé Francesco Cavalli, with his keen ear for poetry and the varied affective mood of his Venetian operas, could not overcome the tedious regularity of the six-syllable verses on offer from his librettists. The moment that fascination with exploring the emotional reactions of the participants was allowed to dominate, the search for purely musical ways to convey the action was lost. A notable strength of Monteverdi and Cavalli (but one not shared by many of the next generation of composers) was to allow this affective reaction to fuse with and *become* the action, just as it would do in due course in many of Bach's cantatas and Passions.

From the middle of the seventeenth century onwards, the Venetian theatres, without the limitless resources that the Barberini family were throwing at operatic productions in Rome at around the same time, bobbed up and down on the tide of free-market forces and the threat of incipient bankruptcy. Under the twin pressures of the demand by a paying public for novelty and constant innovation on the one hand, and the inflationary fees paid to the leading singers on the other, Venetian impresarios began to urge composers (who were normally paid half the fees of the singers – just a one-off sum as opposed to nightly pay-cheques) to extend both the number and the length of the arias they provided. Singers now travelled with 'suitcase arias' that they were expected to sing on their perambulations, regardless of the composer or the opera for which they had been hired. What earlier had been an exception – the momentary suspension of the narrative for the insertion of an arietta for a minor character or for a strophic aria – now became a commonplace. By 1680 the *da capo* aria was the dominant form; ten years later its hegemony was complete. The result was that *dramma per musica* developed into an increasingly two-paced affair. A damaging cleavage was opening up between the dull patter of recitative and the drama-sapping nonsense of *da capo* arias. Recitative became more and more perfunctory, its phrases increasingly and predictably grouped into tonally closed paragraphs mirroring the sectional articulation or shape of the poetry. It was now the principal means to propel the action forwards, but then, at the point where an aria was called for, things came to a juddering halt.

In the generation immediately prior to that of our Class of '85, a few conspicuously musicianly composers like Alessandro Scarlatti fought against this rigidity and predictability of form and took pains to vary it and invested *secco* recitative with as much musical interest as possible; but they were fighting a losing battle: the recitative/aria pairing was now merely a prop on which to hang a star-based drama. Public opera had became formulaic, repetitive and, from a musico-dramatic perspective, unrecognisable. Arias henceforth provided moments for characters to step outside the unfolding drama: to reflect or give lyrical expression to a particular mood or 'affect', or to inhabit the expanded moment. More and more they became opportunities for vocal exhibitions of grace, charm and virtuosity; but now in sharply defined units (known to musicologists as 'closed form'), which by their nature were less conducive to subtle gradations of feeling. Gone was the flexible pattern of weaving in and out of arioso and aria and back into recitative, the fine gradations of feeling characteristic of Monteverdi and, later, of Purcell, in which states of mind are explored before our eyes and ears. For composers obliged to concentrate all the musical interest in arias, one way round this problem was to contrive stark juxtapositions of mood: 'My heart is grieving' (A) . . . but 'I will seek revenge' (B) (section quicker and in a different key) . . . and yet (cue for *da capo*) 'my heart is [still] grieving' (return to A) or 'grieving still more painfully' (cue for emotionally charged embellishments of the vocal line). A structural balance mirroring various codified 'affections' was thus gained at the expense of tracing in music the living growth of emotion within an operatic character.

A new formal and inventive challenge to the composer began to emerge when the instrumental contribution of the orchestra, once confined during Cavalli's heyday (1640–60) to introductory or linking ritornelli within strophic arias, was allowed to spread across the entire aria.* Parallel to this was the gradual disappearance in Venetian heroic opera of ensemble numbers, since the main concern became not the way characters interacted, but how they expressed their emotional experience after the event. This absence of a chorus was one key factor in speeding up the process whereby music and drama became uncoupled, as market forces more and more dictated the shape of this increasingly popular form of entertainment – sublime at one moment, vulgar or preposterous the next. The initial pursuit of the ideals of music in Greek drama cherished by the early Florentine pioneers, together with respect

* Gracefully proportioned A-B-A structures were to grow lopsided in the 1720s and 1730s as the music of the A section expanded and the first stanza came to be repeated eight times, in contrast to the B section, which was heard only the once.

for poetic texts and for the Aristotelian unities, was now forgotten in the transition from one-off court events to public opera governed by the rules of a commercial venture ruled by impresarios. As we saw in Chapter 1 (p. 14), the idea of 'the work' as such barely existed. It would be oversimplifying – but not greatly – to imply that what once emerged like some brilliant culinary invention, tested and then perfected in mouth-watering recipes by the master-chef Claudio Monteverdi, degenerated after his death in a matter of generations into a standardised 'tourist' menu.* It is salutary to tot up the number of towering seventeenth-century composers, born musical-dramatists to a man, and to weep at the missed opportunities: Monteverdi (three aborted operas), Carissimi (restricted to short biblical oratorios and cantatas), Schütz (perpetually thwarted by the non-payment of fees owing to his musicians), Charpentier (kept under by Lully) and Purcell (prey to a chauvinist Restoration culture, with its aversion to sung speech).† One is left musing on what these men might have achieved if they had been given a free rein (always supposing they had such a conception) to expand the genre and develop it, while staying true to the principles of 'imitation'.

But that is only part of the story. The other is that of the mutant forms – those variants of the genre that became the outlets for irrepressible musico-dramatic impulses. While these only rarely achieved widespread recognition or influence at the time and are not part of the mainstream, to dig them out of the archives is one of the most rewarding activities of a twenty-first-century musician. As we shall see, the first thing that strikes one about them is the extraordinary economy of means: the best instances of mid-seventeenth-century music-drama, so different from the opulence and extravagance of the later Baroque and of opera in general, are characterised by their compression and intensity of expression, often calling for very few notes and a precise placement of a dissonance to project a particular 'conceit'. The majority of these

* The spread of opera-theatres – first within Italy, from Palermo in the south to Milan in the north, in the second half of the seventeenth century, and then right across Europe – was not unlike the chains of pizza houses that opened from St Petersburg to Manchester during the 1980s (thirty years after they had started in America), not always with native Italians as resident dough-masters.

† England in the late seventeenth century was not the fertile ground for opera that many had hoped, mostly because, as one contemporary put it, 'our English Genius will not Relish that Perpetual singing' (a correspondent in the *Gentleman's Journal* (1691/2) – sometimes attributed to John Dryden).

'deviants' have nothing to do with the opera-theatre, either courtly or public. They did not need the frame of a proscenium arch and the width of an orchestral pit to ensure that the action being presented was separate and different from that of 'real' ordinary life. Mostly they belonged in churches and chapels (especially in the Catholic south – as the last gasp in the dominance of religious music before it became totally swamped by secular forms), and as a result managed to sidestep the commercial distortions that leading singers brought with them. So-called spiritual 'madrigals' and dialogues in recitative style, such as those that Giovanni Francesco Anerio composed for the Oratory of Filippo Neri in Rome, constituted what he called a 'winter theatre of the Gospels and Holy Scriptures, with the *laudi* of all the saints'.[15] By providing a poetic paraphrase of biblical verses sung in Italian, Anerio's music reached out to a large congregation, a means of critical exposition similar to the sermon, and punctuating the liturgical calendar in ways that are curiously prophetic of Bach's Lutheran cantata cycles.

* * *

Another antidote to the secular opera during Carnival was the sequence of five Latin oratorios performed annually in Rome on the five Fridays of Lent – soon to become receptacles for the creative theatrical imaginings of Giacomo Carissimi. Only two years after Venice had opened the first of its celebrated public theatres for the performance of opera, an itinerant French musician reported from Rome that in the Oratorio del Santissimo Crocifisso he heard two musical settings of biblical stories in which 'the voices would sing a story from the Old Testament in the form of a spiritual play, such as that of Susanna, Judith and Holofernes, or David and Goliath. Each singer represented a character of the story and expressed the force of the words . . . the singers imitated perfectly the different characters whom the Evangelist mentioned. I could not praise enough that recitative music; one must have heard it on the spot to judge well its merits.'[16] The enchanting *historiae* Carissimi later composed on themes suitable for Lenten meditation, such as Jonah and the Whale, Jephtha and his Daughter, and the parable of Dives and Lazarus, were confined to non-liturgical performance before an exclusive club of Roman aristocrats and foreign dignitaries in San Marcello or at the German College where Carissimi was *maestro di musica*. In essence these were miniature sacred operas, with solo and choral music of picaresque charm, vivid drama (the storm scenes in *Jonas* and the battle scenes in *Judicium extremum*), or wringing pathos (the final chorus of *Jephte*).*

The only composer to persist in writing a quantity of Latin oratorios in the style of Carissimi was his French pupil, Marc-Antoine Charpentier, equally committed to using musical rhetoric and dramatic means to arouse religious belief in the listener. Charpentier's thirty-six surviving works, called variously *dialogi*, *cantica* and *histoires sacrées* (never oratorios), were composed not for Oratory meetings but for use in the main Jesuit church in Paris, known as *l'église de l'opéra*. Such success as they enjoyed in France in the second half of the seventeenth century owed more to a temporary enthusiasm for music and the arts in general and to all things Italian in particular than to any lasting response to the intrinsic beauty of Charpentier's music. His lustrous vocal writing is typical of the French Baroque in its meshing of recitative (more varied in pitch than that of Carissimi, and features the use of wide intervals and rhythmic patterns), expressive ariosi and (more rarely) airs constructed either out of simple dance measures or as rondeaux – in which the main 'affect' is clearly defined, then elaborated upon in episodes before returning to clinch the message or mood.†

But what lifts Charpentier's *histoires sacrées* above the work of all his contemporaries with the exception of Purcell (see below) is the prominent and dramatic role he gives to the chorus. As in the Passions of Bach that lie a generation ahead, at one moment he requires his chorus to function as the crowd and to intervene directly in the action, and at another to stand outside it: either to provide a release of tension or to point the moral. Also like Bach to come, Charpentier is totally at home in writing free, florid counterpoint for his chorus often in as many as eight parts and with concerto-like subdivisions between *soli* and *tutti*,

* The contrast with Italian vernacular oratorio could hardly be greater. Hugely popular all over Italy in the second half of the century, oratorios were normally performed every Sunday all through the winter season. Dispensing with a narrator and often with biblical words, they display a vapid and sentimental response to the Scriptures, in stark contrast with the imaginative verve and devotional fervour of early-seventeenth-century Italian church music and with the Latin oratorios of Carissimi.

† In this Charpentier clearly avoids the dramatically stultifying effect of Italian *da capo* arias, since in his treatment 'the dramatic meaning of the text lies precisely in its singleness of thought, and since that thought is stated in its purest affective form in the opening sentence, the recurrence of the sentence can only intensify the dramatic power of the text' (H. Wiley Hitchcock, 'The Latin Oratorios of Marc-Antoine Charpentier', MQ, Vol. 41, No. 1 (Jan. 1955), p. 50).

and then in building up overlapping layers of sound with rich dissonant harmonies. A telling instance of this from *Extremum Dei judicium* points directly to Mozart (the finale of Act I of his *La clemenza di Tito*, where the horrified crowd watches as Rome's Capitol goes up in flames) and even to Berlioz. This occurs just before the Chorus of the Damned sings the despairing line 'It would have been better had we never been born!' There is an ironic similarity to the phrase 'It would have been better to have left nothing at all', the scathing Italophobic criticism of Charpentier's music 'which the public and time have declared pitiable'.[17] Sadly, it confirms that the diversity of invention which Charpentier himself considered to be 'the highest goal of music' and the creative imagination he expended on bringing Old Testament figures like Joshua, Esther, Judith, Saul and Jonathan to life, failed to reach out beyond the closeted preserve of his patroness, the Duchesse de Guise, and her guests. Perhaps he drew a wry satisfaction in presenting to the assembled law lords of the French *Parlement* his *Judicium Salomonis* in 1702. Its subject matter – Solomon's ruling in the quarrel between two harlots each claiming to be the mother of a single living child – was 'singularly, almost mischievously, appropriate', given as it was before an institution shorn of any political clout and confined to purely judicial affairs.[18]

Despite Germany having been reduced to a battleground for a third of a century, its lasting fascination for all things Italian provided more fertile soil for the grafting on of these shoots of music-drama than France or anywhere else in Europe. As we saw earlier, Heinrich Schütz, having twice spent time in Italy, was by far the best placed among German musicians to bring this about, even if he had no opportunity at the Dresden Court to stage operas. On his second trip to Venice in 1628–9, Schütz sought out Monteverdi so that he might experience at first hand how the expressive vocabulary of music had been expanded to the point at which 'music had reached its final perfection.'‡ He immersed himself, he told the Saxon Elector, 'in a singular manner of composition, namely how a comedy of all kinds of voices can be translated into declamatory style and brought to the stage and enacted in song'. The important thing here is the huge

‡ This comes from Schütz's preface to his *Symphoniae sacrae II* (1647), but Monteverdi in fact makes no such claims in the preface to his eighth book of madrigals (1638), though Schütz had stated that he did so. 'Schütz may have been privy to some earlier version of it which, perhaps out of modesty, his Italian mentor decided eventually not to publish' (Basil Smallman, *Schütz* (2000), p. 116).

development that had come about since Schütz's first visit fifteen years earlier: due to Monteverdi's impact 'the style of musical composition has somewhat changed . . . and the old laws have been to some extent abandoned in the attempt to charm the ears of today with new titillations.'[19] A chance to escape for a while from the demoralising war-torn atmosphere of Dresden came four years later, when he was hired to supervise music for the marriage of Crown Prince Christian of Denmark to the Elector's daughter in Copenhagen – an opportunity to put into practice the new theatrical style he had learnt in Italy, techniques that 'to the best of my knowledge are still completely unknown in Germany'.*

Schütz, in common with Monteverdi, Charpentier and Purcell, was quick to scent any musical opportunities for dramatic treatment of scenes from the Scriptures. He himself described the process of musical composition as the 'art of translating the text into music' – and this may be one key to our unlocking Bach's purpose in following the same process and his future treatment of it. Schütz's early *Psalms of David* (1618) are full of arresting examples of his imaginative response to the rhythmic sounds and accentuations of the German vernacular, similar to what Monteverdi was doing at around the same time.† Time after time

* Following in the footsteps of Albrecht Dürer, who had been lured at the end of the fifteenth century to develop his draughtsmanship in Italy, German-born musicians from Heinrich Schütz on were drawn to Italy, with Venice and Rome as the twin magnetic poles. It mattered not one jot to musicians of their degree of curiosity that they could be accused of supping with the Devil. The physical risks in travelling across the Alps, particularly once war had broken out in 1618, were immense; but to the intrepid the artistic rewards evidently justified the perils faced. Those that made it to Italy and back besides Schütz (1628–9), included Kaspar Förster (1633–6), Johann Caspar Kerll (before 1656), Christoph Bernhard (1657) and Johann Philipp Krieger (1673–5). One of the most talented, Johann Rosenmüller, having been held on suspicion of homosexuality, escaped from prison, travelling to Venice – which he liked so much he stayed for the next twenty-four years. What these seventeenth-century German composers learnt and assimilated during their time in Italy is still in the early process of re-evaluation, dependent on the fragmentary and scattered works that have survived and then, crucially, tested in live performance. All were formative in propagating new musical cultivars.

† We still need to account for the exceptional effect Schütz's German-language music seems to have on listeners past or present. Thrasybulos Georgiades analysed the intimate symbiotic relationship between the music and the rhythms of the written or spoken German word – the remarkably close links between the natural accentuation of German words (semantic in origin) and their actual meaning, which is so much more personal than Latin for example. 'Here the [musical] stress . . . is nothing other than the emphasis [or ictus] given to the syllable that carries the meaning . . . [By this means] it [i.e., the musical stress] conveys the meaning' (*Musik und Sprache* (1954), p. 55).

he found music overwhelming in the pathos of its rich harmonic vocabulary, and still more in the force of its rhetoric, the intensity of its syllabic reiteration and rhythmic potency. There is little more poignant in all seventeenth-century music than Schütz's setting of the verse *ich bin so müde von Seufzen* ('I am weary with my groaning') from Psalm 6 (*Ach Herr, straf mich nicht*), expressing the stiff and painful movement of someone in the throes of grief; or the heartbreak he finds in the repeated *bricht mir mein Herz* (from *Ist nicht Ephraim*), from which he extracts the maximum feeling by the smallest figural means. But if I had to choose a single instance of Schütz's flair for the unexpected, it would be the extended use of unmeasured choral recitation (*falso bordone*) in his setting of Psalm 84, where at a given signal it is as though the entire congregation sinks to its knees to whisper this most solemn prayer: *Herr, Gott Zebaoth, höre mein Gebet, vernimm es, Gott Jakobs, Sela* ('O Lord, God of hosts, hear my prayer: give ear, O God of Jacob. Selah'). Although this belongs to a psalm-setting and is in no sense an opera, it anticipates by almost 200 years the mood of collective remorse and the suppressed, muttered homophony of the Prisoners' Chorus in Beethoven's opera *Fidelio*.

But it is not so much the particular felicity of word-setting, however inspired, that is so original in these works: it is the ability to turn sacred texts into convincing mini-dramas. We do not find it in Schütz's proto-cantatas, nor in the austere late Passions, nor even in the haunting *Auferstehungshistorie* (*Resurrection History*) (1623). The biblical texts that inspired him were the same ones that stimulated Carissimi (and perhaps still more Charpentier) as well as painters such as Caravaggio and Rembrandt – the grief of David over the death of his son Absalom, the encounter of Jesus and Mary Magdalene in the garden, the conversion of St Paul. These miniatures survive in the form of Schütz's biblical *scenas* and dialogues, giving us a precious glimpse not just of his exceptional theatrical flair but also of the irrepressible vitality of mutant opera, which jumped formal tracks.

Direct speech is all that concerns Schütz when treating the subject of St Paul's conversion, *Saul, Saul, was verfolgst du mich* (SWV 415). Implied, however, in this quite stupendous work – a 'sacred symphony' lasting less than five minutes – is an imaginary *mise en scène*: of Paul on the road to Damascus, 'breathing out threatenings and slaughter against the disciples of the Lord . . . Suddenly there shined round about him a light from heaven: and he fell to the earth, and heard a voice saying unto him, Saul, Saul, why persecutest thou me?' It was a masterstroke by Schütz to confine his setting to the sixteen words of the invisible Jesus that ring in Paul's ears. He marshals his ensemble of six soloists (or *favoriti*), two obbligato violins, two four-part choirs with optional instrumental reinforcement not just to depict the scene with pictorial effects, nor to fill in the textual gaps by means of apt rhetorical figures, but to create a compelling psychodrama compressed into eighty bars of music. The result is an astonishing portrayal, every bit as striking in its way as Caravaggio's altar painting of the same subject in Rome's Santa Maria del Popolo. But where Caravaggio captures the bolt-out-of-the-blue moment – the blinding light from heaven which fells Saul like a poleaxe – and savours the physical threat to him from the raised foreleg of his colossal horse, he gives nothing away about Saul's state of mind (in fact Saul has his back to the viewer and his eyes are closed). Schütz's main concern, by contrast, is to probe the psychological turmoil caused by the apparition and the personal transformation from Saul into Paul.

True to past practice when setting Christ's words, Schütz employs his voices in pairs. They emerge from mysterious depths as a barely audible mutter in a four-fold repetition of Saul's name, separated by rests, before transferring to the next terraced pair, each climbing through the space of an octave before evaporating in a wordless violin extension (or is it a symbol of the divine incandescence which blinds Saul?). What began as a quiet reproach, the voice of conscience, now grows into an accusation, the monosyllable punched out and tossed between the two halves of the double choir – to encircle and disorient the now-enfeebled Saul before the *Was verfolgst du mich* is sped up in dizzying contracted rhythmic patterns and terraced echoes. Schütz's purpose is to make sure that the listener gets caught up in the process and becomes equally disoriented. In performance (especially in a church with a long reverberation and with the musical forces deployed spatially) it can amount to an aural bombardment with a disturbing resemblance to the amplified noises of the torture chamber directed at the target from all sides, in all pitches and volumes.

Playing on the listener's expectations, Schütz sets up a regular-seeming alternation of the Saul appellations and the two halves of the main *Spruch*, only to dash them by bringing back his big guns before the phrase has quite finished.[20] The torsional pressure – on Saul and the listener – now begins to increase as one of the tenors detaches himself from the rest (still chanting *Was verfolgst du mich*) and starts bawling out Saul's name in long emphatic notes – three times and at rising pitches, hoisting the whole ensemble upwards. From this climax, with all fourteen voices baying at full volume, the music gradually subsides to a whisper, leaving the protagonist and the listener all at sea, having witnessed what seems like the authentic voice of God. What Schütz did here made it possible for future composers to make a single word stand out with sudden monumental significance, so that a hundred years later Bach could break in on Pilate's questioning with a savage shout of 'Barrabas!' and a hundred years after that Verdi 'could disturb a tense pool of silence in his Requiem by dropping into it his muttered "Mors ... mors ... mors"'.[21] Neither of these works can truthfully be claimed as an 'opera'.

* * *

The sense of missed opportunity – of what might have been – is most pronounced in the case of English Restoration music-drama. In Italy, as we have seen, once opera had gone public, commercial pressures effectively derailed any organic development of the original form; in France, centralised political power dictated the agenda of opera; and in Germany, debilitating warfare lopped off the shoots of operatic enterprise. But in England, three key elements, which would have allowed a successful transplant of the Italian form, were already in place: a long musical Elizabethan and Jacobean tradition of plays rich with interpolated music, a promising precedent for integrating music with dramatic spectacle in the shape of the English court masque; and, after years of Puritan austerity, a dam of theatrical activity ready to burst. Added to this was the emergence of one of the handful of seventeenth-century musicians to warrant the term genius: Henry Purcell. Yet, just at the moment when it looked as though English opera might establish itself after all – though more by accident than design – Purcell was not involved.

Passing from Schütz to the much younger Purcell, one is struck by the greater harmonic licence and astringency in the tonal language of the Englishman – those 'uncouth and antiquated' traits and harmonic 'crudities' that so upset Charles Burney later on, but that constitute so much of Purcell's appeal to other musicians. It is like watching two highly skilled craftsmen at their workbench, each equally adept and at ease working in his own vernacular style. Both were intent on exploring the musical gestures and rhetoric that grow spontaneously out of the text to be set, while avoiding the distraction of an excess of pictorial effects in the interests of overall form, neither willing to cheapen the desired impact of their words and music by submitting them to the caprices of theatrical performance. Yet, where with Schütz one sees somebody writing to keep up his courage in the maelstrom of a debilitating war, with Purcell one senses a different perspective: a generally lighter spirit reacting to the austerity and moral earnestness of the puritanical Interregnum and now free to express, or to 'act out', the extremes of penitential grief, righteous wrath or divine transport.*

Purcell had shown theatrical flair – the ability to encapsulate a mood, to mesh music with words with amazing skill – as early as the Latin motet *Jehovah, quam multi sunt hostes* (*Jehovah, how many are mine enemies*) or his monologue *Mad Bess*. One turns with high expectations to the court odes he composed for the birthdays and homecomings of the royal family or to those that mark St Cecilia's Day. Here, in these panegyrics, there is musical exuberance, brilliant choral writing, evidence of tonal planning and ingenuity aplenty, and brave attempts to overcome clumsy, platitudinous verse; but his music flatters to deceive and cannot disguise that these are essentially *pièces d'occasion*. They are false scents – like looking for examples of embryonic opera in Bach's secular cantatas, his *drammi per musica* that, despite their title, invariably turn out to be less 'operatic' than some of his church cantatas. Purcell excelled in what Dryden defined as 'a kind of tuneful pronunciation, more musical than common speech, and less than song'.[22] Where his celebrated works like *Dido and Aeneas*, *The Fairy Queen* and *King Arthur* reveal what Purcell's contemporaries meant by his 'genius for

* Eric van Tassel suggests that 'at a time when sectarian fervour had lost many lives, one may imagine the [Anglican] church tolerating, even encouraging in the choir stalls an emotional directness that would have been impolitic in the pulpit.' This may partly account for the hectic, self-conscious tone of some of Purcell's verse anthems. 'There seems so much to say, so little time or room in which to say it: the hearer is exhorted and seduced and swept along on a rising current of musical events more varied and perhaps more energetic and colourful than in the church music of any other era' (Michael Burden (ed.), *The Purcell Companion* (1995), pp. 101, 169, 174).

expressing the energy of the English language',[23] it is not in them that we find the revolution of seventeenth-century music on display.*

One of Purcell's most intensely dramatic works had absolutely nothing to do with the English stage. Faced with an opportunity to write a piece to celebrate King William's victory at the Battle of the Boyne in 1690, Purcell chose to set words that, at a superficial glance, jarred horribly with the occasion and overall mood of relief that the country must have been feeling at this latest defeat of the menace of resurgent Catholicism. With religious and political feeling running so high all through the seventeenth century in England, it is not surprising that scriptural parallels were sought for the heroes and bogeymen of the day. Hugely promising in this respect, and able to lend itself to different interpretations, is the scene in the Book of Samuel where King Saul, out of favour with Jehovah and poised to do battle with the Philistines, enlists the services of a witch to raise up his old mentor Samuel.† *Saul and the Witch of Endor* has been variously described as biblical dialogue, church cantata, mini-oratorio, dramatic *scena* or conversational piece for three characters. Certainly it was a genre Purcell had neither tried before nor was ever to attempt again, and intriguingly it reveals common features with two of the 'mutant' examples already discussed: with Monteverdi's *Lamento della ninfa* (see footnote on p. 108) it shares a triptych form,

* As Imogen Holst wrote 'there was no need for Purcell to go through Peri's laborious process of deciding when the recitative needed a new bass to support it. The experimental stage was over.' She observed that 'His tunes were not meant to be coupled lovingly to lines that were already brimful of their own verbal music. He needed verses that could be torn in shreds and tossed into the air.' That is, of course, exactly what he did with Nahum Tate's doggerel, so we can see that 'the characters in *Dido and Aeneas* talked in harmony because it was their native language, with the rise and fall of their voices clearly expressing their feelings . . . Recitative such as this can slip easily in and out of the arias without destroying the scene.' No wonder that Gustav Holst, according to his daughter, had his 'great awakening . . . on hearing the recitatives in Purcell's *Dido*'. Holst the composer once asked how Purcell 'managed *straight away* to write the only really musical idiom of the English language we have yet had?' (Imogen Holst, *Tune* (1962), pp. 100, 103, 104, 157).

† Mary Chan has shown that the text was used in the 1650s as Royalist, anti-Puritan propaganda with David associated with the future Charles II, then in exile, and possibly Cromwell as Saul and Charles I as Samuel's ghost. But then, with an almost Shostakovich-like ambiguity for political allegiance or sympathy, the tables are turned during the 1670s, the anti-Puritan propaganda now directed against the Catholics in general, with Saul standing in one instance for Louis XIV but more usually for James, Duke of York, once he had been outed as a Catholic (Mary Chan, '*The Witch of Endor* and Seventeenth-Century Propaganda', *Musica Disciplina*, Vol. 34 (1980), pp. 205–14).

the core of the *scena* being framed by choruses for three voices; and with Schütz's *Saul, Saul*, an intensely dramatic encapsulation of a single moment in biblical history.

Purcell himself encapsulates the conversion of Saul as a solo declamatory song; here, in the *Witch of Endor*, he deliberately sets up an interplay between three contrasted voices.* Like the other works *in genere rappresentativo* in this chapter, this work of Purcell's needs no staging to help it achieve its dramatic impact. It opens with an eerie chromatic chanting by the three voices: 'In guilty night, and hid in false disguise, / Forsaken Saul to Endor comes and cries.' The music is evocative and chilling, with Purcell intent on squeezing every last drop of pathos from the words. He has adapted Italian *seconda prattica* technique to his inimitable way of setting English words to music, thus creating a brilliant hybridisation. Listening to this music in Westminster Abbey, King William III would surely have understood Purcell's subtext – that, like David, with Saul in his power, refusing 'to stretch forth his hand against the Lord's anointed', he had overruled his advisers and decided to spare James, his own father-in-law, so as not to have the ex-king's blood on his hands.[24] In the ten-bar epilogue, Purcell starts out with the same chromatic ground bass that underpins Dido's 'Lament':† not just the most celebrated of Purcell's grounds, but itself a by-product of Monteverdian *ostinato*, and a paradigm of so much seventeenth-century pathos-ridden music. Through its extreme concision, its emphasis on witchcraft, and its historic, histrionic characterisation and implied gesticulation, this little work by Purcell channels the full force unleashed by the discovery of 'opera' in the 1600s and sums up his refusal, and that of a select body of other composers, to be tied down by the conventions or constraints of opera-theatre. It is in moments like these that one

* Basil Smallman suggests that, in choosing this paraphrase of Samuel so often set to music during the seventeenth century, Purcell may have been aware of the 'special tradition that evolved through presenting the scene of Saul and the Witch of Endor, perhaps even with stage action and costume', though it seems doubtful whether Purcell would have required scenery, costumes and staging in Westminster Abbey on this occasion. Smallman traces this back to versions by John Hilton the younger and Robert Ramsay given at Trinity College Cambridge during the 1630s, witnessed by Andrew Marvell and later transferred to London, 'gaining considerable popularity' (Smallman, 'Endor Revisited', *Music & Letters*, Vol. 46, No. 2 (1965), pp. 137–45).

† There are thematic and musical cords that tie this sacred *scena* to *Dido and Aeneas* – 'a troubled monarch tangles with a witch, but discovers that the spirit raised by the witch only speaks the monarch's doom' (R. Savage in *The Purcell Companion*, op. cit., p. 254).

recognises that Monteverdi's true heirs were not his immediate Venetian successors,[25] but Schütz, Charpentier and Purcell.

* * *

Connected to these gradual shifts in the patterned organisation of public commercial opera were changes in the nature of music itself in the course of the seventeenth century. By the time our Class of '85 had attained their majority, it now existed in a hugely expanded world that had begun to be been opened up by sea-faring merchants and charted by cartographers, in which a city like Amsterdam, for example, had become 'an inventory of the possible', storing 'all the commodities and curiosities one could wish for'.[26] While its citizens needed little imaginative effort to see their path to instant riches, for artists and writers realism was the key to such acquisition by other means. Music had shown that it could now articulate, reflect and project a sense of an established secular order – hence allowing the absolutist polemics of Lully's court operas – and yet also be the mouthpiece of a radical sense of often beleaguered individuality. By 1700 music had developed techniques capable of dividing and ordering time and of holding the attention of its listeners in ways that would have been impossible a century earlier. Thanks to the lead given by Monteverdi and the other monodists in Italy, by the metaphysical poets and lute-song writers in England and by the religious composers of the war years in Germany, musical discourse had now expanded to the point where it allowed composers to penetrate to pre-linguistic regions of the psyche as well as to give powerful and nuanced expression to the whole gamut of human passions – and, as we have seen, in unexpectedly different ways, formats and contexts. In particular, the experimental dramatic music we have been discussing was beginning to open up new ways of listening and a new type of consciousness, whereby differing components of musical experience and the memory of them had the potential to collide, interact and infect one another in a 'dialectic in time'.* This would soon be momentously realised in the 'sound dramas' of Bach, in which, for example, we will encounter arias assigned not as in opera to characters in a fictitious drama but to proxies for different kinds of human beings going through different types of crisis. Having set before us displays of

* The phrase is John Butt's.

human turmoil and postulated a path of redemption, Bach then draws all the strands together by means of sung chorales that take us into a cultural present in ways that opera never could.

Of course it is not known, nor would it be possible to establish, just how much of the music discussed here was really known to our '85ers. These mutant types may have remained hidden from them, or only vaguely figured in their musical awareness. Yet, when it came to career trajectories and opportunities to build on the achievements of the previous century, our '85ers as individual composers were spoilt for choice. Take the conventional route – Italian opera as it had been adapted, say, in Hamburg in 1700 – and you could end up a Mattheson or a Telemann, composing music of a softly focused geniality heading towards the *galant* style of the mid to late eighteenth century. Pick up the salient features of *opera seria* (notably the basic *da capo* aria/recitative division) and, intrinsically compromised as a vehicle for continuously unfolding music-drama though it was, you could make a brilliant success of it, as Handel was poised to do. He would buck the trend by means of a series of superbly crafted *opera seria*, whose chief glories lie in the way that he penetrates to the recesses of his characters' minds. Later in life Handel would come to realise that the presence and active participation of a chorus was helpful, perhaps even essential, to his expressive aims; the result – the matchless dramatic oratorios and masques he wrote in English for the Protestant English between 1735 and 1752.*

On the other hand, you could adapt its Lullian, Gallicised structure into a vessel for the transmission of sung drama in almost through-composed form, as Rameau would eventually do, setting the door ajar, first, to the 'reforms' of Gluck and then to that first great Mozartian synthesis of music, drama and action, *Idomeneo* (1781). Adopt it in the modern Neumeister form applied to church cantatas, as Bach was soon to do, and it could lead initially to a diminished fluidity and naturalness of form. For Bach, this was superficially a rejection of much of what he had inherited from the composers within his family circle, from Schütz

* Winton Dean summarises this transition and the effect of Dr Gibson (Bishop of London) banning theatrical performances of works based on Holy Writ: 'It is likely that Handel's highest and longest dramatic flights . . . originated as a sort of compensation for the absence of the visual drama, which drove him to concentrate the action within the music itself' (*Handel's Dramatic Oratorios and Masques* (1959), p. 37).

and back from him to Monteverdi – but it also allowed him to embrace fresh compositional challenges and to open doors leading to new, unthinkably fruitful dramatic opportunities.

As we shall see, a strong thread running through Bach's creative life – parallel to that of Handel and less obviously of Rameau – is his coming to terms with these seemingly opposed manifestations of music-drama and his finding new ways to extend its range, while staying essentially true to the spirit which informed its birth in the early 1600s. Aged eighteen to twenty, these three had the goods to reinvent Baroque music-drama. One might in the end prefer the 'sound', the style or the solutions of one, but one can hardly deny the genius of the other two. What will make their music-drama so potent – so much *more* potent than contemporary *opera seria* – is their ability to internalise and then dramatise the situation of the individual believer, spectator or hearer. Bach will soon have the answer to Gottfried Ephraim Scheibel's rhetorical observation: 'I do not know why operas alone should have the privilege of squeezing tears from us; why is that not true in the church?'[27] With never an opera to his name, Bach will be the one to work his way towards uncovering and releasing a dramatic potency in music beyond the reach of any of his peers, the leading opera composers of his day; and, as it turns out, beyond that of any composer until Mozart. For back in 1703, of the Field of '85, no one spotted the eventual winner.

5
The Mechanics of Faith

Man is made by his belief. As he believes, so he is.
– *Bhagavad-Gita*[1]

Pastor Robscheit of Eisenach welcomed us warmly into his church.* Eisenach, he insisted, is *the* place where 'Bach meets Luther'. Both Luther and Bach had once stood as boy choristers exactly where we were now standing as honoured guests invited to lead the singing of the *Hauptgottesdienst*, or main service, on Easter Sunday 2000. From our position in the choir loft high up at the back of the late Gothic Georgenkirche, arranged like a three-decker galleon, we had an unimpeded view of its two most prominent physical symbols: the pulpit in which Martin Luther preached on his return from Worms in 1521 and the baptismal font where Bach was christened on 23 March 1685. (See Plate 1.)

For many people the hallmark of Bach's music lies in the lucidity of its structure and the mathematical satisfaction of its proportions. These contribute to the fascination it holds for professional composers and performers; but they might also account for its proven attraction to mathematicians and scientists. Nevertheless, that secular and appealing clarity originated in a fundamentally religious outlook. As we have seen, a high proportion of Bach's music, unlike that of his peers, was addressed

* We should have come here ten years ago, the pastor said; for then, under the GDR, there was so little contact with the outside world that the only way his parishioners could pick up hints of Bach performance practice elsewhere was via the radio or CDs smuggled over the border by friends and relations. Still, it was good that we had chosen to stop here for the Easter weekend on our cantata pilgrimage.

to a church congregation, rather than a lay audience. Religion was central not just to his upbringing and his education but to the locus of his employment and to his general outlook on life. For him it went beyond dogma, having a practical as well as a spiritual application, and was underpinned by reason. The mechanics of Bach's faith – the structured and systematic way he applied his religion to his working practices – is something that anyone searching to understand him either as a man or as a composer needs to address. The dedication of his art to God's glory was not confined to signing off his church cantatas with the acronym *S[oli] D[eo] G[loria]*; the motto applied with equal force to his concertos, partitas and instrumental suites. And Eisenach, his birthplace and the site of his first encounter with Martin Luther, the founder of his inherited version of Christianity, is clearly a good place to start.

It was not hard for us to imagine Bach here in the town where he had spent the first nine and a half years of his life, one of the cradles of Lutheranism and outwardly so little changed. Hewn out of the same wooded landscape, both he and Luther had attended the same Latin School and both had had some of their earliest experiences of music in this church. Luther's presence is most strongly to be felt in a tiny room with a high ceiling in the Wartburg, the medieval castle that towers over the town, skirted by woods where he used to pick wild strawberries as a boy. (See illustration p. 27.) After his challenge to religious authority and his dramatic appearance before the Diet of Worms in April 1521, this most talked-about man in Europe, so accustomed to seeing himself as the leading actor in God's own drama, had become an outlaw. He spent the next ten months here hidden away, lonely, troubled and desperately constipated.* Years later he recalled how he had been haunted in his confinement by visions of Satan as a poltergeist snatching walnuts off his desk and flinging them at the ceiling all night long. Once he found a dog in his bed. Convinced that it was the Devil in disguise, he hurled the poor beast out of his window into the night.†

Luther called the Wartburg his Patmos – a reference to the barren

* 'The Lord has struck me in the rear end with terrible pain. My excrement is so hard that I have to strain with such force to expel it that I sweat, and the longer I wait, the harder it gets . . . My arse has gone bad' (WA BR, Vol. 2, Nos. 333, 334).

† In his Reformation cantata BWV 79, Bach's anonymous poet invokes God's protection as 'our sun and shield' against 'a blasphemous barking dog' – perhaps a reference to Luther's nightmarish vision (WA TR, Vol. 5, No. 5,358b).

island where St John supposedly wrote the Book of Revelation with its stirring evocation of the cosmic battle between Satan (the 'Beast') and the Lamb. His initial response to these terrors was to write furious polemical diatribes against his enemies; but soon he was launched on his ground-breaking translation of the New Testament. Using Erasmus' Greek text as his base, he worked feverishly and in three months he had completed a first draft. He searched for a tone that would be comprehensible to as many people as possible across the different German-speaking regions. In the end he took as his standard the chancery language of Prague and Meissen, in which he was fluent, but changed its style drastically: in place of the stilted prose of lawyers, with its baffling tendency to pile syllable on syllable in clusters of compound nouns, he brought the translation closer to his own oral delivery – vigorous and colourful, direct and impassioned – and to the thought patterns and colloquial ways of speaking people used in their homes or in the marketplace here in the heart of Thuringia.*

This was the same sturdy German prose with which he clothed the Easter Day hymns we were due to sing – linked to tunes that were at least as old as the Georgenkirche itself – *Christ ist erstanden* (*Christ is risen*) and *Christ lag in Todesbanden* (*Christ lay in death's prison*) – and then given a further twist by Bach through his stupendous four-part harmonisations. The sense of Easter as the pivotal feast of the liturgical year was inescapable here – from its origins as a pagan spring sacrifice, to the ancient Jewish ritual of Passover and the feast of Unleavened Bread, that Canaanite agricultural festival adopted by the Hebrews after their settlement there – all re-rooted by Luther in this unchanged, sylvan landscape. We were both participants and observers in this predominantly sung celebration, one in which the pastor and congregation responded to each other in fluent dialogue. At one point in the service

* The spread of Luther's Bible had colossal implications for the German language, previously divided into many regional dialects. Luther wrote, 'I have so far read no book or letter in which the German language is properly handled. Nobody seems to care sufficiently for it; and every preacher thinks he has a right to change it at pleasure and to invent new terms' (quoted in Philip Schaff, *History of the Christian Church* (1910), Vol. VI, pp. 6, 10) – not that he himself was immune to this tendency. But in popularising the Saxon dialect and adapting it to theology and religion, Luther enriched the vocabulary with that of earlier poets and chroniclers and transformed it into the common literary language from which later writers and poets such as Klopstock, Herder and Lessing traced their stylistic origins. A contemporary of Luther, Erasmus Albertus, called him the German Cicero.

we were suddenly joined in the gallery by a group of local men who sang a short litany in Thuringian dialect and then left.

It was difficult to gauge the congregation's response to these sixteenth-century hymns – so plain but evocative and to us extraordinarily moving. We were all singing from the same *Eisenachisches Gesangbuch* of 1673 that was in use when Bach sang here as a chorister between the ages of four and nine, and whose tunes and illustrations may have combined to forge a link in his mind between the town, the family of musicians into which he was born and the dynasty of musicians who served King David in the Temple (see Chapter 3 and Plates 2a and b). In the reverence of the ceremony one could catch a glimpse of the way Luther, and probably therefore Bach after him, regarded the Eucharist – as a ritual in which the believer, like some character in a play of redemption, is called on to cast aside his doubts, ready to meet the immanent Christ in tangible form. For Luther, the Eucharist was as much physical as spiritual, and baptism was a physical sacrament of death and resurrection (justifying the font's central position in the church), the means whereby the tension between fear and faith, which permeates Christian life, is resolved.

Here was first-hand evidence of a perceptibly close synergy between Luther and Bach, though separated by almost two centuries. The bond between them was established at birth: by geography, by the coincidence of their schooling and membership of the Georgenschule choir and the extracurricular singing for bread.* It was reinforced by the thoroughgoing ways that Luther's hymns and theology impregnated Bach's school lessons (as we saw in Chapter 2): they really were the principal means by which he imbibed and assimilated knowledge of the world around him. By the time Bach reached his early twenties Luther's teaching had become all-pervasive in his musical training, and now formed the very clay from which he modelled his first music for use in church. Three remarkable cantatas, all composed in quick succession during his year in Mühlhausen, provide an early snapshot of his musical intelligence and its mathematical application at work, showing us how he had already begun to deal with the faith he was required to expound

* Luther admonished those who looked down on the *Currende* ('busking choristers'): 'I too was such a crumb collector ... we were singing in four voices from door to door in the villages [surrounding Eisenach]' (LW, Vol. 46, No. 250; WA, Vol. 30, No. 576).

and support. Giving close scrutiny to each of them will show us that Bach, by inheriting Luther's late-medieval concept of the course of life being a daily battle between God and Satan (BWV 4), assented to the basic tenets of Luther's eschatology (BWV 131): the need to make a good fist of life and to face death courageously, joyously even, with hope and faith (BWV 106). In each of these early works Bach comes up with a fresh and compelling exposition; each one propounds a highly original musical solution to biblical exegesis. Within the mechanics of faith, music is there first and foremost to praise God and reflect the wonders of the universe.

The specific task of music, as defined by Luther, is to give expression and added eloquence to biblical texts: *Die Noten machen den Text lebendig* ('The notes make the words live').[2] As two of God's most powerful gifts to humanity, words and music must be forged into one invisible and indivisible force, the text appealing primarily to the intellect (but also to the passions), while music is addressed primarily to the passions (but also to the intellect).[3]* Luther maintained that without music, man is little more than a stone; but, with music, he can drive the Devil away: 'It has often revived me and relieved me from heavy burdens,' he admitted. This belief was to give fundamental justification to Bach's vocation (*Amt*) and craft as a musician, lending credence to his professional status and comfort to his artistic goals, while his emphasis on a 'vocal' delivery of Scripture would later help to provide his *raison d'être* as a composer of church music.

Luther is often said to have asked why the Devil should have all the good tunes. To make sure that he didn't, Luther and his followers appropriated secular melodies that everyone in his congregation knew, redirecting the candid earthiness and bawdiness of folksongs to the service of faith, for 'the whole purpose of harmony is the glory of God', he

* On this point Bach's contemporary Johann Mattheson wrote, 'A right-minded cantor, by the function of his holy vocation [*Amt*], proclaims ... God's Word. *Verbum Dei est, sive mente cogitetur, sive canatur, sive pulsu edatur* [the Word of God is uttered by the thinking of the mind, by singing and by playing (lit. = striking)], as expressed in the words written by Justin Martyr' (*Critica Musica II*, p. 316). But Robin A. Leaver has shown that this is based on a mistranslation (*Luther's Liturgical Music* (2007), pp. 287–8). Despite Joseph Kerman's warning that 'Baroque composers *depict* the passions, Romantic composers *express* them' (my italics) (Joseph Kerman, *The Art of Fugue* (2005), p. 100), it seems to me Bach goes a long way further here than merely 'depicting' the passions.

claimed; 'all other use is but the idle juggling of Satan.'* From this it is clear that Luther saw human emotions as free-floating *Affekte* ('affects') that can be pressed into service – for good or improper use. Not surprisingly he had no truck with co-reformers like Calvin, who banned instrumental music from worship, or Zwingli, an accomplished musician in private life, who, in his insistence on private prayer, would not allow any music at all, not even unaccompanied singing, in church. Evidence that Luther's ideas were still working well in the Protestant heartlands more than a century and a half later can be found in Bach's clear familiarity with the chorales, which, as we shall see, were to play a central role in his church cantatas – and in those very hymns, refashioned by Luther, we sang in Eisenach on Easter morning.

Luther's magisterial hymn *Christ lag in Todesbanden* brings the events of Christ's Passion and Resurrection dramatically to life, depicting both the physical and spiritual ordeal Christ needed to undergo to bring about man's release from the burden of sin. Christ is evoked simultaneously as the conqueror of death and as the sacrificial Paschal Lamb. The way Luther unfolds this gripping story has something of the tribal saga about it, full of graphic imagery and incident. If, as seems likely, Bach first heard this hymn in this church and in this season, he could have found no clearer formulation of the way in which Luther's faith sprang from early Christian roots: from the Old Testament portrayal of Christ as the Easter Lamb; and the appropriation by the early church of pagan rites in which the essence and embodiment of life was connected to light (the sun) and food (bread, or the Word). As every farmer and stockbreeder knows, Easter is a critical time of year when the border between life and death is at its most slender, so to Luther's Thuringian congregation these connections were easily made: '[Luther's]

* Yet, contrary to popular misconception, we have just one example of Luther himself composing a *contrafactum* (a parody of a secular song with a substituted religious text): he took a secular 'riddle' song ('Ich komm aus fremden Landen her') and made it the basis of his first version of the Christmas hymn 'Vom Himmel hoch, da komm ich her' that appeared in the Wittenberg hymnal of 1535. But he was dissatisfied with the result and decided to compose a new melody for it – the one that has become inseparably linked to it ever since. Research by Robin A. Leaver (op. cit., pp. 88–9) does much to explode the myth surrounding Luther's alleged support for the use of popular music in church. In his own words, Luther was keen to 'wean [the young] away from love ballads and carnal songs and to teach them something of value in their place, thus combining the good with the pleasing' (LW, Vol. 53, No. 316; WA, Vol. 35, Nos. 474–5).

genius seized on the fears of ordinary folk in a world full of evils and terrors, and helped his congregations roar away these terrors in song.'[4]

Bach, by choosing this particular hymn as the basis of a celebratory *Kirchenstück* (BWV 4), was asserting his kinship with Luther. Aged twenty-two, Bach was making his first attempt, in what was probably his second (or third) cantata, at painting narrative in music. It marked a significant expansion in his development – from acknowledged organ virtuoso in his first post, in Arnstadt (1703–7), to composer of figural music of amazing precocity and daring in his second. Most likely composed for his probationary audition for the position of organist at Mühlhausen at Easter 1707, it was in effect his tender for the directorship of the city's musical life. No mere *jeu d'esprit*, it is a wonderfully bold, exuberant piece of concerted music-drama. Bach sets all seven of Luther's verses (*per omnes versus*) verbatim and without additions; following a line of distinguished seventeenth-century composers including Samuel Scheidt and Johann Schelle, he uses the chorale tune as the basis for all movements, each beginning and ending in the same key of E minor, yet without a trace of monotony. At each step of the narrative Bach shows that he is alert to every nuance, scriptural allusion, symbol and mood in Luther's hymn.

Bach drew on the whole reservoir of his learning to date: habits of communication and performance, music he had learnt by heart, the family's rich archive of motets and *Stücken*, the music put before him as a chorister in Lüneburg, as well as works that he had studied or copied under the aegis of his various mentors. His approach seems to exemplify the advice given to budding composers by the Bavarian music theorist Mauritius Johann Vogt (1669–1730): 'to be a poet, not only so that he recognise the metre of the verse, but that his themes also be inventive and, like a painter, place the beautiful or frightful images lifelike before the eyes of the listeners through the music'.[5] There were also techniques borrowed from the ancient art of rhetoric to help him on his way. The theorist who did most to make rhetoric an integral part of German *musica poetica*, with everything directed towards grasping and then sustaining the listener's attention, was the Lüneburg cantor Joachim Burmeister (1564–1629).[6] To the potentially overwhelmed student Burmeister advised: study the text, match it with appropriate musical devices and 'the text itself will prescribe the rules.'[7] A specific and indispensable aid for giving such vivid expression to the idea of the text was the application of *hypotyposis*, 'when a person [or a] thing . . . is depicted through written or oral expression in such a fashion that it is perceived as though the described person was present or the event was personally experienced.'[8] While we cannot know whether Bach was familiar with the terminology, this is exactly what he achieves in *Christ lag in Todesbanden*, as he was later to do in his Passions. Thus he connects with a theological strategy that began long before the Reformation: the process of humanising Christian verbal iconography by vivid narration and dramatic presentation such as in the medieval Mystery Plays.

Next in importance for textual expression comes *pathopoeia*, 'a forme of speech', according to the seventeenth-century English author and musician Henry Peachum, 'by which the Orator moveth the minds of his hearers to some vehemency of affection, as of indignation, feare, envy, hatred, hope, gladnesse, mirth, laughter, sadnesse or sorrow'[9] in such a way 'that no one remains untouched by the created affection'.[10] Bach shows his ability to incorporate these and other rhetorical and pictorial devices that characterized the 'modern' style of Heinrich Schütz (though dated, of course, by Bach's day), itself drawn from Monteverdi's *seconda prattica*, in which music serves the words (rather than vice versa), and the listener is invited to experience the imagery and emotions generated by words and music welded together. By this token there are both flashes of modernity in Bach's musical treatment of *Christ lag* and traces of a distinctly medieval flavour to its ritualized drama.

This is all very well for the present-day Lutheran listener, but not for those without the familiarity that comes with regular hymn-singing or an understanding of the many musical-rhetorical figures that were the church musician's stock-in-trade; he or she may feel a bit at sea trying to understand Bach's terms of reference or the subtle connotations his music carries. By utilising so many rhetorical figures, one might imagine that Bach's music runs the risk of being remote, formulaic or pedagogically dull.* In fact it is anything but. What we encounter here is a youthful refusal to be tied to a single methodology, either of form or of rhetoric. Then, by making room in his composition for his own startling improvisatory skills as a performer, Bach draws us into the distinctive

* In 1708, only a year after Bach's Mühlhausen audition, his colleague and cousin, J. G. Walther, wrote, 'the music of today is to be compared with rhetoric on account of its multitude of figures' (*Praecepta der musicalischen Composition*, MS 1708, p. 152), a phrase that was lifted straight out of Christoph Bernhard from about sixty years before, though it is not immediately apparent whether Walther is being factual or slightly derogatory.

sound patterns of his world and a mode of musical expression that (among other things) is underpinned by its strong rhythmic outline. In his imaginative response to Luther's text, Bach makes us aware that music can do much more than merely mirror the words from start to finish: he shows that it can hold our attention and captivate us by metaphors that strike like lightning. As long as we are willing to let go and allow him to describe the world to us as he sees it, we are soon provided with a first point of entry.*

Luther's narrative begins with a backward glance at Christ in the shackles of death and will end with his jubilant victory and the feast of the Paschal Lamb.

> Christ lay in the bonds of death,
> Sacrificed for our sins,
> He has risen again
> And brought us life;
> For this we should rejoice . . .

So much excitement is generated by the inexorable forward propulsion of Bach's music that, as listeners, we are caught up in the exuberance – especially at the point where the fantasia goes *alla breve*. Who else (Beethoven? Mendelssohn? Berlioz? Stravinsky?) would think of rounding off such a section with a fleet-footed canon based on the simplest of tunes – five descending notes, shaped as a syncopated riff?

That mood of unbridled joy is short-lived, however. Luther takes us back to the pre-redemptive era, reminding us of a time when Death held humanity captive:

> No innocence could be found.
> Thus it was that Death came so soon
> And seized power over us –
> Held us captive in his kingdom,
> Alleluia!

This is a grim evocation every bit as enthralling as those late-medieval 'Dance of Death' friezes mentioned in Chapter 2 or, closer to our own

* V. Ramachandran has researched the phenomenon of cross-activation between adjacent areas of the human brain: not just among synaesthetes (who see letters as expressing colours) but in any normal people who have a heightened sense of metaphor and are able to link seemingly unrelated concepts in their brains (BBC Reith Lectures, 2003).

time, the allegorical chess game played between a medieval knight and the personification of Death in Ingmar Bergman's film *The Seventh Seal* (1957). Timeframes overlap here: first that of pre-regenerate man, then those of the Thuringians of both Luther's and Bach's day, scarred by their regular brushes with pestilential death. Bach uses his falling semitone in two-note fragments – segmented and desolate – as an exchange between soprano and alto in a grief-laden, rocking motion suspended over the basso continuo playing the same two-note interval in diminution but with octave displacement.

The music is spellbinding. It conjures up humanity in the grip of death, helpless and paralysed, awaiting what Luther called the 'most serious and most horrible' penalty of death – God's judgement against sin. On to this bleak stage Death now makes a stealthy approach, seizing mortals in his bony hands. Twice Bach freezes the music, first on the words *den Tod . . . den Tod*, handed back and forth four times between soprano and alto, and then on the word *gefangen* ('imprisoned'), where the voices are locked in a simultaneous E/F♯ dissonance – the captive state just prior to the onset of rigor mortis.* The surprising word *Halleluja* – so dulled by overuse – follows, as it does at the end of every stanza, but always with a different slant. Here its mood is elegiac and unremittingly sad, as though to convey the idea that God must be praised even at the moment of death. After the merest flicker of promise in the last phrase, the music sinks back in resignation.

In the starkest contrast of mood the unison violins herald the coming of Christ: sin is overthrown and Death's sting is plucked out. Bach uses the violins symbolically as the flail with which Christ slashes at the enemy to nullify the power of Death. There is something Miltonic about the way he dispatches the rebellious angel to the depths as the continuo line spins down to a bottom E: 'plumb down he drops / Ten thousand fathom deep, and to this hour / Down had been falling . . .' Death's power is snapped in two. The music comes to a complete stop on *nichts*: 'naught remained' – the tenors

* Something similar to Bach's use of the reiterated B/F♯ to convey the thraldom of death recurs in the music of an otherwise unlikely follower – Hector Berlioz, when, in *Les Nuits d'été*, he came to set 'Au Cimetière' (from Théophile Gautier's *La Comédie de la mort*, published in 1838): the harmonically ambiguous resolution of G to F♯ and back to the words *passe, passe*). In his setting of Gautier's words (*Un air maladivement tendre / À la fois charmant et fatal, / Qui vous fait mal*) Berlioz portrays death as a curiously voluptuous occurrence, a momentary distraction from the gruesome reality in the struggle of light over darkness, life over death.

slowly resume – 'but Death's mere form', Death now a pale shadow of himself. Here Bach etches the four-note outline of the Cross with great deliberation, before directing the violins to resume with their concerto:

BWV 4, Versus III, bb 27–28

By now it has become a festive display of prowess, a victory tattoo heralded by the addition of the tenors' celebratory *Hallelujas*. At the hymn's core is an evocation of the *wunderlicher Krieg* – that 'wondrous battle' waged between the forces of life and death, the old season and the new, the spring corn about to burst through the earth's wintry crust: 'It was a marvellous battle when Death and Life struggled.' The only instrumental support is that provided by the continuo, as groups of onlookers voice their reactions to the bout that will determine their fate. Yet they sing from the vantage of knowing the outcome already – for it was 'foretold by the Scriptures ... how one death gobbled up the other', reflecting Lutheran dogma that Christ's resurrection signals the defeat of death itself.

For this Hieronymus Bosch–like scene Bach sets three of his four voice parts in hot pursuit of one another, a fugal *stretto* with entries just a beat apart, while the fourth voice (altos) trumpets out the now-familiar melody. One by one their voices peter out, devoured and silenced: 'Death has been turned into a joke.' Back comes the falling semitone that he has used from the very beginning, still the emblem of death, now spat out with derision by the crowd: *Ein Spott!** Again there are strong

* Heiko Oberman identifies Luther's language as 'so physical and earthy that in his wrathful scorn he can give the Devil "a fart for a staff"' (WA TR, Vol. 6, No. 6,817): 'You, Satan, Antichrist, or pope, can lean on it, a stinking nothing.' Thus 'a figure of respect, be he Devil or pope, is effectively unmasked if he can be shown with his pants down' (H. Oberman, *Luther: Man between God and the Devil* (1989), pp. 108–9).

Miltonic overtones – a parallel with Satan's return to Pandaemonium, boasting to his minions of his success against man,

> ... expecting
> Their universal shout and high applause
> To fill his ear, when contrary he hears
> On all sides, from innumerable tongues
> A dismal universal hiss, the sound
> Of public scorn.[11]

All four voice parts round off the scene with the *Halleluja* refrain, each section reflecting on a separate facet of the battle scene: the sopranos with curious, sighing appoggiaturas – a moment of pathos recalling Death's former power to inflict hurt; the altos more matter of fact (a plain rounding off of the tune); the tenors almost manic in their glee (articulated in jagged staccato quavers); and the basses descending through nearly two octaves before coming to a point of rest. It suggests a stage direction – *exeunt* – as the commentators file off stage.

Returning as celebrants in the ritual Easter Mass the basses intone the fifth stanza over a descending chromatic bass line redolent of Purcell's music for Dido's 'Lament' in its solemnity. At this point a tense seriousness descends on the scene: it feels as though a mystical link has been established between the Paschal Lamb foretold by the prophets and Christ's sacrificial death. Halting the harmonic movement for two bars, Bach requires each instrumental voice to pause symbolically on a sharp (in German, *Kreuz*, also the word for 'cross'), while, once again, he inscribes each of the four points of the Cross: the basses in parallel tenths with the violins, then the continuo and lastly the violins – painting and re-painting the very symbol to which faith clings ('burned in ardent love') up to the point of death – like the Emperor Constantine's battle cry, *In hoc signo vinces* ('In this sign conquer!'). The text then refers to the mysterious way 'blood marks our door.' Bach inscribes the new symbol several times (just as the doors of the enslaved Israelites in Egypt were marked): four separate attempts (basso continuo, bass voices, strings, then voices again) to launch the tortuous search for a means of escape, conveyed by means of an angular melisma. At the moment when faith is subjected to its greatest test, Bach forces his basses to plunge down by a diminished twelfth to a low E♯. Finally, to mirror the challenge Luther throws at the Devil (described as 'the strangler [who] can no longer harm us'), Bach requires his singers* to sustain a high D at full force for nearly ten beats until the air drains from their lungs. This is music of magnificent defiance.

This cantata never palls, and, as far as we know, it was the only one of his early cantatas that Bach chose to revive (in Leipzig eighteen years later). Performing it on Easter Sunday 2000 in the Georgenkirche in Eisenach brought a strong sense of its joint authors' presence and personalities, as well as a fresh awareness of the medieval musical roots of their vision. Their concept of a cosmic battle between the forces of life and death links it not just to *Paradise Lost* but even to the writings of such different twentieth-century authors such as H. G. Wells, Charles Williams and Philip Pullman.† It shows us how Luther can imbue complex theological concepts with everyday experience, making them spring to life and become instantly more accessible. Then, totally faithful to the spirit and letter of Luther's epic hymn, we see Bach do the same, and in the process reveal a basic similarity of temperament. The fiery personality that gave Luther the courage to break with Rome and to launch a new

* Yes, plural, for in all the later cantatas there are no instances of Bach writing like this for a solo voice. Although we have no means of knowing precisely how many voices he intended – or were assigned to him – for the first performance of this piece in Mühlhausen (and it may have served a useful purpose for him in assessing the abilities of his new choir), its communal, hymn-like nature and the way Bach responds to Luther's evocation of a many-voiced crowd in the middle verse suggest more than one voice per part. Its challenges are also technically more easily manageable with several per line. Of course not everyone agrees.

† While it is true that in H. G. Wells's science fiction novel *The War of the Worlds* (1898) good and evil appear to be evenly balanced and the defeat of the Martians does not involve any kind of direct divine action (the insane clergyman's attempts to relate the invasion to some kind of biblical enactment of Armageddon seem only to reinforce his mental derangement), that is not the case either with Charles Williams (a close friend of J. R. R. Tolkien and C. S. Lewis) or with Philip Pullman. Three of Williams's best-known novels are *War in Heaven* (1930), *Descent into Hell* (1937) and *All Hallows' Eve* (1945). T. S. Eliot, who wrote an introduction for the last of these, described Williams's novels as 'supernatural thrillers' because they explore the sacramental intersection of the physical with the spiritual while also examining the ways in which power, even spiritual power, can corrupt as well as sanctify. In his re-telling of Milton's epic in *His Dark Materials* (1995–2000), Pullman inverts its conclusion, commending humanity for what Milton saw as its most tragic failing. What he most admires about *Paradise Lost* is 'the sheer *nerve* of Milton's declaring that he's going to pursue "Things unattempted yet in prose or rhyme", to "justify the ways of God to men".' Isn't that similar to what we have to admire also in Luther – and still more in Bach?

vision of Christianity is rekindled in Bach in this work.* We will see it re-surface in his cussed determination to withstand opposition and criticism all through his professional life and in his tenacity in devoting the first four years as Thomascantor in Leipzig (1723–7) to composing year-long cantata cycles and two monumental Passions that chart the bumpy course of doubt and fear, faith and disbelief, in life's pilgrimage.

We see, then, that the impact of the reformer Luther on the impressionable young Bach was immense: it shaped his view of the world, bolstered his sense of vocation as a craftsman-musician and tied that vocation to the service of the church – far more profoundly than was the case with his German peers, Telemann, Mattheson and Handel. For, although they, too, had strong Lutheran roots that shaped their music-making, religion for them was tempered early on by wider exposure to the sophisticated world of opera, as we saw in the previous chapter. With Bach, on the other hand, you feel it was more a case of natural necessity. The Italian philosopher Vico could be speaking for Bach in his belief that 'man's nature and potentialities, and the laws which govern him, had been bestowed on him by his Creator to enable him to fulfil goals chosen for, and not by, him.'[12] His particular goal at this stage of life he would very shortly define as a 'well-regulated church music to the Glory of God'.[13] (See illustration p. 180.)

Bach's achievement in *Christ lag* is to draw the listener, regardless of his or her religious beliefs, into this drama of faith – by the techniques of the apprentice rhetorician and the compelling skill of his precocious artistry, but most of all by the basic honesty of his approach. Here, too, he set down a marker for his future accommodation between words and music, showing how, with a minimum of critical reappraisal, music can be used to interpret text in a way that is not just theologically compliant with Luther but profoundly empathetic towards him – as evidenced in Bach's shared love of paradox and urgency of utterance, and in his pre-

* The professional historian, according to Richard Marius, would have us believe that 'Luther's insights came chiefly from the intellect and not from the gut – an attitude as wrongheaded as any effort to define Luther by psychology alone' (*Martin Luther: The Christian between God and Death* (2000), p. 21). The same, I feel, could be said of those 'positivist' musicologists who seem intent on proving that Bach's music was the consequence of prodigious cerebral control, thereby disregarding or diminishing the role of an emotional and spontaneous response to the devotional texts he was setting.

sentation of a dichotomy in human nature between the spiritual and fleshly.*

It is instructive to set this work beside one that Handel wrote at around the same age when he was in Rome – his vivid rendition of Psalm 110, *Dixit Dominus* – overwhelming proof that he, too, was a dramatist in the making. Where Bach is yoked to Luther, Handel, decidedly more of a man of the world even at this stage, shows us why he was so drawn to Italy, responding, like Dürer and Schütz before him, and Goethe later on, to her landscape, her art in all its vitality and vivid colours, and of course her music. Where we saw Bach seizing on the physicality of the crucial contest between life and death in ways that anticipate some of the crowd choruses in his two great Passions, Handel re-lives for us the wrath of the Old Testament God, giving drastic pictorial expression to the psalm text ('He shall . . . smite in sunder the heads') by pounding staccato repetitions of a single word – *con-qua-sa-a-a-bit* – in all voices and instruments. What we might respond to as 'dramatic' in both these compositions has very little to do with the theatre. The drama is all in the mind – conjured up experimentally by musical techniques both new and old, which in Bach's case vivify biblical incident, and in Handel's demonstrate the exercise of raw power bubbling just below the surface of the psalm text. Both works give us a foretaste of how these young Saxons would go on to play such a profound and innovative role in shaping the development of mutant opera, as outlined in Chapter 4. And even at this stage there are pointers to the divergent future preoccupations of these two giants: love, fury, loyalty and power (Handel); life, death, God and eternity (Bach).

* * *

A month after Easter 1707, the parochial council of the Blasiuskirche in Mühlhausen met to appoint their new organist. The burgomaster, Dr Conrad Meckbach, asked 'whether consideration should not first be given to the man Pach [*sic*] from Arnstadt, who had recently done his trial playing at Easter'. Since no other name was put forward, the town

* Here is an early instance of Bach's ability to capture the imagination, so that 'what the listener gets, then, is a span of musical time in which the fleetingness of the narrative moment is suspended, and by which the overall drama acquires an increased depth of field' (John Butt, 'Do Musical Works Contain an Implied Listener?', JRMA, Vol. 135, Special Issue 1 (2010), p. 10).

scribe, J. H. Bellstedt, was instructed to communicate with the candidate. Bach replied that he would require a salary of 85 florins – the same as 'he received in Arnstadt' – slightly rounded up. Although this came to 20 florins more than his predecessor had received, Bach stipulated the same payments in kind: 54 bushels of grain, two cords of wood (one of beech and one other) and six times threescore faggots – all delivered to his door.[14] He further requested the use of a wagon for all the chattels he had accumulated in his three years in Arnstadt – musical instruments, scores, music and books as well as clothes and furniture. The Parish Council did not demur. Bach asked for the agreed terms to be put in writing. These he received the next day (15 June), and the agreement was sealed with a handshake.

Two weeks earlier, a colossal fire had swept through the lower town, destroying 360 dwellings; the church, too, had nearly gone up in flames. Three of the council's deputies, still too shaken by the calamity to focus their minds on matters such as music,[15] could find neither pen nor ink to sign Bach's appointment. Once they had righted themselves, the burgomasters recognised the need for a commemorative service of penance, and it's more than likely that they commissioned their new organist to compose a cantata for the occasion. This may have been BWV 131, *Aus der Tiefe* (*Out of the deep*) – a work we know from an autograph inscription in the original score to have been requested not by Superintendent Frohne, Bach's immediate superior at the Blasiuskirche, but 'at the desire of pastor Eilmar', archdeacon at the Marienkirche.[16] Bach chose to set the complete text of Psalm 130, a prayer for forgiveness of sins, in Luther's translation.*

This is the second of three early cantatas (BWV 4, 131 and 106) we explore in this chapter that display three successive, linked approaches to the mechanics of faith and how they operated within Bach's music-

* That in itself calls for comment, seeing that Luther, who, as a former Augustinian friar, testified to the transformative power of chanting the psalm-tones, called it a process in which the 'affections' seem to 'pluck' the 'strings' of the psalmist's words, causing them to vibrate and be transformed into divine affections. Luther claimed *vox est anima verbi* – 'the voice is the soul of the Word': Scripture reaches the listener as words to be not 'interpreted', but 'captured' or 'incorporated' in sound via the body's chamber of resonance. There is every reason to suppose that Bach was familiar with Luther's theology of the Psalter and that he pondered how he might apply it to a figural, concerted setting of the psalm (see Bernd Wannenwetsch, '"Take Heed What Ye Hear": Listening as a Moral, Transcendental and Sacramental Act', JRMA, Vol. 135, Special Issue 1 (2010), pp. 91–102).

ally active mind during his early twenties. On this occasion there was no simple structural device in BWV 131 for Bach to fall back on, such as the omnipresent chorale melody that unifies all seven stanzas of *Christ lag* and so providing a bedrock for his musical realisation. Here the psalm text demanded a more complex meshing of words and music, pointing to sharper contrasts of style, form and fluidity of expression. Bach's solution was to spread the eight verses symmetrically over five interlinked movements and to leaven the psalm with two pieces of 'troped' commentary. These insertions, two stanzas of a chorale by Bartholomäus Ringwaldt (1588), *Herr Jesu Christ, du höchstes Gut*, closely mirror instructions for confession and repentance by a theologian, Johann Gottfried Olearius (1611–84), author of the five-volume *Biblische Erklärung* (1678–81), a copy of which Bach was later to own:[17] that man should repeat daily these five words –

i. *God . . .,*
ii. *show . . .*
iii. *me . . .,*
iv. *a sinner . . .,*
v. *mercy.*

These five words open one section of Luther's catechism, whose whole is almost mirrored in Bach's five movements. Striving for an optimal characterisation of the text led Bach to a new music of powerful, if perhaps unequal, eloquence. He establishes three choral movements as the pillars of his structure. What stands out in the first movement, constructed on the model of an instrumental prelude and fugue, are the liberties Bach takes to permit rhetorical expressivity: the subtle way he places motivic links in the *adagio* prelude for oboe and strings that anticipate the shapes of the words that follow, how the voices then respond fugally in *stretto* with the instruments, how the whole flows seamlessly into the second verse, a choral fugue marked *vivace*, and how this concludes with a triple echo (*f*, *p*, *pp*) incidentally very similar to Handel's practice in the sixth movement of *Dixit Dominus*, and in turn sets up motivic anticipations of the bass arioso that follows without a break to form one overarching unit.

Bach picks up and develops for the first time what has been called Luther's 'penitential exaltation',[18] a thread running through many psalm settings by German composers who had either lived though the Thirty Years War or suffered in its aftermath. Schütz's settings of Psalm 6 (*Ach Herr, straf mich nicht*) and Psalm 130 (*Aus der Tiefe*) from the *Psalmen Davids* (1619), written at the outset of the war (as well as many individual compositions written during its course), are all touched by this spirit. If there is something a little contrived about the opening to the cantata, as though Bach were striving to strike the right attitude, by the time he gets to the central chorus it has vanished completely. This is the most telling portion of the work, set to the words 'I wait for the Lord, my soul waits, and I rest my hopes on His Word.' Announced by three full-blooded affirmations in block harmony followed by little cadenza flourishes for two individual voices, it opens out into a slow, long-arched fugue. The emotional tug of the music (indeed, its penitential exaltation) is lodged in a succession of diminished sevenths, major and minor ninths that Bach strategically places on strong beats to emphasise the 'waiting' or 'yearning' sentiment. Each successive fugal entry gains in poignancy and heightened delivery as a result; each voice has a musical personality very much its own and really 'sings'.

Chord for chord, there is nothing so far that could not be traced back to the harmonic syntax of an inventive mid-seventeenth-century composer such as Grandi, Carissimi, Schütz or Matthias Weckmann; it is the instrumental fabric – Bach's way of interlacing oboe and violin (and later violas and even bassoon) in decorative counterpoint to the impassioned voice-leading of the chorus – that gives this movement its distinction.* Animating the wordless was a significant new strategy in an age in which the 'word' had become so dominant at every level. It suggests that Bach may have already intuited a still more authentic *logos* residing in instrumental 'speech', which was there to glorify God and celebrate His universe just as powerfully as music linked to biblical or devotional words.

An original feature of *Aus der Tiefe* is not so much Bach's utter faithfulness to the words, as the way he consistently adjusts his themes to the *shapes* of the sung words, their inflection and punctuation: changes of metre, tempo and texture enable him to characterise each verbal phrase

* Expressive gestures such as these and a detectable strain of mysticism in this cantata suggest if not an influence, then an affinity with another noble setting of the *De profundis* by the French composer Michel-Richard de Lalande, composed in 1689. Bach's and Lalande's versions share an overall sobriety of expression and, in particular, parallel ways of layering voices and instruments in dense contrapuntal webs of exceptional intensity.

and to change the *Affekt* almost instantly. So, for the impressive chorus that concludes the work, he constructs a mosaic-like sequence made up of four distinct but interlocking segments:

'Israel'	*adagio*	three assertive blocks of open harmony
'hope in the Lord'	*un poc' allegro*	imitative counterpoint with instrumental interjection
'for with the Lord there is mercy'	*adagio*	hymn-like, with decorative oboe *cantilena*
'And with him is plenteous redemption'	*allegro*	a vigorous imitative treatment with antiphonal figures in *suspiratio*

This leads without a break into an independent fugal sequence, its theme and counter-theme skilfully adjusted to reflect the dual character of the final sentence:

'And he shall redeem Israel'	*allegro*	a brief head-motif with an extended melismatic 'tail' for the word *erlösen* ('to redeem')
'from all his iniquities'	*allegro*	chromatically rising counter-subject

In this final section, culminating with this extended fugue subject and its chromatic answer, Bach finally distances himself from the earlier motet-like structures of his forebears' music and reveals that, though certainly no modernist, he is au fait with up-to-the-minute devices taken from contemporary Italian practice that were being transplanted around this time by north German composers such as Johann Theile (1646–1724), Georg Österreich (1664–1735)* and Georg Caspar Schürmann

* The final fugal section of Österreich's *motetto concerto*, *Ich bin die Auferstehung*, composed in 1704, is constructed on similar lines. Bach could have encountered other examples of Österreich's music in the Lüneburg library. Despite the neglect of these composers today, thanks to collectors such as Düben and the Lüneburg cantors, and tireless copyists including Österreich himself, enough of their music has survived in manuscript for us to gain an inkling of their originality, their versatility and, above all, their ingenuity in adapting Italian Catholic music for use within the Lutheran liturgy.

(*c.* 1672–1751).* Obscure, shadowy figures today, all three composed German *concertato* motets and cantatas considered state-of-the-art in terms of style that stand out by the quality of their invention and craftsmanship. Though their innovative choral repertoire still languishes in obscurity, there are grounds for thinking that Bach's music would have developed differently but for their example. This is not the same as saying that their music provided the immediate point of departure for his imagination; it may have acted more like a slow-release bolus, emitting its influence gradually and at successive stages in his development. But it is significant that at the point of taking his first experimental steps as a composer of figural music Bach was operating in a milieu close to the cosmopolitan cultured atmosphere of north German courts, where composers such as these were being encouraged to use their ingenuity and direct their experiments in music towards the edification (*Erbauung*) of believers. By choosing for musical treatment texts that combined a familiar chorale with a story taken from Scripture, they signalled a robust new approach to positioning the traditional Gospel message within the context of contemporary Lutheran worship and illuminating it in the manner of a musical sermon. Such powerfully affective music was underpinned by sophisticated fugal writing with tonally orientated themes (often with a chromatic counter-subject), an extended development of sequential harmony and the pronounced use of *ostinato* basses, particularly the 'walking bass' variety and those comprising a stepwise descent of four notes. They gauged how a personal response to core Christian beliefs could be teased out of their complex musical interweaving of biblical texts, contemplative poetry and Lutheran chorales, and probed new ways of drawing the listener in.

* * *

In reflecting on his own beliefs later in life, and having acquired his own copy of Abraham Calov's Bible commentary, Bach wrote *Nota bene* in the margin and underlined two almost identical passages: *Ich will dich nicht*

* After a year's study in Venice, Schürmann was given a free transfer for four years as composer and Capellmeister to the court of Meiningen, where he met Bach's cousin Johann Ludwig, who succeeded him in 1706. There he composed the most intriguing of his liturgical music: nine cantatas in which the characteristic alternation of recitative and aria developed in Italian opera – and these now included *da capo* arias, as Bach was to do ten or more years on – were now applied to church music by a German composer perhaps for the first time. Each cantata concluded with a chorale setting, treated in a variety of ways likely to have attracted Bach's attention.

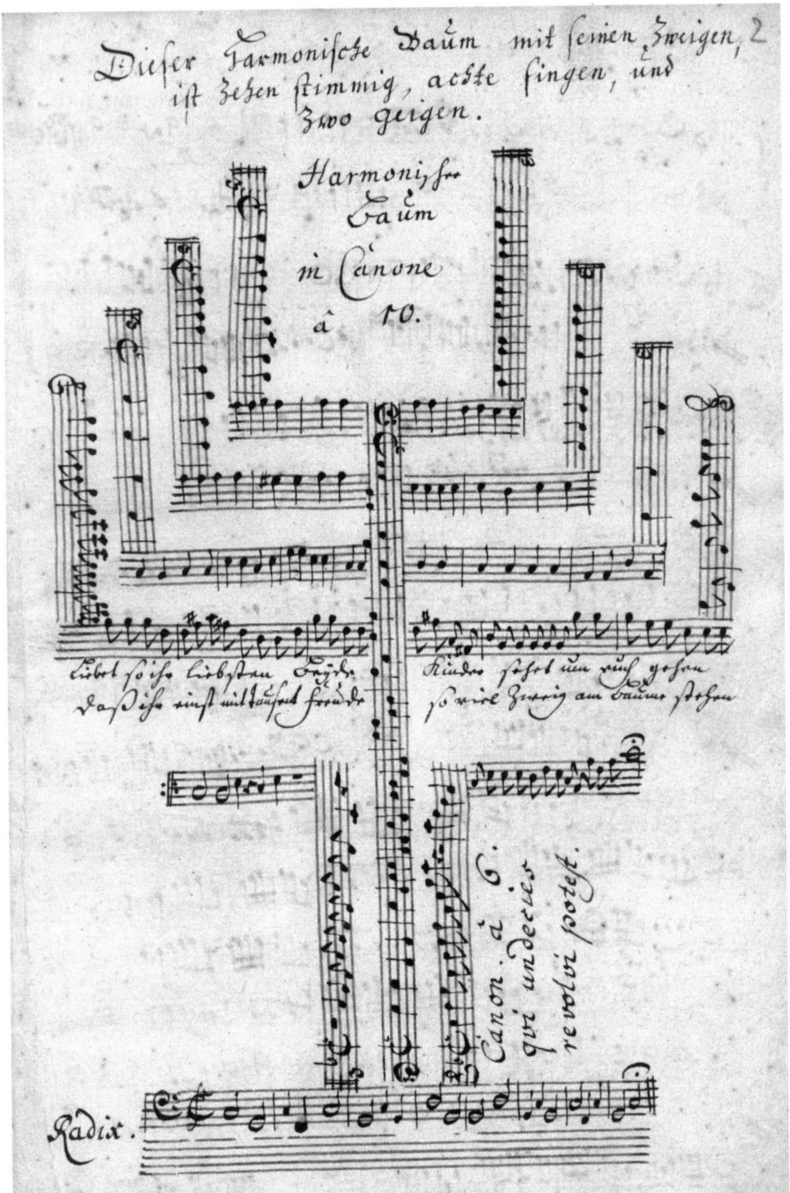

The Harmonischer Baum, *a ten-part canon in the form of a tree, from the treatise* Musicalisches Kunst-Buch *by Johann Theile (1646–1724), known to his contemporaries as 'the father of contrapuntalists'.*

verlassen, noch von dir weichen ('I will not forsake you nor stray from you') and *Ich will dich nicht verlassen, noch versäumen* ('I will not forsake you nor abandon you'). One would dearly like to know how much of that confident assurance – of not being entirely alone in the world – Bach already possessed when he became an orphan, and how much of his grief returned twelve years later when he sat down to compose the work known as the *Actus tragicus*, or *Gottes Zeit ist die allerbeste Zeit* (BWV 106) (*God's own time is the very best of times*). That we do now know the answer should not tempt us into applying a speculative post-Freudian psychoanalytical framework to assess his state of mind – postulating resentful thoughts towards his parents, anger, wish fulfilment, guilt, the search for an alternative father figure and so on.[19] Such an approach to measuring the permanency of Bach's psychological scars (if any there were) is just as inexact and unhistorical as applying adult thought patterns retrospectively back into childhood. What is beyond dispute is that all through his lifetime Bach had frequent and painful encounters with death, which scythed through his family: neither of his parents lived beyond the age of fifty, and he lost twelve out of twenty of his own children before they had reached the age of three – well beyond the average, even at a time when infant mortality was ubiquitous.

To what extent did Bach share Luther's overwhelming terror of death – a fear shared and admitted by many of his followers and theologians – 'the one misery that makes us more miserable than all other creatures'?[20] Indeed, to what degree was he truly convinced by Christian dogma, especially the kind that emphasised personal faith and the rewards of salvation? If he was, when did it begin? Beyond his links to Luther by geography, schooling and circumstance, was he drawn to the founder of that theology by real conviction?* These are questions to which no very convincing answers can be found in the archives. We

* The first generation of Lutherans regarded their founder as the *Wundermann*, one who was called for, and sent, by God. Nearly 200 years on Robert L. Marshall concludes that 'there can be little doubt that Bach revered Luther, strongly identified with him, recognized him as a supremely towering figure, as a truly "great man", and venerated him almost to the point of obsession' (*Luther, Bach, and the Early Reformation Chorale* (1995), p. 10). Peter Williams suggests an interesting alternative role model here: Luther's close colleague Philipp Melanchthon: 'orphaned (aged eleven), expressed fidelity to his fatherland and place of origin, was headstrong, and educated himself by assiduously studying what others had written' (*The Life of Bach* (2004), p. 9).

need to look elsewhere. Once again, some of Bach's early works provide fertile evidence of a kind, none more so than the *Actus tragicus*.

Even to his most ardent admirers Bach can seem a little remote at times: his genius as a musician – widely acknowledged – is just too far out of reach for most of us to comprehend. But that he was a very *human* human being comes across in all sorts of ways: not so much from the bric-à-brac of personal evidence such as family letters and first-hand descriptions, which are few and far between, but from chinks in his musical armour-plating, moments when we glimpse the vulnerability of an ordinary person struggling with an ordinary person's doubts, worries and perplexities. One such is the *Actus tragicus* – a funerary piece that Bach probably wrote shortly after *Christ lag*, when he was still only twenty-two, just twelve years from the time he was orphaned, and when he was preparing to set up house with his wife-to-be.

No one has so far been able to pinpoint the exact occasion for which the *Actus tragicus* was composed. There has been conjecture that it was written either for his uncle Tobias, who died in August 1707 and whose legacy of 50 gulden (amounting to more than half a year's salary) allowed him to marry his second cousin, Maria Barbara, in the village church at Dornheim, a mile or so outside Arnstadt, on 17 October. Another possibility is that it was composed in memory of Susanne Tilesius, the sister of Bach's friend and ally Pastor Eilmar of Mülhausen. Susanne was thirty-four when she died, leaving a husband and four children, just as Bach's own mother had done twelve years before. Might the *Actus tragicus* in some way be a cathartic musical outpouring of his own unresolved grief? It is possible that Susanne and his mother are both being invoked and commemorated in the solo soprano's entreaty 'Come, Lord Jesus', which is repeated over and over again at the very centre of the work. On this evidence the subject of death was a preoccupation, or at least a recurrent theme; it is supported by the significant proportion of books he amassed over time in his library devoted to the Lutheran *ars moriendi*.[21] Precociously, he seems to have learnt how the colossal force of faith embodied and enacted in music could deprive death of its powers to terrify, as though concurring with Montaigne (whom he certainly never read), 'Let us banish the strangeness of death: let us practice it, accustom ourselves to it, never having anything so often present in our minds than death: let us always keep the image of death in our imagination – and in full view.'[22] Luther, too, had insisted, 'We should familiarize

The battle with death from Heinrich Müller's Himmlischer Liebes-Kuss *(1732), one of several tomes in Bach's library advocating constant preparation and training for the unexpected, arbitrary hour of one's death.*

ourselves with death during our lifetime, inviting death into our presence when it is still at a distance.'[23]

Many of his later works, including the two great Passion settings, deal with the same subject as a dichotomy between a world of tribulation and the hope of redemption – quite standard in the religion of the day. But none does so more poignantly or serenely than the *Actus tragicus.** This extraordinary music, composed at such a young age, is never saccharine, self-indulgent or morbid; on the contrary, though deeply serious, it is consoling and full of optimism. Unlike some of Bach's busier contrapuntal inventions, it has good 'surface' attraction, no doubt as a result of its unusually soft-toned instrumentation: just two recorders, an organ and a pair of violas da gamba. With this restricted palette Bach manages to create miracles: the opening sonatina comprises twenty of the most heart-rending bars in all of his works. From the yearning dissonance given to the two gambas, to the ravishing way the recorders entwine and exchange adjacent notes, slipping in and out of unison, we are being offered music to combat grief. Jean-Philippe Rameau once implored one of his pupils: *Mon ami, faites-moi pleurer!*[24] Listening to Bach's sonatina, we are shown what Rameau meant and are moved. The whole work lasts less than twenty minutes and flows seamlessly through several switches of mood and metre. As often in the best music, there is a brilliant use of silence. After inserting a sequence of pleas for release from this world in which the soprano sings 'Yes, come, Lord Jesus!' several times over, Bach ensures that all the other voices and instruments drop out one by one, leaving her unsupported voice to trail away in a fragile arabesque.† Then he notates a blank bar with a pause over it. This active, mystical silence turns out to be the exact midpoint of the work.

This is just one example of deliberate and effective planning by Bach.

* It is here, too, that we see that his approach to death, as reflected in his earliest choral music, seems to differ from that of others within his immediate family circle. Life seen as a 'vale of tears' was the inherited seventeenth-century view, exemplified by Heinrich Schütz's composing throughout the Thirty Years War, an outlook that resurfaces in the music of Bach's elder cousin Johann Christoph Bach, whose *Mit Weinen hebt sichs an* (first performed in Arnstadt in 1691 when Johann Sebastian was six) describes the three Ages of Man in decidedly nihilistic terms, serving to guide the listener and charting the miseries of youth, middle and old age.

† There is a parallel here with the deeply affecting conclusion of Johann Christoph Bach's five-voiced motet, *Fürchte dich nicht*: at the point where the soprano enters with words *O Jesu du, mein Hilf* (from a funeral hymn by Johann Rist) there is a momentary intertwining of the two common words *du* and *mein* – as though a halting contact has just been made from one world to the next (see p. 71 above). This expression of the 'freedom' of the Gospel expressed in the free-flying soprano line (with no basso continuo to tie her down) is in marked contrast – and with intentional theological purpose, one can only assume – to the strict fugal exposition of the Law and its demands (*Es ist der alte Bund*).

The more you peer below the surface, the more complex the *Actus tragicus* turns out to be – considerably more so than the two cantatas we examined earlier. Composite texts had come into fashion in northern Germany from the 1670s onwards, the idea being to elucidate and interpret the Scriptures by juxtaposing different passages on a single theme. In all likelihood Bach got the idea of selecting seven biblical quotations and interleaving them with familiar Lutheran chorales from the aforementioned theologian Johann Gottfried Olearius. Through the text's particular disposition and arrangement, we are presented with a clear juxtaposition of Old Testament Law and New Testament Gospel. Luther put it this way: 'The voice of the Law terrifies because it dins into the ears of smug sinners: "In the midst of earthly life, snares of death surround us." But the voice of God cheers the terrified sinner with its song: "In the midst of certain death, life in Christ is ours."'[25] The timing of any individual death was God's secret: it is He who 'sets the clock' of human life and orders matters according to His own timetable.[26] Luther's underlying purpose is to prepare the believer 'to die blessedly' and to comfort the bereaved with the notion that life is essentially a preparation for death: acceptance of this provides the only reliable way of coming to terms with our humanity and the futility of our endeavours. In his Bible commentary Olearius makes room for an image (by Christian Romstet) of St John the Baptist at the gate of Heaven and, behind him, Jesus tending his garden, entitled *This is the Tree of Life*. (See Plate 17.) There is a parallel here in the visual arts with the cycles of painting known as *paysage moralisé* that link the ages of man with the times of day, the seasons of the year and the eras of biblical history.[27] Seen as a symbol of the way the human spirit attempts to create a harmony with its environment (though one in which the natural wilderness had been tamed and brought to heel), such works could be used allegorically to move the viewer to the contemplation of 'solemn things'. The duty and purpose of art in the face of death was to represent the recently deceased to those left behind on earth, to console them in their grief and to facilitate communication and discourse about the unutterable. In conveying emotive and complex themes that depend on the interplay of past and future, hope and despair, music may often be more effective than painting.

The way Bach matches his musical design to the theological principles outlined is breathtaking. As with *Aus der Tiefe*, he has to impose his own musical structure. To mirror the theological division between Law and Gospel, he sets out a symmetrical ground-plan, the individual movements arranged so that, as listeners, we can trace in music the journey of the believer progressing via Old Testament Scripture (with its bald statements about the inevitability of death) downwards to his lowest ebb and then, through prayer, upwards again to a more spiritual future. The solo interventions on both sides of the divide are arranged in contrasted pairs, making it easy to follow the chiastic pattern and the deliberate contrasts. So, for example, of two solos for bass the first is an authoritative Old Testament injunction to 'set thy house in order, for thou shalt die, and not live.' This is answered by Christ's words from the Cross to the malefactor, 'Today shalt thou be with me in paradise.' Overlapping the second of these solos is Luther's version of the Song of Simeon, *Mit Fried und Freud ich fahr dahin . . . Der Tod ist mein Schlaf worden* ('In peace and joy I now depart . . . Death has become my sleep'). If Bach intended a musical representation of physical extinction anywhere in the piece, it must be here, as the two gambas peter out at the end of the chorale, a reminder to the devout listener that the hour of death can unleash an intensification of the Devil's wiles. And, as if he had not done enough already to mirror Scripture with music, Bach goes a step further, allegorically leading the believer to understand and accept the pattern of his life by providing a progression of keys, modulating downwards from E♭ (the home key) to B♭ minor (the remotest flat key in the circle of fifths, used by Bach later for the description of the Crucifixion in the *John Passion*) and back to E♭ again (see illustration in Chapter 10, p.372). So again we have a symmetrical design: a descent from E♭ via C minor and F minor for those grim Old Testament injunctions, via that nadir of silence to B♭ minor, then rising with the comfort of the Gospel texts via A♭ and C minor back to E♭. The pattern is perhaps intended to prod the listener into reflecting on the successive stages of Christ's own life, through birth, crucifixion, death and resurrection.

Yet the most impressive feature of Bach's fusion of music and theology occurs in that central silent bar to which we as listeners are irresistibly drawn. Bach's final, masterly coup – to illustrate the believer's crisis of faith and overwhelming need of divine help – is to leave the soprano's immediately preceding notes tonally ambiguous – her voice just evaporating into that desperate cry. There is no resolution, not even a partial closure that might carry the harmony towards a stable cadence: so it is up to *us* how we interpret it in the silence that follows. If we hear it at face value as a weak perfect cadence (a *tierce de Picardie* in F minor), that would indicate death as a kind of full stop. But perhaps we are being gently nudged to hear the final oscillation between A and B♭ as leading note and tonic respectively, in the key of the movement which follows, B♭ minor. In that case Bach's message is one of hope, the tonal upswing indicating that Christ's intervention guarantees death is only a midway point on our journey, the beginning of whatever comes after. This planting of uncertainty, or rather ambivalence, is not the same as toying with our expectations, a use of hiatus that Bach (along with many other composers) employs on other occasions to hold our attention and keep us guessing.

Bach's *Actus tragicus* is music of extraordinary profundity. It comes closer to piercing the membrane of awareness that separates the material world from whatever lies beyond it than any other piece of music in this immensely fecund *fin de siècle* period. Again there are pointers to what he might have learnt from cousin Christoph, some of whose compositions also seem to inhabit and explore that shadowy borderline between life and death: vitally expressive on the one hand, fragile to the point of imminent extinction on the other. Of course one can no more define the emotional charge – or, for that matter, the pain or the pleasure – that Bach's music affords us than a neuroscientist can distinguish between stimuli of reality in the brain and those of fantasy.

* * *

The proportional lucidity of the *Actus tragicus* gives a deceptively simple feel to it, but it also makes for great complexity – of thought, structure and invention; both point to the same sense of trembling on the brink of understanding. Perhaps the unobtrusive complexity of mathematical structure that underpins much of the music draws in people of a certain type of mind, even if they are not wholly aware of what is taking place. For the rest of us for whom the mathematics embedded in the music appeals only on a subconscious level, if at all, we can content ourselves with the consoling beauty of the sounds on offer.

The *Actus tragicus* also raises the delicate issue of religious belief – whether the partial or total presence (or absence) in the listener can influence receptivity to music. It would be invidious to insist that a person needs to hold Christian beliefs in order to appreciate Bach's church music. Yet it is certainly the case that without some familiarity with the religious ideas with which it is imbued one can miss so many nuances, even the way his later music can be seen to act as a critique of Christian theology. For many, the path towards enjoying, say, an opera by Mozart is obviously much smoother and less troublesome than that to a Bach cantata or Passion: in the former you have recognisable human emotions, a rollicking good story, spectacle, comedy and drama (even though some of their morally dubious characters pose pleasurable dilemmas). All these elements are present in Bach, too, but in a covert form. The texts he sets do not always coalesce to create a smoothly integrated dramatic form such as we find in the Act finales to Mozart's operas. The later cantatas are often laden with lurid imagery – of leprous sin, pus and boils – which, together with the thickets of theology, can create an impenetrable barrier to the uninitiated, to the point where part of what Bach may have meant gets lost in transmission. Something of the initial unveiling of the mystery is required to help the listener resist the temptation to drop (or shun) the religious content altogether because of the absurdity of the imagery, and to provide reassurance that the immense craft and complexity *can* be penetrated. In order to reach the human core of Bach's church music, my contention is not that we are obliged to place the music back in its original liturgical context (opting for a cold church pew, instead of a padded theatre seat) – though that is what evangelical Lutherans were urging throughout the twentieth century. We do need, however, to be aware of its place in the liturgy, the original purpose of its composer and of the church authorities in commissioning it (not necessarily the same thing), and the peculiar dialectical relationship Bach seems to forge between his music and the word (which we will explore in depth in Chapter 12). Once these onionskins have been peeled, the rewards far outstrip our initial superficial response to the music.

The problem is hardly new. In a letter to Erwin Rhode (1870) Friedrich Nietzsche wrote, 'This week I heard the *St Matthew Passion* three times and each time I had the same feeling of immeasurable admiration. One who has completely forgotten Christianity truly hears it here as Gospel.'[28] Yet in 1878 he was to complain, 'In Bach there is too much crude Christianity, crude Germanism, crude scholasticism . . . At the threshold of modern European music . . . he is always looking back towards the Middle Ages.' Nietzsche points to the conflict some people experience in relation to Bach's church music: put off by the harshness of some of the language, they are nonetheless in thrall to the music and the way it carries the conviction of his faith.

In the process of reconciling these opposite responses one can empathise with William James on the subject of religion in general – using 'every fibre of his intellectual energy to defend and justify freedom of the will' and, in his phrase, 'the right to believe'. Religion, he recognised, 'like love, like wrath, like hope, ambition, jealousy, like every other instinctive eagerness and impulse . . . adds to life an enchantment which is not rationally or logically deducible from anything else'.[29] At the same time it can embrace the torments of the 'sick soul' finding consolation in conversion, as seen in Augustine, Luther and Tolstoy, and the fascination of the divided self, as seen in John Bunyan – and indeed Bach.[30] With him, music inspires a religious sensibility that is very common but not necessarily tied to a specific dogma. Just as there are many non-religious *aficionados* of Bach's church music, so there are atheists among Bach-loving professional musicians. One of the most widely revered figures among contemporary European composers, György Kurtág, recently confessed, 'Consciously, I am certainly an atheist, but I do not say it out loud, because if I look at Bach, I cannot be an atheist. Then I have to accept the way he believed. His music never stops praying. And how can I get closer if I look at him from the outside? I do not believe in the Gospels in a literal fashion, but a Bach fugue has the Crucifixion in it – as the nails are being driven in. In music, I am always looking for the hammering of the nails . . . That is a dual vision. My brain rejects it all. But my brain isn't worth much.'[31]

* * *

In September 1742 Bach, then aged fifty-seven, bought a *de luxe* edition of Martin Luther's complete works in seven volumes. According to a little note in his own hand[32] about 'these German and magnificent writings of the late D.[octor] M.[artin] Luther' that had previously belonged to two distinguished theologians, Calov and Mayer, he had paid ten thalers for them. On his shelves he already had fourteen fat folios of Luther's writings, including the *Tischreden*, plus a Second Quarto volume of his *Hauß-Postilla*, besides many volumes of sermons, Bible commentaries and devotional writings by other authors, most of whom cited Luther generously. So why the new purchase? Was it just because this was the new Altenburg edition, whereas he already had the Jena version? Bach's working library, estimated to have contained at least 112 different theological and homiletic works, was less like a typical

1. (previous page) Georgenkirche, Eisenach
Built at the end of the twelfth century, and after incurring heavy damage during the Peasants' Revolt, the Georgenkirche was restored and three galleries were added. Both Martin Luther and Bach had deep, formative connections to this church as quondam pupils of the Latin School linked to it and as members of its *chorus musicus*.

2a & b. (above left & right) Neues vollständiges Eisenachisches Gesangbuch, 1673
Early exposure to this book with its iconic chorale tunes and emblematic depictions of musicians in the Temple of David and Solomon cemented the connections Bach would go on to make between music and theology, and between the ancient Temple musicians (seen in the left-hand engraving), the landscape of his home town (at its foot) and the choir of his own day (in the right-hand engraving).

3a. (opposite, above) The Whole World in a Cloverleaf
Map of the world as a cloverleaf, from Bünting's *Itinerarium Sacræ Scripturæ* (1592) – 'a travel book over the whole of Holy Scripture'.

3b. (opposite, below) Buno's Dragon
One of an ingenious series of illustrations from Johannes Buno's *Idea historiae universalis* (1672), the dragon symbolized the fourth millennium AD and includes smaller images of historical personages and incidents that provide memorable historical nuggets for school pupils to retain.

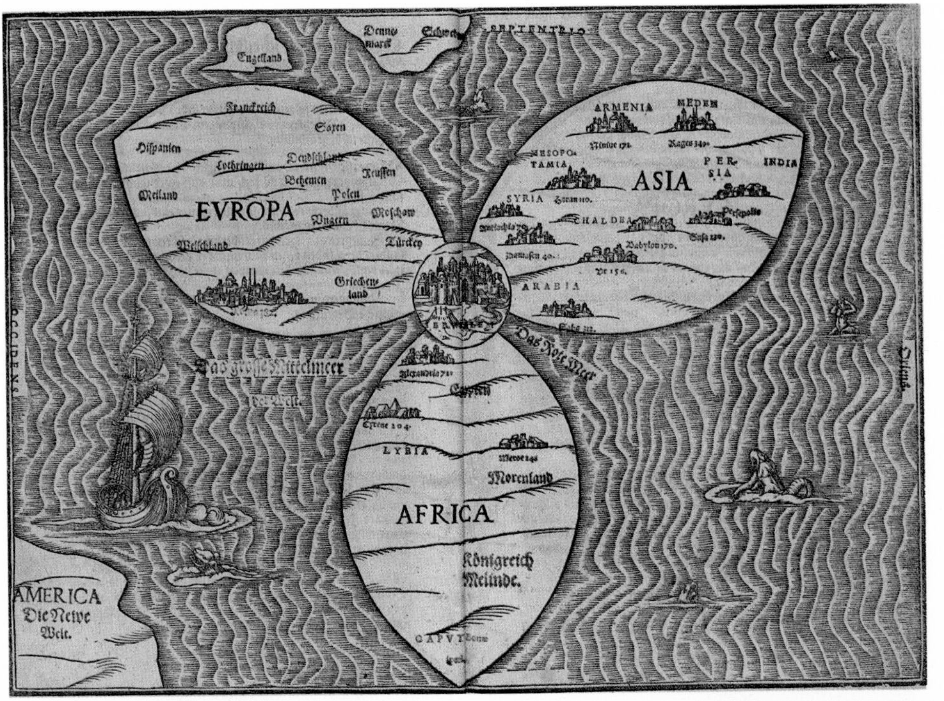

SEPTENTRIO
Engelland
Franckreich
Saxen
Hispanien
Lothringen
Deudschland
Reussen
Behemen
Polen
Meiland
EVROPA
Moschow
Ungern
Welschland
Türckey
Griechenland
ARMENIA
MEDEN
MESOPOTAMIA
ASIA
PERSIA
INDIA
SYRIA
CHALDEA
ARABIA
Das Rote Meer
LYBIA
Morenland
AFRICA
Königreich Melinde
AMERICA Die Newe Welt

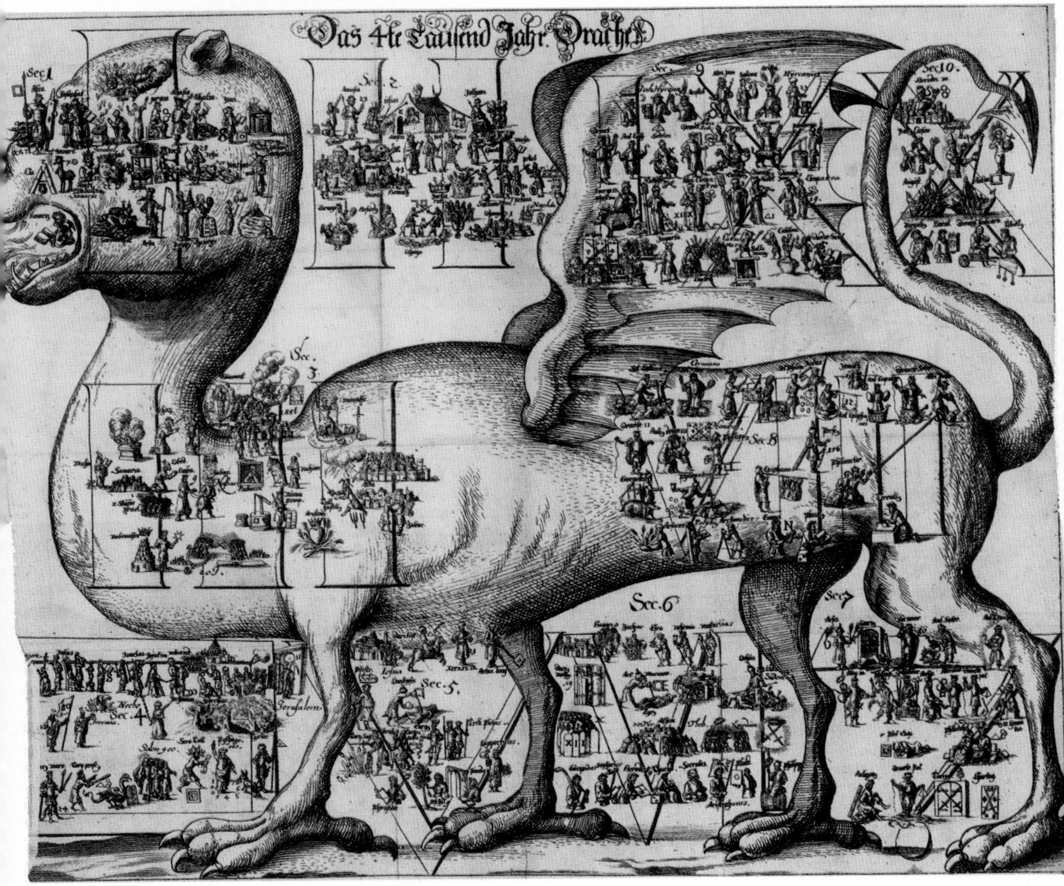

Das 4te Tausend Jahr. Drache
Sec. 1
Sec. 2
Sec. 3
Sec. 4
Sec. 5
Sec. 6
Sec. 7
Sec. 8
Sec. 9
Sec. 10

4. *Heinrich Schütz (1585–1672)*
This portrait in oils by Christoph Spetner (*c.* 1660) is of the most influential of Bach's German seventeenth-century predecessors, a brilliant composer and wordsmith similarly committed to exploring ways that music could expound and underpin Lutheran teaching.

5a & b. Organ Tablature Transcriptions
Among the most spectacular discoveries of *Bachiana* of the past decade, these two transcriptions by the teenage Bach of important organ works by Buxtehude (*Nun freut euch, lieben Christen g'mein*, BuxWV 201) and by Reincken (*Am Wasserflüssen Babylon*), were discovered in 2005 in the Duchess Anna Amalia Library in Weimar by Michael Maul. Together with Peter Wollny (the acclaimed specialist in identifying Bach's handwriting), he established without reasonable doubt that the first fragment (*below*) was copied out by Bach as a twelve or thirteen-year old in Ohrdruf when under his elder brother's tutelage. At the bottom of the second (*right*) is a note announcing *â Dom. Georg: Böhme descriptum ao. 1700 Lunaburgi* – 'written out at the home of Herr Georg Böhm in the year 1700 in Lüneburg', when Bach had just turned fifteen.

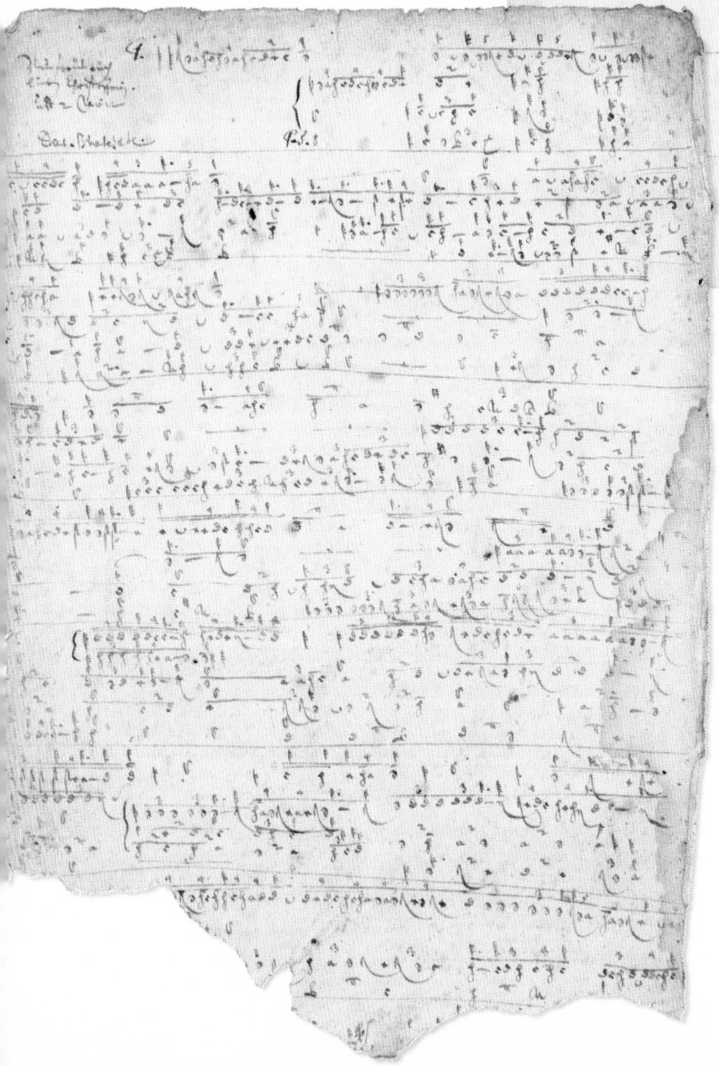

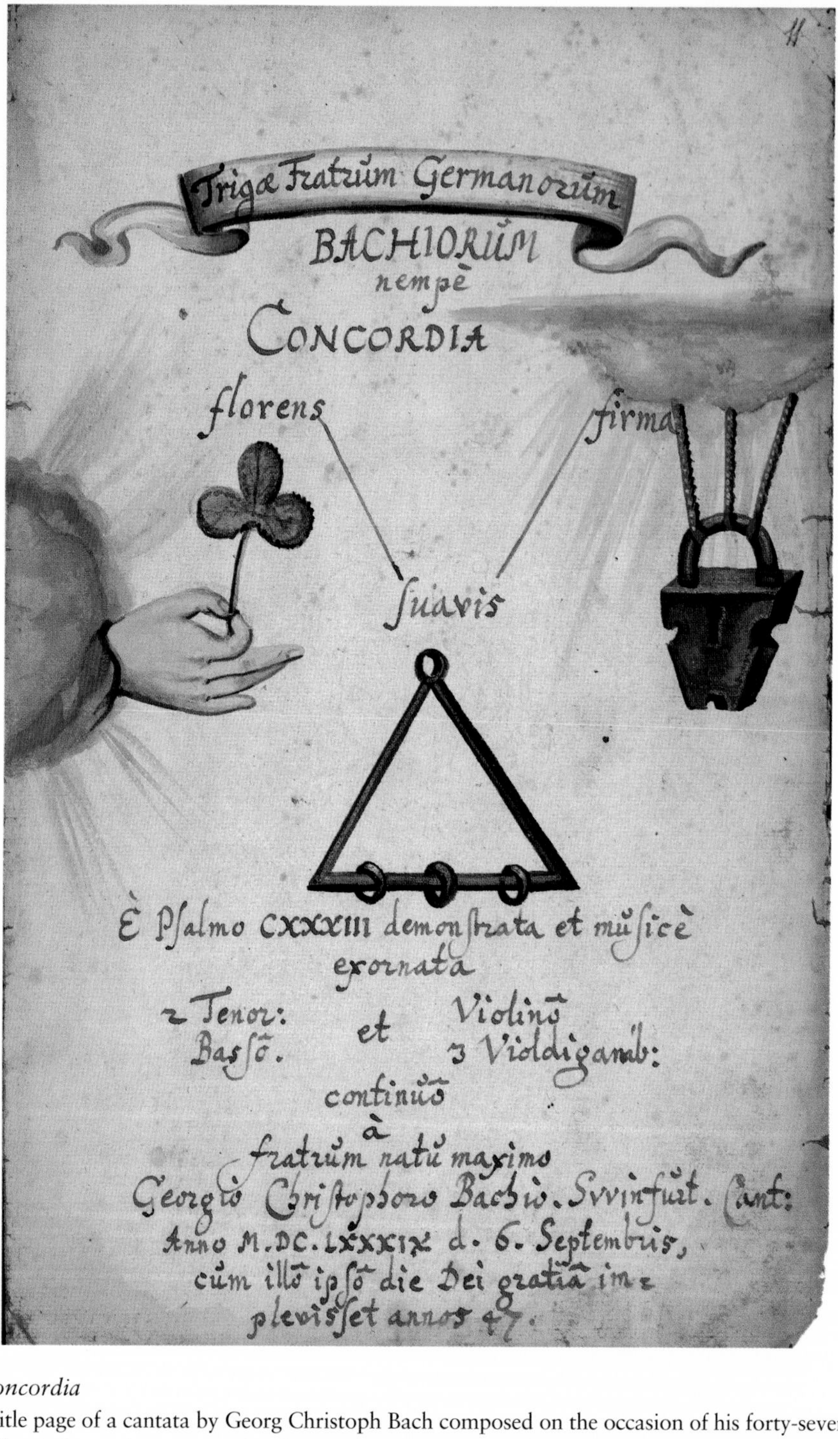

6. Concordia

The title page of a cantata by Georg Christoph Bach composed on the occasion of his forty-seventh birthday (6 September 1689), when his twin younger brothers (Johann Christoph and Johann Ambrosius) visited him in Schweinfurt, it illustrates the *concordia* that existed between the three of them together with its attributes: *florens* ('flourishing'), in the form of a three-leaf clover; *firma* ('firm'), shown as a padlock binding three chains; and *suavis* ('sweet'), illustrated by a triangle with three jingling rings attached.

7a & b. The Dukes of Saxe-Weimar
Bach's twin employers at the court of Saxe-Weimar from 1708 to 1717 were the nephew and uncle team of Duke Ernst August (1688–1748) (*left*) and Duke Wilhelm Ernst (1662–1728). As co-regents they occupied separate palaces, employed the same musicians and feuded constantly.

7c. Wilhelmsburg, Weimar, c. 1730
This view of the Wilhelmsburg (the palace occupied by the elder duke, Wilhelm Ernst) was painted from the perspective of the Rote Schloss (occupied by his nephew, Ernst August). It shows the ramparts, the spire of the Himmelsburg and the wooden footbridge that connected the two palaces.

8. Himmelsburg (interior), c. 1660
Short for *Weg zum Himmelsburg* ('The Way to the Castle of Heaven'), the name referred to the painted cupola depicting the open heavens in the palace church of the Wilhelmsburg, the centre of Duke Wilhelm Ernst's devotions. Destroyed along with the court music library in the great fire of 1774, it was of unusual design – a tall, three-storeyed structure with a balustraded music and organ gallery (just 13 feet by 10, and 65 feet above floor level), from which 'heavenly' sounds would float down upon members of the ducal families, courtiers and guests.

church musician's and more what one might expect to find in the church of a respectably sized town, or that 'many a pastor in Bach's day would have been proud to have owned'.[33] It is slightly odd, too, that the price that Bach claimed he had paid for these new volumes appears to have been obliterated and rather clumsily altered to ten thalers from a figure likely to have been twice or even three times as large – in the same month a Leipzig bookseller, Theophil Georg, published a four-volume catalogue of new and old Luther editions which quoted twenty thalers for the Altenburg edition.[34] Was Bach too embarrassed to admit to his wife the full price he had paid – amounting to perhaps half a month's salary? If this little deception is evidence of a midlife crisis, it did not amount to very much – it is not as if he had splashed out, say, on a new edition of a forbidden titillating work like the *Decameron* of Boccaccio or of Spinoza's banned and allegedly atheistic *Ethics*. What it does reveal, beyond his personal piety, his lifelong reverence for Luther and the central importance of Luther's writings in both his personal and professional capacities, is that 'Bach was evidently deeply – and apparently uncritically – immersed in a mindset that was at least two hundred years old.'[35]

There may indeed have been further cantatas composed during his first postings in Arnstadt and Mühlhausen that Bach felt no need to preserve once he had reached Leipzig in 1723, since they belonged to that 'former style of music [which] no longer seems to please our ears'.[36]* Yet he might have agreed with Schoenberg when he said of his early pieces 'I liked them when I wrote them' – and, in the case of BWV 4, *Christ lag*, this was still true in his forties. Those that have survived show that Bach had charted an initial course for his music – not merely to articulate, support and interpret these doctrinal positions, but to go beyond them in actualising the position of religion in people's everyday lives. In his hands, music is more than the traditional analogue of a hidden reality, more even than an instrument of persuasion or rhetoric; it encapsulates the role of religious experience as he understood it, charting the ups and downs of belief and doubt in essentially human terms and in frequently dramatic ways, and rendering these tensions and quotidian struggles vivid and immediate. These early works show him exploring music's power to provide aural, sensory comfort for life's hardships, softening

* One such composition may have been a second *Ratswechsel* cantata for Mühlhausen in 1709 after he had left, which may have been printed, like BWV 71, *Gott ist mein König*, but is now lost.

the impact of grief, like new skin over a wound. Aligning his music with the Lutheran conception of death as a reward for faith perhaps provided him with the means by which to subsume his own early pain of grieving. What it could not deliver was any softening of his attitude towards authority, as we shall see in the next chapter.

* * *

As we filed out of the Georgenkirche at the end of the Mass on Easter Sunday, the pastor invited us to visit what remains today of Bach's former school and the old Dominican monastery. We walked with him past the old town wall to the cemetery known as the *Gottesacker* ('God's acre'). Somewhere here are the unmarked graves of Bach's parents. As a member of the local *chorus musicus*, the youngest of the Bach sons would have been expected to sing at his father's interment and obliged to witness the ritual: the tolling of the funerary bell, the solemn procession of clergy, choir, family and mourners to the *Gottesacker.* There, on a small wooden dais, covered by a roof projecting from the town wall that was designed to give protection to the mourning family, Sebastian and the other Bach orphans would have foregathered.[37] In the middle of the cemetery stood a timber hut – hardly more than a garden shed – and a small pulpit from which Magister Schrön gave the graveside sermon. While the coffin was lowered the cantor and his choristers intoned the medieval funeral hymn in Luther's version: 'Mitten wir im Leben sind'.*

* Four hundred and fifty miles to the west, in London's Westminster Abbey, another musician would soon be laid to rest, one who had composed settings of these same sombre funerary sentences: Henry Purcell – 'In the midst of life we are in death . . . Thou knowest, Lord, the secrets of our hearts.' These words, from the funeral service in the Book of Common Prayer, are taken almost verbatim from Miles Coverdale's version of the *Media vita*, but they were translated not from the Latin but from Luther's 'Mitten wir im Leben sind'. The connection with Luther could therefore hardly be any stronger (see Robin A. Leaver, *'Goostly Psalmes and Spirituall Songes': English and Dutch Metrical Psalms from Coverdale to Utenhove 1535–1566* (Oxford Studies in British Church Music) (1991), p. 133). It suggests the possible existence of a common human condition extending right across Europe at this time, and even of something that links Bach (who never travelled abroad) to a living English tradition.

6
The Incorrigible Cantor

He shows little inclination to work . . . he is not even willing to give an explanation of the fact . . . a change will be necessary, a break will have to come soon . . .[1]

– Court Councillor Adrian Steger

In August 1730 relations between Bach and his municipal employers in Leipzig reached breaking point. The council minutes merely report: 'He had not conducted himself as he should.' But behind that opaque generalisation lay a long list of criticisms and alleged misdemeanours, different in detail but not in substance to those that had blighted relations between the young Bach and the Arnstadt Consistory nearly thirty years earlier (see below p. 174), and were now sticking in the Leipzig councillors' collective craw. He had recently dismissed a choirboy and sent him back to the country without apprising the governing burgomaster of this fact. Then he himself had gone away without leave – 'for which he must be reproached and admonished', they noted – just as he had done twenty-five years earlier on his seminal four-month visit to Buxtehude in Lübeck.* Not only was the cantor 'doing nothing' in the fulfilment of his teaching duties, nor giving obligatory singing lessons, but then, most vexatiously, 'he is not even willing

* In 1729 he had, on his own admission (NBR, p. 132), been absent for three weeks in Feb., possibly commissioned to compose and perform a birthday cantata for Duke Christian of Weissenfels. This was followed the next month by his visit with Anna Magdalena and Wilhelm Friedemann to Cöthen to perform a large-scale funerary ode (BWV 244a) containing seven arias and two choruses recycled from his *Matthew Passion* at a memorial service for his former patron, Prince Leopold, on 23–4 Mar.

to explain himself,' Burgomaster Steger (see Plate 11c) declared. This was now the third time in his life that Bach flatly refused to work, the first time being in Arnstadt, the second in 1717 in Weimar after he had been passed over as Capellmeister. Meanwhile other complaints were mounting up: 'a change would be necessary, for matters were bound to come to a head sooner or later, and he would have to acquiesce in the making of other arrangements.' Even Burgomaster Gottfried Lange, Bach's most vocal and longest-standing protector, had to admit, 'everything was true that had been mentioned against the Cantor.' So the council resolved to hit him where it was guaranteed to hurt: by cutting back his incidental income. They were exasperated by his non-compliance and taciturnity. In brief, they concluded, 'The Cantor was *incorrigible*.'

What had brought things to such a pass? It was all part of an increasingly acrimonious series of disputes between Bach and the council that had been simmering for the past seven years, and a classic example of the conflict that arises when an artist is placed in public office – expected to be both 'a genius and an obedient subject'.[2] On one side was an irascible man, passionate in defence of his craft and bristling at any perceived threat to his right to practise it unobstructed. On the other was a formidable alliance of secular and religious powers whose methods of subjugating employees had been honed over time and who were expert at making life difficult for successive cantors. The conflict also points to a deep contradiction in the make-up of Bach's personality: tacit acceptance of the hierarchical order that came with his time and his religion; and, opposed to that, as we will explore in this chapter, signs of constitutional truculence and a recurrent refusal to accept authority. To account for Bach's curmudgeonly behaviour in 1730 we need to trace these patterns back to his earliest brushes with authority, and from there explore how his attitude to authority in general appeared at different stages in his career.

* * *

First we need to take a look at the peculiar circumstances of the Leipzig cantorate. Back in 1657 negotiations were taking place between Adam Krieger and the council when, as organist of the Nikolaikirche, he applied (unsuccessfully) for the post of Thomascantor. Krieger made his attitude clear from the start: he should not have to 'both labour in the school and act as cantor' like the previous incumbent* – 'not out of any [personal] ambition [such as] to cast aspersions on the school position, but because this effort, along with the *studio compositionis*, would be too burdensome, considering that one who works himself to the bone in the school subsequently has little desire to put together concerted music [in church], and if he lacks desire for composing, it tends to turn out poorly'. He added that the previous incumbents, burdened with school duties, had 'become stiff with indignation and ill humour and suffered poor health'.[3] Unwilling to teach Latin, Krieger was never to reach an accommodation with the councillors, who then, as in later years, refused to countenance a division of teaching and composing roles into two separate offices. Krieger's analysis is strangely prophetic of the problems Bach was to face seventy years later, which narrowed on the questions of who had the final say in the discharge of the cantor's duties and, in particular, who set the boundaries between him and the rector of the Thomasschule as regards pupil admissions and the appointment of prefects.

The stark truth is that, by the time of Bach's Leipzig appointment in 1723, the best days of the Thomasschule, once considered the pacesetter among choir schools in German-speaking lands, were long since past. Standards and conditions had been heading downwards for at least a generation, from the time when Johann Schelle had been cantor in the 1670s. The old system of pooling resources to create a 'Concert of forty or fifty voices' made up of town musicians, choirboys, students and other music-lovers had long ago ceased to function. From around the turn of the century there was a marked dip in the musical quality of the *Alumnen*, the boys who boarded. Added to this was a shortage of funds sufficient to attract university-student musicians, who helped to plug the gaps in the performing ensemble of Thomaner, when they could very well play at the opera house. A glance at Johann Kuhnau's petitions to the town council shows us that the problems Bach was about to face – in recruiting and training a musical ensemble capable

* The Lübeck cantor, Caspar Ruetz, who looked somewhat longingly at Leipzig as being one of the few cantorates in Germany 'where one can make an ample livelihood only through music', deplored the way things were going: 'cantors are [stuck] in the school and are buried for ever under [a mountain] of school work' (Michael Maul, *'Director musices' . . . Zur 'Cantor-Materie' im 18. Jahrhundert* (2010), pp. 17–18).

Engraving of street music performed by Leipzig University students in 1729.

of tackling his music and rising to its exceptional technical demands (far in excess of Kuhnau's) – had already bedevilled his predecessor's musical ambitions for the whole duration of his cantorate (1701–22).*

On 4 December 1704 Kuhnau complained to the council that, since Telemann had arrived to take over the music at the Neukirche, music at the Nikolaikirche and the Thomaskirche, the two major city churches, had suffered, 'especially on feast-days and during the [trade] fairs ... when I should be making the best and strongest music'. This, according to Kuhnau, 'causes the greatest mischief, for the better students, as soon as they have acquired, at the cost of infinite pains to the cantor, sufficient practice, long to find themselves among the *Operisten*', participating in the avant-garde activities at the Neukirche, where the music (at this stage under Melchior Hoffmann) 'had degenerated and become operatic in character, which naturally scandalised those members of the congregation who appreciated and loved the true style of church music'.[4] So, while the Neukirche creamed off his best musicians, Kuhnau was left with boys 'who shouted themselves hoarse outside in the street, or were sickly and crabby, together with some town musicians, apprentices and none-too-competent ad hoc musicians'. The situation deteriorated further all through his cantorate, to the point where Kuhnau could no longer put on 'full-voiced music', let alone music for two or more choirs, and had to make do with *a cappella* motets, since he could not locate 'a few well-trained students' to help out at services in the city's two main churches. He petitioned the council to re-introduce supernumeraries (in effect, four or five extra pupil

* Kuhnau himself may unwittingly have contributed to this problem. Shortly before his appointment as cantor, Councillor Johann Alexander Christ, commissioner for the Thomaskirche, pronounced that the coffers of the two main churches could no longer stretch to so many handouts for student helpers in church music as previously. As a result, Kuhnau undertook (or was obliged to undertake) that in future he would exchange tuition to students in return for their participation in church services. In other words, it was a cost-saving device compounded by the fact that in the following years the number of churches in Leipzig doubled and the musical competence of the students could suddenly no longer be taken for granted; further, Telemann had far greater pulling power over students at the Neukirche and in the opera house. On top of this, the new form of the cantata, which Kuhnau went on to compose – Bach still more so – entailed a larger choir and a more varied orchestra. In essence, by 1700 the system by which the Thomaner had previously functioned had broken down. (Michael Maul, '*Dero berühmbter Chor': Die Leipziger Thomasschule und ihre Kantoren 1212–1804* (2012), pp. 97–8, 129–32, 149–50).

places) and to ban the students from singing at the Neukirche, but with what success we do not know.[5]

Kuhnau's chief bugbear was, of course, Telemann, who in his student days (as we saw in Chapter 4) had been the very epitome of this counter-culture. It is faintly ironic therefore that twenty years later he should have expressed interest in succeeding Kuhnau as Thomascantor. Along with two other favoured candidates, Christoph Graupner and Johann Friedrich Fasch (both of whom had been Thomaner in its heyday), he knew at first hand how problematic it would be to navigate the bureaucratic swamps of Leipzig and achieve anything worth while there. Judging from the evidence from Kuhnau's tenure, one can only conclude that by the early 1720s the cantorate had become something of a poisoned chalice. Sensing this, after weighing up the Leipzig offer, all three men preferred to stay in their current posts – proof that eighteenth-century Capellmeisters often postured like today's football managers: hoodwinking their current employers and playing on their fears that they were about to leave just in order to lever a raise in salary.

Bach himself was not exempt from this, turning down the offer of an attractive post at Halle in 1713 and gaining himself a boost to his income at the Weimar Court (see below, p. 184). But when the prospect of the Leipzig post materialised ten years later his first consideration was for loss of status: 'it did not seem at all proper to me to change my position of Capellmeister for that of Cantor,' he later reflected.[6] Not having been a Thomaner himself and having never previously worked in Leipzig (as far as we know), he had no inside information as to the potential obstacles other than via professional hearsay or gossip. The allure of the Thomaner choir and the quality of its music-making might have been suggested to him by Adam Immanuel Weldig, who had been a prefect in the 1680s under Schelle, when the choir was in its prime, and later became Bach's landlord and fellow musician at the Weimar Court. If so, this rosy image could have been shattered when Bach and Kuhnau met face to face in April 1716 as joint assessors of a new organ in Halle. We have a detailed menu of the sumptuous dinner that they consumed at the Golden Ring tavern,[7] which, together with the lavish quantity of wine and beer set before them, may have been enough to loosen Kuhnau's tongue as to the pitfalls of the job – the paucity of musical resources, the back-stabbing and the wearisome challenges to his authority.

Then again, a visit to Leipzig itself (a lucrative commission to examine a newly completed organ at the university church in December 1717) may have added a fresh layer of impressions – favourable ones for the most part. Leipzig held the prospect of a prestigious university education for his sons, but its main attraction for Bach was its rich urban life – its thriving book trade, the presence of printers, the network of foreign agents and the cosmopolitan aura the city acquired with the flood of visitors attending its three annual trade fairs. For others it was probably the novelty and exoticism of things on offer: we are told 'visitors could savour a cup of imported Turkish coffee or purchase an ivory crucifix from Florence, a wool sweater from England or even tobacco from America. They could also expect to encounter street musicians, jugglers, tightrope walkers, fire-eaters, giants and midgets, snake charmers and a great menagerie of animals – elephants, apes, tropical birds etc.'[8] No wonder, then, that before deciding to leave Cöthen after five and a half comparatively untroubled years as Capellmeister at the court of Prince Leopold, Bach prevaricated. It was fifteen years since he had last worked as a civic employee, and to walk away from the protected (though at times stifling) environment of courtly life in the provinces to begin working again under public scrutiny suggests that he needed to quell deeply embedded fears – a premonition even – of what a return to municipal employment might entail. 'I postponed my decision for a quarter of a year,' he later told his old schoolfriend Georg Erdmann.[9] Throwing in his lot with civic employment meant Bach was now leaving behind him a twenty-year pattern of shuttling between church and court, exchanging the uncertainties of aristocratic caprice for a drop in salary and status, and the frustrations of municipal atrophy.*

Meanwhile the long – and, to some councillors, dispiriting – search

* Johann Beer (the novelist and quondam singer and concertmaster at the Weissenfels Court) devotes a whole chapter of his *Musicalische Discurse* to the dilemma that confronted professional musicians of the time. In answer to the question: 'What advantages did republics or city states have over courts in organising good music-making?' Beer makes the following points:

i. Aristocratic love of sensual pleasure means that courts are normally likely to support the personnel and infrastructure for music to a much higher level than in towns. 'It is known that music in its pure form flourishes more at court,' so the financial rewards are accordingly better.
ii. Court life has its own disadvantages, however. Many musicians prefer municipal to court employment, since dukes, princes and counts tend to be very capricious, and one's standing is therefore much more precarious. Also, life there is frenetic, with everything geared to satisfying princely pleasure. Those who value stability

for Kuhnau's successor led to months of uncertainty at the Thomasschule and a disruption of its musical functions. Once Bach, after Telemann's withdrawal as the third choice for the cantorate, had finally decided to answer the call, he did so on the basis of reassurances from Burgomaster Gottfried Lange (see Plate 11b), who described the post to him 'in such favourable terms that finally (particularly since my sons seemed inclined towards [university] studies) I cast my lot, in the name of the Lord, and made the journey to Leipzig.'[10] We have no means of knowing what really went on in those discussions. Ten months after Kuhnau's death, he was duly elected. By the time of his appointment Bach had already been required to pass through several hoops: first, to apply formally and audition for the post (7 February), then to sign an undertaking to take it up within four weeks (19 April). Once elected on 5 May, he was presented to the consistory court three days later and sworn in on the 13th; the starting date of his salary was set two days later. He and his family were reported to have arrived from Cöthen on the 22nd and, according to a Leipzig chronicle, the *Acta Lipsiensium academica*, he performed his first music on 30 May in the Nikolaikirche, two days prior to his formal installation, 'mit guten *applausu*'.[11]

Bach would soon have discovered that the days were long gone when the presence of a genuinely music-loving burgomaster, together with a headmaster sympathetic towards consolidating the musical standards of the Thomaner, had allowed earlier cantors such as Calvisius, Schein, Knüpfer and Schelle to select the most promising recruits on the basis of a musical entrance exam. That had started to change during Kuhnau's time, when the city councilmen, divided in their political allegiances, held conflicting views on the way the school should be run. Sometimes clashing with the leading church officials of the city, those with Pietistic leanings now began to question the role of music in church and at bap-

---

choose to work in cities where an urban code of honour prevails. [Perhaps that is what Bach hoped for – and failed to find.]

iii. Though the pay is better at courts, in cities one has better chances of finding stipends for one's children.

iv. At court, rivalries between musicians for princely favour lead to strategies to block one another's progress and careers. This problem is particularly acute for those with exceptional talent.

Beer's *Musicalische Discurse* was written in 1690 but not published until 1719 (reprinted in his *Sämtliche Werke*, Vol. 12, Parts 1 and 2 (2005), pp. 305–6).

tisms and funerals.* Clear signs of their burying their differences in a pact of silence have recently come to light, showing that they conspired to conceal from Bach the dysfunctional reality he was now expected to deal with.[12] At the point when he formally pledged to comply with 'the School statutes now in effect or to be put into effect', Bach might reasonably have assumed that he was committing himself to the old regulations – 'not to take any boys into the School who have not already laid a foundation in music, or are not at least suited to being instructed therein, nor do the same without the prior knowledge and consent of the Honourable Inspectors and Directors'.[13] That was not the case, and he had every reason to feel that he had been misled and tricked, since he had no means of knowing at the time of his pledge that the recruitment process had already been tilted away from musical criteria and that his potential earnings from *Akzidentien* (freelance fees) due to him as cantor had been reduced.

These moves had been discussed in council meetings as early as 1701 and were certainly in the air when a commission and working party were appointed in 1717 to recommend revisions to the school statutes. Although their findings were known to councillors at the time of Bach's appointment, they were not issued until 13 November 1723 – six months after he had been sworn in.† Besides the points made above they exhibited increasing pressure on the school to match up to the higher academic standards of its nearest rival, the Nikolaischule, while at the same time strengthening its status and image as a charity school with an increased commitment towards the children of the underprivileged and paupers of the city. To further this, a key paragraph was struck from the statutes which had specified, 'a boy, regardless of [his]

* The school's teachers, and foremost Johann Heinrich Ernesti, the elderly headmaster, may unwittingly have done more damage than good by their stubborn opposition to the proposed new statutes as well as by the deep fissures that had opened up between upper and lower teachers in the school over the apportionment of salaries. The reputation of this, the first of two co-rectors bearing the name Ernesti, was further damaged by the fact that his authority in the school had eroded almost completely and by the criticism he incurred for holding down a university teaching post as well.

† As we shall see later in this chapter all of this came to a head at the time of his dispute with Johann August Ernesti (headmaster of the Thomasschule) in 1737 when Bach made a direct appeal to the consistory for protection against the application of the 1723 school regulations: these, he argued, were invalid, having never been ratified by the consistory, and were greatly disadvantageous to him 'in the discharge of my office as well as in the fees accruing to me' (BD I, No. 40/NBR, pp. 194, 192).

social origin, may be admitted as *alumnus* only if [he is] highly proficient in music.'[14] At a stroke serious damage was dealt to the musical standards and prestige of the Thomasschule. Henceforth the specialist musical caucus of the school (the *Alumnat*), with pupils recruited largely from outside Leipzig, came to be seen almost as an optional appendage – a sop to the musically minded lobby and an irritant to the academics. Inevitably this meant a lowering of the musical quality of the intake at a time when less civic money for *beneficia* (fees in cash) was available to pay student extras or supernumeraries, who were frequently needed to plug gaps in the Thomaner apparatus.

On the face of it, then, Bach's dispute with the Leipzig Council was little different from the battles that earlier cantors such as Krieger and Kuhnau had fought with the same town council in defence of their authority to provide good music, and typical of other clashes between cantors or organists and councils in other German cities (still continuing today), except for this new, initially hidden, throttling of the supply of new recruits.* To this extent it was independent of any quirks in Bach's character. But the more one probes the underlying causes of his sequence of disagreements with the Leipzig Council, the clearer it becomes that after fifteen years' employment at ducal courts, he was ill-equipped to deal with a situation where his capacity to deliver church music of a high quality was fundamentally compromised by the organisational arrangements with which he was working. Nevertheless his part in exacerbating an already tense situation may be traced back to his ancestry: the Bachs' traditional view of themselves as a privileged and untouchable guild of musicians on a musical mission. Bach's Bible reading strengthened his belief in the scripturally sanctioned bond he

* Luther's creed of music and theology, having been at the very heart of his and Melanchthon's ideas for schooling, is now less sustainable as church music becomes more complex and specialised, to the point where music can no longer be situated at the core of the curriculum. A chasm starts to open between a composer/cantor's needs for a high quality of boy trebles with good voices and all-round musical ability and the academic teachers who consider they have a prior call on the boys' education. Bach arrives in Leipzig thinking that (at last) he should have access to a competent body of musical boys, only to find his hopes dashed and that the recruitment process has been surreptitiously tilted against him. He soon finds himself in the middle of someone else's argument – and that there are some people (like J. A. Ernesti) who, incomprehensibly, simply don't like music. As the organist and choirmaster Robert Quinney has suggested to me, the situation is aptly parallel to what is going on currently in Oxbridge colleges, where choral trials now take place only after academic selection.

had been told existed between him, his family and the musicians who served in King David's Temple, led by Asaph as Capellmeister (as we saw in Chapter 2 and Plates 2a and b). Where modern biblical scholarship views this picture of music in the Temple as idealised and anachronistic, there is every reason to believe that Bach read it as true history.[15] He seems to have been drawn to the particular chapter (I Chronicles 25) that deals with the way music was structured in the Temple, how the musicians there were organised in guilds and set apart in their offices, and how they were given specially allocated roles as composers, singers and instrumentalists. In the margin of his copy of Calov's Bible commentary Bach writes, 'This chapter is the true foundation of all church music pleasing to God.' That King David did not think up this plan on a whim, according to Bach, is clear from other additions in the margin: 'NB. A splendid example, that besides other forms of worship music, too, was especially ordered by God's spirit through David.'[16] It was a brave council, then, that set out to brush aside Bach's conception of his divinely inspired and divinely appointed office.

We saw earlier how successive generations of Bachs, concerned to prove themselves as virtuous citizens, had often clashed with their civic employers, how they had been resented by other musicians and accused of nepotism; how some, like his father, Ambrosius, learnt to work the system to their advantage, while others, like Christoph of Eisenach, failed, and others still, like Christoph of Ohrdruf, skirted around it, managing for years to get out of 'toilsome school duties' in the Lyceum.[17] The aggregate of Bach's provincial roots and his family's status were both a source of strength and, later on, a hindrance in terms of social advancement, as we can see in his obduracy in contractual negotiations. How far did a certain frame of mind, even a congenital problem with authority, predetermine the long series of clashes in which he was embroiled all through his career? The strong impression one gets is of a man almost constantly at odds with someone or something. It should not surprise us, then, if we find that these lifelong problems with anger and authority were incubated in the unsavoury atmosphere and environment of his early schooling and in childhood traumas.

* * *

The picture of lawlessness in the Eisenach Latin School we glimpsed in Chapter 2 left us uncertain which way the eight-year-old Bach faced.

Was he a model pupil, holding himself apart and diligently learning his catechism, his musical rudiments and his ten new Latin words each day – the goody-two-shoes of legend – or did he belong to the 'in' crowd of playground ruffians who chased the girls, the proto-hooligans who lobbed bricks through windows and whose blather disrupted church services? These are, of course, fictional constructions; yet each in its way is plausible. There is no reason to turn our backs on the plentiful evidence of rowdiness and thuggery which caused the Eisenach Consistory so much concern, stoking its fear of a *scandalum publicum*,[18] nor to take it on trust that Bach was a paragon of rectitude. The side of his upbringing often glossed over is the one in which, like Brer Rabbit in *Uncle Remus*, he was 'bred en bawn in a brier-patch'.[19]

Given what has been unearthed about the school conditions prevailing in Eisenach, the statistics of Bach's absences take on a different hue. Faced with the hard evidence of von Kirchberg's and Zeidler's memoranda (see Chapter 2), we have to ask whether the widely reported disorderliness, even the alleged 'brutalisation of boys', had as much to do with these high instances of truancy. In which case, was it Bach or his parents who decided he should regularly miss his school classes? So far the only conclusion one can reach with any degree of certainty is that his less than glittering school record in Eisenach – he came 47th out of 90 in his first year, rising to 14th the next year (his second in the *quinta*) and then 23rd out of 64 in the *quarta* – was marginally better than that of his brother Jacob, who came in two places lower in his final year, despite being three years older. When later in life he was asked 'how he contrived to become such a master in his art', Bach generally replied, 'I was obliged to be industrious; whoever is equally industrious will succeed equally well.'[20] Such an opaque statement leaves us none the wiser as to why such industriousness – training himself for duty, striving for craft, expertise and achievement – really took hold.

Suddenly, after the death of his parents and with his move to Ohrdruf, Bach's school performance improved dramatically. Perhaps there were fewer distractions there – certainly nothing like the hive of musical activity he had been used to in Eisenach as a young boy. Alternatively he may have retreated into himself, simply doing what was required of him – diligence triumphing over adversity. The school records show his grades were excellent: entering the *quarta* in March 1695, he spent two years in the *tertia*, where he was placed fourth in 1696 and first in 1697.

Then came two years in the *seconda*, where he was placed fifth in 1698 and second in 1699. The Ohrdruf Lyceum was regarded as one of the better educational establishments in the region. Yet, on closer inspection, the situation within the school – just as it had been in Eisenach – was far from peaceful or conducive to learning: 'a downright turbulent and disorderly situation [pertaining] in this otherwise respected educational institution'.[21] Contemporary sources reveal a comprehensive menu of chastisements, with both physical punishment and the threat of *die ewige Verdammnis* ('eternal damnation') meted out to pupils convicted of misdemeanour or vice of one sort or another, including bullying, sadism and sodomy. Incidence of all these were common enough at the time to justify graphic description and detailed codes of punishment in J. H. Zedler's *Universal-Lexicon* (1732–54) as well as in contemporary memoirs.

The villain of the piece here was a certain Johann Heinrich Arnold. As cantor of the Michaeliskirche, where Bach sang as a chorister, Arnold was also Bach's form master in the *tertia*. The twelve-year-old boy had unusually close exposure to him. Despite four or five years at university and an unsullied teaching record in Gotha and Erfurt, from the moment Bach arrived in Ohrdruf, Arnold seems to have been an irascible, heavy-handed disciplinarian given to doling out medieval-style punishments of the sort condemned by school reformers such as Comenius and Reyher.* Worse, there was no effective authority able to rein him in, and in the space of two years he managed to engineer the expulsion of three different headmasters of the Lyceum.[22] Luckily the fourth in line, Johann Christian Kiesewetter, seems to have got his measure and managed to stay the course. One of Kiesewetter's first tasks during Bach's first full year in Ohrdruf was to remove three pupils from under Arnold's sadis-

* Medieval theologians considered children capable of mortal sin at the age of six or seven (see Steven Ozment, *When Fathers Ruled: Family Life in Reformation Europe* (1983), pp. 133, 144, 147, 148) – the age when fathers were expected to discipline their children. Luther himself said that too much whipping broke a child's spirit, implying that his parents had almost broken his. The German attitude was that children were beasts to be tamed, an attitude common both at home and at school. '"Some teachers are as cruel as hangmen," he said. "I was once beaten fifteen times before noon, without any fault of mine, because I was expected to decline and conjugate although I had not yet been taught this." Yet late in life when a child relative of his stole a trifle, Luther recommended that she be beaten until the blood came' (Richard Marius, *Martin Luther: The Christian between God and Death* (2000), pp. 22–3).

tic sway,[23] a highly unusual procedure, yet one he considered imperative: Bach, his cousin from Arnstadt, Johann Ernst, and an unknown third boy were singled out for reprieve on account of 'the intolerable punishments' meted out by Cantor Arnold.[24]

As an orphan marked by his brother's alleged authoritarianism, Bach may have bore scars of lasting damage in the year he spent under Arnold's bullying tutelage. With all the chaos around him, Bach needed to be exceptionally resilient. The only thing we know for certain is that Kiesewetter was forced eventually to sack Arnold, to whom he referred as *pestis scholae, scandalum ecclesiae et carcinoma civitatis* ('the plague of the school, the scandal of the church and the cancer of the city').[25] Even so, not all the disciplinary problems at the Lyceum ended with his dismissal, for in 1698 we find Kiesewetter pleading with the consistory for the installation of a detention room in the school in view of the 'frequent and strong commotion'.[26] The school environment was ugly, and any sign of weakness was calamitous. In these circumstances one might reasonably ask how anything positive or productive could have come from Bach's formal education in Ohrdruf – with four different headmasters in as many years – or anything that would stand him in good stead when dealing with authority in his future career, let alone help to explain the training of a mind soon capable of making creative constructs of a bewildering complexity.

Replacing Arnold as cantor was the 23-year-old Elias Herda.* Getting wind of Bach's plans to move to Lüneburg in 1700, and having spent his own teens at the Michaelisschule, Herda could (and perhaps should) have warned him that membership of the Mettenchor there included more than just daily choir practice and the liturgical singing of an exciting new repertoire in a protected environment: that as likely as not it entailed street-singing or busking that often led to fisticuffs.† During the last third

* Herda (1674–1728), a farrier's son from near Gotha where he went to school, went on to spend two years in northern Germany as one of those Thuringian boys much sought after 'for their musical skills' and recruited for the Mettenchor of the Michaeliskirche in Lüneburg. He subsequently trained for the priesthood at the University of Jena and was about to be ordained in Gotha when the call came for him in Jan. 1698 to audition for the cantor's job in Ohrdruf in succession to the disgraced Arnold.

† The larger twenty-strong *chorus symphoniacus* was one of only two Lüneburg choirs (the other being attached to the Johannesschule) which took part in frequent street-singing in front of well-to-do burghers' houses, hopeful of charity – or, if we are to believe one commentator, 'thriving on chance charity passed from the windows to put an end to what was

of the seventeenth century, street brawls between the two choir schools in Lüneburg had developed unchecked while the burghers stood by, impotently wringing their hands. It seems the choir prefects planned the pitched battles, dictating the no-go areas and the territorial division of the town between these embryonic Jets and Sharks or Mods and Rockers. The town council passed innumerable protocols and by-laws in its attempt to bring some sort of order into what eventually erupted into gang warfare, an eight-year *Sängerkrieg* (1655–63). At one point they even contemplated bringing in the army to sort things out.[27] No doubt Herda stressed the standard virtues of boy choristers – *modestia, pietas et diligentia* – and advised Bach to keep out of trouble and set a good example.

But, as already suggested, there are no grounds for supposing that Bach was such a model boy at any stage during his school years – nor for assuming the same of his mentor Elias Herda. In the Lüneburg town archives there is a document labelled 'The Investigation and Punishment of the Schoolboy Herda'[28] based on the sworn evidence of a respectable citizen. Sometime around 1692 Herda had been spotted with an accomplice in a local hostelry looking for trouble – 'undoubtedly with the intention of starting a brawl, as they were thoroughly drunk and had [placed] their daggers on the table, and were arguing about nothing other than slashing and stabbing with [their] dirks and hunting knives'. The plaintiff, who had known Herda for the past three years and previously thought well of him, was incensed by his anti-social behaviour. That evening, making his way home, he was accosted by Herda, who called him a 'rogue, thief and swine' – a felony which in parts of Germany incurred the legal requirement to make a public apology and

---

frequently an irritating noise'. Busking in Lüneburg was initially popular – obviously with the choristers as a desirable perk – in fact it was one of the best sources of supplementary income, though Bach himself started in May 1700 in ninth place with a mere twelve groschen. Initially the citizens welcomed it, too. But what began as harmless rivalry between the two *Currende* choirs soon acquired a nasty competitive edge as they fought over turf, each seeking out the wealthier streets and the most lucrative front doors, reserving the best times of day and squabbling over the distribution of rewards. On one occasion the cantor of the Michaeliskirche himself became embroiled and was pelted with stones by the opposition, the Ratsschüler. On another occasion, the rival Michaelissänger were led by a particularly autocratic prefect called Ferber, who seems to have banned some choristers from the chance to busk and to have dealt blows left, right and centre – even to his own team – before retiring to the nearest hostelry, or *Weinstube*, for hours on end. Yet only a few years on and the same Georg Ferber would re-surface in the respectable role of cantor in Husum and Schleswig.

a six-week gaol sentence. The citizen now wanted satisfaction and proper assurances from the school authorities that Herda would be suitably punished for 'such grievous and bare-faced insults'. The incident reveals a different side to the character of someone who has previously been portrayed as Bach's erstwhile saviour and unofficial godfather, whose motto seems to have been: 'Do as I say, not as I do.' With the example of a former gang-leader-turned-respectable before his eyes, Bach may have followed a similar path. There is certainly sufficient circumstantial evidence here to dent the traditional image of Bach as an exemplary youth, on his way to becoming 'the learned musician', surviving unscathed the sinister goings-on in the schools he attended. It is just as credible that the bewigged cantor-to-be was the third in a line of delinquent school prefects – a reformed teenage thug.

* * *

We now move forward a few years to an episode in Bach's first full-time post – to the saga of the recalcitrant bassoon. On one of the few occasions when Bach actually complied with the consistory's desire for him to compose figural music, he came up with what may have been a first draft of a cantata (BWV 150), or, if not, then something very similar to it, involving a difficult bassoon solo.* Setting the music in front of his raw student ensemble, the twenty-year-old Bach had either seriously miscalculated or was being deliberately provocative. His novice bassoonist, three years his senior, was Johann Heinrich Geyersbach. In rehearsal he evidently made a hash of it, and Bach showed his annoyance. As the son of a municipal music director, Bach would have been familiar with the values shared by Saxony's instrumentalists, who were always told to be wary of *Pfuscher* ('bunglers'), *Störer* ('troublemakers') and *Stümpler*

* Georg Österreich had already begun writing prominent parts for what he called 'bassono obligato' before his move in 1702 to the court in Wolfenbüttel (ninety-three miles to the north of Arnstadt), which housed the largest library north of the Alps. It is possible, though fairly unlikely, that Bach could have come across Österreich's motet *Weise mir, Herr, deinen Weg* (1695) or his *Alle Menschen müssen sterben* (1701), which contains parts for two obbligato bassoons. In all likelihood Österreich had the more versatile, jointed French bassoon in mind, rather than the German *Fagott*, and, even though neither instrument resembled a bundle of sticks, it is likely that Geyersbach, Bach's student *Fagottist,* would have shown up with a primitive prototype – more like a dulcian – consisting of a single yard-long shaft of wood, oval in section, drilled with two bores connected at the bottom so as to form one continuous conical tube – indelicate in tone and a treacherous instrument to master.

('botchers').* If this was the result of having done his best to make music with an unruly lot of what would now be called late-maturing students, it merely confirmed all his misgivings.† Geyersbach, for his part, was *beleidigt* (that superbly expressive German word which signifies both taking offence and feeling hurt), stung by the public dressing down he had received at the hands of a stuck-up young organist, known to be paid exceptionally well for doing remarkably little. The word *Stümpler* may have crossed Bach's mind; instead, he called him a *Zippel Fagottist.* Even in recent biographies this epithet continues to be translated euphemistically as a 'greenhorn', a 'rapscallion' or a 'nanny-goat bassoonist', whereas a literal translation suggests something far stronger: Bach had called Geyersbach 'a prick of a bassoonist'.

A few weeks pass but the insult still rankles, and Geyersbach plots his revenge. On the evening of 4 August 1705 he and five of his comrades, well oiled after attending a christening party, sit waiting for Bach in the market square. Bach is on his way home from Neideck Castle. He passes the town hall when Geyersbach accosts him, cudgel in hand, demanding an apology for the insult. Bach is caught completely unawares. Geyersbach strikes out and hits him full in the face. Bach draws his rapier in self-defence. The situation turns ugly, and there is a scuffle broken up by the intervention of the other students. Eventually Bach dusts himself down and continues on his way. Next day he goes straight to the consistory to lodge a complaint. The clerk reports him as saying that, since 'he did not deserve such treatment and was thus not safe on the streets, he humbly requested that . . . Geyersbach be duly punished and that he

* To defend the honour and morality of their profession 107 instrumentalists from 43 towns in Saxony had joined together to form their own guild, the Instrumental-Musicalisches Collegium, in 1653, submitting their statutes to the Emperor Ferdinand III for ratification, and having them printed and distributed (Spitta, *The Life of Bach*, Clara Bell and J. A. Fuller Maitland (trs.) (1899 edn), Vol. 1, pp. 144–153; Stephen Rose, *The Musician in Literature in the Age of Bach* (2011), pp. 79–81).

† Mostly a year or two older than Bach, as the sons of well-to-do craftsmen and town merchants, these students probably had little musical motivation, unlike the Mettenchoristen Bach was used to from his Lüneburg days. Once again the local archives reveal a picture of endemic student lawlessness. A complaint from the town council to the consistory, dated 16 Apr. 1706, reads: 'They have no fear of their teachers, they fight even in their presence and talk back to them in the most offensive manner. They wear their rapiers not just in the streets but in school too; they play ball during church services and in class, and run about in disreputable places' (Uhlworm, *Beiträge zur Geschichte des Gymnasiums zu Arnstadt*, Part 3, pp. 7–9, quoted in Spitta, op. cit., Vol. 1, pp. 314–15).

[Bach] be given appropriate satisfaction and accorded respect by the others, so that henceforth they would let him pass without abuse or attack.'[29] Ten days go by before Geyersbach is summoned to answer the allegations, together with two of his accomplices. He denies point-blank attacking Bach, claiming that Bach had drawn his rapier first and gone after him with it: Geyersbach has holes in his vest to prove it. Five days later Bach is told he must produce a witness. Meanwhile he is admonished for calling Geyersbach a *Zippel Fagottist*.

Suddenly the consistory switches tack: Bach already has 'a reputation for not getting on with the students', they maintain, 'and of claiming that he was engaged only for simple chorale music, and not for concerted pieces, which was wrong, for he must help out in all music-making'.[30] In effect, Bach's punishment for successfully defending himself against Geyersbach is an order to make concerted music in church with a bunch of incompetent superannuated students. His reply is laconic – neither an outright refusal nor a dismissive criticism of the students' musical shortcomings; in future 'he would not refuse provided there were a Director Musices [present]'. In other words, he is prepared to compose further figural music, but not to direct or conduct, or to play under the direction of a school prefect. This elicits a homily from the consistory: 'Men must live among *imperfecta*; he must get along with the students, and they must not make one another's lives miserable.'[31] Two days later, Bach's cousin Barbara Catharina appears before the consistory and endorses his side of the story, but since neither the superintendent nor any other of the clerics are present, no verdict is reached: Geyersbach walks away with the mildest of reprimands.

The Arnstadt Consistory had publicly failed to back up their young organist. The end result was a moral victory for Geyersbach and his cronies: they had broken Bach's authority over them and knew that if they cheeked or even assaulted him a second time they would probably get away with it. By drawing his sword, even in self-defence, Bach may have been sailing closer to the wind than he knew. Perhaps the rapier he was carrying was more a ceremonial sword than a serious weapon; yet he had clearly threatened to use it. The legal punishment for this (later formulated in 1712) was severe: as we saw in Herda's case, just by verbally insulting Geyersbach, Bach could have been required to make a public apology and sent to prison.[32] Four church services a week, a rowdy intractable student choir, an incongruous cultural milieu at court – these were not sufficient to retain Bach in Arnstadt for long. On the other hand, there was the counter-attraction of Maria Barbara with whom he had recently begun a liaison. She was the youngest of three daughters of the organist–composer Michael Bach (his father's first cousin). Recently orphaned, she was living in Arnstadt in a guesthouse belonging to her godfather Martin Feldhaus, the burgomaster responsible for hiring, and perhaps lodging, Bach.* So the two of them may even have been living under the same roof. Before being able to marry, Bach needed to move to a more secure post, one with less aggravation.

In the late autumn of 1705 he decided to apply for a month's leave, and hired his cousin Johann Ernst to deputise for him at the Neukirche while he travelled 260 miles north to Lübeck – 'on foot' according to the *Nekrolog* (a little improbably) – home to the man he then considered to be the greatest living practical musician, Dietrich Buxtehude, then aged seventy. There he witnessed dazzling concerted music on a monumental scale as well as small-scale chamber music of the most intimate, devotional kind. Memories of these – and of Buxtehude's own special style of playing the organ – would stay with him all his life. His musical imagination had been fired with visions incomprehensible to any petty town official in Arnstadt, as he was to discover on his return there in February 1706. The minutes of his run-in with the Arnstadt Consistory are written in high-sounding jargon peppered with obscure Latin pedantries that may or may not have been understood correctly either by the councillors or by their faithful scribe. Bach's replies are dismissive and proud, almost monosyllabic. To the perfectly reasonable question as to why he had been

* A well-to-do merchant, Feldhaus had been responsible for negotiating a special bonus due to Bach amounting to thirty thalers (= thirty-four florins or guilders and six groschen) for board and lodging payable in cash from St George's Hospital fund – a richly endowed old people's home of which he was the administrator. The hospital accounts show annual living expenses of thirty-four florins and six groschen reimbursed to Bach on 1 Aug. 1704 and 1705; then suddenly an invoice submitted by Feldhaus for the same amount for the year 1706/7, claiming direct reimbursement for Bach's 'food, bed and quarters' (BD II, No. 26). Was Bach living in an apartment belonging to Feldhaus from the start – passing on the full bonus to his landlord – or had he moved in only in the last year (once his relations with his fiancée Maria Barbara were intensifying), leaving the way for Feldhaus to claim the full amount from the hospital fund and to redirect it into his own pocket? In the fullness of time, Feldhaus's questionable business dealings were brought into the open, for in 1709/10 he was summoned to stand trial for 'much incorrectness and embezzlement', demoted as mayor and stripped of all his offices (Andreas Glöckner, 'Stages of Bach's Life and Activities', in *The World of the Bach Cantatas*, Christoph Wolff (ed.) (1997), Vol. 1, p. 52).

absent for four months instead of four weeks, Bach offered the withering riposte 'in order to comprehend one thing and another about [my] art'.* The consistory, now provoked, took the opportunity to pile on its criticisms. Bach was reprimanded for having made 'many curious *variations* in the chorale and mingled many strange tones in it' so that the congregation were confused. In future, if he wished to introduce a *tonus peregrinus* he must sustain it and not shift too swiftly on to something else, as had been his habit, even playing a *tonus contrarius*.[33]

Picture the scene: Bach, still high on his return from Lübeck after the most stimulating professional encounter of his life, is suddenly being given a lesson in how to compose and improvise at the organ by worthy councillors who have never taken a harmony lesson in their lives. Desperate to display their erudition, they in fact show their ignorance of even the rudiments of musical theory and its terminology. They then further attack by deploring the absence of figural music in the Neukirche, laying the blame squarely on him for not collaborating with the students. They push him into a corner on this issue. Bach parries: provide him with a competent director (and not a mere prefect) and he would 'perform well enough [with the students]'. The next episode borders on the farcical. The prefect Rambach is reproved by the consistory for the *désordres* between the students and the organist. Rambach counter-attacks, accusing Bach of improvising for far too long, then, once corrected, of going to the opposite extreme and playing too little, thereby anticipating their next criticism – that he had gone off to the pub during the sermon, leaving Rambach no time to get back to his post before the start of the next hymn, and then causing mayhem by adding cadenza-like flourishes between the verses.

During the next six months the situation deteriorated still further. While organists have always seemed to consider it fair sport to confuse the old dears of the parish by introducing strange harmonic progressions during the verses of a hymn, the impasse with the student choir was more serious, as was his extended unauthorised absence in Lübeck. Bach's final admonition was recorded on 11 November 1706, when, after being asked to declare once again if he was willing to make music with the students as

* This could also have been his way to forestall any attempt by the consistory to impute a covert motive for his visit – to ingratiate himself with Buxtehude as his potential successor – an unlikely scenario, given that it was conditional on his marrying Buxtehude's thirty-year-old daughter, Anna Margareta.

instructed, he said he would give his reply in writing (which was probably never forthcoming). It is easy to see why the Arnstadt authorities, for their part, were so incensed by his attitude, which must have seemed unpardonably arrogant to them. Perhaps they knew that he had been eyeing up another post in Mühlhausen for some time, and it was only the Duke who had given instructions that he should be retained.

The consistory asked him by what right he had invited a strange, unknown, unmarried young woman (*frembde Jungfer*) to make music with him in the organ loft. Women were still not allowed to sing in church at this time and we are left wondering whether this was a private assignation – though it cannot have been with his future wife Maria Barbara, since she could hardly be considered a 'stranger' in Arnstadt – or a deliberate flouting of authority. Bach replied cryptically that he had already 'told Magister Uthe about it'. Instructed to provide a cantata, Bach had obliged, composing one for solo soprano (easier to coach than his allotted student ensemble), which he had rehearsed with her in the organ loft. Tongues obviously wagged, but Bach had the perfect (unspoken) rejoinder: 'You asked for a cantata: here it is!'

Clearly there was no future for him in this stamping ground of his ancestors. As a parting shot he may have found a way to comply outwardly with the consistory's demands while also getting even with Geyersbach. In what many scholars consider to be the first of his surviving church cantatas, BWV 150, *Nach dir, Herr, verlanget mich*, there are three movements which feature an exposed independent part for bassoon, and in one case a fast passage covering a range of two octaves and a minor third – playable by a competent professional but not by a student sight-reading, let alone a *Zippel Fagottist*. Had Bach placed the perfect banana skin and engineered a final public showdown with his nemesis?*

* Possibly hearing on the family grapevine (Bellstedt, the town scribe in Arnstadt and related by marriage to the Bachs, had a brother who occupied the same position in Mühlhausen) that there was soon to be an opening at the Blasiuskirche in Mühlhausen (whose ailing organist, J. G. Ahle, was to die in early Dec. 1706) and that two figural works would be required from candidates (as we know from J. G. Walther, himself a candidate who later withdrew), Bach may have spent his last months in Arnstadt composing BWV 150 and BWV 4. He might have felt that there was no harm in flattering the mayor of the new town in the first of these cantatas by means of an acrostic that spells out the name DOKTOR (Movement 3), CONRAD (5) MECKBACH (7) (see Hans-Joachim Schulze, 'Rätselhafte Auftragswerke: Johann Sebastian Bachs. Anmerkungen zu einigen Kantatentexten', BJb (2010), pp. 69–74) and trying it out first in Arnstadt before his trial at Easter 1707.

A pattern was now beginning to emerge in early adulthood: in his short-fused exchanges with Geyersbach, in his refusal to tolerate slipshod music-making and in his haughty, laconic replies to the consistory (at least as reported), we have evidence of Bach's propensity to flout – or simply ignore – authority and to disregard the rules of ordered society. In his eyes he would never be guilty, no matter what actually happened: the fault would always lie with somebody else. We can link this behaviour to the alternative characterisations of his unruly temperament, his susceptibility to peer-group pressure, and his experience of bullying and harassment in childhood and the rough-and-tumble of life in the successive schools he had attended. We notice a deep reluctance to ingratiate himself (again, unlike all the rest of the Class of '85, who had more worldly success) and a tendency to sulk when confronted by what he saw as bone-headed officialdom. It is almost as if a perverse streak in him was seeking to act out the meretricious side of the music profession as we find it gleefully satirized by novelists of the time like Johann Beer or Daniel Speer.[34] To his employers he was already showing signs of being 'incorrigible'. Small wonder, then, that in later life he should have tried to play down these transgressions in response to questioning by his children. In a letter to his father's biographer J. N. Forkel, Emanuel Bach wrote: 'There are many adventurous stories about him. A few of them may be true, and concern useful pranks. The deceased never liked to hear them mentioned, so pray omit these humorous things.'[35] Aged twenty-one, Bach seems to have been a man of restive intelligence, heading for a life of more or less perpetual 'vexation and hindrance' (his own expression) – of a typical square peg in a round hole.

* * *

By 1 July 1707 Bach was responsible for the music at six services per week in the Blasiuskirche in Mühlhausen, two more than in Arnstadt. He had gone from being organist of the third church in a small town to municipal organist in the main church of a city almost twice its size, the second largest town in Thuringia and, like Lübeck and Hamburg, one of a handful of 'free imperial cities' where councillors were answerable directly to the Emperor in Vienna and not to some local princeling. Here he was now de facto music director, occupying the equivalent position to the one Buxtehude had held in Lübeck. Just as in Arnstadt, his new contract made no reference to participation in or responsibility for vocal or concerted music, though, as before, this was evidently expected of him. Yet he had learnt his lesson in Arnstadt, and one gets the feeling that his artistic priorities had shifted too. This time, instead of trying to concern himself exclusively with the organ – its mechanical workings and the challenges it held for him as a virtuoso performer, improviser and composer – he was now actively engaged in writing innovative *Kirchenstücke* for voices and instruments (see Chapter 5). Having witnessed at first hand what bold musical initiatives an experienced figure like Buxtehude could achieve in such a position, Bach, aged twenty-two, was hoping to be granted the same degree of autonomy to pursue his own similar goals in Mühlhausen.

But something serious must have upset him there, for before the first full year of his contract was up, Bach had bowed out. At this stage he seems to be conforming to the stereotypical itinerant musician as described in Daniel Speer's novel *Ungarischer oder Dacianischer Simplicissimus* (1683), somehow at odds with a hostile society and constantly obliged to 'travel onwards, against his own will'.[36] The traditional explanation is that he was caught in the crossfire between the representatives of the two wings of Lutheranism – Orthodox and Pietist – yet Bach made no mention of this in his letter requesting his release to the burgomaster and parochial *conventus* (church council). Instead he focused on two other bones of contention: pay and conditions. Having thanked the mayor for his 'graciousness in permitting me to enjoy a better living' in Mühlhausen, he went on to say it was simply not enough: 'However frugal my manner of living,' he claimed, 'I have not enough to live on, having regard to my rental and other really necessary expenses.' At no time in his career was Bach shy in bargaining for more pay and was always keen to negotiate the best possible terms for himself and his family, as much as a measure of self-worth as from economic necessity. Now newly married, he had extra responsibilities, as Maria Barbara was expecting their first child. The lure of a raise from 85 to 150 florins (plus benefits), which was what he would receive in his next position at the Weimar Court, represented a hefty (77 per cent!) improvement in his circumstances, and he had found it irresistible.

This was only half the story. The other half concerned the conditions of work in Mühlhausen. In his letter he referred, without going into any detail, to the 'hindrance' he had experienced to his music-making. After the earlier set-back in Arnstadt, in Mühlhausen, Bach had started out with goodwill, determined to improve musical standards and to establish a forward-looking musical regime – and been thwarted. All that had been made available to him – and then only at irregular intervals – was 'an unholy mix of school choirs, non-professional helpers, student instrumentalists, and town musicians'.[37] This is surely the point of his spelling out somewhat tactlessly to the councillors that he had 'received the gracious admission of His Serene Highness of Saxe-Weimar into his Court Chapel and Chamber Music'[38] – meaning a better quality of musical performer than he was ever likely to find in Mühlhausen. Bach could not resist having a parting swipe at the councillors for the low standard of the music-making at the Blasiuskirche by comparing it to that in almost all the surrounding 'villages, where church music is flourishing ... and often better than the harmony fashioned in this place'.[39] One sees what a colossal disappointment this would have been for him. Looking back over the last four or five years, he might have found it ironic that the figural music he had been unwilling to provide in Arnstadt (because of inadequate resources) he had been happy, eager even, to compose and perform in Mühlhausen – but he had been prevented from accomplishing anything worth while by conditions there.*

It is against this background, and in his request to the church council of the Blasiuskirche for his release from Mühlhausen, that Bach defined for the first time an *Endzweck* (artistic goal) – 'namely, a well-regulated or orderly church music to the Glory of God and in conformity to your wishes'.

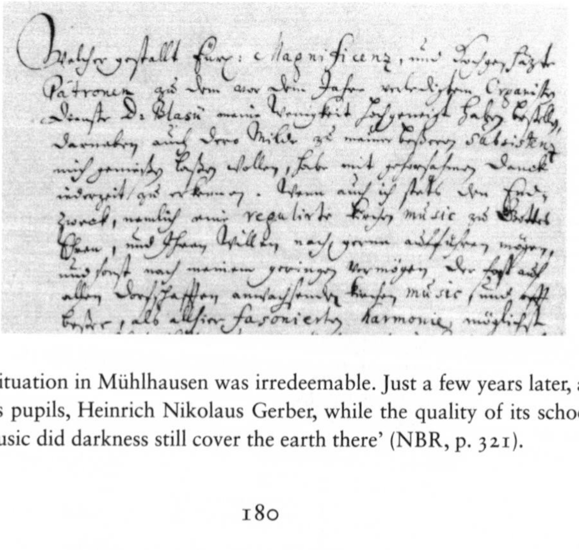

* Perhaps the situation in Mühlhausen was irredeemable. Just a few years later, according to one of Bach's pupils, Heinrich Nikolaus Gerber, while the quality of its schooling was high, 'only in music did darkness still cover the earth there' (NBR, p. 321).

This was the pipe dream that was to become a lifelong obsession – something, he claimed, it had not been possible to accomplish in Mühlhausen 'without opposition'. By moving to Weimar, he explains to the city elders, he now hopes to be able to pursue 'the object which concerns me most, the betterment of church music, free from the opposition and vexation encountered here.'[40] Bach, at twenty-three, had shown himself, on this occasion at least, cooperative and just about polite to his employers, from whom he now parted on reasonable terms. 'Since he could not be made to stay,' they reasoned, 'consent must doubtless be given to his dismissal.'[41] Bach had a burgeoning desire for the freedom and means to make music – but under orderly and regulated conditions that he fully expected to find on his return to the Weimar Court. His move illustrates an uncrushable sense of his own worth as a craftsman and his growing certainty as an artist.

* * *

For the next fifteen years Bach operated in a cultural milieu beyond the arm of civic power and church control. Working within the confines of a provincial middle-German court and in the semi-feudal employ of capricious musically minded aristocrats, while risky and at times combustible, seems to have suited him – at least for quite a while. True, he was moving from a situation where he had been the undisputed leader of civic musical life in a 'free imperial city' to a position at court in provincial Weimar, where, despite an exceptionally favourable salary and a fancy title – *Cammer Musico* and *Hofforganist*[42] – he started off next to last in the professional hierarchy of the court Capelle, which was headed by Johann Samuel Drese as Capellmeister and his son Johann Wilhelm as his deputy. But on the face of it so much was propitious – his young family, the 'better living' he had referred to in his resignation letter to the Mühlhausen Council, the support and enthusiasm of two music-loving dukes, and the clear favour they showed him in his regular increases in salary and in accommodating him within the strict pecking order of court musicians. It would nevertheless require powers of diplomacy, hitherto not much in evidence, to carve out a fulfilling niche for his musical activities within this rigidly stratified and tightly circumscribed milieu. At least it fitted with his deeply embedded sense of hierarchical authority: God first, then His closest representative on earth – King, Prince or Duke.

But what if there were *two*? Ever since an imperial law of 1629 the Duchy of Saxe-Weimar operated under a constitution that vested executive authority jointly in twin rulers. At the time of Bach's earlier employment in Weimar five years before, it was the younger of the two brothers, Duke Johann Ernst III, to whom he had been directly answerable; it was he who had pieced together the court Capelle after its dissolution twenty years earlier and who had made all the main appointments. Bedridden for the past two years (during which his elder brother neither visited nor inquired after him), his decline and loss of appetite accelerated, according to his wife, by tobacco and strong wine (*der starcke Sect und tabac*), he died in 1707 – just a year before Bach's return to Weimar as court organist. The elder brother, Wilhelm Ernst, had been highly impressed by Bach's organ-playing at his audition in June 1708, and it was his decision (as sole ruler momentarily) to hire him on the spot. In his mind, Bach was now *his* man. But friction was inevitable in this feudal edifice from the moment the 21-year-old Ernst August stepped up as co-regent in 1709 and occupied the Rote Schloss ('Red Palace')(see Plates 7a and b). He and his 45-year-old uncle, Wilhelm Ernst, who lived in the adjoining castle, the Wilhelmsburg, were permanently at loggerheads. The uncle arrested his nephew's advisers and decreed that members of the court Capelle could make music over the road in the Rote Schloss only with his express permission or on pain of a stiff fine and even imprisonment; the nephew threatened reprisals if they complied.

How were these 'joint servants' of both ducal establishments supposed to behave? Initially Bach's situation appeared safe, being a clear favourite of both uncle and nephew, each making separate demands of his time and talents. To the uncle he was a musical trophy – his private court organist to be heard twice weekly up in the Himmelsburg,* and in special organ recitals, and to be paraded abroad on diplomatic missions. For the nephew he was primarily a chamber musician and a composer of the highest calibre, fit to consort with his half-brother the

* Short for *Weg zur Himmelsburg* ('The way to the castle of Heaven'), this referred to the painted cupola depicting the open heavens in the palace church in the Wilhelmsburg, the centre of Duke Wilhelm Ernst's devotions. Destroyed along with the court music library in the great fire of 1774, it was of unusual design – a tall, three storeyed structure with a balustraded music and organ gallery (just thirteen by ten feet, and sixty-five feet above floor level) from which 'heavenly' sounds would float down upon members of the ducal families, courtiers and guests (see Plate 8). Probably the nearest equivalent in the area today is the Schlosscapelle in Weissenfels built around the same time, though larger.

prince, Johann Ernst (himself a talented composer), and to impart to him the fruits of his erudition and skill. How was he to satisfy both masters (given the explosive tension between them), to survive the rigid court protocols, rankings and intrigues with the ever-present risk of being flogged if found playing for the 'wrong' duke – which was the fate of the horn-player Adam Andreas Reichardt, who, each time he asked to be relieved of his post, received a hundred blows and a prison sentence? That was the challenge. Having eventually made his getaway, Reichardt was branded an outlaw by Duke Ernst August and hanged in effigy as a lesson to other would-be transgressors.[43]

In the productive years that followed one might expect all Bach's musical activities and the compositions they engendered to be subject to the whims and different musical preferences of these two autocratic paymasters, and to a degree this was the case. The religious-minded Wilhelm Ernst provided serious and discriminating support for Bach's sacred music: according to the *Nekrolog*, 'His gracious lord's delight in his playing fired him up to attempt everything possible in the art of how to treat the organ.' In effect he stood as patron of fully half of Bach's extant organ music – the fraction, that is, to have survived in written form (the majority being the improvisations that emanated from Bach's creative mind, which disappeared instantly into the celestial ether of the Himmelsburg). Over in the Rote Schloss, other priorities ruled. There the younger Ernst August, with whom Bach came to enjoy a far warmer relationship, was known for his enthusiasm for modern secular music, and the excitement he showed when his younger brother Johann Ernst returned from Holland in 1713 with a trunk load of new concertos by Corelli, Vivaldi and others to show to members of the Capelle is reason enough to suppose that Johann Ernst's teacher J. G. Walther and the court keyboardist Bach 'soon had them on their music desks, ready to play'.[44]

Princely courts were reputed by some commentators of the day to be full of scheming 'foxes and wolves', and the life of a court servant no better than that of 'a caged bird', yet at this stage Bach could have reflected that as a rule his family tended to fare better under aristocratic than civic patronage – and that had also been his experience till now.[45] Yet, no matter how much the two dukes admired his skills, at some stage Bach must have realised that the route to full responsibility for the music at court – the way it was organized and the free rein it would give for his creative urgings – was barred to him in Weimar by the presence of the Dreses, *père et fils*. The flow of church cantatas that had burgeoned so promisingly in Mühlhausen was stemmed for some five years, by which time his artistic and stylistic priorities had started to shift. This may help to explain why he toyed with the idea of accepting the invitation to 'present himself' for the town organist's post at the Marienkirche in Halle in 1713, and once elected (after a two-week visit) why it took him so long to sign. Much to the chagrin of the church elders, who felt that he had led them a dance, he eventually turned them down. Bach, predictably denying accusations of skulduggery, put his decision down to their uncompetitive offer of a salary with built-in incidental fees that were impossible to predict, but one cannot help but suspect tactical manoeuvring.

The truth is that the opportunity Halle had offered him – to compose and perform cantatas once a month – was exactly what was lacking in Weimar and was then promptly rectified there. The new title of *Concertmeister*, conferred on him in 1714 (at his own 'most humble request'), and with the equivalent of a Capellmeister's salary to boot, marked a shift in the balance of power at court, giving him increased authority in so far that from now on 'the musicians of the Capelle are required to appear upon his demand.'[46] But not even that could disguise the fact that both Drese as Capellmeister and his son as deputy still stood higher up the professional ladder, as Bach knew full well. When Drese senior died on 1 December 1716, Bach's immediate reaction was to assume full control and – possibly as a bid to be confirmed in the now vacant post – to come up with three first-rate cantatas for three consecutive Sundays in Advent (BWV 70a, 186a and 147a), well beyond his contractual obligation to provide one a month. Tantalisingly the autograph score of the third of these cantatas breaks off abruptly in mid-flow – though whether from sudden illness, pique, disenchantment or Drese junior pulling rank (he was confirmed as court Capellmeister in October 1717), we cannot tell.*

At times when Bach sensed that he might be losing the argument with a higher authority, as now, he had potential recourse to inserting a sliver of mild subversion into his music, which, provided it stayed reasonably

* That was it as far as further cantatas composed by Bach in Weimar go. Not even a major celebration such as the second centenary of the Reformation on 31 October 1717 (the day after Duke Wilhelm Ernst's birthday, on which he had declared a new fund to endow the members of his Capelle) elicited a commemorative cantata from Bach.

subtle, could always be denied and never be proven – neither by the intended target, nor of course by us. A windbag of a preacher was a fair target, for example. Duke Wilhelm Ernst had given his first sermon as a boy of seven, and was given to preaching to his entire entourage at the Weimar Court and to holding spot-check catechisms and interrogations of his staff to see if they had been paying attention to what he had said. The closing aria of Bach's cantata BWV 185, *Barmherziges Herze der ewigen Liebe*, for bass and a continuo strings opens with the words 'This is the Christian's art' and then proceeds to list his various obligations and injunctions. Bach comes up with ingenious ways to overcome the banality of the text by mimicking the rhetorical displays of eloquence of a typically pompous preacher – repeating almost *ad nauseam* the same words with little mitigating musical variety. Whether or not this was an ambivalent piece of mild satire at the Duke's expense, the relationship between them was about to deteriorate rapidly. The final movement of his Christmas cantata BWV 63, *Christen, ätzet diesen Tag*, opens with a one-bar fanfare for four trumpets and kettle drums – ostensibly to announce the portentous arrival on earth of the baby Jesus as King, but it could equally serve as a ceremonial greeting to some dignitary, even Duke Wilhelm Ernst himself. Hard on the heels of this stylised bugle call comes a flippant fragmentary response – a sort of irreverent tittering by the three oboes, then passing like Chinese whispers from them to the upper strings (had he tripped or was his wig askew?).* It points the way to the infinitely more elaborate and cryptic ambiguities of Shostakovich, who once made an impassioned plea, 'I want to fight for the legitimate right of laughter in "serious" music.'[47] Bach might have gone along with that; but even if he found it therapeutic now and again to vent his disgruntlement on an unsuspecting victim, it would be wrong to see him as a full-blown dissident encoding anti-establishment messages in his scores.

Mild satire was one thing; facetiousness was another matter. Performed at the birthday celebrations of Duke Christian of Weissenfels on 23 February 1713, BWV 208, *Was mir behagt, ist nur die muntre Jagd!*, allowed Bach for the first time to adopt wholesale the conventions of

* Later in the same movement Bach inserts a preposterous collective trill extended on a diminished seventh chord on the word *quälen* ('to torture') intended to describe the futility of Satan's attempt to torment us, but graphic enough to cause a shudder in listeners familiar with the Duke's recourse to dictatorial punishments.

Italian opera and the secular chamber cantata and to step aside from the contemporary fuss over just how theatrical a piece of church music was entitled to be.* It was a chance to experiment with recitative without fear of censure, yet in a liberated style far removed from the formalism of all his contemporaries except Handel. After only four bars the rhythmic pulse of free recitation shoots off into a fluctuating arioso over continuous semiquavers in the continuo. Bach saw an opportunity to depict in quick succession the flight of the goddess Diana's arrow (in implied *allegro*), her momentary delight at the prospect of a catch (*adagio*) and the swiftness with which she pursues her prey (*presto*). Here, in a pastoral allegory stretched over fifteen mostly short movements, he could pretend for an instant that he was a Handel or a Scarlatti. Fresh and bucolic, it is a rougher and less charming equivalent to Handel's *Acis and Galatea*. Perhaps this is what recent commentators intend when describing it as a 'pathbreaking work' and 'a milestone in Bach's creative development'.[48]

Salomo Franck's text for BWV 208 is frankly banal. The stock Classical allegorical characters he introduces (besides Diana these are Pales, Endymion and Pan) are little more than cardboard cut-outs. The 'dramatic' plot is simplicity itself. Diana praises hunting as the sport of gods and heroes, to the chagrin of her lover Endymion, who deplores her hunting fixation and the company she is keeping. Once she has explained to him that it is all in a good cause – to mark the birthday of the 'most esteemed Christian, the Pan of the woods' – he agrees to join her in paying homage to the Duke. That leaves ten numbers still to come, all on the same oleaginous theme. The whole thing is a pretext for extolling the attributes of the good governance of Duke Christian, and as such it might have elicited titters and some eye-rolling by the courtiers. There was a glaring discrepancy between this fawning tribute to a solicitous ruler and the Duke's general mismanagement of his lands, which obliged the Elector to set up a royal commission to administer his finances and only a few years later got him hauled up before the Reichsgericht (Imperial High Court).† Could Franck and Bach have known any of this at

* This is corroborated by the discovery of a copy in his hand of an Italian chamber cantata by the Venetian composer Antonio Biffi (Peter Wollny, 'Neue Bach-Funde', BJb (1997), pp. 7–50).

† Michael Maul has found source material showing that the Duke lived far beyond his means, had no grip on his dukedom's finances and was often drunk. His handwriting is crude and barely legible. How much attention he actually gave to the music must be questionable (private correspondence).

the time? Do they imply any irony? Secular rulers were considered to be God's viceroys, ruling on earth in His name and by His grace to preserve the true faith. What today we might consider toadyism was then a generally accepted way of paying tribute to a reigning prince.

At the start of 1716 Bach had provided the music for Duke Ernst August's marriage to the sister of the young Prince Leopold of Anhalt-Cöthen. Deeply impressed, the Prince at some point offered Bach exactly what he had been denied at the Wilhelmsburg: the coveted title of Capellmeister and, as 'director of our chamber music', control of all the music at the court and its newly formed hand-picked ensemble, at a salary of 400 thalers – nearly twice his current earnings and with an advance payment of fifty thalers. Bach was about to discover that it was far harder as a highly prized artist to obtain release from a princely ruler than from a town council. Unlike his application for the Halle job, which seems if anything to have enhanced his standing at Weimar, there seems to have been no response from Duke Wilhelm Ernst, convinced of seeing his nephew's hand in the affair.*

All in all 1717 was a turbulent year in Bach's life. It saw the first printed evidence of his rise to fame† and ended in official disgrace at the Weimar Court. In between, his production of cantatas seems to have come to a standstill – either from choice or, after a show of dissent, because the senior duke had silenced him. Then there were extensive travels: to Gotha to fill in for a sick colleague and compose music at Passiontide; to Cöthen to clinch his new contract; and to Dresden in October where he had been billed as the challenger in a celebrated (much hyped, but never independently documented) bout with the French keyboard virtuoso Louis Marchand. With his opponent scratching at the last moment, Bach returned to Weimar in a black mood, smarting from the non-contest, the affront to his pride and the loss of 500 thalers in prize money somehow embezzled at source. Very possibly

* This was indeed very likely the case, as was the strategy to circumvent the old Duke's intention to promote Drese junior by tempting Telemann (unsuccessfully) to accept a kind of 'super-Capellmeistership' of all three Saxe-Thuringian courts – Weimar, Gotha and Eisenach (see Telemann's account of this approach in Mattheson's *Grundlage einer Ehren-Pforte* (1740), p. 364).

† Johann Mattheson, the most widely read music critic of the day, claimed to have 'seen things by the famous organist of Weimar, Herr. Joh. Sebastian Bach, both for the church and for the hand [i.e., keyboard pieces] that are certainly so constituted that one must greatly esteem the man' (*Das beschützte Orchestre* (1717), p. 222).

he lashed out in some way that broke with protocol enough to incur the wrath of Wilhelm Ernst.[49]

> On 6th November [1717], the quondam concertmaster and court organist Bach was arrested and held at the County Magistrate's house of detention for obstinate testimony and forcing the issue of his dismissal, and finally on 2nd December was informed by the Court Secretary of his unfavourable discharge and simultaneously freed from arrest.[50]

Bach's four-week incarceration or house arrest raises uncomfortable questions over his moral probity. Had there been an ulterior motive to his visit to Dresden – an attempt to go over Wilhelm Ernst's head to win royal support for his transfer to Ernst August? Or was he even making an early bid for a post at the electoral court in Dresden itself? Had he been playing fast and loose with his Weimar employers, taking double pay for a few months?* Then there is the issue of the missing music, if it ever existed – at least there is no trace today of the fifteen or more church cantatas that Bach had been contracted to compose in Weimar. If he had taken them with him to Cöthen (but with no chance of performing them there), he would surely have found ways to revive or recycle them later in Leipzig, and we would know about them. Possibly, like his successor, Johann Pfeiffer, and his 'musical works composed during the tenure of office',[51] Bach was instructed to leave all his compositions in the organ loft of the Himmelsburg, where they were locked away, and what he regarded as his intellectual property returned with the key to the Duke.† Taken together, these incidents seem to indicate that, when provoked, Bach let his sense of propriety fall away. Suddenly, he saw those in authority who lorded it over him merely as his equals, or even as his inferiors. If music was God's gift and he was the master of delivering it, that put him above others.

The perilous events of Bach's final year in Weimar, and the tangled issues of his brushes with authority, now recede into the background. During his next five years at the Calvinist court in Cöthen he appears

* There are at least two mitigating instances of Wilhelm Ernst's decency and show of compassion to senior court musicians – Johann Effler and Johann Samuel Drese (Andreas Glöckner, 'Von seinen moralischen Character' in *Über Leben, Kunst und Kunstwerke: Aspekte musikalischer Biographie*, Christoph Wolff (ed.) 1999, pp. 124–5).

† Meanwhile, according to a report by E. L. Gerber, the son of a former pupil, the *Well-Tempered Clavier* was conceived during his period of incarceration when he was fed up and without access to any musical instrument (BD III, No. 468).

to have enjoyed a complicit and harmonious relationship with his employer, Prince Leopold. This was the first time in his life that he had left the profession of church organist behind him to operate within an almost exclusively secular environment. He was given generous facilities towards realising Leopold's dream of making his Capelle one of the leading ensembles of the day. Bach repaid this trust by concentrating his compositional activity on mainly instrumental works. Besides the first volume of the *Well-Tempered Clavier* some of the most celebrated of his collections were assembled here in sixes: the Brandenburg Concertos, the sonatas and partitas for unaccompanied violin, the sonatas for violin and obbligato harpsichord, the suites for solo cello, and the four *Ouvertures* for orchestra. As a gift to his nine-year-old son Wilhelm Friedemann, Bach filled the pages of a little book with two- and three-part *Inventions* – simple enough for him to play for pleasure yet each with a distinctive character, providing an open door to the mysterious world of counterpoint.

Then came a dual bereavement. Bach travelled to Berlin to buy a new harpsichord for the Prince's household, leaving Maria Barbara, his wife of twelve years, at home and pregnant with their fifth child. The boy, born in November 1718, was named Leopold after the Prince, who stood godfather to him. He died ten months later. Then, on one of his few excursions outside his homeland, Bach left Cöthen with his prince in May 1720 for Carlsbad, a spa town 130 miles to the south. Here for the next two months he led the musical entertainment in what has been described as conceivably 'the earliest summer festival of the performing arts'.[52] While he was away, Maria Barbara suddenly died and was buried on 7 July. Their son Carl Philipp Emanuel, who was six at the time, later described his father's experience of returning home and 'finding her dead and buried, although he had left her hale and hearty on his departure. The news that she had been ill and died reached him only when he entered his own house.' As far as we can tell, theirs had been a close and harmonious marriage ('blissful', according to Emanuel), and she had been both a link to his family roots and a stabilising influence during his unsettled years of employment in Arnstadt, Mühlhausen and Weimar. Within two months of her death, Bach's thoughts were turning towards re-locating to a major city. There was an opening at the Jacobikirche in Hamburg, one which offered him challenges the small Calvinist court in the provinces could not match. Bach played his cards shrewdly – a successful display of his performing and compositional skills, a tactful improvisation on a theme by, and in the presence of, the 97-year-old Hamburg master Adam Reincken – only withdrawing once it transpired that as the successful candidate he was expected to pay a covert bribe of 10,000 marks into the church's coffers.

With four young children to raise, Bach, like his father before him, lost no time in finding a new wife. Aged twenty, Anna Magdalena Wilcke was a professional singer employed at the court of Saxe-Weissenfels and came from musical stock. Their wedding was held 'at home, by command of the Prince', midweek in December 1721, to allow the musicians to get back to their posts in time for their Sunday services after imbibing the copious wine that Bach had ordered at the cost of nearly two months' salary. Other than the fact that Anna Magdalena was fond of gardening (and especially of yellow carnations) and of birds (especially linnets), we know pitifully little about her. Eight days after the wedding Prince Leopold also married – to the Princess of Anhalt-Berenburg, someone who disliked music and was later referred to by Bach as being an *amusa* – a bit of an airhead.[53] The long-term prospects in Cöthen were beginning to look shaky. With a new wife and children to educate, Bach was on the lookout for a new opening. We are coming full circle back to his Leipzig appointment.

* * *

On 15 February 1723 a press report appeared in the Hamburg *Relationscourier*: 'On the past Sunday [7 February] in the forenoon the princely Capellmeister of Cöthen, Mr Bach, gave an audition here [in Leipzig] in the Church of St Thomas in respect of the still vacant post of the cantor, and the music he made on that occasion was highly praised by all those who judge such things.'[54] Some three months later the special correspondent of another Hamburg paper reported, 'This past Sunday at noon, four wagons loaded with household goods and furniture arrived here from Cöthen, belonging to the former princely Capellmeister there, now called to Leipzig as *Cantor Figuralis*. At 2 o'clock he himself arrived with his family in two carriages and moved into the newly renovated apartment in the Thomasschule.'[55] Recently the spicy suggestion has been made that the 'special correspondent' could have been Bach himself.[56] If so, its emphasis on indicators of status and authority – his being 'called' to the Leipzig post, the number of carriages required for his chattels and family, pride in the fact his lodgings had been freshly renovated – must make it one of the earliest recorded examples of 'spin'. These were not trivial matters and they would have weighed with him, as would the opportunities Leipzig offered as a university city to his growing sons.

Bach saw the Leipzig post as his best chance of setting new musical standards in what he hoped was an orderly civic environment and of replicating the levels of performance he had become used to in his last two positions. He intended to introduce a new style of church music to a large urban congregation – one evolved from his Weimar years and therefore both more modern and more sophisticated than anything Johann Kuhnau had composed. On the face of it this was the best chance he had yet had of realising that *Endzweck* that had been three times frustrated: in Mühlhausen (not yet recovered from the fire of 1707), Weimar (where he had been passed over in the succession) and Cöthen (with its Calvinist court).

But even now it was not a straightforward move. From the moment he set foot in Leipzig, Bach found himself caught in the crossfire between rival political factions within the council, a microcosm of an enduring struggle within Saxony itself between the Elector in Dresden, bidding for increased autonomy – in particular the power to raise taxes to finance his foreign policy – and the Estates, made up of the nobility and the cities, determined to hold the Elector in check.[57] Music – since it carried with it a strong element of cultural prestige – formed part of these inbuilt contradictions and tensions between the Estates' city party and the nominees of the absolutist court on the Leipzig council loyal to the Elector. Having started out as their sixth choice as cantor, Bach became the eventual nominee of the latter, led by Burgomaster Gottfried Lange. They were his natural allies, keen to invest his title of *Director Musices* with the authority of a modern Capellmeister so as to fulfil their ambitions for Leipzig as an international city of the arts. On the other side were the councillors belonging to the Estates' city party, who were opposed to anything so radical in aim and independence. They wanted a traditional cantor tied into the school system that they themselves could control. So long as Telemann had been in the running they had been prepared to compromise over teaching duties, because of his reputation, credentials and earlier success in Leipzig.* But Bach, without Telemann's academic qualifications or links to the university and its church, could expect no such favours. They insisted on defining his role as cantor as narrowly as possible by setting restrictive terms on his teaching obligations. Bach's last-minute concession in agreeing to this condition appears out of character when we consider how he had acted in the past, and perhaps suggests an element of desperation. Herein lay the seeds of future discord. A compromise was eventually struck: Bach was elected to fulfil what could be described as an absolutist mandate, yet within a municipal structure that sought to call him to heel. There was no possibility that he could stand apart from the local and political conflicts of the time, though (as we have seen) Lange may have taken him aside and told him privately that as long as he followed the court party's mandate he could count on their support, freeing him from the more onerous teaching and administrative duties of a cantor.†

* Before he declined the Leipzig post in November 1722, Telemann had first made sure that he would also be allowed to resume being director at the university church (just as he had been twenty years earlier) – which, with its close links to the *collegium musicum*, was the main recruiting ground for student musicians. By the time Bach was appointed that position had already been filled.

† Just where things were hotting up in the council deliberations, in Apr. 1723 the minutes unfortunately break off (BD II, No. 127/NBR, p. 101). With none of three finalists (Bach, Schott and Kauffmann) allegedly 'able to teach', the spokesman for the Estates Party, Councillor Platz, made his much touted remark: 'since the best could not be obtained, mediocre ones would have to be accepted.' This is less the woeful misjudgement of Bach's qualifications that has stung his biographers than a last-minute political bid for hiring a solid schoolmaster as cantor. Having come so far, Bach was not willing to see the chance slip from his grasp. Starting at the back of the field, he had made the best impression at his trial on 7 Feb., and with all the Estates Party candidates out of the running, he had leapfrogged into pole position and was now able to negotiate. Did he? What we cannot know, of course, is what took place behind closed doors. Ulrich Siegele no doubt comes close to the mark in suggesting that a deal was struck between the rival coteries on the council: the Absolutist Party eventually got their man but were 'unable to carry out the public and legal act of redefining the office' ('"I Had to be Industrious . . .": Thoughts about the Relationship between Bach's Social and Musical Character', JRBI, Vol. 22, No. 2 (1991), p. 25) – the high price exacted by the conservative wing of the Estates Party. Bach had accepted an absolutist mandate but one hedged around with restrictions imposed by the Estates Party. Its leader, the appeals judge Platz, voted him in 'most especially because he had declared himself willing to instruct the boys not only in music but also regularly in the school'. Cryptically, he added, 'it would remain to be seen how he would accomplish this last' (BD II, No. 130). By the time he took the pledge to the council on 5 May, Bach promised 'faithfully to attend to the instruction of the school and whatever else it befits me to do; and if I cannot undertake this myself, arrange that it be done by some other capable person without expense to the Honourable and Most Wise Council or to the School' (BD I, No. 92/NBR, p. 105).

Although after months of delay he was voted unanimously into office in 1723, irregularities of protocol at his official inauguration threw up a fresh bone of contention between the council and the consistory: which of these bodies had the authority to install Bach as cantor. The situation was almost Ruritanian: teachers and pupils arrived in the school's upper auditorium expecting to greet the new cantor and see him installed, and sing him a welcome song. It was normally the chief town clerk who officiated on such occasions, but no sooner had Herr Menser proclaimed Bach as cantor 'in the name of the Holy Trinity', adding that 'the new Cantor was admonished faithfully and industriously to discharge the duties of his office', than the pastor of the Thomaskirche piped up, brandishing a decree issued by the consistory to the effect that the cantor 'was presented to the School and [so] installed . . . adding an admonition to the Cantor to the faithful observance of his office, and a good wish'. In eighteenth-century German lands, where protocol was at a premium, this was all highly irregular. It seems, then, that Bach was doubly installed as cantor. A public confrontation had somehow been averted, but it would hardly be surprising if, at this point, he was a little confused. Having made concessions to the council in the terms of his contract, here he was caught in the secondary crossfire – a dispute for precedence between the lay and the church authorities. On this occasion he responded graciously, thanking the council for conferring on him 'this office, with the promise that he would serve the same with all fidelity and zeal'.[58]

Bach had won a single point: the right to turn over some of his teaching duties (five hours per week of Latin grammar, Luther's catechism and Corderius's *colloquia scholastica*) to the *tertius* for fifty thalers per year. That still left him with musical classes and individual lessons to teach, and other less specific pedagogical duties. There is no shortage of sources documenting the chaotic situation within the Thomasschule and the illicit goings-on within its four walls (see p. 194). In the new school charter (*Schulordnungen*) of 1723 were rules (restricting the cantor's attendance at theatres, public houses, etc.) and new guidelines for the distribution of incidental fees among teachers and pupils that reduced his income. The cantor's living quarters were situated right next to those of the headmaster and those of the fifty-five boarding students of a '*schola pauperum* endowed to serve the best interests of the poor'. As a teacher Bach was required to act *in loco parentis* to the pupils 'and show each of them paternal affection, love, and solicitude, and be forbearing toward their mistakes and weaknesses while nonetheless expecting self-discipline, order, and obedience'. In reflecting on how well Bach was equipped to provide these functions, one can imagine him musing on the principal figures in his own childhood and the treatment he himself received. Did the shadow of Cantor Arnold, the old sadist from his Ohrdruf past, loom into view?* Certainly there appears to be a continuation in the pattern of bullying we have encountered so far – mostly of younger boys suffering at the hands of older ones. In 1701 a complaint against the older students asserted that they burnt mice over a candle and left the remains on the teacher's chair, that they spilt water on the floor and tables, smashed windows, ripped the blackboards off the wall and swore roundly at the teachers.[59] In 1717, the teacher-assistant Carl Friedrich Pezold complained about rats and mice darting to and fro on the staircases in broad daylight. In 1733 Christoph Nichelmann, then about sixteen, found conditions too rough for someone of his 'gentle and peace-loving nature' and ran away from the Thomasschule, later to become a respected composer and harpsichordist.[60]

After only a few weeks of living at such close quarters to the din and disorder of a boys' boarding school, particularly after the tranquillity of court life in Cöthen, Bach might have felt inclined to do the same. Five years into the job the situation had deteriorated still further: the school was described as being 'in a deplorable condition', with 'the beds ruined and the pupils ill-fed' and the teachers' authority severely undermined. A further report coinciding with the appointment of Burgomaster Stieglitz as school inspector in January 1729 speaks of finding the school 'in great disorder' with three classes amalgamated in the dining room, and the dormitory beds shared by two boys at a time. Under such conditions

* It is just possible that Arnold was among the people who came to Bach's mind years later as he was reading Abraham Calov's Bible commentary. Bach underlined a passage from Deuteronomy (23:4) describing how the Ammonites and Moabites had not been raised to a position of authority because of their hostility towards the Israelites, from which Calov concluded that no one should be raised to a position of authority who has demonstrated his hatred for those he would rule. Furthermore, as Robert L. Marshall points out ('Toward a Twenty-First-Century Bach Biography', MQ, Vol. 84, No. 3 (Fall 2000), p. 525), Calov concludes that 'no one should accept as his leader anyone who has demonstrated such hatred' – a sentiment no doubt shared by Bach, with his constitutional distrust of authority.

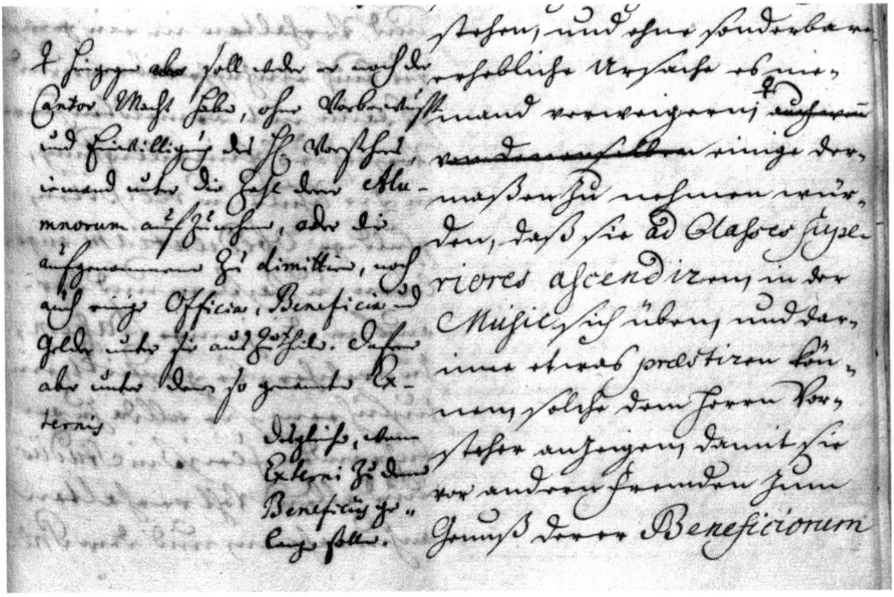

Extract from Chapter 6 of the new Schulordnungen *(school regulations) for the Thomaskirche, 'concerning the recruitment and dismissal of pupils', with marginal commentary by Johann Job, attorney to the town council.*

how, we might ask, was Bach expected to set the boys the example of 'a discreet life'? We can only guess at how he managed to protect his family (indeed to have a family life at all) and, amid all his duties both at school and across town, to find both the time and the calm to compose at the speed and intensity necessary to keep pace with his self-appointed weekly schedule of cantata production.

The significant point about the *Endzweck* is that it was an ideal, not a manifesto: a model framework within which Bach felt he could operate most productively and create orderly church music in conformity with the way the God-inspired Temple music was organised in the time of King David. The orderly framework had so far eluded him – in Arnstadt (short of the basic human resources), in Mühlhausen (conflict and inadequate musical forces), in Weimar (where he was never accorded the necessary authority to carry it out except on an ad hoc basis) and in Cöthen (with no Lutheran liturgy with music at its core). Now that the best opportunity for realising it presented itself in Leipzig in 1723, he showed he was ready to sacrifice status, salary, family and comfort in order to achieve it. For the next three (or, at most, five) years he threw all his energies into the realisation of that dream. His creativity in this field – in the three cantata cycles and two Passions he now composed – was almost profligate and far outstripped in conception, design and quality anything that any other composer of the time was attempting. It is all the more astonishing for having been carried out in a climate of innate conservatism, artistic indifference and discord, while he operated within a creaky structure, undermanned and underfunded.

But then Bach was a misfit in Leipzig from the start. As we shall see (in Chapters 9 and 12) the type of concerted music he would go on to compose on a regular basis was so much richer, more complex and more demanding than what Kuhnau had offered to his congregation, not to mention the easy-listening cantatas of his peer group, the three favourites for his job, Telemann, Graupner and Fasch. Bach's church music requires enormous concentration on the part of both performer and listener: you have to hold the emotion as you play or listen, channelling it, controlling it and letting it loose in the same second. Lest we forget, all this was produced and performed by a heterogeneous medley of musical forces that could rarely have met the technical and interpretative demands of his music; and, as far as we can tell, it was met with a depressing lack of discrimination but with general consternation by clerics and city fathers alike. The increase in the number of musically incompetent children admitted to the Thomasschule, growing from 5 per cent in Schelle's time to more than 15 per cent in Bach's early years, is another indicator of a worsening situation. In 1730 Bach was to report in his 'Entwurff' that of the current alumni only 17 were usable, 20 were not yet usable and 17 were unfit. In such crippling circumstances, we cannot be sure whom he could count on in Leipzig as unequivocal supporters of his musical ambitions, and the choice of godparents for his children clouds the picture still further: Senior Burgomaster Gottfried Lange, both of the two co-rectors of the Thomasschule with the surname Ernesti (Johann Heinrich, the elder, and Johann August, with whom Bach seemed to have got on reasonably well at first before the 'Prefects' War' turned them into implacable enemies), the wife of Burgomaster C. G. Küstner, C. F. Romanus, J. E. Kregel and the wife of G. L. Baudis. How dependable or effective any of these would turn out to be in support of his musical ambitions is open to doubt.

* * *

Lying on Bach's desk in the first week of February 1727 was the text of a cantata (BWV 84) waiting to be set to music: *Ich bin vergnügt mit meinem Stande, / Den mir der liebe Gott beschert* – 'I am content with the office the dear God has allotted to me'. By contrast, in a novel of the time, Johannes Riemer observed that 'nobody is content with his status or honour: even the most humble man seeks to elevate his title.'[61] Bach was no different. As the son of a town piper and in common with many municipal musicians of the day, Bach was engrossed with issues of status. At every stage in his career he was alert to the going rate before putting his signature on a new contract and, ever afterwards, quick to defend each clause at every opportunity. Given his recurrent dissatisfaction with the offices in which he found himself, the insufficient respect accorded to him that came to the surface in pay disputes and other perceived slights to his authority, we might expect him to have found the homily of this cantata's text hard to swallow. It was not often, as far as we can tell, that he intervened to change the texts he was due to set. But here he did so: all it took was the alteration of a single word in the libretto – from *Stande* to *Glücke* – from one's 'office' to one's 'lot in life' – and he changed the whole polemical thrust of the homily, which now focuses on the 'good fortune the Lord confers on me'.* Even with this shift of emphasis, to look for an unequivocal portrayal of equanimity in the long opening E minor aria for solo soprano, oboe and strings would underestimate the ambivalence and complexity of music – especially Bach's music – as a medium capable of giving nuanced depictions of mood. Contentment is in any case a rather static state of mind, whereas Bach's music here suggests something dynamic and fluctuating. The florid intertwining of voice and oboe, the prevalent lilting dotted rhythms and expressive syncopations, the way the opening ritornello returns again and again in various guises, while the soprano initiates fresh motifs – all these contribute to the enchantment of the music and its elusive moods: wistful, resigned, even momentarily elegiac.

* It is of course just possible that Bach was not modifying, but quoting from an earlier version of Picander's text than the one published in 1728/9.

All that we have managed to glean so far from Bach's troubled cantorate suggests a constant struggle between the desire to do his job conscientiously and to the utmost of his abilities, on the one hand (to the glory of God and the betterment of his neighbour, as he would have put it), and, on the other hand, the bother of having to put up with 'almost continual vexation, envy and persecution' (as he described it in a letter to a friend[62]). Music such as this aria helps us to find out how he dealt with these extremes. He differed from his contemporaries – Telemann, in particular, who managed to arrive at some sort of stress-free accommodation with the demands of earning his keep – and in some ways he was temperamentally closer to the Romantics. Despite being both a product of the prevailing absolutism and acquiescent in accepting the hierarchical system of his time,* Bach was a natural dissident – almost a proto-Beethovenian rebel *avant la lettre*. One thinks of Beethoven composing 'between tears and mourning' (Op. 69) or Berlioz's self-description: 'I have found only one way of completely satisfying this immense appetite for emotion, and that's music . . . I live only for music, it's the only thing that carries me over this abyss of miseries of every kind.'[63]

In his copy of Calov's commentary we encounter a passage (which Bach underlined and flagged up with a marginal 'NB') in which Luther makes a distinction between illicit shows of anger and those that are justifiable: 'Of course, as we have said, anger is sometimes necessary and proper, but be sure that you use it correctly. You are commanded to get angry not on your own behalf, but on behalf of your office and of God; you must not confuse the two, your person and your office. As far as your person is concerned, you must not get angry with anyone regardless of the injury he may have done you. *But where your office requires it, there you must get angry, even though no injury has been done to you personally . . . But if your brother has done something against you and angered you, and then begs your pardon*, your anger too should disappear. Where does the secret spite come from which you continue to keep in your heart?' [64] In other words, if you are attacked it is not for you to retaliate if it is personal; but if the attack is on your vocation or profession you are duty-bound to defend yourself or get

* In Bach's view God's authority seeps down into secular authority (the princely autocrat being God's representative on earth, as exemplified by the bass aria 'Großer Herr' from the *Christmas Oratorio*), order being simultaneously 'natural' and 'artificial'. Absolutism is surely artificial, yet for Bach it was natural.

someone to do it for you – exactly what Bach did by hiring Magister Birnbaum to represent him in the Scheibe dispute (see Chapter 7, p. 222). An account by one of his earliest biographers, Carl Ludwig Hilgenfeldt (with connections going back to C. P. E. Bach), confirms this vital distinction:

> Peaceful, quiet, and even-tempered though Bach was whenever he encountered unpleasantness at the hands of third persons so long as it concerned only his own personality, he was however quite another man when, no matter in what form, anyone slighted art, which was sacred to him. In such cases it doubtless happened at times that he donned his armour and gave expression to his wrath in the strongest ways. The organist of St Thomas's, who was in general a worthy artist, once so enraged him by a mistake on the organ during the rehearsal of a cantata that he tore the wig from his head and, with the thundering exclamation, 'You should have been a cobbler!' threw it at the organist's head.[65]

We have now clearly seen how prone Bach was in his dealings with municipal authorities to leap to defend his professional rights, even if the impression one gets from the dry responses reported by the clerk is more of a detached hauteur than of choleric outbursts. Additionally, as one of his modern biographers put it, 'Just as his composer's brain never loses track of a thought once it has occurred to him, his conscience seems to keep a tally throughout his life of his rights and the injustices he has suffered.'[66] One comes across individual movements in the cantatas that show what kind of things made him angry and how he dealt with them in his music. Such a work is BWV 178, *Wo Gott der Herr nicht bei uns hält*, with its dire, sibyl-like mood of warning against hypocrites and prophets ('wicked men . . . conceiving their artful plots with the serpent's guile'). It exhibits such sustained defiance that one asks whether there is a submerged story here – of Bach operating in a hostile environment, of his ongoing conflict with the Leipzig authorities suddenly reaching boiling point, or of a more personal falling-out with one of the resident clergy. How much more satisfying, then, for him to channel all that frustration and vituperative energy into his music, and then to watch as it rained down from the choir loft on to his chosen targets below. There is an equivalent vehemence to the first three movements of BWV 179, *Siehe zu, dass deine Gottesfurcht* – an action in itself, violent and brooding – and in the bass aria (*Weicht, all' ihr Übeltäter*/'Begone, all you evildoers!')

from BWV 135 with its violins behaving like virtuoso storm petrels. This is superb, angry music executed with a palpable fury, with Bach fuming at delinquent malefactors. One can picture the city elders, sitting in the best pews, listening to these post-Trinitarian harangues, registering their intent and starting to feel increasingly uncomfortable as these shockingly direct words – and Bach's still more strident and abrasive music – hit home. In a Lenten cantata, BWV 144, *Nimm, was dein ist, und gehe hin*, Bach's librettist draws the moral from the parable of the labourers in the vineyard: accept and be satisfied with your lot, however unfair it may seem at the time. Bach had found an eloquent but annoying way of fixing in the minds of his listeners the perils of what Germans describe as *meckern und motzen* ('bleating and bellyaching') – the grumblings of dissatisfied labour. As they would have known, behind the mutterings of the aggrieved vineyard workers stands St Paul's injunction to the Corinthians, 'Neither murmur ye, as some of them also murmured, and were destroyed of the destroyer' (I Corinthians 10:10), and, further back, the God of the Old Testament, exasperated beyond endurance by the moaning of the ungrateful Israelites whom He had safely shepherded out of captivity in Egypt: 'How long shall I bear with this evil congregation, which murmur against me?' (Numbers 14:27).

* * *

At the start of this chapter we saw how vexed the councillors had become by 1730 at Bach's failure to carry out his teaching duties and to obey the school authorities. The situation was to deteriorate further with the appointment four years later of J. A. Ernesti as school rector. Bach's junior by twenty-two years, the first thing we hear of him is complaining that Bach was not rehearsing the boys adequately – almost as though the new headmaster felt it was down to him to monitor musical standards in church services. Demarcation of areas of responsibility and the rapidly entrenched positions of two strong-willed men, both laudably concerned to maintain standards in their respective fields – of music and the humanities – lay at the core of their dispute, one that rumbled on for months and then years, and left a long paper trail in the council records. It ended up in a complete breakdown in their personal relations and brought out the worst in both men: stubbornness, self-importance, the overriding need to appear to be in the right; and it led to accusations of insubordination, lying, malice, deceit and vindictiveness. Their

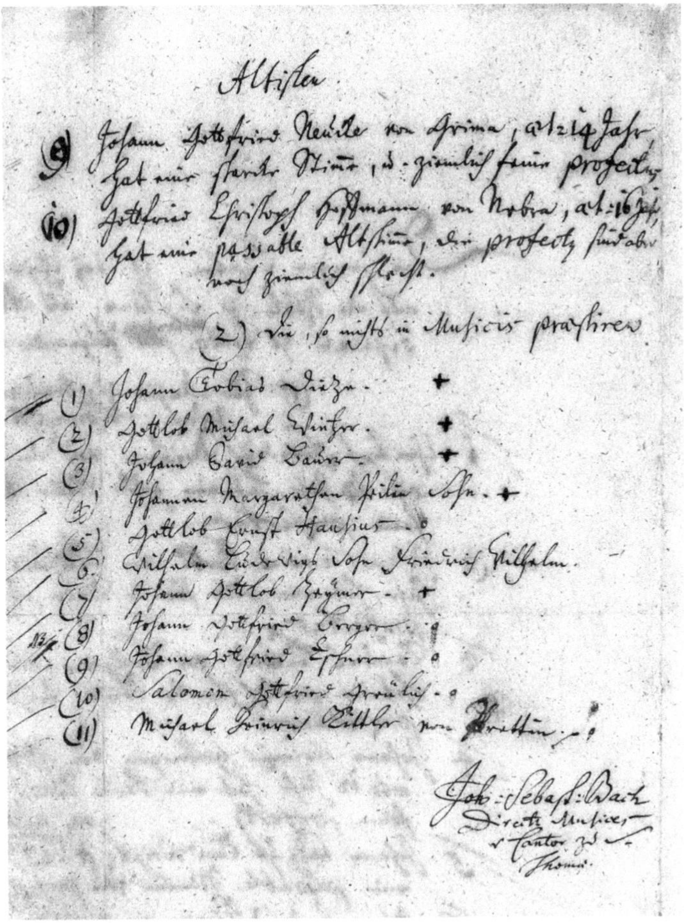

Altisten.

Joh: Sebast: Bach
Direct. Musices,
u. Cantor zu S.
Thomae.

Of the thirteen boy altos who auditioned in 1729, Bach reported: one 'has a strong voice and is a pretty good prefect'; another has 'a passable voice, but is still fairly weak as a prefect'; while the eleven others are 'not presentable in music'.

successive disputes turned initially on an interpretation of the old and new school regulations bearing on the right to appoint school prefects – crucial assistants to the cantor in the supervision of rehearsals and the three ensembles that needed to be on parade in different churches each Sunday or when he was absent. Farcically both men appointed boys with the name Krause – Bach's boy had been sanctioned for some irregularity and disappeared from sight; Ernesti's choice as a replacement was musically 'incompetent'. It became progressively both sillier (the prefects turning up

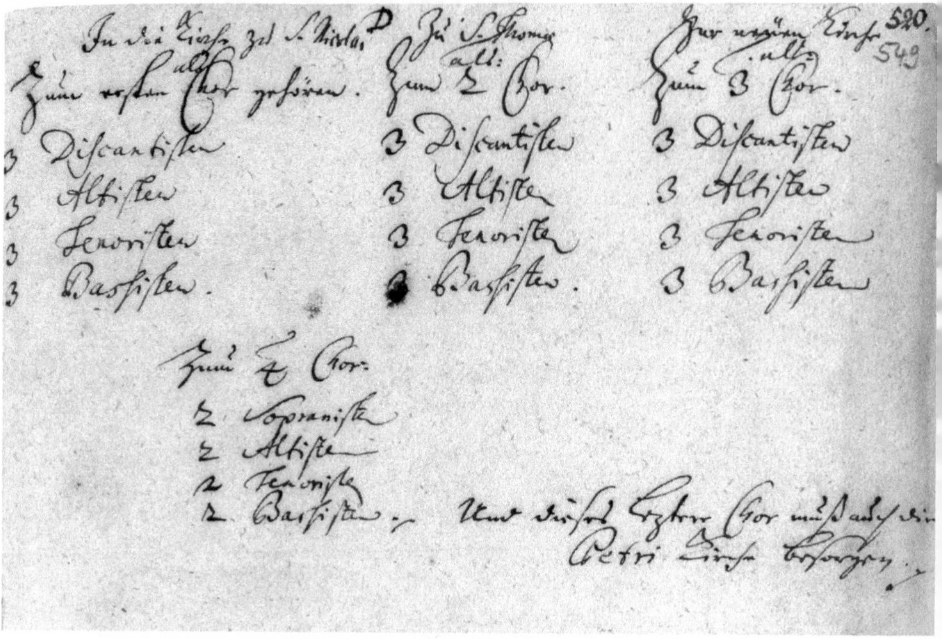

In die Kirche zu St. Nicolai
Zum ersten Chor gehören.
3 Discantisten
3 Altisten
3 Tenoristen
3 Bassisten.
Zu St. Thomas alle:
Zum 2 Chor.
3 Discantisten
3 Altisten
3 Tenoristen
3 Bassisten.
Zur neuen Kirche alle:
Zum 3 Chor.
3 Discantisten
3 Altisten
3 Tenoristen
3 Bassisten
Zum 4 Chor.
2 Sopranisten
2 Altisten
2 Tenoristen
2 Bassisten.
Und dieser letzter Chor muss auch die Petri Kirche versorgen.

Bach's scheme for distributing the forty-four 'necessary singers' (out of a theoretical maximum of fifty-five alumni) to make up the four choirs needed to serve in five city churches.

to serve at the 'wrong' church), more public (with no one competent to direct the motet during Holy Office) and more sordid as Bach hit below the belt with his innuendo that the rector had always had a 'particular liking for the said Krause'.[67] The dispute was never fully resolved.

One of Bach's defining impulses, as we have seen, was a reverence for authority (although it could disappear in a matter of seconds). But now he began to show obsequiousness, a rebarbative toadyism in regard to royalty that was extreme even by the standards of the day. Using his new title at the Dresden Court by appealing directly to the Prince-Elector in October 1737, he played what he thought was his trump card, pulling rank and accusing Ernesti of 'effrontery'. It backfired, the Prince deciding to leave the dispute to the Leipzig authorities to sort out. No more than many distinguished figures who work in the arts and sciences both then and now, Bach was prone to exceptional sagacity in his field of expertise and to exceptional pettiness in his daily social and professional relations whenever he felt unjustly treated, wrangling over minor matters and never letting the matter rest until he could be sure his opponent had fully grasped his point. With his tendency to be irascible and prickly whenever he felt his own authority as musician and chosen servant of the Lord was being challenged, and his in-built shyness holding him back from the network needed for success, it is remarkable that Bach managed to work the system at all, and for as long as he did, in pursuit of his artistic goals. Ever since Peter Shaffer's play *Amadeus* (1979), we have gradually got used to the idea of a disassociation (albeit conjectural) between a puerile jokester in a state of arrested development and the 'divine' musician we revere as Mozart. However much his doting admirers genuflect before Richard Wagner as a composer, even they, sooner or later, have to come to terms with the inconvenient evidence that he was an abominable human being. Similarly, we should debunk once and for all the idea that Bach in his personal and professional life was some kind of paragon, the Fifth Evangelist of his nineteenth-century compatriots, the living embodiment of the intense religious faith and 'real presence' that his music seemed to transmit.[68] Acknowledging Bach's frailties and imperfections, far less heinous than those of Mozart or Wagner, not only makes him more interesting as a person than the old paragon of mythology, but also allows us to see his humanity filtering through into the music, which is far more compelling when we understand that it was composed by someone who, like all human beings, experienced grief, anger and doubt at first hand. This is one of the recurrent features that confer supreme authority on his music.

7
Bach at His Workbench

Mon cher Jacques,
Never correct J. S. Bach's accompanied violin sonatas on a rainy Sunday . . . ! I've just finished revising the above and I can feel the rain inside me . . .

When the old Saxon Cantor hasn't any ideas he starts out from any old thing and is truly pitiless. In fact he's only bearable when he's admirable. Which, you'll say, is still something!

All the same, if he'd had a friend – a publisher perhaps – who could have told him to take a day off every week, perhaps, then we'd have been spared several hundreds of pages in which you have to walk between rows of mercilessly regulated and joyless bars, each one with its rascally little 'subject' and 'countersubject'.

Sometimes – often indeed – his prodigious technical skill (which is, after all, only his individual form of gymnastics) is not enough to fill the terrible void created by his insistence on developing a mediocre idea no matter what the cost!

– Claude Debussy to Jacques Durand,
15 April 1917

In the Bach-Archiv in Leipzig is a scale model of the Thomasschule based on an engraving made by Johann Gottfried Krügner in 1723, from which it is clear that, as cantor, Bach and his extended family had to live cheek by jowl with the school, with direct access to its classrooms and dormitories on three of its four floors. The Bachs' marital bedroom was separated from one of the dormitories by a thin party wall. Bach's composing room (*Componirstube*) was directly adjacent to the *quinta* classroom. The noise at times must have been deafening, impossible to screen out even for someone with his formidable powers of concentration. This was the crucible in which all the stupendous compositions of his last twenty-seven years were to be forged. What concerns us most closely are the two Passions and the back-to-back annual cycles of cantatas composed at breakneck speed in a kind of creative fury during the first three years of his cantorship and in the shabby and run-down cantor's quarters before the renovation of the Thomasschule in 1731–2. The contrast in pace here with the previous five and a half years he had spent in the provincial backwater of Cöthen was enormous. Had Bach had the luxury of time we associate with a composer of the Romantic era like Beethoven, he would have had the chance to assemble and experiment with a large number of ideas from which he would ultimately have chosen the best. Any possibility of that disappeared with his arrival in Leipzig. From now on Bach had to formulate, or, as he might have said, 'invent', his ideas quickly. Robert L. Marshall, who led the scholarly investigation of Bach's compositional processes in the 1970s, wrote drily, 'the hectic pace of production obviously did not tolerate passive reliance on the unpredictable arrival of Inspiration.'*

On the shelves of his studio, therefore, we could expect to find the scores of serenades, birthday cantatas and New Year odes – works that, as a result of his bifocal vision as to the possible destination of his music

* An exact comparison between the pace of production in Cöthen and Leipzig is impossible, since so many of the instrumental and chamber works he composed in Cöthen have vanished, and dating the remainder with utter certainty is problematic. Judging from the few autograph materials and original performance parts we have from these years, Bach, even there, composed under the pressure of time – either because he was in the habit of leaving things to the last moment (when an event or deadline was approaching fast) or because he mulled over a piece for a long time before making the initial step to set it down in notation. Generally accepted by modern scholarship as 'Cöthen works' are the autograph scores of: the *Clavier-Büchlein* for Wilhelm Friedemann (1720), Vol. 1 of *Das Wohltemperierte Clavier* (1722), the *Clavier-Büchlein* for Anna Magdalena (1722), eventually to grow into the set of six French Suites (BWV 812–17), the fifteen Inventions and fifteen Sinfonias grouped together as *Aufrichtige Anleitung* (1723) and the forty-five organ chorales begun in Weimar that made up the unfinished *Orgel-Büchlein*. To this list can be added the solo and ensemble works: the six Partitas and Sonatas for Solo Violin, the six Suites for Cello and the six Brandenburg Concertos. Autograph scores for only two (BWV 134a and 173a) of a dozen occasional secular cantatas composed for New Year's Day and Prince Leopold's birthday have survived, plus one original and incomplete set of parts (for BWV 134a): the sources for the rest are either incomplete or lost, but were later to re-surface as 'parodies' in several of his Leipzig church cantatas.

(the church or the salon), could be plundered for future 'parodied' church cantatas. Next to these was a stack of manuscript paper ready for use: heavier than ordinary writing paper and more expensive, since the sheets needed to stay upright and rigid on the music stands. Sometimes he waited until he had planned the layout of a fresh composition and estimated the space he would need on each sheet, before ruling out the staves. This he did with a special five-nibbed pen called a rastrum. With frequent use his rastra were liable to spread or distort, so that the spaces between the five lines became uneven and led to confusion as to the intended notation (as in the case of the fifth Brandenburg Concerto, where the outer, lowest prong was virtually broken). Occasionally, as in this work, he used rastra of different sizes even on the same page, so as to give extra prominence to the harpsichord part. A quick glance at his composing scores is all that is needed to appreciate how economical Bach was in his use of the page, squeezing new material into the margins wherever practicable. On his desk were inkpots filled with black, sepia and red tints and a supply of copper-gallic ink powder ready for mixing with water. It was the acidity in this ink that was eventually responsible for its bleeding through the manuscript pages and, over time, severely damaging the paper on which he wrote. Also there were quills, lead pencils, knives for sharpening pens and for correcting mistakes once the ink had dried and a straight ruler for inscribing long bar-lines in fair-copy scores. Finally, there was a box of fine sand to blot the ink, though this, as we shall see, was not reliable enough to allow Bach to turn the page and to continue composing without a wait.

Before he could put pen to paper Bach needed to consider a wide range of issues and there were crucial decisions to be made. First came the delicate issue of negotiating with a literary partner, someone whose poetic text lent itself to musical treatment – and, more than that, someone whose poetic imagery would stimulate his creative imagination. He was then required to submit his choice to the senior clergy for approval before composition could legitimately begin.* There is a lot of uncertainty here. We do not know if he assembled any of the texts himself,

* At any one time Bach only had to deal with two of the clergy with respect to his cantatas: Salomon Deyling, superintendent and pastor of the Nikolaikirche, and, until 1736, Christian Weiss I, pastor of the Thomaskirche. After 1736 there was a sequence of four Thomaskirche pastors: Schütz (1737–9), Sieber (1739–41), Gaudlitz (1741–45) and Teller (1745–50).

like his contemporary Gottfried Heinrich Stölzel, an accomplished German stylist who is known to have written a good many of the poetic texts for his vocal works. We cannot tell whether potential librettists were suggested to, or even imposed on, Bach by the consistory, or what happened if he contested their choice. Collaborating with the same (usually anonymous) writer over a number of weeks could have meant that they were able to plan ahead together and submit their texts on a monthly basis. Once these were approved, they prepared booklets for publication, each of which contained around six cantata texts, and put them on sale for the benefit of the congregation.

Next, having determined an overall structure for his cantata, Bach needed to decide whether to apportion its consecutive movements exactly as suggested by the librettist – here a chorus, there a recitative and aria (*da capo* or otherwise) – or according to a separate scheme of his own devising. Thereafter the choice and positioning of the chorale was critical. Normally it came at the end, like the final couplet in a Shakespearean sonnet where, after three quatrains in iambic pentameter, the focus narrows in a funnel-shaped conclusion. Bach needed to give similar prominence to the moment when doctrine, exposition and persuasive musical oratory had run their course and could give way to a communal prayer. This was a vital gathering point in the service, just prior to the sermon. Having set out the stages of his argument, Bach could bind the threads together and thereby create a resolution to lift his listeners into the 'now' of collective singing, drawing on their sense of shared existence and values they held in common.

There was also the make-up of his performing ensemble to consider, its particular strengths and weaknesses: who happened to be sick or unavailable that week, who could be trusted for a particularly demanding solo or obbligato – a perennial dilemma for a music director – a promising alto, a flautist or even a budding exponent of the newly invented violoncello piccolo. Always conscious of the shape of the seasonal and liturgical calendar, Bach gave great importance to the cluster of feast-days at the main turning-points of the year and to the three annual Leipzig trade fairs, when his regular congregation swelled with international visitors whom the city elders were keen to impress. These were festive occasions that cried out for trumpets and drums. But incorporating the Stadtpfeifer into his young band of students was not always straightforward: like brass players before and ever since they operated differently from other musicians, ruled by their own tariffs and following their own arcane practices. Like one of today's football managers, Bach also had to anticipate which members of his regular pool of hard-pressed singers and players might need to rest after the intense pressure of back-to-back feast-days – factors that led to a more modest instrumentation and a reduced choral participation in certain cantatas. In this he may have been responding to notions of the pupil's psychology and stamina. These had became gradually more important in the course of the previous century, thanks to educational reformers such as Jan Amos Comenius (see Chapter 2, p. 45). Comenius had urged the cultivation of a more favourable environment for learning and closer attention to the pupil's ability for self-evaluation within the various stages of instruction[1] – strategies that may have made Bach's demands for virtuosity possible in the first place.*

* * *

While it would be futile to imagine that we can trace with any degree of certainty the sequence of Bach's thought processes that led to composition, there are encouraging things we can glean from studying his composing scores, from sketches, and from descriptions of his procedures left by his sons and pupils. Unpicking the constituent parts of a musical composition can bring us closer to seeing the composer at work, following him as he makes decisions, choosing to go this way or that. There is the element of surprise (because he may have turned a corner in a way you weren't expecting) and the continual wonder (at how he has managed to get from A to Z). We inch forwards in trying to unravel what is by its nature a mysterious, unfathomable process and, crucially, in describing its overall impact on us. It is obvious how much hinged on Bach's powers of *inventio* – his capacity to find the germ or creative spark that would, in large measure, determine the content of a piece. For someone with his great natural gifts and thorough training – surrounded by music from the very beginning and in regular touch with the copying and performing of it – it is reasonable to suppose that for

* This is reflected in the regulations (*Ordnungen*) of the Thomasschule in 1634, which instruct teachers to 'awaken pleasure and enjoyment in learning' and to avoid unfriendliness and tyrannical gestures – though whether this was inserted as a reaction to the evidence of a heavy-handed approach by teachers, which we encountered in the Ohrdruf school of Bach's time (see Chapter 6), is hard to say.

him the invention of ideas was a matter of daily experience. Like Shakespeare, he must have *expected* to find things to write, themes to compose. The presence of an ensemble of singers and instrumentalists or a company of players, a congregation or a theatre audience – these were all external factors capable of forming an armature both of expectation and of reassurance. Alexander Gerard, in his *Essay on Genius* (1774), confirms what most people assume: that 'genius is properly the faculty of *invention*', by which he meant what we mean when we talk about creativity. 'Genius' in Gerard's sense barely pertained in Bach's background, yet *inventio* was important enough to persist under the later model. Bach alludes to invention as 'a strong foretaste of composition'.[2] He was presumably describing the formation of embryonic ideas that rise to the surface of the mind before being captured in notation. His first biographer, Forkel, relates how he obliged his pupils to master thoroughbass and voice-leading in four-part chorales before attempting inventions of their own. Emanuel Bach, who should have known, affirmed that his father considered invention a talent that manifests itself early on in the training of young musicians: 'As for the invention of ideas, my late father demanded this ability from the very beginning, and whoever had none he advised to stay away from composition altogether.'[3] Interestingly, this very ability, the trigger that fired his imagination and set the creative act in motion, does not always appear to have come naturally or fluently to Bach himself.* For him invention was an uncovering of possibilities that are already there, rather than something truly original – hence his view that anyone could do as well, provided they were as industrious. God is still the only true creator.

When he was most under pressure, composing to a tight weekly deadline as with the church cantatas of his first Leipzig years, 'the astonishing mass of [his] unusual and well-developed ideas' might have become choked by the limitations of time – not that they show any lack of fantasy.† This is Johann Abraham Birnbaum, Bach's spokesman, who is talking, and since he is no musician himself these remarks must

* In his pre-Leipzig cantatas it seems Bach experienced few problems finding his opening ideas and more difficulty in working them out (*elaboratio*), whereas in Leipzig, when he was under greater pressure of time, the situation was exactly the opposite (see Robert L. Marshall, *The Compositional Process of J. S. Bach* (1972), Vol. 1, pp. 237–8).

† Birnbaum refers rather enigmatically to Bach's melodic style as 'chromatic and dissonant' and to his 'dissonant wealth' (BD II, Nos. 300, 354/NBR, p. 342).

have originated with Bach. It was a matter of pride for him to fill every available liturgical slot for music and to compose cantatas for every single feast-day in his first three years. Normally his imaginative range was so vast that it disguised the fact that he was drawing on a common stock of material from which to choose. Just occasionally he gets caught out and miscalculates the initial structuring process. When composing only the second of his Leipzig cantatas, BWV 76, *Die Himmel erzählen die Ehre Gottes*, he sketched his first idea for an opening ritornello on the two uppermost staves, but soon realised that its imitative figuration was too formulaic, too short (only six bars before the first choral entry) and leading nowhere. So he struck it through and began again, this time holding back fugal treatment until the second phrase: 'There is no speech nor language, where their voice is not heard.'[4] On the other hand, his knowledge of harmony was so profound that it was practically mathematical in effect. He knew how every single note and key related to each other, what could be done with every chord and with every change of direction. As Emanuel tells us, 'He worked them out completely and dovetailed them into a large and beautiful whole that combined diversity and the greatness of simplicity.'[5]

Most composers need sketchpads, if only to jot down a theme, not necessarily an original one, but one that looks promising.* Very few of Bach's sketches have survived, yet Robert L. Marshall, one of the first scholars to have combed through all the sources, is convinced that Bach worked from preliminary drafts that have subsequently been lost or destroyed.† With music we do not have the luxury of spectrographic images preserved just underneath the surface that reveal the early stages in a masterpiece. Fortunately there are still intriguing thematic fragments that Marshall has been able to recover: sometimes in pencil, sometimes in ink and sometimes tagged on to an unrelated composi-

* The English composer Hugh Wood describes the moment when ideas come into focus: 'You know this is a very valuable moment, and you feel attached to it; where you are presented with *donnée* – something "given" – and you don't know where it has come from. Then the work begins, but without being given something the piece is probably not really alive' (private correspondence).

† This is undoubtedly true in the case of Bach's most complex instrumental music, such as the *Well-Tempered Clavier*, *The Art of Fugue* and so on, whose surviving autograph material consists only of fair or revision copies, whereas relatively few preliminary drafts have survived for most of his cantatas composed under enormous pressure of time (see Marshall, op. cit., Vol. 1, p. 240).

tion. These reveal false starts and Bach's efforts to get back on course. There are two intriguing sightings of Bach at his workbench in the lead-up to the pressurised Christmas period in 1724. For his Christmas Day offering Bach is well launched in composing the opening chorus of BWV 91, *Gelobet seist du, Jesu Christ*, with a festive instrumentation of three separate 'choirs' of horns, oboes and strings. At the bottom of the first page of his composing score Bach has made sketches of movements 1, 3 and 5 – clearly he has given careful thought to the succession of movements from the outset and the cyclical structure of the work. He decides to assign the third movement to a tenor and starts to sketch possible themes in triple metre and in dotted rhythms. It turns out that none of these will eventually be used; but somehow you cannot imagine him formulating dozens of beginnings and then, like Schubert, rejecting them with a cryptic remark: *Gilt nicht* ('Won't do!'). On a separate occasion, poised to compose BWV 133, *Ich freue mich in dir*, he comes across an existing melody evidently new to him that he sketches in at the foot of a separate score – that of BWV 232iii, the *Sanctus*, also composed for Christmas in 1724 – simply using the available space as a notepad as he tries to fit it to the words of the hymn that he intends to use as the basis of this cantata (see overleaf). Then, on the same page, just above the chorale tune, there is a separate instance of his putting a theme to the test – in this case, that for the *Pleni sunt coeli* fugato we recognise from the *B minor Mass* – and underneath it (added later) a reminder to himself that he will need to make a new set of parts since the originals 'are in Bohemia with Count Sporck'.[6]

Whatever went on in his mind in terms of pre-composition or was first jotted down in sketches, Bach's working scores show us how concentrated and economical he was when actually composing. Among twentieth-century composers Shostakovich is reported to have composed his symphonies straight into full score, bypassing even particells, on the basis that he didn't have time to make errors: he simply couldn't afford the luxury of making mistakes. Bach was much the same. We can see this from the composing score of BWV 135, *Ach Herr, mich armen Sünder*, a cantata from his second cycle. Here he is composing directly into score on consecutive folded sheets of a fascicule of ruled paper. At this point he still doesn't know how it will develop or how much space or paper he is going to need. Arriving at the foot of a page he is in full flow. Now he has a dilemma: manuscript paper being so expensive, he

Bach's MS of the Sanctus, BWV 232iii *with a sketched melody for* BWV 133.

cannot just use a spare sheet to notate the continuation of his thought,* so he has to wait for the ink to dry (blotting paper had not yet been invented and sand was not a reliable way of drying ink). It may be as long as five or six minutes before he can safely continue – time perhaps for a coffee with Anna Magdalena, but perhaps also long enough to risk the train of thought (and *inventio*) being broken. His solution is there at the foot of the page: a little mnemonic in tablature – an *aide-mémoire*, squeezed into the bottom-right-hand corner of the page, the immediate sequel of the aria he is composing.

Other than organists, there were not many composers then left who used (or knew how to use) tablature; but for Bach it was an effective

* Robert L. Marshall has found examples of Bach turning the sheet round and starting to write again, or temporarily laying it aside. In this way, a rejected version of a movement can suddenly appear in a much later portion of the same manuscript (as in the case of BWV 117i) or even in the manuscript of another work (*The Music of J. S. Bach: The Sources, the Style, the Significance* (1989), p. 111). This was the situation as regards Bach's revision copies and fair copies, but it definitely was not the norm for the majority of his cantata autographs – certainly not for the vast majority of Leipzig composing scores from the high-intensity period of 1723–7. For those, he (or his assistant) pre-ruled a stockpile of paper in advance clearly before Bach had a definite notion of the specific layout of the work. Marshall refers to this as the 'non-calligraphic principle' in *The Compositional Process of J. S. Bach* (Vol. 1, p. 43, also pp. 47–54).

type of shorthand for capturing his creative thoughts before they flew off the page.*

This is a classic example of Bach being caught up in the process of *elaboratio*, the second stage in the fleshing out of a musical composition as defined by Christoph Bernhard. In his *Tractatus compositionis augmentatus* (*c.* 1657), widely circulated in manuscript during the second half of the seventeenth century, Bernhard brought Cicero's five divisions of rhetoric up to date and in applying them to music reduced them to three: *inventio*, *elaboratio* and *executio*. First, Bach crafts a workable idea (*inventio*), one that opens the door to creative embellishment (*elaboratio*), and then puts it to the test in performance (*executio*). These concepts are complementary and vital. The first two require intense mental activity, but there is a crucial difference between them: whereas invention is work, elaboration is play. Laurence Dreyfus expands on this: 'while invention requires foresight, planning, consistency, savvy, and seriousness of purpose, elaboration is content with elegance, an associative logic, and an eye for similarities.'[7] The latter allowed Bach to explore dormant qualities in composition that most composers of his day would have missed. The hallmark of Bach's skill in *elaboratio* lies in the intricacy and connectedness of his methods, such as variation and parody: these come across as far more refined and distinctive than those of his contemporaries, who, as Dreyfus observes, tend to treat elaboration in a more casual manner. But we are liable to be disappointed and may be trivialising the creative process if we expect to find all the germs of a new work neatly contained in its beginnings and then elaborated in

* Peter Wollny has drawn my attention to the following examples of draft opening movements of Bach's cantatas:

1. in pencil: a fugal exposition (alto, tenor) in the final movement of BWV 68, found on the last page (upside down) of the autograph score of BWV 59.
2. in pencil: a fugue subject for a chorus to the words *Meine Hilfe kommt vom Herrn, der Himmel und Erde gemacht hat* (apparently never realised) found on fol. 13r of the autograph score of BWV 49.
3. in ink and unrelated to the work in which it is found: the beginning of an opening chorus for BWV 149, *Man singet mit Freuden vom Sieg*, an instrumental ritornello (fourteen bars), and the initial entry of the bass voice (only one note and one word – 'Man'), found in the autograph score of BWV 201.
4. in ink and unrelated to the work in which it is found: the beginning of cantata BWV 183 (seven bars assigned to two oboes, two oboes da caccia, basso continuo plus bass solo); the opening of an aria in D major in $\frac{3}{8}$ (also possibly for BWV 183), both found in the autograph score of BWV 79.

logical progression. At certain times this does happen; at others Bach introduces new thematic material that involves discarding or cutting short the trajectory of an opening theme, but in such a way that we would probably not notice that anything was amiss, so accomplished is he at papering over the joins and bringing things to a natural-seeming conclusion. Dreyfus points to the formal oddity of an immensely popular piece, the opening movement of Bach's second Brandenburg Concerto, to illustrate how the formation of its two competing ritornellos is incomplete and in a sense defective. Bach seems to acknowledge the fact by his inability to repeat both of them intact at the end of the movement.[8] Yet the listener is probably not in the least disturbed by the irrationality of its construction, delighting instead in its playfulness, wit and brilliance. What is most valuable about this sort of approach is that Bach could be shown to be at his most creative when his chosen inventive material falls short in some way, or when some sort of irregularity gives rise to ideas that he probably would not otherwise have had. What Dreyfus reveals is that there is a real human intelligence operative here, not some detached Godlike figure who just creates *ex nihilo.**

Once launched, Bach's concerns revolved around harmony. Zedler defined universal harmony as 'the conformity and harmony of all things, for everything in the world acts together in respect to both cause and effect'. Bach himself had this to say: 'The thorough-bass is the most perfect foundation of music . . . that results in a well-sounding *Harmonie* to the Honour of God and the permissible delight of the soul.' Emanuel

* As we can see from the numerous changes Bach made to the duet from BWV 134a, *Die Zeit, die Tag und Jahre macht*, this was a laborious process. First he wrote out the opening ritornello (bars 1–19) notated in minims (time signature: C), and then worked on the shape of the inner parts. The natural flow of the alto and tenor voices is also the result of hard work. Initially the alto moved in quavers (E♭ | E♭ – F – G – E♭ – F – G – E♭ | F – G – A♭ – F). The first climax is reached in bars 21–9, where the strings play almost the entire ritornello superimposed over the voices. Bach achieved this by first entering the strings into his score and then by adding the vocal lines. Double counterpoint comes into play in bars 34 onwards: here Bach simply swapped the alto and tenor parts from bars 29 onwards (transposed by a fifth) and then restored the ritornello, now in B♭. A similar process can be observed in the second vocal section, where the alto and tenor again exchange lines in bars 59–65 and 66–72. The concluding ritornello of the first part of this *da capo* aria is now no longer a problem for Bach: he simply added it into his score for the empty bars 74–88. The insertion of the entire ritornello within the two vocal sections of the A section provided coherence and balance and, by exchanging the two voices via double counterpoint, the beautiful proportions of this duet were achieved. I am grateful to Peter Wollny for drawing my attention to the compositional process involved in this work.

Bach described this preoccupation in similar terms: the defining aspect of his father's engagement with harmony was its *Vollstimmigkeit* (its 'full-voiced-ness') – in other words, the way it incorporated counterpoint. Here is quite literally the crux of the matter: the crossing of vertical and horizontal planes of sound. Certainly no one before Bach (and only a handful of composers since) had used this point of intersection so fruitfully: melody underpinned by rhythm, enriched by counterpoint and coalescing to create harmony, itself a composite of consonance and dissonance that register in the listener's ear.* Looked at another way, it is astonishing how the harmonic motion seems to carry the full freight of melodic ideas on its shoulders. All this is of course highly symbolic from a theological viewpoint and draws attention to the fact that the word *Vollkommenheit*, besides meaning perfection, has an undercurrent of 'completeness'. It was a concept that bemused the most vociferous of Bach's critics, Johann Adolph Scheibe, who thought the aim of a modern composer was 'merely to place accompanying voices under a melody'.[9] Perfection for Bach entailed knowledge of 'the most hidden secrets of harmony'. His skill in discovering them was a passion – almost an obsession – and 'no one was able to arrive at so many inventive and unfamiliar thoughts from otherwise seemingly dry artifices as he was.'[10] The steps to his acquiring these skills can be traced back to the various comments scattered in Emanuel Bach's writings about his father. In essence Emanuel is telling us not so much what produced the initial spark (the *inventio*) in his father's mind as the profusion of ways he expanded it (*elaboratio*):

1. Being essentially self-taught he learnt by observation 'the works of the most famous and proficient composers of his day and by the fruits of his own reflection upon them'.
2. 'Through his own study and reflection even in his youth he became a pure and strong writer of fugues.'
3. 'Thanks to his greatness in harmony' when sight-reading a new piece he was able on the spur of the moment to convert a

* Glenn Gould put it this way: 'The prerequisite of contrapuntal art, more conspicuous in the work of Bach than in that of any other composer, is an ability to conceive a priori of melodic identities which when transposed, inverted, made retrograde, or transformed rhythmically will yet exhibit, in conjunction with the original subject matter, some entirely new but completely harmonious profile' ('So You Want to Write a Fugue', *Glenn Gould Reader*, Tim Page (ed.) (1990), p. 240).

three-part texture into a complete quartet – all this 'on the basis of a sparsely figured continuo part . . . being in a good humour and knowing that the composer would not take it amiss'.

4. 'When he listened to a rich and many-voiced fugue, he could soon say, after the first entries of the subjects, what contrapuntal devices it would be possible to apply, and which of them the composer by rights *ought* to apply, and on such occasions when I was standing next to him and he had voiced his surmises to me, he would joyfully nudge me when his expectations were fulfilled.'[11]

Like a chess grand master, Bach is able to predict all the next conceivable moves. One would like to know whether someone so precise and so obviously comfortable with figures and structures was in the habit of applying these faculties to other areas. (Was there some 'harmony', for instance, in the way he set out his bills and accounts?) Bach seems to have been unique in identifying the elusive divine spark which for him, as Dreyfus suggests, lay at the core of musical and human experience and which he pursued through hard and arduous work.

Another source of the spark of his imaginative ability to 'elaborate', similar to (3) above, comes in an observation recorded in 1741 by someone from Gottsched's circle (see p. 220). Theodor Leberecht Pitschel can only have had Bach senior in mind ('the famous man who has the greatest praise in our town') when he suggests that he 'does not get himself up to speed . . . to delight others with the mingling of his tones until he has played something from the printed or written page, inferior to his own ideas, and has [thus] set his powers of imagination [*Einbildungskraft*] in motion. And yet his superior ideas are the consequences of those inferior ones.'[12] This sounds similar to Handel's practice. Both men borrowed musical ideas as a spur to greater invention, but there is a subtle difference. While Bach adapted Vivaldi's ritornello designs and the permutation fugue subjects of a previous generation, by far his most extensive borrowing came from his own compositions, leading to expansions and transformations, all part of his quest for perfection. Handel, on the other hand, borrowed from his own work mainly, one suspects, to save himself time and bother. He 'stole' from other composers' works far more extensively than Bach did, particularly from his middle years onwards, but had the knack of transforming the originals so radically that they emerged as essentially new. This is what lies behind the description attributed to William Boyce – that Handel 'takes other men's pebbles and polishes them into diamonds'.[13]*

* * *

Each time he was faced with a new poetic text lying on his desk, Bach needed to weigh up its form and the degree to which he felt constrained to replicate it in his musical structures or, alternatively, free to alter it. Unlike Johann Kuhnau, Bach was not a gifted linguist, so that his predecessor's advice – that when faced with the task of setting a prose text, a composer should consider the given words in various other languages and take inspiration from there – was not much use to him.[14] Naturally, where a close understanding already existed between him and his librettist, such issues did not generally arise. His collaboration with Leipzig's young, twice-widowed salon poetess, Christiane Mariane von Ziegler, for example, was intense but did not last long. This may have been because he made alterations to the texts of nine of her cantatas to suit his own purposes (see Chapter 9). She got her own back, however, by publishing them in 1728 restored to their original state.† By far his most frequent literary partner was Christian Friedrich Henrici, usually known by his pseudonym Picander. Either by acquiescing or by negotiation Bach would normally allow the count of Picander's verses to determine the number of movements in which his music was cast and even to let the accentual patterns of the text dictate his choice of metre

* The most blatant and, in some ways, most baffling example of this practice occurs in his great oratorio *Israel in Egypt* (1737). Of its thirty-nine numbers no fewer than sixteen owe a melodic motif (and sometimes a lot more besides) to four other composers – Alessandro Stradella, Johann Kaspar Kerll and two rather obscure Italian composers, Dionigi Erba and Francesco Antonio Urio. Some of their material clashes with Handel's style, while some of it is frankly banal; but it seems to have acted like a trigger, detonating Handel's creative processes. In every case he enriches and surpasses his models. The overall result is one of the most original and dramatically gripping sequences of choral/orchestral writing to have survived from the middle years of the eighteenth century.

† This intellectual daughter of the Burgomaster Romanus is described by a contemporary 'as yet a young widow, who, however, on account of a multitude of circumstances, will hardly marry again. Among other things, her *conduite* is almost excessively womanly, and her spirit far too lively to submit to common male expectations. Her outward aspect is not ugly, but she has rather large bones, a squat figure, a flattish face, a smooth brow, lovely eyes, and she is healthy and rather brown in colouration'(Christian Gabriel Fischer, quoted by H.-J. Schulze in Christoph Wolff (ed.), *Die Welt der Bach-Kantaten* (1998), Vol. 3, p. 118).

or influence the rhythm of his thematic motifs and, less directly, the pitches, tonality and even the instrumentation. These decisions all flowed from Bach's reading of the text and were in basic accord with it. This more or less matches Emanuel Bach's slightly rosy picture of his father's methods when composing *Kirchensachen* ('church things'): 'he worked devoutly, governing himself by the content of the text, without any strange distortion of the words or highlighting individual words at the expense of the overall sense, by means of which ridiculous thoughts often appear that sometimes arouse the admiration of people who claim to be connoisseurs and are not.'[15]

What Emanuel does not describe are the times when his father decided to be less compliant. If his interpretation of the lectionary differed from that of Picander (or any other librettist's poetic paraphrase or exposition) and his own thought patterns suggested an alternative structure, Bach was not always inclined to follow quite so submissively. It is at these moments that he reveals the full extent of his ambitions for music: for it to interpret and find meaning in the world about him. At that point no author or librettist could stop him from using his natural gifts, as Birnbaum describes them, to gain 'imaginative insight into the depth of worldly wisdom'.[16] On such occasions his risk-taking strategies could lead to a total disregard for the conventional rules of propriety in poetic construction: the rulebook is thrown out of the window and ends up in the street below. Some of his critics found these procedures impermissible – proof that he was wilful and headstrong. They puzzled even his most fervid supporters, who subscribed to the conventional notions of the 'natural' and 'reasonable' more readily than he did. There is a grain of bemusement as well as admiration in Emanuel's description of his father's melodies as 'strange, but always varied, rich in invention, and resembling those of no other composer'.*

One such case when Bach took matters into his own hands is the

* Eric Chafe has this to say by way of explanation: 'Bach's melodic lines, often jagged, even distorted-sounding at times, do not permit the sense that they go down like a raw oyster, that they might just as well be disregarded from the musical standpoint, or that projecting a sense of "naturalism" is of foremost importance. They arise from the harmony, of course, and that harmony is often considerably more complex and original than that of any of his contemporaries . . . The complexity of Bach's harmonic thought converges with that of the theological ideas: he must have welcomed the opportunities to unpack the astonishing array of text-musical correspondences we find in virtually every work' (*J. S. Bach's Johannine Theology: The St John Passion and the Cantatas for Spring 1725*, forthcoming).

so-called *Trauer-Ode* (BWV 198). Here he was fulfilling a controversial commission to commemorate the passing of Queen Christiane Eberhardine, Electress of Saxony. There was a political dimension to the occasion. Queen Christiane was widely revered in Saxony for staying faithful to Lutheranism, unlike her late husband and son, who had converted to Catholicism in what many at the time saw as a cynical bid to qualify for the Polish crown. Bach's music is dignified, atmospheric and profoundly moving. Its first movement bears a stylistic and emotive resemblance to the opening chorus of his *Matthew Passion*, which had first seen the light of day only a few months before. The memorial service was held in the university church on 17 October 1727, yet the score of the ode was not completed until the 15th, leaving less than two days for copying the parts and rehearsals. In setting it as a cantata, made up of choruses, arias and recitatives, Bach was treading on dangerous ground. The university church was not one of his usual haunts, and he had set words not by any old cantata hack, but by a respected university professor – Johann Christoph Gottsched, the leading exponent of literary reforms and lionised in Leipzig as a representative of rational literature. The trouble was that Gottsched's mourning ode turned out to be insipid – a potpourri of banalities, mawkish sentiments and bathetic rhymes. Bach chose simply to disregard the formal layout of its strict eight-lined strophes with its regular rhyming scheme (A-B-B-A) and to ignore Gottsched's textual hints as to what kind of setting would be appropriate. His crime was not so much his indifference to the elevated tone of Gottsched's text, but the way that he supplanted and eclipsed it.* Johann Adolph Scheibe, predictably an avid admirer of Gottsched, tells us how Bach ought to have set it – by avoiding excesses of any kind, such as modulating to distant keys or using an 'unending mass of metaphors and figures'. Yet it is precisely these metaphors and figures that make Bach's setting so gripping. On the one occasion when Gottsched provides him with a quatrain that rises above the mediocre – 'The bells' vibrating clang / shall awaken our troubled souls' alarm / through their swung bronze / and pierce our

* For Laurence Dreyfus, 'Bach's music can be said to have savaged the intentions of the poetic text.' Yet, by dividing up some of his stanzas into two numbers, it could be said that Bach was doing Gottsched a good turn by disguising the rhythmic monotony of his nine consecutive stanzas. In doing so, he fell foul of the style police, who expected him to adjust his melodic invention and slavishly follow the strophic divisions, contours and punctuation of Gottsched's verses.

marrow and our veins' – Bach responds memorably. One would expect him to replicate the sound of funeral bells (see pp. 461–2), and here he has an exceptional instrumental palette with which to do so: pairs of flutes, of oboes, and (unusually) of violas da gamba and lutes besides the strings and continuo. But it is what he does with these contrasting instrumental timbres in just eleven bars that is so astonishing. First he builds up the sonic profile by introducing each of the eleven upper lines one by one, each evoking a bell of a different size – from the smallest via the tap-tap chiming of the flutes, to a sustained tolling of middle-sized bells in the oboes and a haze of plucked strings, to the deep, sonorous booming of the larger bells in the gambas and continuo that clang ominously in regular fourths and fifths. By now we have moved from D with a flat seventh in the oboe via a diminished seventh to C minor, a minor ninth on E. Then, below the third inversion of the dominant seventh on C♯, comes an abrupt (and by the standards of the day, impermissible) rocking back and forth from E♯ to A in the bass, before the bells peter out one by one in the same order as they began. What this tonal analysis seems to be telling us is that, as a result of the queen's death, time has stopped working with its normal God-appointed regularity – that with her demise the natural world is out of kilter.

The overall criticism, direct or indirect, that we find in Scheibe and Mattheson, while confined by their conceptual limitations, provides us with a benchmark with which to measure the degree of incomprehension people may have brought to Bach's music: how could he persist so obstinately in ignoring their efforts to rationalise and catalogue appropriate and agreeable styles of composition? We can only imagine how dull Scheibe's own 'correct' response to setting this text to music would have been.* The truth is that stylistic impropriety was a badge of Bach's approach to invention in a culture that was not equipped to deal with its originality. As Birnbaum said of Scheibe, he 'attempted to make Bach's works repulsive to delicate ears'.[17] The imaginative richness of Bach's music – one of the qualities we now admire and savour perhaps as a result of what we have learnt from later composition – clashed noisily with the cultural values of his day and undermined widely accepted ideas of decorum.

* Scheibe's Christmas cantata *Der Engel des Herrn*, for example, is like a pale, student copy of a Bach cantata – a series of fragmentary ideas that run out of steam almost instantly. The impression is of a caged gerbil puffing on its wheel.

From Bach's perspective, what made matters worse as regards the criticism of Mattheson and Scheibe was that both were mediocre composers. Mattheson, after showing early promise (see Chapter 4, p. 95 and footnote), soon drifted away from composition towards theoretical writing. Though some of it is astute and helps to fill gaps in our knowledge of how composers operated at the time, it turned Mattheson into a windbag of stupefying pomposity and self-importance. Scheibe, on the other hand, comes over as an embittered husk of a man consumed by envy, given to satirising and bad-mouthing his colleagues in code. Not even his co-critic Mattheson escaped his disdain, despite advocating a similarly 'scientific' approach to music. Scheibe was only too eager to retract his criticisms the moment any of his chosen targets showed the smallest interest in performing his own music.[18] This all came about after accidentally losing an eye while working alongside his father, a Leipzig organ-builder. Having trained as a musician and failing to land any of the posts of organist for which he had applied (including one in Freiberg in 1731 and for which Bach had recommended him),[19] he decided to become a music critic as well as a composer. In 1737 he published an article, pillorying Bach's music for being 'bombastic' and 'confused' and referring to him pejoratively as a *Musikant* (*Musikus* would have been the correct term – the very one he used in the title of the fortnightly journal he founded, *Critischer Musikus*).

As one of nine of his chosen victims, Bach was an easy target from the moment he became the only one to react publicly to Scheibe's stinging criticism. But, instead of responding in person, Bach chose a professor of rhetoric, Magister Johann Abraham Birnbaum, to act as his counsel. This enraged Scheibe, who returned to redouble the attack, accusing Bach of 'not taking an especial interest in the sciences actually needed by a learned composer . . . [namely in] the rules of rhetoric and poetics'.[20] He mocked Bach for 'never having taken the time to learn how to write an extensive letter.' Actually, he had a point; for, in channelling so much energy into the formulation of organised sounds, Bach was prone to forgetting the simpler forms of written communication.*

* C. P. E. Bach justified it to Forkel in this way: 'With his many activities he hardly had time for the most necessary correspondence, and accordingly would not indulge in lengthy written exchanges' (BD III, No. 308/NBR, p. 400). His most extensive letters are those to his schoolfriend Georg Erdmann (see p. 163) and those that relate to his third son, Johann Gottfried Bernhard, and his misdemeanours (see Chapter 14, p. 534).

Social awkwardness and fear of intellectual engagement other than by means of music were a constant throughout his life.

Bach did of course eventually put pen to paper in the rather awkward and prickly memorandum known to scholars as the 'Entwurff' ('Brief but Highly Necessary Draft of a Well-Appointed Church Music'), which he submitted to the city council in August 1730.[21] (See overleaf.) In it he pinpointed the main differences between himself and his contemporaries when he alluded to 'the present musical taste'. By that he may have meant the *galant* style with which he probably had little sympathy but was perfectly capable of emulating since, according to Lorenz Mizler, another who wrote in his defence, he knew 'perfectly how to suit himself to his listeners' and 'in accordance with the latest taste'.[22] Bach was merely flattering the councillors' sense of themselves as cultural connoisseurs equipped to assess how during the past dozen or so years 'the taste has changed astonishingly'. In the same breath he referred to the shortcomings of the musical resources he was expected to draw on for services held in the four main city churches, the inadequacies in the council's current provision of funds and personnel, and his minimum requirements when it came to musicians able to 'master the new kinds of music, and thus be in a position to do justice to the composer and his work'. At this point he is clearly referring to himself: since his music is 'far more intricate' and more challenging to performers than any other, he needed well-paid specialists of the kind he had been used to in Cöthen or, as he tells the council, the virtuosi employed by the Elector himself: 'One need only go to Dresden,' he tells the council, 'to see how the musicians there are paid by His Royal Majesty. It cannot fail, since the musicians are relieved of all concern for their living, free from *chagrin* and obliged each to master but a single instrument.' (This sounds like a prototype of the modern orchestra, and, given that this pointed to the breakdown of the very versatility and transferability that was part of Bach's success, it is rather ironic.) Bach's pitch is none too subtle: restore the fees (*beneficia*) that a Most Noble and Most Wise Council used to pay his *chorus musicus* and he will instantly 'bring the music into a better state'. They didn't and he couldn't. In fact he never received an acknowledgement, let alone a reasoned reply, to this poignant but blunt manifesto that has since given rise to so much misreading and controversy.

Behind these remarks directed towards improving the pay and conditions (and therefore the quality) of his performing apparatus in Leipzig,

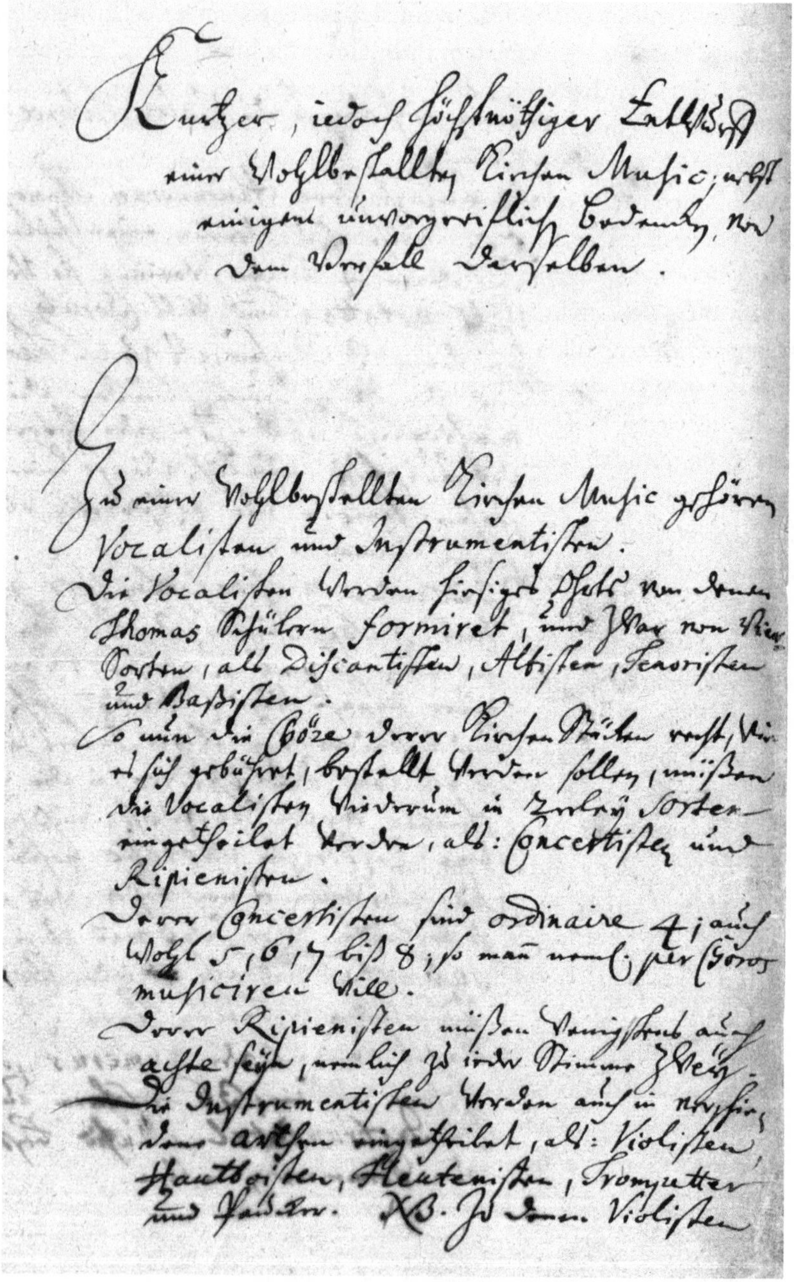

Kurtzer, iedoch höchstnöthiger Entwurff
einer wohlbestallten Kirchen Music; nebst
einigem unvorgreiflichen Bedencken, von
dem Verfall derselben.

Zu einer wohlbestallten Kirchen Music gehören
Vocalisten und Instrumentisten.
Die Vocalisten werden hiesiges Orths von denen
Thomas Schülern formiret, und zwar von vier
Sorten, als Discantisten, Altisten, Tenoristen
und Baßisten.
So nun die Chöre derer Kirchen Stücken recht, wie
es sich gebühret, bestellt werden sollen, müßen
die Vocalisten wiederum in zweyerley sorten
eingetheilet werden, als: Concertisten und
Ripienisten.
Derer Concertisten sind ordinaire 4; auch
wohl 5, 6, 7 biß 8; so man nemlich per Choros
musiciren will.
Derer Ripienisten müßen wenigstens auch
achte seyn, nemlich zu ieder Stimme zwey.
Die Instrumentisten werden auch in verschie-
dene arthen eingetheilet, als: Violisten,
Hautboisten, Fleutenisten, Trompetter
und Paucker. NB. Zu denen Violisten

The first page of Bach's 'Entwurff' – his combative, painstaking and fiercely argued memorandum to the Leipzig Council (1730).

we can sense the weight Bach attached to the act of performance itself – *executio*. The close scrutiny we give to the written notation of his works may distract us from a key component in his creativity: the way performance fed into the very act of composition. Take for example his three sonatas and three partitas for solo violin (BWV 1001–6) or the cello suites (BWV 1007–12). The deliberately restrictive medium teems with interpretative matter implied by, but not containable within, the notation. Their skeletal nature means that the music is festooned with little time-bombs of harmonic potential that tease the listener to speculate on how they might turn out – what chords are really implied, in other words. In order to grasp and 'realise' Bach's harmonic movement, both player and listener are drawn in and required to complete the creative act. Nineteenth-century composers, beginning with Mendelssohn, and with Busoni the most conspicuous, took the bait and sought to capture this in their transcriptions – which simply underscores how unusual and original Bach's chord progressions really are. Something similar happens when we look at Bernini's life-sized marble statue of David in the Villa Borghese in Rome. Unlike Michelangelo's classically poised hero, Bernini's David looks as if has been sculpted in the heat of battle. Like an Olympic discus-thrower, he is coiled up, face contorted, muscles straining, about to release his slingshot at his unseen adversary any moment now. As unsuspecting viewers, walking round the sculpture and observing David's twisting torso, we find ourselves drawn into the dramatic action. By occupying the space where we expect Goliath to be, and sensing the split second when David will release his slingshot, we become implicated in the action and present in the theatre of war; and in this way it is our imaginative response that completes the creative act of viewing the sculpture. In both cases – Bach's and Bernini's – the listener/viewer has to 'work' to constitute the finished article – something relatively new in the age of the Baroque, and not equivalent to mere 'decoding'.*

* * *

Turning to his larger choral works involving several performers, including himself in a dual capacity, one gets the sensation that Bach as composer

* This may have been what Beethoven had in mind when he described Bach as the 'progenitor of harmony', agreeing with Johann Friedrich Reichardt that the violin sonatas were 'perhaps the greatest example in any art form of a master's ability to move with freedom and assurance, even in chains' (*Jenaische Allgemeine Literaturzeitung*, No. 282 (Nov. 1805)).

was constantly in dialogue with Bach the performer, and that performance actively influenced the creative process. Not everyone agrees. Some of the most painstaking modern scholars, equipped with the modernist methodological tools of analysis and textual criticism, shy away from anything connected to performance – though one would hope that they share with music-lovers and performing musicians an underlying conviction in the profound aesthetic experience and worth of the music as it is revealed through performance. Nevertheless, they tend to regard the act of performance as an optional extra – uncontrollable and variable, therefore misleading and potentially damaging to the intrinsic perfection of a composition as preserved in print or in one of Bach's fair copies.* Bach was of course considered supreme as a performer in his lifetime and was celebrated far more as a keyboard virtuoso and for his improvisations than for his compositions, few of which were published or known outside a restricted geographical area; traces of their origins as improvisations are clearly apparent in the earliest of his keyboard fantasias and toccatas. The act of (re-)performance can help to take us back to an original that existed only in his head. As John Butt expresses it, performance can be seen 'as much a part of the past, as of the future, of a newly finished piece'.[23] The unusual amount of detailed figuration Bach includes in his scores relates to his practical experience as a performer, encapsulating in the most remarkable way the different strategies he used to improvise, elaborate and improve on a straightforward initial idea. It would be foolish to ignore the signs of creative synergy in the case of anyone so closely involved in the performance of his own music. We enrich our understanding of Bach's music each time we come across traces of his own interpretation within its complex notation. There is also the bonus of his graceful and expressive orthography, which reveals the way he experienced his music and expected it to unfold – the shapes and gestures suggestive of his phrasing and motion. (See Plate 23.) It is hardly surprising that performers nowadays often play from facsimiles of his autographs in preference to the static and regularised visual image of the printed score.

* One might object to this view of notation as the ideal embodiment of a piece and suggest that, as a static object, it is ultimately stultifying – to which you could legitimately counter, in Birnbaum's words, 'It is true, one does not judge a composition principally and predominantly by the impression of its performance. But if such judgement, which indeed may be deceiving, is not to be considered, I see no other way of judging than to view the work as it has been set down in notes' (BD II, No. 41, p. 355; and Christoph Wolff, *Bach: Essays on His Life and Music* (1991), p. 397).

The *Musical Offering* (BWV 1079) is probably the best-known example of Bach rising to a special occasion and drawing on all his inventive and interpretive resources – of *elaboratio* leading to *executio*. In May 1747 Frederick the Great set him an awkward, chromatic theme (Bach politely called it an 'excellent theme') on which to extemporise, first in three, then in six parts. It became a further test of his skill once he had left Potsdam, where his and King Frederick's views on the purpose of music may have clashed dramatically, since he would have to resubmit. It gave him the chance to reflect and pin down any notational improvements – and further brainteasers – to what had originated as a command performance *jeu d'esprit*. In the end he came up with a puzzling miscellany comprising a trio sonata, ten canons and two very different fugues (Bach called them 'ricercars'): a free one in three parts and a strict one in six parts. In the copy he sent to King Frederick he arranged for the inside page to be inscribed with the words *Regis Iussu Cantio Et Reliqua Canonica Arte Resoluta* ('At the King's Command, the Song and Remainder Resolved with Canonic Art'). Bach was making a pun on the word *canonica* – his way of showing that his 'canons' had been fashioned 'in the best possible way' for the King's amusement. Did Frederick even bother to look at them? Did he realise that the initial capitals of Bach's dedication spelt *ricercar(e)*, meaning 'to search out' and that Bach had deliberately refrained from writing the canons out in full, leaving them for him to discover? Having experienced the dazzling high-wire act of those first impromptu performances, when everyone was 'seized with astonishment', there was no incentive whatsoever for the King to scrutinise the written-out versions of the three main movements or to solve the attached canonic puzzles.*

* * *

* The ten canons in the *Musical Offering* are among the most complicated Bach ever wrote; yet the idea behind them is the same: of a single motif being played against itself, shared between equal voices who imitate the first voice note for note, as in a round. For it to work, each note has to be part of a melody and to be capable of harmonising with each separate occurrence of that melody. One of the most ingenious is the 'Canon a 2 per Tonos', in which the upper line inscribes a variant of the royal theme, while the two lower voices give a canonic harmonisation of a second motif. What makes this canon stand out from the others is that it modulates step-wise in minor keys: from C – D – E – F♯ – G♯ (= A♭) to its conclusion, all in the space of forty-nine bars. Though the piece may be broken off at any point, as the voices arrive at an octave higher than they were at the beginning, theoretically

All the various avenues to composition we have been pursuing – strands of pre-composition, *inventio*, *elaboratio*, word-setting – come together the moment we view them from a hermeneutical angle. Early on in Bach's Leipzig cantatas can be found a striking example: BWV 181, *Leichtgesinnte Flattergeister*. The title refers to the 'frivolous flibbertigibbets' – those fickle and superficial folk who, like the fowls of the air in the Parable of the Sower (Luke 8:4–15), devour the seed that 'fell by the wayside'. It makes them prey to the Devil, who 'taketh away the word out of their hearts, lest they should believe and be saved'. A decision Bach made at the outset was to set the Gospel words not as the usual chorus but as an aria for bass. For its opening ritornello he fashions a fragmented melodic line peppered with trills, then breaks up its rhythmic outline by means of angular little figures that clash with the symmetrical approach to the first cadence. By calling for light, staccato articulation in *vivace* tempo, by the third bar he has already done enough to establish the idea of nervy fluttering movements in the listener's mind and created an image of predatory flapping wings. This is how Albert Schweitzer describes the scene: 'we instinctively see a swarm of crows descending upon a field with beating wings and wide-stretched feet' – an image graphic enough to disturb the sleep of the anxious arable farmer.[24] When he came to revive the cantata *circa* 1743/6,[25] Bach added a flute and oboe to play in unison with the first violins. It might seem a minor adjustment, but their inclusion gives a fresh glint to the upper line: it reinforces the jerky movements of the avian seed-stealers as they vie in their greed for the fallen grain.

In these few brushstrokes Bach has brought together French airiness in the quirky manner of Rameau with hints of the *galant* style now com-

---

it can modulate upwards *ad infinitum*. This explains Bach's note in the margin 'as the notes ascend, so may the glory of the King.' According to Eric Chafe, 'Bach seems here to underscore in a baroque manner what Benjamin called "the disproportion between the unlimited hierarchical dignity with which [the monarch] is divinely invested and the humble estate of his humanity"' (*Tonal Allegory in the Vocal Music of J. S. Bach* (1991), p. 23; Walter Benjamin, *The Origin of German Tragic Drama* (1977), p. 70). Douglas R. Hofstadter, on the other hand, sees this as the first example of what he calls 'Strange Loops'. He traces its re-occurrence in the work of the Dutch graphic artist M. C. Escher (1898–72), emphasising a clash between the finite and the infinite, and in the mathematical discoveries of Kurt Gödel (1906–78) – his Incompleteness Theorem: 'All consistent axiomatic formulations of number theory include undecidable propositions' (Douglas R. Hofstadter, *Gödel, Escher, Bach: An Eternal Golden Braid* (1979), pp. 8–17). Take your pick.

ing into vogue. It is not until bar thirty-five that the link between the first theme and the devouring fowls of the air is connected to 'Belial with his brood'. Instantly the mood changes. Bach sets this B section unconventionally within the thematic web of the surrounding material. Then what sets out as a modified *da capo* of the A section seems to lose its way after only four bars and is abruptly transformed into a modified repeat of B. This is not just highly unusual; it is also destabilising to the listener expecting a normal *da capo*. In place of the tripartite A-B-A structure we now have a four-part structure: A - B (with elements of A) - A (truncated) - B (modified), and in place of the anticipated return of the opening words, back comes *Belial mit seinen Kindern* ('Belial with his brood') with more force than before. This is one of the relatively few cantatas of which the original libretto has survived, and it is obvious that it was Bach, not his anonymous poet, who was responsible for these structural anomalies. Perhaps in the heat of the moment Bach could not resist a further chance to depict this Miltonic Prince of Darkness, demon of lies and guilt. It enabled him to push home the point that it was Belial, a fallen angel, who effectively sabotaged God's plan to make the Word be 'of service' and to underline to anyone who wasn't paying proper attention that the devouring fowls are none other than Satan and his cronies. So what started out as a witty evocation, irresistible in its imagery and skill in word-setting, has by now acquired a sinister Hitchcockian edge.* Yet purely as a piece of mood music it is so atmospheric that in a different context it could serve as the soundtrack to a film of a gaggle of flighty, giggly teenage girls being bundled out of a nightclub by Belial the bouncer.

The moral is now drawn: the seed that falls on stony ground, the alto tells us (No. 4), is like the hard-hearted unbelievers who die and are dispatched below to await Christ's last word, the time when the doors will burst apart and the graves open. The recitative ends with a playful descent in the continuo to describe the absurd ease with which the angel rolled back Christ's tombstone (Look, no hands!) and to ask the rhetorical question 'Would you, O heart, be harder still?' A relatively uneventful soprano recitative then turns the listener's attention from the

* Alfred Hitchcock's horror movie *The Birds* (1963) does not have a conventional incidental score, of course. His usual musical collaborator, Bernard Herrmann, reduced to 'sound consultant' on this occasion, used sparse electronic sounds in counterpoint to calculated silences.

wasted seeds to those that fell on fertile ground. It is God's Word that prepares fruitful soil in the heart of the believer. Bach celebrates this not in the conventional way, with a chorale, but in a concluding movement that unites choir, flute, oboe, strings and, for the first time in the cantata, a trumpet. Despite this festive instrumentation the vocal writing has a madrigalian lightness and delicacy perfectly attuned to the joyous message of the text, suggesting perhaps that this movement borrows from a lost secular ode of Bach's Cöthen years. In this regard it neatly illustrates a point made by Ludwig Finscher when referring to the 'multi-potentiality' of Bach's writing and the 'excess' of musical thought beyond the mere setting of text.[26] They come together perfectly here, as they do in so many of his cantatas. Bach knew, as Shakespeare and later John Dryden did, that 'a continued gravity keeps the spirit too much bent; we must refresh it sometimes, as we bait upon a journey, that we may go on with greater ease.'[27] The degree of workmanship, of formal production, in Bach as a professional composer and performer is sometimes difficult to grasp. There is a two-fold time-specificity to a piece like this: it enacts a duration specific to itself, but it also encompasses the relations between the metronome, the acoustic properties of the building, the complex web that connects the composer to his performing ensemble and to his listeners and the element of recall – a combination that differs with each performance.

Indeed, the process of elaboration seems never to be wholly complete in Bach's work – sustained by his quest for perfection but never free from an entanglement with performance. Peter Wollny (the curator of the manuscript and rare books collection in the Bach-Archiv Leipzig and since 2013 its director) is gathering evidence from the manuscript parts of Bach's chorale cantata cycle that reveal layer after layer of alteration in the successive revisions he made in 1732, in the early 1740s and, for a last time, in the late 1740s. Inexplicably many of these multiple revisions were passed over by various editors of the *Neue Bach-Ausgabe*, with one of two results: either they remain undifferentiated or they are subsumed in a putative, but often spurious, Ur-text. Yet it is clear that there was never any uniformity to Bach's practice spanning these decades. The existence of these revisions raises several questions: whether, for example, the changes of verbal text Bach introduced were suggested to him, were linked to changing tastes in religious literature as the Enlightenment took a firmer hold in Leipzig in the 1740s, or were made entirely of his own volition. Similarly, one longs to know whether the changes in articulation that he now introduced – the slurs, staccato patterns, ornaments* and dynamics that he successively added – were the expression of an initial dissatisfaction with the way things had turned out in 1724/5 in the stressful rush to rehearse and perform them, or an indication of his changing aesthetics, or even a bit of both. This, in turn, raises the question of quite how much performing instruction Bach could initially have imparted to his ensemble by verbal or gestural means just before or even during the performance. Based on contemporary descriptions of his very active conducting (see below) I suspect quite a lot. I believe it is significant that Bach arranged to leave the performing material of this cycle to the Thomasschule, an act showing that he felt this to be his core repertoire; representing the very best of his cantata output, it was the music most closely associated with the Leipzig liturgy (and less exportable, therefore), and the local congregation might in time respond to it with more or the same enthusiasm in the future.

* * *

Where other cantors of the Thomaskirche on taking office had followed the custom of having the council pay the widows of their predecessors to allow them to continue to use their works, Bach had no such intention. Somehow he managed to convince the officials that the money was better spent on hiring two professional scribes – a signal of his ambitions to provide consecutive works of his own for all the feast-days in the liturgical calendar. The pressure on these two paid copyists, Johann Andreas Kuhnau (nephew of his predecessor) and Christian Gottlob Meissner, must have been intense, just as it was on countless pupils and family members dragooned into the process.† The privacy of Bach's composing

* John Butt suggests that, whereas Bach 'may have been brought up to ornament profusely, if not somewhat indiscriminately', he seems to have 'become increasingly prescriptive, frequently adding ornaments to the instrumental and vocal parts of his cantatas' (*The Sacred Choral Music of J. S. Bach: A Handbook* (1997), pp. 52–3).

† There are many other instances of Bach enlisting, besides his regular copyists, the help of the family and of apprentices in a kind of cottage industry, and later of his establishing his own private hire library. It was illegal to use the copyists on the Thomasschule payroll for the hire library, so the family and pupils had to step in to help out. In the case of BWV 41, *Jesu, nun sei gepreiset*, for New Year, there must have been a demand for an out-of-town performance for which an extra set of parts was needed. That would explain why one of the first violin parts is in Anna Magdalena's hand, while the cello piccolo part is in Bach's own matchless hand.

studio was not quite the ivory tower of popular Romantic imagination. In all likelihood Kuhnau and Meissner sat with the master in the *Componirstube*, copying frenetically from his scores and under the closest scrutiny. Only these two were allowed to touch the scores: once they had copied the individual parts they passed them on to junior scribes, who were possibly seated in an adjoining room, for making *doubletten* (the doubling parts). For much of the time and all through Bach's two and a half years things proceeded fairly smoothly. Even though Meissner was prone to making careless mistakes, his hand was so like his master's that it was enough to fool later analysts. Kuhnau, by far the more consistent of the two, also had an impressively clear hand. Working alongside Bach, they were able to convey an instantly legible and comprehensible imprint of the notation to the sight-reading performer – a huge boon to Bach, given the pressure of rehearsal time (there is nothing musicians like better than to bring a rehearsal to a standstill with questions to the conductor like 'Sorry, but I can't make out whether I am to play a B♭ or B♮ in bar 27, and, by the way, is that a dotted crotchet or a minim?'). Kuhnau had the wit to look for the best moments to arrange page-turns – wherever possible to coincide with bars' rest, regardless of the number of players present, so as to avoid holes in performance. Lesser copyists (and that includes those of some reputable publishers today) would simply not have bothered. He was not infallible, however. Once, when setting out the title page of BWV 135, *Ach Herr, mich armen Sünder*, in a moment's aberration he misspells the composer's name and writes *Bacch*. Clearly not amused, Bach must have given his errant copyist a sharp smack: a black smudge appears right across the page – Kuhnau's pen following the trajectory of the chastising biff (see opposite).

But how Bach must have rued his decision to lay Kuhnau off when his contract was due for renewal at the end of 1725. Family loyalties clashed with professional etiquette and the smooth running of the copying laboratory from February 1724 with the arrival in Leipzig of Bach's nephew Johann Heinrich (1707–83), the fourth son of Bach's eldest brother, Johann Christoph, who had recently died. In return for the favour he had received as a ten-year-old orphan when he was taken in by his brother, Bach now accepted the eighteen-year-old Johann Heinrich as a live-in apprentice. After a while, in order to justify his nephew's food, lodging and tuition, Bach dismissed his best copyist and set Johann Heinrich to work in his stead. Things immediately started to go awry.

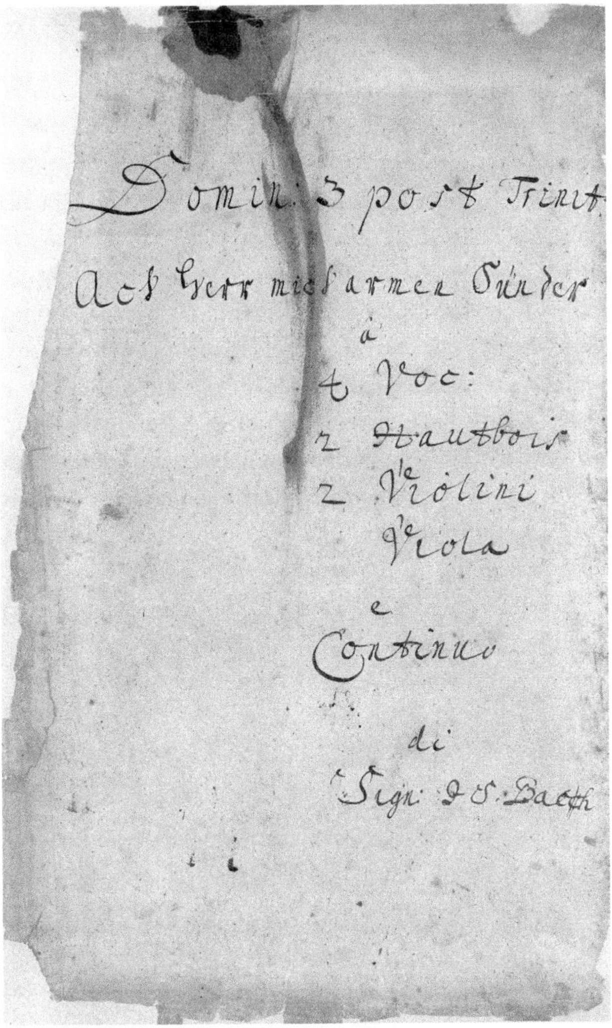

The surviving parts of a cantata for the first Sunday after Easter, BWV 42, *Am Abend aber desselbigen Sabbats*, tell a story that is not hard to interpret. Johann Heinrich is instructed to begin by copying out the second violin part. Perhaps his progress is too slow for the Cantor's liking, for after just three and a half bars Bach summons his fourteen-year-old son, Wilhelm Friedemann, to take over. Friedemann manages to copy out the entire *sinfonia* accurately enough (including the *tacet* indication for movement 2); but again the pace is too slow for his father, who decides to take over himself for the alto aria. That done, he turns back to Johann Heinrich and gives him a second chance – the simple one of copying out the final chorale. Even this is beyond him, it seems: Heinrich wrongly inserts the first violin melody in the concluding chorale, realises his mistake and crosses it out. Now crippled by nerves, he starts again, this time to copy the correct second violin part. Exasperated to find that he has made similar errors here and in other parts, Bach pushes him aside and enters the correct notes.*

On an earlier occasion, when copying BWV 127, *Herr Jesu Christ, wahr' Mensch und Gott*, Wilhelm Friedemann, jittery under parental scrutiny, gets the first note wrong – he is transposing the first violin part into the standard treble clef from a score written in the soprano clef (C on the lowest line) – but after the initial blip he corrects himself. The same happens with the viola part: he makes an initial error in transposing from the tenor clef down a third to the viola clef, but then manages to complete it smoothly and creditably. Meanwhile Bach decides to take over copying the continuo part for the bass arioso himself. He is now really pressed for time. This is a dramatic movement, virtually a prototype of the hurricane ('Sind Blitze') chorus from the *Matthew Passion*. Caught up in the creative frenzy and elation of the moment, Bach

* There is an intriguing sequel to this family anecdote, proving that Bach continued to take an interest in his sons' musical development and even the problems they faced as adult composers. Were we momentarily to fast-forward by some twelve years, by entering some hostelry in central Dresden, we might find two adults engrossed in conversation and poring over a musical document. This happens to be the sketch of a never completed trio sonata by Wilhelm Friedemann Bach, now twenty-six, the organist of the Sophienkirche in Dresden. Discovered in Kiev in 1999, the sketch shows signs of regular interventions in a second hand which Peter Wollny identified as that of J. S. Bach. What this represents, then, is less a tutorial between father and son, and more a dialogue between two professional colleagues, both absorbed by the technical challenges of composing in invertible counterpoint, settling down to work out their different solutions, which cover three dense pages of thirty-stave manuscript paper and representing probably a whole evening's work. Friedemann starts off by showing his working sketches to his father, who makes counter-proposals and suggests fresh approaches to the problems his son is facing. Their exchanges are initially couched in contemporary style, but then move on to passages in *stilo antico*, which at that time was a living concern of Sebastian's (see Chapter 13). We see him outlining different models, Friedemann struggling to produce acceptable themes and counter-themes, and his father responding with an exemplary alternative that shows how it can work in inversion, and then how it lends itself to a treatment using parallel thirds. The full extent of these exchanges, plus Wollny's realisations of them in modern notation, are published in the supplement volume to the NBA (BA 5291) (2011), pp. 67–80.

has to rush to finish. He cannot risk the snail's pace of his son's progress. Perhaps the orchestra was already tuning up. Gone are the elegant curved beams he normally arches over the notes: in their place, scratchy vertical strokes tilting forwards like a forest of bamboos in a force-eight gale.

Several years later, and we find that things have not changed fundamentally. Gerhard Herz selects a late cantata, BWV 140, *Wachet auf, ruft uns die Stimme*, first performed in 1731, to re-create the process. He suggests that in this instance Bach entrusted the copying of parts to one of his star pupils, Johann Ludwig Krebs, instructing him to begin copying 'so that the singers might be able to start learning the extended opening chorus' even before the autograph score was complete, perhaps indicating that there were pre-rehearsals. Private coaching of the week's soloists, sectional rehearsals ahead of the Saturday read-through, any of the time-saving strategies music directors resort to when pressed for time – all this would have made eminently good sense to a resourceful Capellmeister of Bach's experience. At this stage three other copyists are recruited. Bach himself gets involved later as mistakes start to be made through haste. 'Copyist 3 decided to do more than he was supposed to . . . not realising that thereby he bestowed the first violin part upon the viola player. Krebs caught this mistake, scratched out these two wrong lines (with what good Saxon oaths we can only imagine) and wrote out the correct viola recitative himself. Bach then seems to have been drawn into this squabble . . . he took the part away from Krebs and wrote out the final chorale himself, squeezing it on to this page only by the addition of a hand-drawn staff at the very bottom.'[28] (See below.) Taken together, these examples expose the degree of manic activity, of potential error and tension in the quotidian background of Bach's cantata production – not dissimilar to the backstage activities on a TV or film set today.

* * *

Besides all the other multiple activities involved in teaching at the Thomasschule and overseeing the musical life of the city, Bach most likely devoted the first four or five days of each week to composing a cantata for performance on the following Sunday. The copying of parts may, as we have seen, have started while he was still composing and, in any case, would have needed to be finished by the Saturday. Though in the run-up to the major feasts and at the time of the fairs additional time was allotted in the school curriculum on a Friday for extra rehearsal, Saturday was when the only full rehearsal took place and when everything came together in *executio*. With rehearsal time so tight, in practice this meant that a great deal of information needed to be contained in the notation, as we have seen, so that Bach's performers could grasp all the essentials while sight-reading; all the rest had to be transmitted by gesture or whispered instruction in the heat of performance. We have one precious eyewitness account of Bach the conductor by someone who, as headmaster of the Thomasschule in the early 1730s, had the opportunity to watch him at close quarters on many occasions. Johann Matthias Gesner contrasts 'the self-sufficiency of the organ and organist with the fragile interdependence of orchestra and chorus with their conductor, who must not only discharge his continuo function, but also fill holes in the music by singing, signalling, or playing missing parts when his musicians have gone astray.'[29]

> If you could see Bach . . . singing with one voice and playing his own parts, but watching over everything and bringing back to the rhythm and the beat, out of thirty or even forty musicians, the one with a nod, another by tapping with his foot, the third with a warning finger, giving the right note to one from the top of his voice, to another from the bottom, and to a third from the middle of it – all alone, in the midst of the greatest din made by all the participants, and although he is executing the most difficult parts himself, noticing at once whenever and wherever a mistake occurs, holding everyone together, taking precautions everywhere, and repairing any unsteadiness, full of rhythm in every part of his body – this one man taking in all these harmonies with his keen ear and emitting with his voice alone the tone of all the voices . . .[30]

Gesner's description has sometimes been dismissed as a personal eulogy to a colleague and friend. But its legitimacy is supported by a handwritten commentary on school regulations he made in the mid

1730s specifying the cantor's duties in performance: 'It is sometimes necessary for the cantor to delegate the giving of the beat to a prefect, to give him the freedom to move around from one section of the ensemble to another to make sure everything is in good order.' This is backed up by another of Bach's pupils, Johann Christian Kittel, who described the unnerving experience of having Bach loom up behind him when he was playing harpsichord continuo: 'You always had to be prepared to have Bach's hands and fingers intervene among [your] hands and fingers . . . and, without getting in the way . . . furnish the accompaniment with masses of harmonies that made an even greater impression than the unsuspected close proximity of the teacher.'[31] Being on the inside of a Bach-directed performance, like the co-authors of his obituary, C. P. E. Bach and Johann Friedrich Agricola, had a similar effect:

> His constant practice in the working out of polyphonic pieces had given his eye such facility that even in the largest scores he could take in all the simultaneously sounding parts at a glance. His hearing was so fine that he was able to detect the slightest error even in the largest ensembles. It is but a pity that it was only seldom he had the good fortune of finding a body of such performers as could have spared him unpleasant discoveries of this nature. In conducting he was very accurate, and of the tempo, which he took very lively, he was uncommonly sure.[32]

Somehow you would expect Johann Adolph Scheibe, as a professional critic, to comment on those 'uncomfortable noises' that he claimed to be able to identify, things that spoilt Bach's polyphony in performance. But, rather than being due to any 'faults' in the compositions, they are just as likely to have been occasioned by flaws in execution by his under-rehearsed ensemble, or by the background noise within the church, or indeed by deficiencies in Scheibe's own hearing. A sign that things did not always go according to plan comes in Birnbaum's rebuttal to Scheibe, its rather defensive tone suggesting that this is Bach who is speaking:

> Now, when all this is performed as it should be, there is nothing more beautiful than this harmony. If, however, the clumsiness or negligence of the instrumentalists or the singers brings about confusion, it is truly very tasteless to attribute such mistakes to the composer. In music, anyway, everything depends on performance . . . a piece in whose composition one can see the most beautiful harmony and melody can certainly not please

the ear if those who are to perform it are unable and unwilling to fulfil their obligations.[33]

These contemporaneous accounts help us to appreciate not only the diversity of Bach's musical gifts but the evident frustrations he experienced when errors crept into the performance of his works. At another stage Birnbaum (or, rather, Bach putting words in his mouth) expresses his annoyance: 'It is true that there are difficulties, but that does not mean that they are insurmountable.' A system of quite harsh fines was enshrined in the school statutes – 'everyone must be attentive to the signs and beat of the *praecentor*. He who makes a slip or a noticeable mistake in the music will be fined 1 groschen [the equivalent of four pints of beer], but someone who makes a deliberate, mischievous error will be fined 3 groschen.'[34]

After Bach's death there was considerable discussion by the authorities, led by the school chairman Dr Carl Gottfried Winckler, on how best to reduce the extra rehearsal time on a Friday allocated to the cantor in times past for preparing 'Passion music' and works for other red-letter days in the church calendar. The implication is quite clear that, with Bach no longer making such intense musical demands on the student choir and orchestra, a new regularisation of everything within the ordinary curriculum of the Thomasschule was desirable, so that a single rehearsal on the Saturday afternoon should suffice for a normal Sunday, as it had in the past.[35] We simply do not know how Bach used this 'stolen' rehearsal time, or how in general he surmounted the constraints of time and the fallibility of his performers. One obvious way would have been to take principal singers and players aside and rehearse the most technically challenging passages privately, such as long arias with elaborate obbligati. In this, the school statutes are not especially illuminating beyond noting obligatory singing lessons in class, and we are left to fill in the gaps and to intuit what strategies other music directors have recourse to in similar situations.

This rehearsal pattern basically accords with that which we adopted for the Bach Cantata Pilgrimage in 2000. Each week we were confronted by a new clutch of cantatas, and, unlike Bach's regular forces, so used and attuned to his style of music and performing under his direction, it was a repertoire new to most people in the group, never previously having crossed their horizons. It was of course a daunting task, given the sheer quantity of music to assimilate and perform, the fact that the sources are incomplete in many cases, and above all the physical absence of the central figure, the composer as oracle, *fons et origo*, though he was very much present to us in the musical notation. To cope with the constraint of having only two or three days in which to rehearse a full programme of three or four cantatas, we divided up the ensemble into sections. I started rehearsals with just the solo singers (*Concertisten*) with the continuo and obbligato instruments, then moved on to separate sessions, first with choir and then with orchestra, and sometimes to subdivisions such as all the violins rehearsing with their leader. Sectional rehearsals function in a similar way to arranging pieces of a jigsaw puzzle before locking them together: corner pieces here, border pieces over there, sky-blue here, grass-green there, and so on. Eventually comes the *tutti* rehearsal and nearly always there is an exciting additional charge of energy as choir and orchestra perform together for the first time. This is the test of whether the earlier sectional rehearsing, when everyone was working independently, but along parallel lines, has been effective. There is the thrill of the totality now being so much greater than the sum of its individual parts.

This is where the really creative chemistry begins, and the process is similar to baking a cake. It begins with sieving and weighing all the constituent elements (flour, butter, sugar, etc.); but, their human equivalents being alive, you need to ensure that they all react organically to one another, taking responsibility for their respective roles and tasks. Because every musician is responding primarily to a single printed line of music that contains only his or her part, it is also the moment when each needs to switch on their aural radar and establish lateral awareness so that they find out rapidly how their line fits into the overall fabric. We know from Emanuel Bach that 'the placing of an orchestra he [Bach] understood perfectly: he made good use of any space.'[36] An intelligent spatial disposition and layout of both vocal and instrumental components can indeed help enormously in creating little cells of aural complicity, between, say, an obbligato player and a singer, or between larger sectional units such as violins and sopranos, where the meshing of decorative lines is critical. For every instrumentalist needs to know not only what the words of the singers *mean* but also what they *sound* like, so that they, in accompanying them, can match their shape, colour and expressive inflection, or, as Dreyfus points out about the ritornellos to arias: 'only once the words become known . . . will the rhetoric of persuasion become operative.'[37] The process is part cerebral, part physical and sensual, in some ways visual, but mostly, of course, aural. It is a 'freeing up', lifting eyes and ears away from the printed line or score, and responding to the different (almost electrical) impulses that are there to be given and exchanged.

It is at this stage, or thereabouts, that a new process begins. First, there is the gradual coming into focus for all performers of features that previously had been flattened out, or hitherto absent: intersections or collisions of music and text, variations of mood, passing associations with totally different modes of music. These occur only once all the other component elements are fully in place – tempo, balance and cohesive ensemble, close identification with the text and with all the quirks of the music. Then there is that other indefinable process whereby everyone's awareness of all the component elements becomes so acute (the way they differ from one another and yet cohere) that they seem to have gained an enhanced sense of clarity and understanding – or, as Philip Pullman describes it in *His Dark Materials*, 'going so deep you cannot see the bottom, but clear all the way down'. This is a process that cannot be forced. It is associated with the very special type of calm, concentrated attention musicians give and owe to the music. It allows all the many layers of meaning to become clear to the point where you can sense all the intricate connections between them. It is at this stage that you can gain a sense of naturalness or rightness about the way the music should unfold – *that* way and no other. (Tomorrow it may be quite different.) One defining feature of this experience is, of course, the human one: the atmosphere and vibrations set off by separate personalities within the performing group, the sum of various individual and collective initiatives which influence the interpretation and so have a bearing on the 'live' experience of the music (so different from one's detached reading of the score in the initial period of private study, although notation can also remind you of an experience you once had and be almost Pavlovian in its effect). Often it can come down to a single moment, one in which a potentially negative atmospheric charge can be switched in an instant to a positive one. It is like the legendary placement of a single pebble that can redirect the flow of even the strongest river. For if one can feel a connectedness of Bach's music to this degree and intensity when experiencing it at only stage three (*executio*), imagine, then, the force and potency of what it must have been like to experience the music in the hands of the person who created it and realised it first.

8
Cantatas or Coffee?

It is but a pity that in such a famous place [Leipzig], where the Muses have taken up their seat, there are at the same time so few connoisseurs and lovers of true music.

– Lorenz Christoph Mizler (1747)

Res severa est verum gaudium: 'True pleasure is a serious matter' – certainly to the Germans. Seneca's motto was adopted thirty years after Bach's death by Leipzig's famous orchestra and emblazoned on the walls of their Gewandhaus Concert Hall at its opening in 1781. Several rebuildings later it is still up there in capital letters, reminding audiences that listening to music requires giving it due attention. Whether it already applied in Bach's time – sufficient to quell the congenital inattentiveness and rowdiness of his male listeners in the first tier gallery as they gazed down at the ladies walking late into church – it undoubtedly reflected the intricate meshing of the secular and the sacred in his urban world. We see this epitomised in the frontispiece of a popular-song collection published in 1736. At first glance *Singende Muse an der Pleisse* is a portrayal of an elegant social gathering set against a panorama of Leipzig with views across its main river and some of the prominent buildings of the city's skyline. The ambivalence of location – a composite of coffee-house, inner salon and pleasure garden – is no doubt deliberate, designed to show how each is an appropriate and fashionable setting for music, itself a sign of civic wealth. In the middle distance we can pick out Schellhafers Haus,* an upmarket tavern in the

* The engraver was Christian Friedrich Boethius (1706–82); the author was Sperontes, the pen name of the poet Johann Sigismund Scholze (1705–50), who settled in Leipzig in the

Singende Muse an der Pleisse. *In the foreground two allegorical figures are busy making music together. Nearby, a lady plays the*

virginals while a gentleman appears to listen attentively; other couples are playing cards or billiards.

Catharinenstrasse where weekly concerts were held in wintertime, and opposite it, across the river, Apel's sumptuous gardens, later to delight the eye of Goethe ('glorious . . . the first time I saw them I thought I was in the Elysian Fields'[1]). But most prominent is the looming presence of the Thomaskirche, not the main city church (that was the Nikolai), but the symbol of its Orthodox Lutheran faith, with the richest musical tradition of any church within the German-speaking world.

Boethius's panorama depicts three of the main venues for public music-making in Leipzig – the church, the coffee-house and the pleasure gardens – leaving us to imagine the fourth – the market square and town centre where Bach, as the city's music director, put on grand displays of ceremonial music whenever the Elector or members of the royal family came to town and to which the whole city thronged. All in all, it suggests that citizens of Leipzig, like townspeople elsewhere in Europe, were (in the words of one social historian) 'caught between the imperative of appearing *galant* in a newly cosmopolitan world, and an older, still vigorously preached view that luxury and many secular activities were sins that invited divine punishment'.[2] This was the backdrop to the leisure activities of a burgeoning middle class, an urban society in the throes of re-adjusting its religion, intellect, taste, social customs and expectations. Young men of today, some complained, paid only lip service to Christianity and had trouble combining traditional values while cutting a *galant* and worldly figure.[3]

A short publication called *The Well-Designed and Abridged Housekeeping Magazine* appeared in Leipzig in 1730.[4] It aimed to give advice to those who aspired to improve their living conditions and to hoist them into conformity with the new cultural norms of the city. Beginning with the etiquette of serving lavish gourmet meals and the postprandial rituals of drinking coffee and pipe smoking, its author, called simply Bornemann, goes on to discuss appropriate household furnishings. He even selects suitable first-aid kits. Then, without any intended incongruity, he outlines what might constitute a well-stocked library to meet every conceivable material and spiritual need, such as 'for refreshing the spirit', 'for repent-

1720s and wrote plays and *Singspiel* texts. Three further volumes of his song anthology were to follow in 1742–5, comprising 250 poems that depict scenes and activities from everyday life set as simple *galant* strophic songs. Bach has been credited (somewhat unconvincingly) with two of them: 'Ich bin nun wie ich bin' and 'Dir zu Liebe, wertes Herze' (BWV Anh. II 40, 41).

ance, confession and Communion', 'for thorough extermination of all evils and fortification of the true faith'.[5] The recommended books include many by the same authors that are known to have been in Bach's private library, and show us how he attempted to keep pace with current literary fashions. Literature both serious and diversionary rubbed shoulders in such collections with volumes such as the *Serious-Humorous and Satirical Poems* by Picander, Bach's regular literary partner.[6]

Coinciding with the crisis caused by the deteriorating relationship with his employers on the town council (see Chapter 6) came a conspicuous switch of forum for Bach's most prominent musical activities: from the church to the coffee-house (in winter) and its gardens (in summer). To comprehend the social, liturgical and performance background for his public music-making in his Leipzig years, we need to explore these two parallel worlds of music, one sacred, one secular, and these two public meeting places, one over 500 years old, the other relatively new. How well did Bach adjust to these competing environments, how was his music received, and how did his profile change, both on arriving in Leipzig and after a few years in office? To answer these questions we should take into account signs of the *Aufklärung* that were now beginning to impinge on the urban intelligentsia of Leipzig, converging unexpectedly with the late surge in Lutheran Orthodoxy that was affecting all sections of society. Hegel may have stumbled on a truth when he observed that the German version of the Enlightenment was 'on the side of theology' – certainly as it applied to the performing arts.[7] In Bach's day the arts were still expected to impart some explicit moral, religious or rational meaning. It was not until the second half of the century that aesthetic concepts such as 'the Beautiful' and 'the Sublime' began to uncouple the artistic from the scientific and the moral.*

The ease with which music crosses frontiers meant that, even without the heavy investment in star performers that typified the Dresden Court

* Long before it was translated into German by Christian Garve in 1773, Edmund Burke's *A Philosophical Inquiry into the Origin of Our Ideas of the Sublime and the Beautiful* (1757) had an immediate impact on German aesthetics, influencing important thinkers such as Lessing, Kant and Herder. Lydia Goehr has pointed to the successive changes in aesthetic attitude that led theorists 'first, to abandon the belief that music should serve an extra-musical, religious, or social end, and then to adopt, in its place, the belief that instrumental music could be a fine and respectable art in service to nothing but itself' (Lydia Goehr, *The Imaginary Museum of Musical Works* (2007), pp. 146–7).

(inclining first towards French, then, on a change of electoral whim, switching to Italian styles in the 1730s), in Leipzig it could aspire to true cosmopolitan status. Music bolstered the city's image as 'Athens on the Pleisse', its reputation as fashionable 'Little Paris' (as Goethe called it) and even, according to Lessing, as 'a place where one can see the whole world in microcosm'.[8] The city's ability to boast an active opera house gave credence to these cultural pretensions, but with its collapse in 1720 – due as much to disputes over rental arrangements as to its huge operating debts – they were harder to justify. Though the Dresden Court was in favour of preserving it, as was a swathe of Leipzig's intelligentsia, its attractions were not enough to save it. For that to happen, the city's financiers would have needed to pool their resources, apply for a licence from the electoral court, surmount numerous bureaucratic hurdles and appoint a charismatic musical director such as Telemann, able to attract students.* The fact is that, for all its mercantile wealth and cultural aspirations, Leipzig in the middle years of the eighteenth century was no match for thriving, genuinely opera-minded cities like Dresden, Hamburg or London.

In Chapter 6 we saw how, thanks to the peculiarities of local government in Leipzig – entailing, for example, the alternation of mayors and their respective political affiliations – Bach as a municipal servant had to operate in a complex, intensely hierarchical urban environment, and struggle to force a path through the tangle of the city's dense bureaucratic and ecclesiastical regulations for at least the first six years. The city has been compared to an octopus: 'If one wriggles free of one arm, one is promptly seized by another.'[9] To Bach, the title 'Thomascantor' implied a socially inferior position, restricting his musical authority to within the church and school. He, but not the council, favoured the appellation 'Director Musices Lipsiensis'. But it was not until six years after taking up office that Bach could begin to substantiate his claim to the title of main director of the city's musical activities. This was partly a matter of protocol and partly from necessity, because he was devoting

* If things had worked out a little differently Bach might theoretically have found himself at the head of Leipzig's troubled opera theatre, which was closed in 1720 and eventually demolished in 1729. His entry into the world of opera was a lot closer than many have suspected, as Michael Maul has shown ('New Evidence on Thomaskantor Kuhnau's Operatic Activities; or, Could Bach Have Been Allowed to Compose an Opera?', Bach Network UK (2009)).

Seven hundred municipal street oil lamps were installed in Leipzig in 1701, by which 'many sins, especially against the 5th, 6th and 7th commandments, were remarkably checked and strongly hindered' (J. C. Vogler, 1714).

all his energies to composing church cantatas and Passions. In 1729, by taking over leadership of the *collegium musicum* (an independent, not a civic institution), Bach was signalling his bid to free himself from the council's control and to establish a solid independent basis for his activities as Director Musices of the city. The coffee-house and the church were its twin temples, and he could – and *would* – serve in both.* It was no accident that this move occurred just after an acrimonious altercation with the assistant deacon of the Thomaskirche over the right to choose the hymns for the vesper service, the customary prerogative of the cantor. Behind the councillors' dark warnings of a showdown that we encountered in Chapter 6, it is not difficult to imagine their displeasure at his latest bid for artistic autonomy and their contrary resolve to keep him in his place.

* One can almost hear his relief in the note he attached to an otherwise routine testimonial: 'PS. The latest is that the dear Lord has now also provided for honest Mr [Georg Balthasar] Schott [the previous organist of the Neukirche], and bestowed on him the post of Cantor in Gotha; wherefore he will say his farewells next week, as I am willing to take over his *collegium*' (BD I, No. 20/NBR, p. 132).

Of course, had they looked at things slightly differently, they might have acknowledged the palpable benefits to the city and welcomed the musical enrichment of the Sunday service. Finding volunteer instrumentalists good enough to play figural music was an age-old problem, one that had defeated Bach's predecessors as cantors and was to frustrate his successors. What the city most needed, according to Burgomaster Gottfried Lange in 1723, was a musical celebrity able 'to animate the students'[10] – in other words, someone who could attract skilled labour willing to play free of charge at the Sunday services of the two main churches. At last, Lange might have thought, his man was vindicating his support. Wasn't Bach's new access to a number of student or semi-professional instrumentalists prepared to augment the core group of Thomaner and Stadtpfeifer and to play in church from time to time on a quid pro quo basis, exactly what Lange and his supporters on the council had always hoped for? Such a system of exchange was accepted elsewhere as a matter of course and had been tried twenty years earlier in Leipzig in Telemann's time, but its success had depended upon a favourable alignment of the opera, the Neukirche and the *collegium* concerts, and so far it had never worked to the benefit of the two main city churches.

As the newly appointed head of the *collegium musicum*, Bach now had the chance to turn things around. Provided he could trade private lessons for playing at church services or offer a platform to ambitious performers at his coffee-house concerts, it was an arrangement that might prove workable, at least from time to time, since the participation of university students in church services would not then be a drain on council funding. But the problems ran deeper. The tipping point for Bach in his dispute with the council came in early June 1729. On 24 May they had finally agreed to the admission of unmusical *Alumnat* boys to the Thomasschule. In so doing, they had cut off Bach's supply of adequate singers, and from now on he would no longer have vocal forces competent enough to do justice to the intricate figural opening choruses that had been the most dazzling feature of his first two Leipzig cantata cycles.

It was at this point that Bach conceived the idea of a 'protest cantata', an opportunity to make a public and very audible case for changing the basis of church music in Leipzig. On Whit Monday 1729 the newly appointed head of the *collegium musicum* made sure that his best instrumentalists were on parade in the Thomaskirche, giving them a prominent role in a new cantata, BWV 174, *Ich liebe den Höchsten von ganzem Gemüte*, which opened with a quasi-orchestral and harmonically expanded version of his third Brandenburg Concerto. Judging by the surviving performing material, this was a fairly last-minute decision: into the new score, he instructed his copyist to transfer the original concerto lines for nine solo strings (three each of violins, violas and cellos) who now constituted a *concertino* group set against a brand-new independent *ripieno* ensemble comprising two horns, three oboes and four doubling string parts. These last he composed straight into score. Immediately, even with one instrument per part supplemented by violone, bassoon and keyboard continuo, Bach was able to feature a band of over twenty players, one able to provide a magnificent sonic display. With instrumental colours and rhythms even sharper than before, and the strings shining in their solo episodes, this was Bach's ebullient, rather secular-sounding way to open the celebrations to this Whit Monday feast and with not a single singer audible. It was given (presumably) under the approving eye of the man who up to now Bach might have seen as his main ally, Burgomaster Gottfried Lange.

Few of the listeners present, including Lange, could have been in any doubt that this was a polemical statement. In its instrumental opulence the *sinfonia* of the cantata dwarfs all its other movements. It was a defiant demonstration to the council of what was theirs for the taking if only they would cease their niggardly refusal to divert sufficient funds to augment the Thomasschule forces and thereby add musical lustre to the feasts of the church. The cantata's remaining movements comprise just two arias separated by a recitative in which Bach points up the plainness of the vocal writing – clearly intended not to overtax his Thomaner soloists – and follows it with a plain four-part chorale, in marked contrast to the livelier, virtuosic writing for obbligato instruments played by the older *collegium* students. It was the second prong of Bach's demurral: in effect, he was telling the councillors that 'if you cut off my supply of musically gifted boys, you leave me with no alternative but to shrink my vocal and choral contributions to church music.'

* * *

Had Lange or any other of his fellow councillors sought admission to Zimmermann's coffee-house later that autumn, they would have found exactly the same players performing BWV 201, *Geschwinde, geschwinde, ihr wirbelnden Winde*, Bach's new secular *dramma per musica*, entitled 'The Contest between Phoebus and Pan' in the autograph score – a satirical skit on pedantic, ill-informed critics whose utterances are ridiculed through the downward bray of a donkey over an octave and a half. From Bach's perspective, then, there were no insurmountable obstacles for moving from one forum to another or from one genre to another, as the formulations we encounter on the title pages of his publications confirm. Expanding on the celebrated formulation by the fifteenth-century theorist Johannes Tinctoris – *Deum delectare, Dei laudes decorare* ('To please God, to embellish the praise of God') – Bach had defined music's purpose in his *Orgel-Büchlein* as 'For the highest God alone honour; for my neighbour that he may instruct himself from it.'[11] Beneath its flowery surface, we are shown the underlying didactic purpose of his collection, one close to the twin purposes of music in the Lutheran tradition: *die Ehre Gottes und des Nechsten Erbauung*[12] – for giving honour to God (the standard Orthodox position) and for edifying one's neighbour (the slant favoured by the Pietists).

Once Bach is ensconced in Leipzig his views begin to lean towards the more 'enlightened' formulations of musicians such as Friedrich Erhard Niedt,[13] embracing aesthetic pleasure as well as devotion and edification. We now find him adopting in his *Generalbasslehre* of 1738 a different two-fold purpose of music: '*zur Ehre Gottes und zulässiger Ergötzung des Gemüths* – 'for giving honour to God and for the permissible delight of the soul'.[14] He explains, 'And so the ultimate end or final purpose of all music . . . is nothing other than the praise of God and the recreation of the soul. Where this is not taken into account, then there is no true music, only a devilish bawling and droning.'[15] Behind these generalisations lies an assumption, if not exactly a claim, that by its dedication to 'the honour of God' his music would lead to the 'permissible delight of the soul' on the part of his musicians and listeners – as if, as Butt suggests, 'there were a mechanical connection between a sacred compositional intention and a secular, earthly effect'.[16] This was another way for Bach to affirm the unity of physical and spiritual natures, evidence of his awareness of changing public tastes and of living in a culture that was increasingly pluralistic and thus very different from that of his parents' generation.

It would be misleading, therefore, to assume from this two wholly distinct and contrasted styles of Bachian composition, as is implied by the authors of the *Nekrolog*: 'His very serious temperament drew him predominantly to hard-working, serious and profound music [*zur arbeitsamen, ernsthaften, und tiefsinnigen Musik*], but he could also, if it seemed necessary, particularly when playing, make himself comfortable with a light and jocular manner of thinking.'[17] In reality these categories were far from rigid, and we are just as likely to encounter the 'light and playful manner' in Bach's church cantatas as we are 'serious and profound' music in his instrumental concertos. With an interest in French courtly music aroused in his teens thanks to Georg Böhm in Lüneburg, Bach was by no means the first or only composer to introduce dance-derived forms into his church cantatas – and may well have attracted criticism for this even in a city where the French fashion for dancing was well entrenched.* Very possibly his *collegium* concerts at Zimmermann's café sometimes ended with a ball, just as they did at the rival establishment run by Johann Gottlieb Görner at Schellhafer's wine tavern.[18] Nor was Bach averse to making the occasional switch to composing in the new *galant* style, even if one of its characteristics – of sustaining the same tone throughout – curdled somewhat with his instinctive feel for unity through diversity. He was equally at ease providing 'a solemn music, with trumpets and timpani, at Zimmermann's gardens' to mark the Elector's accession to the throne on 5 October 1734, or for the torch-lit processions that led to crowd-filled celebrations in the town square.[19] (See illustration overleaf.)

Perhaps the writers of the *Nekrolog* were inadvertently hinting at a genuinely radical or subversive streak in Bach – his refusal to be tied down by convention to an appropriate *Affekt* in any given genre, something for which both his elder two sons were also later renowned. This is exactly what brings us up short when we come across slow movements of exceptional gravity, as in the Brandenburg Concertos or, at the

* 'Writing in 1752 to defend the use of dance rhythms in church music, Caspar Ruetz, cantor in Lübeck [*Widerlegte Vorurtheile von der Beschaffenheit der heutigen Kirchenmusic*], illustrated this perspective when he wrote, "If we should not bring into the church even the least thing that belongs to dancing, we would have to leave feet and hands, indeed the whole body, at home." For him the dance floor was no dishonourable or sinful place but rather "the school of elegance, courtesy and bodily dexterity". And if church music could promote "hopping and jumping in the hearts of upright Christians", why should rhythms that produce such spiritual pleasure be avoided?' (Joyce Irwin, 'Bach in the Midst of Religious Transition' in *Bach's Changing World*, Carol K. Baron (ed.) (2006), p. 121). Doubtless Pietists would have been apoplectic, but Bach, along with Scheibel, would surely have agreed.

Friedrich August II, Elector of Saxony, receiving the homage of the inhabitants of Leipzig on 20–21 April 1733 in the market square.

other extreme, the palm-court levity of a church cantata like BWV 181, *Leichtgesinnte Flattergeister*, as we saw in Chapter 7. This delightful wrong-footing of the listener, this criss-crossing from the secular to the sacred, while it may be a feature of Baroque culture in general and common practice in a mercantile and university town like Leipzig, turns out also to be a defining characteristic of Bach's compositions. Yet, for every one of his listeners who took issue with him for the inappropriate theatricality of his church music, there may have been others, looking up from their card-tables while sipping their coffee, who objected to the undue seriousness of some of his instrumental music. They might even have agreed with Count Pococurante in Voltaire's *Candide* (1759) that 'this noise can give half an hour's amusement; but if it lasts any longer it bores everyone, though no one dares to admit it . . . Music today is nothing more than the art of performing difficult pieces, and what is merely difficult gives no lasting pleasure.'

* * *

The founding of Leipzig city concerts can be traced back to the 1650s, when an informal gathering of musicians drawn mainly from university students began meeting regularly in the house of Councillor Sigismund Finckthaus under the musical direction of the colourful Johann Rosenmüller. These student *collegia* came and went depending on the initiative and drawing power of successive musical luminaries – such as the head Stadtpfeifer, Johann Christoph Pezel, or Thomascantors such as Sebastian Knüpfer and Johann Kuhnau. Kuhnau boasted of the opportunities his ensemble gave to young *studiosi* 'to refine further their excellent art, and in part, too, because they learn from the pleasing harmonies how to speak together concordantly', adding rather acidly, 'even though these same people mostly disagree with one another at other times'.[20]

But it was with the arrival in 1701 of Telemann as a law student that things really took off. Before then, music had been a leisure-time activity for musically minded students; under Telemann's aegis his *collegium musicum* became a major star in the city's musical firmament. Rapidly redirected towards public performance in three separate venues – in Johann Lehmann's coffee-house (the Schlaffs Haus in the market square), at the Neukirche (which was still at the time also the university church) and at the Leipzig Opera – the ensemble was now successful enough to be put on a professional, fee-paying basis. For as long as the opera house was viable, students keen to supplement their budgets and to gain experience and contacts could now be active in one way or another in all the main musical goings-on of the city.* These multiple performing activities linked by venue and personnel were epitomised by the custom of afternoon run-throughs of selected arias given in Lehmann's café that would be heard on stage at the opera later that evening – advance publicity for the composer and lucrative for *Hofchocolatier* Lehmann, who, besides running the coffee-house in the town centre, had a concession to provide drinks and finger food at the opera-theatre.[21]

Bach's own association with the *collegia musica* may already have begun during his first visit to Leipzig in 1717 while he was still employed

* Even after Telemann's departure in 1705 the tripartite stand of his orchestra's activities remained firm – first under Melchior Hoffmann (with the famous violinist Johann Georg Pisendel as leader and Gottfried Heinrich Stölzel as assistant composer), then under Johann David Heinichen, while a separate, twenty-strong ensemble was led by Johann Friedrich Fasch.

at the Cöthen Court. It was certainly cemented at the beginning of his Leipzig tenure, first as principal guest conductor,* and then from 1729 as director of the larger of the two *collegia*. There was, however, a subtle difference in the rationale of the two groups. Where Johann Gottlieb Görner's university *collegium* was designed to help train future cantors and organists ('ein *exercitium* vor die *Studiosos*'), Bach's saw itself as an elite ensemble of virtuoso instrumentalists who played to divert and delight members of the public.[22] Bach remained in charge of it for the next eight years (1729–37); then after a gap of two years (during which he still guest conducted) he resumed control until at least 1741.† Under his aegis the ensemble performed once a week for two hours all through the year: in summer from 4 to 6 p.m. on Wednesdays in Gottfried Zimmermann's coffee-garden in the Grimmischer Steinweg outside the east gate of the city, and in winter from 8 to 10 p.m. on Fridays in Zimmermann's coffee-house in the centre of town (Catharinenstrasse No. 14).[23] (See opposite.) These weekly performances were doubled during the three annual trade fairs, when the group performed twice a week from 8 to 10 p.m. on Tuesdays and Fridays (each fair lasted three weeks). At

* In the Leipzig academic chronicle of 1 June 1723 Bach is mentioned not just as the new cantor but as 'director of the *collegium musicum*' (*Acta Lipsiensium academica* (1723), Vol. 5, p. 514). Was this a confusion arising from the fact that he also directed music at the university or a slip of the reporter's pen? Further evidence of his early involvement with the *collegium* has recently come to light. The original parts of the First Orchestral Suite (BWV 1066) date from 1724, and Heinrich Nikolaus Gerber reported that during the first six months of his Leipzig sojourn in 1724/5, before meeting Bach personally, he had heard not merely outstanding church music but 'a good many concerts under Bach's direction' (see BD III, No. 476).

† Michael Maul has uncovered evidence to suggest that this little interregnum was not of Bach's volition. His former pupil-turned-tormentor, Johann Adolph Scheibe, was then in the midst of a campaign of self-promotion, paying heavy court to Carl Gotthelf Gerlach, a musician whose competence he had earlier set out to demolish in a coded attack as someone having no knowledge in composition – 'Therefore he must always perform music by other composers, sometimes pretending to be the creator of these works.' Bach seems to have been caught in the slipstream: either there had been a *Putsch* within the *collegium* to dispense with his services, or, thoroughly disgruntled, he left of his own accord (BJb (2010), pp. 153ff.). Had he been a little more sensitive to their situation, he might have seen that besides Gerlach, two other *collegium* colleagues, Johann Gottlieb Görner and Johann Schneider, had been mauled even more savagely by Scheibe – and instructed Magister Birnbaum to include them in his rebuttal. The fact that he didn't probably meant that they in turn were indifferent to his decision to resign from the *collegium musicum*.

Zimmermann's coffee-house, marked 2. Örtelische, *referring to his landlord, Theodor Örtel, who bought the house in 1727.*

these coffee-house events, or *ordinaire concerten*, as they were called at the time, the precursors of late-eighteenth-century public concerts, audiences could hear the latest in *galant* instrumental ensemble music as well as concertos for one or more harpsichords performed by Bach and his sons, and, more rarely, secular Italian cantatas and opera arias performed by touring musicians. Opera lovers – still smarting in disappointment at the closure of the opera house in 1720 and still whistling snippets of arias they had first heard there – had to set aside a whole day's travel to Dresden in order to satisfy their addiction.

Excursus: *The protocol and rules for the Leipzig* collegium musicum *have not survived. The nearest we have is a summary of the rules for one founded in Greiz in 1746 by the Leipzig-born Johann Gottfried Donati. Its members were usually professional or pre-professional musicians, organists and court musicians, lackeys, and two pupils or apprentices.*

1. Rehearsals are from 3 to 5 p.m. Wednesdays (2 to 4 p.m. in winter). At least five works are to be played and rehearsed until there are no more errors, beginning with an overture and ending with a symphony.
2. Members are fined one groschen for every fifteen minutes they are late.
3. Everyone must play his or her appointed instrument unless otherwise directed.
4. If members are not playing in a given piece they should remain quiet or be fined one groschen.
5. Four-groschen fine if you skip a rehearsal unless it is through a summons to perform at court or on account of illness.
6. Keep your instrument in good shape, or be fined one groschen.
7. Fighting or arguing will incur a fine of two groschen.
8. Tune carefully to the Clavecin.
9. The deplorable habit of musicians of doodling [*fantasieren*] on their instruments between pieces, particularly during recitatives in church music, is bad, as it creates a *Mischmasch* for the listeners, causing such an inconvenience to their musical understanding as to give them toothache, or a stitch in the side.
10. Pay close attention to the much loved *piano* and *forte*. Play only the notes the composer wrote and without fancy arpeggios in between them.
11. By failing to learn your part or by making a mess of things you will be fined four groschen the first time and eight the second. After this you may be thrown out.
12. Do not drink or smoke until the time for it is allowed, or be fined one groschen.
13. Any honest person is free to attend the concert, but needs to pay two groschen.
14. The fines and other fees are to be paid into a charitable pot.
15. Every year there is a banquet to celebrate the founding of the *collegium musicum*.
16. Now and then the *collegium musicum* will buy new instruments. Members should not lend them out.
17. All members are obliged to attend church services. The main goal of the ensemble is to serve their masters and neighbours.[24]

It has been estimated that Bach was in charge of sixty-one two-hour *collegium* secular concerts each year for a period of at least ten years, which works out at more than 1,200 hours of music, compared with the 800 hours entailed in providing church cantatas lasting a half-hour or so over his twenty-seven years as Thomascantor.[25] These figures are of course approximate, and, since we have neither detailed programmes for the concerts nor reliable information about Bach's compositional contribution to them, they do not necessarily reflect an unequal distribution of Bach's own creative output across the two categories. But they do raise the question of how Bach prioritised his activities at any given stage – his differing roles as composer, performer and concert promoter. It is possible that he attached more weight to the prestige of leading the *collegium musicum*, to the autonomy of action it afforded him and to the de facto contact it generated with the Dresden Court than was previously thought. At the very least these statistics provide a startling corrective to the slewed image of Bach's activities and output presented by nineteenth-century biographers, who placed an overwhelming emphasis on his church music and who pushed secular music to the margins.

* * *

The first in a string of coffee-houses in Leipzig opened in 1694 in Schlaffs Haus, a property next to the Elector's temporary residence in the Marktplatz, although some claim it was pipped to the post nine years earlier by a rival establishment known as Zum Kaffeebaum, which is still open for custom today. Over the entrance to Zum Kaffeebaum there is sculpture of a cupid handing a coffee cup to a languid recipient, a *galant* Leipzig burgher to the waist and below that something of a Turk. Inside at one time there was a painting of 'an oriental figure with all imaginable accessories ... said to have been a gift from August the Strong, who in 1694 had enjoyed the good coffee (or, as others would have it, the hostess)'.[26] These exotic trappings and the brown beverage's reputation as an aphrodisiac ensured that from then on the city's consumption of coffee increased dramatically, explaining why several of its taverns were converted into coffee-houses. Identified as prime sites for prostitutes to 'establish' themselves, especially at the time of the fairs, the council twice (in 1697 and 1704) passed an ordinance banning all women from entering coffee-houses either for work or to consume coffee on the premises. Patently these had little effect, for a lexicon of the time mentions 'coffee-trollops' (*Caffe-Menscher*) among the regular clientele: 'questionable and dissolute women who serve men in coffee-houses and render them all desired services'.[27] No doubt this was the kind of thing Julius Bernhard von Rohr had in mind when advising his young cavaliers to be on their guard and only to frequent coffee-houses in large towns that stand 'in guter *Reputation*'.[28]

Despite the calls for close regulation and even an electoral ban on new establishments, by 1725 seven more coffee-houses had opened their doors.[29] The frontispiece of a popular local treatise by Daniel Duncan, *On the Misuse of Hot and Fiery Food and Drinks* (1707), shows how upper-class women, in defiant solidarity, formed 'coffee-circles' in their own homes so as to ensure unimpeded enjoyment of the beverage.[30] Duncan then explains that since this sex 'does not have as much to do, [coffee] serves in place of an activity, and women drown their cares in coffee just as we drown ours in wine.'[31] To make sure everyone has got the message, Duncan then has his women say: 'Even if we all drink ourselves into the grave, / it'll still be the fashionable way to behave' (*Sauffen wir uns gleich zu Tode, / so geschiehts doch nach der Mode*). In his *Universal-Lexicon*, Zedler claimed that coffee makes the mind subtler, increases (temporary) vigour and 'can drive . . . the fog from [your head]'. Yet he too points to the potential dangers: it can over-stimulate the senses, weaken the body and create a jaundiced look. Taken to excess, it leads to impotence in men, miscarriage in women and diminished mutual sexual attraction. In London, the damage caused by excessive consumption of cakes and ale was harped upon by the intolerant and zealous high Puritans of Shakespeare's day; so in Bach's Leipzig, Pietist preachers considered overdosing on coffee just as reprehensible as the 'misuse of music' in church. The twin vices of coffee and church music fuelled the Pietists' recoil from the overindulgence prevalent in the secular culture (see Chapter 2, p. 33).

Leipzigers' taste for coffee – now at least as old as Bach himself and threatening to become one of the most talked about foibles of its high society – was a theme ripe for satirical treatment. Bach's so-called *Coffee Cantata* (BWV 211) dates from 1734 – just a few months after a professor of botany at the university had submitted a dissertation on the dangers of excessive coffee-drinking and been promoted as a result. Bach's chosen librettist was Picander, who had provided him with the text of the *Matthew Passion* (see Chapter 11) and countless church cantatas; he was on hand with a ready-made text already set to music by at least two other composers. One of Picander's spoken comedies, *Die Weiber-probe*, published in 1725 and 'designed to uplift and entertain the spirit', introduces two women: Frau Nillhorn ('Mrs Hippo') declares she would rather cut off her finger than miss her coffee; and Frau Ohnesafft ('Mrs Dried-Old-Prune') warns, 'If I must pass a day without coffee, you shall have a corpse on your hands by evening.'[32] Here are the models for young Liesgen (or perhaps her aunts), intent in the *Coffee Cantata* on defying the empty threats of her grumpy old codger of a father, Schlendrian (literally 'lazy bones'). It was an ideal piece for Bach to perform with his *collegium musicum* at their usual concert venue, and for Herr Zimmermann it was obviously excellent publicity. No need for gods dressed up as Baroque royalty or cardboard cut-outs of shepherds and shepherdesses: the domestic peccadilloes and irritations of those around him could provide Bach with all the material he needed. First, get the audience to pay attention – not via an overture but by a direct appeal in recitative: 'Be quiet, stop chattering, and listen to what's about to happen.' As a harassed parent there was nothing he did not know about the vexations of living (and of having to compose) in a house full of querulous children and with a rowdy boys' dormitory overhead or in the next room: the chains of rotating semi-quavers that introduce Schlendrian's bear-like grumbling could almost be the germs of his own musical ideas locked in enforced routine and desperate to break free. Even the cadences on *Hudelei* – an onomatopoeic word that combines 'annoyance' with 'work badly done' (or, in slang, 'masturbation') – spin off in random directions.

For a composer practised at sliding barbed references and covert satirical pen-portraits of his clerical tormentors into his church cantatas, this was a singularly good-humoured portrayal. The father's other aria, 'Mädchen, die von harten Sinnen' ('Stubborn girls aren't easily won over'), shows how well Bach could bridge the worlds of church and café: with its twists and turns, the angular *ostinato* bass line is remarkably similar to the one he had composed in BWV 3/iii that paints 'Hell's anguish and torment'. It gains a comic edge as a result of its sexual innuendo – a temptation to a girl even stronger than her weakness for coffee. But then, from the pretty and disarming music he allots to Liesgen, you feel Bach to be on her side. In the first of her two arias he contrives an ambivalence of verbal stress and metre wavering between $\frac{3}{4}$ and $\frac{3}{8}$, as though she and her accompanying flute, with their heads high in the clouds, are hankering (like Jonathan Swift and his Vanessa) after the sweetness of something beyond mere coffee. It seems that in some way Bach was recalling the rich subtext and multiple double entendres of his cousin Johann Christoph's wedding cantata, *Meine Freundin, du bist schön*, discussed in Chapter 3.

We fully expect the cantata to end once the father Schlendrian has finally trapped his daughter into giving up her addiction by threatening to forbid her to marry. And that is indeed where Picander's published text (1732) finishes – so far, so typical of the male view of women of the time. But that is not what Bach had in mind. He begins composing the ninth strophe on two separate bifolios, as though pointing it in another, rather more interesting direction: in place of a banal truce between father and daughter in a final duet, we have instead the return of the narrator – an invention of Bach's, not Picander's. It is possible that Bach initially planned to set just Picander's dialogue for Liesgen and Schlendrian, and only later decided that an opening recitative was necessary to establish the scene and quell the coffee-drinkers. But from that point on he was pretty well also committed to a final recitative and a *tutti* for all three voices telling the audience that, while old Schlendrian is on the prowl looking for a suitable son-in-law, Liesgen has put it about in town that she will insist on a 'pre-nup' – one that guarantees her the right to drink coffee whenever she wants. The original satire is thus turned on its head. The tenth stanza brings about a sort of reconciliation – a compromise between a conventional outcome and a more radical one for this domestic comedy. In chorus, all three voices (father, daughter and narrator) agree: 'The cat will not leave off chasing mice, maidens will remain coffee-sisters.' They recall that both the mother and grandmother have been coffee addicts – so why should they worry about the daughter? This chimes with the proverb of the day: 'A good coffee must be as hot as the kisses of a girl on the first day, as sweet as her love on the third day, and as black as her mother's curses when she finds out about it.'*

* * *

* Every German child knows the *Kaffee-Kanon* by Carl Gottlieb Hering (1766–1853), which goes: *C-a-f-f-e-e, trink nicht zu viel Kaffee, nicht für Kinder ist der Türkentrank, schwächt die Nerven, macht dich blass und krank. Sei doch kein Muselmann, der das nicht lassen kann!* ('C-o-f-f-e-e, don't drink too much coffee. This Turkish brew is not for children, weakens your nerves and will make you sick and pale. Don't be like a Muslim, who can't keep his hands off it!').

Stepping back for a moment, we can begin to assess what kind of authority was conferred on Bach as a performer-composer by where he and his performers were physically placed at successive junctures in his working life. How might he have presented himself – as organist, harpsichordist and conductor – to his listeners across his vast repertory? All through his career the physical location for his liturgical and public music-making varied considerably. It was one thing for him to play harpsichord while directing hand-picked colleagues in the intimate secular drawing-room setting of the Spiegelsaal at the Cöthen Court, and quite another to perform in a church setting, either as organist or as cantor. Visibility had a considerable bearing on how his music was received. The layout of churches might vary from the barn-like Neukirche in Arnstadt, where in his first post as organist he was in full view and had the whole packed church gazing up at him, to the cramped musicians' gallery high up in the private chapel of the dukes of Weimar cut in the ceiling, where he and his small ensemble were out of sight to the Duke and his guests. This created a vertical sound perspective in which the music floated downwards as though from celestial spheres – a metaphor for the unfathomable perfection of God-directed music and an explanation of the chapel's name, Weg zur Himmelsburg ('the path to the heavenly castle').* (See Plate 8.)

At the opposite extreme, watching at close quarters from up in the organ loft as Bach performed, the twelve-year-old Landgrave of Kassel was so transfixed by the miraculous way 'he ran over the pedals ... as if his feet had wings, making the organ resound with such fullness, and so penetrate the ears of those present like a thunderbolt ... that he drew a ring with a precious stone from his finger and gave it to Bach as soon as the sound had died away'.[33] Public response to Bach's organ-playing in cities such as Dresden, Hamburg, Halle and Potsdam and at all stages

* The layout of the Himmelsburg accords with what Christoph Wolff describes as 'the Hebrew notion of the presence of the invisible prompted by a physical phenomenon' (see *Bach: The Learned Musician* (2000), p. 339) – a concept that appealed to Bach, as can be deduced from the annotation he made in his Calov Bible to a section that deals with the presence of the invisible God at the divine service in the Temple. Verse 13 of II Chronicles 5 ends with the words, 'when they lifted up their voice with the trumpets and cymbals and instruments of music, and praised the Lord ... then the house was filled with a cloud.' At this point Bach added his celebrated comment: 'NB Where there is devotional music, God with His grace is always present.' (See Plate 13.) Wolff explains, 'music prompted the appearance of the glory of God in the cloud, and the cloud demonstrated God's presence.'

in his career seems to have been almost as enthusiastic. In *Bach's Feet*, David Yearsley suggests that Bach was fully aware of the powerful visual spectacle of his extravagant mastery as organist and the impact his playing had on bystanders – the wonderful machinery up there, with him busy doing fiendishly difficult and intricate manoeuvres: 'The feeling of power beyond human scale, enjoyed by all organists at the controls of these giant constructions, is magnified by the visual impression of these stolen, neck-straining views: playing with feet and hands was an often aerobic activity that required a good deal of stretching, swivelling, and balancing . . . a physical feat unparalleled in other modes of music-making.'[34] Indeed, it became the stuff of legend. Ernst Ludwig Gerber, whose father had studied with Bach in Leipzig, marvelled at his superhuman technique:

> On the pedals his feet had to imitate with perfect accuracy every theme, every passage that his hands had played. No appoggiatura, no mordent, no short trill was suffered to be lacking or even to meet the ear in less clean and rounded form. He used to make long double trills with both feet, while his hands were anything but idle.[35]

None of this was on regular display to music-lovers in Leipzig, where Bach spent the last twenty-seven years of his life and where such authority might have given him a boost when he was locked in dispute with his employers. It may have been his reputation as an organ virtuoso that qualified him for the post there as cantor, but it was somebody else's job to play and impress with the organ in church. Leipzig rarely heard Bach, the supreme organist of the day, or saw him rule over 'the most responsive, all-encompassing, powerful, and advanced musical technology . . . [the way] he could impress distant listeners with both his fantastical playing and his polyphonic brilliance'.[36] Directing a choir and orchestra from the west galleries of the two main churches in Leipzig, out of sight of three quarters of the congregation unless they strained their necks, was quite a different proposition. Bach as conductor may have exerted a complete and hyperactive command of his performing ensembles (as witnessed by headmaster Gesner in the last chapter (p. 237) as well as by those wealthy citizens and council members with their reserved pews and boxes close to the choir gallery); but it is small wonder that in terms of public perception less authority (and far less glamour) was conferred on Bach in his roles of choir-master and conductor than on Bach the virtuoso organist.

* * *

The church in Bach's day was still the focal point of Leipzig society. For its citizens it was a meeting place: with God, but also with their neighbour, week in, week out. The three decades following the Thirty Years War had seen a sharp increase in church attendance. Leipzig's two main churches, the Thomaskirche and the Nikolaikirche, had become steadily more crowded on Sundays, and in 1694 the town council authorised the renovation of two dilapidated churches. The deconsecrated Franciscan Barfüsserkirche was reopened for Lutheran use as the Neukirche in 1699 and soon became the centre for avant garde church music, followed a decade later by the re-modelling of the Paulinerkirche. The Georgenkirche was built around the same time, and finally the fifteenth-century Petrikirche was extended in 1712. By now Leipzig, as a church ordinance put it, had become a 'city of churches'[37] in which there were twenty-two Lutheran services with sermons to choose from every week, with new midweek Communion services and even more prayer services. Doctrinal teaching each Sunday was given from 'six pulpits in six separate houses of God',[38] with plenty of variety in the fare on offer in the two largest churches and the smaller more peripheral ones; the university church occupied yet another niche and provided services slanted towards different sectors of society.[39] There was protracted power play between the consistory and the council over pretty well everything: disputes arose about major building works, the precise shape and content of the different liturgies, the nature of the congregation whom they were supposed to be addressing, right down to the choice of hymns and how best to conduct catechism sessions. To this already complicated situation, periodic interventions by the electoral authorities in Dresden added a further layer of conflict – a sign that secular categories of status, gender and property had already spilt over into the religious arena.

The main service, or Hauptgottesdienst, which alternated Sunday by Sunday between the Thomaskirche (the church favoured by the court party) and the Nikolaikirche (the Estates Party's preferred church), constituted the principal religious and social event of the week, beginning at 7 a.m. and lasting up to four hours. Even today the phenomenon of around 9,000 of the urban community (from a total population of *circa* 30,000) convening on a Sunday at the Hauptgottesdienst in one of the two main city churches – and, once full, spilling over into the minor churches or obliged to attend later services – would have the power to impress us. Throughout the year (except during Lent and Advent) it provided Bach with the largest audiences he was ever to address – up to 2,500 congregants seated in pews with additional seats and standing room for a further 500, and 'common women' seated on the stairways that led up to the balconies or galleries.* Yet how many people were actually present in church when the moment came for the cantata to be performed? As we shall soon see, this was the moment for which many worshippers timed their entrance with theatrical panache.

The two main churches in Leipzig were laid out like opera-theatres, according to social rank. The more prestigious seats (individual *Stühle* or *Stände*, equipped with locks and keys) were arranged in rectangular blocks, as opposed to the simpler benches (*Bänke*). Right up to the 1760s they were handed down as debenture seats to successive generations of a family by the rules of secular inheritance (just as they do today in the major Italian opera houses, in London's Royal Albert Hall and at Wimbledon), and could be rented out or sold for considerable sums of money. There was separation by class, profession and gender – with women on the ground floor, the most coveted seats being closest to the preacher in his pulpit, and the men mostly in the balconies (exactly the opposite to synagogues). In this way the leading citizens and polite families were split up and scattered around the church; for *hoi polloi* there was standing room only at the back.

Though technically the property of the church, pews were valued as status symbols – home ownership was a prerequisite to 'holding' a pew, and there were elaborate regulations surrounding the passing of title from one holder to the next. From the 1660s areas traditionally kept for the unpropertied classes were gradually appropriated by newly powerful city councillors, who enclosed groups of already existing pews and constructed their own private Capellen, often with separate entrances, so that they and

* These numbers do not include servants and other workers whose choices for attendance were limited to a shorter midday service, 'since they were prevented from attending the early service either because of lack of sitting- or standing-room or because of necessary and permissible work' (Adam Bernd, *Eigene Lebens-Beschreibung* (1738), pp. 96–7).

their families could sit together without having to interact with ordinary parishioners – in violation of the Lutheran injunction to worship God in the company of one's neighbour. Far from constituting a single meeting of the faithful, a priesthood of all believers in which everybody is spiritually equal before God, the interior design of the two main churches and the social stratification of the seating arrangements operated directly against the notion of a united Lutheran congregation brought together for the sole purpose of communal worship. Over thirty Capellen were built in each of the main churches, some furnished with their private libraries and stoves and acting almost as second homes to members of the social elite. Adam Bernd describes how prominent citizens could disrupt a sermon by talking at the tops of their voices or even laughing out loud from their secluded positions in their Capellen. Presumably they did the same during the performance of the cantata. One female character in Gottsched's *Die vernünfftigen Tadlerinnen* (*The Reasonable Tatleresses*) (1725) cattily comments about another, 'I doubt whether she would even go to church if she did not have her own Capelle in which she could take shelter from the vulgar odours of the common people by closing the windows.'[40]

The main Sunday service was structured in such a way as to involve the public at all the traditional points, such as the move to the altar for the Communion, the cue to stand for congregational hymns and the passing round of the collection bags with jingling bells attached – a suggestive and perhaps effective way to prise coins from pockets and purses. The quality of congregational hymn-singing seems to have varied from the sublime (Ulm in 1629) to the really deplorable (Bautzen in 1637). In 1703, according to one contemporary source, 'it is frequently in utter disarray: some sing quickly, some slowly; some pull the pitch upwards, some downwards. Some sing at the second, others at the fourth, this one at the fifth, that one at the octave, each according to his own pleasure. There is no order, no rhythm, no harmony, no grace, but for the most part pure confusion.'[41] By the time that first Kuhnau and then Bach were at the helm in Leipzig, standards there were probably well above average; but we cannot be sure. What remained of the old Pietist mantra: that elaborate figural music shut worshippers out, turning them into passive bystanders so that their minds wandered, whereas congregational singing made them active participants and therefore more devout? Some still turned back to St Augustine for support: 'When it happens that the singing entertains me more than what is sung moves

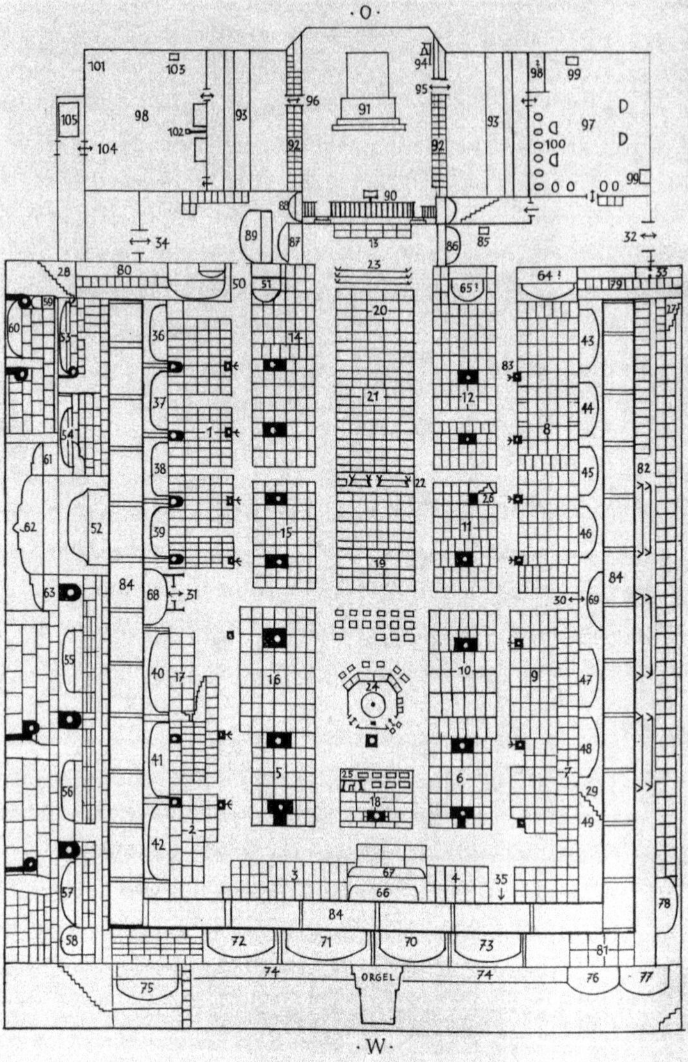

Abb. 11a: Schema nach dem Gestühlplan von 1780. Zeichnung von Lotte Schumann

58

This reconstruction of the seating arrangements shows rectangular blocks of debenture pews and the wide bays allocated to the choristers (Nos. 70–73). (From Arnold Schering, Johann Sebastian Bachs Leipziger Kirchenmusik, Studien und Wege zu ihrer Erkenntnis, *Breitkopf & Härtel, 1954. Reproduced by permission.)*

me, then I am culpable and would much rather never have heard the song.'[42] Modern advocates of figural music could not refute this outright: its purpose, they maintained, was 'to instruct the audience in a genteel and agreeable manner' (Bokemeyer), 'to edify the audience' (Scheibe) and to move their emotions (Mattheson). In 1721 Gottfried Ephraim Scheibel put the case for stylistic unity succinctly: 'The musical tone which gives pleasure in the opera can do the same in the church, just with a different object of the pleasure'[43] – a view by no means universally shared. The vast majority needed to be enticed to come to church – and here, Scheibel insisted, was one effective inducement. Further objections – not necessarily by Pietists – to the intrusion of styles of music linked to popular entertainment seeping into church can be found all through the 1720s. The Berlin-based cantor Martin Heinrich Fuhrmann fulminated against composers 'who pour Italian operatic "soft cheese" [nonsense, in other words] into church music'. He likened the resulting pieces to 'pork-veal roasts' and 'Italian spiritual *cervelas* sausages' made of rotten donkey or mule meat in order to poison the German Protestant church.[44]

More problematic still was the widespread habit of congregants arriving late and leaving early. The Leipzig churches were 'quite empty' at the start of the service, Johann Friedrich Leibniz noted in 1694, and, according to Christian Gerber, this was still the case nearly forty years later right across Saxony. To combat this, church ordinances were issued; ushers were appointed to stop people from rushing out 'like cattle' after the sermon; and preachers were instructed to admonish those who failed to enter church in time for the singing and hung about outside until the signal was given that the preacher was about to mount his pulpit. It seems that the more chic members of the municipal elite of Leipzig – especially its womenfolk – took pride in arriving anything up to an hour late. According to Gerber, this was because they were too lazy to get out of bed earlier and, unlike the 'common people' who did their work before going to church, these ladies spent too much time dressing, grooming themselves and drinking coffee.[45]* Making their

* Tanya Kevorkian (*Baroque Piety: Religion, Society, and Music in Leipzig 1650–1750* (2007), p. 24) refers to the inappropriate kinds of luxury and fashion on display in the Leipzig churches. In 1742 councillors voiced their concerns about a particular style of dress, the *Reifrock*, with skirts so wide that women could injure themselves by falling off the plinth next to the baptismal font ('Kirche zu St. Nicolaus Verordnungen und Nachrichten . . .' (1740–83), Stadtarchiv Leipzig, Stift. IX.B.4).

ostentatious entrance just in time for the sermon and under the full gaze of the men seated in the galleries inevitably led to elaborate attendant rituals of greeting – hat-removal, bowing, hand-shaking, etc. The consequent hullabaloo coincided exactly with the performance of the *Predigtmusik*, the Sunday cantata specially composed by Bach.

Gottsched satirises a young woman taking snuff and offering it to her male admirers from her pew,[46] while von Rohr scolds the young bucks for the way they parade their ill manners: they too arrive late, talk, sleep, disturb their neighbours by groaning and sighing during prayers, reading their letters or newspapers – behaviour they themselves would abhor in the opera house.[47] Congregants were in the habit of talking during the music, with the large population of soldiers and day labourers standing at the back of the church on any given Sunday taking most of the blame (as 'transients' they were forbidden by law from renting pews). There are visual parallels here in the paintings by Dutch artists such as Emanuel de Witte and Hendrick van Vliet, who portrayed dogs urinating in the whitewashed Oude Kerk in Delft. Against this background of people-gazing and running commentary, paper darts and other objects being thrown from the gallery on to the women seated below, the ogling of eligible young ladies and even the presence of dogs running amok in church, one might think that the music stood little chance of being heard.*

Of the many different shock techniques Bach developed in his church cantatas to grab the attention of his unsuspecting listeners while all this was going on, two instances stand out. Sunday, 15 October 1724, saw the first outing of BWV 5, *Wo soll ich fliehen hin?* A robust aria for bass with a ferociously demanding trumpet obbligato set against the

* In 1722 an electoral decree, reissued twice in the following years, attempted to counter the threat of a *turbatio sacrorum* brought about through 'inappropriate walking to and fro during the sermon and by throwing [objects] from the galleries on to the women beneath' (Christoph Ernst Sicul, *Annalium Lipsiensium*, Sectio XVII (1724), pp. 207–8). A Pietist writing to his father confessor wrote that 'during services and especially during Communion, a public disgrace and abomination is carried on through excessive opulence in dress, *alamodische* styles and manners, fleshly shoving for precedence, and the envy and jealousy awakened by all of these' (Johann Christian Lange in Archiv der Franckeschen Stiftungen, Halle, D57: 42–77, 55 (1695)). One councillor complained of 'youth and other useless riffraff' retiring to spaces behind the Capellen to make noise. These are among the documents examined by Tanya Kevorkian relating to this theme of congregational disruption (op. cit., p. 34).

rest of the orchestra, it describes measures intended to repel the 'hordes of hell' (*Höllenheer*). Bach might have reckoned that this assertion of liberation and triumph, with its repeated injunctions of *Verstumme! Verstumme!* ('Be silent!'), would be enough to arrest any late-comers engaged in making a grand entrance or going through the rituals of greeting their neighbours. Six months later he gave a more subtle twist in the tail to an elaborate double-chorale fugue that concludes the Whit Monday cantata BWV 68, *Also hat Gott die Welt geliebt.* Following St John's bald division of the world into believers and sceptics, Bach's contrapuntal working-out is full of pent-up energy and invention. Towards its conclusion he suddenly assigns the first musical subject to a new accusing text: 'because he hath not believed in the name of the only begotten Son of God' – sung once loud, once soft. This abrupt ending seems calculated to give a sharp jolt to any congregation expecting, but not getting, the traditional chorale to round things off and to bring them comfortably back to earth after a stern homiletic reproof. Bach had delivered a sucker punch.

* * *

To the authorities the insertion of 'the music' into the service carried with it the fear that if it were too long (or in the eyes of the clergy too entertaining, too frivolous or too 'operatic') it could be a distraction from God's Word and provide a pretext for disorder and unruly behaviour of one kind or another. Further evidence of this fear of a breakdown in civil order comes from the official decree that on all Sundays and feast-days the city gates were to be kept closed throughout the day, thus bringing wheeled traffic to a standstill and restricting comings and goings to pedestrians. As late as 1799 we hear that 'during the service iron chains in the streets and alleys close the approaches to the churches in order to prevent all disturbance'[48] – though it is not clear whether this was ostensibly to ensure a peaceful ambience during the service itself and to 'promote devotion'[49] on those official 'days of fasting, penitence and prayer' or from fear of public disorder stirred up by those who were unable (or unwilling) to attend church. Was Bach being sly when he wrote in 1728 to the council, 'It may be added that when, in addition to the concerted music [i.e., the cantata], very long hymns are sung, the divine service is held up, and all sorts of disorder would have to be reckoned with'[50] – first, pandering to their known dislike of long services prolonged by music, and, second, to their fear of crowd disturbance?*

* * *

Our modern patterns of concert hall listening and of church service decorum inherited from nineteenth-century conventions are of no help in evaluating the way Bach's music was received at the time. They give us a false perspective on the customs of Bach's Leipzig congregation, for whom neither punctuality nor silent listening was considered de rigueur. Yet the founder of their brand of Christianity, Martin Luther, had unequivocally sanctified the listening process: the Word of God was not text, he insisted, but sound, or, rather, voice – to be heard and listened to: *Vox est anima verbi* ('The voice is the soul of the Word'). But, he regretted, 'we do not listen, even when the whole world and all creatures cry out to us, and God is addressing us with His promises.'[51] He was equally critical of those who just 'sing along or read the psalms as though they had no business with us; rather we should read them and sing them in such a way that we are thereby bettered, our faith is strengthened and our conscience is consoled in all sorts of trouble.'[52] Genuine listening is therefore a sacramental activity and brings us in touch with divine grace: 'in listening to a piece of music, we listen not only to the musicians, but also to the sound of our own body resonance, as a way of responding to the spirit of the piece and its truth that claims and seeks to transform us.'[53] One wonders whether the clergy of Bach's day were equally emphatic on the subject. To anyone in their congregation spotted paying more attention to the cantata than to the sermon, the pastors, one suspects, might have replied that the preaching of the Word was the summit of religious activity, whereas music, though it was to be welcomed, was its (not always biddable) handmaiden.

As a composer addressing a captive audience, Bach appears to have stretched every imaginative muscle in his body to engage with his listeners. Counting on their active participation, he must have found signs of

* Two and a half centuries later, in Oct. 1989, the Nikolaikirche saw 700 Party members and Stasi, prepared and armed for a riot, enter its walls. Surprised by their arrival, Pastor Christian Führer welcomed them to his church and treated them to an eloquent address on the subject of 'The Sermon on the Mount' ('Blessed are the peace-makers'). It is a matter of conjecture whether the Stasi were more surprised by the sermon or by the peaceful candle-carrying procession that ensued.

inattention desperately frustrating. From his own experiences Mattheson wrote, 'Most musical listeners are uninformed people with respect to art. What a great deed I have done when I know how to disguise an art-piece [*Kunst-Stück*] from their ears, so that when they hear it they don't even notice at all. What a miracle! – just as when a peasant-farmer unknowingly swallows along with his sauerkraut a roasted canary that cost him six thaler, and, having done it, he would far rather have stuffed himself with roast pork!'[54] To use artifice because of contempt for his listeners was not Bach's way. Unlike Mattheson, he was probably not especially concerned if they were able to perceive the complex workings of his music just so long as they were not distracted from its content. And he was perfectly capable, when so minded, of providing his congregation with music that was easy on their ears, as certain of his cantatas show us.

There is a strange irony here. Keen listeners and music-lovers, one might suppose, as well as serious believers, would have been irked by the general rowdiness of the church service, their enjoyment further quelled by disapproving looks from those of the clergy with a Pietist outlook. In the coffee-house, however, a secular and, some might argue, morally questionable environment, a more select and discerning audience listened and paid attention to music.* It might also be the case that the coffee-house concert gave birth to the strand of secular German morality encapsulated by Seneca's aphorism and later adopted by the Gewandhaus Orchestra. From the protocol of other *collegium* concerts in nearby Delitzsch, we know that listeners were expected to 'remember (and without special admonition) that good manners demand that they refrain from playing cards or pursuing other pleasures that might disturb the *collegium*'.[55] A student at the University of Jena was most concerned lest his pleasure at hearing his friends play in the local *collegium musicum* would be compromised by 'giving room for inhuman boozing, which always produces total disgust in me'.[56] Listeners there could expect to be treated to 'the most pleasant moments' in which 'Music sounds sweetly in the stillness. / Here rules a silenced will, / Quietness often imposes itself.'[57] There is a further irony in that Bach's

* They may have included members of the congregation who, as in Augsburg, felt that they needed more music (or a more silent ambience) than was usual in church, as Christian Gabriel Fischer reported after his visit there in 1731 (Nathanael Iacob Gerlach, *Zwölffte Reise durch die mehresten Kreise Teutschlandes . . . Hoffe durch Christian Gabriel Fischer vom 3 April 1731 bis 12 Octobr 1731*).

music has almost always been appreciated within a secular concert environment that has posthumously co-opted some of the trappings of religion. This includes the halo of religious reverence accorded by German listeners to Bach's music ever since the nineteenth century, both in and out of church (and at organ recitals even to this day).

Clearly there is no simple distinction in contemporary listening habits to be made here, then, between 'absorption' (in church) and 'amusement' (in coffee-houses), or between inattention and attentiveness. The well-established concept of *Affektenlehre*, the doctrine that the role of music is to stir the feelings of composer, performer and audience alike, held regardless of venue.[58] Just because attendance at musical performances was sociable, it does not necessarily follow that the listening was shallow;[59] nor, since many were connoisseurs (*Kenner*), was there automatically a high degree of holy attentiveness (though some who attended may have assumed that this was the appropriate attitude). There was a bit of this and a bit of that, as we learn from Johann Andreas Cramer's account after attending a performance of Leipzig's Großes Concert founded by 'sixteen persons, some noble and some bourgeois' on 11 March 1743:

> This society gathers together once per week in the winter, and once every fourteen days in the summer. The decorations in the room in which their meetings take place are so tasteful, that the eyes are pleased without being distracted, and an equal degree of care is taken in every other way to make sure that participants feel at ease. According to connoisseurs, the society does itself honour both in the selection of its members, who further the delight of the group with their musical strengths, and in the selection of pieces to perform, which are composed by the most famous and greatest masters. Though the organization does not allow the entire city to participate in their events, good manners and *politesse* are welcome, and the way in which one allows them to take part is as selfless as it is *galant*.
>
> The attentiveness to music that pervades society gatherings deserves mention here. All arts, which appeal through the beauties of harmony, and arouse various passions of the heart, require attentiveness, so that their effects are not disturbed. Only silence during musical performances can satisfy those who have ambitions as listeners. To a connoisseur whose musical ear does not wish to miss a single bowstroke from [Carl Gotthelf] Gerlach's violin, every noise – however small it may be – is intolerable. In

a masterpiece there are no tones or sounds that are unimportant, and a single measure misheard can rob one of a large part of the pleasure intended by its composer. I am so offended by people asking me questions while I am listening it is as though they are mocking me, and I mercilessly judge those who are inattentive to music as lacking sensitivity and taste.

I could not hide the annoyance aroused in me by my neighbour at a recent concert, and I cannot forgive him even though (without recognizing me) he has praised my writing in other contexts. His having shared distracting thoughts while the music was playing destroyed all of my confidence in his praise. I sat there listening like one whose entire soul had been brought to order by music, so that pleasure could find a totally open path, and crawl into every crevice of my being. A solo, which Mr Landvogt played on the flute, put me in an enraptured state of mind, and I was poised to be completely intoxicated with the music, to be lost in joy, when this immodest neighbour suddenly moved over and got close to my ear, putting the gentle and ingratiating tones to flight, and asked me with a knowing expression: 'Have you heard that Bochetta has once again been taken, and the Turks are expected to gather together in the European provinces?' Furious that my quiet rapture had been disturbed, my answer probably gave him a poor impression of my knowledge of political science. I said to him with as much haste as possible: 'No!'[60]

Cramer's account, tendentious as it is, is just the kind of thing we lack for Bach's church music and the way it was received at the time. But at least it serves to remind us that music is ultimately dependent on a degree of silence and the capacity of the listener to *hear*. John Butt divides listening into three interlocking categories. The first exemplifies the 'general hearer-orientated nature of virtually all music'; the second 'the many types of music that are specifically listener-orientated'; while the third relates to 'the type of listener who creates a specific sense of self over the duration of the listening experience'. Cramer clearly fell into this category. Though more elusive, contentious and harder to define, this third category points to 'the notion of an "internal" or "implicit" listener, someone latent in the way the music seems to have been put together'.* This

* As we shall see in the next chapter and in the context of Bach's church cantatas, we can conclude with John Butt that 'music possesses an independent narrative function only when it does something exceptional, something that runs counter to the demands of the existing narrative' (John Butt, 'Do Musical Works Contain an Implied Listener?', JRMA, Vol. 135, Special Issue 1 (2010), pp. 8–10).

seems particularly true of Bach and the impact he may have had on some of his listeners at the time and ever since. 'Most aspects of Lutheran worship,' Butt maintains, 'were designed to dispose the listener not only to a direct experience of the biblical events, stories or doctrines appropriate for the day, but also to make connections and to take to heart specific lessons learnt from Christ's sacrifice.' The music, as we saw earlier, seems 'tailored to a sense of the listener's presence'.[61]

It took many decades following Bach's death before the habit of the devout enjoyment of music moved from the church (if indeed it had ever existed there with any degree of consistency) to the concert hall. Before Goethe and others taught audiences what we would think of as good musical manners and habits of silent inwardness (what Peter Gay calls 'the nineteenth-century ideal of self-control for the sake of the exquisite, if postponed, psychological rewards'), composers as different as Gluck, Mozart, Rossini and Spohr all had to learn to put up with the flow of talk, card games and the slurping of sorbets, as well as frequent comings and goings while their music was being played. Meanwhile much aristocratic scorn was poured on the bourgeois habit of earnestly attending musical events to listen, nothing being 'so damnable as listening to a work like a street merchant or some provincial just off the boat', as one French author wrote at the time.[62] Is it entirely natural to sit stock still when listening to music, or does the practice of giving 'undivided silent attention to a musical performance [do] violence to basic human impulses' – the sublimation 'of the urge to become actively involved'? Gay maintains that 'listening awakens the urge to mimic marked rhythms, march-like sonorities, stirring crescendos.'[63] One can very well imagine the varied types of inward struggle going on among Bach's first listeners between conflicting urges – to listen intently, pass comment, beat time, hum along with it, or to ignore it completely.

* * *

Some commentators in the past half-century have claimed that around 1729–30 Bach became disillusioned with the task of church-cantata composition and may have become creatively spent or even suffered some kind of crisis of faith. These claims represent one type of reaction (or overreaction) to the forensic research carried out in the 1950s by Alfred Dürr and Georg von Dadelsen, who between them proposed a radically new chronology of church-cantata composition based on watermark analysis, showing it to have been concentrated in the first three years of Bach's Leipzig cantorate and to have fallen off over the following two years. 'A landslide has taken place in the wake of the new chronology,' proclaimed the German Protestant scholar Friedrich Blume to the International Bach Society in Mainz in June 1962. He dared to ask, 'Did Bach have a special liking for church work? Was it a spiritual necessity for him? Hardly. There is at any rate no evidence that it was. Bach the supreme cantor, the creative servant of the Word of God, the staunch Lutheran, is a legend. It will have to be buried along with all the other traditional and beloved romantic illusions.'[64] That Blume overstated his case is now widely accepted, and must be obvious from the contextual reconstruction and the shards of biographical evidence we have attempted to assemble in previous chapters. Blume was making a laudable attempt to readjust the inherited image of Bach in the light of the new chronology and to warn us against basing our view on only those works to have survived the passage of time. His reasoned corrective to the conventional image of Bach was that 'he is more down-to-earth, more human ... a man bound up with his own age with every fibre of his being, a man who warmly welcomes the trends that point promisingly to the future, but who dutifully devotes all his powers to the traditional office of cantor when it devolves upon him: a man standing on the boundary between two epochs who is aware of the fact.' It is difficult to argue with that. Nor can he be faulted for suggesting that 'the Cantor's resistance to the narrowness of the ecclesiastical regime grew deeper.'[65] But there could be other explanations of the falling off in cantata composition besides those he proposed. In the first place, Bach may have felt that by 1729–30 he had provided the main Leipzig churches with a sufficiently rich repertory of cantatas to meet most future needs.

We are now better placed than Blume to trace the strategies Bach developed for stepping off the weekly treadmill of cantata composition.[66] During the mid 1730s, for instance, he regularly substituted generally slighter and less demanding cantatas by other composers such as Telemann and his own cousin Johann Ludwig Bach, and in 1735/6 an entire annual cantata cycle, *Das Saitenspiel des Herzens*, by Gottfried Heinrich Stölzel, having already performed the latter's Passion oratorio (*Ein Lämmlein geht und trägt die Schuld*) in 1734. To feature these and other composers' music in place of his own, while still in fulfilment of his cantor's duties, must have come as a relief; there may also have been a hint of disgruntlement, as if to say to his congregants, 'Well, you couldn't bother to make the effort to listen to my music or give it a modicum of attention, so here is some *Gebrauchsmusik* by other composers better suited to your tastes and levels of concentration.'

Even without such a hint of defiance, Bach may have begun to sense that the communality of belief and convention he once shared with his congregation was now starting to alter, or even to break down. There probably never was a full consensus about the sacred nature of music per se, neither among the Leipzig clergy (divided, as we have seen) nor among his employers on the council (equally divided as they were), even if a slightly rickety understanding between Bach and (some of) his congregation was negotiated between them, once the more conservative members had got over the initial shock of his cantata style. Bach may have looked differently on his church music of these middle years, placing more and more value on its craftsmanship and inherent musical qualities rather than on its contingent usefulness. This put him still more out of step with theorists, theologians and the new breed of 'enlightened' aestheticians who favoured the *galant* style.

Corroboration for this shift of attitude can be detected in the trilogy of interrelated oratorios he wrote for Christmas, Easter and Ascension during the mid-to-late 1730s, all of them originating in secular *drammi per musica*. In 1725 Bach had hastily adapted one such *dramma* recently composed for the Weissenfels Court, BWV 249a, into an Easter cantata: he transposed, not wholly convincingly, four shepherds and shepherdesses from a theatrical Arcadian setting into Christ's disciples hurrying to the empty tomb. There were no chorales. A decade later his oratorio adaptations take on a different hue and are painted on a much broader canvas. Returning to the same Easter cantata around 1738, the *Easter Oratorio* (BWV 249) now emerged, a more polished effort, expanded and re-scored, and then subjected to a further revision between 1743 and 1746 (its last performance occurring on 6 April 1749) with the opening duet expanded to a chorus. The earlier identification of the vocal parts with the roles of the two Marys, Peter and John was now virtually expunged. Bach's intent here was manifestly to eliminate the theatrical flavour of the cruder cantata version and to give a more consistently meditative emphasis to the scriptural narrative, in which the expression of human emotional responses to the Resurrection is paramount.

To base a biblical oratorio celebrating the birth of Christ as ruler of heaven and earth on the story of Hercules, famous in myth as the strongest man in the world – and therefore a flattering encomium for the crown prince of Saxony, for whom it was written in 1733 – was hardly a risk-free strategy. Whether his first listeners spotted (or were the slightest bit concerned by) the wholesale recycling of material from BWV 213, *Herkules auf dem Scheidewege*, into the *Christmas Oratorio*, that Bach bridges the secular, divine and mythological worlds so smoothly gives a modern quasi-'Enlightened' flavour to the transplant that is very much of a piece with the prevailing *Zeitgeist*.

Another possible explanation for Bach's decision to switch genres and the forums of his activities during these watershed years could have nothing to do with twentieth-century allegations of a diminished religious fervour, or a loss of complicity with his audience. Instead it might relate to a desire for pastures new (even within Leipzig's city walls) and a wish for contact with a new group of listeners unencumbered by church protocol. Here were solid reasons for his assuming control of the university *collegium musicum* in 1729. From this laboratory he could achieve several things: he could reinforce ties to the university musicians and trade favours with them; he could offer his two eldest sons and other leading pupils a platform and valuable experience before they went off to take up positions elsewhere; and he could expand his production of congratulatory cantatas for the Saxon royal family and act as artistic intermediary between them and the university. In addition he could cement ties with the intelligentsia of Leipzig and attempt to meet some of their cultural needs. It seems likely that, in this secular urban culture, Bach also made several other deliberate choices – typical of his curiosity and of those abrupt shifts of compositional genre one comes across at separate stages of his career: to get acquainted with instrumental works by contemporaries such as Benda, Graun and Telemann; to feature works by his own two eldest sons written 'in an advanced, popular style';[67]and to perform selected Italian cantatas and arias by opera composers such as Porpora, Scarlatti and Handel. These provided him with a fresh critical starting-point and were a spur to his own compositions in the fashionable genres of the day (BWV 203 and 209).

* * *

Over the course of his career Bach composed for a variety of listeners – in fulfilment of his official duties, out of a moral obligation to his 'neighbour' and, though he would not have put it in such terms, to satisfy his own creative urge. We search for anything, even passing references in diaries and letters from those who attended church services, to bridge the deplorable gaps in our knowledge of how audiences of the day reacted to his music. The euphoria and fervour of response by audiences in our own day – clear signs of how deeply Bach's music continues to affect people of all ages, religions and backgrounds – is in itself no guide to how people at the time responded to Bach's own performances of his music. However, I am convinced that at some stage in the next few years the sharp-eyed sleuths in Leipzig's Bach-Archiv will alight upon correspondence, perhaps in the more obscure provincial libraries of eastern Germany, and we will then get the direct testimony we have been looking for all along. Bach's music simply cannot have been passed over with indifference: delight, astonishment, bafflement, even dislike – all of these, but not with a mere shrug of the shoulders.*

Meanwhile it is misleading in the extreme to see Bach exclusively as a composer for the church, switching to secular composition only when circumstances turned against his creative contributions to the liturgy. Indubitably his view of his craft was that it was God-given and secure, as well as vocationally and dynastically preordained (as we saw in Chapters 3 and 5), but there is no reason to suppose that he considered his secular music in any way inferior to his church music. That said, catch him in a certain mood and he might have agreed with his predecessor Johann Kuhnau that in church music 'the sacred place and text call for every possible artistry, splendour, *modestie* and devotion; here, in secular works, good pieces may appear next to bad, droll, ridiculous, and melodies may creep in that excessively hop about and transgress the rules of art.'[68]

That might help to explain Bach's lack of enthusiasm for conventional opera and the dismissive (or at best ironic) remark about the 'pretty little ditties' he witnessed in Dresden, and for his never composing in that genre.† This diffidence extended to the secular chamber

* As a foreign conductor invited to perform Bach's church music in his homeland and leading a predominantly English choir and a thoroughly cosmopolitan group of instrumentalists (misleadingly called the English Baroque Soloists), I have been struck time and again by the exceptional attentiveness of German-speaking audiences, both in the former GDR and in the Federal Republic. Three hundred years after its inception, one senses this is still *their* music.

† This appears in Chapter 8 of Forkel's biography, when he describes how courteously Bach was received on his visits to the Dresden Opera with his eldest son: 'He used to say in jest,

cantatas and the congratulatory odes termed *drammi per musica* that have survived from his first years in Leipzig (BWV 201, 205 and 207), a genre described by Gottsched as 'little operas or operettas' which, however, 'seldom find their way to the stage'. Significantly, in complaining about the bad habits of poets and musicians, Gottsched singles out Hurlebusch and Handel for praise, but not Bach.[69]

The truth is that, for all their technical accomplishments, Bach's *drammi per musica* are a good deal less dramatic than a number of his church cantatas, and it seems to be far harder for us, curiously, to reconstruct a living context for Bach's congratulatory music than for his church music despite the complications of belief. They evoke the pastoral environs of Leipzig prettily but less vividly than in his unselfconscious transfer of rural imagery to contemplative religious texts. In a predominantly agrarian society like eighteenth-century Saxony, there was a close linking of the seasons to the patterns of everyday life and the concerns of Christianity, and even to Bach's urban audience there would have been nothing peculiar or quaint in hearing pastoral music as a metaphor for their own Lutheran community watched over by Jesus as the Good Shepherd. Belief is the motor for this pastoral music, Bach's purpose being to demonstrate that, with Christ's help, the 'meadow of heaven' is not a lost Arcadia but a realistically attainable destination.

There is none of that in the secular cantatas of his Leipzig period.* Rather, we find the equivalent in French Baroque art – painters such as Pater and Lancret struggling to get beyond the pretty conventionalities of form and to reproduce the enchanted world of their master Watteau, whose *fêtes galantes* often suggest a profound and simple longing for something out of reach and beyond belief. One senses in these and other

some days before his departure, "Friedemann, shan't we go again to hear the pretty little ditties?" Innocent as this joke was in itself, I am convinced that Bach would not have made it to anybody except his son, who, at that time, already knew what is great in art and what is only pretty and agreeable' (J. N. Forkel, *Ueber Johann Sebastian Bachs Leben, Kunst und Kunstwerke* (1802), p. 86).

* Why was he apparently unable to replicate, let alone build on, the unfeigned pastoral beauty of the *Hunt Cantata* composed in his Weimar years (BWV 208)? There, in the most famous of all of his pastoral mini tone-poems, 'Schafe können sicher weiden', known to English listeners as 'Sheep May Safely Graze', he succeeds (not without a dash of sentimentality) in bridging the secular and sacred, so that behind the flattering homage paid to the beneficent aristocratic rule of Duke Christian of Weissenfels stands the caring image of Jesus the Good Shepherd.

works that Bach was being sucked further into the world of *galant* music espoused by his sons than was altogether natural for him. While it was his second son, Carl Philipp Emanuel, who in due course became known as the most celebrated proponent of the aesthetics of *Empfindsamkeit* ('sensibility'), Johann Sebastian proved equally adept at forging a direct emotional connection with his listeners when he had the will to do so.

* * *

The context for Bach's public music-making in Leipzig was multi-layered, with commercial, political, liturgical and social aspects all vying for inclusion. It illustrates the growing secularisation of German society in the mid eighteenth century – the interweaving of pressing social concerns in a fast-expanding urban community and the grass-root effects of the *Aufklärung*, or Age of Reason, labels under which we otherwise abstractly subsume the century. In the public ceremonial events given al fresco in the town centre, Bach had a relatively free hand in the choice of musical styles and literary partners, even if he had to adopt a conventional tone when acting as master of musical ceremonies during visits to Leipzig by the Elector and his family (which led eventually to a prestigious and much coveted court title, a counterbalance to his thraldom to the town council). Then the coffee-house *collegium* concerts exposed him to a broad range of styles which remind us of the protean side of his character. His music was transformative, the *galant* being just one of many elements he was willing to absorb and embrace in his own work, from which he created a synthesis that transcended all its parts. Additionally he was eager to study the music of others, willing to engage with different kinds of listener and be open-minded in giving opportunities to other composers and performers (not necessarily kindred spirits).

Whereas in his coffee-house rehearsals and concerts he could stake out a degree of autonomy, when we follow him back into church we see that his room for manoeuvre was far more restricted. There he needed to tread a fine path to avoid giving unwitting offence to the doctrinal scruples of the local clergy on the one hand, while satisfying his civic paymasters on the other. For the clergy the role of the cantata was to inspire devotion among the congregation and to provide a calming atmospheric foretaste of the main event – the sermon. What most concerned the town councillors was that church music should avoid causing civil unrest, and then to guarantee a prestigious 'show' with which to dazzle visitors to the trade fairs. For Bach, there were artistic standards to defend, often in the face of clerical meddling and councillor opposition, a degree of public indifference and boorish behaviour, as well as squabbles with, and petty criticism from, disaffected ex-pupils to contend with. To assist a diverse congregation coming to church with widely different expectations of the role of music there, Bach had the texts of his cantatas printed and put on sale. Even then there were marked differences in people's ability to 'hear' the music he provided. To a professional critic like Scheibe there were those 'uncomfortable noises' that he claimed to be able to identify, spoiling Bach's polyphony. But these are just as likely to have been occasioned by flaws in execution by Bach's under-rehearsed ensemble, or by the ambient noise within the church, or indeed by deficiencies in Scheibe's hearing abilities, as by any faults in the compositions themselves. Bach's aim, after all, was to write music designed to praise God and to inspirit and captivate his listeners.* He had set out in 1723 with ambitious plans to compose five integrated cycles of cantatas, each with a Passion as its central jewel. It is to these that we now turn.

* We saw in Chapter 6 how Bach was drawn to the passage in I Chronicles 25 that relates to the elaborate use of music in Temple worship, seeing it as 'the true foundation of all God-pleasing *Kirchenmusik*' (Robin A. Leaver (ed.), *J. S. Bach and Scripture: Glosses from the Calov Bible Commentary* (1985), pp. 93–6).

9
Cycles and Seasons

Rituals in Time are what the habitation is in Space. For it is good that the flow of time should not appear to us to wear us away and disperse us like a handful of sand, but should complete and strengthen us. It is right, too, that we see Time as a building-up. So I move from one feast-day to another, from anniversary to anniversary, from harvest-time to harvest-time, just as I went as a child from the council chamber to the bedroom within the thick walls of my father's mansion, where every footstep had purpose.

– after Antoine de Saint-Exupéry, *Citadelle* (1948)

On the face of it, there is little reason for us to bother about Bach's cantatas today. Never intended to be performed or listened to other than as part of a lengthy church service, they were composed (and rehearsed) each week at great speed to act as a foretaste of the Sunday sermon. The genre is essentially a bastard obsolescent form, 'cobbled together from multiple styles of writing'.* Bach's examples of the form were structured in an ungainly lopsided sequence – typically a long opening chorus, followed by pairs of exhorting recitatives and chastising arias, and then a closing hymn to wrap things up. Their texts (mostly anonymous) seldom rise above poetic doggerel, while the underlying

* Johann Mattheson describes its succession of recitatives and arias as belonging to the 'madrigal style' (by which he probably meant the current operatic style), its polyphonic choruses and fugues to the 'motet style', accompaniments and interludes to the 'instrumental style', and finally its chorales to the 'melismatic style' (Johann Mattheson, *Der vollkommene Capellmeister* (1739), Ernest C. Harriss (trs.) (1981), p. 215).

theology is at times unappetising – mankind portrayed as wallowing in degradation and sinfulness, the world a hospital peopled by sick souls whose sins fester like suppurating boils and yellow excrement. What is one to make of a cantata (BWV 199) that opens with the words 'My heart swims in blood, for sin's brood turns me into a monster in God's eyes . . . my sins are my executioners, as Adam's seed robs me of sleep and I must hide from Him, He from whom even the angels conceal their faces'?[1] Perhaps it comes as no surprise to find that only one cantata was published during Bach's lifetime – BWV 71, *Gott ist mein König*, written for the inauguration of the Mühlhausen Town Council in 1708 – while at his death the bulk of them were distributed among four of his sons and his widow, but with scores and parts separated. Some cantatas lingered on for a while in the repertoire of his successors, a few were revived in bowdlerised form, many were sold, and an uncountable number disappeared into the recesses of church libraries or were lost for ever.* Some were used to light fires.

So what is all the fuss about? If we are to believe the late Charles Rosen, 'the fashionable placing of the cantatas as Bach's principal achievement has only been harmful: it has led to an overemphasis on extra-musical symbolism.' Great pianist that he was, Rosen not surprisingly felt 'it is time to return to the old evaluation of Bach's keyboard music as the centre of his work.'[2] However, he failed to explain why the writers of the *Nekrolog* placed 'five full annual cycles of church pieces [*Kirchenstücke*],† for all the Sundays and feast-days' right at the head of Bach's work-list of unpublished pieces if they – and Bach himself – had not believed them to be of huge importance. Bach saw himself as belonging to a line of north and central German organist–composers who considered themselves representatives of modern music within the life of the Lutheran church. Cycles were to be a vital component of his cantatas and were a constant theme and presence throughout his œuvre,

* Christoph Wolff estimates that nearly two fifths of the cantatas were lost one way or another because the estate was split up (*The World of the Bach Cantatas* (1997), Vol. 1 p. 5).

† *Kirchenstück* was just one of several names (including *Stück* or just plain *Musik*) given to what for convenience scholars and musicians have called 'cantatas'. From the strangely promiscuous descriptions Bach appended to his earliest works – *actus* (BWV 106), *concerto* (BWV 61), *motteto* (BWV 71) – with the appellation *cantata* confined to just two early works, both for solo voice (BWV 52 and 199), we can see that the title was manifestly not of primary significance.

beginning with the *Orgel-Büchlein*, an unfinished collection of jewel-like chorale preludes crafted and adjusted to the rhythms of the entire church year. While the challenge for him was always to make every composition a complete and harmonious work in itself, composing in cycles gave him the possibility of moulding a single idea in multiple ways and of extending its expressive range beyond the horizons visible to any other composer of his time. Anton Webern grasped the significance of this in 1933 when he wrote, 'You find everything in Bach: the development of cyclic forms, the conquest of the realm of tonality – the attempt at a summation of the highest order.'[3] In terms of music intended for use in church, cycles opened up an inviting route for him to stretch his skills in mirroring the fullness and harmoniousness of God's creation and in engaging deeply with what was essentially an ancient cosmology. For, as John Butt notes, 'cyclic time is essential to a liturgical, ritualistic approach to religion, in which important events and aspects of dogma are celebrated within a yearly cycle.'[4]

When the opportunity finally came for him to compose church cantatas on a monthly schedule at the Weimar Court, he met the challenge almost as though he were in training for more extended future ones. If we take, for example, the three cantatas he wrote for the Advent and Christmas season in 1714 and a fourth composed two years later, we see that they join naturally to form a plausible mini-cycle. Hearing them in sequence is a bit like opening the doors of a child's Advent calendar: each is a brilliant cameo, a story linked by the underlying metaphor of the old year as the time of Israel and the new year as the time of Christ. The first, BWV 61, *Nun komm, der Heiden Heiland* (for Advent Sunday), addresses the hopes and fears of the Christian community in the context of Jesus' birth as the beginning of God's plan for our salvation. The second, BWV 70a, *Wachet! Betet!*, focuses on Christ's second coming as judge of the world, beginning with an exhortation to watch and pray, and then alludes to Israel's captivity in Egypt and the destruction of Sodom and Gomorrah; dire warnings that 'this is the end of time' are, however, mitigated by a vision of release and final reconciliation. By way of contrast, BWV 63, *Christen, ätzet diesen Tag*, celebrates Christmas itself as the long-awaited day of the fulfilment of God's promise and the end of Israel's captivity. Placed at the heart of this cantata's symmetrical structure is the word *Gnaden* – the grace that comes with Christ's birth and, with it, the release of humanity from sin and death – the very word that sanctifies music-making when two or three are gathered together with the right spirit: 'Where there is devotional music, God with His grace is always present.'*

Another word, *Stein* ('stone'), lies at the centre of BWV 152, *Tritt auf die Glaubensbahn*, for the first Sunday after Christmas: it symbolises the cornerstone of faith set by God in Jesus' incarnation, but also the way human inclination can take the form of a stumbling block to salvation. Bach and his librettist Salomo Franck make much of this duality – between humanity's initial fall and the need for spiritual abasement, and the triumph of faith and the soul's attainment of the crown as the terminus of the *Glaubensbahn* (the path, or 'train', of faith). It is constructed as an allegorical dialogue between Jesus (bass) and the Soul (soprano), an intimate chamber piece in which three archaic instruments – a recorder, a viola d'amore and a viola da gamba – standing for the old order (the Rock of Ages reinforced still more tellingly by the 'old-fashioned' counterpoint) are juxtaposed with a 'modern' oboe and basso continuo representing the new. You sense the evident pleasure Bach takes in the mixing and blending of these instrumental timbres before their final convergence to reflect the unity of Jesus and the Soul. Residual flaws in the genre itself seldom proved insurmountable for Bach, and he was rarely stumped for ways of getting round the problems of the texts in front of him – even when dull, peculiar or simply over the top. Indeed, there is such an astonishingly rich diversity and quality to these Weimar works that, had Bach never composed another cantata – that is, the 150 or so that have survived from his Leipzig years – he would still qualify as the most innovative composer of church music of his day. We have twenty-two immensely varied church cantatas

* This, as we have already mentioned, was an annotation (see Plate 13) Bach made in the margin of his copy of Abraham Calov's *Die Deutsche Bibel* (see *The Calov Bible of J. S. Bach*, Howard H. Cox (ed.) (1985)), catalogued in his library in 1733. But since this and other equally illuminating personal marginal notes reveal to us the biblical foundations of his vocation as a church musician, some scholars think that Bach could have been familiar with Calov's commentary at a much earlier date – when his activity in composing church cantatas was at its most intense. Bach clearly prized Calov's commentary greatly. When he bought at a book auction in 1742 a copy of the seven-volume Altenburg edition of Luther's *Schriften* that had once belonged to Calov, he added a note saying that he felt this was what Calov 'probably used to compile his great *Tütsche Bibel*' (see Robin A. Leaver, *Bach's Theological Library* (1983), p. 42). The three Calov volumes were the first to be listed in the inventory of his estate drawn up after his death in 1750.

from these years: sparing and resourceful in their use of musical material, exuberant and sometimes dramatic in their response to their texts. His subsequent move to the Calvinist court at Cöthen in 1717 brought no further responsibility for church music. But if the next six years formed a period of Lutheran hibernation, they were far from wasted in terms of glorifying God: he was building up a rich store of secular works, admirable in themselves, and that had all the potential for recycling and transforming on to a higher level in years to come.

* * *

The opportunity to resume composing cantatas, but on a far more regular basis than in the past, was one of the factors that weighed with Bach and a main reason why, after months of hesitation, he applied for the cantor's job in Leipzig. Clearly he saw this as the chance to fulfil his *Endzweck* – the 'ultimate goal' of a 'well-regulated church music to the glory of God' (see Chapter 6, p. 180). Indeed, it is as though he had reached a point where his desires as an artist were so imbued with strong religious leanings that he had to find an immediate outlet for them: there is no other logical explanation as to why he concentrated all his energies on composing cantatas over such a short period of time and to the virtual exclusion of all else. For, from the moment of his official induction as Thomascantor in Leipzig in the early summer of 1723, Bach set off at a pace of weekly church-cantata composition so furious that probably no one – not even he, with his extraordinary reserves of creative energy and powers of concentration – could sustain it for more than a couple of years (as indeed he didn't). There is a sense of him saying to himself: 'This is my time: I can do this.' Far from being fallen wood-shavings from the great man's workbench, the cantatas Bach went on to compose are substantial independent works in their own right. Now approaching the zenith of his powers, Bach poured some of his most striking creative energy into their individual shaping, voicing and content. What has come down to us is not just a residue of *œuvres de circonstance*, a splutter of glorious blazes ready for re-ignition in occasional performances today, but a procession of gripping musical works of exceptional worth.

On assuming office in 1723 Bach was evidently determined to set out his compositional stall as quickly as possible. At the back of his mind may have been the consistorial jibe he received in Arnstadt at the very outset of his career about his failure to provide figural music, the frustrations he experienced in finding adequate musicians there and in Mühlhausen, and then the years he had to wait in Weimar before the chance came to string together a monthly cycle of cantatas. Now, as Leipzig's newly appointed Thomascantor, with the chance to provide figural music for every Sunday and festival in the church year, he set off as though stung into action. Such zeal went far beyond any contractual obligation to compose and perform music to adorn the liturgy of the Lutheran church. No one, least of all the sceptical mayoral committee that had appointed him (see illustrations of burgomasters in second inset), would probably have expected him to produce a new composition for every single one of the sixty annual feasts of the church; that he would need to have occasional recourse to the works of past or contemporary colleagues would have been understood. Certainly no previous Thomascantor had done so, nor had any of his peers ever attempted such an ambitious, pressured undertaking – at least not on an equivalent scale or level of musical complexity. But then, as he was later to insist to a bemused city council, 'most of my own compositions are incomparably harder and more intricate [than those of other composers].'[5]* Their success was wholly dependent on highly skilled musicians capable of persuasive performances under his direction. For, as he is reported to have said, 'in music, anyway, everything depends on performance.'[6] A lot more was at stake for Bach: an endeavour that was to prove among the sternest challenges in his life as a creative and performing artist.

Cantatas were called for on saints' days and feast-days, in addition to the regular Sundays, and were distributed unevenly across the year in the Leipzig liturgy: rare periods of passivity (the so-called 'closed' seasons of Advent and Lent, when no figural music was allowed in the city churches) were followed by sudden bursts of frenetic activity

* This was anathema to those who, like Scheibe, preached the gospel of new music, advocating the replacement of 'artificial' polyphony by simple, easily comprehended melody. Bach was soon accused of being the victim of his own unassailable skill: he expected his young singers and players to replicate the complex sounds that he could produce on the organ; and his habit of annotating even the most minute ornaments not only took 'away from his pieces the beauty of harmony but completely [covered] the melody throughout' (BD II, No. 400/NBR, p. 338). Scheibe simply misunderstood. It is the test of any Bach interpreter to avoid this happening: the skill lies in giving judicious weight to the individual lines so that they converse on an equal footing. The opening bars of a Bach cantata are an invitation to enter – and complete – a separate world of rhythm and harmony, complex yet lucid, transparent yet utterly mesmerising – an enthralling river into which the imagination can plunge.

around the main festivals of Easter, Whitsun and Christmas. (See diagram of the Lutheran Liturgical Year, Plate 14.) To follow the chronological elaboration of his cantata cycles in linear sequence, just as his Leipzig audience experienced them week to week, is to be dazzled by the fecundity of his invention, his extraordinary consistency, and the rich diversity of texture, mood and form he managed to achieve. Furthermore, exploring Bach's cantatas sequentially can help us to understand how these intense agglomerations of work could have precipitated the crises – of both creation and reception – in his first two years, particularly (as we shall see) in the build-up to Good Friday, when a Passion performance was due, with the result that his plans for a given cantata cycle were disrupted. Donald Francis Tovey's view that 'the main lesson of the analysis of great music is a lesson of organic unity' is exemplified by Bach's approach to cyclical cantata composition, showing him to be flexible and capable of widely differing responses from one year to the next.

Following his cantatas in their seasonal context also allows us to notice how Bach, like Janacek two centuries later, often brings to the surface pre-Christian rituals and forgotten connections that reflect the turning of the agricultural year – the certainty of the land, its rhythms and rituals, the unerring pace of its calendar and the vagaries of rural weather. Saxony in the eighteenth century was still a predominantly agrarian society in which these seasonal events and happenings were closely linked to the concerns of religion – reminding us how, in today's predominantly urban society, many of us tend to lose contact with the rhythms and patterns of the farming calendar and even with perceptions of the basic cyclical round of life and death which feature prominently in so many of Bach's cantatas. There we find rural imagery permeating contemplative religious texts and the poetic elaborations of the lectionary for each successive feast-day.* For Bach to remind his

* The Lutherans adopted the historic lectionary that goes back to St Jerome in the fifth century AD and was standardised 300 years later by Charlemagne's spiritual adviser Alcuin, who shortened both the Gospel readings and the Epistles so that they dealt with a specific topic each week. With the establishment in the thirteenth century of Trinity Sunday as a major festival of the church, so-called 'Propers' were then assigned for the entire year. Penitentiary texts predominate in the second half of the Trinity season and extend to its very end – the Lutherans adding Propers for Tr + 25 and + 26 as eschatological lessons designed to connect the end of human life with the end of all things.

urban audience of Leipzig burghers of the patterns of seed-time and harvest existing just beyond their city walls was nothing unusual, and the rhythms and rituals of the agrarian year frequently seep through into his music, giving it topicality and currency as well as a layer of simple rusticity. So when Bach expands on Jesus' Gospel words from the Sermon on the Mount – 'By their fruits ye shall know them' (Matthew 7:15–23) – in a cantata from his first cycle, BWV 136, *Erforsche mich, Gott, und erfahre mein Herz*, he could count on his congregation knowing that Christ's words referred to the terrifying Old Testament warning 'Cursed is the ground on your account . . . thorns and thistles shall it bring forth to you' (Genesis 3:17–18). This is just one of the perennial worries of the arable farmer at this time of year, along with corn-flattening summer storms (BWV 93/v), bird damage (BWV 187/ii) or the threat of it (BWV 181/i), and crop-failure (BWV 186/vii) – all this despite good seed-bed preparation and timely sowing (BWV 185/iii). At these moments he seems to be drawing on his own childhood memories of country customs, of life close to the Thüringerwald, as we saw in Chapter 2, inspired by the view from his study in the Thomasschule across the River Pleisse to the pleasure gardens that Goethe later compared to the Elysian Fields, and beyond them the rural chequer-board of villages, spinneys and fields being worked by farmers.

A year-to-year comparison of Bach's cantata cycles reveals, too, how strongly they are linked to the rhythms of the geophysical year. This is most apparent at those seminal points when church festivals such as the Annunciation and Palm Sunday coincide with the spring equinox (BWV 1 and 182), or at Easter (BWV 4, 31 and 249), or at the beginning (BWV 75, 20 and 39) and closing (BWV 60, 26, 90, 116, 70 and 140) of the Trinity season, or, the clearest of all, at the winter solstice with its proximity to the ending of the calendar year itself (BWV 190, 41, 16 and 171). These turning-points form an essential backdrop in Bach's measuring of the ups and downs of the liturgical calendar; his braiding of the two conveys the simple idea of an inevitable progression from beginning to end and thence to a new beginning. The difference between the Greek concepts of *kairos* and *chronos* has a direct bearing on Bach's concept of time and how it plays out in his cantatas.* In the Koine

* The major languages spoken by both Jews and Greeks in the Holy Land at the time of Jesus were Aramaic and Koine Greek (and, to a limited extent, a colloquial dialect of

Greek of the New Testament, *chronos* signifies time in general – both stretches of time passing and waiting time (such as Advent). But, whereas *chronos* marks a continuous line indicating duration, *kairos* is a moment marked somewhere along that line. The phrase *en kairo* means 'at the right moment' (such as Pooh Bear's 'time for a little something'). The New Testament *hoi chronoi kai hoi kairoi* ('the times and the seasons') is a key to understanding what might have been Bach's concept of time – his way of locating and encapsulating music in precise moments and in the appointed season. By localising the event and occasion to which his music was attached, one might think that he risked reducing its impact and future accessibility, but the reverse seems to be true – its universality lies in the very specificity of its origins.

One of the features that registered most strongly with me and with many of the musicians who were exposed to Bach's cantatas in their seasonal succession in 2000 was the periodic emphasis he gives to the idea of cyclic return, of a journey from a beginning to an ending – or, in the theological language of his day, from Alpha to Omega. In replicating the rhythms of Bach's own practice and experiencing the cantata cycles at their appointed times, we gained a sense of *kairos* through this seasonal unfolding. We became aware of indissoluble connections between the music and its place in the season and often between the music of one week and that of the next, like arcs of a circle being drawn and re-drawn. It felt as though we were reconnecting to the seasonal progression and rhetorical ambit implied in Bach's music – a continuously unfolding rhythmic pattern, but one that normally goes unnoticed. As a result it allowed us to be drawn into the (re-)creative process and active edification implied in Bach's music. This was markedly different from the conventional practices of music-making we were accustomed to in concert halls, which, however persuasive, cannot help but carry resonances foreign to the intrinsic purpose of the music.

More than half of all Bach's sacred cantatas to have survived were composed in his first three to four years as Thomascantor. This is how the Leipzig cantatas break down:

Mishnaic Hebrew). All the books that were grouped together and eventually formed the New Testament were originally written in Koine Greek.

- In Year 1 (1723/4) he composed forty new cantatas. This first cycle also included fourteen adaptations or expansions of Weimar cantatas and five 'parodies' of secular Cöthen cantatas for the period after Easter 1724 that may not have been part of his original plan (see below).
- In Year 2 (1724/5) he composed fifty-two new cantatas; three of these (BWV 6, 42 and 85) are structurally identical to cantatas composed in the February of the previous year and could therefore be considered casualties of a crisis associated with the first performance of his *John Passion* on 7 April 1724. (See diagram of Bach's First Leipzig Cycle, Plate 15.)
- An equivalent disruption to his plans for Good Friday the following year could be linked to the abandonment of the chorale-based cantata cycle after Palm Sunday 1725, and may account for the inclusion of a revival (BWV 4) and a parody (BWV 249) on Easter Sunday; it may also have contributed to the realisation of a new sequence for the 'Great Fifty Days' between Easter and Pentecost. This last now comprised twelve cantatas: three (BWV 6, 42 and 185) whose texts may have been taken from a collection originally reserved for the first cycle, and nine cantatas with texts by Christiane Mariane von Ziegler (BWV 103, 108, 87, 128, 183, 74, 68, 175 and 176). It seems, then, that Bach planned this new sequence as a way of completing his first cycle in a more satisfactory way than had been possible in the spring of 1724, this time mirroring the liturgical character of the 'Great Fifty Days' unified by the preponderance of texts drawn from St John's Gospel.
- The rate of production of cantatas slows down by almost 50 per cent in 1725/6 to twenty-seven new works, and slower still to just five in the following year, a sign of the mounting problems Bach was facing in finding good-enough musicians from his available Thomaner performing ensemble. This meant that this third cycle ended up being stretched over two years (1725/7).
- This, in turn, is followed by the so-called 'Picander Cycle' of 1728/9 that may have been intended by Bach to be apportioned among himself (eight new works), his two elder sons and selected pupil-composers.
- There are around a dozen 'late' cantatas to have survived from the 1730s and 1740s.

Evidence that from the outset Bach planned on a broader scale than individual works and feast-to-feast is clear from his opening salvos for the first four Sundays after Trinity in both of his first two annual Leipzig cycles. Compared to Advent, the real beginning of the liturgical year, the first Sunday after Trinity might not seem a particularly significant day to begin a new cycle, but in fact it marked both the beginning of the academic year of the Thomasschule and the midpoint of the Lutheran liturgical year: the crossover from 'the time of Christ' (the *temporale*) to 'the era of the church' (the long Trinity season) dominated by the concerns of Christian believers living in the here and now under the guidance of the Holy Spirit. Bach therefore had good reason to emphasise this important seasonal change – which was coincidentally when he and his family arrived in Leipzig – and to establish it as the launching pad of two successive cantata cycles, the first beginning on 30 May 1723 with BWV 75, *Die Elenden sollen essen*, and the second a year later with BWV 20, *O Ewigkeit, du Donnerwort*, which set the tone for a completely new stylistic orientation and a more radical approach (see below, p. 313). Add to these the third of his surviving cantatas for this feast, BWV 39, *Brich dem Hungrigen dein Brot*, composed in 1726 (see Chapter 12), and we have three contrasted large-scale bipartite works all for the same liturgical occasion that afford us a basis for comparison.

Bach announced himself to the congregations gathered in Leipzig's Nikolaikirche and Thomaskirche in 1723 in an opening sequence couched in wide-ranging musical styles and full of exegetical allusions. His two debut cantatas, BWV 75 and 76, composed for consecutive Sundays (Tr + 1 and Tr + 2), are formed like identical twins in the way they present a musical interpretation of Scripture spread across fourteen movements (with the same unfolding pattern of movements of arias and recitatives) – seven to be performed before and seven after the sermon and during the distribution of the Communion. Evidently much thought had gone into both works – discussions with an unknown librettist and possibly with representatives of the Leipzig clergy at the time of his audition in February – before the style, tone and narrative shaping were set. The thematic link between the two works was prompted by the two set Epistles – the injunction to love God (1 John 4:16–21) and one's brother (1 John 3:13–18) – with the implicit insistence that brotherly love is the principal means by which the believer can honour God (BWV 76, Part 2). Such a comprehensive double exposition of the two New Testament commandments – to love God and one's neighbour – was in perfect accord with the definitions Bach gave at various times of his musical goals: glory to God and service to his neighbour (see Chapter 8, p. 252). Here was the perfect opportunity for Bach to make plain his future intentions to his congregation, and using his own identifying number* – fourteen – in the number of movements of these consecutive works may have been Bach's symbolic way of conveying a personal message to his congregation.[7] As his first official Leipzig cantata on assuming office, BWV 75, *Die Elenden sollen essen*, was performed eight days after he and his family arrived in Leipzig, and two days prior to his formal installation.† Judging from the neat appearance of the autograph score and the non-Leipzig paper on which it was written, it seems that Bach had given himself a head start by finishing it while he was still in Cöthen. (By contrast, the autograph of its sequel, BWV 76, *Die Himmel erzählen*, is a working score with multiple corrections, showing clear signs of haste.) The contrast between poverty (*Armut*) and spiritual riches (*Reichtum*) is used as a metaphor not just for the impermanence of earthly wealth but also for the spiritual privation of the Christian up to the moment that he is enriched by faith. Reduced to its essentials, BWV 75 presents the following message:

* Bach's cousin Johann Gottfried Walther (*Musicalisches Lexicon* (1732), p. 64) was the first writer to draw public attention to Bach's frequent use of B-A-C-H in his compositions to express his surname – a cryptographic use of the simplest number alphabet, where A = 1, etc., with B in German standing for B♭ and H for B♮, so both expressing the musical notes B♭-A-C-B♮) and the numbers 2-1-3-8 = 14.

† There is an alternative scenario in which Bach announced himself to his Leipzig public on Whit Sunday 1723 (16 May), two weeks before his reported arrival in the city. Alfred Dürr states categorically that the autograph of BWV 59, *Wer mich liebet, der wird mein Wort halten*, was written for Whit Sunday 1723 at the latest (although the surviving performing parts date from the following year). It is possible that before leaving Cöthen, Bach drew on some earlier material and assembled this four-movement cantata just in time for a 1723 premiere at Leipzig's university church. This hypothesis is supported by a passage in one of his letters of complaint to the Saxon king in which Bach claimed that he 'entered upon my University functions [in Leipzig] at Whitsunday, 1723' (*The Cantatas of J. S. Bach* (2005), p. 350; BD I, No. 12/ NBR, p. 124).

Part I

1. Appearances are deceptive, but those who suffer in this life will one day, like Lazarus, be recompensed (*opening chorus as prelude and fugue*); for
2. riches and worldly pleasures are transitory (*accompanied recitative for bass*),
3. whereas unreserved devotion to Jesus (*aria as polonaise for tenor with oboe and strings*)
4. can lead to joy in the next life (*tenor recitative*).
5. So endure patiently like Lazarus (*aria as minuet for soprano with continuo*)
6. and you can live with a clear conscience (*soprano recitative*);
7. for whatever God does, is for the best (*chorale*).

Part II

8. *Sinfonia (for trumpet and strings)*
9. Poverty of spirit (*accompanied recitative for alto*)
10. is made rich by Jesus (*alto aria as* passepied *with violins and continuo*);
11. so practise self-denial (*bass recitative*)
12. and you will be warmed by Jesus' flame (*dramatic aria for bass with trumpet and strings*);
13. so take care not to forfeit it (*tenor recitative*),
14. for whatever God does, is for the best (*chorale*).

The Gospel's 'theme of the week' – the idea that the lowly shall participate in the kingdom of God as conveyed through the Parable of Dives and Lazarus (Luke 16:19–31) – is summed up in the stirring hymn 'Was Gott tut, das is wohlgetan' that concludes both parts of Bach's opening cantata, not in a conventional four-part arrangement, but with the voice lines loosened in polyphony and placed in an independent orchestral fabric:

> Whatever God does, is well done:
> To this I shall be constant
> Though I be cast on to a rough road
> By affliction, death and misery.

There is something both poignant and prophetic in Bach's assent to the principle these words describe – his constancy in embarking on a divinely inspired assignment and the rough road he had taken towards fulfilling it. Bach was later to complain to a friend that, in fulfilling his duties in Leipzig, he had been scarcely helped by the authorities, whom he had thought 'odd and little interested in music'. But for the moment all is optimism while he focuses on his work with a white-knuckled energy.

BWV 76 is clearly more than just a sequel to the previous Sunday's cantata: together they form a diptych reflecting the dualism of the two segments of the church's year, while also ensuring a thematic continuity extended over two weeks, their texts replete with cross-references between the two set Gospels and Epistles. Thus the injunction to give charitably to the hungry (BWV 75/i) is balanced a week later by the parable of the great banquet to which all are invited 'from all the highways' (BWV 76/vi). Bach chose to open the latter with the same psalm (19:1, 3) that Heinrich Schütz had set so memorably seventy-five years before when he included it in his *Geistliche Chormusik*, dedicated to the same choir of the Thomaskirche in Leipzig:

> The heavens declare the glory of God;
> and the firmament sheweth his handywork.
> There is no speech nor language,
> where their voice is not heard.

The idea of the entire cosmos celebrating God's rich creation was a gift to a composer of Bach's conceptual ability. It allowed him to contemplate and expound the meaning of infinity, a concept that was largely sidestepped throughout the Middle Ages, of the cosmos being aware of itself, of how 'nature and grace speak to all of mankind', showing us how as humans we can marvel about our own ability to do so. Bach's vision is reflected in his choice of instruments: regal trumpets in Part I to symbolize God's glory; a viola da gamba, that ancient instrument he uses at moments of the most intense feeling, to underline the human potential for faith and love in Part II. Treating the poverty/riches antithesis would have been enough for most other composers. Instead Bach and his unknown librettist (could it have been Gottfried Lange, the poet–burgomaster, who was acting almost as his patron in these early years of his cantorate?) looked for ways to enrich the connective tissue. In his First Epistle, John focuses on the meaning of love for humanity – conveyed by Bach in a majestic aria for bass and trumpet (BWV 75/xii) – and then, the following week, on brotherly love (*die brüderliche Treue*) as the basis of worldly life, the means by which mankind gives honour to God (BWV 76/xi).

Bach extends his theme over four consecutive Sundays, for at some point he must have realised how aptly two of his Weimar cantatas (BWV 21 and 185) could be re-worked to round it out. In reviving BWV 21, *Ich hatte viel Bekümmerniss*, which had already grown into one of his more impressive works, Bach was able to enrich the duality of love of God and one's neighbour with a vision of eternity as man's eschatological goal. Remembering how the librettist Salomo Franck of BWV 185, *Barmherziges Herze*, had written that 'the art of the Christian' is 'to know only God and myself, to burn with true love, not to judge unduly, nor nullify another's deeds, not to forget one's neighbour and to mete out ample measure', Bach saw an opportunity to recycle this modestly scored work for four voices and strings with just an oboe and clarino in support. A further advantage to including these two earlier works was that it allowed him to display to his congregation a wide range of compositional styles painted on canvases of strikingly different sizes. It was a means, too, for him to gauge his listeners' preferences.

Bach's task all through this First Leipzig Cycle (see diagram, Plate 15) was to keep pace with the weekly demand. In the process he created forty new cantatas, binding them thematically in subunits to provide continuity and clarity, while remembering which earlier pieces could fit comfortably into the weave of this unfolding tapestry without stylistic disturbance. There was the copying out of parts and guiding his (as yet) untried group of young musicians in how to negotiate the hazards of his startling and challenging music with a bare minimum of rehearsal – tasks we explored in the previous chapter. Come the day, there was first a long, cold wait in an unheated church, then a single shot at a daunting target. Then, without a backward glance, on to the next, maintaining a relentless rhythm. For all the invention and originality of these initial works, this was a sequence to allay the fears of the Leipzig authorities, so suspicious of anything 'operatic' being heard in church; in comparison with the works he would go on to compose, there was at this stage nothing to alarm them.

With the long Trinity season stretching from late May to late November came a persistent thematic emphasis in the Lutheran lectionary on sin and sickness in mind and body. 'The whole world is but a hospital' declares the tenor at one point in BWV 25, *Es ist nichts Gesundes an meinem Leibe*: Adam's Fall has 'defiled us all and infected us with leprous sin'.* Sickness, raging fever, leprous boils and the 'odious stench' of sin are described in detail in the text of this cantata, making no concession to the listener's delicacy of feeling or potential queasiness. Although the unknown librettist builds to an impassioned appeal to Christ as the 'healer and helper of all' to cure and show mercy, it is Bach's music that completes the spiritual journey for us. As listeners we sense this happening, but it is difficult to say *how* he affects a change in our perception of what the words are saying. Take the opening chorus with its gloomy description of a sin-ridden world: 'there is no soundness in my flesh because of Thine anger; neither is there any rest in my bones, because of my sin' (Psalm 38:3). Having set things in motion to underscore the words by every corroborative means he could devise (two-voiced canons, sighing motifs and unstable harmonies modulating downwards), Bach had, one might imagine, exhausted his expressive arsenal, but not so. In the fifteenth bar he brings in a separate 'choir' made up of three recorders, a cornett and three trombones to intone the familiar 'Passion Chorale',† one phrase at a time. Bach has added an independent commentary of his own which gradually works its magic, instilling the idea of hope and consolation. Here he reaches out to his listeners, his music serving as a kind of spiritual blood transfusion, in which the critical agency in the healing process emanates from the music, not the words.

Time and again in these early Leipzig works we notice how Bach's most persuasive cantata-writing is all about helping listeners to see what choices they have in life, in showing them an ideal ('heaven'), then focusing on the real world and how to deal with it – in terms of

* BWV 25 was first performed on 29 Aug. 1723, the last of seven consecutive, interrelated cantatas all based on stern homiletic injunctions giving further expression to the core doctrines of faith already adumbrated in the first four Sundays of the Trinity season. They follow an identical ground plan: chorus – recitative – aria – recitative – aria – chorale.

† So-called on account of Bach's five-fold use of it in the *Matthew Passion*. Its famous tune by Hans Leo Hassler (1564–1612) was originally that of a love-song but was adapted to several hymn-texts. Probably the one Bach had in mind here was that based on Psalm 6, 'Ach Herr, mich armen Sünder' by Cyriacus Schneegass, whose fifth stanza sends a clear message of hope and relief. Apart from this, Bach's weaving of this chorale into his contrapuntal fabric is an extraordinary technical feat, and the only time, incidentally, when he uses trombones other than to bolster the voices and add colour.

attitude, behaviour and conduct. This explains why his cantatas appear to escape their historical and liturgical confinement and reach out to us today. Thoughts and feelings that we have had find expression through Bach, but with so much more candour and clarity than we can ever muster. Then he draws together all the strands of exegetical gloss he has given to the devotional themes in the course of the work in a closing chorale (usually but not always) perfectly adjusted to its situation within the emotional scheme. This was a moment of comfort for his listeners, bringing them back to the here and now of their quotidian concerns – to a 'sane' present. For, however strange or complex the new cantor's music was in the opening movements of his cantatas, the chorale was a familiar point of reference – a return to territory to which they could respond either by singing along with the melody or just by following inwardly.

Successive penitential cantatas follow, maintaining this seasonal campaign of catechismal strafing, sometimes reinforced, sometimes tempered, by Bach's music. We become accustomed to the way the human actor is positioned by the librettist in scenarios of faith and doubt, sin and Satan. The curious thing is that all this heavy theological attack neither blunts the audacity of Bach's musical response nor diminishes the humanity of his sympathy with the faithful. For, although Bach is habitually required to deal with such towering universal themes as eternity, sin and death, he shows he is also interested in the flickers of doubt and the daily tribulations of every individual, recognising that small lives do not seem small to the people who live them (just as such lives come to seem enormous the instant they are richly imagined and minutely observed by novelists such as Tolstoy or Flaubert). In this he exemplifies what Vico called *fantasia*: a faculty of imaginative insight or a capacity to get into the skin of others, or what Herder later called *Einfühlung* ('empathy').[8]

This comes to the surface in a work like BWV 105, *Herr, gehe nicht ins Gericht*, in which the penitent servant rues 'the errors of my [his] soul'. Bach turns to a device, a commonplace Baroque representation of anxiety, the *tremolo*, requiring his string players to make pulsated reiterations by twos or fours under a single bow stroke (a technique sometimes called 'bow vibrato')* and uses it astutely in three of

* This is just one device that Bach could have learnt from Buxtehude, perhaps from his motet cycle *Membra Jesu nostri* or from his elder cousin Johann Christoph, who used it in his superb lament for bass, *Wie bist du denn, O Gott*.

the cantata's six movements: first to represent the 'unjust steward' waiting nervously, knowing that he is about to be dismissed for failing to collect his master's dues (Luke 16:1–9), then to represent the quivering conscience of the sinner, fixing the idea in the listener's ear by means of the persistent thrum of semiquavers assigned to the two violins and the quaver-pulsed viola line tapping out a light but inescapable symbol of mental distress: 'How the thoughts of sinners / Tremble and reel / As they accuse / And then dare to excuse one another / Thus is the anguished conscience / Torn asunder by its own torture.' There is both a crystalline fragility to this soprano aria and a fragmented lyricism in the melodic line, first for oboe, then for the voice. They exchange tentative proposals and reticent retractions – two 'voices' echoing one another within a single mind manifestly at odds with itself. Bach avoids all melodrama. Where another composer might have seized on the obvious opportunities for vivid mimesis of the 'anguished conscience', Bach instead opts for a subtle and essentially human approach, varying his chromatic and diatonic harmonies to convey the mood-swings of a mind in a state of constant vacillation: tempted, resisting, succumbing, resisting again, achieving repose only with the final cadence (which even so we sense is only provisional). Then, in the finale chorale, to convey the progressive stilling of the sinner's troubled conscience, he returns to the *tremulant* device of the cantata's opening movement. First he plants pulsating semiquavers in the instrumental lines, then slows them down to triplet, then duplet quavers, then slower still to tripletised crotchets, and finally to plain crotchets chromatically descending – a gradual winding down to the point where both voices and continuo fall silent. It is a brilliantly graphic and original means to describe the release of the spirit from its earthly encasement.

At this distance it is easy to empathise with the deeply human way Bach lays out the various choices we all have to face at different stages in our lives – the blind alleys we pursue, the temptations and the price we often have to pay for following or giving in to them, the various ploys for easing our troubled consciences. While the word-painting here is subtle and the imagery generally easier to grasp than in several other cantatas (much helped by the atypically high quality of the libretto), the real pleasure comes in following Bach's prodigious musical inventiveness as it develops: those ideas which sparked his fantasy in the first place, and then the techniques used in presenting and elaborating them.

The relationship between this cantata and that for the following Sunday, BWV 46, *Schauet doch und sehet*, is far too close to be accidental. It goes beyond the obvious facts that they share warnings against sin, fear of reprisal in the shape of God's harsh judgement and the same (by no means unique) symmetrical six-movement layout (chorus – recitative – aria – recitative – aria – chorale). For example, both draw on *bassetchen* texture (105/iii, 46/v) and both have highly unusual final movements in which the chorale is embedded within an independent orchestral setting, with interludes for upper strings (105/vi) and two recorders (46/vi), in both cases unsupported by continuo. Even the *tremulant* device, such a prominent feature of BWV 105, reappears (perhaps to jog the listener's short-term memory) in the second part of a storm-scene bass aria (BWV 46/iii), changing the mood of martial menace to one of anxious waiting for God's vengeance to strike – and marked to be performed *pianissimo*. Most importantly, both cantatas announce themselves in grand opening movements structured as a chorale prelude and fugue to mirror the sentence divisions of the biblical text.

There are signs here of the way Bach was already thinking ahead to Passiontide, the two choruses revealing features we associate with the opening tableau of the *John Passion* (see Chapter 10, p. 357): in BWV 46, the same pronounced sighing figure in the violas; and, in BWV 105, imploring choral shouts of *Herr! Herr!* linked to similar harsh suspensions in the upper instruments, and the same throbbing bass line and G minor tonality. BWV 46 begins as a lament over the destruction of Jerusalem in the words of Jeremiah (Lamentations 1:12). Jesus' prophecy of the Roman destruction in AD 70 is recounted in the Gospel of the day (Luke 19:41–8), and both on this Sunday and on Good Friday in the Leipzig churches there were annual readings of the Roman historian Josephus' account of the event as well as John's Passion narration. By alluding to it here, Bach's musical narrative is able to span separate historical eras – from that of the Old Testament prophet Jeremiah to that of Jesus – and brand these successive catastrophes in the believer's mind, giving them the form of metaphors for his self-inflicted woes, just as there is a similar spanning of time zones in his Passions.

It might have taken him nine or ten Sundays to get fully into his stride and develop these elaborate contrapuntal choruses, but from this point on there is no turning back. Bach had set out to develop a new cantata style in Leipzig, distinct from the works he had written earlier, and by reviving four Weimar cantatas in previous weeks he had given himself additional time to reflect and elaborate on it. BWV 105 and 46 are the result. Preference for one or the other of these imposing cantatas is a matter of personal choice, but one could easily be seduced by the richer instrumentation of BWV 46 – two recorders, two oboes da caccia and a slide trumpet added to the normal string ensemble – and by the fact that its first ('Prelude') section came to be re-used to the words *Qui tollis peccata mundi* in the Gloria of the *B minor Mass*, evidence of how highly Bach himself valued it.* Taken together, one senses that Bach intended the cantatas of these two weeks to form a musico-theological climax to this early Trinity season.

With summer giving way to autumn, the focus of the appointed texts for each Sunday is on the hazards of living in society – with warnings against false prophets and hypocrites and how to live righteously in a sin-affected world. One could choose any of the thirty cantatas he included from the start of his first cycle up to Christmas to illustrate this progression. Midway through BWV 93, *Wer nur den lieben Gott lässt walten*, Bach has his tenor exclaim, 'There is death in the pots!' – an allusion likely to have puzzled even his Bible-reading congregation. (It turns out to be Elisha's reaction in a time of death to an unappetising dish prepared for him which he somehow makes edible 'for the people' (II Kings 4:40–41) – an apt metaphor for Bach's skill in regularly converting the hard doctrinal crust of this unpromising Trinitarian fare into something both palatable and varied.) Having already acquired the knack of how to vivify a doctrinal message and, when appropriate, of delivering it with a hard dramatic kick, he is now exploring ways of how and when to balance it with music of an emollient tenderness, humouring and softening the severity of his texts while in no way blunting their impact. Time and again one senses Bach's exceptional level of engagement with the words, his music going far beyond literal mimesis

* The recorders also have a prominent role in the sequel – to illustrate Christ's 'brimming streams of tears', set high above the sustained strings who inscribe nine successive bars without a common chord – and in anticipation of Jerusalem's fall and Christ's mercy in protecting the devout in a *bassetchen* aria for alto with oboes da caccia. They replicate that mood in episodes played between the lines of the final chorale – with the same cascade of semiquavers as well as melodic gestures recalling the opening chorus.

or the codified use of conventional figures and symbols. (Bach's complex braiding of words and music will be the subject of Chapter 12, where we will encounter more of his inaugural Leipzig cantatas.)

* * *

As autumn passes to winter the themes of the week become steadily grimmer as the faithful are urged to reject the world, its lures and snares, and to focus on eventual union with God – or risk the horror of permanent exclusion. From week to week this dichotomy appears to grow harsher, with the stress on sin and guilt deepening as the weather worsens. To convey the inner conflict between belief and doubt in BWV 109, *Ich glaube, lieber Herr, hilf meinem Unglauben!*, we find him assigning two opposing 'voices', sung by the same singer, one marked *forte*, the other *piano*. (How Schumann – the creator of Florestan and Eusebius, who hated to express himself in a single unified voice – would have loved this.) Polarity of a different kind is suggested in BWV 90, *Es reißet euch ein schrecklich Ende* – between the terrifying outcome that awaits sinners at the Last Judgement and the protection God guarantees to 'His elect'. Bach opens with a 'rage' aria of unflagging energy – with *tirades* and flourishes of fourteen consecutive demisemiquavers, big jumps in tessitura, curtailed phrase-endings and dramatic pauses mid-word (*schreck . . . lich*). This is as theatrically extreme as anything his listeners (and performers) might have encountered during the years when Leipzig had its own opera house (1693–1720)[9] – and not what they would normally expect to hear in church – and the first time he had risked this flagrant breach of protocol.

For his final cantata of the Trinity season, BWV 70, *Wachet! betet! betet! wachet!*, with its play on words, Bach increases the voltage. In flanking *accompagnati* now added to his earlier Weimar cantata, with their repeated semiquavers hammered out in Monteverdi's *stile concitato* (the 'excited style'), Bach anticipates by many years the inherently operatic outbursts of two of Handel's most formidable stage heroines: Dejanira, the unhinged wife in *Hercules* (1745) ('Where shall I fly?'), and Storgè, the outraged mother in *Jephtha* (1752) ('First perish thou!'). But it is not merely the full-throttle openings of these dramatic scenes that beg comparison with this cantata: Bach is a match for his Saxon contemporary at every step – in the power of his vocal declamation, in the vividly supportive orchestral accompaniment he invents to portray the cataclysmic destruction of the world and in the seraphic transition he achieves as Jesus finally guides the believer to complete 'stillness, to that place of abundant joy'. In these two cantatas that bring the Trinity season to a close, Bach seems – presumably unintentionally – to have taken on his peer group of Italian-opera composers and beaten them at their own game. (This is all part of the evolution of a mutant form of opera proposed in Chapter 4.) In the process he manifestly broke the pledge he had given to the council barely six months previously – not to make compositions that were 'too theatrical' or of the kind he had composed in Weimar. As we shall soon see these were not momentary slips but by now a habitual transgression – hugely entertaining and to be relished by a congregation numbed by cold and four hours on a hard pew.

With Bach's approach to his first Christmas season in Leipzig the mood lightens. After the Advent *tempus clausum* comes a collective intake of breath, followed by an explosion of festive music. A cluster of brand-new works suddenly appears on the music stands of the Thomaner – nine major pieces for them to master and deliver over the next sixteen days in three of the city's churches. In his mind Bach must have set aside this first break in the cycle as the time to accelerate his speed of weekly composition.* In less than a month he would need to complete music for seven feasts, from Christmas Day through to the first Sunday after Epiphany: six new cantatas – BWV 40, 64, 190, 153, 65 and 154 – and two Latin works in a separate but equally challenging idiom – a compact *Sanctus* in D (BWV 238) and the *Magnificat* in E♭ major (BWV 243a), more familiar nowadays in its later D major version (BWV 243). These two were to be performed in tandem with his grand Weimar cantata BWV 63, *Christen, ätzet diesen Tag*, on Christmas Day. A glance at the schedule reveals the immensity and relentlessness of the assignment Bach set for himself and his performing ensemble:

* From the evidence of the hastily copied part-books for the cantatas, Bach was rarely able to compose ahead of schedule. However, his last newly composed work before Advent was BWV 90 on 14 Nov. Most of BWV 70 the following week had been pre-composed in Weimar and all of BWV 61 performed on 28 Nov., so that one could reason that he had almost six weeks in total to compose the *Magnificat*, his largest-scale vocal composition to date, and all the other works due for performance as part of his first Christmas festival.

Christmas Day, 25 December 1723			
7 a.m. Mass	Thomaskirche	BWV 63	*Christen, ätzet diesen Tag*
		BWV 238	*Sanctus*
9 a.m. Service	Paulinerkirche	BWV 63	*Christen, ätzet diesen Tag*
1.30 p.m. Vespers	Nikolaikirche	BWV 63	*Christen, ätzet diesen Tag*
		BWV 243a	*Magnificat*
Second Day of Christmas, Feast of St Stephen, 26 December			
7 a.m. Mass	Nikolaikirche	BWV 40	*Darzu ist erschienen*
		BWV 238	*Sanctus*
1.30 p.m. Vespers	Thomaskirche	BWV 40	*Darzu ist erschienen*
		BWV 243a	*Magnificat*
Third Day of Christmas, Feast of St John, 27 December			
7 a.m. Mass	Thomaskirche	BWV 64	*Sehet, welch eine Liebe*
New Year's Day, Feast of the Circumcision, 1 January 1724			
7 a.m. Mass	Nikolaikirche	BWV 190	*Singet dem Herrn*
1.30 p.m. Vespers	Thomaskirche	BWV 190	*Singet dem Herrn*
Sunday after New Year's Day, 2 January			
7 a.m. Mass	Thomaskirche	BWV 153	*Schau, lieber Gott*
Epiphany, 6 January			
7 a.m. Mass	Nikolaikirche	BWV 65	*Sie werden aus Saba*
1.30 p.m. Vespers	Thomaskirche	BWV 65	*Sie werden aus Saba*
First Sunday after Epiphany, 9 January			
7 a.m. Mass	Thomaskirche	BWV 154	*Mein liebster Jesus*

One marvels at how he and his performers could have met these challenges. We shall of course never know how well they acquitted themselves and just how well the music was performed under such pressure.* Signs that Bach had anticipated the problem of cumulative fatigue may be found in his use of *colla parte* instruments to bolster the choral lines of several opening choruses and the absence of soprano solos in five cantatas (BWV 40, 190, 153, 65 and 154). Open any one of these scores at random or listen to them and you cannot fail to be impressed by the stupefying scale of Bach's undertaking and the technical demands he made of himself and his performing ensemble in composing and performing such a cornucopia of Christmas music at breakneck speed: one is left with what Dreyfus calls 'inchoate feelings of awe'.[10]

As Bach emerged from this punishing schedule, there was the need to think ahead, to plan and plot, scrabbling for time to conceive and then to flesh out his first Passion oratorio. We have already seen evidence of preparatory sketches for his *John Passion*, but how much of it had been completed at this stage? Already at Christmas-time we start to find signs of him preparing his listeners for shocks to come and giving hints of what lay in store for them. For example, he gave what might seem to us a curiously unseasonal theological twist to three consecutive works for the three days of Christmas. Bach provides none of the usual themes we are used to from his (later) *Christmas Oratorio*: no song of the Virgin, no music for the shepherds or for the angels, not even the standard Christmas chorales. The exception is the well-known *Magnificat*. In this first version in E♭ Bach introduced so-called *laudes*. Mostly delightful, sometimes rather peculiar, these pieces are quite intricate for mere cradle songs and were apparently intended as a sop to local custom, to be sung by a separate 'angelic' choir from the swallow-nest gallery of

* Scholars have been quick to point to the smaller scale of a few works such as BWV 153 and 154 – so as 'not to strain the choir unduly' – requiring the choir to sing only simple four-part chorales or to have the help of instrumental doubling (BWV 64). But when was that ever a 'compensation for the lack of rehearsal time'? (Christoph Wolff, *Bach: The Learned Musician* (2000), p. 264). In my experience, instrumental doubling by cornets and sackbuts, such as Bach uses in several of his *stile antico* opening movements, while providing the singers with a safety net, also requires extra time to ensure balance and good intonation. The truth is that this Christmas sequence comprises some of the most hair-raisingly difficult music in his whole œuvre: the succession of difficult tenor arias, the tempo changes mid movement in BWV 63, the opulent orchestration of BWV 65, the acrobatic *Fecit potentiam* fugue in the *Magnificat*, etc.

the Thomaskirche. Inserted between the verses of Mary's song, they form a summary of the Christmas story in miniature.

Elsewhere he presents us with a decidedly Johannine view of the incarnation – as God's descent in human form to save man and to bring joy through His defeat of the Devil – in clear anticipation of the message of his *John Passion*, now only a few months away. In three thrilling Christmas cantatas – BWV 63, 40 and 64 – Bach gives strong emphasis throughout to John's depiction of Jesus as *Christus victor*.* Since the third day of Christmas is also the Feast of St John we see why Bach might have chosen to emphasise a division between the world 'above' (full of truth and light) and the one 'below' (full of darkness, sin and incomprehension). God *descends* in human form to save man from the sin that has poisoned him ever since his first encounter with the Devil (represented by a snake). Man's aspiration is to *ascend* to a plane where he can be included as one of God's children. But before this ascent can begin Jesus must first undergo his Passion and then, by his resurrection, defeat sin, death and the Devil. It is of course all too easy to describe Bach's music mainly in terms of text and then forget why we were interested in it in the first place. In the cases of BWV 40, 64 and the glorious Epiphany cantata BWV 65 that follows ten days later, there are little pointers in the way many of the words and images seem to spring so easily from the biblical quotations and chorales and are then fused so naturally with the music, enough to suggest that Bach himself might have written their texts, or at least had a preponderant influence on their author.

* * *

* While this Johannine slant could be said on this occasion to come from the Christmas Gospel (John 1: 1–14), there is unquestionably a detectable Johannine emphasis all through the cantatas of Bach's First Leipzig Cycle that cannot be attributed to the Gospel formulations alone and must therefore have formed part of Bach's overall design and the way he prepares his listeners for the 'big event' – his first Passion setting. Leaving aside the Passion narratives, there were thirty-four Gospel lections taken from Matthew, compared to twenty-one from John, or (in terms of verses) 319 verses from Matthew against 203 from John. (I am grateful to Robin Leaver for these figures.) On the other hand John's Gospel marks the crucial start of key segments of the liturgical year, and this is reflected by Bach in his first cycle, where he favoured a biblical citation as the text of twenty-eight out of forty of his newly composed cantatas.

In Bach's time the period between Christmas and Epiphany was called *Raunächte* – literally 'rough nights' – the German equivalent to the Roman Saturnalia and of similar pagan tradition. Yet there was no respite for him: there were nine weeks from Epiphany to the beginning of Lent for which six new cantatas were needed (with three earlier Weimar works available for revision) plus one for the Feast of the Purification (2 February). For Epiphany + 4, what must count as Bach's most 'operatic' cantata bursts into life: BWV 81, *Jesus schläft, was soll ich hoffen?* Here he gives his listeners a foretaste of the enthralling music they could expect when his imagination was torched by a particularly dramatic incident. Based on Matthew's description of Jesus' calming a violent storm on the sea of Galilee that threatens to capsize the ship in which he and his disciples are sailing, it makes a sea voyage into a metaphor for the Christian life. It begins with Jesus asleep on board ship, the backdrop to an eerie meditation on the terrors of abandonment in a godless world – cue for a pair of old-fashioned recorders added to the string band for an aria for alto, the voice Bach regularly uses for expressions of contrition, fear and lamenting. Here he challenges the singer to a serious technical (and symbolic) test of endurance: to hold a low B♭ without quavering for ten slow beats and then to negotiate a series of angular leaps and twists (through diminished and augmented intervals) to evoke the gaping abyss of approaching death. Life without Jesus – his somnolent silence lasts all the way through the first three numbers – causes his disciples, and of course Christians ever since, acute anguish and a sense of alienation that rises to the surface in the tenor recitative with its dislocated, dissonant harmonies. In the background of the night we hear the words of Psalm 13 – 'How long wilt thou forget me, O Lord, for ever? How long wilt thou hide thy face from me?' – and the image of the guiding star precious to all mariners and to the magi.

Suddenly the storm bursts. A continuous spume of violent demisemiquavers in the first violins is set against an unabated thudding in the other instruments. It reaches a succession of ear-splitting cracks on diminished seventh chords conveying the rage of 'Belial's waters' beating against the tiny vessel. It is similar to one of Handel's powerful 'rage' arias, demanding an equivalent virtuosity of rapid passagework by both tenor and violins, but imbued with vastly more harmonic tension – what *Paradise Lost* might sound like if set as an opera. Three times Bach halts the momentum mid-storm for two-bar 'close-ups' of the storm-tossed mariner. Though it feels intensely real, the tempest is also an emblem of the godless forces that threaten to engulf the lone Christian as he stands up to his tormentors. It is extraordinary what a vivid *scena* Bach has created from its beginning in a simple $\frac{3}{8}$ *allegro* in G major for strings alone. Jesus, now awake (as if he could possibly have slept through all the mayhem), rebukes his disciples for their lack of faith. In an arioso with straightforward continuo accompaniment, almost a two-part invention, the bass soloist assumes the role of *vox Christi*. After the colourful drama of the preceding *scena* the very sparseness and deliberate repetitiveness of the music is striking. One wonders whether there is a pinch of dramatic realism here, of yawn-induced rebuke (the repetition of *warum?*) or even of mild satire – one of those occasions when Bach may be poking fun at one of his Leipzig theological task-masters. There follows a second seascape, almost as remarkable as the earlier tempest, this time as an aria for bass, two oboes d'amore and strings. The strings are locked in octaves, a symbol of order to show that even the pull of the tides, the undertow and the waves welling up can be checked just as they are about to break by Jesus' commands *Schweig! Schweig!* ('Be silent!') and *Verstumme!* ('Be still!').*

When might Bach, a landlocked Thuringian, have witnessed a maritime storm? It could only have been on the Baltic during his brief stay in Lübeck in 1705, if ever. However, one of his favourite authors, the seventeenth-century theologian Heinrich Müller, certainly did. Müller lived in Rostock on the Baltic coast and commentated eloquently on this particular incident in Matthew's Gospel. For the true believer to travel in 'Christ's little ship' is, metaphorically, to experience the buffetings of life and bad weather but to come through unscathed: 'the paradox of total peace in the midst of turbulence'.[11] Müller's tropological interpretation of this biblical event – one to give moral guidance to the listener – may have prompted Bach's exceptional treatment, a fore-

* Neither Bach's autograph score nor the original parts contain any indication of articulation, which of course does not preclude their introduction in his performances. Experimenting with different slur-permutations and with localised *crescendi* aborted one beat earlier than their natural wave-crest, I found that this worked both idiomatically and pictorially, as did the final ritornello played smoothly and softly, as though now obedient to Christ's commands. The stilling of the storm is also implicit both in the alto soloist's concluding recitative and in the final chorale, the seventh verse of Johann Franck's hymn 'Jesu, meine Freude' – a perfect conclusion to this extraordinary work.

taste of the equally dramatic story-telling in music in his *John Passion*, whose premiere was fast approaching. No doubt it ruffled the feathers of Leipzig councilmen like Dr Steger, who, nine months earlier, had voted for Bach as cantor with the explicit proviso 'that he should make compositions that were not too theatrical'.[12] A work such as this suggests what kind of opera composer Bach might have made if he had been so inclined, for there is nothing in his secular cantatas (despite their titles as *drammi per musica*) that is as remotely theatrical as this amazing cantata.

Assuming that he had a pre-eminent role in the choice of poetic texts and selection of chorales in the period leading up to Lent, it seems that Bach was carefully preparing the congregation for the communal response that the chorales were soon to fulfil in his first Passion setting, making sure also to establish a connection in their minds between a bass voice and the voice of Christ. That left Lent, its forty days interrupted by the Feast of the Annunciation (25 March), in which to complete the *John Passion* in time for Good Friday (7 April). This, as it turned out, would be his one opportunity to stamp his mark on the shape, style and purpose of music for this red-letter day with impunity. We can piece together the links in the narrative from the council minutes. In the lead up to Holy Week 1724 Bach had forged ahead, posting announcements, printing and issuing libretti of his *John Passion* scheduled for performance in the Thomaskirche. To the dismay of some in the council offices it must have seemed as though the new cantor simply did not grasp the elementary protocol of how things were done in Leipzig. Was he not aware of the local 'tradition' (established just three years before, in 1721) of alternating the Good Friday service between the city's two main churches? The council minutes state that the cantor had been notified in advance that this year it was the turn of the Nikolaikirche. He was duly summoned to appear before the consistory to explain why he had flouted their instruction and to be told in no uncertain terms to 'pay attention' (*darnach achten*) and 'to take better care in future'. The town clerk's minutes indicate that Bach's response was (surprisingly) measured and co-operative: 'He would comply with the same [agreeing to switch venue to the Nikolaikirche in other words], but pointed out that the booklet had already been printed . . . [and] he requested at least that a little additional room be provided in the choir loft, so that he could place the persons needed for the music; also that the harpsichord be repaired.' To this 'The Honoured and Most Wise Council' duly agreed, and a new leaflet announcing the change of venue was printed.[13] That should have been the end of the matter, but it clearly wasn't: there was still the clergy to deal with, as we shall see in the next chapter.

Bach's best-laid plans seem to have gone awry. The first performance of the *John Passion* on 7 April 1724 manifestly interfered with the subsequent unfolding of his first cantata cycle, though we can only guess whether this was because Bach had received a stern theological reproof or was simply a consequence of his having overextended himself. Fifteen church feasts remained for the 'Great Fifty Days' from Easter to Whit Sunday and its sequel, Trinity Sunday, before the cycle was complete, and with dense three-day pressure points at the Easter and Whitsun weekends.* For whatever reasons Bach was not able to keep to his original plan for a through-composed sequence, and as a consequence we find him being forced into makeshift solutions – resorting to four previously composed cantatas (BWV 31, 12, 172 and 194) and then recycling material from secular works composed in his Cöthen days (BWV 66, 134, 104, 173 and 184) for another five. That still left five new works leading up to Whit Sunday for him to compose. Their overall quality is consistently high, and here again he casts them to form a mini-cycle.

The first in this sequence, BWV 67, *Halt im Gedächtnis*, is especially impressive: the music vibrates with a pulsating rhythmic energy and a wealth of invention. Bach's task here is to depict the perplexed and vacillating feelings of the disciples, their hopes dashed after the Crucifixion. He conveys the palpable tension between Thomas's doubts and the need within the group to keep faith (the corno blasts this out as a sustained single note in the opening chorus, an injunction to 'hold' Jesus in remembrance). Later, what starts out as a poised and chirpy gavotte for tenor, oboe and strings fragments abruptly in its second bar: 'But what affrights me still?' juxtaposes these contrary *Affekts*, one fretful, the other affirmative. He successfully captures the jittery mind-frame of the beleaguered Christian, his alto soloist exhorting the choir to keep their spirits up by

* Overall the cycle contains sequences where formal structures recur: a pattern for ten cantatas in the Trinity season that use a scriptural dictum and a closing chorale to act as bookends to two recitative/aria pairings, a further scheme at Christmas that interpolates a second chorale at the midpoint, and a third of pre-Lenten works similar to the second, only dropping the first recitative.

singing the iconic Easter hymn 'Erschienen ist der herrlich Tag'. Then at the climax of the cantata comes a dramatic *scena* in which the strings work up a storm to illustrate the raging of the enemy without. The three-voiced choir of stricken disciples, augmented by the *furioso* strings, conveys a sense of alienation of the Christian community in the here and now. Like a cinematic dissolve, Bach blends this into a slower, gently dotted triple-rhythm sequence for his three woodwind instruments – cue for Jesus' sudden appearance to his disciples who are huddled together in a locked room. Three times their anxiety is quelled by Jesus' beatific utterance *Friede sei mit euch* ('Peace be unto you'). At its fourth and final appearance the strings abandon their storm-rousing and symbolically melt into the woodwind's lulling rhythms. In this way the scene ends peacefully, the concluding chorale acknowledging the Prince of Peace as 'a strong helper in need, in life and in death'.

* * *

Now, without so much as a week to reflect or take stock, Bach plunges ahead with his Second Leipzig Cycle on 11 June 1724 (see diagram, Plate 16). There is an unmistakable shift in his approach but not the slightest diminution in quality. The first cycle was boldly experimental – in the diversity of its forms, in its varied instrumentation and in the huge challenges it posed to Bach's performing forces – but the second is, if anything, bolder still. The technique of his players and singers is to be stretched still further, the new music demanding an instant responsiveness to the pulse and mood of the moment: singers need to match the instruments for precision and agility; players reciprocally need to shape and inflect their lines like singers. There will also be fewer concessions to his listeners' scruples. That much is clear from the outset of his first cantata, BWV 20, *O Ewigkeit, du Donnerwort*. It is an astonishing piece, one that sets the tone for the whole cycle and sums up so many of the original features we will encounter – a new range of expression, the use of operatic technique to enliven the doctrinal message and wild contrasts of mood. In this instance Bach takes his lead from the Epistle's plea for 'boldness in the day of judgement' (1 John 4: 16–21) to fire his imagination and powers of musical invention. We seem to be already in the death-throes of the Trinity season, not at its start – but then Bach's was an age that had the taste for apocalypse, and the theme crops up regularly and unexpectedly.* While the tune of Johann Rist's hymn was familiar enough to his congregation, Bach's treatment of it was novel and shocking. Where the previous year's vision was of a faith-propelled anticipation of eternity in BWV 21, fear, rather than comfort, is now the subtext of BWV 20 – the chilling prospect of an eternity of torture and pain. It is the spur to man to save his soul: the only way towards salvation is for him to renounce sin. The hymn tune dominates all three segments of the opening chorale fantasia (*fast – slow – fast*). Bach saw to it that the combined energies of the Thomaner trebles were channelled into the rising melodic *cantus firmus* (*O Ewigkeit*) ('O eternity') and reinforced by the martial slide trumpet propelling the three lower voices in its wake before they splinter off in the sharply dotted style of the instruments (*du Donnerwort*) ('thou thunder-word'). Powerful cross-accents and a huge upward sweep for the basses on *Traurigkeit* ('grief') characterise the double fugue. Abruptly the orchestra screeches to a halt on a diminished seventh. Only a bold dramatist would risk stopping the forward momentum to convey trepidation – personal and petrifying – and Bach had good reason to be proud of this. (Any late-coming worshippers entering at that point would have been frozen to the spot, their neighbourly greetings silenced.) Out of the ensuing silence, terse and angular fragments are tossed from oboes to strings and back again in anticipation of the choir's resumption: 'My terrified heart quakes' – with actual breaks in the voice – 'so that my tongue cleaves to my gums.' Disjointed discourse of this intensity seems unimaginable in a pre-Beethovenian world. Bach understood the physiology of the voice far more than he is given credit for and makes it very much part of the expression. Suddenly we realise why he has chosen a French overture form as the structural basis of this movement:† far from its traditional evocation

* One need only reflect on how many of Bach's children died in infancy and how both his parents had died on reaching the age of fifty to appreciate how human mortality and death were a constant reality for him – hence the continuing significance of eschatology. One of the books in his library was Martin Geier's *Zeit und Ewigkeit* (*Time and Eternity*), a fat quarto volume of sermons on the Gospels throughout the church year (1664) in which each Gospel is expounded for its significance for time and eternity, now and then, showing that eschatological themes were explored at all times during the year.

† Back in his Weimar days Bach had found what a powerful setting a French overture could make for a chorale *cantus firmus* in his Advent cantata BWV 61 – how Louis XIV's most regal and ceremonial manner provided a naturalistic way to announce the arrival of Christ on earth.

9. Thomasschule and Thomaskirche, 1723

This engraving by Johann Gottfried Krügner illustrates the close proximity of school and church. Bach's private apartments were a mere stone's throw away in the school building on which his duties as Cantor were centred. But as the town's *director musices* these extended equally to the larger Nikolaikirche, the official town church, some seven minutes' walk away, and to more distant arenas of music-making within and just outside the town walls.

a. Abraham Christoph Platz (1658–1728)
Leader of the Estates' city party, commissioner for the Nikolaikirche, Platz became mayor in 1705 until his death. He opposed Bach's candidacy as Thomascantor and was the force behind the new Thomasschule statutes and the admission of poor children regardless of musical ability. A philanthropist and Pietist, Platz was a close ally of August Hermann Francke.

b. Gottfried Lange (1672–1748)
Leader of the absolutist court party in Leipzig, commissioner for the Thomaskirche from 1719 to his death, Lange became the senior burgomaster after Platz's death. Initially a staunch supporter and patron of Bach, godfather to his first Leipzig-born son, later, suffering serious illness, he proved to be a lot less supportive.

c. Adrian Steger (1662–1741)
Ten years older than Lange and belonging to the same absolutist court party, Steger, as mayor, always stood in Lange's shadow. He opposed Bach's candidacy and was his sternest critic, predicting in 1730 that since 'the cantor did nothing … a break would have to come sometime.'

10. Thomasschule and Thomaskirche, 1749
This coloured engraving shows the renovated and enlarged Thomasschule (1731–2) in the distance, just to the left of the church.

11. (below) Six Leipzig Burgomasters

d. Christian Ludwig Stieglitz (1677–1758)
As a lawyer Stieglitz was appointed inspector of the Thomasschule in 1729, pushed through the new rules for school admissions and was instrumental in appointing J.A. Ernesti (a close ally, and tutor to his children) as co-rector and later rector. He succeeded Steger as burgomaster in 1741.

e. Jacob Born (1683–1758)
Born succeeded Platz in 1728 as leader of the Estates' city party and as commissioner for the Nikolaikirche. In 1730 he led a campaign to clip Bach's independent wings by reinstating his teaching duties at the Thomasschule on the grounds that he showed 'little inclination to work'. Born succeeded Lange as senior burgomaster in 1748.

f. Gottfried Wilhelm Küstner (1689–1762)
Küstner was initially the Elector's favourite to succeed Steger in 1741, and only became burgomaster in 1749, successfully blocking Stieglitz's reappointment as inspector of the Thomasschule. His wife was godmother to Bach's daughter Elisabeth Juliana Friderica.

J. N. J.

Die Heilige Bibel

nach S. Herrn D. MARTINI LUTHERI

Deutscher Dolmetschung/ und Erklärung/

vermöge des Heil. Geistes/

im Grund-Text/

Richtiger Anleitung der Cohærentz,

Und der gantzen Handlung eines jeglichen Texts/

Auch Vergleichung der gleichlautenden Sprüche/ enthaltenen

eigenen Sinn und Meinung/

Nechst ordentlicher Eintheilung eines jeden Buches und Capitels/

und Erwegung der nachdrücklichen Wort/ und Redens-Art

in der Heil. Sprache/

sonderlich aber

Der Evangelischen allein seligmachenden Warheit/

gründ- und deutlich erörtert/

und mit Anführung

Herrn LUTHERI deutschen/ und verdeutschten Schrifften/

also abgefasset/

daß der eigentliche Buchstäbliche Verstand/

und gutes Theils auch

der heilsame Gebrauch der Heil. Schrifft

fürgestellet ist/

Mit grossem Fleiß/ und Kosten ausgearbeitet/

und verfasset/

von

D. ABRAHAM CALOVIO,

Im Jahr Christi cIↄ Iↄc XXCI.

welches ist das 1681

5681ste Jahr/ von Erschaffung der Welt.

Zu Wittenberg/

Nicht uns HERR/ nicht uns/ sondern deinem Namen gib Ehre/

umb deiner Gnade und Warheit!

Gedruckt in Wittenberg/ bey Christian Schrödtern/ der Univ. Buchdr.

JSBach 1733

12. (opposite page) Calov Bible

The prominent seventeenth-century Orthodox theologian Abraham Calov (1612–86) was the editor of *Die Heilige Bibel*, a detailed commentary on the Scriptures based on Luther's writings and translations. It has not so far been established exactly when Bach acquired his copy of the 1681 edition, which was rediscovered in 1934. The monogram 'JSBach 1733', in the bottom-right corner of the title page, might simply indicate the date he entered when re-cataloguing his library.

13. (below) Devotional Music and God's Grace

From his annotation of passages in Calov's *Heilige Bibel* it is clear that Bach selected passages that gave biblical justification for his chosen profession and for the art of music itself. In response to a section of 2 Chronicles 5, which Calov introduces with the words 'How the glory of the Lord appeared upon the beautiful music', Bach adds a comment on the metaphysical dimension to music-making: 'NB. Where there is devotional music, God with his grace is always present.' The very act of music-making, in other words, elicits God's presence, provided it is *andächtig* – devotional and mindful. *(Images of the Bible commentary of Abraham Calov owned and annotated by J. S. Bach courtesy of Concordia Seminary Library, St Louis, Missouri {all rights reserved})*

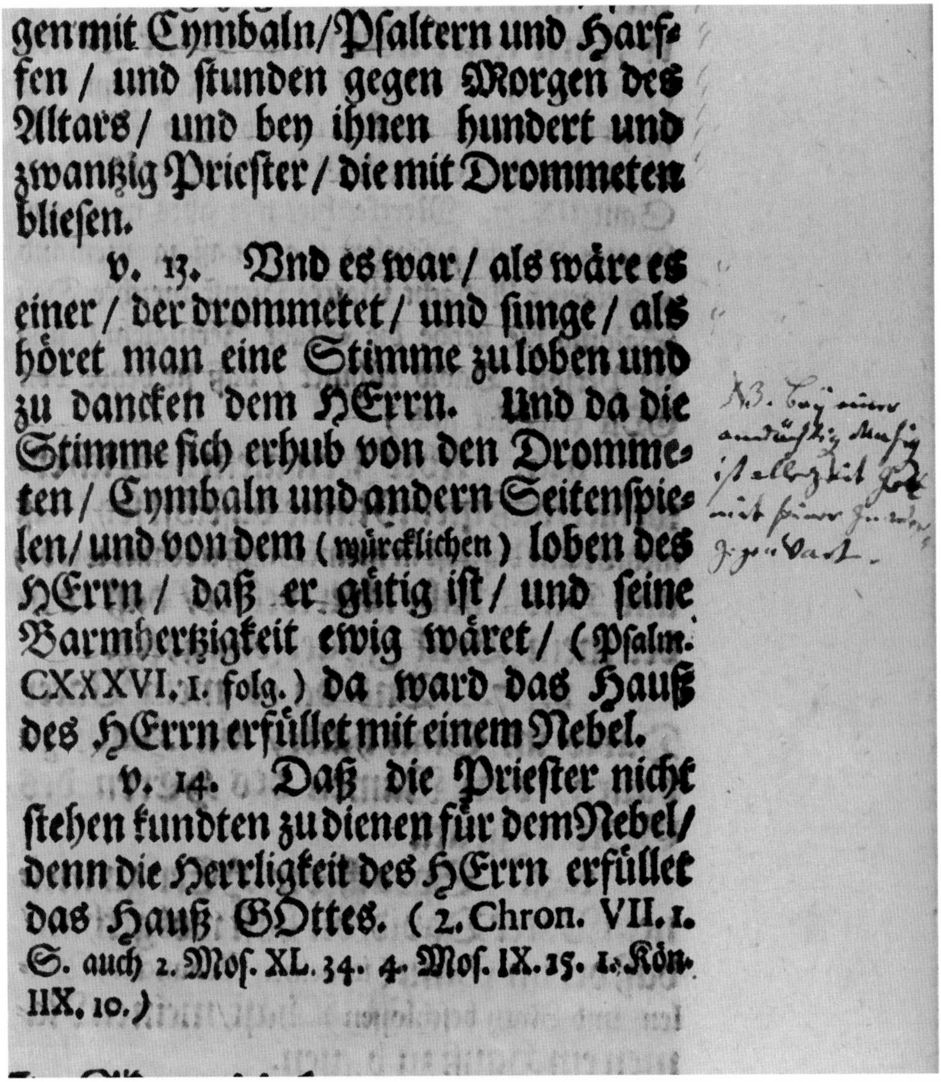

gen mit Cymbaln/Psaltern und Harf-
fen / und stunden gegen Morgen des
Altars/ und bey ihnen hundert und
zwantzig Priester / die mit Drommeten
bliesen.

v. 13. Und es war / als wäre es
einer / der drommetet / und sünge / als
höret man eine Stimme zu loben und
zu dancken dem HErrn. Und da die
Stimme sich erhub von den Drommeten / Cymbaln und andern Seitenspie-
len / und von dem (würcklichen) loben des
HErrn / daß er gütig ist / und seine
Barmhertzigkeit ewig wäret / (Psalm.
CXXXVI. 1. folg.) da ward das Hauß
des HErrn erfüllet mit einem Nebel.

v. 14. Daß die Priester nicht
stehen kundten zu dienen für dem Nebel /
denn die Herrligkeit des HErrn erfüllet
das Hauß GOttes. (2. Chron. VII. 1.
S. auch 2. Mos. XL. 34. 4. Mos. IX. 15. 1. Kön.
IIX. 10.)

NB. Bey einer andächtigen Music ist allezeit Gott mit seiner Gnaden Gegenwart.

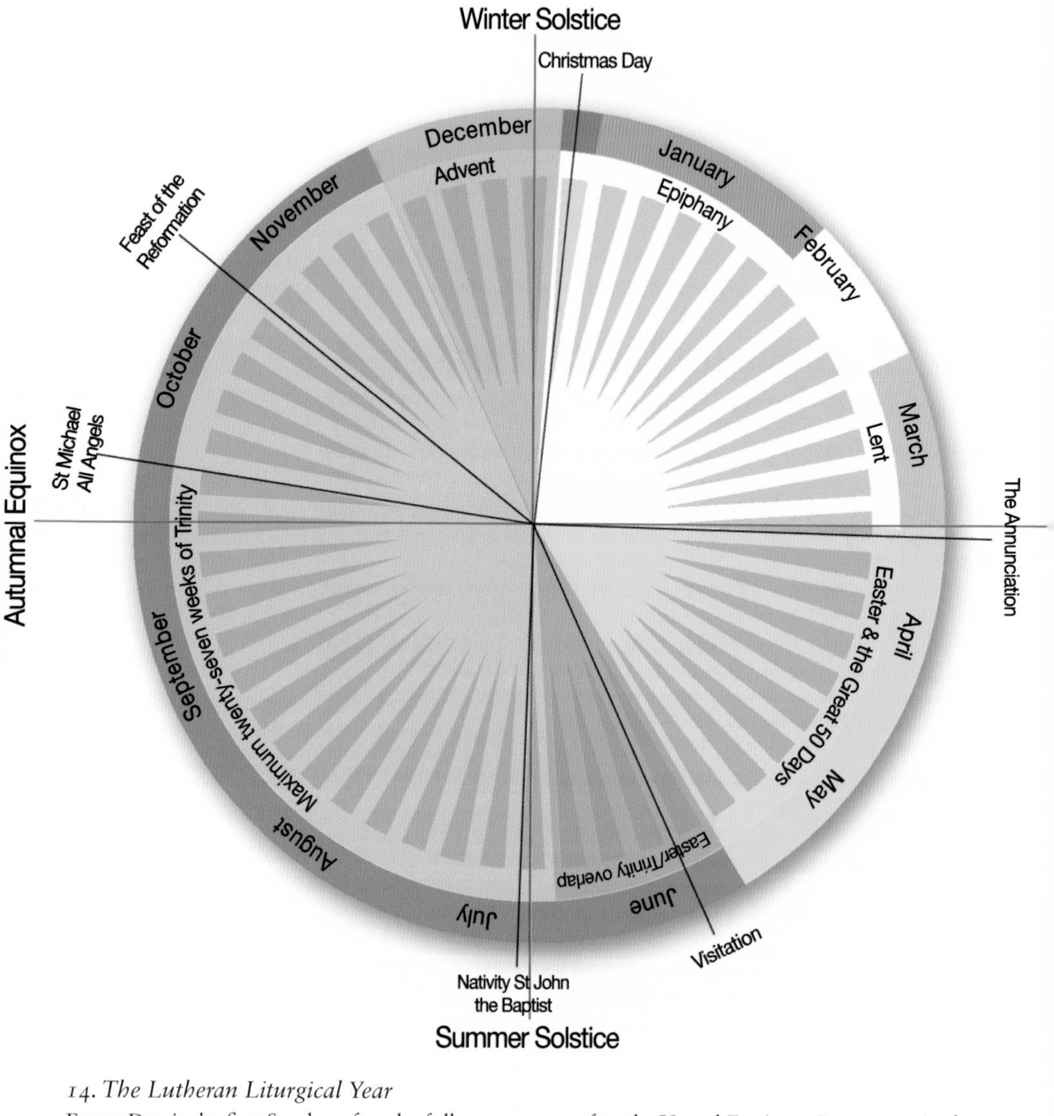

14. The Lutheran Liturgical Year

Easter Day is the first Sunday after the full moon on or after the Vernal Equinox. It can vary in date from 22 March to 25 April, and in turn determines the dates of Ash Wednesday, Lent, Holy Week, Ascension and Pentecost. Advent starts on the fourth Sunday before 25 December, the Sunday from 27 November to 3 December inclusive.

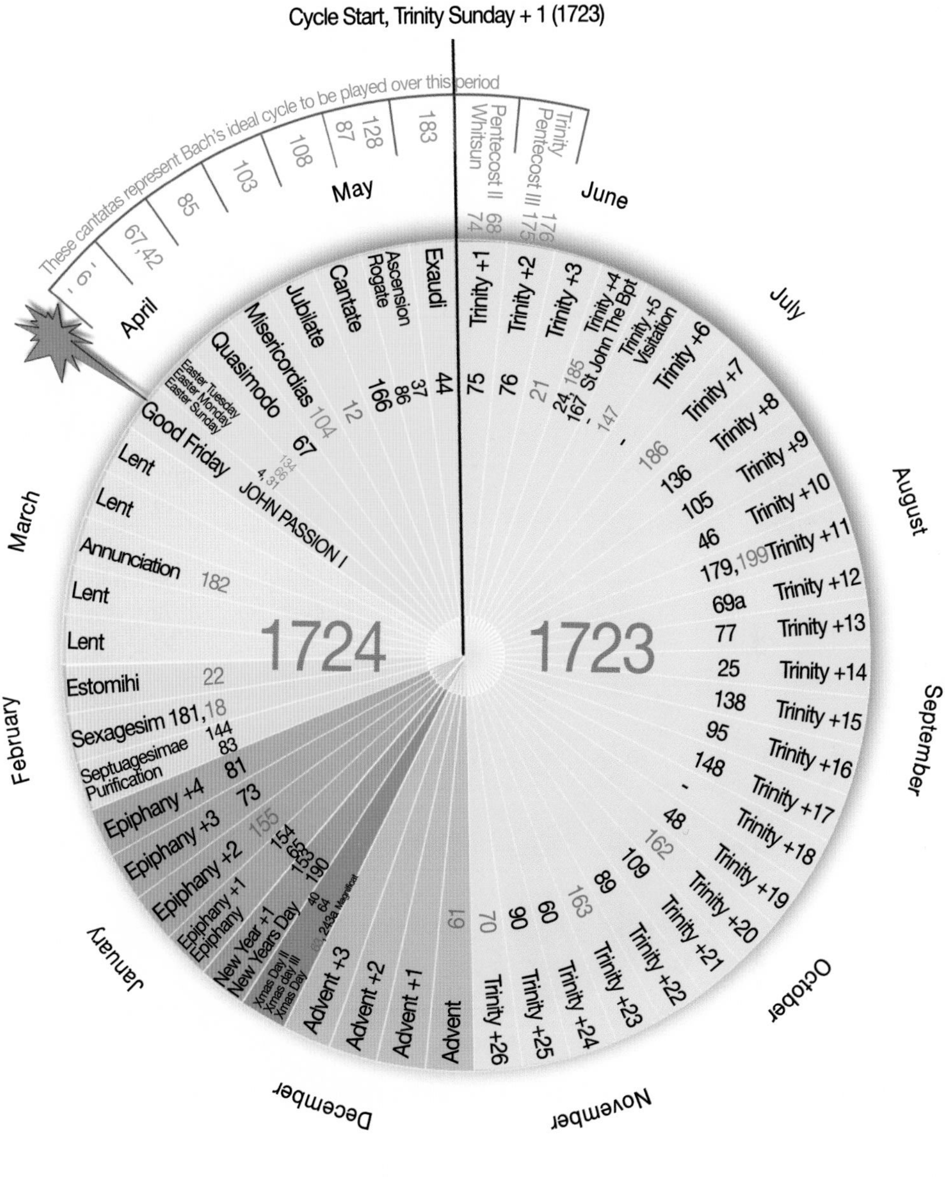

15. Bach's First Leipzig Cantata Cycle, 1723/4

Easter coming late in 1724 meant that Whitsunday and Trinity Sunday overlapped with the Trinity +1 and 2 of the previous year, leaving the following cantatas needing to be included for the cycle to be complete:

Whitsun	1724	172, 59
Pentecost II	1724	173
Pentecost III	1724	184
Trinity	1724	194, 165

The green outer segment represents cantatas that Bach later considered as belonging to (and completing) this first cycle after its original disruption around Easter 1724.

Key

The BWV numbers are in different colours:

Black	Newly composed works
Blue	Earlier works revived
Red	Parodies of secular cantatas composed in Cöthen
Green	Bach's ideal cycle works

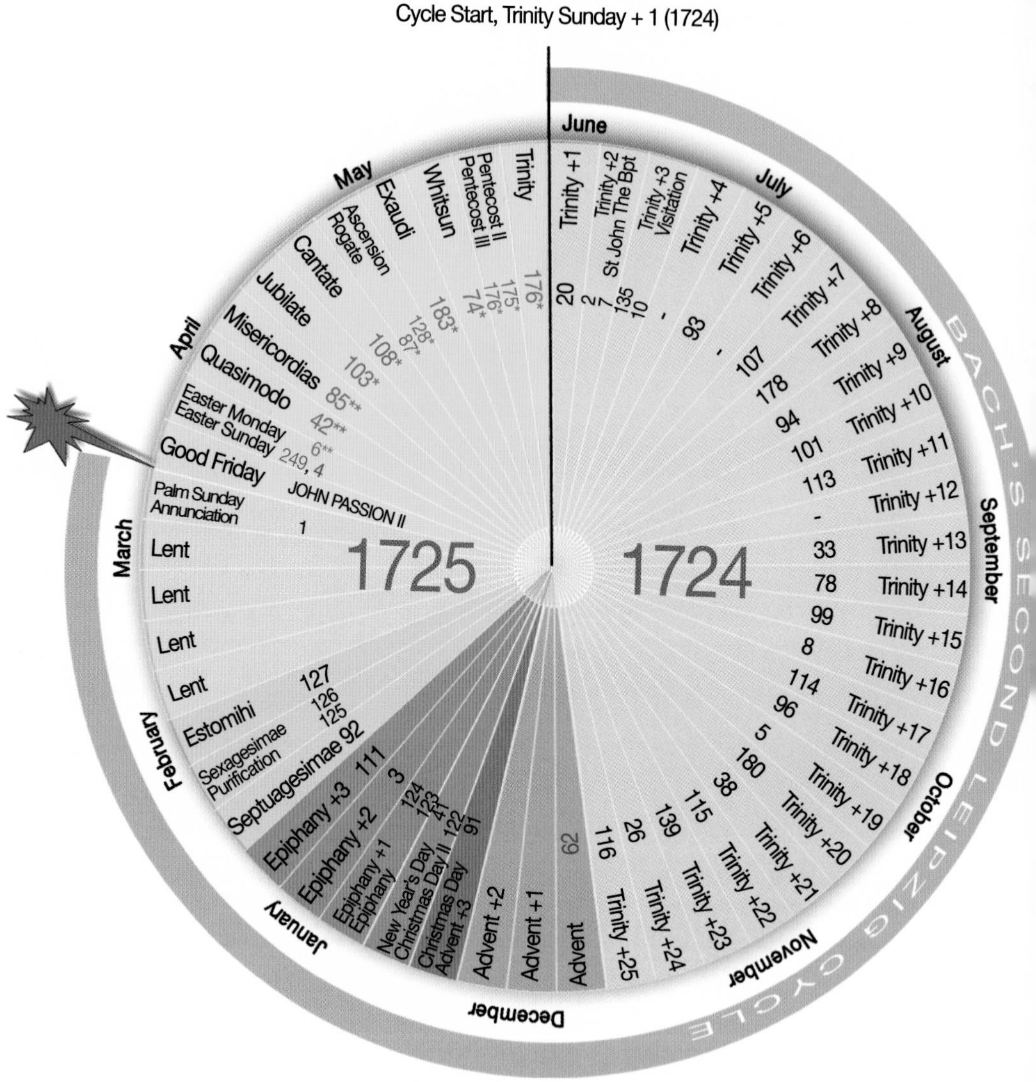

16. *Bach's Second Leipzig Cantata Cycle, 1724/5*

Key

The BWV numbers are in different colours:

Black	Newly composed works
Blue	Earlier works revived
Red	Parodies of secular cantatas composed in Cöthen
Green*	Series of nine cantatas with texts by Christiane Mariane von Ziegler most probably planned to follow on from the *John Passion* (1st version) after Easter in 1724 but only completed by Bach in the spring of 1725
Green**	Three new cantatas that bear a striking affinity to five for this period in 1724 but not set to music till now

of order and grandeur, the jagged dotted rhythms and extravagant rhetorical gestures that typify the form delineate here a world disintegrating. Once underpinned by destabilising harmonies, the effect gains in potency – still more so when the pace quickens to *vivace*. Bach makes us instantly aware that the region of eternal condemnation will be peopled by ghoulish minions of the Devil, herding and spearing the souls of the damned into a subterranean corral.

Nor does the apocalyptic vision fade at the close of this opening tirade. A tenor soloist steps forward and piles on the agony: 'there is no redemption from the pain of eternity . . . it drives on and on in its play of torment.' Bach draws on a varied armoury for this aria – long notes and undulating quavers to imply eternity, tortuous intervals paired in quavers to suggest trepidation, broken fragments, chromatic and syncopated, for the quaking heart, wild coloratura runs for 'flames that burn for ever', sudden silences to underscore the terror. This profusion of dramatic imagery is seamlessly integrated into his overall design. The turbulence of the bass line is a destabilising feature of the entire cantata (we need only glance at the original basso continuo part to see how exceptionally angular are its gestures).

Climbing back into his pulpit, the bass delivers the harrowing prospect of 'a thousand million years with all the demons'. Then, as he moves from recitative into aria, he abruptly changes tack and tone. We appear to have been shunted into the world of *opera buffa*, or, rather, of ducks – three of them (all oboes) and a bassoon (a token drake?) – quacking in genial assent as the singer declaims *Gott ist gerecht* ('God is just') over and over again. The mood seems to jar horribly. Was it not a prototype of Beethoven we were listening to a moment ago? Have we been misled by all the fire and brimstone? Perhaps Bach could see no further way to develop the theme of eternity before offering a speck of hope to the Christian soul now thoroughly battered and bruised. He reminds us that the solution to life's problems is childlike in its simplicity: all it takes is to put one's trust in God. It is a deliberate ploy to dissipate the gloom and tension – like opening a window in a smoke-filled room. Having cleared the air, you can almost picture him sitting back in his favourite chair, lighting a fresh pipe and contentedly blowing smoke circles.

Bach's depiction of hell is far richer and more polychromatic than that of any other composer before Mozart and Berlioz. So much of his richness comes from the dissonance that runs from the smallest to the largest levels.* The reprieve he allows us, however, is only temporary (after all, would we really want to achieve a serene eternity characterised by ducks?). The sequel he has planned is a strange aria for alto and strings – 'O mankind, save your soul, flee from Satan's slavery' – presented with extravagant rhythmic dislocation, regular $\frac{3}{4}$ bars alternating with single or double hemiolas in $\frac{3}{2}$ as metaphors for Satan's slavery. Stranger still is the way that he repeats the singer's second phrase with orchestra alone – in a reflective coda which takes up exactly half of the whole aria's duration.

The sermon was designed to follow at this point, ushered in by a pessimistic, even nihilistic, hymn stanza – 'Torment shall never cease: men shall be plagued, by heat and cold, fear, hunger, terror, fire and lightning ... This pain will end when God is no longer eternal', thus effectively undoing the repair work achieved earlier by the bass soloist. What words coming from a preacher's mouth could now add anything meaningful to this musical bombardment? A logical choice for his theme would have been the call to the lost sheep to wake up and throw off the sleep of sin (Ephesians 5:14), the subject of the electrifying bass aria with trumpet and strings which opens Part 2 – Bach's answer, as it were, to Handel's 'The trumpet shall sound' from *Messiah* – a taxing piece for both singer and trumpeter, requiring dramatic delivery and technical control. As if that were not enough, the alto soloist now blasts off in a tirade against the carnal world, much along the lines of an Oxford Street sandwich-board-wearer: 'Repent before it's too late: the end is nigh.'† And with this message comes a twist calculated to bring the listener up short: 'Consider ... it could be this very night that the coffin is brought to your door!' It is not very often that Bach resorts to lurid pictorialism of the Hieronymus Bosch kind; yet, in the ensuing duet delivered

* It evokes Leibniz's spectre of the 'best of all possible worlds', one that contains necessary and perfectly balanced dissonance, though Bach might have agreed with Spinoza's twist to this: that 'this is not the best of all possible worlds; it is the *only* possible world'. Leibniz apparently claimed to have lived by the Roman playwright Terence's famous saying *homo sum: humani nil a me alienum puto* – 'As a man I consider nothing pertaining to human affairs outside my domain.' Leibniz was a true polymath, as Bach was not. But it is instances such as these that suggest not just that he might have endorsed Terence's aphorism, but that he included it within the purview of his cantatas and Passions.

† Richard Stokes's translation of the original is: 'O mankind, save your soul / Flee from Satan's slavery / And free yourself from sin / That in the pit of sulphur / Death, which plagues the damned / Shall not for ever gnaw at your soul / O mankind, save your soul' (*J. S. Bach: The Complete Cantatas* (1999), pp. 31–2).

to the errant pilgrim as though by Bunyanesque angels (alto and tenor), he treats us to a ghoulish cameo of 'howling and chattering teeth', of the ominous approach of the hand-drawn hearse as it clatters across the cobbled street. Successions of first inversion chords over a disjointed bass line in quavers with parallel thirds and sixths in the voice parts give way first to imitative and answering phrases, then to an anguished chromaticism evoking the bubbling stream and the drop of water denied to the parched rich man. The voices join for a final flourish. We hear the gurgling of the forbidden water and the continuo playing a last furtive snatch of the ritornello. Then, dissolve . . . fade out . . . silence. Extraordinary.

Only in the final chorale of this gripping work does Bach revert to being the congregation's spokesman, this time voicing their plea to be spared life's torments and temptations and the hideous spectre of eternal damnation. A small ray of light is offered at the conclusion of this lurid tableau, one in which what Laurence Dreyfus calls Bach's 'subversive pleasures' can be experienced.* Were they relished or wasted on Bach's first listeners? One somehow doubts if they left church whistling the hymn tune or any of Bach's melodies. Were we ever to recover even snippets of testimony as to how his cantatas were received at the time, it would help us gauge how, if at all, the reactions of his congregations affected the way he approached his weekly task. Was public opinion in any sense a spur or encouragement to his trying out different approaches, or did he just decide such strategies on his own and stick to them determinedly – this week a modern Italian concerto movement or a prelude and fugue, next week a polyphonic motet or a medieval *cantus firmus*, the following week elements of a modern French dance suite? Did he adjust to public reaction in the way, for example, that Dickens did when writing his novels in serial instalments? Might one or two adverse, even waspish, comments overheard from the congregation as it filed out of church on that Sunday morning on 11 June 1724 goad him towards his own brand of dare-devilry and to still bolder experiments? We simply have no idea. But one thing we can say for certain – a paradox, in fact: that what Bach undertook from duty (though in excess of

* 'The power of music, especially Bach's music, surely extends beyond what words or pictures or gestures can signify, which is why, at best, Bach seduces us with his subversive pleasures as much as he challenges us with his unique insights' (from a lecture given at the Lufthansa Festival, London, 14 May 2011).

his contract) stirs our emotions as strongly as anything prompted by his artistic desire to create. As Jack Westrup writes, 'In fulfilling a duty which must often have been tedious, and sometimes intolerable, Bach not only satisfied the demands of his own age: he enriched ours.'[14]

* * *

Bach's decision to ground his Second Leipzig Cycle on Lutheran chorales was by no means arbitrary: it was a key difference between this and the first cycle, in which a scriptural dictum (or *Spruch*) had provided the opening to most of his pieces. All through year one Bach had adjusted both to a new congregation and to a strong local liturgical tradition, while putting a new group of performers to the test. To an extent he had needed to live hand to mouth. For someone of his ordered and systematic way of thinking that cannot have been what he meant by a 'well-regulated church music'. As a corrective, and ever conscious of past precedent, he may have decided to give a new twist to a practice going back to Ludwig Senfl in the sixteenth century of setting chorales (and sometimes chorale variations *per omnes versus*) as a musical framework for what were known as 'chorale sermons' (*Liederpredigten*). This would also reinforce a more recent tradition: in 1714, unusually for a pastor of the Thomaskirche, Johann Benedikt Carpzov III had given a sermon extolling the virtues of concerted music. When he had finished expounding 'a good, fine old Protestant and Lutheran hymn', it was then sung by the congregation. Carpzov told them that what they had heard earlier was the result of the Cantor Johann Schelle having 'undertaken willingly to set each hymn in a charming piece of music, and let it be heard before the sermon'. It could have been the bicentenary of Luther's three hymnals in 1724 which prompted Bach and Salomon Deyling (who, as superintendent of the Nikolaikirche, was responsible for overseeing Bach's duties as Director Chori Musices) to put their heads together in a similar harmonious collaboration and to revive Schelle's practice of writing a complete chorale-based cycle.*

At all events, to plan a full cycle grounded on hallowed and iconic

* Alternatively the idea may have been hinted at discreetly, or even imposed, by the clergy, as a corrective to what they saw as Bach's overtly Pietistic leanings in some of his first cycle works. Alfred Dürr questions darkly whether Bach might have 'needed any special inducement' (op. cit., p. 30). Perhaps what he had in mind was the *Zusatz* – the supplementary fee paid by the Stadtrat to an earlier Thomascantor, Sebastian Knüpfer, for composing a cho-

Lutheran hymns was one of Bach's most courageous decisions as a composer – one that he sustained for the next nine and a half months with extraordinary consistency. His commitment to using them as the structural thread for substantial compositions lasting between twenty and thirty minutes each meant that, were inspiration to flag, he could no longer rely on his own earlier pieces to plug the gaps – or on anyone else's come to that – so distinctive and specific was his chosen genre. The varied fare of Christmas the previous year, when cantatas had rubbed shoulders with Latin canticles and Mass movements, was no longer possible. Previously there had been a strong presence of chorales in all the cantatas, serving as a perpetual confirmation of his self-set challenges, and perhaps even affirming his self-definition as a composer, performer and teacher, in terms of the skill he showed in combining melody, harmony and instrumentation more inventively than anyone had before. Now, at the beginning of the Trinity season in 1724, for the first time the chorales move centre-stage. For the next year Bach stuck limpet-like to these hymns: a total of fifty-two new cantatas used them as their starting-point and, once elaborated, gave them fresh currency. From here onwards they stand out with the glint and regularity of brass studs on a leather-upholstered chair.

The sheer intellectual and experiential brio of these early second cycle cantatas leaps off the pages of their scores with a palpable sense of physicality. Rehearsal time with his trebles could be cut to a minimum if all that they had to do was to sing a familiar tune (often doubled by a horn, a cornett or a slide trumpet) within an otherwise elaborate opening chorus. Meanwhile choral fantasias, recitatives and arias, all extending Bach's demands and expectations of the human voice and of his chosen obbligato instruments, develop afresh as he strikes out in new directions.

As in the previous year the first four in this crop of early Trinity season cantatas constitute a mini-portfolio of discrete works, differing in their treatment but connected by doctrinal twine (not unlike the six component parts of the later *Christmas Oratorio*, with its 'unity in variety'). Each work opens with an elaborate setting of the unaltered first strophe of the hymn on which the whole cantata is built. The

rale cantata cycle in 1666/7 – something that Bach would surely have welcomed – but there is no evidence that he was similarly rewarded.

following movements – recitatives, arias and duets – are textual paraphrases of the inner verses of the hymn, before the cantata concludes with a four-part harmonisation of the final strophe. Each of the four has a striking hymn tune emblazoned in its opening movement, its *cantus firmus* migrating each week to a different voice: soprano (BWV 20), alto (BWV 2), tenor (BWV 7) and bass (BWV 135). Each is couched in a distinct stylistic idiom: that of a French overture (BWV 20), an archaic motet without independent obbligato instrumental lines (BWV 2), an Italianate *concertante* movement featuring a solo violin (BWV 7) or a chorale fantasia (BWV 135). In all except the second of these, the principal test for Bach lay in combining a chorale melody with an instrumental concerto or ritornello form. He had previous practice of embedding chorales within a ritornello structure (as we saw in the conclusions to both parts of BWV 74 and 75) but on a far smaller scale than these imposing introductory movements. The corrections we find in Bach's surviving autograph scores reveal the colliding priorities of two unconnected structures and of his solutions in reconciling them – all under the pressure of time. This was a poser of far greater complexity than the Rubik's Cubes of the previous year. Here we see a great composer at the height of his powers meeting the challenges of a self-imposed regimen week by week and adjusting his choice of form, his approach and his tone of voice to each underlying theme, each symbol and each metaphor arising from the texts laid out in front of him. There can be no doubt as to the magnitude of the task or the rapidity with which his skill developed as he did so.

* * *

One disadvantage to exploring even such a coherent cycle as Bach's second *Jahrgang* in linear sequence (just as his Leipzig audience experienced them) is that it can insulate one from the equally striking connections from year to year. Just as 'vertical' and 'horizontal' tastings of fine wines and whiskies have their respective value, so a 'slice-wise' comparison of one cycle to another, and of the different approaches Bach adopted to the same occasion and the same lectionary prompting, can bring insights into his creative personality – as it did for those of us who took part in the Bach Cantata Pilgrimage in 2000. Suddenly he ceases to be a fixed Godlike figure located outside time and emerges as someone flexible and prone to widely differing responses from one year to the next. We saw how the Gospel account of Jesus weeping over the fate of Jerusalem dominated BWV 46, Bach's first cantata for Trinity + 10 (see pp. 302–3), yet it barely gets a mention the following year in BWV 101, *Nimm von uns, Herr, du treuer Gott*. This is because as a chorale cantata it is based squarely on the primary hymn for this Sunday, written during a time of plague and sung to the melody of Luther's German version of the Lord's Prayer. The relentlessness of Luther's *Vater unser*, and the way the chorale is a strong, audible presence in all but one of the movements, including the recitatives, is matched in the opening movement by Bach's use of yet *another* of Luther's hymns as the thematic basis of a chorale fantasia, one associated in the congregation's mind with the Ten Commandments (*Dies sind die heil'gen zehn Gebot*). The wages of sin, the overwhelming power of retribution visited upon those tempted to stray from the Lord's path, prompted Bach to subject his first listeners to a twin-barrelled doctrinal salvo and to compose what the pianist and scholar Robert Levin described to me as 'the most crushing work of Bach's career'.

It starts out ruminatively with an independent continuo line supporting a trio of oboes exchanging the 'Ten Commandments' theme with the upper strings. But before long sharply accentuated dissonances over a dominant pedal are introduced, the first in a succession of hammer blows to convey the *schwere Straf und große Not* ('grave punishment and great distress') of the hymn text.* These contribute to the unsettling mood of this remarkable tone poem, sounding at once so archaic in the doubling of the voice parts by old-fashioned cornetto and trombones (as though Bach were intent on reconnecting to Luther's time) and yet so modern in the way, for example, wrenching harmonies only begin to make sense as passing events in contrapuntal terms at a specific tempo. (This is just one of its interpretative challenges.) Bach elaborates a seven-part orchestral texture and then proceeds to expand it to eleven real parts. If that were not extraordinary enough, there is no thematic correspondence with the chorale tune: the orchestra functions independently of the choir throughout, as though fixated on this war-scarred

* This was an anonymous adaptation of the chorale of 1584 by Martin Moller, and it reads like a penitential cry from the Thirty Years War: 'Protect us from war and famine / Contagion, fire and grievous pain ... Sin has greatly corrupted us / The Devil plagues us even more / The world, our very flesh and blood / Leads us astray incessantly / Such misery, Lord, is known to Thee alone / Ah, let us be commended to Thee.'

landscape. In fact, the influence inverts the usual practice – with the lower voices occasionally borrowing instrumental themes in preparation for the re-entry of the hymn tune. A persistent feature is a three-note 'sighing' figure tossed between the instruments, appoggiaturas that resolve normally but are approached from above and below by a variety of initial preparatory intervals that appear to grow wider and wider to convey the inescapability of punishment, the fate that we 'with countless sins have truly merited' (indeed, the word *allzumal* – 'ineluctably' – comes in for vehement reiterated protestations by the three lower voices). Over the final tonic pedal Bach engineers a disturbing intensification of harmony and vocal expression for the words *für Seuchen, Feur und großem Leid* ('contagion, fire and grievous pain'). Here we sense Bach working his chosen motifs as hard as he possibly can, a trait we associate more readily with Beethoven and Brahms.

The antithesis between God's anger and mercy is clearest in the fourth movement, where Bach sets himself the challenge of interpolating a 'rage' aria for bass within each line of the chorale, now sung, now played and at three different speeds: *vivace – andante – adagio*. He has three oboes to help him – three *angry* ducks on this occasion, transformed into a kind of latter-day saxophone trio. There is a single moment midway, enough to strike horror in the listener, when Bach makes an abrupt Mahlerian swerve from E minor to C minor on the word *Warum* [*willst du so zornig sein*?]. Not even Purcell, with his penchant for a calculated spot-lit dissonance, was capable of matching this when setting the same words in his anthem 'Lord, how long wilt Thou be angry?' Sudden juxtapositions of sacred text and personal commentary are a potent new dialectical weapon in Bach's expressive arsenal.

With its imploring gestures in *siciliano* rhythm, a flute now acts in counterpoint to the chorale tune first assigned to, and then exchanged with, the oboe da caccia. One wonders whether it was this particularly affecting combination of obbligato instruments and its association with the Saviour's love and compassion shown to the sinner at the moment of 'Jesus' bitter death' that planted the seed in Bach's mind for 'Aus Liebe', the great soprano aria from the *Matthew Passion*. If so, this duet served as a preliminary sketch for the Passion, which, I suggest, was still very much alive as the culmination of his second *Jahrgang*, planned for Good Friday 1725. (See below, p. 331.)

At all events, BWV 101 was a cantata that Bach rated very highly.

Reviving it a last time in 1748 (or possibly 1749), he intervened in the part-copying process with thick pen-strokes that by their pressure reveal his urgent intent as much as they do his failing eyesight. It had taken him three or four previous attempts to arrive at his ideal in terms of textual underlay, and at this point he drastically reduced the number of word repetitions. A whole fresh layer of minutely differentiated articulation and dynamic markings now appeared to enable him and future musicians to realise the precise nuances present in his imagination. Deciding to write out a new flute part for the musical highpoint of the cantata, the soprano–alto duet, and as economical as ever with manuscript paper, he wrote it on the back of the cornett part – a sign that for this final revival he intended to dispense altogether with the old-fashioned cornett/trombone *colla parte* choir – while adding far stronger contrasts of *legato* and *staccato* phrasing. Elsewhere mutes are introduced, pizzicato marks added in the bass line (technical matters that could have been indicated by a simple gesture in earlier performances), even cautionary *tacet* (bars' rest) marks are revised. Nothing is to be left to chance. The impact of these detailed instructions goes beyond mere adjustment to the more delicate (*empfindsam*) stylistic taste of the 1740s. It is a vital testimony to Bach's quest for perfection, for completion, and a paradigm of the style of performance he continued to strive for during the last years of his life.

* * *

The theme of the hidden granting of faith returns later in the season in BWV 38, *Aus tiefer Not schrei ich zu dir*, for Trinity +21, based on Luther's paraphrase of Psalm 130: he describes the cry of a 'truly penitent heart that is most deeply moved in its distress . . . We are all in deep and great misery, but we do not feel our condition. Crying is nothing but a strong and earnest longing for God's grace, which does not arise in a person unless he sees in what depth he is lying.'[15] Bach would have known that Luther's hymn was linked to a time-honoured Phrygian tune, one so perfectly suited to archaic treatment in motet-style that it is hard to imagine him setting it in any other way. In an opening chorus in severe *stile antico* he etches each line of the melody in long notes sung by the sopranos and anticipated imitatively by the lower three voices, just as he was to do in his later six-part organ setting of the same chorale in *Clavier-Übung III* (BWV 686). Once again he doubles each of the four voices with a trombone – a technique one might associate more readily with Schütz or even with Bruckner than with Bach. Besides their unique burnished sonority, these noble instruments bring a sense of ritual and solemnity to the overall mood. Bach seems intent on pushing the frontiers of this movement almost out of stylistic reach through the abrupt chromatic twists he gives to its modal tune. By reordering the vocal entries at each juncture he creates a powerful evocation of this Lutheran *De profundis* in the clamour of imploring voices.

All three of the cantata's final movements are equally stern and uncompromising. Bach marks the recitative for soprano *a battuta* – unusually, to be sung in strict tempo – while the continuo thunders out the old tune as if daring the believer to give in to doubts in a magnificent reversal of usual practice, the singer's weakened faith scarcely having time to express its frailty. Signs and wonders abound. The very word for signs (*Zeichen*) is given expressive, symbolic expression – a diminished seventh chord in the soprano recitative, formed by all three 'signs', one sharp (F♯), one flat (E♭) and one natural (C♮).* In place of a second aria Bach inserts a *terzetto* for soprano, alto and tenor to describe how soon the rise of the 'morning of comfort' succeeds 'this night of distress and cares'. Chains of suspensions precipitate a downward cycle of fifths through the minor keys (D, G, C, F then B♭ major), whereas the dawning of faith reverses the direction upwards until the idea of the troubled night turns it back again. Different as they may seem, these three final movements flow easily from one to the next. As with his cantata for this Sunday from the previous year (BWV 109), he delays the provision and granting of help until the last possible moment. With all the voices given full orchestral doubling (including those four trombones), this chorale is not simply impressive, it is even intimidating in its Lutheran zeal – especially its final Phrygian cadence, with the bass trombone plummeting to bottom E.

Less than a month later the need for comfort in times of distress is unchanged, but Bach's musical treatment is radically different. The

* There is a clear explanation for this: 'since St John's Gospel is known as the *Book of Signs*, and since the tonal plan of Bach's *St John Passion* appears to have been conceived as a form of play on the three musical signs (i.e., sharp, flat and natural key areas), this important detail in the plan of *Aus tiefer Not* perhaps possesses a wider significance, relating it to Bach's tonal-allegorical procedures in general' (Eric Chafe, *Tonal Allegory in the Vocal Music of J. S. Bach* (1991), p. 320).

instrumental ritornello to the opening chorale fantasia of BWV 26, *Ach wie flüchtig, ach wie nichtig*, is a stupendous musical confectionery illustrating the brevity of human life and the futility of earthly hopes. Long before the first statement of the hymn tune, Bach establishes the likeness of man's life to a rising mist that will soon disperse. Fleet-footed scales, crossing and re-crossing, joining and dividing, create a mood of phantasmal vapour – a brilliant elaboration of an idea that first came to him ten years earlier in Weimar when composing an organ chorale (BWV 644) to a simplified version of this hymn. In his second stanza Melchior Franck (*c.* 1579–1639) compares the course of human life to rushing water shooting down a mountainside before disappearing in the depths, an image dear to the Romantic poets. Did Goethe have Franck's hymn in mind when he wrote his marvellous 'Gesang der Geister über den Wassern' ('Song of the spirits over the waters') in Weimar sometime in the 1780s? Schubert set it to music for male voice choir on four separate occasions. There does seem to be a proto-Romantic *Gestalt* to the way Bach set it as an aria for tenor, flute, violin and continuo: each musician is constantly required to change functions – to respond, imitate, echo or double one another – while contributing to the inexorable forward motion of the tumbling torrent and a brief episode of falling raindrops. Human life first as mist and spray, then as a mountain torrent; next, Bach turns to the inevitability of beauty's withering like a flower and the moment when man succumbs to earthly pleasures and 'all things shatter and collapse in ruin.' He scores this for three oboes and continuo supporting his bass soloist in a mock *bourrée* that develops into a grim dance of death. Where one might have expected this trio of oboes to establish a mood of earthly (even evangelical) pomp, with the stirring entry of the singer their role becomes rapidly more subversive and realistic: first in the throbbing accompaniment that seems to undermine the fabric of those 'earthly pleasures' by which men are seduced; then through jagged figures to represent the tongues of flame which will soon reduce them to ashes; and finally in hurtling semiquaver scales of $^6_4$ chords for those 'foaming floods' that will tear all worldly things apart.

* * *

With seven new cantatas and a *Sanctus* to compose for seven feast-days within twelve days, Christmas 1724 cannot have been any less frenzied than the previous year. The celebrations on Christmas Day itself began with BWV 91, *Gelobet seist du, Jesu Christ*, Bach's majestic setting of Luther's hymn, whose opening ritornello has the special sense of expectation that is the hallmark of Bach in Christmas mode: fanfares for the horns and running G major scales in the oboes that suggest the dancing of angels. In the unselfconscious abandon of his setting of *das ist wahr* ('this is true') and the syncopated *Kyrie eleis!* (reminiscent of a similar word-setting in the *Zwiegesänge* of Michael Praetorius), Bach's seventeenth-century roots are exposed; and this mood persists in the soprano recitative interwoven with the second verse of the hymn and in the festive tenor aria set for three oboes swinging along in genial accompaniment. But even at Christmas-time Bach would not be Bach without a reference to the 'vale of tears' from which the newly incarnate Christ will lead us. He duly obliges with a slow, chromatic *accompagnato* (No. 4) for bass and strings in contrary motion, calculated to bring the listener up short. An extended duet for soprano and alto postulates the poverty that God assumed by coming into the world and the 'brimming store of heaven's treasures' He bestowed on the believer.

When Bach came to re-work this cantata during the 1730s, in order to illustrate the human aspiration to sing (and, by implication, dance) like the angels, he added lilting syncopations to the vocal lines that clash with the violins' dotted figure. The polarity between them is reinforced by means of upward modulations, once in sharps (as if to symbolise man's angel-directed aspirations), once in flats (as if to represent Jesus' humanity). The music brings to mind the vivid imagery of Botticelli's dancing angels or Filippino Lippi's angelic band in full cry on the walls of the Carafa Chapel in Santa Maria sopra Minerva in Rome. As with the *Sanctus* that followed in the same Christmas Day Mass, surely the most imposing of all of Bach's D major choruses, he may have been inspired by the vision of St John Chrysostom (*c.* 347–407), which he surely knew – those 'thousands of Archangels and ten thousands of Angels . . . six-winged, full of eyes, and soar aloft on their wings, singing, crying, shouting, and saying *Agios! Agios! Agios! Kyrie Sabaoth!* Holy, Holy, Holy, Lord God of Hosts! Heaven and Earth are full of Thy Glory! Hosanna in the Highest!'[16]

Bach adopts a wholly different strategy for its sequel the next day. More than in any other cantata you sense a primitive root, an early Christian origin for the Marian text of BWV 121, *Christum wir sollen loben schon*, one of the oldest-feeling of all Bach's cantatas. Luther had appropriated and translated a famous fifth-century Latin hymn, 'A solis ortus cardine' ('From the rising of the sun'), used for Lauds during the Christmas season, and Bach sets its opening verse in motet style, the voices doubled by a cornett and three trombones in addition to the usual oboes and strings. There is something mystical about this tune, not least in the way it seems to start in the Dorian mode and end in the Phrygian (or, in the language of diatonic harmony, on the dominant of the dominant). Replacing the portrayals of dancing seraphim are images of those angular, earnest faces that fifteenth-century Flemish painters use to depict the shepherds gazing into the manger-stall at the *reinen Magd Marien Sohn* ('little son born of a spotless maid'). The archaic feel of the opening chorus seems perfectly attuned to the mystery of the Incarnation.

Unequivocally modern, however, is the startling enharmonic progression – a symbolic 'transformation' no less – at the end of the alto recitative (No. 3) describing the miracle of the virgin birth. This is the tonal pivot of the entire work and, appropriately, it occurs on the word *kehren* ('to turn or reverse direction'); with *wundervoller Art* (Bach's play on words is his cue for a 'wondrous' tritonal shift) God descends and takes on human form, symbolically represented by the last-minute swerve to C major. It is the perfect preparation for the bass aria (No. 4), where bold Italianate string writing and solid diatonic harmonies are used to describe how John the Baptist 'leapt for joy in the womb when he recognised Jesus'. Bach's design for this cantata mirrors the change from darkness to light and shows how the moment when Christians celebrate the coming of God's light into the world coincides with the turning of the sun at the winter solstice. Beyond that, his purpose is to emphasise the benefit of the Incarnation for mankind and (again) that the supreme goal is to join the angelic choir (cue for a tough audition for the lead treble, who is required to reach a top B in the penultimate recitative). Any other composer would have been tempted to set the final chorale in some glittering stratospheric tessitura; instead, by returning to the cantata's opening tonality (E major with its ambiguous and inconclusive modal twist to F♯), and by retaining the coppery timbre of the cornett and trombones to intensify the choral sound, he finds other, subtler ways of achieving a luminous summation. It is the believer's hope – not the certainty – of eternal life Bach evokes here.

* * *

One of the crowning glories of Bach's first Christmas season was BWV 65, *Sie werden aus Saba alle kommen*, for Epiphany 1724, and it is fascinating to observe him attaining the same peak the following year in BWV 123, *Liebster Immanuel, Herzog der Frommen* – but via a different route. One of the keys to this lies in the instrumentation. Where the atmosphere of the earlier work is oriental and pageant-like, the second opens with a graceful chorus in $\frac{9}{8}$, a little reminiscent of an Elizabethan dance, with paired transverse flutes, oboes and violins presented in alternation. Its choral interjections form a Mendelssohnian love-song that sticks in the mind days after the music has ended. For the earlier 'Saba' cantata, by contrast, Bach uses high horns to convey majesty and antiquity, recorders to represent the high pitches traditionally associated with oriental music and, still more, oboes da caccia so redolent – to the modern ear – of the Macedonian *zurla*, the *sahnai* of Hindustan and the *nadaswaram* from Tamil Nadu in the southernmost part of the Indian Peninsula (which surely qualifies as the world's loudest non-brass acoustic instrument). With their haunting sonority these 'hunting oboes' seem to belong to the world of Marco Polo – of caravans traversing the Silk Route – and it remains something of a mystery how a specialist wind-instrument-maker, Herr Johann Eichentopf of Leipzig, could have invented this magnificent modern tenor oboe with its curved tube and flared brass bell around 1722 unless he had heard one of these oriental prototypes played by visitors to one of Leipzig's trade fairs (see Plate 21).

Bach was clearly intrigued by this new apparition (rather as Berlioz was a century later when Adolphe Sax was inventing the saxhorn), and was to make extensive use of it in at least thirty of his choral works, not least in the opening ritornello to BWV 65. Here he shows off the glittery sheen of his exotic orchestra to advantage, so that even before the voices enter in canonic order he succeeds in parading before our eyes the stately procession of the three magi and the 'multitude of camels' (Isaiah 60:6) laden with gifts. This imposing fantasia concludes with a restatement of the octave unison theme, this time by all the voices and instruments spread over five octaves, as the caravan comes to a halt in front of the manger. Now there is a sudden shift in scale and mood, from the outward pomp of the royal procession to the intimacy of the simple stable and the oblations offered to the child in the crib, as the choir intone the sober German version of the Latin 'Puer natus in Bethlehem' traditionally sung in Leipzig at this feast.

We can be so taken and dazzled by the glamour of these cantatas' opening movements as to be in danger of overlooking those in the middle. The earlier work features a *secco* recitative exemplary in its word-setting, its arching melodies and its rich chromatic harmonies, culminating in an affecting arioso. This leads to an aria for bass (No. 4) in which the two oboes da caccia engage in a triple canon with the continuo, evidently to portray the gifts of gold, incense and myrrh. To depict 'the most abundant wealth' (*des größten Reichtum*) mentioned in the recitative (No. 5), Bach draws on a most opulent scoring for this entrancing triple-rhythm aria for tenor (No. 6). Pairs of recorders, violins, horns, and oboes da caccia operate independently and in consort, exchanging one-bar riffs in kaleidoscopic varieties of timbre.*

The quality of the arias in BWV 123 is more telling still: a tenor aria (No. 3), with two oboes d'amore, describes the 'cross's cruel journey' to Calvary with heavy tread and almost unbearable pathos belying the words '[these] do not frighten me.' Four bars in a quicker tempo to evoke 'when the tempests rage' dissolve in a tranquil return to the *lente* tempo as 'Jesus sends me from heaven salvation and light.' This is followed by what is surely one of the finest, but also loneliest, arias Bach ever composed, 'Lass, o Welt, mich aus Verachtung' ('Leave me, O scornful world / To sadness and loneliness!'). The fragile vocal line, bleak in its isolation, is offset by the flute accompanying the bass singer like some consoling guardian angel trying to inspire him with purpose and resolve. Even the B section ('Jesus ... shall stay with me for all my days') offers only a temporary reprieve because of the expected *da capo*. Here voice and instrument are intimately linked, but with the wordless flute left to complete what the singer cannot bring himself to utter. A year later Bach returned to this mood of Epiphany blues with a second hugely demanding bass aria, 'Ächzen und erbärmlich Weinen' from BWV 13, *Meine Seufzer, meine Tränen*, describing how 'groaning and piteous weeping cannot ease sorrow's sickness.' With the white, sepulchral sound of twin recorders playing an octave above a solo violin, Bach seems determined to impress on his listeners the full misery and wretchedness of life here

* To English ears the main melody has more than a passing similarity to the nursery rhyme 'Lavender's blue, dilly, dilly', while the fervent concluding chorale (Verse 10 of Paul Gerhardt's 'Ich hab in Gottes Herz und Sinn'), set to a secular French sixteenth-century melody, is familiar as the hymn 'O God, Our Help in Ages Past'.

below. Just where the text mentions a 'beam of joy' appearing, Bach momentarily lifts the shroud of dissonant angular harmony prior to a full-scale recapitulation in the subdominant, the music plunging again into darkness as though intent on exploring new agonies of mind and soul. With pulse and mind slowed down, our senses sharpened, we become alert to each tiny detail of Bach's mood-painting.

* * *

Quinquagesima, the last Sunday before Lent, held a special significance for Bach, for it was on this Sunday in 1723 that he had performed the twin trial-pieces (BWV 23 and 22) that were to clinch his appointment as Thomascantor, and he revived BWV 22 on the same Sunday the following year. Quinquagesima 1725 was his last opportunity to present a cantata to his Leipzig audience as a foretaste of a Passion performance and the biggest musical event in the Lutheran calendar, and, in this last regard, BWV 127, *Herr Jesu Christ, wahr' Mensch und Gott*, occupies a crucial role, for Bach placed a 'chorale Passion' like a jewel at its centre, just as he had done the year before. There are features of BWV 127, a strikingly experimental cantata, that function in the same way. The first occurs in the elegiac chorale fantasia that opens the work: here Bach weaves together no fewer than three chorale tunes – an instrumental presentation of the Lutheran *Agnus Dei* with its clear reference to Christ's Passion, a funeral lament by the French composer Claude Goudimel (1565), and finally several strains of a chorale melody we recognise as that of the Passion chorale, *Herzlich tut mich verlangen*, which will feature so prominently in the *Matthew Passion*. Next, it is noticeable that the following recitative for tenor links the individual's thoughts of death to the path prepared by Jesus' own patient journey towards his Crucifixion. Most telling of all is the fourth movement, a grand, tableau-like evocation of the Last Judgement, part accompanied recitative, part aria, made up of three alternating sections: a restless *accompagnato*, with no discernible tonal centre, an arioso in G minor (*Fürwahr, fürwahr*) quoting Goudimel's choral melody on which the whole cantata is based, and finally a wild $\frac{6}{8}$ section signalling man's rescue from the violent bonds of death.

It is in this last segment, with trumpet fanfares and scurrying strings, that we come across a glaring instance of self-quotation unique in Bach's church music: for the solo part for bass is identical with the four choral entries of the spectacular double chorus 'Sind Blitze, sind Donner', one of the highpoints of the *Matthew Passion* and rightly identified as 'one of the most violent and grandiose descriptions of unloosed passion produced in the Baroque era'.[17] A comparison of the two settings suggests that the Passion chorus was composed *before* the cantata aria. (We caught a glimpse of Bach's stressful preparation of the performing material of this number in Chapter 7.) Though not conclusive proof in itself of a planned premiere for Good Friday, 30 March 1725, this 'pre-echo' of the 'Sind Blitze' chorus in BWV 127 suggests a consistent frame of mind and an indication that up to this point the *Matthew Passion* was still on course.

Those who attended Mendelssohn's famous revival of the *Matthew Passion* in Berlin in 1829 were told that they were celebrating the exact centenary of its first performance on Good Friday 1729. Since 1975 that date has been brought forward by two years.[18] But if, as suggested, Bach was actively engaged in preparing the *Matthew* as he was composing his second cantata cycle of 1724/5, the point at which it became clear to him that he would not have it ready for performance on Good Friday 1725 remains to be established. Had he miscalculated the time needed to allow him to bring it in on schedule? Was it simply a case of exhaustion, or had there been further dispiriting disputes with the clergy during the past year? No one has so far come up with convincing answers, and it could well be that the truth lies in a combination of all of these, with the decision to abort made very close to Holy Week 1725. By failing to complete the *Matthew* on time for Good Friday, Bach found himself boxed in. We do not even know at what point he officially informed the consistory of his solution to the problem of providing a Passion for that year – or whether the decision to fill the vacuum with a substantially revised version of the *John Passion* was imposed on him by the consistory with instructions to adjust its doctrinal tone (see Chapter 10). One new aria in particular, 'Zerschmettert mich, ihr Felsen' for tenor, has echoes of the climactic sequence of BWV 127, suggesting that Bach still had the material of that cantata in his mind when he sat down to compose this revision, as though determined to salvage something of its intended pre-announcement.

From all this confusion there is one thing to emerge with near certainty: it looks as if Bach's initial intentions at Leipzig were even more grandiose than scholars have generally supposed, and that at his appointment in 1723 he had set himself the task of presenting his *own* music, mostly newly composed, some of it re-cast from his Weimar years, for at least the first two *Jahrgänge*, each cycle culminating with a Passion setting – radically new by Leipzig standards, theologically controversial in the case of the *John* in 1724, and ground-breaking and more time-consuming than he had expected in the case of the *Matthew* (in which he took a bigger swing at the ball), thus necessitating a deferral for a further two years.

In the midst of all this uncertainty Bach's Second Leipzig Cycle came to a premature close on 25 March 1725 with the jubilant springtime cantata BWV 1, *Wie schön leuchtet der Morgenstern* (see diagram, Plate 16). This year, there was a rare coincidence of Palm Sunday (a movable feast) with the Feast of the Annunciation (with a fixed date). It needs little imagination to gauge the importance of this dual celebration to Leipzig worshippers, coming as it did towards the end of the forty days' fasting period of Lent, during which they had heard no music in church. One hundred and twenty-five years later this was the first cantata to be published in Vol. 1 (out of forty-five) of the *Bach-Gesellschaft* (Bach Society) edition (hence its singular numbering), more than half of which was devoted to vocal music for the church. The subsequent numbering of the cantatas by BWV prefix was totally random and had nothing to do with the chronology of their composition.* Both Schumann and Brahms were enthusiastic subscribers, and one wonders what they made of the inventive and masterly way Bach wove his contrapuntal textures around one of the most stirring of Lutheran hymns. The scoring is opulent and regal, redolent of the Epiphany cantata BWV 65 both in its 'eastern' instrumentation – horns, oboes da caccia and strings (but no recorders this time) – and in metre: a dignified $^{12}_{8}$ ceremonial in F major for the opening chorale fantasia in which a grand choral proclamation of Nicolai's tune is given out in long notes by the sopranos and the principal horn. As with Bach's only other cantata for Palm Sunday (the skittish and much smaller-scale Weimar cantata BWV 182), the crowd's greeting is stirring and jubilant. A measure of what Bach had achieved by this time in his handling of this form comes with

* The Society's grand, well-intentioned project came to a close in 1900, by which time all the available cantatas, both sacred and secular, including some that were not by Bach at all, had been published – an invitation to performance that was taken up only selectively and then with drastic re-orchestration, thick wads of organ accompaniment and what seems to have been a characteristically lugubrious delivery. There has been another whole century of trial and error, fierce debate over the ways to resuscitate them (in or out of the liturgy), historical research, critical appraisal of the source material, variably successful attempts to fill the gaps in the threadbare sources, heated arguments over Bach's original performing forces and practice – and still the cantatas remain on the fringes of many Bach lovers' knowledge of his œuvre.

the movement's climax, his setting of the last line, *Hoch und sehr prächtig erhaben* ('Highly and most splendidly exalted'), full of majesty and splendour. The effect is overwhelming – inspiration underpinned by unobtrusive skill.*

The reasons for Bach leaving the chorale cycle incomplete at this point are unclear, but, whatever the cause, it was a breach he tried to repair in subsequent years by the insertion of appropriate chorale cantatas for this final segment, such as BWV 112 and 129. Meanwhile, for Easter Sunday 1725 Bach revived the earliest of his chorale cantatas, BWV 4, a worthy but by now old-fashioned addition to the cycle, and probably performed it in the university church; while for the two main churches he made a hasty parody of a (lost) Weissenfels pastoral cantata (BWV 249a) as *Kommt, gehet und eilet*, later to be revised as the 'Easter Oratorio', *Kommt, eilet und laufet* (BWV 249) – which, in the meditative beauty of its slow second movement (with its aura of a Venetian oboe concerto) and its long soprano aria with flute obbligato, catches the sense of loss at Christ's death and the feeling that the use of spices and embalming ointments could now be superseded by the power of musical prayer. Resurrection has not yet fully registered in the believer's mind.

After Easter he then resumed his production of cantatas by setting a group of texts, including nine by the Leipzig-born poet Christiane Mariane von Ziegler that may have been planned as sequels to the *John Passion* the previous year.† What appeared to be a makeshift solution

* Philipp Nicolai's hymn is known to English churchgoers as 'How brightly shines the morning star'. When we performed Bach's elaboration of it in Walpole St Peter's on Palm Sunday 2000, there seemed to be enough audience familiarity with the tune to elicit that 'invisible circle of human effort', as Yo-Yo Ma describes it, when performers and listeners alike are engaged in a collective or communal act. It was a feeling that returned twenty-four hours later during a rock concert in the Royal Albert Hall in which Sting exchanged snatches of familiar songs with his adoring audience in a kind of spontaneous litany. It is in moments like this, when there is a particularly strong bond between musicians and listeners, that one gets a sense of how these cantatas might have been received in Leipzig at the time of their creation – or at least of how Bach would have hoped they might be received.

† Dürr noticed that the last of the five newly composed works in Bach's first cycle, BWV 44, *Sie werden euch in den Bann tun* (his first version of a cantata of this title), shares with three other post-Easter cantatas from the *following* year's cycle (BWV 6, 42 and 85) a similarity in overall design (biblical *Spruch* – aria – chorale – recitative – aria – chorale) and in the emphasis placed on Christian suffering in the world. This leads to the conclusion that Bach originally intended those three cantatas to be incorporated into his First Leipzig Cycle along with BWV 44 (see Plates 15 and 16), but they had not been set to music until now – casualties of the fallout from the *John Passion* in 1724 (Dürr, op. cit., p. 33).

turned into a post-Resurrection sequence of twelve outstanding works, all beginning with biblical *dicta*, all with poetic texts that turned out to be more closely interrelated than any to be found in his other cantata sequences, and reflecting the liturgically unified character of the 'Great Fifty Days'.[19]

* * *

The 'Great Fifty Days' from Easter to Whitsun were rooted in the Jewish tradition of marking the seven weeks plus one day between Passover (the Feast of Unleavened Bread) and Pentecost/Shavuot (the Feast of the Weeks, and also the Day of the Ceremony (Bikkurim) of First Fruits – harvest, in other words). They signalled the completion of Jesus' work on earth, his last appearances to his disciples, his valedictory message to them to bolster their faith, and his promise to protect them through the coming of the Holy Spirit. It is thus a season of contrasts – of joy at Christ's resurrection and reappearances, clouded by the prospect of his departure and the adversarial pressures of life in the temporal world. This duality between a world deprived of Jesus' light and physical presence and a world of increasing spiritual darkness is very palpable in Bach's cantata for Easter Monday, BWV 6, *Bleib bei uns, denn es will Abend werden.* One senses that Bach had the final chorus of his *John Passion*, if not on his writing desk then still ringing in his ears when he sat down to compose this cantata, with which it shares in its opening chorus both the sarabande-like gestures of 'Ruht wohl' and the key of C minor with its characteristic sweet-sad sonority. (Since this chorus was omitted in the revival of the *John* in 1725, as we shall see, it strengthens the argument that BWV 6 and its two sequels belonged in Bach's mind to the previous year's cycle – and were perhaps even sketched then.)

But where the Passion epilogue is elegiac and consolatory, the cantata is tinged with the sadness of bereavement. Its tender pleadings for enlightenment become ever more gestural and urgent in a darkening world from which Jesus' presence has been removed. It manages to be both narrative (evoking the grieving disciples' journey to Emmaus as darkness falls) and universal at the same time (the basic fear of being left alone in the dark, both literally and metaphorically). The overall mood is one of descent and abandonment, a direction reversed by the subtle weaving in of a theological message to the faithful – to hold on to the Word and sacrament, those mainstays of Christian life in the world after Jesus' physical departure. Bach finds a way of 'painting' these two ideas by juxtaposing the curve of descent via trajectories of downward modulation with the injunction to remain steadfast – threading twenty-five Gs, then thirty-five B♭s played in unison by violins and violas all through the surrounding dissonance. This device is linked to the disciples' pleas to Jesus to remain, intoned nine times during the ensuing choral fugue. We might see in the collision of these two ideas an affinity with Caravaggio's first portrayal of the *Supper at Emmaus*: beyond the obvious parallel of contrasted planes of light and darkness is the further dichotomy of serenity and reassurance on the one hand – Christ in the act of blessing the meal affirms his identity and presence and seems to extend his hand of comfort right out of the canvas towards the viewer – and on the other, urgency, evident in the impulsive, theatrical gestures of the two disciples painted directly from life. It is religious drama presented as contemporary quotidian life, rather as if Bach were seeking to capture, here and in the next two movements, the disciples' despondency in the Saxon twilight he observed outside his study window.

* * *

One of Bach's most engaging habits we encounter in these cantatas is his turning to individual instruments, either alone or in various combinations, for expressive ends. In his hands they do a great deal more than just create special effects or moods, and it has been argued (by Eric Chafe and others) that they serve to underpin abstract theological ideas and associative links from work to work. But above all their presence creates immediacy in the listener's consciousness. We come across heart-stopping moments in arias of both cycles where Bach's chosen obbligato instrument – most often oboe or violin and, on rare and wonderful occasions, flute – complements the voice and adds a new layer of expression and meaning, beyond the reach of words.*

* A later instance – far too good not to mention – is an aria for solo oboe, strings and bass soloist from BWV 159, *Sehet, wir gehn hinauf*, from the so-called 'Picander' cycle of 1729, which opens with the same words as the celebrated 'Es ist vollbracht' from the *John Passion*. That Bach should have set these words twice, both so memorably and each time with such overwhelming but distinctive pathos, is something to marvel at. In this cantata version in B♭, time seems almost to stand still – even when the singer's words are 'Now shall I hasten' – radiating a solemn peace achieved through Christ's resignation to his fate. This may be partly a function of the exceptional richness of Bach's harmonic language – a frequent stressing of the subdominant key, even the subdominant of the subdominant.

Particularly noticeable in these final dozen cantatas is the rich and prominent use he gives to two specific instruments, each with a unique timbre and compass: the violoncello piccolo and the oboe da caccia (see Plates 21 and 22). With its beguiling, wide-ranging sonority the violoncello piccolo has a smaller soundbox than the normal full-sized cello and (sometimes) a fifth string that extends its treble range. Both instruments are used wonderfully in successive movements of BWV 6, the da caccia as the chief agent in a dance-like appeal for Jesus' continued presence (No. 2), the cello piccolo in a wide-ranging, mediating role between voice and continuo (No. 3). Bach is so enamoured of them that he uses the oboe da caccia in six and the cello piccolo in five of the twelve cantatas from the final segment of his second cycle, deliberately seeking out roles for their qualities that are central to his poetic and interpretative approach. Both have a plangent sonority in the tenor register that seems to tug on the listener's heartstrings, but where the sound of the little cello suggests something essentially benign and consoling, the oboe da caccia tends to be used to convey suffering and anguish. As we shall see, Bach turns to it in the *Matthew Passion* at intense moments of suffering – for the Agony in the Garden ('O Schmerz'), his innocence in the Roman trial ('Aus Liebe'), his Crucifixion ('Sehet, Jesus hat die Hand') and burial ('Mache dich, mein Herze, rein'). Bach does something equally compelling in the D minor aria 'Vergib, o Vater' ('Forgive, O Father, all our sins and be patient with us yet') from BWV 87, *Bisher habt ihr nichts gebeten in meinem Namen*, by drawing on paired oboes da caccia to merge with his alto soloist against ascending arpeggios in the continuo. In this way gestures of grief and entreaty are registered concurrently – and primarily by instrumental means. A fortnight earlier, in BWV 85, *Ich bin ein guter Hirt*, he had used the cello piccolo in a meditation on Christ the Good Shepherd, profiting from the special glow it brings both in range and in harmonic function. You sense that with this mantra-like sound, any 'lamb' would feel confidently armed against the sheep-rustler – wolf, fox or human. At the start of the calendar year, in BWV 41, *Jesu, nun sei gepreiset*, Bach had composed for the five-string model (with a range extending from its lowest string, C, up to B♮ three octaves above in the treble clef) as though to encompass the duality of earth and heaven and to mirror God's control of human affairs both physical and spiritual (see Plate 23).

Jubilate (the third Sunday after Easter) in Leipzig marked the start of the Ostermesse, the Easter trade fair, when, for three weeks, a flood of visitors – book dealers, craftsmen, hawkers and international commercial travellers – swelled the resident population to some 30,000 citizens. Bach, who timed the publication of the four sets of his *Clavier-Übung* to coincide with these fairs, would have understood the need to provide special music for this Sunday (when no trading was allowed), 'since visitors and distinguished gentlemen [would] certainly want to hear something fine in the principal churches', as his predecessor Kuhnau had pointed out.[20] All three of Bach's surviving cantatas for Jubilate (BWV 12, 103 and 146) concern themselves with the sorrow surrounding Jesus' farewell to his followers, with the trials that await them in his absence, and with joyful thoughts of seeing him again. Each is a journey, a musical and emotive progression – from profound gloom and anguish to euphoric celebration – based on the Gospel for the day: 'Ye shall be sorrowful, but your sorrow shall be turned into joy' (John 16:20), from which BWV 103, *Ihr werdet weinen und heulen*, takes its title. It seems a little strange, therefore, to find that it opens with a glittering fantasia for a *concertante* violin doubled on this occasion by another unusual instrument – a soprano recorder in D, known as a 'sixth flute'. These two are pitted against a pair of oboes d'amore and the rest of the strings, who engage in (apparently) festive dialogue. Only with the entry of the four vocal *concertisten* to an angular fugal theme (comprising an augmented second and an upwards seventh) do we realise that we have been caught unawares: Bach's bubbly instrumental theme represents not the disciples' joy at Christ's resurrection but the sceptics' jeering laughter at their distress – hence the malicious cackles of the high recorder.

With Pentecost only ten days away, Bach conspired with Frau von Ziegler to review and reassemble in BWV 183, *Sie werden euch in den Bann tun*, many of the themes that together they had brought to the surface in the past five weeks through their collaboration: worldly persecution (No. 1), suffering mitigated by Jesus' protection (No. 2), comfort afforded by Jesus' spirit (No. 3), surrender to the guidance of the Holy Spirit (No. 4) and the Spirit's role in pointing to prayer as humanity's means to obtain divine help (No. 5). In a terse and dramatic curtain-raiser, a five-bar *accompagnato*, Bach assigns the opening *Spruch* to four oboes (two d'amore and two da caccia), a permutation unique in his output outside the *Christmas Oratorio* and drastically different from his solution the previous year when for the identical line in BWV 44 he took eighty-seven bars for a duet and a further thirty-five bars for a chorus. This time the *Spruch* is dwarfed by its sequel, a hugely demanding aria in E minor for tenor with four-stringed cello piccolo, in which the singer insists that he does not fear the terror of death, while every ornate, feverish syncopation and rhythmic sub-pattern belies it. Meanwhile, the cello maintains its serene and luminous course with sweeping arpeggios. It is an intimate *scena* in which we can follow the believer in his struggles to overcome his fear of persecution and eventual extinction, sustained all the while by the soothing sounds of his companion, the *Schutzarm* (Jesus' protective arm) referred to in the text – the cello piccolo.

Whit Sunday might seem a strange day for a graphic depiction of hell. That, however, is the purpose of the alto aria 'Nichts kann mich erretten' from BWV 74, *Wer mich liebet, der wird mein Wort halten*, which makes demands of a solo violin at the opposite end of the expressive spectrum usually associated with Bach's writing for that instrument. He seems determined to convey to his listeners with stark realism the image of hellish chains being rattled by Jesus in his struggle with worldly forces. Accordingly he sets up battle formations for his three oboes and strings, asking his violinist to execute fiendish *bariolage*, with the lowest arpeggiated note falling not on, but just after, the beat. The effect is both disjointed and invigorating. Soon the vocal line embarks on arpeggios that appear trapped within the vehement dialectic, as though it were trying to work itself free from the hellish shackles. At times this search for belief is plaintive, with cross-accented phrases reinforced by the oboe and solo violin against a menacing thud of repeated semiquavers. In the B section victory seems assured and the singer 'laughs at Hell's anger' against stabbing accents in the winds and colossal smashing chords for the upper strings in triple and quadruple stops. The gloating comprises chains of tripletised melismas and a descent of an octave and a half before the *da capo*. Bach draws on illustrative techniques from opera, though not gratuitously: they serve an impeccable theological purpose, while the results, you would think, must have been vastly entertaining to members of the Leipzig intelligentsia still grieving for the loss of their opera house. Perhaps one day we will know more about how the dichotomy between late-burgeoning Lutheranism and secular, enlightened thought played out – and about music's pivotal role in these conflicts.

Mouldering away somewhere in the attics of its citizens there still could be letters holding what we so sorely lack – direct testimony to the varied responses by members of Bach's listening public to the music he put in front of them.

* * *

By Pentecost Bach was nearing completing his ambitious design for the twelve Sundays leading up to Trinity Sunday, based on biblical citations. His settings of John's words are full of purpose, never more so than in the final chorus of BWV 68, *Also hat Gott die Welt geliebt*, when, in place of a chorale, he puts to his listeners the chilling choice between salvation and judgement in the present life: 'He that believeth on him is not condemned: but he that believeth not is condemned already' (John 3:18). Bach's setting is as uncompromising as the text: a double fugue whose two subjects describe the alternatives, the voices doubled by his familiar alliance of archaic brass instruments, a cornett and three trombones. The second day of Pentecost may have been a time of celebration, elation and relief brought by the Holy Spirit (and that indeed is the tenor of the cantata's earlier movements), but in projecting a world starkly divided between believers and sceptics, Bach would have left the congregation pondering.

Ziegler's poetic contributions needed to be fitted to two pre-existing movements (Nos. 2 and 4), both festive in character, adapted by Bach from his *Hunting Cantata* (BWV 208) of 1713. Sometimes in Bach we come across a joyous inner spirit barely contained by a law-abiding artistic intellect. For example, the soprano aria 'Mein gläubiges Herze', one of his most unbuttoned expressions of melodic joy and high jinks (the polar opposite of those slow, extended meditations of the beleaguered Christian we encountered in the Epiphany season). In its original secular form the leaping dance-like bass mirrors the sheep gambolling as they are turned out to pasture every spring. The continuo line is once again allocated to a five-string violoncello piccolo, Bach's chosen vehicle for announcing Jesus' presence in the physical world – his second incarnation within the believer's heart. On the last page of the manuscript he appended an instrumental coda, adding an oboe and violin to the piccolo cello and its continuo. At twenty-seven bars this occupies nearly three quarters of the length of the aria, almost as if the singer's words were inadequate to express the full joy at the coming of the Holy Spirit. In the second of the arias Bach succeeds in fitting Ziegler's paraphrase of Verse 17 of John's Gospel to music he previously assigned to Pan, the god of woods and shepherds, who 'makes the land so happy / that forest and field and all things live and laugh'. The retention of a trio of pastoral oboes is the key to the grafting process by which Bach externalises the message of joy caused by Jesus' presence on earth.

Trinity Sunday marks the last in the sequence of nine cantatas to texts by Christiane Mariane von Ziegler. The title of BWV 176, *Es ist ein trotzig und verzagt Ding*, translates as 'There is something stubborn [or defiant or wilful] and yet fainthearted [or despondent or despairing] about the human heart.' All the permutations of these adjectives apply to Bach's setting, an arresting portrayal of the human condition – and might also reflect his own views, particularly as regards the intractable attitude of the Leipzig authorities. By interpreting the story of Nicodemus' furtive nocturnal visit as a general human tendency Ziegler, working in cahoots with Bach, it seems, had given him the opportunity to set up a dramatic antithesis between headstrong aggression and lily-livered frailty. He opens with a defiant, indignant presentation of this *Spruch*, a terse, four-part choral fugue set against a string fanfare reminiscent of the fifth Brandenburg Concerto. That applies to the first half only, with a rushing melisma up to the minor ninth on *trotzig* ('defiant') and then, at its peak, a melting and sighing figure over sustained strings to underscore the *verzagt* ('despondent') side of things. This ascending and descending contour persists throughout the fugue, two and a half expositions without ritornellos, the voices doubled by the three oboes, while the strings alternate between the vigorous Brandenburg motif and plaintive, sustained counterpoint.* The exploration of these twin facets of human behaviour persists all through this cantata: the juxtaposition of Nicodemus (night) and Jesus (day) presented in the alto recitative (No. 2) is implied in the soprano gavotte aria in B♭ (No. 3), in which the timid, hesitant yet happy believer is singled out as a contrast with the rebellious mind portrayed in the opening chorus. Nicodemus is personified in the bass recitative (No. 4), to which Bach adds the words 'for

* As with his other collaborations with Ziegler there is evidence of a productive dialogue between them (often sadly lacking when he was confronted with a set text), although there are signs that from time to time he may have changed Ziegler's text without consulting her, for, as we saw in Chapter 7, p. 218, her printed versions differed sometimes quite strikingly from those that Bach actually set to music.

whosoever believes in Thee, shall not perish' to Ziegler's text and sets them as an extended arioso to underline their significance. In the final aria, 'Ermuntert euch, furchtsam und schüchterne Sinne' ('Have courage, fearful, timorous spirits'), a trinity of oboes in symbolic unison accompanies the alto. Just when the unwary might imagine Bach is going to end there on the subdominant, he breaks the symmetry by adding two more bars. With the dénouement (No. 6) at a far higher pitch, he asserts the essence of the Trinity – *ein Wesen, drei Personen* ('one essence, three persons') – and the remoteness of God in His relationship to humankind. And so in this way he signs off this mini-cycle of twelve cantatas spanning the period between Easter and Trinity Sunday 1725 with a cantata crammed with provocative thoughts and musical exegesis. Bach had come full circle.

* * *

In the opening stanza of his *Choruses from 'The Rock'* (1934) T. S. Eliot berates modern society for losing faith in God, casting it in non-Christian symbols:

> The Hunter with his dogs pursues his circuit.
> O perpetual revolution of configured stars,
> O perpetual recurrence of determined seasons,
> O world of spring and autumn, birth and dying!
> The endless cycle of idea and action,
> Endless invention, endless experiment,
> Brings knowledge of motion, but not of stillness;
> Knowledge of speech, but not of silence;
> Knowledge of words, and ignorance of the Word.
> All our knowledge brings us nearer to our ignorance,
> All our ignorance brings us nearer to death,
> But nearness to death no nearer to God.
> Where is the Life we have lost in living?
> Where is the wisdom we have lost in knowledge?
> Where is the knowledge we have lost in information?
> The cycles of Heaven in twenty centuries
> Bring us farther from God and nearer to the Dust.

The pity is that Eliot did not know Bach's cantata cycles (though he might have heard individual movements). If he had, he might have appreciated that in Bach's music the cycles of Heaven can bring us closer to God. They could also be telling us that the Dust is not the enemy, but part of our daily existence.* At that point Eliot might genuinely have agreed with Thomas à Becket, when he has him say,

> I have had a tremor of bliss, a wink of heaven, a whisper,
> And I would no longer be denied; all things
> Proceed to a joyful consummation.[21]

* This again is a tangential reference to *His Dark Materials*, by Philip Pullman, who may have had this image in mind when he formulated his concept of Dust. Bach's music reminds us of a need to re-embrace Christian orthodoxy (quite the opposite of Pullman's view, therefore), but more than this, it points to a godhead beyond petty human self-representations.

10
First Passion

What passion cannot Music raise and quell?
– John Dryden, 'A Song for St Cecilia's Day' (1687)

The house lights are dimmed, the conductor enters the pit, the orchestra is poised to begin. There is that unique mood of expectancy you find only in a darkened theatre at the beginning of an opera before the music starts to weave its particular magic and the drama to unfold. No opera overture of the first half of the eighteenth century that I know comes closer to anticipating the moods of those to *Idomeneo* or *Don Giovanni* than the opening of Bach's *John Passion*; nor is there a better direct ancestor to Beethoven's three preludes to *Leonore*. For pictorial vividness and tragic vision, the turbulent orchestral introduction is without parallel. Like a true overture, it beckons us into the drama – not in a theatre, but in a church or, nowadays, often in a concert hall. The tonality – G minor – is one that from Purcell to Mozart usually implies lamentation. The relentless tremulant pulsation generated by the reiterated bass line, the persistent sighing figure in the violas and the swirling motion in the violins so suggestive of turmoil, even of the physical surging of a crowd – all contribute to its unique pathos. Over this ferment, pairs of oboes and flutes locked in lyrical dialogue but with anguished dissonances enact a very different kind of physicality, one that can create a harrowing portrayal of nails being driven into bare flesh.

So far one could interpret this as a highly charged representation of the Crucifixion, one in which each of these motivic elements seems to call attention both to itself and to the way it impinges on all the others. But then the bass line, static for its first nine bars, begins to move downwards chromatically, and the music starts to well up and intensify. (Three years later Handel will do something similar, though to vastly different expressive ends, for the coronation of George II – in the monumental build-up to the first choral entry of 'Zadok the Priest'.) With the entry of the chorus something of unprecedented, shocking power occurs: in place of words of lamentation Bach introduces a song of praise to the universal reign of Christ, 'O Lord, our Lord, how excellent is thy name in all the earth' (Psalm 8),* a unique occurrence in Passion settings of the time.[1] The voices enter together in three isolated stabs: *Herr! . . . Herr! . . . Herr!* The impression of a dual *Affekt* could hardly be clearer: an evocation and portrayal of Christ in majesty like some colossal Byzantine mosaic, but one who is looking down on the maelstrom of distressed unregenerate humanity below. Bach has found a way of matching the stark duality of ideas so often cultivated by John: light versus darkness, good against evil, spirit and flesh, truth and falsehood. In the course of this movement we soon realise that the duality takes the form of a vertical section – between the Godlike Christ 'lifted up' on the Cross and drawing all men to him – and his abasement, 'brought low' for the sake of humankind. Jesus' majesty is thus proclaimed, as one Pietist contemporary of Bach's put it, 'behind the curtain of his sufferings'.[2]

There was a time, not far distant, when public familiarity with Bach's church music was confined to the canon of his three most substantial chorale works: the *B minor Mass*, the *Christmas Oratorio* and the *Matthew Passion*. Bolder choral societies might tackle his Latin *Magnificat* now and again (in spite of being chorally one of the most technically demanding of all Bach's works), yet strangely would pass over the *John Passion*, perhaps assuming it to be little more than a rough draft for Bach's 'Great' Passion. Ever since Mendelssohn's hugely acclaimed restitution of the *Matthew Passion* in 1829, *that* became the work, practically definitive of Bach's genius, to command universal respect bordering on awe. Next to it the shorter *John Passion*, though also revived by Mendelssohn in 1833, tended for long to be regarded as its poor relation – cruder, less finely honed and essentially 'far inferior to

* Bach's startling use of opposites here – between Jesus' glorification (*Herrlichkeit*) and his abasement (*Niedrigkeit*) – can be traced back to Johann Arndt's three sermons on Psalm 8 (*Auslegung des gantzen Psalters Davids* (1643)).

the *St Matthew*', according to Philipp Spitta, the first in a line of Bach specialists who considered that 'as a whole it displays a certain murky monotony and vague mistiness'.[3] Not to Robert Schumann, however. After conducting the *John Passion* in Düsseldorf in 1851, Schumann found it 'in many ways more daring, forceful and poetic' than the *Matthew*: 'How compact and genial throughout, especially in the choruses,' he exclaimed, 'and of what art!'[4] It would take until the second half of the twentieth century before Schumann's enthusiasm for the earlier work –'one of the most profound and perfected works of Bach' – began to prevail and some sort of parity between the two Passion settings started to emerge.*

I am convinced that Schumann was right. Far from being dwarfed by its epic companion piece, the *John Passion* is the more radical of Bach's surviving Passion settings. Indeed, it packs a more powerful dramatic punch than any Passion setting before or since, an impression strengthened by its greater popularity and frequency of performance in the late twentieth century. Given a storyline so intrinsically strong and so familiar, Bach may instinctively have gauged that his listeners would be susceptible to the proven devices of fiction. He uses suspense and the satisfying arc of traditional narrative, including conflict, crisis and resolution, and sustains it at a pitch of musico-theatrical intensity beyond that of any opera score of the period. To make his narrative as vivid as possible, Bach is perfectly happy to rifle through the conventions of representation that opera had been developing for the past century, and now formalised in his day. The cast-list includes clear-cut villains, a hero-cum-martyr, and secondary characters either likeable but flawed (such as Simon Peter) or merely flawed (Pontius Pilate); and yet, emphatically, it is not an opera. Its conventions and its purposes are not those of the opera house, nor did Bach ever imagine for a second that it could be performed with theatrical apparatus and accoutrements. It is as bold and complex an amalgam of story-telling and meditation, religion and

* John Butt suggests that in Britain, at any rate, 'the public disgrace of not performing in the "approved" historical style was simply too heavy to bear for cash-strapped orchestras; moreover, the *Matthew Passion*'s traditional outing on Good Friday began to make much less sense as the public grew ever more indifferent to the notion of such a Friday. Greatly valued and still performed the *Matthew Passion* might be, but no longer as an unquestioned part of the mainstream repertoire' (John Butt, *Bach's Dialogue with Modernity: Perspectives on the Passions* (2010), p. 18).

politics, music and theology, as there has ever been, and a climactic manifestation of that 'spirit of music-drama' whose emergence we traced in Chapter 4. And since he is not catering for a 'passive' opera-theatre audience but rather a Lutheran congregation eager for spiritual nourishment, Bach can count on a degree of active participation from his listeners as they find themselves inexorably drawn into the fabric of the drama. This allows him to set tough questions for them.

Avoiding any glib 'operatic' characterisation of his biblical cast, Bach instead encourages individual singers and players of his ensemble to step forward at given points – to voice their thoughts, prayers and emotions as contemporary witnesses to the re-telling of Christ's Passion (and in his own performances even to swap roles). This was an experimental way of creating a fresh experience for his listeners, one outwardly geared to their spiritual edification but unprecedented in its dramatic intensity. What must have been so shocking to Bach's first listeners was that all this was heard and being played out in *church*. It is entirely possible that such a unique fusion of music, exegesis and drama might have perplexed its original biblically saturated listeners, just as much as it seems guaranteed to pass over the heads of an often biblically disabled modern audience, who do, nonetheless, still find it so gripping. We need to find reasons why a music so theologically impregnated and so fixed in what looks like a parochial version of Lutheran Christianity seems to 'slip its historical moorings'[5] to reach out and enthral audiences in so many different parts of the world almost 300 years after its inception. This, in turn, is the place to look for the renewal and expansion of the principles that inspired the founding fathers of opera, Monteverdi principal among them, whose central objective was to harness music's powers to move the passions of their listeners.

* * *

We saw how, from the outset of his cantorate in Leipzig, Bach had set himself the herculean task of composing (as far as conditions and time allowed) new music each week for all the festivals in the church year, his initial target (most likely) a minimum of three annual cantata cycles, each with a Passion setting as its climax. Accordingly, the *John Passion* was to become his first major 'planet' encircled by its co-orbital 'moons' – the cantatas he had fashioned so far in his first season. To re-approach it through familiarity with the cantatas that surround it, even nearly three centuries after its creation, changes and enriches our experience of it as performers or as listeners: it emerges as a work in which Bach crystallised ideas and techniques he had systematically been developing over the preceding year – different ways of combining choruses, chorales, recitatives and arias, of alternating the action of the narrative with the contemplative, and balancing vivid, dramatic scene-setting with stretches of the most beautiful and persuasive exposition of its meaning for the listener. Judging by the regularity with which he revived it in later years in the face of what seems to have been adverse criticism by the consistory and attendant pressure to alter its tone and theological slant, Bach must have attached a high value to it. It was his largest-scale work to date, one comprising forty separate movements and lasting over one hundred minutes, greatly exceeding any liturgical needs or directives, and one of a small selection of works that would occupy his thoughts at intervals for the rest of his career. It is significant that for two last performances in the year of his death and one the year before, he reverted in all essentials to its original state.[6] Perhaps this was his way of seeing that justice was done to the exceptional artistic effort he had expended in planning and shaping one of the most elaborate designs of any of his major works.

We referred in Chapter 9 to the unstoppable creative flow of his first year in Leipzig, the subtle and resourceful means he found to reflect and adumbrate the theological themes particular to each church feast, the cantatas thematically linked by twos and threes (and in once case six) to provide continuity and coherence from week to week. We saw him give an unseasonal theological twist to two successive Christmas-time cantatas (BWV 40 and 64), in which he played down the Nativity story and instead gave a persuasively Johannine view of the Incarnation as God's descent in human form to save man and to bring joy through his defeat of the Devil – in clear anticipation of the message of the *John Passion*. To the same end, in his choice of cantata texts and in his selection of chorales in the period leading up to Lent, Bach carefully prepared his listeners for the communal response which the chorales were soon to fulfil in his first Passion setting. He had even given them a foretaste of what type of music they could expect of him when faced with an extended passage of Scripture and with his imagination fired by a particularly dramatic incident such as Matthew's description of Jesus' calming a violent storm on the sea of Galilee (BWV 81), as we saw in the previous chapter.

As they assembled in the Nikolaikirche on that Good Friday afternoon, the congregation must therefore have had a pretty good idea about the kind of music that was in store. They had had almost a year in which to become accustomed to a style of music which Bach himself later freely admitted to the authorities was 'incomparably harder and more intricate' than any other music performed at the time. Now, for the first time in his cantorate, and with the spoken elements of the liturgy shrunk to a minimum in the Good Friday service, his music could legitimately occupy the centre-stage and constitute what Telemann once described (of his own cantata cycles) as a veritable 'harmonious divine service' in itself. Here was his opportunity to show on a large canvas what sort of input modern music – *his* music – could have in defining and strengthening Christian belief. None of his peers, and certainly none of his predecessors, had ambitions for exegetical music of an equivalent complexity or scale. None could match the depth of his elaborately patterned music – his meshing of narrative and reflection, of scriptural chronicles and theologically shaped poetic texts. In a university city famed for its theological faculty, it was a courageous – some might have called it a brazen – statement, coming as it did from someone who was not a theologian and who did not even have a university degree.

> Fifty and more years ago it was the custom for the organ to remain silent in church on Palm Sunday, and on that day, because it was the beginning of Holy Week, there was no music. But gradually the Passion story, which had formerly been sung in simple plainchant, humbly and reverently, began to be sung with many kinds of instruments in the most elaborate fashion, occasionally mixing in a little setting and singing of a Passion chorale in which the whole congregation joined. And then the mass of instruments fell to again. When this Passion music was performed for the first time – with twelve stringed instruments, many oboes, bassoons and other instruments – many people were shocked and did not know what to make of it. In the pew of a noble family in church, many ministers and noble ladies were present, singing the first Passion chorale out of their books with great devotion. But when this theatrical music began, all these people were thrown into the greatest bewilderment, looked at one another and said, 'What will come of this?' An old widow of the nobility said, 'God save us my children! It's just as if one were present at an Opera comedy.'

> But everyone was genuinely displeased by it and voiced many just complaints against it. There are, it is true, some people who take pleasure in such idle things, especially if they are of sanguine temperament and inclined to sensual pleasure. Such persons defend large-scale church compositions as best they may, and hold others to be crotchety and of melancholy temperament – as if they alone possessed the Wisdom of Solomon and others had no understanding.[7]

While some scholars have suggested that this account by the Lutheran theologian Christian Gerber referred to an event in Dresden rather than Leipzig, it nonetheless voices what may have been a typical reaction to Bach's presentation of his *John Passion* in the Nikolaikirche on Good Friday 1724. Leipzig, in the early decades of the eighteenth century, was a conservative environment where political and religious life was conditioned by tradition and precedent. Its citizens might have grown accustomed to having their own opera house – and for the city fathers this was living proof of their cultural open-mindedness at the three annual trade fairs. But 'operatic' Passion music in church was quite another matter. Merely by setting it as concerted or figural music, Bach was straying into a potential minefield. In the absence of any direct testimony, Gerber's is the best account we have to help us gauge the public response to Bach's first Passion – or at least that of his more vigilant and pious listeners. The presiding clergy, too, may have been disconcerted, ever alert to the danger of music stealing their thunder, disturbing their congregation's Good Friday meditations and threatening to swamp the liturgy altogether. In the relations between church authorities and musicians there was (and usually still is) always an element of suspicion.* As the musical climax of his first year in Leipzig, the Passion carried with it the certainty of impact and the likelihood of a drastic ruffling of feathers.

How could it have been otherwise? While there were identifiable local traditions and preferences for marking the anniversary of Christ's

* Nevertheless there was a tradition of support for concerted music within the liturgy by some of the Orthodox clergy in Leipzig, including August Pfeiffer (1640–98), who enthused about the importance of music in worship, even though he was stone deaf (his *Apostolische Christen-Schule* (1695) was in Bach's library), and Johann Benedikt Carpzov III, archdeacon of the Thomaskirche between 1714 and 1730 and whose family had connections to the Bachs (see Chapter 9, p. 318). We should not rule out the possibility that some of the clergy may well have been bowled over by the scale of Bach's *John Passion*, which was unprecedented in its length, drama and rhetorical force.

Passion in different communities throughout the German-speaking world, and even from one part of a town to another, ultimately this was a personal matter in which one man's meat was another's poison – though some kind of meditation on the Passion was essential for the devout Lutheran.* In Leipzig a rich theological symbolism operated within the liturgy of its two main churches, which in turn had an impact on the choice of texts and on the way music for Good Friday was assembled, presented and received. The sermon and the musical Passion-setting, whether monophonic or figural, were different but complementary means of fixing people's attention on particular moments in the unfolding of the story – an aural Lutheran equivalent to the Catholic Stations of the Cross. For some, the very act of congregational hymn-singing was cathartic and sufficient to guide their thoughts, while others may have welcomed the experience of a vivid musical re-enactment of the Passion story to put them in the appropriate devotional frame of mind (not least, perhaps, because the hallowed tradition of the medieval Mystery Play, though rejected by Luther, still cast a long shadow). No doubt there was considerable variety between these two extremes, even before taking into account the style and complexity of the musical realisation.

Opinions about the role of music in church had probably been divided for at least a generation before Bach's arrival in Leipzig, a factor guaranteed to stoke any resistance to the novelty of his musical and religious thought. Georg Philipp Telemann had a lot to answer for in this regard. We have already traced his mirific musical activities as a student and noted how during his four years in the city (1701–5) he refused to let them be curbed by the town's arbitrary divisions and structures. This legacy continued to disturb the tranquil surface of the town's musical life long after he had left – his innovations deplored by some and welcomed as overdue by others. Leipzig's pretensions to elevated cultural status as a university city could not disguise its innate conservatism and provinciality. It seems, for example, to have been largely impervious to the vigorous attempts by north German composers over the past hundred years to transplant Italian recitative style – and all that went with

* In his 'Meditation on Christ's Passion', Luther had stressed its central importance for the believer: 'It is more beneficial to ponder Christ's Passion just once than to fast a whole year or to pray a psalm daily, etc.'; 'Unless God inspires our heart, it is impossible for us of ourselves to meditate thoroughly on Christ's Passion' (*Eyn Sermon von der Betrachtung des heyligen Christi* (1519) in LW, Vol. 42).

it in terms of boldness of harmony and a vivid delivery of the text, as we saw in Chapter 2 – into German soil. The systems that Telemann had put in place at the Neukirche continued to siphon off the best students and freelance musicians in town years after his departure in 1705.* The church also acted as a magnet to the more progressively minded communicants, causing ripples of disapproval and envy among those who continued to worship in one of the two main city churches. Here was exactly the type of competition to put the ageing and defensive-minded Thomascantor, Bach's predecessor Johann Kuhnau, on his mettle.

* * *

Meanwhile, the new figurative style of Passion music was being ushered in, not in Leipzig, but in Hamburg in Holy Week 1712, when Barthold Heinrich Brockes invited 500 guests to his large town house for a performance of his own poetic Passion meditation, *Der für die Sünde der Welt gemarterte und sterbende Jesus* (*Jesus, martyred and dying for the sins of the world*) – set to music by the city's opera director, Reinhold Kaiser. Four years later Telemann, by now director of church music in Frankfurt, performed his own musical version of Brockes's text in the Barfüsserkirche, attended by 'several of the most famous foreign musicians [in town]'. At a further performance of this Passion setting, Telemann claimed in his autobiography, 'the church doors had to be manned by guards not to let anyone in who didn't have a printed copy of the Passion [libretto].'[8] Brockes's text ran to more than thirty editions between 1712 and 1722; at the height of its fame Johann Mattheson arranged for four consecutive performances in Hamburg during Holy Week 1719 in settings by Keiser, Handel, Telemann and himself. Ostensibly this was for the edification of the city's pious intelligentsia, but in reality it was an excuse for a public contest in concert form between these rival composers – the kind of spectator sport eighteenth-century Germans could not resist. Brockes's particular brand of mawkish religiosity was just what many of its citizens wanted for their spiritual nourishment. By providing a series of pre-set reactions

* Telemann's student ensemble, the *collegium musicum*, continued to give concerts of church music in the university church on feast-days and during the fairs, while at the Neukirche, under Telemann's successors (Hoffmann, Vogler and Schott), music impregnated with the Italian operatic style went on being performed there during the first two decades of the eighteenth century.

and responses to the story, he took away the effort of having to imagine or reconstruct the events of Christ's Passion in the mind's eye. Yet the cloying imagery of its verses was all that it took to whip up a gushing response.* Again, the court preacher at Gotha helps us to understand the attraction: 'The Passion, movingly presented and sung on Good Friday, a day worthy of every devotion, takes us every year into the open court rooms in which the just God pronounces the blood-judgement on his beloved and obedient Son, for our sins, and lets it be executed, which Mary and John, standing contritely and faithfully at the accursed wood [i.e., Cross] . . . never could bear to hear. The same, then, also without doubt, will be done this year, on this day, by those who love God.'[9]

Could the Leipzig pastors have written in this vein? It seems unlikely. If we were to take an overview of what was on offer at Passiontide, say, in 1717, we would find that at the Thomaskirche, the age-old rituals still prevail, deemed adequate to the needs of the more traditionally minded parishioners. Here, in time-honoured fashion at the morning service, the Thomaner are quietly delivering the responsorial setting of the *John Passion* traditionally attributed to Luther's musical adviser, Johann Walter.† The congregation, we note, remain standing all through the performance and are ready to return to church a second time for

* All that was missing were the operatic sets and costumes. Brockes's was the most celebrated in a genre called Passion oratorios, set to a completely original and non-liturgical poetic text that was distinct in purpose and structure from the oratorio-like Passions, which faithfully adhered to the biblical text (normally confined to one of the four Gospels but sometimes synthesising their accounts), even when varied with meditative aria-interpolations and, of course, chorales. His sentimental literalism has much in common with the sculptures to be found in Bavarian Catholic churches of the time, which, at their worst, degenerate into a zealous but dismal kitsch, a pageant of often sado-masochistic imagery. Basil Smallman draws attention to the paradox that 'these libretti [by Brockes and others] were part of a reaction again the Pietist cult of simplicity . . . their tasteless imagery and their preoccupation with the grosser physical aspects of pain and suffering – traits which were characteristic of Pietist poetry' (*The Background of Passion Music* (1971), p. 76).

† This was a practice going back to 1530 in which, at the main service on Good Friday, in place of the Gospel, John's account of the Passion story was chanted in front of the lectern in the chancel 'by an alumnus as Evangelist . . . [while] a deacon had the role of Christ and the choir that of the people' (*Bildnisse der sämmtlichen Superintendenten der Leipziger Diöces* (1839), p. 54). The fact that as late as 1722 a new set of parts of Walter's Passions were written out for the *turba* chorus – simple four-part chordal responses, in contrast to the monophonic delivery of the biblical narrative – is an index of this enduring tradition (H.-J. Schulze, 'Bachs Aufführungsapparat' in *Die Welt der Bach-Kantaten*, Christoph Wolff (eds.) (1999), Vol. 3, p. 148).

afternoon Vespers: with astonishing stamina and piety, they sing all twenty-three stanzas of Sebald Heyden's Passiontide hymn 'O Mensch, bewein dein Sünde groß' or the twenty-four verses of Paul Stockmann's hymn 'Jesu, Leiden, Pein und Tod'. On the other side of town, at the Neukirche, a figural Passion oratorio with instrumental accompaniment is being performed for the first time in the city's history: Telemann's setting of Brockes's Passion. Telemann's enduring reputation and the lure of highly approachable music may account for the exceptionally large congregation, for 'the people would surely not have arrived at church so early and in such numbers for the sake of the preacher', according to the young theology student Gottfried Ephraim Scheibel: 'I was amazed at how attentively people listened and how devoutly they sang along. The moving music contributed most to this. Although the service lasted over four hours, everyone stayed until it was finished.'[10]

Meanwhile, several miles to the west of Leipzig, in the castle church at Gotha, none other than J. S. Bach himself, travelling from Weimar to deputise for the indisposed resident court composer, is leading a performance of up-to-the-minute Passion music. Neither the music nor the text has been recovered; but other Passion settings from the next few years provide us with a clue to the tastes then prevalent at the court of the Duke of Saxe-Gotha and at similar courts throughout Germany.* In 1719 a versified meditation on the Passion said to be by Reinhard Keiser to a libretto by Christian Hunold was performed at Gotha, and in 1725 the new Capellmeister, Gottfried Heinrich Stölzel, presented his setting of a Passion oratorio, again in Brockes's version. Hunold and Brockes share a similar linguistic style – physically explicit, garish and saccharine by turns – corresponding to a type of non-liturgical devotional literature in vogue at ducal courts and in cosmopolitan cities such as Hamburg. Through their drastically realistic descriptions of Christ's torture, and passages of calm exposition alternating with bursts of outrage by the disciples, they aimed to enlist the deepest sympathies of the listener.[11] How far Bach went down this road in his Gotha Passion of 1717 (if such a work ever existed) is hard to say, though some scholars

* We learn that Bach was paid twelve thalers for this guest appearance and that twenty copies of the libretto of that particular Passion setting were printed for use by the courtiers; but we do not know whether the fee was paid for composing, as opposed to supervising the performance of someone else's music (A. Glöckner, 'Neue Spuren zu Bachs 'Weimarer' Passion', Leipziger Beiträge zur Bach-Forschung, Vol. 1 (1995), p. 35 NBR, p. 78).

think that movements from it were recycled in his second version of the *John Passion* in 1725 (see below).

It was not until 1721 that Bach's future patron, Burgomaster Gottfried Lange, having taken stock of the popularity of the Telemann/Brockes Passion oratorio and the way this resulted in lower attendances at the Thomaskirche and the Nikolaikirche, finally succeeded in persuading the consistory to give in and to authorise the performance of figural music there at Good Friday Vespers, though they still insisted that the morning service stayed as it had always been. The Thomascantor, Johann Kuhnau, now frail, held out against the new fashion almost to the end, though he then allegedly 'very much wanted to perform the Passion story in figural style'.[12] Only a fragment of his *Mark Passion* has survived* – not enough to judge whether it was a genuine endeavour to regain the initiative or merely bowing to pressure and fashion. Its disappearance also deprives us of an immediate comparison with which to gauge the degree of continuity or novelty represented by the first appearance of Bach's *John Passion* in Leipzig three years later. Still, Kuhnau provided Bach with a precedent for a Leipzig Passion that relied on unadulterated biblical narrative as its core, and, apparently, punctuated by 200-year-old chorales, several *turbae* and arias set to new texts of lyrical commentary.†

* A 'short' conducting score survives in a later copyist's hand, extracts of which appeared in Arnold Schering's *Musikgeschichte Leipzigs* ((1926) Vol. 2, pp. 25–33) – enough to demonstrate Kuhnau's mastery of recitative style but not a lot else besides. Johann Adolph Scheibe evidently knew Kuhnau's *Mark Passion*: 'sometimes he succeeded in writing deep and poetic music [as] shown by . . . his last sacred works, especially his Passion Oratorio which he finished a few years before his death . . . We see how clearly he understood the employment and laws of rhythm, we see too how careful he always was to make his sacred works melodious and flowing, and in many cases really affecting' (*Critischer Musikus* (1737), Vol. 2, p. 334). Against this, Schering's study of the surviving Kuhnau fragment elicited disparaging observations upon it: its overall value is 'astonishingly limited in terms of fantasy . . . narrow in its musical horizon . . . a mosaic of backward-looking forms in terms of style and expression' (Schering, op. cit.). Yet the sexton of the Thomaskirche, Johann Christoph Rost, marked down the premiere of Kuhnau's Passion in his diary as a red-letter day: 'On Good Friday of the year 1721, in the Vespers service, the Passion was performed for the first time in concerted style [*musiciret*]' (BD II, No. 180/ NBR, p. 114).

† Standing behind Kuhnau's experiment was a century and a half of varied attempts at Passion oratorios and oratorio Passions beginning with Antonio Scandello's *John Passion* (1561), in which plainsong alternated with short bursts of polyphony. To me by far the most intriguing of these prototypes are the three modally structured settings by Heinrich Schütz: his *Luke Passion* of 1664, his *John* of 1665 and his *Matthew* of 1666. Restricted to a small

What is clear from this brief survey is that all across the German Lutheran world an appetite had grown for Passion meditations in music in a variety of forms during the early decades of the eighteenth century. For sections of the clergy, the musical innovations in Holy Week were cautiously welcomed in so far that 'devotion . . . must always be renewed, animated, and as it were, fanned, otherwise sleep will be the sequel.'[13] Introducing Stölzel's setting of Brockes's Passion in 1725, the court preacher in Gotha wrote, 'This story is so diligently presented, that Christ seems to be portrayed before its hearers' very eyes and crucified again now among them.'[14] And that was surely the point: new music was now being attached to texts in which the Passion story was paraphrased and retold in lurid terms, with periodic eruptions of communal outrage and protest – a kind of heckling by the contemporary witnesses – built into the narration. Against this was a whole swathe of conservative opinion opposed to the theatricality of the Passion oratorio and to attempts to draw the listener in as a fictional witness to Jesus' suffering and passion. 'There is no edification to be hoped for here,' complained Georg Bronner, 'other than that the ears are somewhat tickled by the music.'[15]

Even in the early stages of the *Aufklärung*, Lutheran Christianity was very much alive, informing and influencing the patterns of thought of the overwhelming majority of German citizens of Bach's day, as we saw in Chapter 2. It is a measure of an era inching its way towards modernity that, despite the shattering scientific discoveries of the previous century, faith was solid and moving in parallel – at least during Bach's lifetime. Clearly there were good opportunities for composers to meet

---

a cappella vocal ensemble, Schütz evolves his own idiosyncratic style of recitation, one that proves far more expressive than that of many of his successors, balancing it with brief but striking choral interventions. Between Schütz and Kuhnau probably the most notable examples are those by Thomas Selle – his *John Passion* (1641) being the first to include instrumental interludes, and four *Matthew* Passions: by Christian Flor (1667), in which there is the embryo of orchestrally accompanied *turbae*; by Johann Sebastiani (1672), the first to include simple chorales; by Johann Theile (1673), in which the Evangelist is accompanied by viols; and by Johann Meder (1701), in which Jesus' words are set in arioso. Here at last there are signs of expressive tension at the more dramatic junctures as well as a few well-crafted strophic arias. But only in Schütz's Passions does one encounter a strong creative imagination flying free of the liturgically imposed restrictions, although in a more etiolated style than that of his successors, opening the door to a rich world of biblical exegesis. Performances today of any one of his three settings still prove capable of holding an audience in their spiritual and emotional grip.

this demand, just as in the previous century there had been for painters positioned either side of the denominational divide. The key figures then, of course, were Rubens and Rembrandt, similar in the way that each took advantage of the continuing preoccupation with faith in their choice of subject matter, yet separated by an aesthetic and denominational divide. Futhermore, whereas Rubens's preoccupations were centred on the human body – its sensual physical musculature and tactility, Rembrandt was intent on exploring the inner emotional and spiritual temperature and the essential humanity of his subjects. To press the analogy with German theological scripts of the early eighteenth century may be going a step too far – not least because Brockes's audience were solid Lutherans, not Counter-Reformation zealots. One cannot overlook the fact that musicians as much as painters were held in contempt by the more conservative wings of religious opinion – and here the distaste shown by Lutherans of Pietist bent to music linked to Brockes's inflammatory imagery is strikingly similar to the Dutch Calvinists' disgust at the opulent fleshiness and gratuitous physicality of Rubens and his school. It was not the gushing texts alone that were offensive to the Pietists – how could it be since they themselves were lampooned by the Orthodox for their mawkish religiosity? – but rather their combination with musical settings featuring elaborate instrumentation. In an earlier age Erasmus had urged, 'let us give up this business of wailing . . . unless we do it on account of our sins, not His wounds. We should rather be joyfully proclaiming His triumph' – but not everyone paid attention to him.[16]*

* * *

It is obvious that, like so much of the greatest Western painting and music of the last millennium, Bach's *John Passion* was conceived not just as a work of religious art but as an act of worship in itself. How else are we to explain the extraordinary seriousness and devout sense of purpose that it exudes? The sheer conviction of Bach's vision, its vivid particularity, inspired by John's eyewitness account of the Passion story,

* In his comparison of the two painters' *Descent from the Cross*, Simon Schama suggests 'where the emphasis in the Rubens is on action and reaction, in Rembrandt's version it is on contemplation and witness . . . doers are perforce replaced by watchers' (*Rembrandt's Eyes* (1999), pp. 292–3). That, too, is the main difference, albeit oversimplified, between Bach's *John* and *Matthew* Passions.

is thus apparent from the very beginning in the choral prologue, 'Herr, unser Herrscher', which seems to sweep all before it. Even approaching it from the vantage point of the preceding church cantatas with their astonishing array of distinctive opening movements, each of which seems to portend the essence of the ensuing work, this grand tableau is unprecedented both in scale and in *Affekt*. In common with the prologues to two later works, the *Matthew Passion* and the *B minor Mass*, the opening bars carry within them the seeds of the entire work. As a conductor, one senses that the inexorable unfolding of the successive narrative and contemplative movements of the work is predicated upon – or at least implicit in – that initial downbeat. The way one gives it can determine much more than just the pacing of the movement: it can affect the tone and mood of the entire work and the degree of success it may have in pulling the listener into active participation in the performance and widening the terms of reference beyond the pre-existing meanings and connotations that Bach may have intended for it. The *da capo* structure that Bach adopts is no mere formality or structured conceit, as so often in contemporary opera: it is a metaphor for the entire Passion story in miniature. In the A section we are shown Christ glorified as part of the Godhead ('Glorify thou me with thine own self with the glory which I had with thee before the world was', John 17:5). The B section then refers to his abasement and anticipates the way he is destined to lay down his life for mankind. Finally, the reprise of the A section serves to mark Christ's return to his Father in glory and majesty (Jesus prayed earlier that his disciples 'may behold my glory, which thou hast given me', John 17:24).*

* Spitta is the first in a line of commentators who fail to detect in Bach's opening chorus any of the 'ideas of tenderness or love' we associate with John's Gospel. I feel this is wrong. A lot, of course, hinges on interpretation. To my mind the B section beginning *Zeig uns durch deine Passion* ('Show us through your Passion') implies tender, *dolce* singing, while the upward skipping A minor scale of the sopranos (bars 77–8) signifies the joy and release implicit in Christ's atonement. That the road to victory for humankind is shown to be bumpy and hard-going is evident from the sharp contrasts between these positive upward arpeggios (*zu aller Zeit*/'at all times') and the dissonant re-descent in *piano* (*auch in der größten Niedrigkeit*/'even in the greatest abasement'). The synchronisation of a spirited vocal melisma (*verherrlicht worden bist*/'you have been glorified') with the turbulent movement of the upper strings is a brilliant association of opposed ideas, one that he had already adumbrated in the final chorale of BWV 105, *Herr, gehe nicht ins Gericht* (see Chapter 9, p. 301).

This is just the first in a series of structural devices Bach puts in place to articulate and complement the structure of John's account. Theologians have drawn attention to John's way of inscribing a pendulum-like curve for Christ's presence here 'below' in the world. Beginning at the point of its downward swing with his Incarnation, it reaches its nadir with the Crucifixion, which is itself the start of the final upswing to his Ascension and return to the world 'above'. Bach is at pains to replicate this pendular swing in the tonal planning of his Passion – and also to go beyond it. As we shall see, at the midpoint Bach places his longest aria, 'Erwäge' (No. 20), which evokes the rainbow, the symbol of the ancient covenant between God and Noah after the flood. In so doing, he inscribes a symmetrical arc to match the pendulum swing of Christ's presence on earth to form an ellipse (see Plate 20).

In Chapter 14 of his Gospel, John makes it clear that consolation (*Trost*) and joy (*Freude*) are the eventual outcome of Jesus' victory over death. Bach's plan is to chart the course of this hard-won victory through a re-telling of John's eyewitness account of Christ's Passion, staying utterly faithful to the New Testament – not paraphrased, as with Brockes or Hunold – inserting only two short passages from Matthew's Gospel account, and then punctuating the narration with spiritual commentary by means of ariosos, arias and chorales, the last serving as a vehicle for moments for collective contemplation.

John's account is stretched over three 'acts'. Act I (John 18:1–27) opens with the arrest and interrogation of Jesus at dead of night in the Sanhedrin court and comes to a head with Peter's denial. Act II (18: 28–40 to 19: 1–16) then deals with the Roman trial in seven scenes on a split stage: the Jewish clergy and the mob outside the Praetorium, Jesus within and Pilate hovering from one to the other. It culminates with the passing of the death sentence. In Act III (19:17–42) the action shifts to Golgotha for Jesus' Crucifixion, death and burial. With a sermon to accommodate at some point, it looks at first glance as though Bach intends to replicate John's tripartite structure by placing it at the end of John's Act I – his Part I, closing with the crowing of the cock in a verse from Matthew (26:75) which he interpolates to voice Peter's remorse and bitter weeping. Thereafter, as we shall see, the act or scene divisions are far less clear, and the structural complications begin to pile up – hotly debated between theologians and musicologists. This is the result of Bach's design for Part II of his Passion operating on two levels simultaneously: on a literal or historical level, which obliges him to replicate John's physical narration; and on a spiritual or metaphysical level, which allows him the scope for a more abstract design in which to draw theological meaning from the events.[17] While there are no rigid divisions demarking either level, there are numerous correspondences between movements that suggest geometric patterns encasing a symmetrically arranged core. The musical ordering of what has been described as Bach's 'symbolic' trial[18] is slightly out of sync with the narrative divisions and changes of locale, and favours the spiritual dimension that Bach, in following John, seeks to extrapolate for the attentive listener.

For this most crucial day in the liturgical year, then, Bach evolves a structure with a subtle balance between the narrative and the contemplative, which only one composer seems previously to have attempted. Long attributed to Reinhard Keiser, this *Mark Passion* (1707) was the Passion oratorio Bach knew best, and so exceptionally 'modern' that he and an assistant copied and performed it in Weimar in 1712.* Following its lead, Bach establishes a triple alternation of utterance between Evangelist, Jesus, the minor characters and the crowd. The sheer pace and intensity of Bach's narration, which of course telescopes the actual timeframe of its historical occurrence, seems fast at times, but never breathless, let alone perfunctory. Prompted by the almost spoken, declamatory style of Keiser, Bach's is always poised to rise to moments of a far more persuasive lyricism.† Though his listeners would by now have been familiar with Bach's recitative style from hearing his cantatas over the past nine months, here the narrative fluency and dramatic

* Daniel R. Melamed has shown that the attribution to Keiser is found 'in only one source not connected with the early performances [in Hamburg] and is open to question' (*Hearing Bach's Passions* (2005), p. 81). Bach brought the performing parts of this *Mark Passion* with him to Leipzig in 1723. Don O. Franklin makes a persuasive case for viewing this work (often cited as a model for Bach's *Matthew Passion*) as an important source for the *John Passion*: 'Bach drew extensively on [it] . . . in compiling the libretto for his first oratorio passion' – 'in general contour and style' – and there is indeed a striking 'similarity in the overall proportions of the two works' ('The Libretto of Bach's John Passion and the Doctrine of Reconciliation: An Historical Perspective' in *Proceedings of the Royal Netherlands Academy of Arts and Sciences*, A. A. Clement (ed.), Vol. 143 (1995), pp. 191–2, 195). That Bach held this score in high regard is given further proof in his decision to work on it further in a revival he gave of it in Leipzig in 1726.

† None other than Bertolt Brecht was fascinated by Bach's 'exemplary gestural music'. He admired Bach's precision in defining locality from the outset, in the very first words of the Evangelist: 'Jesus . . . went forth with his disciples over the brook Cedron' (John 18:1).

vehemence of the Evangelist's line, tied to the fluctuating, harmonic tension between voice line and supporting continuo (and so different, too, from the 'holy' spoken tones habitually adopted by preachers), would have come as a surprise. Kuhnau's Passion cannot have been anything like this. Bach was not merely filling Kuhnau's shoes, or even those of the fashionable Telemann: his style of story-telling in music was immeasurably stronger and musically richer than theirs.

For years I was struck by the way Bach seems to show an instinctive feel for knowing exactly when to interrupt the narrative and slow the pace down, when to intercalate solo arias in order to attach personal relevance to the unravelling of events, and when to insert 'public' chorales in which his listeners could voice (or hear voiced) their collective response. There were sound theological precedents for his scheme in the way Lutherans were instructed first to read their Bible, then to meditate on its meaning, and finally to pray – in that order.[19] But it now seems that Bach had a useful guide close to hand, a commentary on John's Passion account in the form of ten lectures given by the Pietist theologian August Hermann Francke (1663–1727) and published in 1716.[20] Francke's commentary reveals unmistakable co-occurrences: in the structural paragraphing, and in the placing and thematic content of Bach's meditative insertions. So, for example, in Bach's Part I, we can see how

- The first theme of Francke's opening lecture is the same *Herrlichkeit* – Jesus' divinity – we have already noted in Bach's opening chorus.
- This, in turn, derives from his love for the Father and for mankind in general, mirrored in Bach's placement of his first chorale, 'O große Lieb'/'O great love' (No. 3).
- Francke points to the moment that Jesus, when offered the chance to avert the course of the Passion, rebukes Peter for using his sword and accepts his 'cup' of suffering; Bach responds with his second chorale, 'Dein Will gescheh'/'Thy will be done' (No. 5).
- Francke chooses to round out his first lecture at the point where Caiaphas advised the Jews that it would be good that one man should be put to death for the people, stressing the benefits of Christ's voluntary self-sacrifice for humanity: not in

a literal but in a spiritual sense, to accentuate the opposition between Caiaphas's evil intent and God's goodness. Bach inserts his first and very personal aria, 'Von den Stricken' (No. 7), at this juncture – a description of Jesus being bound 'with the ropes of my sin' in order to 'unbind me' and 'to heal me fully'.

- Francke urges the believer to emulate Peter in his eagerness to follow the master; Bach adopts the same very positive tone in his first major key movement, the soprano aria 'Ich folge dir gleichfalls' (No. 9).
- In the scene where Jesus is dishonoured in the High Priest's courtroom, Francke insists on his innocence and exhorts the listener to reflect on his own guilt. In perfect synchronism Bach places the chorale 'Wer hat dich so geschlagen' (No. 11) here to voice in successive verses, first, the believer's bewilderment at Jesus' mistreatment and then his or her implication in the process: 'I, I and my sins, which are as the grains of sand on the seashore, they have caused you the sorrow that strikes you and the grievous host of pain.'
- With Peter's denial and tortured self-reproach, Francke urges the need for individual penitence, a theme poignantly and vehemently expressed in Bach's explosive aria 'Ach, mein Sinn' (No. 13).

What is so striking is that Bach, in assimilating many of the themes outlined by this Pietist theologian, took such great care in structuring his first Passion, rooting it in the strong dramatic opposition between the vengeful mob and the serenity of the prisoner Jesus, whose eventual triumph is manifest in the lifting up of the Cross on to which he was nailed. The interpenetration and sheer depth of Bach's fusion of theology and music is there for all to see and hear. Indeed, one explanation for the overwhelming impression that Bach's music can make on the listener is, paradoxically, due to the unemotional, 'pure' theology of John's narrative account. Today, from our less theologically nuanced perspective, it seems incomprehensible that there should have been any qualms about the theological complexion of Bach's *John Passion*. More troubling in our post-Holocaust world is the demonising of the Jews in both Passions that is sometimes laid at Bach's door. Yet traces of anti-Semitism, utterly deplorable per se, are an integral part of the

Gospel accounts: they are not attributable to Bach, and his Passion is noticeably free of the egregiously anti-Jewish reflections to be found in Brockes's text as set by other leading German composers of the time.[21] As in all heroic myth the presence of evil malefactors is a dramatic device, providing the essential background to justify (or at least facilitate) the emergence of the hero, or, in the case of the Passion story, the Saviour of humankind. Bach was setting to music a version of events intrinsic to the Lutheran tradition – certainly not to be condoned, but no different in essence from the demonising of the Egyptians in the Book of Exodus, as portrayed by Handel in his oratorio *Israel in Egypt* (or of the Babylonians as portrayed by Verdi in *Nabucco*). One could object even more strongly to the targeting of the Papists and Turks in Bach's settings of Luther's litany, as in BWV 18, since they were not part of hallowed Scripture, but gratuitous topical demons – the sworn enemies of Luther's Reformation – whom Bach chose to treat with a degree of humour, almost as pantomime villains.

This leaves us with the question, how could Bach's graphic characterisation of a bloodthirsty mob in the Gospel account, lumped together as *die Jüden*, coexist in his Passions with heartfelt expressions of Lutheran piety? The answer lies in the explicit admission of collective guilt in the contrite response of Christians in the chorales, symbolised by Bach's requiring identical singers to double as the frenzied mob and the community of the faithful. That the very persecutors of Christ from whom we recoil with outrage and disgust are *us* makes the experience of his Passions all the more emotionally harrowing. For this very reason, when I conduct these choruses, while respecting Bach's stylised forms (fugue, sequence and the use of imitation and *figura corta*, etc.), I do not hold back in drawing out expressions of the utmost self-importance, legalistic point-scoring and sheer blood-thirstiness from the *turbae*; nor in bringing to the surface the overwhelming sense of remorse and self-incrimination in the following chorales. Heard in close succession, they mirror both reprehensible human patterns of behaviour and our horror-struck response to them, which, as Bach so poignantly reveals, often go hand in hand – one generation of out-and-out victims becoming, with tragic irony, the next generation's perpetrators of similar atrocities.

So, after the action-filled narration and, in particular, the unremitting interventions of a deranged mob, the chorales stand out as islands of musical sanity – and indeed that may have been the way Bach himself viewed them. As everyone familiar with either of Bach's surviving Passions knows, participating either from the outside as a listener or from the inside as a performer, the placement of the chorales is central to the overall experience – pulling the action into the here and now, confirming, responding to or repudiating what has just happened in the narrative, and obliging one to consider its significance. Even if the consensus among today's scholars is that they were not intended to be sung congregationally, the chorales certainly provided a cultural framework and moments for the contemporary listener to make instantaneous connections between the unfurling of biblical events and the reassuring recognition of familiar verses and melodies which were accepted as the most direct forms of address between the believer and his God. Their tunes are solidly crafted and peculiarly satisfying in their regular paragraphing. Marvellously lucid, Bach's harmonisation lifts the often humdrum words of the hymn-writer on to a higher level, giving equal emphasis to depth of feeling and humanity. It is fruitless trying to separate out their harmonic richness from the exquisite shaping of all three lower lines, each one a credible melody in its own right.* The intersection of these vertical and horizontal planes is crucial – in the earliest etymological sense of the word – to one's experience of them.

* * *

Equally important to the articulation of John's Passion account is Bach's strategic placing of his arias. At key moments they draw together the threads of the underlying doctrinal significance, establishing an active engagement with the listener yet without diminishing the inexorable

* Another indicator of the potency of Bach's use of chorales in the *John Passion* lies in their homophony: by adding instruments to double the vocal lines Bach tilted the balance in favour of the top and bottom, the extra edge of the oboes adding to that of the violins but softened by the flutes, the bassoon functioning the same way and supported by double bass and organ – the effect is rich but never opaque. None of this serves any purpose, of course, if there is not a total identification and understanding of the text by the instrumentalists, even to the point of imitating the exact word-shapes and vocal inflections of the hard-working singers. Bach's music is full of instances when his singers are called on to emulate the agility and technical fluency of the instruments in the interest of clearly articulated running passages and percussive rhythms. Whereas in the *turba* choruses they are stretched to the limit, here in the chorales the players are required to return the compliment: to add colour and depth but never to mask or overwhelm the singers nor to reduce the hieratic impact of the sung delivery of the text.

unfolding of the drama. Bach has sometimes been criticised by twentieth-century commentators for placing the first two arias of Part I cheek by jowl (with only three bars of recitative between them); but this is to misunderstand his purpose. Here is one of several occasions when we sense his creative impulses, in this case producing a contrasting diptych taking its lead from Francke's reflections and working to convey successive images: in the alto aria, Jesus, newly fettered and manacled, his bonds serving to 'unbind' and free man from the 'bonds of sin'; and in the soprano aria, the contrite believer hurrying to follow him – to the ends of the world if necessary, or at least as far as the High Priest's courtroom. In the first case he seizes on the punning references to bondage – 'to free me from the *bond* of my sin, my Saviour is *bound*' – and in this opening ritornello motif he devises a subtle braiding of the two oboe lines to symbolise the 'bonds' in what Germans call the *gebundener*, or 'bound', style: a falling, perfect fifth (second oboe) answered in canon by a diminished, or 'diabolical', fifth (first oboe), Christ's 'bond' – willingly endured for man's 'bonds of sin' and – piling on the symbolism – 'tied' over the bar-lines. Bach's instruments in the second aria are a pair of transverse flutes, who engage in canonic exchanges with the soprano.* A single flute might have given a breathless credibility to the love-chase, but with two players sharing the same part and thus able to alternate, or 'stagger', their breathing to ensure an unbroken line, the impression of a spinning- (perhaps prayer-) wheel is more pronounced. The effect is strengthened by Bach's use of a palpitating melismatic descent for the word *ziehen* (a reference to the Crucifixion – 'when I am lifted up I will *draw* all men to me'). At all events the success of this entrancing piece – a *passepied* in B♭ major – is to convey the eager innocence of willing participation and companionship. It makes the ensuing account of Peter's fall all the more poignant. 'Ich folge dir' is very much in a Bachian genre of naive, faithful, trusting, even blissful soprano arias, often the last number of a cantata before the final chorale.

John's eyewitness account of Jesus' appearance before the High Priest Caiaphas has the flavour of a tense courtroom drama (the more significant Roman trial follows in Part II). Aggression and suspicion are in the air –

* Wilfrid Mellers makes a suggestive parallel here to William Blake: this is a 'Song of Innocence' to complement the preceding 'Song of Experience' (*Bach and the Dance of God* (1980), p. 103).

the prisoner in the dock, the self-possession and reason of his answers enough to infuriate his accusers. That this is a kangaroo court is clear from the gratuitous blow to Jesus' face by the High Priest's servant: as John Drury observes, it is 'all he can do by way of reaction to him'. The narrative never slackens its pace, though the recitation moves in and out of third-person reportage and emotionally charged lyricism. The drama of a sideshow at the back of the courtroom is equally gripping: Peter ushered in by John, the narrator – a case of discreet string-pulling – is recognised and identified as an accessory after the fact. As the accusations grow nastier, Peter's laconic denials become progressively more emphatic.*

Bach brings things to a head by means of a gossipy fugal chorus – in his world, it seems, even busybodies conversed in fugues – ending with a shouted homophonic taunt. We can almost see their gargoyle-like profiles inches away from Peter's face, akin to those Flemish and German paintings of the Renaissance, especially by Matthias Grünewald. Inevitably we suffer with Peter; but the uncomfortable question Bach asks us to consider is, would any of us have emerged from his ordeal with greater credit? The tension in the courtroom mounts with the glance that Jesus gives Peter at the moment when the cock crows.† And then, by inserting Matthew's account of Peter's weeping at this point, Bach abandons all objectivity with a momentary shift in both the perspective and the identity of its narrator. For Peter, the pain of betrayal and the reminder that he is not the 'special loved one' are excruciating. Bach constructs a melisma that changes key every two beats and never seems to stabilise, so that the distress is self-perpetuating. This is the prelude to an aria that encapsulates Peter's pain and that experienced on his

* Peter's twin denials (*Ich bins nicht*) were understood in the Lutheran tradition and by subsequent theologians to be the 'negative counterparts' of Jesus' earlier insistence (*Ich bins*). Bach sets both as strong dominant-tonic cadences, but in Peter's case he adds an emphatic appoggiatura to the word *nicht*. Significantly the modulations confirmed by Peter's cadences, first in G, then in A, have already been established in the transitional recitatives: as Eric Chafe observes, by making Jesus 'the agency of the modulation to sharps', Bach ensures that we understand that he is also the agency of Peter's redemption (*J. S. Bach's Johannine Theology: The St John Passion and the Cantatas for Spring 1725* (forthcoming)).

† Actually this glance is described neither in Matthew's nor John's account: it comes in Luke (22:61) and is paraphrased in the tenth verse of Paul Stockmann's hymn that Bach uses here as the culmination of Part I. Bach possessed a copy of Heinrich Müller's sermons on Christ's Passion (*Von Leyden Christi*) in which he says 'The Saviour's glance was like the sun, warming Peter's cold heart' (*Der Blick des Heylandes war gleichsam die Sonne, / die das kalte Herz in Petro erwärmete*).

behalf by John and all subsequent witnesses, even if it is not explicitly assigned to him. Up to this point Peter has been sung by a bass. When in performance the tenor soloist who sings the Evangelist also sings the ensuing aria (which may have been Bach's intention anyway); the sense of dual identity – Peter and the Christian onlooker (*us* in other words) – is thereby intensified, especially when he refers to *die Schmerzen meiner Missetat*, 'the agonies of my misdeed'.

For those who detect only a cool cerebral control in Bach's music, this aria (No. 13, 'Ach, mein Sinn') is the perfect riposte. Bach summons all his available instruments to participate in this finale to Part I of his Passion – full of tortured self-reproach, but widened to convey Peter's lesson to all humankind and to induce in the listener 'a state of violent shock'.[22] What is most unusual for this expression of remorse is his choice of the French heroic style – normally associated with pomp and circumstance – and the way he fuses it with Italianate structural techniques, whereby every single bar excepting the three-bar epilogue is derived from the opening ritornello.[23] Three features contribute to the effect: the choice of key – F♯ minor, known to the French as 'the key of the goat'; the construction of a descending chromatic bass line over which grating dissonant harmonies are elaborated; and the decision to set it as a fast chaconne. One bonus of using a French-style dance as the basis of this aria was the licence it gave Bach to vary the internal shaping of the dotted rhythms – here smoothly 'swung' in conjunct motion for lyrical passages (as in Blues singing), there sharply over-dotted for outbursts of fiery arpeggios (*wo willt du endlich hin*), the vocal phrases constantly varied in consequence, now reinforcing the characteristic second beat of the chaconne, now contradicting it by means of hemiolas bestriding the bar-line. Here, then, he has assembled all the ingredients to make an impassioned statement.* The energy and emotional

* Mellers (op. cit., p. 109) claims it is 'the most humanly passionate music Bach ever wrote', and one can hardly disagree with that. But in the process, as Laurence Dreyfus astutely observes, Bach plays fast and loose with the poetic structures of the text and ignores 'certain sanctioned doctrinal views so as to highlight aspects of the experience he found more compelling'. Unconventional as Bach's word-setting is here, its very disjointedness is, I believe, a deliberate ploy – a way of conveying despair and choking remorse. If one has done something reprehensible (like betraying one's idol) one does not necessarily speak or sing in rhyming couplets. Dreyfus recognises this: that Bach, 'in his anti-literary way, is busy focusing on a peculiarly personal and pointedly self-authorised reading of the text'. But to state 'most [of the words] are drowned out by the music, by all the attention Bach has paid to the

temperature are high and the vocal compass is stretched to the limit: in its frenzy and self-reproach it looks forward to Beethoven's Florestan (and there is indeed proto-Romantic extravagance of imagery embedded in the text, with its references to Christ's prophesy of the day when the faithful 'shall say to the mountains, Fall on us; and to the hills, Cover us'). Implicit beneath the turbulent surface of the music Bach has devised to convey Peter's horror at the realisation of his betrayal is the need for forgiveness. That Bach understood this perfectly is clear from the underlinings he makes at this point in his copy of Calov's Bible commentary. Calov writes, 'The highest and finest apostle, Peter, falls more shamefully than the other apostles, and yet recovers. If I were able to describe or depict Peter I would write over every hair on his head "forgiveness of sins", because he is an example of this article of faith – forgiveness of sins. This is how the Evangelists portray him, for no section of the entire Passion story is described in so many words as the fall of Peter.'[24]

Was coming across this in Calov the impetus for Bach to make the inspired switch from John to Matthew at this point?* The effect is not (as in so many arias in a Passion oratorio of the period and indeed in many of Bach's Passion arias) to take us reflectively out of 'real-time' – witness the way he manipulates the ritornelli to confuse our expectations of the

---

ritornello' would indicate to me signs of a poorly conducted performance ('The Triumph of "Instrumental Melody": Aspects of Musical Poetics in Bach's *St John Passion*', *Bach Perspectives*, Vol. 8 (2011)). Indeed, it is the very subjectivity of Bach's interpretation and the explosively expressive force of his music that makes it so compelling to *us*. This aria in particular is one in which, like Monteverdi before him, Bach aims to move the passions of his listeners. To arrive at this (again like Monteverdi) he himself needs to be moved. Bach is manifestly stirred by Peter's desperate situation and is utterly true to its underlying disclosure of human failings. Proof of his success here comes via the mysterious transformative processes known to all theatre people (and some performing musicians): those experiences of actions and conditions shared between performers and audiences that seem to vault over temporal, cultural and linguistic barriers. This is the phenomenon for which the Italian neurophysiologist Giacomo Rizzolatti claims to have found a biological explanation. His discovery of 'mirror neurons' suggests that we are capable of an instantaneous understanding of the emotions of others through neural imitation, and that there are cognitive processes that allow us to interpret sensory information as laden with a particular emotive significance (G. Rizzolatti and C. Sinigaglia, *Mirrors in the Brain* (2008)).

* In this Bach was following the tradition of seventeenth-century Passion sermons, as Elke Axmacher points out ('*Aus Liebe will mein Heyland sterben*' (1984), p. 155), in which Peter's denial and the second Matthew interpolation (the 'earthquake' scene – see below) were introduced in order to reinforce the need for repentance.

aria's structure, where a more 'rounded' design might have seemed more settled within itself and consequently less 'implanted' in the action.

As the final bars of the tenor aria fade away – appropriately with a speeded-up recall of Peter's weeping theme and the recurrent motif used to convey his shivering at the back of the courtroom – Bach brings us gently back to earth, to our present. His choice of chorale to draw the lessons from Peter's story is both strategic and tactful: Paul Stockmann's 'Jesu, Leiden, Pein und Tod', one of the hymns most often sung by the Leipzig faithful on Good Friday, its stately melody by Vulpius marvellously soothing at this juncture (No. 14). The words refer us again to Jesus' 'serious' glance and the forgiveness of sins it offers to the contrite. With the sermon due to follow at this point, it is hard to believe that not much more than a half an hour has gone by – less than the time needed for one of Bach's double-decker cantatas, yet with so much action compressed within its timespan and music of such blistering intensity. According to Leipzig custom, the Good Friday Vespers sermon drew on the Old Testament texts that presage the Crucifixion (Isaiah 53 and Psalm 22 in alternate years). But, unless the role of the sermon was reduced to something equivalent to a 'translation' or the provision of subtitles, what, we might ask, was Superintendent Deyling to preach that had not already been said for him already by his cantor in music of such impassioned eloquence and persuasiveness?

* * *

After the sermon the action and the tonal shifts speed up, reinforcing the authority of the first-person voices. Once again, as in Part I, Bach shows a similar approach to that of Francke's Passion lectures, although here the symmetrical design of his 'symbolic trial' does not coincide quite so neatly with Francke's boundaries.[25] Chorales frame the sermon like bookends, an impression scarcely diluted by the liturgical requirement of a 'pulpit Lied' and organ chorales at this point. But the first chorale in Part II actually carries the narration forwards: vicariously we experience the way Jesus was 'seized like a thief in the night . . . taken before unbelievers, falsely accused, derided, spat upon and vilely mocked'. In constructing music for this central scene of Jesus before Pilate – the Roman trial – Bach traces the outline of John's Gospel very closely. The sheer theatrical dynamism is here unprecedented. Not even the lake-storm in his cantata BWV 81, *Jesus schläft*, can match this for sustained dramatic momentum. Crucial to its effectiveness, again, is the physical deployment on an imaginary stage set: Christ as prisoner, immobile (perhaps immobilised) in the judgement hall, the crowd holding back in the outer court, 'lest they should be defiled', Pontius Pilate the go-between.*

The contrast between the uneasy public confrontation of the Roman governor with the mob and their spokesmen on one side, and Pilate's attempts at man-to-man dialogue with Jesus on the other, is immensely strong. Even the subject matter is different: arguments about law, custom and political authority in the outer court, questions of a more philosophical nature (including the nature of truth itself) bandied between the two men in the judgement hall. Underlying both is the question of identity: who exactly is Jesus? The whole Passion narrative revolves around this issue. Resolving it one way or another will determine whether Pilate will bow to mob pressure and pass the death sentence on Jesus; it will also point to the wider ramifications this has for humankind. Two opposed concepts of kingship are being debated here: the spiritual, revealed when Jesus tells Pilate that his kingdom is not of this world, and the secular, culminating with the crowd's rebuttal – 'We have no king but Caesar.' Once that option has been twisted and construed as opposition to the colonial power, Rome, releasing Jesus proves to be impossible. Reading and re-reading John's account of the trial scene (Chapters 18 and 19), and then living on the inside of Bach's musical exegesis over many years and performances, I cannot avoid sensing that the faith which undoubtedly supports both accounts, whether read, spoken or sung, has less to do with dogma and far more with a quest to lay bare the human condition and to find ultimate meaning in life.

In each situation Bach seems to find a vivid response and an appropriate tone – for every charge and counter-charge, accusation and riposte – and to keep a tight control of the overall pacing. Though concerned to maintain the momentum and to preserve the remorseless uncoiling of events and arguments, especially in the central trial scene, again he shows an unerring sense of when to freeze the frame, when to interpose moments for reflection and commentary and when to sum up,

* The Jews regarded Gentile houses – and these of course included the Roman Praetorium – as unclean, and purity was at a premium at Passover.

thereby creating space for the story to register with the listener. His aim being to extrapolate and clarify the meaning of the events of the Passion for the listener (in ways that are out of reach for the preacher), he establishes a whole network of lines, constantly checked, to connect each point in the unfolding of the dramatic action with the basic biblical data that account for it. Thus time is always moving on two planes, the present implying (as well as reacting to) the past and the past conditioning the present. Once more it is the judicious choice and placement of chorales that provide the essential scaffolding and punctuation of the narrative and that simultaneously articulate the underlying theological themes. You could of course remove them (together with the meditative arias) and the piece would still make sense at one level; but to do so would break the circuit – obliterating the connections to Bach's time and to ours. What was left would be equivalent to a Greek tragedy without the chorus.*

Recent commentators, lulled by the ease with which it is possible to identify the way-markers Bach leaves along his trail – the plethora of thematic links and recurrences, the progressions, cross-references and self-quotations – claim to have detected purposeful symmetrical designs underpinning Bach's musical structure. At first their findings look promising but soon run into problems. In the first place they cannot always agree exactly where these symmetries occur in the work, and, as one might expect, Bach himself has nothing to say on this subject. Then, the singling out of one or two discernible structural patterns runs the risk of giving each a disproportionate significance – as though *it* was the

* To get an idea of quite how successful Bach is here in his dramatic pacing, one need only compare his setting of the Roman trial with the equivalent portion in Johann Mattheson's Passion oratorio, *Das Lied des Lammes* (1723), a work Bach may have known. Both composers draw on a common literary source, a libretto by Christian Heinrich Postel; both divide John's narrative at the same points; both begin with the chorale 'Christus, der uns selig macht'; both use Postel's text for 'Durch dein Gefängnis' (Mattheson as a duet, Bach as a chorale); and both place it midway through Verse 12. Quite apart from the enormous discrepancy in musical style and substance, the main difference is one of pacing and proportion. As Don O. Franklin observes (op. cit., pp. 188–9), where Mattheson, following Postel, places his greatest emphasis on the arias – seven of them being lengthy ariosi for Jesus and Pilate – Bach breaks the flow of the action only three times (for 'Betrachte/Erwäge', the pseudo-chorale 'Durch dein Gefängnis' and the dialogue aria 'Eilt') and is thus able to drive the action forwards, focusing our attention on the intense interaction between Jesus, Pilate and the crowd – something beyond Mattheson's capabilities – and framing the entire scene with two chorales.

most important aspect of the music.* It seems to me far more likely that Bach, in arriving at his overall design for the work, employed several organising principles at once. To pick on just one as holding the key to our understanding is to devalue the way his creative process may have operated at different levels simultaneously. Any single pattern, whether rudimentary or complex, is likely to provide a distorted and reductive view of a piece whose deeper significance is embedded in its very specificity – of text, style, grammar and, above all, of concept and intent. Indeed, Bach seems regularly to be drawing our attention away from the overall, or 'macro', structure and towards the highly specific, and to the particular details of text and *Affekt*. A common feature distinguishing all his major church compositions is the way they drew from him the full resources of his craft, something he valued as a sacred trust. It was his skill in identifying musical means to mirror mathematical images of God or Nature that gave Bach's music its extraordinary force, and as a result these patterns and images are registered on our unconscious listening habits in multiple ways. But the question remains, does our awareness of them actually enrich our experience of the *John Passion* in performance?

For me their significance registers more on the retina than on the ear, more on paper than in performance.† This is distinct from, but perhaps parallel to, the clearly audible modulatory patterns which Eric Chafe has identified as dividing the work by tonal 'ambitus' – in nine differentiated key regions (see figure below). These he traces back to Johann David

* Part of the trouble here, as Chafe notes, is that 'contemporary theologians interested in Bach and historical Lutheranism, who are the likeliest to understand why Bach might have done what he did in the *John Passion*, have seldom had much grounding in music, whereas musicians [or, rather, musicologists, I suggest] almost never have sufficient involvement in the necessary theological modes for his decisions. Thus questions of symmetry in the design of the Passion are continually addressed as a "problem" of musical form, and one, it seems, that can be speculated on with no particular knowledge of its theological correlates. Such interpretations give very much the sense of being pulled from a hat' (*J. S. Bach's Johannine Theology: The St John Passion and the Cantatas for Spring 1725*).

† To this Chafe's very reasonable response is that 'the boundary between the "audible" and the "inaudible" is not a certain one, that the whole person is a compound of intellectual and affective qualities whose separation does violence to the whole. In this respect, what Bach achieved in the design of the *St John Passion* is what most sets him apart from his many lesser contemporaries.' Earlier in the same chapter he conceded that 'sometimes there appear to be multiple, even overlapping patterns, or partial patterns, no one of which can be considered to represent the "structure" of the work' (*J. S. Bach's Johannine Theology: The St John Passion and the Cantatas for Spring 1725*, Chapter 5).

Heinichen's concept of a *Musicalischer Circul* (1711), or circle of keys,[26] which 'served as the new paradigm of tonal relationships' just before the hugely significant emergence of twenty-four major and minor keys in Bach's time and the well-tempered tuning 'that made their use possible'. Chafe argues most persuasively that the successive use of the 'ambitus' is a deliberate device by Bach to control and organise the music of the *John Passion* on such a large canvas. Furthermore, he suggests, Bach employs it to underscore the fundamental oppositions within John's theology; so that, for example, Jesus' sufferings are associated with flat keys, their benefits for humankind with sharp keys:[27]

Fig 2.

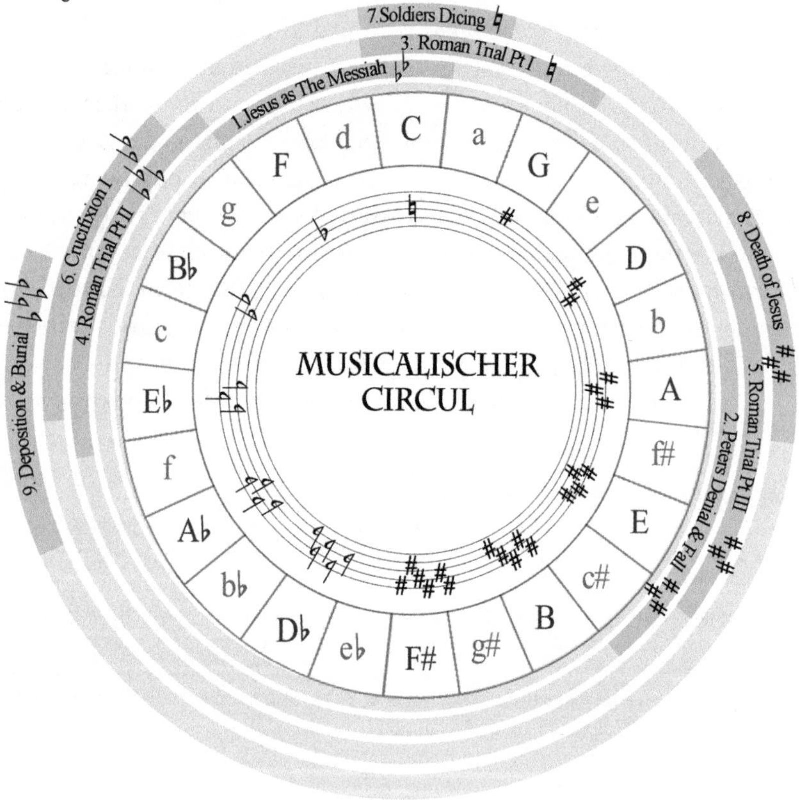

The listener's ability to 'clock' all these modulatory excursions as they progress – and as Bach would have assumed – can enrich the experience, but is not essential. Similarly, while recognising that this is what is happening in the music, we can 'enjoy' the Passion without becoming embroiled in all the paraphernalia of contemporary Lutheran theology and the way it interconnects with the formal patterns and gestures of Bach's music – or is, at times, even at odds with it. My feeling is that there is so much intrinsic human as well as musical substance here that, although Bach's incidental exegetical purpose was undoubtedly to vivify and augment his first listeners' meditation on the implications of the Gospel story, it is his music – and the inexplicable but nonetheless powerful effect it can have on us – which is always the dominant force. So replete in its unique sense of order, coherence and lyrical persuasiveness, it has proved that it can survive the passage of time and cross all boundaries, denominations or absences of belief. But, at the same time – and central to this book's argument – is the conviction that, in order to discover more about the man (as well as to deepen our understanding of the Passion itself), we need to explore beneath the surface of his music: to try to unearth the roots of its inspiration.*

Here we find, as so often in his church music, Bach is Janus-faced: glancing back as he draws inspiration and stimulus from the music he had learnt as a treble, from a time when German music was still in the first flush of excitement, playing at matching vernacular words to Italian-liberated recitative and continuo-based harmony, a time when 'Lutheran music followed the very grain of the text';[28] and also forward-looking in the new complexity and inventiveness of his art. Even if we accept that he took as his starting-point the groundplan of any of the Passion Histories of the previous century – by Selle, Flor, Sebastiani, Theile or Meder, or even the great Schütz (see footnote on p. 355) – these are not necessarily the most significant models in terms of musical materials and language that he was intent on re-working and perfecting.

For a single example one need only point to the way Bach takes over Monteverdi's *stile concitato* (his codification of ways that music can imitate the 'warlike' emotions) and uses it with devastating impact both

* John Butt concedes that theological inquiry into the inspirational roots of Bach's Passion music 'could be useful if it suggests thought processes that are of a piece with the thinking behind the music as an aesthetic art' ('Interpreting Bach's Passions: Outline of Proposed Scheme of Research' submitted to the Leverhulme Foundation (2005)) – balancing different forms of complexity, 'heard' and 'unheard' elements, the counterpointing of ideas, speakers and historical times.

for the belligerent clamour of the *turba* and for the celebration of Christ's immanent victory over death and the Devil in the middle section of 'Es ist vollbracht' (No. 30). Already in Part I we have observed his habit of constructing an opening movement of symphonic proportions that looks forward to the age of *Sturm und Drang*, that of his sons' generation. We had a foretaste of his newly developed recitative style in the way it both reflects the most minuscule inflections of the Gospel text and creates significant frictions with it, and how the harmonic motion 'carries the countless melodic events on its shoulders, so to speak' while allowing Bach opportunities 'to unpack the astonishing array of text-musical correspondences we find [here and] in virtually every work'.[29] We also experienced the strategic placement of the chorales.

Now, in Part II, the pace, tone and structure shift on to the bigger screen, with Jesus face to face with Pilate, who alone has the power to determine the final outcome. In this work, much more so than in the *Matthew Passion*, Pilate emerges as an intriguing and not wholly unsympathetic figure – a beleaguered provincial governor cowed by the mob, yet still demanding better evidence for the charges of sedition against Jesus. In today's performances, especially when Pilate is well characterised, one senses that listeners are drawn to his equivocation and to the dilemma he faced, shuttling to and fro between Jesus, whom he clearly sees as innocent, and the crowd.*

Two features of the trenchant crowd choruses immediately stand out: the rising chromaticism of the four voice lines in canonic imitation, and a manic whirling figure – usually in the flutes, once in the first violins, several times in both – that attached itself to the 'mob' ever since

* Perhaps more than might have been the case in 1724, this may be more a function of our own agnostic age than of Bach's portrayal of the man. The question 'What if he'd done the right thing and set Jesus free?' lurks somewhere in the background of our response to him nowadays. He, of course, 'stands at the centre of the Christian story and God's plan of redemption. Without his climactic judgement of Jesus, the world would not have been saved. Without Christ's death ... there would have been no Resurrection, no founding Christian miracle' (Ann Wroe, *Pilate: Biography of an Invented Man* (2000), p. xii). As head of the occupying forces in the troublesome province of Judaea, and with an estimated 6,000 legionaries to control a population of approximately 2.5 million, Pilate faced a major problem of governance, particularly at the explosive time of the Jewish Passover, the key festival of the foundation of the nation, when many congregated in Jerusalem to celebrate it. (John Drury, 'Bach: John Passion', pre-concert talk, 22 Apr. 2011, Snape Maltings, p. 1).

they first sent a search party out to arrest Jesus in Part I. Readily identifiable, too, is an incipient dactylic figure (long-short-short) first associated with the 'delivering up' of Jesus to Pilate but soon to be used with obsessive insistence – first by the Evangelist to convey (harshly) the whip-lashing ordered by Pilate and then (tenderly) in the long tenor aria meditation on that scourging. This figure will soon become the motto of the two fanatical *Kreuzige* choruses; but in those its remorseless bellicosity is welded to grinding dissonance, the product of fugal entries that have sprung out of the original oboe/flute collisions we noted in the opening chorus. The ferocity and sheer nastiness of these outbursts is chilling, especially as it reflects on us all (not just on the Jews and Romans): in Luther and Bach's view we are all *simul iustus et peccator*, both sinless and sinning, and therefore inescapably implicated in the mob frenzy and mindless brutality that saw an innocent man condemned to be crucified.

Bach finds two very different but equally compelling strategies to round out this portrayal: a sarcastic triple rhythm piece for the Roman guard ordered to stage Jesus' mock coronation (with another of those twirling-whirling figures in the woodwind suggestive of a grotesque game of Blind Man's Buff); and a pompous swaggering fugue-subject – of the kind that Handel was soon to use in his English oratorios to characterise his Old Testament baddies. Bach uses it to capture the self-righteous laying down of the secular law by the High Priest and his cronies – a clear trap for Pilate. Painters from Giotto to Hans Fries and Pieter Bruegel the Elder had found ways of bringing a vernacular realism to biblical scenes and to faces contorted by hatred. But no composer had previously come near to Bach in rendering the subtleties of irony and sarcasm with such penetrative insight. It would require a Hector Berlioz – and a hundred years of musical history – to patent a more garish portrayal of mockery and *grotesquerie* in music.

In all, there are eight choruses for the Jews and one for the Roman guard distributed across the trial scene, to which Bach added a tenth ('Sei gegrüßet'), perhaps to make a symbolic connection between the secular law and the Ten Commandments. There are variants, cross-references and repetitions aplenty. These are easy to identify and can be shaped into synoptic or symmetrical chiastic patterns almost at will. There is also an immensely significant cranking up of tonality in the course of the scene. So, for example, the flute figure identified with the pair of 'Jesus of Nazareth' choruses heard in Part I reappears on five more occasions during the trial scene, travelling upwards from G minor in Part I to a screeching B minor (the flute at the very top of its range) at its last appearance – in the chorus 'We have no king but Caesar' (No. 23f). Such is the intrusive dominance of the crowd's presence throughout this scene – peering into the judgement hall from the outside and, in effect, pulling Pilate's strings – that we may not be conscious of what else might be going on here.

Among contemporary Bach scholars, only Chafe to my knowledge has detected the way Bach has introduced a palliative element embedded within these *turbae*. He argues that, through the association of 'Jesus of Nazareth' with the easily identifiable whirling flute motif, Bach is constantly inscribing Jesus' name 'in situations where the identity of the King of the Jews is called into question' and attaching it to texts 'all associated with the *denial* of Jesus' Messianic identity by the crowd'. Next he points to the way each of the five *turbae* encompasses the full span of chords associated with the 'ambit' of each particular key in which they are set and finds here 'a striking resemblance to the ancient idea of Christ as Creator-Logos binding all things together into a cosmic system, or *systema*' (see p. 372). In other words Bach has hit upon a miniature harmonic formula which stands for John's image of the incarnate Word, which he uses to reinforce the structural devices in his portrayal of Jesus of Nazareth that are hidden beneath the surface of the music. It culminates with the ironic inscription Pilate orders to be affixed to the Cross, proclaiming Jesus as King of the Jews in several languages. Finally Chafe identifies Bach's way of threading the message of this inscription all through the central portion of the Passion by establishing a pattern of transposition with alternate rises of a fourth and falls of a third: G minor, C minor, A minor, D minor, B minor. 'While the physical events of the narrative tend downward leading towards the death of Jesus . . . the ultimate direction is upward, suggesting John's perception of the Crucifixion as a lifting up.' Thus 'the overarching allegory in the "Jesus of Nazareth" choruses is unquestionably the ability of faith to see the truth through appearances': 'Jesus' divine identity is veiled beneath its opposite.'

What we have then is, simultaneously (1) Jesus' true identity being insistently re-emphasised by thematic association in the memory of the listener; (2) a harmonic formula which stands for Jesus in the closed, circular 'ambit' inscribed within each of the successive *turbae*; and (3) what

Chafe refers to as a 'tonal allegory' of Christ's journey on earth, which ends with his being hoisted up on the Cross, his victory emblazoned by the royal inscription. It is as though Bach, faithful to John's habitual use of irony in making a true statement under the guise of its opposite, is intent on subverting the negative connotations of the mob's denunciations by implanting simultaneous formulae to the contrary. For, while the words in their mouths may be derisory and antagonistic – matched by Bach with appropriately violent rhythm and dissonance – in the very act of singing them they are also, consciously or not, giving vent to their opposite meaning through their insistent affirmation of 'Jesus of Nazareth', of the Word and of its triumphant progress. Thus the more virulently they denounce him, the more credence his detractors give to his authority and true identity. How could anyone other than a religiously attuned and probing 'listener' like Bach have conceived such an ingenious and comprehensive strategy of code and symbol? Should we conclude that it was anathema to leave any foul-mouthed vilification of his God unchallenged? And did any among his first listeners spot the subtext? And, finally, when – and if – he was challenged and asked to explain his choice of texts and chosen style of composition, did Bach even try to elucidate his aims and strategy to the Leipzig clergy? Or did he just walk away, shrugging off their objections with incomprehension, fulminating against their obtuseness?

Having established this web of interconnections and theological subtexts – clear to Bach, if not to everyone – and having presented his intensely vivid setting of John's account, he might have considered that he had done enough to draw in his listeners and to stress the contemporary significance of these events to the faithful of Leipzig. For in his eyes his music was incomplete unless it constantly posed questions that drew an engaged response from his public. This, surely, was what lay behind his decision to interrupt the flow at three points: once in response to Jesus' definition of his kingship by means of a chorale re-affirming the believer's allegiance ('Ach großer König', No. 17); once in response to Pilate's giving the order to scourge Jesus; and once at the point just before the crowd's final baying for blood when Pilate 'sought to release him'.

It is the last of these – the insertion of the pseudo-chorale 'Durch dein Gefängnis' (No. 22) – which has attracted the most scholarly comment ever since Friedrich Smend identified it as the centrepiece of the trial scene.[30] Smend drew attention to the presence of several symmetrical patterns underlying Bach's structure at key points, by far the most significant being a *chiasmus* (derived from the Greek letter X, the 'sign of the cross') centred on this intersection: not just the midpoint in the trial scene, but the 'inner heart' (or *Herzstück*) of the whole Passion. Bach placed this chorale here to enable the congregation to latch on to the central theological message, the paradox whereby 'freedom has come to us' as a result of Christ's capture and self-sacrifice.* It is located between two flanking *turbae* ('Wir haben ein Gesetz' and 'Lässest du diesen los') set to the same music but with each in a different key (Nos. 21f & 23b). He turns the first of these into a chorus of strutting arrogance – 'We have a law, and by our law he ought to die' – a whopping send-up of ecclesiastical pomposity, satirical to the point of being comical. Then, by modulating to sharp keys for the second, he winds up the tension as the Jews seek to drive a wedge between Pilate and Caesar – 'If thou let this man go, thou art not Caesar's friend.'

These choruses, in turn, are framed by further pairings of *turbae*, and, moving outwards in both directions, by arias, and, at the extremities, by two chorales ('Ach großer König' and 'In meines Herzens Grunde'). The second of these has a particular magic – not least on account of its luminescent E major tonality and the intensely individual way Bach has harmonised it. Beyond that it occupies a pivotal position in Bach's deliberate tonal shift from flat to sharp keys. Yet, as the centre of an overarching symmetrical structure, it is more readily appreciated on the page than in performance. The comparison frequently made between architecture and symmetrical design in Bach's music is misleading. The unfolding of music in time creates a foreshortened perspective very different from the panoramic impression of symmetry registered by the eye, say, by a Baroque palace. My experience is that in performance this chorale, despite the ravishing cadence that precedes it, as though to herald a reflection of great importance – of fate having been ordained – does not register either as the axis of the trial scene or as the hub of the entire Passion.

That prerogative goes to the immensely impressive tenor aria 'Erwäge' (No. 20) – a meditation on Christ's self-sacrifice in which, after the escalating savagery of the *turbae*, we are offered the metaphor of 'the most beautiful rainbow' reflecting the blood and water on Jesus' flailed back as a reminder of the ancient covenant between God and Noah after the

* By altering a single word of Postel's text – *ist* in place of *muss* – Bach alters the entire meaning of the chorale in line with his *Christus victor* theological stance. Man's freedom is no longer a fond hope but an accomplished fact.

flood.* Significantly Bach has placed it precisely to straddle the chapter division in John's Gospel: immediately after the mob's insistence on Barabbas as the prisoner to be released and culminating in the scourging of Jesus, one of two exceptional moments when Bach lays aside the Evangelist's narration and gives theatrical specificity and horror to the gruesome reality of Jesus' flogging by the Roman soldiers. This is one of the most shocking juxtapositions in the whole work: the Evangelist's outraged and outrageous burst of loud melismatic 'rage', followed immediately by the dulcet tonality of the ensuing arioso ('Betrachte, meine Seel', No. 19). One moment we see Jesus' back torn and blood-streaked by flogging, and the next we are encouraged to see it as something beautiful – as the sky in which the rainbow appears as a sign of divine grace – close to what J. G. Ballard had in mind, perhaps, when he refers to the 'mysterious eroticism of wounds'.[31] That Bach attached exceptional importance to this arioso and its succeeding aria is manifest both from their length (with the full *da capo* of the aria, the scene runs to more than eleven minutes) and its highly unusual scoring – for two violas d'amore and a continuo of (implied) lute, gamba and organ.† Outwardly

* Chafe refers us to 'the traditional image of Christ in majesty portrayed . . . seated in judgement on the rainbow, a sword protruding from one ear and a lily from the other – symbols of the division of humanity that John continually emphasizes' (*Tonal Allegory in the Vocal Music of J. S. Bach* (1991), pp. 316–17). According to Roland Bainton, 'Luther had seen pictures such as these and testified that he was utterly terror-stricken at the sight of Christ the Judge' (*Here I Stand: A Life of Martin Luther* (1950), pp. 22–5).

† Perhaps taking his cue from Albert Schweitzer, who found 'an indescribable felicity' in these two movements (*J. S. Bach* (1911), Vol. 2, p. 181), Wilfrid Mellers (op. cit., pp. 118–24) waxes lyrical on the deceptive 'balm-dispensing repose' of the preceding bass arioso – outwardly calm due to the soothing combination of lute and viole d'amore, but tonally unstable. He connects it to the Orpheus myth (which had eventually been validated by the Christian mystics and by medieval Platonists), both in the singing and via the lute – as post-Renaissance substitute for Orpheus' lyre. If at this point Bach was consciously tapping in to the perceived analogy between Orpheus and Christ, it would make sense of a kind – the balm of the seven-stringed lyre the means by which the Christian soul (while contemplating its 'highest good' as a result of Jesus' suffering) makes its journey heavenwards, returning 'to the origin of music's magic, that is, to heaven' (Macrobius, *Commentary on the Dream of Scipio*, quoted by Joscelyn Godwin, *Harmonies of Heaven and Earth* (1987), p. 61). Tenuous as is the link here, one might speculate on how far Bach might have agreed with Johann Mattheson's attempt to prove that there must be music in heaven, far superior to anything we can imagine, that it existed before the creation of Man, just as it will last for ever (*Behauptung der Himmlischen Kunst* (1747), pp. 3, 6, 19). From here it is but a short step to considering how, as on other occasions already explored in the course of this book, Bach sought here to emulate 'heavenly' music, and the extent to which it embodied a type of therapeutic wholeness and perfection (see illustration p. 553).

this looks like a high-risk strategy: to halt the gripping dramatic forward momentum of the Roman trial scene with its layers of political posturing, collusion and refutation. Yet Bach's instinct was sound. This, the nadir of Jesus' physical degradation, was precisely the moment to halt the motion and to reflect and meditate on its consequences for mankind – to balance an arioso and aria of moving subjectivity in response to the overall objectivity of John's account. The listener is led by means of suggestive (and theologically loaded) metaphors – and still more by beguiling musical textures – to contemplate the lacerated body of Jesus, rather as Grünewald does in his Isenheim Altarpiece and Hans Holbein does in his *Dead Christ in the Tomb*, with *ängstlichen Vergnügen* ('anxious pleasure') in so far as it leads to a pained, uneasy gratitude.* The eruptive force, sensuality and eroticism in Bach's expression of religious sentiment in this central aria may have been another moment to unsettle the Orthodox clergy of Leipzig and turn them against him. In the arioso that follows we are presented with the equivalent of Dürer's Passiontide woodcuts in which flowers, in this case *Himmelschlüsselblumen* (primroses or cowslips), bloom from the crown of thorns. Bach is ultra-precise in his choice of instruments here: a pair of violas d'amore, the most tender, consoling instruments in his locker, with their 'sympathetic' strings, contrasted with the lute (or, in a later version, harpsichord) to suggest the pricking of the thorns, and serving to point up the contrast by very obvious tonal means – a tritone leap in the voice from C to F♯ on *Schmerzen* to instigate sharpened harmonies whose raised pitches and upward tritone give instantly recognisable musical equivalence to the thorns, with the ensuing celestial relaxation going to the flat keys (G minor) for the blooming of the 'key-to-heaven-flower'. The impression is made all the stronger by manifest visual imagery: one need only glance at the even curve of the bridge† of the

* Here, as John Drury notes, 'ambiguous subjectivity could not be more extreme. Quite clearly the texts of both arioso and aria are conscious of their ambivalence between grief and pain, delight and grief . . . the ambiguity . . . rooted in the ancient institution of sacrifice, whereby the innocent victim bears the suffering, even death, which would otherwise fall on the votaries. The affliction of the victim is their deliverance' (op. cit.). In other words, Bach and his librettist are injecting a strong dosage of the 'satisfaction' theory (see p. 389) to balance the Johannine image of Jesus in glory.

† Normal violin and viola bridges are not evenly elliptical: the curve is more pronounced to accommodate the two lower and thicker gut strings. Given the ravishing timbre of the viola d'amore (quite apart from their symbolic appropriateness) it is puzzling to find Bach

six- (or sometimes seven-) stringed viola d'amore (with a further and highly symbolic row of six or seven 'sympathetic' strings) to muse whether it was this gentle ellipse which put the idea into Bach's head for using a pair of these rare stringed instruments as the means to evoke the rainbow – or was it its iridescent tonal colour or a combination of both? Then a glance at the score reveals that the lined pattern of the opening phrase of the aria – three notes up and three down above and across the stave – suggests to both eye and ear the arc of the rainbow (See Plate 20.). On top of this, Bach furnishes other ascending and descending figures that mirror the shape of the firmament – and conceivably of Jesus' trial – all contributing to the image of his humiliations as signs of God's grace emanating from above.

To this one could add its exceptional difficulty for the singer – never (as we have seen on a number of previous occasions) a matter of oversight let alone wilfulness on Bach's part, but intrinsic to his philosophical purpose. The stupendous technical effort required by the tenor – with virtually no time to breathe – to emulate the mellifluous and weightless fluency of the superhuman violas demands that we ponder human fallibility. The dactylic motif sung by the Evangelist when describing Jesus' scourging returns and permeates the entire aria – insistent enough to remind us that it is the weals on Jesus' back that are here being evoked, but now softened and curved in such a way as to suggest the promised rainbow. Then, early in the B section, after the tenor sings the scourging rhythm for the first time and the instruments strain to delineate the 'flood-waves of our sins' deluge', Bach parts the clouds and suddenly the rainbow miraculously appears. To bring this off in performance requires, besides stamina, imagination and a rock-solid technique, a combination of tensile strength and lyricism never easily achieved.

* * *

John's way of introducing the final section of his Passion account is surprisingly succinct: no sooner has Pilate issued the death warrant than

---

replacing them in movements 31 and 32 with muted violins (and substituting organ or harpsichord in place of the lute) in later revivals. As Dürr rather drily comments, 'It seems appropriate to review the replacement of the original instruments as a makeshift solution to which the modern performer should adhere only if he finds himself confronted with the same problems as Bach' (*Johann Sebastian Bach's St John Passion: Genesis, Transmission and Meaning* (2000), p. 112).

Jesus is bound and 'led away . . . bearing his Cross' (19:16–17) to Golgotha. With few words to work with, Bach elongates the narration by a series of drastic modulations – from B minor (using sharps for the last of the *turbae*) through a symbolic and tortuous shift back to flats* and eventually to G minor, the key in which the Passion started, in the process pushing the tonal system of his day beyond its normally accepted boundaries. During a break in the narrative the faithful are now urged to seek solace in Jesus' Crucifixion and to hurry to Golgotha, where his pilgrimage will be fulfilled. For this new tableau, Bach, or his unknown librettist, adjusts Brockes's text – with its unsavoury injunction to the Jews to leave their 'dens of murder' – to make it clear that it is *our* 'besieged souls' which are here being called on – to hurry to 'embrace the wings of faith' at the foot of the Cross. He substantiates this shift in emphasis by allowing the timorous souls to break into the aria (No. 24) with their repeated *Wohin?* . . . *Wohin?* . . . *Wohin?* to express their yearning for redemption. (Perhaps we are meant to recall the tenor's – Peter's – despairing *exclamatio*, *Wohin?* in 'Ach, mein Sinn' at the end of Part I.) He will use the same rhetorical figure (a detached series of rising fifths and sixths) again for *O Trost* in 'Es ist vollbracht'. Once more Bach uses a theatrical device – protagonist and chorus, foreground and background – to help us to experience simultaneously the evolving historical action and the sense that it is also happening now. He takes only what he needs from Brockes's paraphrased text, modifies, edits it and re-tells the story from a contemporary perspective. These vignettes – a lone soloist with a choral interjection behind – are all the more potent for their rarity.

This last section of Bach's *John Passion* is stamped by its rapid juxtapositions of mood. First we are presented with the narration of Christ's Crucifixion and Pilate's insistence on the royal inscription being translated into several languages. Then the crowd, in a final puff of self-importance, appropriates the music which Bach had given earlier to the Roman soldiers when they staged Jesus' mock coronation. This time it is to dispute Jesus' right to the title of 'King of the Jews', Pilate's sole gesture of mitigation and one that he now refuses to withdraw. The

* In the process he inscribes the symbol of the Cross in the Evangelist's melodic line, just as he had done as a 22-year-old in BWV 4 – see Chapter 5, pp. 135, 136), using it like a branding iron in order to fix it in his listeners' consciousness.

scene closes with the chorale 'In meines Herzens Grunde' (No. 26): a radiant affirmation of the fusion of Jesus' 'name and Cross', it marks the arrival of the faithful at Golgotha (in response to the bass's earlier exhortation).

From here there is a momentary descent into levity, given a decidedly sinister twist, as the Roman soldiers squabble over the division of Jesus' clothes. Like the gravediggers' scene in *Hamlet*, this is little more than a sideshow; but, by injecting a dose of ordinary life at this point, it somehow carries over into the more essential components of the concluding drama that are happening centre-stage. In Bach's overall tonal planning it has a significant part to play: being set in neutral C major means that it marks the boundary between the 'ambit' of flat keys used by Bach in the Crucifixion and for the royal inscription, and the sharp keys he will then turn to for Jesus' last words and death. This in itself could be a clue to its disproportionate length, for it needs to balance the equivalent 'ambit' in C (and its closely related keys) used at the beginning of the trial scene. As the only 'ambit' to stay firmly within a single key, it gives an ironic twist to the soldiers' words 'Let us not divide'. Purely as a composition it is an intriguing piece, one which makes virtuoso demands of the chorus. Rhythmic elasticity, agile coloratura and gleeful syncopations are all called on to illustrate the argument over who will have the right to make off with Jesus' cloak, like scurrying rats. At the same time the singers must ensure that their lines synchronise with the Alberti bass line, itself a depiction of the dice being shaken. It is all highly effective: parodistic, naturalistic and theatrical at the same time, but also grotesque, like a scene from Hogarth, culminating in the sopranos' leap up the octave to a top A in the penultimate bar as a ghoulish shriek. Bach's use of an infectious, toe-tapping rhythm in such debased surroundings suggests to me that, in his view, this is rock-bottom human behaviour, lower even than the politics of hate.*

Symbolically we have been shown a world divided between 'goats' and 'sheep' – the squabbling soldiers and the faithful standing at the

* Another way of looking at it (as suggested to me by Robert Quinney) is that the behaviour of the soldiers is strangely neutral and disengaged, set as it is: it is almost as if we step out of the narrative proper, cutting away to a scene which, though it is actually happening at the foot of the Cross, could be a million miles away. The very lack of engagement of the soldiers in the momentous events taking place around them might provoke the faithful listener to even greater involvement and (self-) reflection.

foot of the Cross. From the crowd now emerge the three Marys and the narrator, the disciple 'whom Jesus loved'. Bach rises to new heights in the sensitivity of his word-setting and the way his recitative flows in and out of lyrical arioso, yet quite free of histrionics. For the second time in the Passion he turns to Vulpius' memorable tune, here to acknowledge Jesus as the faithful son who makes provision for his mother's care.

Most poignant of all is the way his last words – *Es ist vollbracht* – are carried through, imitated and transposed by the viola da gamba in the celebrated alto aria (No. 30). The use of this already old-fashioned instrument, with its highly individual and plangent sonority, an etiolated reflection of the human voice, is a calculated device – one that he had used only once previously, in his first cantata cycle (BWV 76) and was to use again in the *Matthew Passion*. Again, as in 'Ach, mein Sinn', Bach adopts the majestic gestural language of the High French style, but here with the opposite effect: where in Peter's aria it was speeded up to convey extreme agitation, here it is dirge-like to explore the borderline between life and death.* In the B section the gamba's tone and melody disappear completely in the wild arpeggiation of the string band – a cameo image of Christ as the hero of Judah. The clarion call of open strings, the adoption of Monteverdi's martial style, the D major tonality – it is hard to imagine a more dramatic articulation of John's view of the Crucifixion as the supreme victory. Yet, with the abrupt cadence on a diminished seventh, Bach draws a halt to this outburst, and suddenly a question mark is attached to the words *und schließt den Kampf* ('and ends his victorious fight'). The return to the ornate and elegiac gamba melody, to Jesus' last words ('It is finished') matched in their melodic outline by the singer and then, in a total break with conventional practice, repeated one last time over the gamba's dying cadence, is a clear sign that no empty triumphalism is intended here. This aria is Bach's strongest yet most balanced way of interpreting John's account – as both a meditation on Christ's suffering and as the victorious affirmation of his identity, the hidden God revealed through faith on the Cross. It is also a way of insisting that comfort and consolation (*Trost*) are availa-

* Bach's use of the extreme dotted rhythms associated with Lully's majestic style is only superficially 'heroic'. As Michael Marissen says, 'only on the page, which listeners do not see, does the music appear majestic. As Bach's music has it, then, Jesus' majesty is "hidden" in its opposite, which is very much a Lutheran approach' (*Lutheranism, Anti-Judaism, and Bach's St John Passion* (1998), p. 19).

ble for those 'besieged' (*angefochtnen*) or 'afflicted' (*gekränkten*) souls who have been addressed in these last two arias.

A mere two bars – to describe the death of Jesus – separate this aria and the next. Bach's gently falling melodic line is the perfect match for John's words (*Und neiget das Haupt und verschied*/'and he bowed his head, and gave up the ghost'). Now comes the second of Bach's dialogues for bass and chorus (No. 32), and it arrives at a terrible moment. At first it seems perplexing that he should open with such a bold swinging melody in D major for the solo cello after the ethereal timbre of the gamba. The heroic lion of Judah now seems to prance and paw the air, where in the middle of the previous aria he roared his way to victory; but as soon as the voice enters it is clear from the angularity of the main theme, and attempts by the singer to counter its falling sixths and sevenths with upward leaps, that this is a feint to disguise a profound unease. A succession of questions are addressed to the *teurer Heiland* ('precious Saviour') voicing the fears and doubts of the whole community of the newly bereaved. What does it signify? Was it all worth it? Has death been overcome? What will be the upshot for humanity? Amid these concerns the four-voiced choir murmur a deathbed chorale to the same Vulpius tune-setting, but now a fifth lower than just a few minutes earlier. The interleaving of two poetic texts, one rhetorical and the other an answering chorale, is a dialogic device we have already come across in the cantatas, and one that Bach will expand still further in the *Matthew Passion*: words and music juxtaposed in two different timescales – the cultural or actual 'present' of a communal act of hymn-singing slowed down to synchronise with the 'subjective' time of the individual reflecting on these perplexing issues.

Now for the second time Bach interrupts John's account with an interpolation from Matthew – again for a specific purpose. Earlier it was to describe Peter's tears and to reinforce the way he stands for the individual suffering a crisis of belief. Here it is to rectify or preserve the balance he has tried to maintain from the outset – between the suffering and eventual triumph of Christ. He follows Matthew's description of the earthquake, and the veil of the Temple being 'rent in twain from the top to the bottom' (27:51–2) with a dramatic arioso for tenor which, while staying within the expressive gamut of the Evangelist's style, expands on this vision of apocalyptic disturbance. This leads without a break into the soprano threnody 'Zerfließe, mein Herze' (No. 35). At first the elegiac tone and human pathos of this aria seem out of place in this Passion-setting so strong in its emphasis on Christ's kingship; but soon we realise that it is the perfect foil for the earlier soprano aria, the carefree 'Ich folge dir' (No. 9) of Part I, marking the distance that the journey has taken us in the interim. For a final time Bach hits on a startlingly original selection of instruments* ideally adjusted to the mood – one of deepest sorrow and grief. He combines a transverse flute and a tenor oboe – the oboe da caccia, so called because of its open hornlike bell made of brass – with the soprano over a throbbing basso continuo, and weaves them together in a four-part linear discourse. Again, for this final arioso/aria pairing he has turned to Brockes's text, but purges it of some of its worst excesses. By now one is so used to the myriad ways Bach finds for easing grief and soothing the battered heart, it comes as a shock when he paints a tableau of unalloyed mourning. This is keening with an incomparable depth of feeling, and the overall effect is achingly beautiful.

* * *

The emotional temperature now has to come down. The coda of the Passion remains elegiac but devoid of sentimentality. The final utterances of the Evangelist are the two longest in the work. (This encourages the tendency by some modern evangelists to sing them as though they were the final words of Schubert's *Winterreise*, forgetting in the process that they are primarily story-tellers responsible for getting things going and keeping them moving, and not part of the story itself.) In the first of them John is at pains to explain those Jewish customs and traditions which by the time he was writing had become unfamiliar to his widely flung readership. The most physical moment in the *John Passion* is when 'one of the soldiers with a spear pierced his side, and forthwith came there out blood and water' (John 19:34). One senses that Bach wants his Evangelist to grasp the attention of his listeners at this moment – to reinforce John's insistence that he was a witness to this action, and that what he is saying is the truth.† The

* Admittedly this was only at its revival in 1725 when he came to make his first of four revisions. Prior to that the sources indicate that both flute and oboe da caccia were to be doubled, while in the fourth version the flute was doubled by a muted violin (see Alfred Dürr, op. cit., p. 114).

† 'It is a very odd thing about St John that while much of the time he is Platonic and Greek and high-minded, just occasionally, and particularly with Christ's wounds (as with Thomas,

fervour of their assent can then find its voice in the chorale 'O hilf, Christe, Gottes Sohn' (No. 37), though it rather drains away in the modally ambiguous final cadence; is this F major or the (implied) dominant of B♭? The very last recitative recounts the deposition and burial. Its harmonies are just as explorative as before, but now they extend the Evangelist's lower range: suddenly there are five bottom Cs for him to negotiate, when there have been only two others elsewhere in the entire Passion. They are there for a purpose and show once more Bach's skill in establishing mood and specific colour in his setting of individual words. There is a new tenderness in his description of the binding of Jesus' body in linen clothes appropriate to the way it reminds us of the swaddling clothes of Jesus' infancy. That tenderness remains right to the end.

Coming to the *John Passion* by way of the cantatas that precede it, one might expect a final chorale at this point – and of course it will end this way, but not before Bach has balanced his monumental opening chorus with another of matching spaciousness. 'Ruht wohl' (No. 39) may owe something to the Hamburg Passion oratorios, which often ended with a choral lullaby, but if there is any closer model for this choral rondo – at least in the melodic shape and rhythmic ambiguity of its opening – it is a rondeau, the second movement from his B minor flute suite, BWV 1067, the 'Ouvertüre' No. 2. That piece surely gives us an idea of what Bach intended here – a chorus that is simultaneously song and dance, with its individual lines woven together to imply a gentle choreography.* One has to turn to Brahms for an equivalent meshing of textures and rhythmic lilt. The expressive tone manages to be collective yet intensely personal, the lines lyrical and more singer-friendly here than practically anywhere else in Bach's writing for chorus. Significantly this is one of only two occasions (the other being the last in each set of *Wohins* in No. 24) where Bach calls for an unaccompanied chorus – or at least one undoubled by instruments. A sense of ritual – of the deposition and of a reverential lowering of the body into the grave – permeates

who puts his finger into them), there are occasional bursts of quite disconcerting physicality in his Gospel account' (John Drury, private correspondence).

* Wilfrid Mellers singles it out as 'a dance of God . . . fulfilling the vision of the early Christian mystics who saw the lyre- or viol- or flute-playing Christ as "leader of the dance; he knows how to touch the strings, to lead from joy to joy, with cherubim and seraphim the soul dances in the round"' (*Bach and the Dance of God*, p. 148).

the chorus. 'Be fully at peace' is the invocation, deliberately repeated again and again, always in the same key, with a soothing poignancy; but the way the final C minor cadence is approached (by means of a high A♭ in the sopranos) undermines and belies that peace.

Bach's decision to follow 'Ruht wohl' with a chorale (No. 40) has come in for criticism; but the truth is that in performance it *works*, returning us to the here and now – in *this* church and on *this* day – removing the last vestiges of grief and reminding us of a future of uncertainty. This is but the latest example of the immense care Bach lavished on the chorale harmonisations of his *John Passion.* Its first half focuses on the grave's repose and is suitably understated, but at the mention of the 'final day', the resurrection of the body and the life of the world to come, Bach increases the tension. Spaces between the four voices begin to open up, and he hits his most magisterial stride. Six of the next seven cadences are 'perfect' and in the major, imbuing the music with colossal strength with the repeated plea *erhöre mich . . . erhöre mich . . . erhöre mich* ('hear me . . . hear me . . . hear me'). Easter is still two days away, but the affirmation here is nonetheless conclusive.

That conclusive cadence may have been Bach's final grievous error in the eyes of the Leipzig clergy: for to anticipate the Resurrection, or the 'final day', in this chorale and elsewhere in the course of the *John Passion* was to jar with the prevalently sombre mood of long-established Good Friday commemorations in Leipzig. Bach could have countered that he had allowed for the traditional singing by the choir of the funerary motet *Ecce quomodo moritur iustus* by Jacob Gallus and the congregational hymn 'Nun danket alle Gott', in line with liturgical practice since 1721, when, according to the sexton of the Thomaskirche, the Passion was performed for the first time in concerted style (see note on p. 354).[32] By this means he brought his listeners back to the contemplation of the events of Good Friday and created a final symmetry with his closing chorus, 'Ruht wohl'.[33] The thing is, we cannot be certain that Bach had cleared the text of his *John Passion* with the clergy in advance. On this occasion he could have slipped his Passion text under the radar of consistorial scrutiny; but in the process he may inadvertently have put the churchmen on their guard. Even before they had heard a note of his music, just reading the printed libretto might have been enough to antagonise them. Then hearing and experiencing Bach's Passion music for the first time, they could have been disturbed by the eruptive force with which it expresses religious sentiments (the charge of blasphemy always seems to come from orthodox guardians of faith whenever spiritual or emotional power takes them by surprise). The sensuality and eroticism of the central aria, 'Erwäge', could have exposed Bach to the charge of irreverence (though the clergy were apparently happy to swallow eroticism in the sermon poetry of the day).

More likely to offend, perhaps, was the Passion's weak overall emphasis on penitence, its close resemblance to Francke's Pietist sermons, the failure of its interpolated movements (except for 'Erwäge') to interpret the Passion as God's act of atonement for man's fallen state and, above all, the 'sheer intensity of the Johannine world view' that Bach portrays.[34] In contrast to the image we gain from Matthew and the other synoptic Gospel writers, who give repeated emphasis to Christ's humanity and his suffering, John portrays Jesus as someone with preternatural powers of insight: serene and magisterially in control of his destiny – and, ultimately, a victor.[35] In this, Bach is utterly faithful to John, showing Jesus to be seemingly unaffected by the vicissitudes of his trial, carrying out the mysterious will of the Father in full knowledge of what awaits him. His very dominance and confidence stands out above the typically human squabbling that surrounds him, a contrast that makes Bach's setting so extraordinarily dramatic. Such an approach reveals a perfectly respectable pedigree, which theologians have traced back to the early Greek fathers' view of the atonement, and one endorsed by Luther himself, who claimed that 'the gospel of John is unique in loveliness . . . the one fine, true and chief gospel . . . far, far to be preferred over the other three and placed high above them.' In it one finds a 'masterly account of how faith in Christ conquers sin, death, and hell; and gives life, righteousness and salvation'.[36]

Why, then, might this have been a controversial approach in Leipzig in 1724? According to the Swedish theologian Gustaf Aulén,[37] Luther was often misunderstood in this regard by his contemporaries and by later theologians, who saw in his teachings an unequivocal preference for the 'satisfaction' theory of the atonement – the one articulated for example by Matthew and given further emphasis in Paul's epistles – whereby Jesus offers himself for punishment and sacrifice on behalf of sinful humanity and to win freedom from God's wrath, as opposed to from the power of evil.* The view probably prevalent among the Orthodox Leipzig clergy of Bach's day, and passed on by them to their congregation, was that only the 'satisfaction' theory was legitimate. Bach, on the other hand, judging from the contents of his library (which, besides two editions of Luther's works, included a three-volume Bible with extensive theological commentary, and all the basic texts of both Pietism and Orthodoxy), seems to have understood and accepted the legitimacy of both views on the theory of atonement and their coexistence in Luther's work. His intention was evidently to give a balanced expression to each of these competing views in successive works – first in his *John Passion* and later in the *Matthew*. In constructing two such comprehensive but contrasted musico-theological statements – something not attempted by any contemporary composer –† Bach was behaving less like a musician and more like a painter, showing the same subject from two different angles, each with validity and conviction.[38] Was this just bravado on his part? Was he intentionally defying local susceptibilities? From our later perspective we see that the two Passions were designed to fit into – and indeed encapsulate – his two complementary cantata cycles adjusted to the Leipzig liturgy of the day. But to the consistory it may have looked like a deliberate flouting of their authority, made worse by his refusal to explain his aims in language that they could understand.

There is no direct testimony for any of this. But some kind of negative reaction seems to have been the precursor of further, more heated and, for the most part, undocumented disputes surrounding his *John*

* Where John celebrates Jesus' triumph over the forces of evil and the law (which he describes as a 'curse' or 'wrath'), Matthew underscores Christ's work of atonement to God's 'satisfaction'. That Luther left no clearly defined statement on the subject of atonement does not mean that he necessarily held a preference for one of these two different, though not mutually exclusive, theories, or that the two could not have coexisted in his theology. Aulén's view is that over time Luther was gradually drawn back to the far older Johannine (*Christus victor*) view 'with a greater intensity and power than ever before'. As he says, 'we have only to listen to Luther's hymns to feel how they thrill with triumph, like a fanfare of trumpets.' This is equally true of Bach's settings of them in his cantatas.

† Telemann, for example, who was required to compose a new Passion for each year he was musical director of Hamburg's five main churches (1721–67), did not seem to have felt the need to differentiate the theological leanings of the four Gospel writers. On the other hand, he adopted a technique much used by Bach in his cantatas, that of inserting a parallel Old Testament text as preparation for each of the five sections into which he divided up the Passion story.

Passion over the next fifteen years, causing Bach to revise it no less than four times: twice with major readjustments to its contents and doctrinal slant; once, in 1739, to abandon the work altogether for ten years; and then, in one last hurrah, to revive it a final time restored more or less to its original state. We can come close to gauging the clergy's reaction to Bach's first version of the *John Passion* by observing the drastic revisions he made to it exactly a year after its premiere. Out went the epic opening chorus ('Herr, unser Herrscher') and the offending closing chorale ('Ach Herr, lass dein lieb Engelein'), to be replaced by the chorale fantasia 'O Mensch bewein dein Sünde groß', planned and later used by Bach to conclude Part I of his *Matthew*, and a more elaborate concluding chorale, 'Christe, du Lamm Gottes', the final movement of the cantata he had presented at his Leipzig audition (BWV 23). Not without a certain creaking of its joints, the *John Passion* was adjusted to its new position as the climax of the chorale cantata cycle. Gone, too, was the tenor aria 'Ach, mein Sinn', to be replaced by 'Zerschmettert mich' and a bass dialogue with soprano chorale 'Himmel reiße, Welt erbebe'. Perhaps the most draconian substitution of all was a new tenor aria, 'Ach, windet euch nicht so', in place of the magical 'Betrachte/Erwäge' pairing, the keystone of Bach's original design for Part II. By any purely musical criteria, while the overall quality of the new numbers is consistently high, it would be hard to argue that these were 'improvements'. Taken as a whole, the effect was to dismember the initial patterning and structure of the original, as well as to alter its theological tone by giving greater prominence to the Pauline theology of justification by faith.

Only a strong consistorial rebuke can explain why Bach agreed to unpick key elements of his initial design and to jettison the consistent Johannine view of Jesus' atonement for humanity, and the far weightier importance he gave in each of the substituted movements to the acknowledgement of human guilt. If the consistory insisted that the Passion oratorio should give greater emphasis to the Orthodox 'satisfaction' theory (see footnote, p. 406), so be it: he would comply by introducing new music to match the sin-drenched imagery and the emphasis on God as 'strict judge'. One of the effects – but surely not the motivation – of the 1725 revisions to the *John Passion* was to bring it into line with the tone of the chorale cantata cycle that he had been presenting for the past ten months (as we saw in Chapter 9). A more drastic result was to destroy what seems to have been his plan, stretched over two years, to make the two Gospel accounts and the two theories of atonement the pinnacles of his cantata cycles through successive and contrasted expression. By failing to complete the *Matthew* on time for Good Friday, Bach found himself boxed into a corner. Version 2 of the *John Passion* was a *pis aller*. By the time he next came to perform it, some five years later, all the interlopers had gone and the opening chorus was back in place, as was the 'Betrachte/Erwäge' pairing. But now strangely excised were the insertions from Matthew and the final chorale. An aria no longer extant replaced 'Ach, mein Sinn' and an instrumental *sinfonia* took the place of movements 33 to 35 (the veil of the Temple recitative, the tenor arioso 'Mein Herz' and the soprano aria 'Zerfließe').

Perhaps the conflict never really died down. We know for example that in March 1739 an emissary from the town clerk came to tell Bach that 'the music he was planning to perform on the following Good Friday was not to be played until he had received due permission to do so, whereupon the latter replied that it had always been done so, it was of no particular interest to him, for he got nothing out of it anyway, and it was only a burden. He would notify the Superintendent that he had been forbidden to perform it. If there were objections to the text, why, it had already been performed several times before.'[39] What pain and hurt and simulated indifference lie behind those words in that civil service reported speech! It took him a further ten years to cease to smart over the injustice; and it was only when he had two years left to live that he brought the *John Passion* back with the original 1724 version restored in all its essentials.

If ever there was proof of the importance Bach attached to the work and, significantly, to its initial conception and design, it is the recently discovered evidence of consecutive performances in the last two years of his life: that on 4 April 1749 was perhaps the very last performance conducted by him. An autograph testimonial for Johann Nathanael Bammler (a former Thomaner prefect who helped Bach with the copying and textual revisions to the final version of the *John Passion*) dates from 12 April 1749, a week later; Bach's hand there[40] is noticeably steadier and more fluent than in the late entries in the performing parts for the Passion, which previously had been thought to be his last. The sudden, temporary collapse in his health seems to have occurred in the second half of April; but by June, though clearly weakened, he was back at work – on the *B minor Mass* and on the first set of proofs for *The Art of Fugue*. Based on the evidence of his handwriting, the last autograph entries in the performing material of the *John Passion* could not have been made before the spring of 1750. That performance took place on 27 March, perhaps under the direction of the senior prefect, one day before Dr Taylor operated on Bach's eyes, the Saturday before Easter.[41] Had he at last reached some sort of accommodation with the consistory or was this a final act of defiance, a flouting of a consistorial decree, and an insistence that he had been 'right' all along? At all events he prepared a fresh score of the Passion in which he himself wrote out the first eighteen folios before turning the remainder over to a copyist. By endorsing the original version, this last version brings 'Fassung Erster' and 'Letzter Hand' into alignment.

There may have been other factors besides those of theological difference behind the enforced revisions of 1725 and 1729 that might help to explain Bach's ultimate return to his initial version of the work – perhaps more fundamental reservations about the music itself, a sensitive nerve touched in the ongoing debate about the very nature of music's role in worship. For, whereas the Leipzig clergy might have found it hard to find anything deliberately subversive in Bach's creative endeavour (it is surely beyond reproach in its fidelity to John's Gospel), it certainly reveals what they might have recognised as a dangerous strain of artistic autonomy. It points up the essential differences between the Logos as spoken word and as set to – and transmogrified by – music.* Quite apart from whether they were interested in, or even capable of discerning, the veiled patterns Bach constructed behind the obvious foreground ones (such as his juxtaposing worldly and spiritual perspectives on Jesus' identity, etc.) – the very qualities which set his *John Passion* apart from those of his contemporaries – they could hardly have failed to notice the compelling emotive power unleashed in his music. Tactlessly, perhaps, Bach was doing the preacher's job more effectively than it could possibly be done by words alone. We might speculate

* Even here the textural alterations to the restored 1724 movements show signs of theological decree and perhaps reflect changing literary tastes as well: the fresh joyousness of the original 'Ich folge dir' soprano aria is diminished by a reference to 'my anxious path' and the need to 'suffer in patience'. The arioso 'Betrachte' loses its metaphor of heaven's primroses flowing out of the crown of thorns, and refers now more closely to the scourging of Jesus. The tenor aria 'Erwäge' loses its glorious rainbow simile for something much blander, though the new words 'Mein Jesu, ach!' are slightly easier to sing.

whether the dialogues between Pilate and the crowd, Pilate and Jesus, things we find particularly poignant today, were perhaps uncomfortably theatrical – just too 'operatic' for what in their view was suitable as church music (though it is interesting that they never succeeded in getting him to tone this aspect down in subsequent revisions). By returning to the work in the last two years of his life and by restoring his initial conception of it, Bach was powerfully reasserting his position on the role the music of his *John Passion* could play in directing people's thoughts to the meaning of Christ's Passion in their lives.

* * *

Let us return one last time to view the work from our own standpoint. There has to be an explanation why, in our secular age, listening to the *John Passion* seems to provide so uplifting an experience for so many people. I would suggest that the multilayered structure underpinning Bach's Passion can be 'felt', if not immediately seen or heard, by the listener, in the same way that flying buttresses, invisible to the visitor when entering a Gothic church, are essential to the illusion of lightness, weightlessness and the impression of height. In fact, the longer you study them the more numerous seem to be the geometric patterns of repetition, symmetry and cross-referring, varying in the sharpness or thinness of their outlines. To change the analogy, it is akin to the experience one gets when looking down on to the gravelly bed of a shallow stream through the filmy refractive prism of water constantly but subtly shifting these outline definitions. Only by looking beneath the surface do the patterns become clear, and at that point the inherently unstable relationship between words and music, and the dialectical one between voice and instrument, singer and player, can come into focus. Potentially every performance moves through this process of deciphering and clarification towards an unknown goal. Any fragmentary contextual knowledge we can piece together will not – cannot – recapture the experience of listeners at its first performance, though it might serve to sharpen our response each time we encounter the music now. Although its original habitation is irretrievably lost, the work carries with it a potential novelty for those who themselves are open to novelty; for 'this is a music that seems supremely wedded to a world of certainty and interconnectedness, yet its results, for many listeners at least, seem to be utterly unexpected and transformative.'[42] Musicians (who of course have a vested interest here) tend to believe that what Bach expressed in his first Passion – and indeed the manner of its expression – has a perennial validity and therefore merits re-application in every new performance. While we might aim to produce something that is close to Bach's performance, it will inevitably manifest itself differently on every occasion and in each new context. There is a sense that the musical material he has left us is both complete and unfinished, and in thinking about the meaning of our performances we should recall the emphasis T. S. Eliot placed on 'a perception, not only of the pastness of the past, but of its presence'.[43] It is by anchoring it in our time that we re-connect with the timeless fertility of Bach's imagination.

The springboard of his achievement is his direct interaction with the Gospel itself – its underlying themes, its antitheses and symbols – here more perceptibly than in the following *Matthew Passion*. The symbols spring to life every time the music is performed and help us to make sense of the outrage and pain of suffering, the contradictions and perplexities of the Passion story. Bach connects all along with the underlying human drama in John's account and brings it to the surface with the sympathetic realism of a Caravaggio or a Rembrandt. The equivalent to their masterly brushwork is his highly developed sense of narrative drama and his unerring feel for an appropriate scale and tone for each and every scene. Akin to the priority both painters gave to the play of darkness and its opposite is the way Bach's music is suffused with a translucency exceptional even by his standards. When speaking of Rembrandt's religious paintings, Goethe implied that the painter not so much 'illustrated' biblical events as took them 'beyond their scriptural basis'.[44] That is exactly what Bach does here: but rather than pigment it is the musical substance that is 'shone through'.

It is peculiarly difficult for us to grasp the prodigious craftsmanship and palpable sense of purpose in a work as complex as the *John Passion*. Bach seldom draws attention to the technical workings that underpin his compositional skills. Yet, like Brahms, he would have been quick to acknowledge that 'without craftsmanship, inspiration is a mere reed shaken in the wind'.* Whether this can mean that his music was spir-

* This phrase may be apocryphal, coming as it does from an account of a conversation with Brahms and Joachim in the autumn of 1896 (German-American violinist Arthur M. Abell, *Talks with Great* Composers (1995), pp. 9, 13–14, 58). Much scholarly scepticism sur-

itually inspired (or, as some might claim, divinely engendered) depends of course on how we choose to reflect on the sources of his inspiration. When questioned further about the source of *his* inspiration, Brahms pointed to John's Gospel and to Jesus' words: 'the Father that dwelleth in me, he doeth the works . . . He that believeth on me, the works that I do shall he do also; and greater works than these shall he do' (14:10–12). Bach's answer could have been identical. The *John Passion* holds our attention from beginning to end – its music stirring, disturbing, exultant and profoundly moving. In this work Bach found his own first triumphant vindication of Luther's injunction that 'Christ's Passion must be met not with words or forms, but with life and truth.'

rounds Abell's transcript of this probing of the religious sources of musical inspiration. Nevertheless, even though Brahms, like Bach (except in his Calov Bible annotations), hardly ever spoke of religion, the phrase attributed to him by Abell sounds plausibly in character.

11
His 'Great Passion'

Whatsoever is harmonically composed delights in harmony; which makes me much distrust the symmetry of those heads which declaim against all Church-Musick. For my self, not only for my obedience, but my particular Genius, I do embrace it: for even that vulgar and Tavern-Musick, which makes one man merry, another mad, strikes in me a deep fit of devotion, and a profound contemplation of the First Composer. There is something in it of Divinity more than the ear discovers: it is an Hieroglyphical and shadowed lesson of the whole World, and creatures of GOD; such a melody to the ear, as the whole World, well understood, would afford the understanding. In brief, it is a sensible fit of that harmony which intellectually sounds in the ears of GOD.

– Thomas Browne, *Religio medici* (1642)

Bach's autograph manuscript score of the *Matthew Passion* is a calligraphic miracle. It is by far the most precious survivor of that 'big pile of Passion music'[1] entered into the second catalogue of Carl Philipp Emanuel Bach's estate in 1805.[2] Phenomenal elegance and fluency of notation characteristic of Bach in his forties contrasts with passages made in the crabbed, rigid handwriting of his later eye-damaged years, with corrections entered on glued-on strips of paper meticulously inserted. The care and the effort it cost him are everywhere to be seen. In common with a handful of other composers (Rameau, Debussy, Stravinsky) Bach plans every part of the page and leaves a minimum of unused staves, all signs of a resolve to capture every polished detail of this immense creation. Uniquely among his autographs, he uses red ink – but generally only for the Gospel words, which thus stand out from the rest like some medieval missal and from the brown-black sepia that was his norm. Twice in its existence the manuscript has been damaged. Once, in his very last years, Bach himself repaired sections which had frayed through accidental use. Then, during the early years of the Second World War, ominous signs appeared that the paper itself had begun to thin – the gallotannate ink had started to oxidise, making the paper brittle. In 1941, in an ingenious labour of love, the Berlin restorer Hugo Ibscher stretched the finest chiffon silk over each of the damaged pages to hold it in place by means of rice starch. It worked – for quite some time, but now the red ink has begun to fade.

The impression of a meticulously constructed autograph score, worked over, revised, repaired and left in a condition aspiring to some sort of ideal, is at one with the monumental scale of the work itself. Yet, with only this fair-copy score dating from the mid 1730s and one set of performing parts to go on, generations of Bach scholars have so far been unable to trace the inception, planning or successive stages of the Passion's evolution with any degree of certainty. There are single-part books for the two four-voiced ensembles which identify the tenor and bass lines in Choir 1 as *Evangelista* and *Jesus* respectively, as well as separate copies for the minor characters and the *soprano in ripieno* required for 'O Lamm Gottes, unschuldig', the German *Agnus Dei* in the opening chorus. We do not know exactly who took part in any of the performances given under the composer's direction – neither the make-up of his vocal and orchestral forces, nor their precise number, nor how they were deployed in the western choir loft of the Thomaskirche (though we have a reasonable idea – see illustration on p. 405). And we have no contemporary reaction to it – not the smallest shard of evidence of what people thought about it at the time.

So what *can* we say with confidence? From the evidence of the autograph score, that the work is unique in its scope and grandeur, that Bach had an enormous personal investment in its composition, and that he had prepared himself for its unprecedented compositional challenges with typical thoroughness. But that does not begin to account for the overpowering experience of the work in performance. We have already suggested that he had prepared his audience for it by means of unmistakable musical anticipations and adumbrations of theological themes in the cantatas leading up to Good Friday 1725 (see Chapter 9). There is, as we have also seen, a distinct possibility – but no proof – that the *Matthew Passion* was planned as part of his second annual cycle of Leipzig cantatas, that of 1724/5, sharing with it an emphasis on chosen chorales as the basis or focal point of each cantata. The Passion could have been designed for – and would have fitted perfectly at – its centre, like the boss of a shield. Yet it was not to be: its first airing was delayed by a further two years. We saw how the problems he had completing it in time in 1725 had a knock-on effect on the post-Resurrection cantatas, disrupting the completion of the chorale cantata cycle (see 'Second Leipzig Cycle' diagram, Plate 16). Nevertheless, I believe that we stand to gain in our understanding of the *Matthew Passion* – draw closer to its purpose, its fine braiding together of musical and theological themes – if we approach it not as an isolated work but from the perspective of that cantata cycle. Bach went on modifying it in the course of the 1730s and 1740s, never as drastically as he did the *John Passion*, but always meticulously and with unflinching resolve. Again, simply from the appearance of the autograph score, we gain the strongest impression of an intention to leave the music in a state that could surpass and outlive its original liturgical function – of an aesthetic entity *sui generis* and entrusted to posterity. This impression is supported by the potency the *Matthew Passion* has had ever since Felix Mendelssohn's famous revival in 1829, and remains undiminished by time.

After two consecutive outings in 1724 and 1725 of the fast-paced *John Passion* in two very different versions, and the controversy that seems to have surrounded that work, Bach appears to have been minded to come up with something which gave his listeners more time to reflect and contemplate between scenes in the Gospel accounts. The acid test for him, then, was whether his new Passion music – conceived on a still grander scale – would hold their attention for over two and a half hours. The very length of the *Matthew Passion* and the complexity of its musical elaboration can be daunting even to those hearing it for the second or third time – and we should not forget, as John Butt points out, that 'one of the greatest ironies about Bach's Passions is that their original audiences were far less familiar with the genre than we are; moreover – as is the case with all Bach's most celebrated music – we might have heard them many more times than did the original performers or even Bach himself.' This is especially true of the *Matthew Passion*:

when approached with the expectations or the memory of the *John Passion* it is easy to be wrong-footed, puzzled – even to feel excluded. As a listener, your primary focus is on the linear progression of the story. Where this is interrupted by extended movements of contemplation, the stop-go nature of the twin timeframes of reported speech and the contemporary response to events can be perplexing. Where are we now? Is this an historical event or a reaction to it? If the latter, by whom: Jesus' disciples, the 'Daughter of Zion', the Christian community or mankind as a whole? And when are things occurring? In the first century AD, in the Lutheran timeframe of the chorale, in the 1720s, 1730s and 1740s of Bach's Leipzig congregation or in the present, as they affect us now? Despite the captivating beauty of individual numbers, the overall impression can be one of a juddering rhythm: no sooner are you launched into the story of the betrayal and trial of Jesus than the forward momentum is halted.

One clue to Bach's structure lies in the effectiveness of its pacing, which is comparatively more stately and measured than that of the *John Passion*, and the success of any interpretation hinges on the degree to which it connects to – and replicates – that pacing in performance without loss of dramatic momentum. Individual performers, being wholly caught up in the interpretative challenges of successive movements – those spokes fanning out from the compositional hub – can easily lose sight of the work's overall shape. But if the pacing is right, the listener is helped to take each of the twenty-eight scenes (see below p. 411) as it comes, and to re-live and relish the re-telling of it. So, instead of waiting impatiently for an aria to end and the story to resume, we begin to value the voice urging us to identify with the remorse, the outrage and the outpouring of grief articulated by individual spokesmen and women in the course of the drama, and by the entire community voicing its contrition in the chorales. Once as a listener you have adjusted to its structural rhythm and sheer length, Bach's *Matthew Passion* can in some ways be an easier ride than the *John*. There, as we saw, everything is breathlessly dramatic, but also so unremittingly Johannine in its theology: you feel you are being taken by the scruff of the neck (as indeed one is by John's Gospel) and required to confront big issues – the nature of kingship, of identity, or of what happens when truth faces falsehood.

Here in the *Matthew Passion* Bach adopts a less polemical tack, dictated in part by Matthew's approach, and is set on making much more room for the listener to process the drama, giving him time to reflect and to digest. Whereas in the *John Passion* the arias are distributed unevenly – two short ones in rapid succession near the start, a third to provide a shattering conclusion to Part I, the lone peak of 'Erwäge' at the midway point (where time seems to stop before a fast resumption of the drama), and four more clustered towards the end – here he ensures a greater overall sense of regularity and stability. He agrees with (or even instructs) Picander at the outset that most arias should be preceded by an arioso – to form an intermediate stage, as if to prepare the listener for the contemplative space which the aria will occupy. Now there is enough time to savour the prodigious beauty of each one in turn, the subtle colouring of the obbligato accompaniments, and the expanded range of emotional and meditative response that they encompass. Any diminution of the vivid scene-painting and the inexorable dramatic thrust we relish in the *John Passion* is compensated for in the *Matthew* by Bach's cunning way of personifying these various 'voices' – the allegorical ones who sing arias as well as those caught up in the drama itself (these he often locks in dialogue) – and the way he maintains all these consecutive, almost simultaneous time-shifts in a state of productive tension. The unity of its pacing is one of the *Matthew Passion*'s greatest achievements: Bach knows exactly when and how to modify *da capo* form, when to elide and override the natural breaks in the text by ensuring that there are no false stops, no unnecessary cadential breaks, so that the forward momentum is maintained. Unlike Telemann, who fills in the *da capo* form compliantly and is not particularly concerned about building climaxes, Bach repeatedly reinvented the *da capo* form, much as Mozart and Beethoven were to re-cast the sonata form in endlessly creative ways.

It is Bach's capacity to see all the possibilities of the material simultaneously and to clasp so many threads together at any one time which is so impressive in the *Matthew Passion* – his ability to combine judgements of a practical kind with considerations of structure, theological exegesis and narrative pacing, even down to the particular tone of voice he chooses to adopt when addressing his specific congregation of listeners on this crucial day in the church's calendar. With the liturgy pared down to just a few prayers and hymns to open and close proceedings, and the sermon, for all its considerable length, coming at the midway point, this was the ultimate test for him to justify Luther's great claim for music – that its notes 'make the text come alive'.[3] This was his opportunity to show, as the poet Hunold (his former colleague in Cöthen) put it, how 'beautiful music can implant a better impression in people's hearts.'[4]

Inevitably this takes us back to the question of how effective Bach was in holding his listeners' attention: of course they *heard* everything, but did they take the trouble to *listen*? How much did they absorb and how much did they assent to his approach, and how would any of this have differed from the way their contemporaries reacted to other Passion music elsewhere in Germany or in the Catholic south? Naturally, we have no exact way of knowing. We saw earlier how Leipzigers clung to their old Good Friday rituals – those plainchant meditations and the prolonged strophic hymn-singing – and resisted the fashionable tide of concerted Passion oratorios until late in Kuhnau's cantorship. Within a year of Bach's arrival the Good Friday Vespers service had suddenly turned into the musical highpoint of the year. Bach's *Matthew Passion* was in essence one long *concert spirituel.**

In the previous chapter we contrasted the situation in Leipzig with the phenomenal popularity of Brockes's Passion libretto elsewhere in Germany, particularly in the more cosmopolitan ducal courts and mercantile seaports such as Hamburg. We saw how there was no literary device or explicit poetic image that Brockes missed in his graphically realistic evocation of Jesus' pain, nor a rhetorical trick he avoided if it could serve to intensify the listener's response. Yet, even though Bach chose to paraphrase and incorporate some of Brockes's verses in his *John Passion*, his approach was fundamentally different to that of, say, Telemann or Stölzel – not because of any diminution in rhetoric, but because of a greater concentration of musical substance, as exemplified by his *Matthew Passion*. But then his listeners in Leipzig's two main churches were probably of another breed from those who thronged Hamburg's famous Drill Hall, eager to sample the contrasting ways four rival composers had set Brockes's libretto to music. Without even the semblance of liturgical function, there was an element of spectator

* There is a parallel to be drawn here with listeners today, some of whom look for immersion in a single cultural unfolding, such as the *Matthew Passion* certainly provides – one that creates space and time away from the fidget of perpetual sound bites and being constantly bombarded by noise coming in short sharp stabs.

sport to these successive evenings of 'spiritual' entertainment. In any case, who were these *Stadtbürger* of Hamburg? It is claimed that they were cultivated, literate and discriminating, 'aware of the Protestant tradition [yet] no longer satisfied by its traditional ecclesiastical form ... no longer blindly accept[ing] religious truths [but] needing to regain them through emotional experience'.[5] With his urbane Hamburgers, Brockes felt that he was free to play on a phenomenon that would soon characterise much of Enlightenment Europe, fanning the embers of faltering faith through his unabashed emphasis on the physical aspects of the suffering of Jesus, which he describes in lurid detail. The typical *Stadtbürger* of Leipzig in Bach's day was, by contrast, a more conservative and straightforwardly pious individual, one who had no need for a high dosage of such psychedelic stimulants. He was dependably to be found in his assigned pew, a member of a self-consciously stratified and provincial urban society. No doubt familiar with all the biblical words and scriptural allusions, and most if not all the chorales that were included in Bach's figural music, in his hands were the *Texts to the Passion Music according to the Evangelist Matthew at the Good Friday Vespers in the Church of St Thomas* by the poet Christian Friedrich Henrici, alias Picander, Bach's most regular literary collaborator.*

The question, then, is whether our *Stadtbürger* was willing to accept and embrace Bach's Passion music in its successive formulations and capable of the prolonged concentration required to come to terms with its complexities. In his autobiography, Pastor Adam Bernd wrote, 'It is said that people are hindered in their devotions by thoughts of wishing to be elsewhere because they didn't know the hymn and couldn't sing along ... Isn't this just a gripe against new-fangled hymns, a citizen once asked on his way home?'[6] Should we take this at face value or ask whether a feeling of partial exclusion may have been at the root of it? Certainly a work as extended and challenging as either of Bach's two great Passion settings was a feat of endurance for any listener sitting

* This was included on pp. 101–112 in Vol. 2 of his *Ernst-Scherzhaffte und Satyrische Gedichte*, first published in 1729 – a date used by earlier Bach scholars as evidence of the first performance of Bach's *Matthew Passion*, whereas this 'well-established' date 'rests on nothing more than an unverifiable guess', as Joshua Rifkin maintained in 1975: 'the work could just as well have originated in 1727 as in 1729', he concluded ('The Chronology of Bach's Saint Matthew Passion', MQ, Vol. 61, No. 3 (July 1975)) – or, as I have suggested above, as early as 1725, but not completed on schedule.

passively on hard wooden benches in an unheated church in late March. Knowing all eight of the different chorale tunes Bach wove into it may have been reassuring, but in any case as a member of the congregation you were not expected to sing along as in the old days (and if you did, you would probably have been a little confused by the strange keys, the sometimes unfamiliar yoking of verse to melody, or by the sheer complexity of Bach's harmonisations).

* * *

Without any concession to theatrical gimmickry Bach provides his audience with a magnificent display of dramatic re-enaction. Building on the techniques he used in the *John Passion* and the more dramatic of his church cantatas, Bach approaches his task with the flair of the born dramatist. The Ancient Greeks watched their theatrical rituals from stone theatre benches; Bach's eighteenth-century Saxons sat for almost three hours in their wooden pews while his musical missiles rained down on them. Just as educated Greeks, intimately familiar with the tragedy of Oedipus – its goriness, its moral outrage and the degree of its hero's affliction and degradation*could still be gripped by the slow, controlled progression of Sophocles' account as though experiencing it for the first time, so Bach's Leipzig listeners, who knew every inch of the road to Calvary, could still be intensely moved by it. The foundations of the city are laid bare, whether it is Athens in the fifth century BC or Leipzig in the 1720s, in the same ritual acknowledgement of fault, re-told and stabilised through its performance and transformation into art. In the same way that we buy tickets for *King Lear* and come away chastened, sobered and put in our place, so Leipzigers (with their opera house closed for the past six years) flocked to the Thomaskirche on a Good Friday, hoping that the excitement and harrowing uncoiling of the human drama would still hold them in thrall, knowing full well that

* This is a feature that Stravinsky, hyper-aware of the banality lurking in so much nineteenth-century opera, captured in his superb two-act 'opera-oratorio' *Oedipus Rex* (1927), a work which reveals his affinity to the spirit of music-drama outlined in Chapter 4 – a 'concept of theatre, and beyond that of music itself, as ritual – something, that is, which is re-enacted rather than simply enacted . . . the feeling that the characters are in the grip of inexorable forces' (Stephen Walsh, *Stravinsky: Oedipus Rex* (1993), pp. 36, 48). This sentiment is reinforced by the choral writing, which at times resembles the formalised barbarity of Bach's *turbae*, and at others the sense of emotionally choked valediction we hear in the Pietistic final choruses to both the Passions.

A reconstruction of the north-west section of the Thomaskirche in Bach's time shows one of the two facing balustraded galleries for the instrumentalists and, to the right, private box pews reserved for the councillors.

they would be distressed (and perhaps disappointed if they found they weren't).

The question was, could Bach's Passion music re-animate the conventions of the Easter story and, by extension, of tragic myth, and re-kindle those 'habits of imagination and symbolic recognition' which are essential to the way music-drama functions?[7] Performing from the organ gallery at the west end of the church, he and his musicians were only partially in view of the congregation, the singers in the middle divided antiphonally by choir, the winds in a raised gallery to the north, the strings in the equivalent to the south, responding and listening to each other, and locked in dialectic exchange. The Thomaner were not a troupe of actors, not a circus act, nor of course did they wear masks or theatrical costumes. Yet neither the absence of a stage nor the peculiar architectural configuration of his performing space could disguise the fact that Bach's was essentially dramatic music: music intended to appeal to – even occasionally assault – the senses of his listeners.

From the very beginning Bach had been warned off from writing operatic music,* yet his purpose was unimpeachable: to re-enact the Passion story within his listeners' minds, to affirm its pertinence to the men and women of his day, addressing their concerns and fears and directing them towards the solace and inspiration to be found within the Passion narrative. As a Lutheran he knew that it was not by acts of contrition, nor by 'good works' nor even by means of the Mass (which Luther described as a 'dragon's tail' – a challenge would have to wait for another day) that the believer could approach or celebrate Christ's sacrifice on his behalf at Calvary; it was by re-living the painful events on each and every anniversary of that sacrifice, something that his music was unsurpassed at helping his listeners to achieve.† It was a sentiment

* The proceedings of the Leipzig Council for 22 Apr. 1723 are worded in such a way as to make it absolutely clear that a condition of Councillor Steger voting for Bach as cantor was that 'he should make compositions that were not too theatrical' (BD II, No. 129/NBR p. 103). We have repeatedly seen in earlier chapters how Bach in his cantatas and Passions comprehensively flouted this injunction.

† Bach's occasional librettist, the Pastor Erdmann Neumeister, maintained that 'what we read about the suffering and death of Christ in the Passion story, and what we hear about this in sermons during this Lenten season – that we must all take as having happened for us and as having been done as an act of satisfaction' (preface to *Solid Proof that Christ Jesus has Rendered Satisfaction for Us and Our Sins*, quoted in Jaroslav Pelikan, *Bach among the Theologians* (1986), pp. 94–5).

captured by the chorus in Bach's setting of the words *Drum muss uns sein verdienstlich Leiden / Recht bitter und doch süße sein* ('Thus for us his most worthy passions / must be most bitter and yet sweet' – No. 20). For Bach's *Matthew Passion* moves beyond dogma and far beyond sectarian doctrine, towering above the liturgy that first legitimised its existence.

As with the *John Passion*, primacy is given to the biblical words. Bach balanced the central thread, Matthew's re-telling of the Passion story, with instant reactions and more measured reflections by concerned onlookers, so as to bring it into the present. Like any good story-teller, Bach knew exactly how to play on his listeners' expectations – how to hold them in suspense, how to tell and then re-tell the story from different angles. Like novelists from Flaubert to Arundhati Roy, Bach provides a succession of subjectivities to help the reader/listener to experience the drama from shifting perspectives. In the earlier *Passion* it was John's special eyewitness account that gave the work its authenticity and edge, while the irregular placement of arias and chorales reinforced this suspense. With Matthew's version comes a larger cast and the added human pathos of Jesus presented as 'a man of sorrows'. It would be hard to better it as an essentially *human* drama – one involving immense struggle and challenge, betrayal and forgiveness, love and sacrifice, compassion and pity – the raw material with which most people can instantly identify. At times Bach's music suggests an almost physical engagement with the bones and blood of the story that gives life both to Matthew's account and to the horrified response of its imagined commentators, so that 'we tremble, we grow cold, we shed tears, our hearts race, we can barely breathe.'*

* * *

* This comes from the article 'As Flowers in Sunlight' (*Guardian*, 23 July 2005) in which Philip Pullman made an impassioned plea for theatre for children and the art of adapting stories for the stage. Only in the theatre, he maintains, can you find 'strong stories with vivid characters and existing events' which 'will always find an audience whether young or old'; so that directors are 'quite right to ransack the whole of literature in search of them'. 'The importance of cherishing and preserving a physical, sensuous connection with things was something I laid great stress on in *His Dark Materials*, and I meant it. Such experiences are profoundly important to our full development as human beings.'

What could Bach possibly now produce in his opening movement to match the powerful vision of Christ-in-majesty of his *John Passion*? His vision this time was of a different order, an allegorical one of the faithful climbing Mount Zion on their way to the holy city of Jerusalem. As with so many of the cantatas from his Second Leipzig Cycle, Bach constructs it as a chorale fantasia, but with a throbbing pedal in the style of a French *tombeau*.[8] One can view it as an *exordium*, a metaphorical 'lifting up' in anticipation of the way Christ will soon be hoisted up on the Cross, an appeal to the devout listener to 'open up' and, as in Homer, an invocation to the poetic muses. One senses Bach's wealth of experience in cantata composition that had been crammed into two or three frenetic years, but also his striving to surpass everything that he had previously written. This powerful and evocative lament, reminiscent in its grandiloquent musical gestures of BWV 198, the *Trauer-Ode* (see Chapter 7, p. 220), turns out to be a microcosm of the new Passion, encompassing both its particular theological slant and the musical structure that Bach gives each of the ensuing movements. We cannot tell if it was his or Picander's idea to link the traditional interpretation of Christ as the allegorical bridegroom (Song of Songs) with that of his identity as the sacrificial lamb – 'He is brought as a lamb to the slaughter . . . so he openeth not his mouth' (Isaiah 53:7). What we do know is that Bach's starting-point – one that he must have discussed and agreed with Picander at the outset – is the concept of dialogue, a device he had already tried out fruitfully in two movements of his *John Passion* (between his bass soloist and the remaining singers (see above, p. 385), and now developed to the point where it led logically to an eventual division into two choirs, each with its own supporting instrumental ensemble.

Once again, the obvious literary model for this was Brockes's Passion libretto of 1711, which calls for exchanges between 'the Believers' and 'the Daughter of Zion'; yet, interestingly, none of the composers who had set Brockes's text (Keiser, Handel, Telemann, Mattheson or Stölzel) picked up on this opportunity to compose for antiphonal choirs. What is intriguing here is the way Picander, while manifestly influenced by Brockes, switches the pronouns: in place of Brockes's 'Believers' he places 'the [individual] Soul' – to whom he assigns an 'aria' – in an exchange with the 'Daughters of Zion'. Evidently Bach sensed a need to turn this prologue into a *communal* lament – for plural forces, in other words. However it was originally or eventually constituted, Bach intends that his first choir should speak for the whole community of believers – to voice a self-accusation by humanity at large – as well as for the individual soul and for the bride of the Song of Songs, who must forfeit her bridegroom on her wedding day. Meanwhile, the 'Daughters of Zion', sung by his second choir, also appear in his musical treatment to stand for that 'great company of people, and of women, which also bewailed and lamented him' – those who followed Jesus all the way to Golgotha (Luke 23:27). Implied, but not set to music by Bach, are Jesus' words, 'Weep not for me, but for yourselves and your children.'*

Viewed in this way, Bach's opening chorus is presented to us as an immense tableau – an aural equivalent, say, to a grand altarpiece by Veronese or Tintoretto – in which, with Albert Schweitzer, we can discern Jesus being led captive through the city and along the *Via crucis*, the voices of the crowd calling to one another in tragic antiphony.[9] The music seems entirely complete – an architectural structure with a chorale prelude superimposed upon an autonomous four-voiced chorus (Choir I) – and we marvel at how smoothly he makes room for a series of antiphonal exchanges between his two choirs and orchestras. But there is still more to come: at the moment when the first choir refers to Jesus as a 'bridegroom', and then 'as a lamb', Bach brings in a third choir with the chorale 'O Lamb of God, unspotted' in an abrupt expansion of the sound spectrum: G major within an E minor context.† Sung in unison by a group of trebles (*soprano in ripieno*) placed in the 'swallows' nest' organ loft in the Thomaskirche – then (but now, alas, no longer) situated a whole nave's length east of the main performing area – the effect must have been stunning – a magical use of space and

* As Eric Chafe writes, 'Luther referred to this passage often – twice in the Passion sermon – to point out that the Passion was intended to awaken consciousness of sin in the believer, not mere lamentation over Jesus' sufferings or outcry over the treachery of Judas' (*Tonal Allegory in the Vocal Music of J. S. Bach* (1991) p. 364).

† Robert Levin observes that 'Bach's decision to combine the G major chorale with the E minor principal material will engender a deliberate wrenching effect as the tonal exigencies of these discrete components of the piece pull in opposite directions.' He shows convincingly that Bach is 'striving not for circularity [the thesis of Karol Berger's *Bach's Cycle, Mozart's Arrow* (2007), pp. 45–59] but *continuity*, in which the sense of both timing and time itself seems caught up in a drama of relentless forward motion' (JAMS, Vol. 63, No. 3 (1 Dec. 2010), p. 665). 'As to [Berger's] notion that the work as a whole suspends time by folding past, present, and future into a single level of Now, is this not ultimately true of every performance, whether a play, an opera, a ballet, or a piece of instrumental music, and regardless of style?' (p. 666).

acoustic, quite the equal of those celebrated Venetian polychoral antiphonies developed in the late 1500s by Andrea and Giovanni Gabrieli to exploit the mysterious spatial configuration of St Mark's Basilica. Yet Bach's purpose is not confined to a spatial expansion of sonorities. By choosing to superimpose on to his choral tableau the timeless *Agnus Dei* of the liturgy in its German versification – which would already have been heard earlier that day at the conclusion of the morning service – he was able to contrast the historic Jerusalem as the site of Christ's imminent trial and Passion with the celestial city whose ruler, according to the Apocalypse, is the Lamb. The repeated acknowledgement of guilt – *auf unsre Schuld* in Choir 1 – is answered down along the Gothic vault by the children – *All Sünd hast du getragen* ('All sin hast thou borne for us . . . have mercy on us, O Jesus'). This is the essential dichotomy – the innocent Lamb of God and the world of errant humanity whose sins Jesus must bear – which will underlie the whole Passion, the fate of the one yoked to that of the other. Bach here gives it an added symbolic tonal form: E minor for the main chorale fantasia, G major for the *Agnus Dei* – distinct, coexisting, colliding, yet never resolved. He has set out his stall. Now the biblical narrative can begin.

From the outset we are offered stark new juxtapositions of texture and sonority – wide-arching *secco* recitative for the narrator, a 'halo' of four-voiced strings surrounding each of Jesus' statements, tense antiphonal interventions by the crowd (sometimes divided, as in No. 4b, between chief priests and scribes), a reduction to single choir for the disciples (No. 4d) and a coming together again for collective prayer. Soon we can discern a series of trifoliar patterns emerging: biblical narrative (in recitative), comment (in arioso) and prayer (in aria). Gradually these begin to take on the appearance of an ordered sequence of discrete scenes, as though borrowed from contemporary opera, each one building towards either an individual (aria) or collective (chorale) response to the preceding narration. Here was ample precedent for dividing up the Gospel narrative into separate 'acts'. Johann Jacob Bendeler, for example, proposed a division of Matthew's account into six principal 'actions':[10] the preparation of the Passion; the Garden (*Actus hortus*); the Sanhedrin trial (*Actus pontifices*); the Roman trial (*Actus Pilatus*); the Crucifixion (*Actus crux*); the Burial (*Actus sepulchrum*). Although Bach's autograph indicates no such clear-cut subdivisions, this may be a helpful way of tracing the Passion's structural outline – as one would a *tragédie lyrique* by Bach's French contemporary, Rameau, one comprising a prologue and five acts, each divided into scenes:*

Part I

EXORDIUM

Chorus: 'Kommt, ihr Töchter'		No. 1

PROLOGUE – The preparation of the Passion (Matthew 26:1–29)

Sc. i	Jesus foretells his Crucifixion	Nos. 2–3
Sc. ii	The plot to kill Jesus	Nos. 4a–4b
Sc. iii	The anointing at Bethany	Nos. 4c–6
Sc. iv	Judas' betrayal	Nos. 7–8
Sc. v	The preparation of the Passover	Nos. 9a–10
Sc. vi	The Last Supper	Nos. 11–13

ACT I – ACTUS HORTUS – 'The Garden Act' (Matthew 26:30–56)

Sc. i	The Mount of Olives I	Nos. 14–15
Sc. ii	The Mount of Olives II	Nos. 16–17
Sc. iii	Gethsemane: Jesus warns his disciples	Nos. 18–20
Sc. iv	The Agony in the Garden I: Jesus' first appeal to God	Nos. 21–3
Sc. v	The Agony in the Garden II: Jesus' second appeal to God	Nos. 24–5
Sc. vi	Jesus' betrayal and arrest	Nos. 26–27a
Sc. vii	The dispersal of the flock	Nos. 28–9

* Picander's libretto – which was available on sale to the congregation – was published as the second volume of his *Ernst-Scherzhaffte und Satyrische Gedichte* (Leipzig, 1729). It contains his own madrigalian verses, but none of the biblical texts and only two chorales; yet, in the captions to his aria texts, he refers to events that have just happened in the Gospel narrative (for example, 'after the woman had anointed Jesus' and 'after Jesus' capture'), thus indicating his ideas for the structural scaffolding of the Passion. There are a few gaps and miscalculations, such as at the end of Part I, where by placing the 'Sind Blitze, sind Donner' as its climax – a thrilling idea in itself – Picander shows he had forgotten that there is an extended speech for Jesus (Matthew 26:52–4) to fit in at this point (see p. 416; and see Ulrich Leisinger, 'Forms and Functions of the Choral Movements in J. S. Bach's *St Matthew Passion*' in *Bach Studies*, Daniel R. Melamed (ed.) (1995), Vol. 2, pp. 76–7).

THE SERMON

Part II

EXORDIUM

Aria: 'Ach! nun ist mein Jesus hin!'	No. 30

ACT II – ACTUS PONTIFICES – 'The High Priests' Act' (Matthew 26:57–75)

Sc. i	Jesus before Caiaphas	Nos. 31–2
Sc. ii	Deposition by false witnesses	Nos. 33–5
Sc. iii	False accusation and mockery	Nos. 36a–37
Sc. iv	Peter's denial	Nos. 38a–40

ACT III – ACTUS PILATUS – 'Pilate's Act' (Matthew 27:1–29)

Sc. i	Judas' remorse	Nos. 41a–42
Sc. ii	Jesus before Pilate	Nos. 43–4
Sc. iii	Pilate confronts the mob	Nos. 45a–46
Sc. iv	Pilate's dilemma	Nos. 47–9
Sc. v	Pilate succumbs to the mob's demands	Nos. 50a–52
Sc. vi	Jesus' mock coronation	Nos. 53a–54

ACT IV – ACTUS CRUX – 'The Act of the Cross' (Matthew 27:30–50)

Sc. i	Via Dolorosa	Nos. 55–7
Sc. ii	Golgotha	Nos. 58a–60
Sc. iii	The death of Jesus	Nos. 61a–62

ACT V – ACTUS SEPULCHRUM – 'The Act of the Sepulchre' (Matthew 27:51–60)

Sc. i	Earthquake and revelation	Nos. 63a–65
Sc. ii	The entombment of Jesus	Nos. 66a–66c

CONCLUSIO

Recit.: 'Nun ist der Herr zur Ruh gebracht'	No. 67
Chorus: 'Wir setzen uns mit Tränen nieder'	No. 68

As with Baroque opera, each 'act' implies a scene-shift or change of location and a shuffling of the principal players. The individual 'scenes' into which Bach appears to divide the five 'acts' of Matthew's narration are of variable length. For example, the purely narrative element in the fourth scene of the *Actus Pilatus* – the turning-point of Part II, when Jesus' fate hangs in the balance – is a mere two bars long (No. 47). But for him each 'scene' evidently required some punctuation and comment, as though he, as an implicated onlooker, had temporarily to avert his eyes from the action: sufficient time for him – and for us – to ponder its implications. These were the critical junctures at which he enlisted Picander: to gloss the long Passion story with poetic reflections with which the congregation could easily identify, and then to fill those reflections with contemplative music or to round off the scenes with a chorale at moments (there are fourteen in all) when Bach considered a congregational reflection was apposite. In this way his listeners could assent or respond to the feelings expressed by the singer in the previous number by means of reassessing hymns with which they were familiar.

The type and mood of the contemplative commentary inserted by Picander and set to music by Bach vary enormously, both in tracing the way of the Cross and at the same time in articulating the three stages of Luther's 'Meditation on Christ's Passion': first, recognition and acknowledgement of sin; second, the growth of faith through love and the unburdening of one's sins in Christ; and third, seeing Jesus' Passion as the model for Christian love.[11] Thus the opening arioso/aria pairing in Part I – 'Du lieber Heiland, du' (No. 5), followed by 'Buß und Reu' (No. 6) – establishes the emphasis on guilt not in an abstract way external to the action, but in response to the disciples' bickering over the 'waste' of precious ointment. Even at so early a stage Bach succeeds in bringing the action and reaction into the present, bolstering the sense of guilt (*Buß*) and remorse (*Reu*) by the contours of the aria's melodic line – short epigrammatic phrases with variable emphases, having little in common with the flutes' ritornello, indeed giving the impression of being a spontaneous response to it. Bach finds an initial means to impart the crunching (*knirscht*) of body and spirit that will become such a feature of his *Matthew Passion*.

The second aria, 'Blute nur' (No. 8), points to the direct connection between Jesus' innocence and suffering and the way man has been instrumental in his betrayal. It takes up the theme of the sacrificial Lamb of the opening chorus – of innocent blood spilt – and adds to this the image of the serpent suckled at a mother's breast. The figure of Judas, a leader in the community and a favoured friend of Jesus poised to betray him, is implied, but so are all of us by association. The third interpolation, in total contrast, moves from tears at the prospect of Jesus' imminent departure (the arioso 'Wiewohl', No. 12) to gratitude for the institution of the Eucharist (the aria 'Ich will dir', No. 13). Fittingly, it is the only genuinely joyful music in the Passion; it is also overtly sexual in its imagery – the idea of merging or 'sinking myself into thee.'

The fourth pairing – 'O Schmerz' (No. 19) and 'Ich will bei meinem Jesus wachen' (No. 20) – comes at the midpoint of Part I and again is constructed as a dialogue. Responding to Jesus' injunction at Gethsemane to watch and pray, the tenor stands for the night watchman – observing Jesus' tortured soul and determined to stay vigilant (just as generations of Bach's ancestors had done professionally as *Türmer*). Yet, as the answering soft-voiced chorus makes clear, he is helpless and cannot alleviate the burden of sin, which, Luther insisted, mankind places on Jesus' shoulders through faith in his resurrection. This imbues it with a mysterious quality, almost as though a muted drama is taking place at a distance from the main action – Christ's 'Agony in the Garden' and his acceptance of his role as Saviour.

The fifth pair (Nos. 22 and 23), a reaction to Jesus' agonised appeal to his Father to be spared the cup, voices the believer's eagerness to participate in Christ's suffering and to accept Luther's injunction to follow the way of the Cross. Bitterness and sweetness – of taste and experience – are juxtaposed; but, in accepting to drink from the 'cup of death's bitterness', Jesus renders it sweet and offers it to humanity at large. The aria's melodic line lurches in intoxicated imitation of the chalice draught: with here a yodel-like upward seventh, there a chain of drunken emphases on a single word (*gerne*/'gladly'), and a constantly shifting beat swinging across the bar-line, it barely stays within the proprieties of Baroque gracefulness. But it does divert our attention from the banality of Picander's rhyming couplet, provided, that is, the singer flows through Bach's crafty hemiolas and ignores the poet's line-divisions: *Gerne will ich mich bequemen, / Kreuz und Becher anzunehmen* ('Gladly will I,

Square brackets have been added to highlight Bach's way of swinging the beat across the bars in order to preserve the correct verbal emphasis.

fear disdaining, / Drink the cup without complaining'). The B section of the aria irons out some of the earlier inebriated irregularities (apart from *des Leidens herbe Schmach*/'sorrow's bitter taste'), but throws a fresh challenge to the singer to inflect the melody without losing the overall triple-rhythmed shape and line (see above).

Part I culminates with the third strategically placed dialogue, 'So ist mein Jesus nun gefangen' (No. 27a). Here the cello and bass – the bed-rock of the music – are silent, leaving the upper strings as the *bassetchen* to portray the stumbling and faltering steps of Jesus, nudged and prodded by the armed pressgang all the way from Gethsemane towards the courtroom, where he will shortly face trial by the Sanhedrin. The soprano and alto of Choir 1 join in a desolate lament for the captive (and in so doing indulge in that 'wrong way to meditate on the Passion' against which Luther warned), while an eerie conjunction of flute and oboe in mixed pairings enact an obsessive circling overhead like dragonflies. The open texture of the music allows one to pick out the disciples (Choir 2) in the middle distance moving from tree to tree through the darkened olive grove, affronted but impotent, not daring to intervene, but bold enough to voice from time to time their muttered protest – to stop molesting Jesus.

This bleak, spellbinding tableau runs counter to the Baroque doctrine which allows for only a single *Affekt* to be portrayed at any one time.

Rather than engineer a collision, Bach sets his two unequally constituted ensembles to work on different planes simultaneously, their two *Affekts* being offset in sophisticated dynamic tension like two separate planets rotating on different trajectories around the same sun. Their opposition is thrown into relief the moment both ensembles, now equal and at full strength, converge and unite to voice the outrage of the whole Christian community at Jesus' capture: 'Sind Blitze, sind Donner' (No. 27b). With its quick-fire exchanges calling on the forces of nature to erupt and destroy Judas and the High Priests' mob, this is double-choir writing of bristling excitement and power. While it could be said to spring from the Venetian tradition of *cori spezzati*, no German composer had come up with anything like this since the days of Hans Leo Hassler and Schütz in the previous century. It is characteristic of the amazing vigour and amplitude Bach brings to his double-choir writing even in quite short *turba* choruses depicting the threat of mob violence (No. 4b), the hideous reality of it (Nos. 45b and 50b), and the cold-blooded mocking of its principal victim (No. 58b).

Having introduced the preceding dialogue with the words 'after Jesus' capture', Picander, in his printed libretto – which includes none of Matthew's words (assumed to be familiar) nor any of the chorales except those woven into his verse – ends at this point. One musicologist muses 'what an enormous effect this savage chorus would have made had it come at the very end of the first part',[12] which is certainly true; ending *Don Giovanni* at the conclusion of the banqueting scene might have had (and can have) a similar effect. But this is not a 'curtain' as in real staged opera, and I doubt whether Bach would have been seriously tempted to conclude Part I in this way. In the church cantatas he composed in Leipzig, and indeed in his *John Passion*, his usual practice was to end with a prayer – a chorale to focus the mind on all that has happened so far – and that is exactly what he does here. Besides, there was an extended speech by Jesus at this juncture in response to a physical intervention by his disciples (the incident of Peter and Malchus' ear), after which Matthew concludes with the line 'Then all the disciples forsook him and fled.' If Bach had even momentarily wavered from setting this line at the conclusion of Part I, the preacher would surely have brought him quickly to order, for that might often have constituted his sermon text – the scattering of the flock.* Bach's initial musical bridge to the sermon was a straightforward harmonisation of the chorale 'Jesum lass ich nicht von mir'. When he came to revise and copy out the score in the mid 1730s, he must have seen that this fell a long way short of balancing the structural mass of his opening chorus after the emphatic double-choir movement 'Sind Blitze, sind Donner'. Now came the decision to replace it with the far more elaborate chorale fantasia, a setting of Sebald Heyden's Passiontide hymn 'O Mensch, bewein dein Sünde groß' (No. 29). A matching pillar to the grand chorale prologue was now in place, and as a conclusion to Part I it provided the ideal meditative opportunity for the Christian community to unite in contrition, drawing out Luther's meaning of the Passion story and acting as a direct response to Jesus' last words about 'fulfilling' the Scriptures. Outwardly the 'fit' seems perfect and is confirmed by little details such as the fluttering semiquavers in the flutes to illustrate the scattering of the flock. Just at the point where the preacher mounts the pulpit stair, the 'flock' disappears from view as the music trails off into the ether. Bach's tact on this occasion ensures a seamless join to the Good Friday sermon.

For years every scholar assumed this chorus to be an integral part of the *Matthew Passion*, yet it was in fact skilfully shoe-horned into it nine years after its first performance, having originated – at the very least – some ten years before that. There is nothing intrinsically odd about his desire to find a new home for one of the grandest and most impressive of his chorale fantasias, one that would be validated in its new position. Not many of us are disturbed, for example, by the frequent side-by-side placing in the *B minor Mass* of movements whose provenance is separated by thirty years or more (as we shall see in Chapter 13). Nonetheless, despite the details that suggest its appropriateness here, in the context of the *Matthew Passion*, where the music in its variety of forms is of phenomenal stylistic coherence, this chorale fantasia draws attention to itself. Each time I conduct the Passion I sense a structural shift at this

* Indeed it may well have been the clergy who decided precisely where to break the musical narration for the sermon. It could so easily have come at the end of the Matthew's Chapter 26 – with Peter's denial and remorse – just as it did in the *John Passion*; but here (see the schema above) it results in a more equal length between parts I and II.

point, a momentary change of gears: it lasts only a few seconds and then all is well again.*

* * *

With the resumption of music after the sermon, it takes a second or two to realise where we have got to in the story. Superficially nothing appears to have changed. The scene is still Gethsemane, now after nightfall. The Daughter of Zion is found distractedly searching for her captured lover, though Jesus, bound hand and foot, has long since gone, taken to face trial in front of the High Priests. To understand why this allegorical figure is re-introduced at this point by Bach and Picander, we need to remind ourselves of the huge appeal to their audiences of the imagery of the Song of Songs and the vigour of the tradition (which goes back to Origen in the first half of the third century AD) by which the male and female spouses symbolise Christ and the Christian soul. The palpably erotic language of the Song of Songs had long been legitimised by the Roman church, was adopted enthusiastically by the Protestant reformers in the guise of an *unio mystica*, and had been extremely popular with composers for the past 150 years in both Italy and Germany (see pp. 35 and 76). The Daughter of Zion equates with the bride of Christ and symbol of the Christian church, while the soul (*anima*) passionately

* This may just be a consequence of Bach's plan to concentrate and unify his antiphonal ensembles at this juncture into a single orchestra and choir. Even the *soprano in ripieno* (assuming that the line was allocated to a group of trebles) are drawn in and welded to those in Choirs 1 and 2. Did they physically move from the 'swallows' nest' to the west gallery, or did a sub-conductor – a Thomaner prefect – relay Bach's beat to them there, as was the practice in St Mark's Venice under the Gabrielis and Salzburg Cathedral during Biber's time? Either way, any physical separation of forces in this movement – particularly of the flutes, oboes and continuo, who have most of the semiquaver passagework – can be troublesome in performance and requires special vigilance. But there could be another explanation for its slight awkwardness – its early provenance. Arthur Mendel was the first Bach scholar to propose an original of Weimar provenance (*c.* 1714–16) for this movement ('Traces of the Pre-History of Bach's *St John* and *St Matthew* Passions' in *Festschrift Otto Erich Deutsch zum 80. Geburtstag*, Walter Gerstenberg, et al. (eds) (1963), pp. 32–5) and expressed his surprise at finding that 'what seems like a mature masterpiece should have been written so early'. I suggest that it could have originated earlier still – perhaps by as much as a decade – in that period when Bach was first flexing his creative wings as a composer of figural music and producing seminal works such as BWV 106, the *Actus tragicus*. I have no formal proof of this – just a strong sense that it belongs stylistically to the earlier period marked by Bach's first concerted setting of words by Martin Luther (BWV 4), at the time he was employed in Arnstadt and headed for Mühlhausen (1707).

yearns for union with Christ. The day of their wedding is the first day of Christ's Passion – the day on which he demonstrated his willingness to become the sacrificial offering in atonement for man's sins. This is why the Daughter of Zion figures in the prologue to both parts of the *Matthew Passion*: so that the contemporary believer could grasp that his own thwarted love for the suffering figure of Jesus is his lot or fortune (*sein Glück*). The dialogue movements (which are strategically placed throughout the *Matthew Passion*) articulate this perceived need for a coherent relationship to Christ, even if it means losing him now to regain him later in another form. So, in this new exordium (No. 30), the role of the second chorus questioning the distraught bride in words borrowed from the Song of Songs (6:1) – 'Whither is thy beloved gone, O thou fairest among women?' – is to proffer comfort on behalf of the community of believers. Their music is madrigalian, light and amiable in contrast with the sobbing anguish of the alto soloist's reference to her 'lamb [caught] in a tiger's claws'. Again, Bach has found a clever way of combining dual *Affekts* of drastically different character, yet linked by an identical dance metre in triple time.*

With the action now shifted to the Sanhedrin court, Bach can no longer rely on John's eyewitness account, but succeeds nonetheless in bringing the trial and its blatant miscarriage of justice vividly into the present via the tenor arioso 'Mein Jesus schweigt' (No. 34) and its sequel, the aria 'Geduld!' (No. 35). Jesus' silence in answer to his accusers is reflected in the thirty-nine ominous detached beats of the oboes, which allude to the second line of Psalm 39 – 'I will keep a muzzle on

* The madrigalian style Bach adopts for the second chorus here shows sufficient affinity with that of Heinrich Schütz in his biblical dialogue SWV 339, *Ich beschwöre euch* – a miniature scenic masterpiece – to make one wonder whether Bach had come across it and took it as a point of departure, or, was it the nuptial dialogue of his cousin Johann Christoph Bach, *Meine Freundin, du bist schön* (see Chapter 3, p. 74) lodged in his memory which inspired his setting of these words? He himself had already prepared his Leipzig audience for the close association between the Daughter of Zion with the King's daughter or bride by reviving his Weimar cantata BWV 162, *Ach, ich sehe, itzt, da ich zur Hochzeit gehe*, in his First Leipzig Cycle, and in his Annunciation cantata BWV 1, *Wie schön leuchtet der Morgenstern*, first given on 25 Mar. 1725, which also refers to 'my king and my bridegroom' and was the last music to be heard in Leipzig before Good Friday. However, as we saw in Chapter 9, it was BWV 127, *Herr Jesu Christ, wahr' Mensch und Gott*, that formed a bridge over the Lenten period and may well have been intended by Bach as a deliberate 'flyer' to announce his *Matthew Passion*, which in the end had to be held back for another two years (see p. 330).

my mouth, so long as wicked men confront me' – after which they too fall silent. With just continuo for support, the focus shifts to an individual bystander (the tenor Concertist) in his battle for self-control. Denied the calm needle-stitch of the cello's opening bar for his own melody, he begins with self-admonishment – with a vocal phrase that sounds more like an anguished outcry than the start of an aria. 'Patience!' he tells himself with his very first word (*Geduld!*), only to lose it the very next moment as 'false tongues sting me.' The melodic line lurches in and out of a recitative-like naturalism with moments of passing lyricism, wholly independent from – yet reactive to – the cello pursuing its own private tussle between forbearance (steady quaver pairings) and protest (jagged dotted rhythms). The energy of Bach's invention leaps off the page in every single phrase and varied sub-phrase of the voice line – something that in performance a smoothed-out or anodyne delivery by the singer can quickly snuff out. Bach allows us to experience and identify with this struggle between moral outrage and the tactical imperative to remain silent as it continues to churn within the tenor's mind – even in the vocal rests and particularly in the premature return of his opening plea, *Geduld!* (bars 39–43), and the way his final outburst seems to subside resignedly. This dual portrayal of Jesus' stoicism and the bystander's struggle with himself to emulate it seems psychologically astute and extraordinarily modern. It has a resonance for beleaguered humanity at all times and in all places – from instances of false accusation in private or domestic life to the outrages under regimes of torture – and perhaps goes some way to explain the symbolic importance attached to the *Matthew Passion* in the German-speaking world throughout the twentieth century.

But, aside from this, there seems to be a special edge to this particular aria that goes beyond the formally illustrative or exegetical. In his copy of the Calov Bible, Bach singles out two verses from Matthew (5:25–6) to underline: 'Make friends quickly with your accuser, while you are going with him to court, lest your accuser hand you over to the judge and the judge to the guard, and you be put in prison; truly, I say to you, you will never get out till you have paid the last penny.' Bach, as we have seen, had direct experience of imprisonment, and by the time he had finished writing out the score of the *Matthew Passion* in 1736, he was battle-scarred from successive professional disputes with the Leipzig authorities. Extraordinarily pertinent here are the words and passages he picked out from Calov on Matthew's verses on the distinction between anger on your own behalf and anger in defence of your office (see Chapter 6, p. 198). They are a sign of those tussles of conscience which this aria exemplifies so poignantly: anger suppressed but always close to the surface, bursting out in the cello's dotted figure, the singer's plea for *Geduld* uttered through gritted teeth. The underlinings confirm what we hear in the music: taken together they provide us with rare insights into Bach's private struggles and leave us clues to his temperament.

Coming at the climax of what we have designated 'The High Priests' Act', the next pair of arias (Nos. 39 and 42) gives expression to the essential difference between Christian repentance and remorse: in the first, extreme contrition is sung as though from a kneeling position, and in the second it is delivered with vehement hand-wringing. While they are closely associated with the two disciples Peter and Judas, who, in their separate ways, have both denied Jesus, the singers assigned by Bach to these roles in the narrative do not actually perform 'their' arias and are absent from the High Priest's courtyard. Peter, for example, is a bass, but his guilt is transferred to another singer – an alto – for 'his' aria, as though to underscore the Lutheran idea that as individuals we are *all* culpable and fallible. Although Judas and the singer who sings 'his' aria are both basses, the aria occurs after Judas' suicide. Bach was very particular about this, even writing Judas' direct speech into a separate part-book for a singer who stands aside from the rest and never appears in any of the arias or choruses. The bass singer of the aria acts as an intermediary – binding the listener into the story's progress urging him to identify with the issues of loyalty and betrayal and to extrapolate subjectively their meaning for himself.[13]

Bach makes much of the polarity between the two arias, even as regards the style and tonality of these concerto-like movements and the way they are placed within the narrative. Emerging out of the Evangelist's poignant melisma that re-creates Peter's weeping in the audience's present time, the solo violin enters with the eight-bar introduction to 'Erbarme dich' (No. 39) and wordlessly extends the identification with Peter's state, exposing the nerve-endings of grief, sorrow and repentance with ineffable tenderness. In a lilting *siciliano* rhythm, the violin floats above the sustained *cantabile* of the middle strings and over a pulsating bass line (organ continuo with pizzicato cello and bass), but with passing appoggiaturas that grind against the unornamented versions of the same note in the vocal line. The only times we hear this haunting melody actually complete are when it is played by the solo violin; we expect the singer to follow suit, but, having essayed the opening gesture, the voice line heads off in another direction, returning with a simplified echo – a mere shadow of the decorously embellished violin tune. Bach has found an audible symbol of human frailty – a falling short, just as Peter, when accused, has just fallen at the first hurdle. As Naomi Cumming explains, 'Language is not essential to this moment, or even adequate to it. A verbal penitence is expressed by the alto voice, but the violin articulates a more universal distress.'[14] It is this raw expression of human failings that makes 'Erbarme dich' so compelling, so heartbreaking – those brave attempts in which an alto voice (speaking in the first person without revealing who he or she is, but with whom we can identify) seeks to emulate the violin and join its line, yet manages just segments of the melody (for it lies outside the alto's vocal compass). The emotional tug of Bach's music on the listener springs from a recognition of those dashed dreams and failed endeavours to live up to a Godlike ideal.

In the starkest of contrasts 'Gebt mir meinen Jesum wieder' (No. 42) is an outburst of Christian remorse to match that of Judas: a peremptory demand for the release of the captive Saviour by the very man who betrayed him. A robust Italianate concerto movement in G major, it, too, is highly charged emotionally, but in a more pictorial way. The violin *bariolage* seems to trace the motion of Judas' wrist as in self-disgust he flings down on the Temple floor coins that have been devalued – thirty notes for thirty pieces of silver. For once in the Passion the singer behaves conventionally at first, entering with the same melody as the violin ritornello, but is soon launched into Picander's second phrase, *Seht, das Geld, den Mörderlohn* ('See the price, the murder's wage'). This properly belongs to the B section of this, the most succinct aria of the Passion, though we are still in the A section (so that technically this becomes a 'through-composed' aria). We can dismiss this as yet another instance of Bach finding his own reasons to play fast and loose with the accepted symmetry of the *da capo* form, until we realise that this particular brand of subversion aptly expresses the disorientation that underlies Judas' – and our – distress at the consequences of blood money.

We cannot fail to be struck by the juxtaposition of unpalatable hectoring and violence, first in the two almost adjacent mocking choruses

(Nos. 36b and d) and then in the ensuing chorale (No. 37), where Bach finds the means to take the sting out of the aggression by interjecting great tenderness and quiet outrage at the maltreatment of a blameless prisoner. Later, after the chilling shout of *Barrabam!* and the first of the blood-lust choruses, 'Lass ihn kreuzigen!' (No. 45b), he requires his singers to switch – with only a minim's rest – from acting as a vindictive hysterical mob to voicing the anguished bemusement of the faithful community of believers (No. 46). One could interpret this as just a filling out of the established structure, or one could see it as Bach's resolve to keep something much darker at bay – to prevent the level of blood-lust from welling up beyond the point of endurance. Bach finds the ideal way to lance the boil – by a heartfelt expression of contrition voiced in a chorale (No. 46) by the united chorus on the listener's behalf and as an admission of complicity in the crime: 'How awe-inspiring is indeed this punishment . . . The master pays the debts his servants owe him, and they betray him!'

Occupying a central place akin to that of the 'rainbow' aria ('Erwäge') in the *John Passion*, is the soprano aria 'Aus Liebe will mein Heiland sterben' (No. 49). It provides a phenomenally poignant and meditative contrast to the coiled-up tension of the Roman trial, which has now arrived at its turning-point. Cowed by the mob's insistence that he release Barrabas and crucify Jesus, Pilate has been alerted to the dangers of becoming embroiled in Jesus' trial by his wife's presentiments, and lamely asks, 'Why, what evil hath he done?' The silence lasts a mere crotchet's rest, but in that time (and before the crowd can find the voice to renew its blood-lust) the soprano steps forward and in measured recitation insists that 'He has done *good* to us all' (No. 48). An air of timeless healing and benediction emanates from the music of this most sublime of arias and acts as an oasis of temporary sanity in a deranged world. Bach's acute sense of instrumental colour guides him towards an unusual choice of instruments – using twin oboes da caccia to underpin the plangent exchanges between voice and flute. Their weightless pulse allows the ethereal grace of the flute arabesques to fly free and simultaneously to cushion the pure timbre and fragility of the soprano. These tenor-ranged oboes featured first in the *accompagnato* (No. 19) describing Jesus' tortured soul in Gethsemane, when they were doubled by recorders, before yielding to the soprano-ranged oboe with its more forthright sonority appropriate for the watchman's call (No. 20). By giving increased prominence to these 'hunting oboes' as the Passion advances, Bach creates an association in the listener's mind with the dual ideas of suffering and love – not love in the abstract, but as here in 'Aus Liebe', the supreme protective love of Jesus that shields the believer from the wages of sin; the power of evil cannot touch those who repent even in the last moments before death, when passing from searing pain to serenity. In the absence of the habitual basso continuo, the hypnotic throbbing of the da caccias serves to isolate Jesus' message from the baying of his persecutors. These vital components can be overwhelming in performance – the sense of love being present yet also vulnerable, especially at the point where the mob bursts in again with redoubled brutality – 'surely one of the most disturbing moments in the history of western music'.[15]

The next interpolated pairs provide emotional responses to Jesus' degradation – his scourging (Nos. 51 and 52) and the carrying of his Cross (Nos. 56 and 57), each seen from a fresh angle. Both feature pervasive dotted rhythms but in patterns so different that any underlying similarity is obscured: harsh whiplashes in the recitative (No. 51) (not dissimilar to Handel's 'He gave his back to the smiters', the B section of 'He was despised' from *Messiah*) that melt into convulsive sobs in its sequel, the alto aria 'Können Tränen' (No. 52). Then the full range of the seven-stringed viola da gamba encompasses the depth of human sorrow and the tottering gait of Jesus burdened by the weight of the Cross. Even if many of the original audience could not actually see the physical appearance of the gambist's extravagant, effortful string crossings, they could have heard them in the sound, with all the struggling arpeggiations, the many cross figures keeping the listener's mind focused on the symbol of the Cross and on the figure of Simon of Cyrene. Once again, the preparatory ariosi in each pairing provide invitations to us – via individual singers who speak for us – to intervene, even to protest, in an attempt to bring events to a standstill so as to spare Jesus from so much suffering, whereas in the arias the singer seems to take a step backwards and contemplate the events from a more oblique perspective.

This is a major departure from Bach's normal practice in his cantatas, a proto-cinematic technique in which he engineers an abrupt shift of focus from the narrative to the commentator elbowing his way into the frame, then softening and widening as the arioso dissolves into the ensuing aria. In the case of 'Erbarm es Gott!' (No. 51) it is not just the hard edge to the rhythms which softens the bridge to the aria 'Können Tränen', but the extreme instability of the underlying harmony, made up of chains of seventh chords, which veers from sharps to flats, back to sharps and (just when you expect a final cadence in F♯ minor) makes a last-minute enharmonic swerve to flats – to G minor. Picander's arioso text refers to a 'vision of such pain' (*der Anblick solchen Jammers*). The visual impact of violin and viola bows lashing the strings adds greatly to Bach's evocative portrayal of Jesus' scourging, putting one in mind of Caravaggio's *Flagellation of Christ* (Naples, 1607), in which the soldiers' muscles are tense with the effort of strapping him to a column.

As the *Passion* moves towards its climax, Bach's strategy of pulling us into the action (in ariosi), and then arranging the angles from which we can contemplate its application to ourselves (in the arias and chorales), becomes ever clearer. By settling on a specific voice and selecting a specific obbligato timbre for each aria – whether solo violin, flute, oboe or viola da gamba – he determines the most appropriate accompaniment: this might be for the full string ensemble from either left or right, or subtle combinations of sonorities, as we saw when the oboes da caccia struck up such a fruitful and intriguing partnership with both soprano and flute in 'Aus Liebe'. In the preceding arioso the two oboes da caccia were centre-stage and then moved into a more subservient role once the aria began. With these arioso/aria pairings, for all their apparent oppositions of mood, the chosen instrumental timbre is the common denominator: a linking of voice and narrative thread. The kaleidoscopic permutations of instrumental colour that Bach finds seem to be boundless. So, for example, although the flutes occupy the foreground in 'Ja freilich' (No. 56), the viola da gamba – which will be the solo obbligato instrument in 'Komm, süßes Kreuz' (No. 57) – is already present, discreetly arpeggiating in the background. It is also intriguing in theatrical terms to observe how Bach has evolved a fluid movement of instrumental *dramatis personae* jockeying for position, ready to advance or retreat, or simply awaiting their turn. The moment a 'bit part' player steps forwards he or she suddenly assumes an enhanced significance as the context shifts. Then, when a dialogue is struck up with another player or singer, we, as listeners, gain a vivid sense of separate human subjectivities locked in animated dialogue just as we might encounter on the pages of a novel.

Now, with the crisis of the Crucifixion – which really *is* a crisis here, not the triumphant 'raising up' we witness in Bach's setting of John's Gospel – the oboes da caccia rise to a position of prominence in the pairing 'Ach Golgotha' (No. 59) and 'Sehet, Jesus hat die Hand' (No. 60). Their initial impact as they imitate the sombre tolling of funerary bells – not the light, high-pitched variety, the *Leichenglocken* we will encounter in the mourning cantatas (see Chapter 12), but dark sonorous ones in a jangled peal – is the first Christian response of protest to the Crucifixion and the curse (*Fluch*) of Jesus' imminent death. The twisted harmonic convolutions of this extraordinary recitative, part of the awkward modulatory shift from E minor (*Ich bin Gottes Sohn*) to E♭ major (*Sehet*), press home the Lutheran message of human guilt being the root cause whereby the 'guiltless have to die guilty'.

With the start of the aria now in the serenity of E♭ major, the mood shifts from the horror of Golgotha to one of pastoral benediction, turning the earlier 'curse' into a blessing. It is hard to say quite how the ominous bell-tolling sonority of the da caccias has suddenly become congenial, even radiant. Now for the first time they are displayed in their full glory as melody instruments – the epitome of the love emanating from the Cross and from Jesus' outstretched arms that offer a haven to the sinner, gathering in the faithful like 'lost chicks' (*ihr verlass'nen Küchlein*).* Here the exoticism of the da caccia timbre lies not in the long stretches of euphony in which they glide together over a staccato bass line, but in the bars (2–4) in which they launch into trill-decorated ascents and quirky syncopations – perhaps in anticipation of those abandoned chicks soon to be enfolded, but also redolent of Near Eastern instruments that exploit the cavity resonance of their flared brass bells (see p. 328 and Plate 21). The transformation in sonority from arioso to aria is of course not haphazard but reflects the change from guilt to love in which Bach, following Luther, draws out the principal benefits of faith to the believer. This is to underscore that 'comfort to the conscience' (*Tröstung des Gewissens*) in the Passion story which the Daughter of

* The great conductor Bruno Walter, who revered the *Matthew Passion* and performed it every year during a ten-year period in Munich, wrote with great insight about the work. He saw this aria as an intimation of the Resurrection, allowing us 'to partake in the vision of a soul that directs the glances of its fellows to where its own are aiming: to the resurrected One'. But this does not mean, I feel, that in doing so Bach 'stepped outside the work that he had laid down in collaboration with Picander' (*On Music and Music-Making* (1961), p. 189).

Zion points out to the community (Chorus 2): *in Jesu Armen sucht Erlösung, nehmt Erbarmen, Suchet!* ('Seek redemption in Jesus' arms, receive mercy, seek!').

After the anguish of the Crucifixion these floating exhortations of both singer and da caccias exude warmth and balm. But the ultimate validation of these rather magical instruments and the special role that Bach assigns to them in the Passion comes in the final aria, 'Mache dich, mein Herze, rein' (No. 65), when they are re-absorbed into the orchestra, adding a burnished gentle colouring to the halo of string sound associated hitherto with Jesus and now with this aria (in Bach's performances the singers of both were one and the same).* The voice line is all of a piece both with the instrumental material presented at the outset and with its texture – Christ's death, having brought atonement, is now entombed in the believer's heart. The aria is in itself a celebration of the transforming potency of music as a means to reflect on, and draw lessons from, the re-telling of the Passion story. As the only conventionally functioning *da capo* aria in the *Matthew Passion*, it is both exuberant and calming by turn, spacious yet onward flowing, and is one of the most inherently satisfying and consoling arias in all Bach's works. There is one remarkable skittish bar (52) – the bridge back to the A section – which seems to sum up the preceding message, 'World, begone, let Jesus in', in a moment of unalloyed joy.

Though the story of Christ's entombment and the imposing double chorus for a deputation of High Priests and Pharisees sent to lobby Pilate is still to come, this magnificent bass aria marks the beginning of the end. The last notes are performed in an accompanied recitative for four solo voices perhaps representing the four Gospel-writers searching for an elegiac summing-up of their personal testimony, like family mourners. The second choir's response is folk-like in its simple valediction in preparation for the sacral dance of the epilogue. Where in the *John Passion*, Bach ended with a choral rondo ('Ruht wohl') as a reverential accompaniment to the laying of the Saviour's body in the grave – and therefore suggestive of a full stop of a sort – here, to conclude the *Matthew*, he chooses a sarabande similar in motivic gesture and key to the one in BWV 997, the Suite in C minor. The sensation is one of continuous movement,

* 'The rhetorical force of someone singing about henceforth containing Jesus, when he has just indeed been acting through the last moments of his saviour's life, is undoubtedly very strong' (Butt, *Bach's Dialogue with Modernity: Perspectives on the Passions* (2010), p. 207).

as though the entire ritual of the Passion story has now been heard in the listener's conscience and will need to be re-lived every Good Friday hereafter. A final reminder of this comes in the unexpected and almost excruciating dissonance Bach inserts over the very last chord: the melody instruments insist on B♮ – the jarring leading tone – before eventually melting in a C minor cadence.

* * *

Looking back at the conclusion of the *Matthew Passion*, one is struck by how the character of Jesus – a much more human figure than the one portrayed in the *John Passion* – is delineated powerfully and subtly, even when reduced, as in the whole of Part II, to three lapidary utterances: his final *Eli, Eli, lama asabthani?* ('My God, my God, why hast thou forsaken me?') and prior to that *Du sagest's* ('Thou hast said') – once to Caiaphas, once to Pilate. Other than that, Matthew tells us, 'he answered him nothing.' Yet there isn't a single moment when we are unaware of his presence. How can this be? Bach gives such a strong imprint to his interventions – always (apart from that very last cry from the Cross) with their distinctive nimbus of string sounds – that from early on (the instigation of the Eucharist during the Last Supper and the Agony in the Garden in Part I) his presence never ceases to loom over the narration; indeed, it is constantly insisted upon by references to him in reported speech and still more by the way the arioso/aria singers invoke it. We see him reflected in the eyes and voices of others, most of all in the moving summation 'Truly this was the Son of God' (63b) – two of the most emotionally charged bars in all of Bach's œuvre, in which the music magnifies Christ's presence at the very moment of his physical absence/disappearance. As always, the music is the place to find Bach himself too. Much as his whole endeavour is to give a voice to others – the protagonists, the crowd, the Gospel writer – his own is always present in the story. We hear it in his fervour, in his empathy with the suffering of the innocent Christ, in his sense of propriety, in his choices and juxtapositions of narrative and commentary, and most of all in the abrupt way he stems the tide of vengeful hysteria, cutting into Matthew's narration and interrupting it with a chorale expressive of profound contrition and outrage.*

* Bruno Walter claimed that: 'we hear [Bach's] own voice and perceive his own heart in the singing of those pious, compassionate figures of the work's second dimension . . .[by] sing-

There is not a single *opera seria* of the period that I have studied or conducted to compare with Bach's two Passions, in terms of the intense human drama and moral dilemma that he expresses in such a persuasive and deeply poignant way. No other German Passion oratorio or a single opera that has come down to us from these years can compare with them as sustained music-drama. Of that brilliant Class of '85, only Handel, vastly experienced composer of operas that he was, showed in the glorious succession of biblically inspired dramas he composed in the 'Oratorio Way' for London audiences between 1737 and 1752 that he was capable of producing persuasive dramatic masterpieces away from the stage and in a theatre of his own imagination. Bach knew perfectly well what opera was and seems to have decided quite early in life that it wasn't for him. What most distinguishes his Passions from operas of the time is the way he does away with the convention of a fixed point of reference for the audience, rejecting the idea of a listener who surveys the development of the dramatic narrative more like a consumer – entertained, perhaps moved, ingesting spoon-fed images, but never a part of the action. Bach took his cue from Luther, who, knowing from direct experience what it was like to be persecuted, insisted that Christ's Passion 'should not be acted out in words or appearances, but in one's own life'.[16] That is exactly what Bach does – by addressing us directly and very personally, by finding new ways to draw us in and towards acting it out in our own lives: we become participants in the re-enactment of a story which, however familiar, is told in ways calculated to bring us up short, to jolt us out of our complacency, while throwing us a lifeline of remorse, faith and, ultimately, a path to salvation. Even when pinching some of the clothes of opera in the process, Bach always avoids anything that smacks of theatrical representation. On the occasions when we can identify discrete 'scenes' in both Passions – semi-realistic ones in the case of those when Jesus is on trial before Pilate or the High Priest – even in these he breaks up the narrative and interpolates moments of reflection or reaction.

So where do they belong? In his book *The Death of Tragedy*, George Steiner maintains

ers [who] are nameless – and yet Bach's *faithful heart* has filled these supra-mundane figures with the pure, warm life-blood of his music, thus personifying them on their own, lofty plane' (op. cit., pp. 175–6).

> there has been no specifically Christian mode of tragic drama even in the noontime of the faith. Christianity is an anti-tragic vision of the world ... The Passion of Christ is an event of unutterable grief, but it is also a cipher through which is revealed the love of God for man ... Being a threshold to the eternal, the death of a Christian hero can be an occasion for sorrow but not for tragedy ... Real tragedy can occur only where the tormented soul believes that there is no time left for God's forgiveness. 'And now 'tis too late,' says Faustus in the one play that comes nearest to resolving the inherent contradiction of Christian tragedy. But he is in error. It is never too late to repent, and Romantic melodrama is sound theology when it shows the soul being snatched back from the very verge of damnation.[17]

This, of course, is the crux of Byron's portrayal of his hero Manfred in his dying moments:

ABBOT: ... Give thy prayers to Heaven –
Pray – albeit but in thought, – but die not thus.
MANFRED: Old man! 'tis not so difficult to die. [MANFRED *expires*]

When he came to compose his sublime incidental music to Byron's 'dramatic poem' some thirty years after it was written, in 1848, Robert Schumann followed these spoken words with a short but poignant choral requiem and so the work ends. Schumann had been present at Mendelssohn's celebrated revival of the *Matthew Passion* in Berlin in 1829, and it is possible that he recognised and learnt from the latent melodramatic features of Bach's score – the sense of going straight for the emotional jugular with its 'man of sorrows' approach.

Significantly, Steiner makes no passing reference to the Passions of Bach, perhaps because he considers they do not qualify as true tragedies, since 'the Christian view knows only partial or episodic tragedy. Within its essential optimism there are moments of despair; cruel setbacks can occur during the ascent toward grace.' True, it is impossible for the Christian story to follow the trajectory of a classical tragedy, since Jesus is both the chief protagonist and to a degree the author of his Passion. Of the two accounts Matthew's comes the closest, in that he borrows certain tragic conventions and gives a highly emotive account of the unjust treatment of the wholly good Jesus by wicked men, whereas in John's Gospel the quasi-tragic figure appears to be in control of and compliant with his fate. My contention, however, is that in both of his

Passions Bach proves that music really *can* 'animate the conventions of tragic myth and tragic conduct which had lapsed from the theatre after the seventeenth century', an achievement which Steiner attributes in the first place to Mozart, with his 'total command of the dramatic resources of music', and then to Wagner, with his 'genius for posing decisive questions: could music-drama restore to life those habits of imagination and symbolic recognition which are essential to a tragic theatre but which rationalism and the era of prose had banished from Western consciousness?'[18] While in no way diminishing Mozart's role in this (Wagner's is in any case self-inflated and can comfortably survive a prior claim), I see it as one of Bach's great achievements. Building on the non-operatic foundations of music-drama (see Chapter 4) as it had evolved during the past century outside the theatre, and often in church – between, say, the publication of Monteverdi's *Vespers of the Blessed Virgin* (1610) and the first airing of the *John Passion* (1724) – Bach set in motion a new burgeoning of the genre, leading his listeners to confront their mortality and compelling them to witness things from which they would normally avert their eyes. Perhaps Steiner might concede that, in this regard, such is the mythic charge to Bach's two great Passions, they could be considered the natural sequel to the spoken dramas of Racine and the English early-seventeenth-century writers, in so far as their themes resonate far beyond their temporal and liturgical borders, demonstrating that 'context of belief and convention which the artist shares with his audience'.

* * *

While there is enough documentary evidence to make it possible to reconstruct the original liturgical setting of Bach's Passions,* we can-

* Daniel R. Melamed (*Hearing Bach's Passions* (2005), p. 135) provides a table showing the liturgy of the Good Friday Vespers (starting at 1.45 p.m.) in Leipzig's principal churches in Bach's time:

Hymn: 'Da Jesus an dem Kreuze stund'
Passion (Part I)
Hymn: 'Herr Jesu Christ, dich zu uns wend'
Sermon
Passion (Part II)
Motet: *Ecce, quomodo moritur iustus* [Gallus]
Collect prayer
Biblical verse: 'Die Strafe liegt auf ihm' (Isaiah 53:5)
Hymn: 'Nun danket alle Gott'

not of course recover the way people experienced them at the time. Since they have proved that they can survive treatments as different as the old massed-choir Victorian rituals (with their strong whiff of sanctimoniousness) and, at the other extreme, the minimalist nostrums of historically informed practice (HIP) – and still move people – we can be certain there is no one definitive way of interpreting them, whether in church, in concert halls or within the secular embrace of the theatre. The search for the most effective ways to present these hugely demanding works – when, where and how, and to whom – has led, in many instances but by no means universally, to a timely abandonment of the starchy reverential rituals of oratorio performance, where once befrocked singers sat in a row at the front of a concert platform rising only to perform their solo numbers. One can understand why stage directors have wanted to deconstruct Bach's Passions and to explore different ways of experiencing these powerful music-dramas with their deep human undercurrents. That Bach chose to deploy not one but two orchestras and (momentarily) *three* choirs in his *Matthew Passion* is indicative of drama being intrinsic to the work. Yet to build on this and to treat either of his Passions as unfulfilled operas concerned with 'representation' of one sort or another runs up against many obstacles, such as trying to accommodate the mercurial switches of time and multiple characterisations that are implicit in their unusual structure. Such approaches are likely to give an enhanced sense of the singers' individual identities as biblical characters, whereas Bach's concern was to do the exact opposite, taking pains to transfer their emotional reaction to non-specific singers (who, let us remember, were out of sight to all except the richer pew-holders in the side galleries of the original venues) as they voice their grief, remorse or outrage while speaking on their own and our behalf. Similarly, the chorus – however skilfully they manage the rapid switches between their allotted roles as disciples, bystanders, soldiers or the baying mob and become meditative commentators in a trice – are liable to be seen in a dramatised treatment as belonging to a world *separate* from that of the audience.

The besetting danger here is the creation of a distraction from the mechanics and inexplicable force of the music, something Jonathan Miller managed to avoid in his revelatory 'activation' of the *Matthew Passion* (first given in London in 1993 and in many parts of the world since), doing just enough by spatial juxtaposition and separation (singers moving among and around the instrumentalists) to suggest different gradations of dialogue – now confrontational (as between separate choirs of believers and mobsters), now intimate, as when the singer of an aria and the obbligato player were placed in close proximity unencumbered by scores and music stands. My own approach is based on the conviction that a similar negotiation between action and meditation can be achieved equally well through a considered deployment of the musical forces in a church or on a conventional concert platform, without replacing one set of rituals with another. While many of us might rejoice at the passing of the old oratorio rituals as the cracking of a great ice floe of misplaced reverence, I see no overwhelming advantage – nor any inherent need – to define and localise the dramatic essence of Bach's Passions by staging them as proxy operas. On the contrary, the moment the drama is freighted with extraneous aesthetic baggage, it risks being flattened out and the music ends up diminished as a result. It is the intense concentration of drama *within* the music and the colossal imaginative force that Bach brings to bear in his Passions that make them the equal of the greatest staged dramas: their power lies in what they leave unspoken. We ignore that at our peril.

12
Collision and Collusion

Blest pair of sirens, pledges of Heav'n's joy,
Sphear-born harmonious Sisters, Voice, and Vers,
Wed your divine sounds, and mixt power employ
Dead things with inbreath'd sense able to pierce,
And to our high-rais'd phantasie present,
That undisturbèd Song of pure concent . . .
– John Milton, *At a Solemn Musick*

'People often complain that music is too ambiguous,' wrote Mendelssohn in 1842. Everyone understands words, of course, but listeners do not know what they should think when they hear music. 'With me,' he said, 'it is exactly the opposite, and not only with regard to an entire speech but also with individual words. These, too, seem to me so ambiguous, so vague, so easily misunderstood in comparison to genuine music, which fills the soul with a thousand things better than words. The thoughts which are expressed to me by music that I love are not too *indefinite* to be put into words, but on the contrary, too *definite*.'[1] It is a startling statement, one many musicians would subscribe to but the very opposite of what some others would expect. The relation of music to language is as complex as that of language to thought. Language can elucidate, but it can also throttle sensibility in the process of its transmission (see footnote on p. 29). Music, on the other hand, when it is performed, allows that channel of transmitted thought and sensibility to flow with total freedom: it might not be very good at expressing our everyday mundane transactions, but the thoughts it does express are conveyed more clearly and fully than they would be by words. So what happens when you put the two together – as has happened from the beginning of time until the latest pop song? Any opera or cantata by necessity places text and its musical voicing in a symbiotic relationship, one that creates both opportunities and constraints for the composer.

It is, I hope, obvious from the previous three chapters that in Bach we are dealing with a composer who was never satisfied just to 'set' religious texts, whether cantatas, motets or Passions. Emanuel Bach told Forkel that his father 'worked diligently, governing himself by the content of the text, without any strange misplacing of the words, and without elaborating on individual words at the expense of the sense of the whole, as a result of which ridiculous thoughts often appear, such as sometimes arouse the admiration of people who claim to be connoisseurs and are not'.[2] That may well have been the impression Emanuel wanted to give – that his father did not normally flout eighteenth-century conventions of text-setting. But the truth is that Bach's texted music is far from compliant: it opens the door to all-encompassing moods, which he evokes far more powerfully and eloquently than words could alone, particularly as his textures are so often multilayered and thus able to convey parallel, complementary and even contradictory *Affekts*. Poring over the texts that he set to music gives us the liturgical context but in itself tells us nothing reliable about the music or of course how it came to be formed in his imagination. With him we soon find music is far from being a neutral outer shell for the words it encases. Bach dealt with textual specificity – sometimes by reinforcing it with music of a parallel definiteness, sometimes by countering it with music of a competing and, in Mendelssohn's sense, superior definiteness. The words impart an extra dimension to the music and vice versa, so that their conjunction is greater than the sum of the individual parts; but even when music surrounds the text with a code of emphasis or matching mood it does not always fuse with language to achieve a perfect synergy. The process is either of collusion at one extreme or collision at another, or some combination of the two. There are of course many gradations in between, including a halfway house (perhaps the most interesting stage) where music seems to absorb a meta-textual component. This chapter highlights some of the more striking examples of Bach's wide-ranging practice in his cantatas and motets – instances where his approach was markedly different to that of his contemporaries, even laying him open to the charge of inappropriateness.

Though he never admitted as much, Bach might have recognised that he was somehow swimming against the tide of current fashions in church music, and that he was aiming at something way beyond that of other composers of his day. This is immediately clear if we compare his results to Telemann's when both are faced with setting an identical text, dating from a time (1708–12) during which the two were in regular contact: Bach in Weimar, Telemann – who gave his middle name to his godson C. P. E. Bach – in Eisenach. The comparison shows how radically their paths had already diverged. As one of the pioneers of the new cantata style founded by Erdmann Neumeister, Telemann was widely admired for his skill in grafting the techniques of contemporary opera on to the old cantata rootstock. The libretto of *Gleichwie der Regen* was even written specially for him by Neumeister in 1711, and his cantata based on it was performed in Eisenach shortly afterwards, and perhaps also in Weimar, where Telemann was held in high esteem by Bach's employer Duke Ernst August.

From the opening solo, in which Isaiah compares the seed (55:4–15), and the impact of the weather on its germination and growth, to the Holy Word, it is obvious that Bach's setting of 1713 (BWV 18) is going to be the more adventurous – and more excitable, too, at moments when he disregards the 'correct' declamation of the words. Where in the second movement the poet combines warnings of the dangers to God's Word in the style of a sermon with four lines of prayer from a litany by Luther, Telemann strives to blur the distinction between psalmody and speech-like recitative and to avoid extremes of expressivity, his music operating modestly as the mere handmaiden of the words. Bach does the exact opposite: relishing the contrast between archaic psalm tone (initiated by the soprano but completed by the full ensemble) and modern operatic recitative style (of which he shows total mastery, even though this is the first time he uses it), he sets his tenor and bass free to voice their personal pleas for faith and resolve in the face of 'devilish guile', with virtuosic displays of coloratura, ever-wider modulations and vivid word-painting on *berauben* ('to rob') and *irregehen* ('to wander off course'), while reserving the most extravagant fifty-five-note run for the word *Verfolgung* ('persecution'). In fact he turns this movement into the centrepiece of his work – a through-composed tapestry made up of four stretches of accompanied recitative, unique in his cantatas.

Where Telemann's instrumentation is the standard one of four-part strings, Bach's is improbable and strikingly original – four violas and basso continuo including a bassoon, bringing a magically dark-hued sonority to the overture and to later movements. The quick responsiveness of his music to the changing sentiments of the text allows him to describe, first, those who renounce the Word and 'fall away like rotting fruit' (in a decorated instrumental phrase, fluttering down) and, a moment later, how 'another man may only tend his belly'. All contribute to a lively Bruegel-like portrayal of rural society at work – the sower, the glutton, the lurking Devil, and some pantomime villains in the form of Turks and Papists. Typical of litanies, the linking passages are unvaried musically (might they contain a whiff of satirical fun-poking at the monotonous intoning of the clergy?), except for the continuo part, which goes ballistic at mention of the Turks and Papists 'blaspheming and raging'. With Telemann, on the other hand, we miss a sense of engagement with the text or of his using the full resources of music, as Bach does so masterfully, to lift it and its underlying message into his listener's consciousness with a huge increase in musical substance, subtlety and interest.

From his Weimar years onwards Bach's procedure in setting poetic commentary rarely fits into a conventional expository mode. His arias, for example, are seldom presented as a sermon of the time would have been, as ordered exegesis, and in shaping them to fit their particular context he takes liberties, following his own private logic. As Laurence Dreyfus has shown, 'he develops selective ideas from his texts that spark a dominating instrumental melody, but he also attaches signs, genres and styles foreign to the text that impose, by way of a kind of performance or execution of the text, an obscuring palimpsest on the poetry.'[13] Take the Easter cantata BWV 31, *Der Himmel lacht*, first performed in Weimar on 21 April 1715. Faced with a verse of undiluted dogma, beginning 'Adam must decay in us, if the new man shall recover', with no discernible emotion and no opportunity for word-painting, Bach sets in motion a pulsating full-blooded string texture suggestive more of rites of spring than of man's resolve to turn over a new leaf. This disregard for the rules of musical propriety would have been enough to make a pernickety theorist like Johann Mattheson wince – for, strictly speaking, the music is not the direct outcome of the text and it is certainly not set in sober syllabic style. It is an early instance of the collision that so often characterises Bach's response to the genre, and which gives the emerging music such lasting vitality. The way he addresses a given text or doctrinal theme and the personal, very human gloss he puts on it tell us a lot more about his character than the self-depreciating words about being 'obliged to be industrious' that he used to describe the permissive basis of his approach to composition. This simply cannot constitute the full story of someone of his stature. At the outset of this book I hinted that viewing Bach as some kind of subversive might provide a point of entry to an understanding of his achievement, which, in common with other great artists, was 'attuned to the most subtle manipulations and recasting of human experience'.[4] Here we are coming across instances that seem to substantiate that claim.

Abstract music provides us with emotions purified of prescribed narratives and untethered from any pressing reality. We get the sadness of loss without loss itself, the sensation of terror without any object of terror to which we have to respond, the luminescence of joy that melts away as we perceive it.[5] Something quite different occurs once music is conjoined with poetry, even poetry of low intrinsic value. At this point there is a delicate balance between sound and sense: the music now *becomes* the loss and the terror just as much as the words do. Paul Valéry called poetry 'a language within a language' – but isn't that also an accurate description of the way music and poetry negotiate with each other? The effect of music on verse goes beyond just adding a layer of *impasto*, thickening the physical presence of the words that convey meaning. It is the equivalent of metaphor: it puts a brake on the flow of speech and recited verse and sets it into a differently structured rhythm and tempo, one that if successful allows the listener to engage with the composer's own reading of the words.*

Theology is traditionally expressed through words, while music, Bach's habitual form of expression, obeys rules that override word-driven considerations – in procedures that Dreyfus shows to be quite

* Valéry saw music as constituting the ideal of poetry because of the way we experience musical works. In hearing music, he wrote, 'I am made to generate movements, I am made to develop the space of the third or fourth dimension, I have been communicated quasi-abstract impressions of balance, of moving of balance' (Paul Valéry, *Œuvres* (1960), Vol. 2, p. 704).

anti-literary at times.[6] In the interplay – even friction – between words and music in his church cantatas, a strong sense emerges of Bach reaching for the definitive, summative formulation of meaning.* In the process he seems constantly to be challenging his listeners to consider what it means to be a Christian (freighted with obligations as well as joys). He uses music both to draw new meanings out of the Gospel texts and to hint at others that occur to him, perhaps subconsciously, in the process of composing and performing.

The danger with Bach was always one of overload: he simply had too much to say – too much, at any rate, for the comfort of the waiting preacher – and too many different ways of saying it, supported by skills and techniques that were much greater than those of the majority of his peers. One suspects that this is what lay behind the strictures of less successful composers who had turned themselves into pundits, men such as Johann Adolph Scheibe and Johann Mattheson. Bach was one to push boundaries – boundaries of accepted taste, of what music could do to expand its formal and expressive vocabulary, of how it can convey human emotions, praise God and edify his neighbour, in excess of anything he himself had previously accomplished. Despite his limited geographical travels, like Shakespeare reaching out far beyond the borders of his own native experience, Bach transports us to places scarcely mapped and to regions far beyond the intellectual reach of his critics. Attacking him anonymously, Scheibe deplored Bach's habit of 'taking away the natural element in his pieces by giving them a bombastic and confused style', darkening their beauty with what he called 'an excess of art'. Furthermore, he took him to task for expecting 'that singers and instrumentalists should be able to do with their throats and instruments whatever he can play on the clavier'. To this Bach (via his spokesman

* It is as though on occasion he is tacitly agreeing with Beaumarchais's disreputable quip 'If a thing isn't worth saying, you sing it.' Beaumarchais was passionately fond of music and even ended his play *Le Mariage de Figaro* with the line *tout finit par des chansons*. Mozart took note. Rossini went even further. A composer, he said, 'should not bother about the words, except to see to it that the music suits them without, however, deviating from its general character. He will operate in such a way that the words are subordinate to the music rather than the music to the words . . . If the composer sets out to follow the meaning of the words with equal steps, he will write music that is not expressive by itself, but is poor, vulgar, mosaic-like, and incongruous or ridiculous.' Italian music had travelled a great distance away from Monteverdi and the old ideal of *prima la parola, dopo la musica* (see Chapter 4, pp. 104–5).

Abraham Birnbaum) countered, 'It is true that there are difficulties, but that does not mean that they are insurmountable': you just have to find solutions – so that singers and instrumentalists engaging in harmonious dialogue can give added significance to a simple reading of a text, and can 'work wonderfully in and about one another, but without the slightest confusion'.[7]

Bach, then, was up against not just the complacency of the style police of the day, but a fundamental misreading of his intentions and practice: his moving towards a radical re-working of the materials of music, his exploration of new ways for music and text to complement but also to rub up against each other, his fostering of an unprecedented interaction between his different singers and players, and finally his probing of the effects all this could have on the listener.[8] Naturally he would have resisted the kind of school-masterly approach epitomised by Mattheson's insistence that when 'instruments and voices collaborate, the instruments must not predominate'. Bach was unwilling to have his orchestra reduced to the role of a docile accompanist simply laying down material in an opening ritornello that the singer would later develop and embellish. On the contrary, for him the opening instrumental strains of a cantata are a bidding to enter an ordered world of rhythm and sounds separate from quotidian noise or daily life and thence to mesh with the singer in fruitful dialogue.

Mattheson would have none of this. 'Many a beautiful painting is obscured in this way when fitted with a gold carved frame which alone diverts the eye and detracts from the painting. Any connoisseur of painting will prefer to choose a dark over a bright frame. The same thing applies to instruments, which provide no more than a frame for the words set to music.'[9] Mattheson seems to hanker for a musician to be compliant in the same way that a painter gathers what he wishes to portray into a rectangle, frames it and brings it indoors, thereby domesticating the seeing eye so that the distance between the actual landscape and the viewer is widened. Strict obedience to the 'frame' in his cantata arias and choruses would have stemmed that flood of invention that brims over in Bach's music. With far greater ambition than that of any of his contemporaries, he binds a vast quantity of material together in ways that require – insist upon – our active attention and engagement. That does not turn him into a musical van Gogh or Howard Hodgkin, artists who paint right over the frame of their pictures; for, although he shrugged off concerns of propriety and public approbation, he is of course ultimately compliant to the strictures of form.*

We saw in Chapter 5 how in his very first church cantatas, BWV 4, 131 and 106, Bach was staking out new territory for music, using it both as a point from which to view the universe and as a kind of critical megaphone. By examining the music we can discern the delicate path he treads between a theologically dutiful underpinning of texts and an individual glossing of them – and a whole range of ambivalent gradations in between. We know that Bach's music does not fuse smoothly with language to create an integrated dramatic form such as we find in, say, the operas of Monteverdi or, much later, of Mozart. Instead, time after time, we encounter the peculiar dialectical relationship Bach seems to forge between his church music and the word – in particular the vernacular word, which since Luther's day had become so dominant in the German consciousness.† Bach has the knack of being able to vivify a doctrinal message and, when appropriate, of delivering it with a hard dramatic kick – and the next moment balancing this with music of an exceptional tenderness. He can both soften and humanise the frequent severity of the words while in no way diminishing their impact. He refuses to be cowed by the solemnity of the liturgy, willing to look behind the curtain of religion and, like any practised man of the theatre (which by any conventional definition of course he wasn't), ready to use

* In comparing the dynamics of painting and music, there is another aspect that immediately stands out. With painting the viewer is always free to pick out and scan features at will and not in some time-oriented fashion. Music, on the other hand, carries with it an innate obligation on the part of the listener to follow in real time (unless of course you are silently following it in the score): it does not permit the promiscuous dipping in and out that visual art does. Just as paintings offer us glimpses for their own purely visual sake, so music is available for listening as pure sound. But there is a difference: music creates an appetite for a resolution of a kind – that it can and will itself provide – something it shares with literature but not with painting. Without simplistic representation music presupposes an ability and willingness on the part of the listener to string together a succession of related events not dictated by the material world, nor in Bach's case by an artificial division of it between raw nature and total artifice (see John Butt, 'Do Musical Works Contain an Implied Listener?', JRMA, Vol. 135, Special Issue 1 (2010)).

† Dreyfus makes the pertinent observation: how 'music could be coaxed into a genuinely new form of commentary' – even a critique of his age and the music of the early Enlightenment in its 'facile hedonism' and the rejection (as well as cooption) of music as a branch of metaphysics (Laurence Dreyfus, *Bach and the Patterns of Invention* (1996), pp. 242–4).

wit and even satire if it helps to open his listeners to the realities of life, to the world and its ways.

'Meta-language' is the term sometimes used to describe language describing itself. Between the area I call 'collusion', where Bach's music is in effect compliant with the text, and 'collision', where it clashes with it directly, there is a middle state akin to what Walter Benjamin in a parallel context calls a 'dichotomy of sound and script':[10] here it can comment on, expand on, speculate about, agree or disagree with the text from a position of equality. That is what Bach sometimes does, and that is what interests me here.

* * *

The typical libretto of a Bach cantata has a moral that is fleshed out in a variety of forms. Take BWV 169, *Gott soll allein mein Herze haben*, composed in October 1726, the last and most consistently beautiful of his cantatas for alto solo. Here we find Bach approaching a text in his most collusive manner, formulating a rondo motif to match the motto-like phrase extrapolated from the Sunday Gospel (Matthew 22:34–46): 'God alone shall have my heart.' This simple idea (the *propositio* in rhetorical terms) provides the basis for an overarching unity, while permitting an implied dialogue between this figure – the repeated self-offering to the love of God – and the gloss (*confirmatio*) given to it by poet and composer. This is about as close as Bach ever came to a straightforward 'setting' of words, with music that matches every gesture and inflection of the text in front of him. Its mood of gently insistent piety, based on observing Christ's twin commandments – to love God and your neighbour – is in extreme contrast with his stern laying down of these laws in BWV 77 (see below, pp. 449–52). Almost as compliant is the hauntingly beautiful Christmas cantata BWV 151, *Süßer Trost, mein Jesus kömmt*. To match the solace of the words ('Sweet comfort: my Jesus comes, Jesus is now born'), Bach constructs the opening aria as a G major *siciliano* in $\frac{12}{8}$ marked *molt' adagio* for soprano, obbligato flute and strings, with an oboe d'amore doubling the first violins. His only gloss here is to imply by association and by means of this *berceuse* that it is the Virgin Mother herself singing a lullaby to her newborn child. Ineffably peaceful in mood, it contains musical anticipations of both Gluck and Brahms, while the arabesques of the solo flute suggest something folklike – perhaps Levantine or even Basque in origin. Any

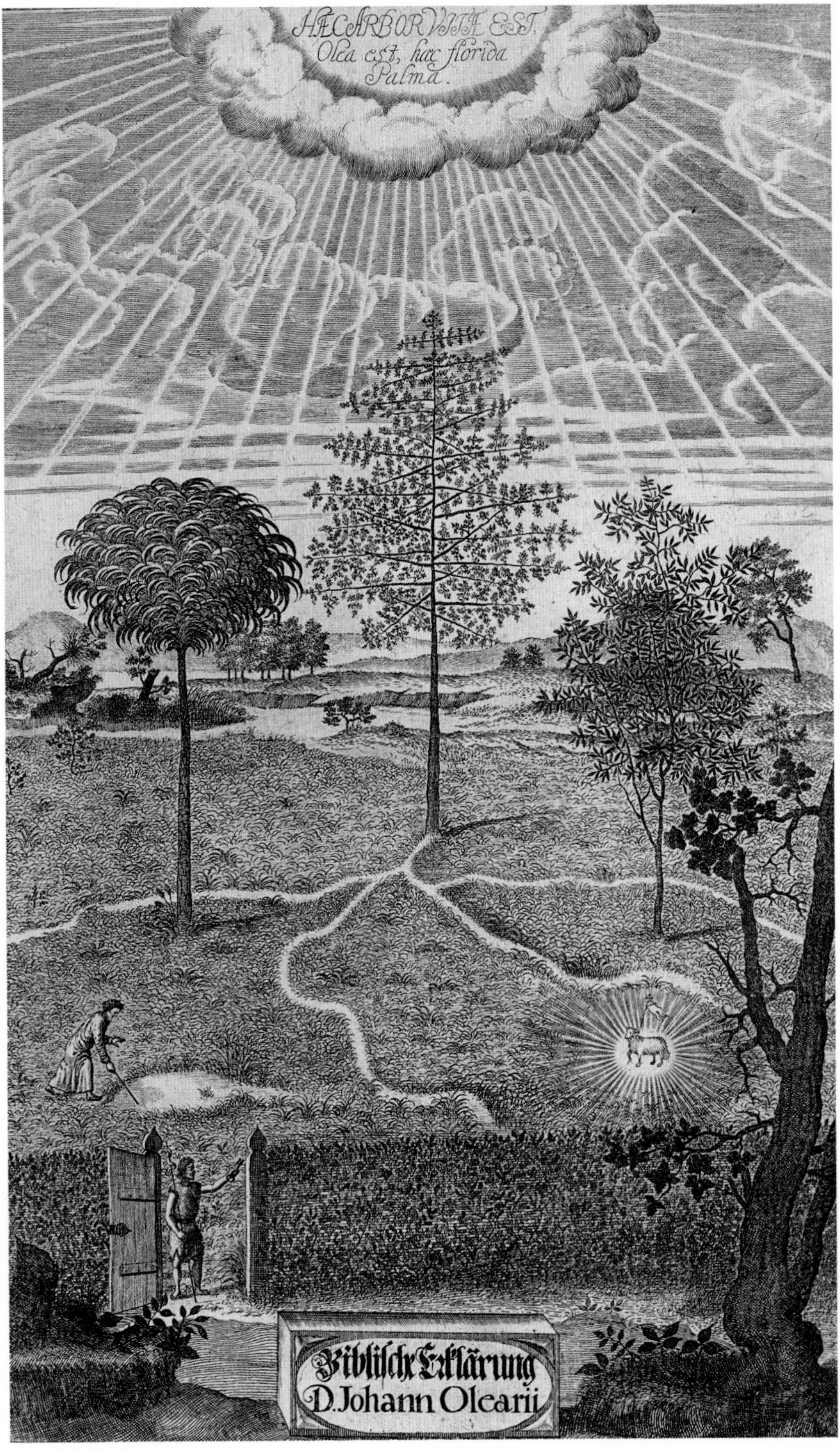

17. The Tree of Life
This image by Christian Romstet (1640–1721), with Jesus tending his garden, accompanies the *Biblische Erklärung* by Johann Olearius (1611–84), of which Bach owned a copy. Bach used learned counterpoint as a means of reflecting on the subject of death.

18. & 19. Elias Gottlob Haussmann: Two Portraits of Bach
Haussmann was the official painter to Leipzig's Town Council. Dating from 1746, the above is the first of only two fully authenticated portraits of Bach. Located in the Stadtmuseum, it has been restored at least four times: after layers of over-painting the canvas is a ruin and the original paint has disappeared in several places. The later and better preserved of the two portraits (*opposite*), was gifted to Emanuel Bach by his father in 1749. Listed in the catalogue of Emanuel's effects (*c.* 1798) it turned up in a curiosity shop in Breslau (*c.* 1820), and travelled to England in a rucksack (1936). For the past sixty years it has belonged to William H. Scheide, of Princeton, New Jersey.

Canon triplex à 6 Voc.
per J. S. Bach

20. Viola d'amore

This instrument, praised for its 'tender and languishing effect' (Mattheson), is by Sebastian Kloz of Mittenwald (1767). It has six playing strings supported by the curved bridge (more elliptical than that of a violin) and six 'sympathetic' strings threaded through the bridge and under the fingerboard. Bach's motif for the central aria in his *John Passion*  replicates the shape of the sacred rainbow, like the instrument itself.

21. Oboe da caccia
Played by Michael Niesemann, principal oboe of the English Baroque Soloists, this tenor 'oboe of the chase' is a copy of one made by J. H. Eichentopf in Leipzig around the time of Bach's arrival there as Thomascantor. It consists of a leather-covered wooden body ending in a flared brass bell. The bore and outward profiles are first created on the lathe; then a series of saw kerfs are made through the bore from the side, which becomes the inner curve. The instrument is then bent over steam and a slat glued on to the inside curve to hold it in place.

22. *Violoncello piccolo*

By A. & H. Amati, Cremona, *c.* 1600, played by David Watkin, principal cello of the English Baroque Soloists. By virtue of its fifth string, its distinctive lighter sound and wide-ranging agility, the cello piccolo allowed Bach, who was forever seeking out different ways of shaping the inner parts of his vocal and instrumental writing, to explore new sonorities in nine of his surviving church cantatas.

23. *Violoncello piccolo obbligato from* BWV 41 Jesu, nun sei gepreiset
Bach is concerned to convey the all-encompassing nature of Jesus as *Alpha and Omega* – hence his choice of the wide-spanning five-stringed cello piccolo in this tenor aria. Viewed purely as a graphic image Bach's handwritten part is a thing of extraordinary beauty; but it is also a wonderfully practical guide to the player – how to shape each musical gesture and phrase.

24. Mendelssohn watercolour of the Thomascantorei, 1838
Mendelssohn was gifted at everything he turned his hand to, including watercolours. He painted this view of the Thomasschule and Thomaskirche under snow during the same winter that as principal conductor of the Gewandhaus Orchestra he introduced a series of four 'historical concerts' – a brief history of music in sound. His advocacy of Bach can be traced back to 1823, when his maternal grandmother gave him a copyist's manuscript of the *Matthew Passion*, a score that seized his imagination and led him to conceive the idea of presenting this totally forgotten work in performance in 1829 in Berlin and in 1841 in Leipzig.

passing association with the musing Madonna is, however, quickly dispatched the moment the *vivace* B section bursts out in an ecstatic *alla breve* dance of joy, part gavotte, part gigue – 'Heart and soul rejoice.' Flute, soprano and the first violins (momentarily) exult in elegant triplet *fioriture* – similar in style and mood to the kind of secular music Handel wrote as a young man when he first encountered the works of Scarlatti and Steffani in Italy – before the opening cradle song returns. There is of course no reason why the Blessed Virgin should not have responded in this spontaneous girlish way, but it is not part of the biblical account of how 'Mary kept all these things, and pondered them in her heart' (Luke 2:19). Bach can hardly be faulted for making this passing link in the listener's mind, and indeed a strict, straight text-setting in this instance might have been as unenlightening – charming but trite – as the pastoral Christmas concertos of Italian composers of the time – Corelli, Manfredini and others – a miniature genre which Bach himself adopted and transformed in the introduction to Part II of his *Christmas Oratorio*.

Earlier, in his Weimar years, Bach had composed the first of several outstanding cantatas for a solo singer, BWV 199, *Mein Herze schwimmt im Blut*, a work that exhibits enough operatic know-how and sensibility to suggest that he may have had a particular opera singer in mind, one of a kind unknown in Weimar (where only falsettists were employed) – perhaps a diva such as Christine Pauline Kellner, who regularly trod the operatic stage in nearby Weissenfels as well as in Hamburg and Wolfenbüttel. What Bach gives us here is not so much a sermon as a portrayal of the complex psychological and emotional transformation of the conscience-struck individual. The underlying theological message based on the parable of the Pharisee and the publican (Luke 18:9–14) is still present but now couched in personal terms. A Christian consumed by self-horror and knowing that her sins have turned her 'into a monster in God's eyes' is racked by grief (opening accompanied recitative). Agony turns her dumb (A section of first aria); tears testify to her remorse (B section); a momentary flash of self-observation (extremely unusual C section interpolation in *secco* recitative) leads to a rhetorical outburst and a return to 'silent sighing' (A repeated). More self-immolation follows (*accompagnato*), culminating with the repentant cry of the publican in the parable: 'God have mercy upon me!' Next, without a break, comes an aria of deep humility and contrition (A), the confession of guilt (B) culminating in a plea for patience (tempo slowed to *adagio*) prior to a renewed expression of repentance (A repeated). This is the turning-point (a two-bar recitative). Now the sinner makes a further act of contrition, casting her sins into Christ's wounds (chorale). Henceforth this will be her resting place (*accompagnato*) whence she can sing an ode to joyful reconciliation (A), blessing (B) and renewed joy (A repeated).

What Bach is striving for here is a lucid presentation of the text, or rather of the ideas that lie behind it, offered to the listener from several vantage points and in a highly individual style of his own devising. Not for him the mechanical patter of contemporary operatic recitative; instead, he develops a musical declamation flexible enough to burgeon into arioso at moments of heightened significance and adjusted to the rise and fall of the verbal imagery. Every recitative acts as the spring-board to the following aria and thus to each change and expression of mood. Bach weaves such an amazingly vivid atmospheric web for each aria that words – even such overtly emotional ones as those written by Georg Christian Lehms – are not really needed to convey the specific *Affekt*. You could almost remove them and remain confident that the inflections and emotional contours would still be understood – which is almost what Bach himself does in the first aria, 'Stumme Seufzer'.

Faced with a text that postulates the limitations of verbal expression ('my mouth is closed'), Bach shifts the expressive burden on to the instruments, so that the oboe expresses the turmoil of the sighing soul through its poignant *cantilena* as eloquently as the voice, perhaps even more so. The emotional charge is then redoubled when the voice returns later to incorporate fresh material into the oboe ritornello, a technique known as *Vokaleinbau*. Again, Bach may have been subverting conventional operatic practice where the singer is the primary focus: the very fact that she is musically contextualised might have provoked religious criticism to such a secular convention. Similarly you do not need to know that the second aria begins 'Bent low and full of remorse I lie' when the melodic arch of the strings of this spacious sarabande suggests prostration so graphically and the stretching of its phrases across the bar-line conveys the gestures of supplication. The success of this strategy depends a great deal, of course, on the oratorical skill and empathy of the individual singer – the ability to touch and literally 'affect' the listener, and not by vocal pyrotechnics alone.

* * *

Bach's implanting of words and vocal material into an existing structure often results in a collusion of sensibility and emotional expression, but nowhere does he do it more impressively than in two contrasted works, one for Christmas, one for Jubilate (Easter + 3). The most festive and brilliant of Bach's Christmas Day cantatas is his third, BWV 110, *Unser Mund sei voll Lachens*, composed in 1725. Its opening movement is identical to that of the overture to the Fourth Orchestral Suite in D, BWV 1069, with the addition of a pair of flutes to the first oboe line. Here he takes its French overture structure (slow – quick – slow) and uses the ceremonial outer sections to frame the fast fugal segment, but with a four-part chorus newly worked into the instrumental fabric. As a paraphrase of Psalm 126 the piece emerges new-minted, alive with unexpected sonorities and a marvellous rendition of laughter-in-music, so different from the stiff, earnest way it is often played as orchestral music. When they are suddenly doubled, as here, by voices singing of laughter, instrumentalists have to re-think familiar lines and phrasing. Reciprocally, the singers need to adjust to the instrumental conventions of a French overture. To an existing structure with an already implied antiphony between separate instrumental groups Bach was later keen to add differentiated *concertante* effects. For one of the cantata's revivals (in either 1728 or 1731) he wrote out new *ripieno* parts for the upper three lines (the bass part is lost) so as to reinforce the contrast between solo and *tutti* sections. The whole piece has irresistible swagger, saved from degenerating into a peasant stomp by its elegance and lightness of touch.

This effect of illuminating a familiar original through engrafting was achieved still more impressively six months later. What started out as a violin concerto (now lost) and later took shape as the famous Concerto in D minor for clavier (BWV 1052) re-surfaces in the opening two movements of BWV 146, *Wir müssen durch viel Trübsal*, first performed at Jubilate in 1726. The first is an imposing introductory *sinfonia* (though it is not entirely obvious what such a vigorous and gritty concerto movement is doing here announcing the Gospel text 'We must through much tribulation enter the Kingdom of God'), and the second is a fully formed choral setting of those words superimposed on existing material, with both featuring the organist as soloist. In performance enormous restraint and control are required by both singers and players to sustain the hushed, otherworldly atmosphere of the latter movement over eighty-seven slow bars. This would be impressive enough as a piece of exceptionally clever implanting, if that is what it was, for we may never know for certain whether Bach had foreseen this particular solution at the outset, or whether, with the text in front of him, the possibility of a twin layering suddenly occurred to him, allowing him to anticipate many possible permutations of future moves.* As Glenn Gould said, 'The prerequisite of contrapuntal art, more conspicuous in the work of Bach than in that of any other composer, is an ability to conceive a priori of melodic identities which, when transposed, inverted, made retrograde, or transformed rhythmically, will yet exhibit, in conjunction with the original subject matter, some entirely new but completely harmonious profile.'[11]

* * *

We now turn to instances in Bach's multilayered approach in which music and text end up pointing in different directions, when instead of thoughts driving moods and emotions, moods and emotions suggested by music start driving thoughts, and as a result alter the way set ideas wear grooves in the mind. Bach's individual 'take' on the Gospel text, while it was intended to announce and bolster the sermon that it preceded, on occasion gave that sermon an alternative, unexpected slant. We have seen how rarely the musical setting of a cantata movement is driven exclusively by the semantic sense of the words. Instead, Bach often surrounds them with his own private code of emphasis, of matching *Affekts*. From a handful of cantatas that give the strongest sense of his music charting its own course at an oblique angle to that of the text, BWV 103, *Ihr werdet weinen und heulen*, stands out. We saw in Chapter 9 (p. 337) how its misleadingly festive opening is an example of a Bachian instrumental ritornello clashing with the sense of the text that follows, and how it can throw the listener off balance. A more conventional approach might have been to leave the antithesis of the two opening clauses intact with, say, a gloom-laden slow movement (as in BWV 12 and 146 for the same feast-day), followed by some form of chuckling *scherzo*. What Bach actually does is altogether astonishing. Anticipating by a century the 'Heiliger Dankgesang' of Beethoven's A minor string

* By this I mean the way, for example, the four vocal lines were liable to intersect with one another at certain moments, and at the same time collide with the right-hand embellishments of the organ solo in the concerto's *adagio* movement. Admittedly, Bach gave himself a wonderfully solid basis for the twin processes of invention and elaboration by means of an *ostinato* bass line heard six times in the course of the movement.

quartet, Op. 132, Bach plans to combine these opposite moods, binding them in mutual contingency while emphasising that it is the same God who both dispenses and then ameliorates these states of mind. Slowing abruptly to *adagio e piano* the bass soloist intones *Ihr aber werdet traurig sein* ('And ye shall be sorrowful') with sustained and tortured harmonies. Then, just when joy seems most distant, it comes bounding back with the return of the fugal subject, the earlier mock-festive theme now transformed into genuine delight – not just extraordinarily clever, but enlightening into the bargain.

There are numerous occasions when Bach's music provides a variety of interpretative twists that would not emerge from a simple reading of the text alone. In Chapter 9 (p. 329) we came across two bass cantata arias whose words imply a silver lining to the harshness of life, but where Bach's music nonetheless seems entirely sombre, impregnated with pain and an inconsolable sadness. Exactly three years from the start of his cantorship and for the important first Sunday after Trinity that marked the beginning of his first two Leipzig cycles, we find ourselves pitched into a world of natural disasters and charitable appeals: BWV 39, *Brich dem Hungrigen dein Brot*, was Bach's second use of a text from the court of Meiningen, where his cousin Johann Ludwig was employed. The Meiningen pattern entailed the quotation of two biblical texts: from the Old Testament for the opening movement, 'Deal [or break] thy bread to the hungry' (Isaiah 58:7–8), and from the New Testament, 'But to do good and to communicate forget not' (Hebrews 13:16), the common thread being an injunction to help the poor.

The opening chorus is multisectional and immense: at 218 bars it occupies more than a third of the whole cantata's length. Bach sets out almost tentatively in an introductory *sinfonia* with repeated quavers tossed from paired recorders to paired oboes to the strings and back over stiffly disjointed quavers in the continuo. German scholars from Spitta to Schering and Dürr claim that it 'unmistakably depicts the gesture of breaking bread'.*[12] Schweitzer rightly counters by saying that

* They base their interpretation on a literal interpretation of the first word, *brich*, from the German verb *brechen*, meaning to break, as opposed to 'deal', or the more metaphorically implied 'share' in English (or *partager* in French). The New English Bible (1970) gives the verse as 'Is it not *sharing* [my italics] your food with the hungry, taking the homeless poor into your house, clothing the naked when you meet them, and never evading a duty to your kinsfolk?'

'no one who listens to the music can take it to be a picture of the breaking of bread . . . it depicts the wretched ones who are being supported and led into the house.'[13]* That is certainly the image that comes to mind at the point when the choir enters after thirteen bars and from the way Bach pairs off his singers with broken phrases in thirds. Theirs are imploring gestures, emotionally choked, their pleas breaking and stuttering. This leads to sustained chromatic phrases – *und die, so im Elend sind* ('and those that are in misery'), then a semiquaver passage in thirds for *führe in's Haus* ('bring [in]to thy house') with weaving melismas. Just where you might expect an Oxfam appeal, you get the begging bowl itself. Bach writes his chorus not from the position of the Appeals Director but from that of the famine victim, in other words he is engineering a movable role for his choir – from members of a cast (here aligned in a famine queue) to biblical instructors laying down rules for appropriate, charitable behaviour.

The tenors now embark on a new condensed fugal theme with prominent A flats and D flats that has a pathos all of its own, especially when for eight bars it is joined in imitation by the altos. After ninety-three bars the time signature changes to common time. The basses begin unaccompanied with the words 'When thou seest the naked, cover him; and hide not thyself from thine own flesh' and are then answered by all voices and instruments very much in the old style of Bach's Weimar cantatas, with a florid counter-subject to suggest the 'clothing' of the naked. Clearly there has been a shift in the voices we are hearing: now no longer the hungry suffering, but the charity spokesmen. Bach is back to colluding again with the text. At bar 106 the time changes once more, this time to $\frac{3}{8}$ (again a Weimar feature) as the tenors lead off in the first of two fugal expositions separated by an interlude with a coda. The sense of relief after the stifling pathos of the opening sections is palpable

* This interpretation does not automatically turn this into Bach's 'Refugee Cantata' as some have maintained by linking it to a service to mark a cause célèbre – the banishing of around 22,000 Protestants from Salzburg by its archbishop in 1732 and their move to Prussia as part of King Frederick William I's *Peuplierungspolitik* (see Tim Blanning, *The Pursuit of Glory: Europe 1648–1815* (2007), p. 88). The cantata was first performed six years earlier, in June 1726, though it is conceivable, as Dürr makes clear, that this cantata could have 'found a new purpose . . . anticipated by neither librettist nor composer' when it was revived in 1732 (Dürr, *The Cantatas of J. S. Bach* (2005), p. 394).

and comes to a sizzling homophonic conclusion with *und deine Besserung wird schnell wachsen* ('and thy health shall spring forth speedily'). The basses now instigate a second fugal exposition, and, after so much pathos, the final coda led by the sopranos, *und die Herrlichkeit des Herrn wird dich zu sich nehmen* ('and the glory of the Lord shall be thy reward'), releases the pent-up energy in an explosion of joy.

Coming as the climax of a series-within-a-cycle in his first *Jahrgang*, BWV 77, *Du sollt Gott, deinen Herren, lieben*, was an opportunity for Bach to give resounding, conclusive expression to the core doctrines of faith already adumbrated in the first four Sundays of the Trinity season. His aim is to demonstrate by means of every musical device available to him the centrality of the two 'great' commandments of the New Testament and how 'on these two commandments hang all the law and the prophets'. This leads him to construct a huge chorale fantasia in which the chorus, preceded by the upper three string lines in imitation, spells out the New Testament statement. At this point he decides to encase the sung New Testament Commandments with a wordless presentation of the Lutheran chorale melody 'Dies sind die heilgen zehn Gebot' ('These are the holy Ten Commandments') to demonstrate how the entire Law is contained within the commandment to love. Calculating that he can count on his listeners to make the link between tune and text, he introduces it in canon, a potent symbol of the Law, between the *tromba da tirarsi* (slide trumpet) at the top of his ensemble and the continuo at its base – a graphic device to demonstrate that the Old Testament serves as the bedrock of the New, or rather that the entire Law is understood to frame, and be inseparable from, Jesus' injunction to love God and one's neighbour.

That is just the start. Bach then proceeds to extrapolate the vocal lines from the chorale theme so that they emerge audibly in what is a retrograde inversion of the chorale tune in diminution. One way to grasp his procedure is to imagine it as a giant Caucasian *kilim*, with the geometric design and decorative patterning all of a piece. Your eye is drawn first to the elegant weave of the choral lines, but you then begin to discern a broader outline – the same basic design, but on a far bigger scale, bordering the whole and with its pattern developing in the opposite direction. That is the equivalent of the canon in augmentation, the bass line proceeding at the lower fifth at half-speed (in minims), symbol of the fundamental Law. Bach's construct allows the trumpet (in crotchets) to deliver nine individual phrases of the chorale and symbolically, in a tenth, to repeat the entire tune for good measure, so that at the climax of the movement the 'old' and the 'new' are unambiguously fused in the listener's mind.*

The strange thing is that whenever the chorale tune stops (in fact even before it gets going) the music reveals a searching, almost fragile quality – a quiet innocent introit without the usual eight-foot bass. Then comes a loud stentorian entry of the commandment theme (guaranteed to grab the attention of his congregation, you would think) and the choral voices thunder out 'Thou shalt love the Lord thy God' like so many evangelising sculptors chiselling the words out of the musical rock face. Suddenly a huge chasm in pitch, structure and dynamics opens up between the gentle interweaving of the imitative contrapuntal lines and the full, impressive weight of the double canon. Some find it helpful to hear this emphatic representation of height and depth as a spatial metaphor for the divine and human spheres – distant, yet interconnected. Beyond the obvious meshing of Old and New Testament commandments, the former strict in its canonic treatment, the latter freer and more 'human' in the working through of its vocal lines, is the symbolic separation of God's control of the spheres of 'above' and 'below' (five statements of each, making ten in all). The music at this point is stupendous, the voices first in downward pursuit, then in upward, under the canopy of the trumpet's final blast of the chorale tune. This is one of those breathtaking, monumental cantata openings that defies rational explanation. The end result is a potent mixture of modal and diatonic harmonies which leaves an unforgettable impression and propels one forwards to the world of Brahms's *German Requiem* and beyond, to Messiaen's *Quartet for the End of Time* – both overpowering works in which their very different music takes on Bach's mantle of extending the biblical message through music to answer to the ultimate questions of fear and faith.

* The tune itself, at least thirteenth century in origin, began as a pilgrimage hymn to the words *In Gottes Namen fahren wir*, chosen by Luther, or those close to him, as an appeal to God for protection, particularly at the start of a sea voyage in which Christ was the chosen captain or pilot. Other than BWV 80, *Ein feste Burg*, no other canonic treatment of a *cantus firmus* in a Bach cantata has quite the same air of monumentality or hieratic authority as this.

What follows is a meditation on how ineffectual the believer's will proves to be when attempting obedience to God's commandments, and a foretaste of eternal life. Deceptive in its apparent simplicity and intimacy, an aria for alto is couched in the form of a sarabande, its weak phrase-beginnings and feminine cadences holding up a mirror to man's proneness to fall short. As a foil to the singer, Bach decides at this point to recall his principal trumpet – so assured and majestic in the opening chorus, but now single and unsupported except by continuo alone. His role here is to convey human imperfection (*Unvollkommenheit*) in the baldest terms. If he had set out to write an obbligato melody for the natural (or valveless) trumpet, Bach could hardly have devised more awkward intervals and more wildly unstable notes – recurrent C sharps and B flats, and occasional G sharps and E flats, which either do not exist on the instrument or else emerge painfully out of tune. In other words Bach is putting on display the shortcomings and frailty of mankind for all to hear and perhaps even to wince at.

To be the agent for illustrating the distinction between God (perfect) and man (flawed and fallible) is a tough ordeal for any musician unless you are a sad, white-faced clown, accustomed to playing your trumpet (badly) at the circus. But before jumping to the conclusion that Bach is being sadistic here, we should look beyond the surface of the music. Richard Taruskin claims that on occasion he 'seems deliberately to engineer a bad-sounding performance by putting the apparent demands of the music beyond the reach of his performers and their equipment'.[14] For that to be true, Bach would have had to allow for no remedial action to be available to his trumpeter using his large mouthpiece to 'bend' or 'lip down' (or 'up') the non-harmonic tones so as to make them slightly more acceptable, or to ask him to play the part on a *tromba da tirarsi* such as he often calls for in other contexts. The point is the *effort* Bach is concerned to illustrate as part of the music,[15] and then, in blatant contrast, the *ease* with which, in the B section of the aria, he coasts through a ten-bar solo of ineffable beauty made up entirely of the diatonic tones of the natural trumpet without a single accidental: like some gleaming aircraft he emerges from a cloud bank into pure sunlight. Suddenly we are permitted a glorious glimpse of God's realm, an augury of eternal life, in poignant juxtaposition to the believer's sense of difficulty, incapacity, even, in executing God's commandments unaided.* The device might be a bit drastic, but it is brilliantly effective. It requires the in-built unevenness of the natural trumpet to make its impact, which is simply lost when played on a modern chromatic valved trumpet. This is just a single example of the advantages historical instruments can bring to Bach performances. The techniques he uses in this cantata are extreme in their sophistication – in the first chorus by laying down the Law and in this aria by presenting the harsh dichotomy between God's perfection and man's efforts to imitate it. We are left wondering how an over-worked church musician, locked into numbing routines, could have come up with anything so inventive – and not as an isolated work but, as we saw in Chapter 9, as part of a coherent and highly impressive cantata cycle.

* * *

What can have spurred Bach to invent music of such density, vehemence and highly charged originality that it holds us spellbound? It is a question that has exercised scholars from the very beginning. Was it genuine religious fervour and the kind of single-minded dedication he exhibits on his title pages and in signing off each cantata with 'SDG' ('To God alone the Glory'), or rather his innate sense of drama and an imagination instantly fired by strong verbal imagery?† You feel you know the answer – that it was sometimes one and sometimes the other – then along come the latter-day theologians sure of identifying an encoded doctrinal message embedded in the cantatas, and close on their heels the

* According to the seventeenth-century German theorist Andreas Werckmeister, whose works were known to Bach, there was a crucial theological distinction between the pure diatonic scale of the *clarino* octave (composed of harmonic numbers and musical consonances), which he interpreted as 'a mirror and prefiguration of eternal life', and those chromatic departures from it which reflect, allegorically, man's fallen state. In other words what we loosely refer to as 'Baroque' music, from the moment it set out to affect and stir the emotions (*Gemütsbewegung*), had, in Werckmeister's theologically coloured view, imperfection embedded in it in terms of 'tempered' intervals. One has only to think of the bass aria 'The trumpet shall sound' from *Messiah* to appreciate how Handel, too, used the natural, God-designed properties of the trumpet and the prevalence of octaves and fifths to express the final stage in human redemption through Christ (see Ruth Tatlow, 'Recapturing the Complexity of Historical Music Theories', Eastman Theory Colloquium, 28 Sept. 2012).

† By no means confined to Bach; musicians of the time used this phrase quite widely to round off their church compositions; according to Heinrich Bokemeyer (1679–1751), 'in their hearts they think *Soli Musico Gloria*, which in reality means *soli carni, mundi & diabolo victoria*' (reported in Mattheson, *Critica musica* (1722), Part 4, Section 26, p. 344).

sceptics who insist that we forget all about religion when we interpret Bach, or literal-minded musicians who insist on keeping their music and Scripture separate. But even if we assume that Bach's Lutheran zeal was sincere (and there are no grounds to believe that it wasn't), does that automatically turn him into a theologian or mean that these cantatas must be interpreted in predominantly theological terms? Surely not: as we have already seen, theology is expressed primarily through words, while Bach's natural form of expression and his musical procedures have their own logic, one that overrides word-driven considerations. Yet Gottfried Ephraim Scheibel, for example, insisted that 'anyone who wants to compose sacred poetic texts must be a good theologian and moralist. For it does not just depend on one's notions; they must also be in accord with Scripture. Otherwise our music in church will consist of empty words that, like empty shells, have no kernel, and it will be mere noise in which God takes no pleasure. A spirit-filled text and a moving composition must be combined.'[16]

However, we should not condone the tendency of theologically motivated commentators to treat the cantatas as doctrinal dissertations, as opposed to discrete musical compositions, any more than accept the glee with which aggressive atheists try to debunk any theological basis for Bach's musical exegesis. In the final analysis nothing can gainsay or diminish the overwhelming transformative force of Bach's music, the very quality that makes his cantatas so appealing to Christians and non-believers alike. When we are presented with thoughts and feelings in music, with far more candour, clarity and depth than we would otherwise be capable of, this can bring a huge sense of relief. We might at first feel preached at or lectured, and resist. But you realise that you can let go – you are not being obliged to subscribe to a doctrine, for Bach's approach, even at his most vehement, is not a moral fitness programme imposed on us *de haut en bas*. Instead, the defining quality lies in how he conveys his understanding of exactly what it is to be human – with all our faults, fears and blind spots – interpreting the word to us like a great novelist, capturing the sense of life itself.*

* * *

* Where the author and poet Blake Morrison uses these and other, similar words to describe the effect of poetry on the reader, others might make equivalent claims for the novel.

There are times, however, when Bach's musical treatment is so compliant and so close to collusion it feels as though he has decided to follow for a change the admonitions of contemporary music theorists – to 'grasp the sense of the text' (M. J. Vogt, 1719), with the goal of 'refined and text-related musical expression [being] the true purpose of music' (J. D. Heinichen, 1711). But, just when you sense their vote of approval, Bach takes the law into his own hands and creates extreme contrasts of *Affekt* in successive movements of a single cantata, guaranteed to startle and perhaps sow confusion in the minds of his listeners.

BWV 78, *Jesu, der du meine Seele*, opens with an immense choral lament in G minor, a musical frieze on a par with the exordia of both his Passions for scale, intensity and power of expression. Bach casts it as a *passacaglia* on a chromatically descending *ostinato* with the 'ground' acting as a counter-balance to a hymn tune, and weaves all manner of contrapuntal lines around it. Where you might expect the three lower voices to provide a respectful accompaniment to the *cantus firmus*, Bach gives them unusual prominence, mediating between *passacaglia* and chorale, anticipating and interpreting the chorale text just as the preacher of a sermon might do. Indeed, such is the power of exegesis here, one questions whether Bach was once again inadvertently stealing the preacher's thunder by the eloquence of his musical oratory. It is one of those opening cantata movements in which you hang on every beat of every bar in a concentrated, almost desperate attempt to dig out every last morsel of musical value from the notes as they come within earshot.

Not in one's wildest dreams, then, could one envisage a more abrupt sequel to this noble opening chorus than the delicious, almost frivolous duet that follows – 'Wir eilen mit schwachen, doch emsigen Schritten' ('We hasten with weak but diligent steps'). Any straightforward reading of the text itself would not suggest a piece of such irreverence and frip-

Mikhail Bakhtin, for instance, in his essay 'Discourse in the Novel' (1934–5), suggests that, unlike all other genres which are in some way fixed and completed, the novel always brings with it the sense of a new era and comprises a living utterance which 'cannot fail to brush up against thousands of living dialogic threads' in any particular present (*The Dialogic Imagination* (1975), p. 276). Most tellingly, John Butt relates these observations to the church music of Bach, proposing that as listeners we experience a cantata or Passion 'more like a novel in sound than a straightforward theatrical representation'. Bach 'managed to combine traditional operatic practice with the type of active participation he would have presumed of a Lutheran congregation, thus engineering the experience as a way of cultivating faith' (*Bach's Dialogue with Modernity* (2010), p. 189).

pery: you expect something dutiful, and instead you get a playful romp. With its *moto perpetuo* cello obbligato there are echoes of Purcell ('Hark the echoing air') and anticipations of Rossini. Bach's wizardry encourages you to smile, tap your foot or nod in assent to the plea 'May thy gracious countenance smile upon us.'

The reprieve is only temporary, however. With the tenor's recitative, unusually marked to begin *piano*, we are back to the Miltonian concept of 'leprous sin', which Bach expounded in several other post-Trinitarian cantatas. The vocal line is angular, the expression pained and the word-setting exemplary: almost an extension of Peter's remorse in the *John Passion*, which he had introduced to his audience six months earlier. Redemption lies through the shedding of Christ's blood, and, in the aria with flute obbligato (No. 4), the tenor claims confidently that, though 'all hell should call me to the fight, Jesus will stand beside me that I may take heart and win the day.' We might expect a trumpet, or at the very least the full string band, to evoke this battle with the forces of evil, but Bach is more subtle. What interests him more is the capacity of the flute's graceful figuration to erase or 'strike through' man's guilt, and, by adopting a catchy dance-like tune, to paint the way faith can cleanse the soul and make 'the heart feel light again'. For the *vivace* section of an *accompagnato* ('When a terrible judge lays a curse upon the damned'), Bach instructs his bass to sing *con ardore* – 'with passion'. For this is passion music with both a small and a capital *P*, strikingly similar in technique, mood and expressivity to the *John Passion* and to that other inimitable setting of the words in 'Es ist vollbracht' from BWV 159 (see Chapter 9 p. 335fn.). Passion in a Bach performance is a rare commodity in today's climate of antiquarian purity and musicological correctness, but its absence jars with the miracle of Bach's technical expertise, his mastery of structure, harmony and counterpoint, and his having imbued them with such vehemence, meaning and – exactly that – passion.

Though we are accustomed by now to Bach's original, dramatic and sometimes wayward settings of words to music, we occasionally stumble across a movement that seems misconceived or indicative of a rare lapse of concentration. Take the melody of the soprano aria 'Lebens Sonne, Licht der Sinnen' from BWV 180, *Schmücke dich, o liebe Seele*, for instance. It starts out attractively, but after nineteen consecutive bars in which the singer continues to repeat the same words over and over again

('Sun of life, light of the mind'), it risks becoming unbearable. The aria 'Ich bin herrlich, ich bin schön' from BWV 49, *Ich geh und suche mit Verlangen*, is not much better. It feels like an early draft of 'I feel pretty, oh, so pretty' from *West Side Story*; but, unlike Bernstein's (and unlike, say, 'Nur ein Wink' from the *Christmas Oratorio*, where one welcomes each repetition), Bach's tune does not have enough intrinsic interest beyond a certain surface attraction to warrant so many repetitions of the same words. In BWV 134, *Ein Herz, das seinen Jesum lebend weiß*, faced with the task of 'parodying' one of the most joyous of his Cöthen cantatas, Bach first had the vocal parts of the original copied out without text; then he wrote in the new 'sacred' words himself, note for note, making a few adjustments to the music as he went along. Obviously rushed or distracted, the recitatives (normally exemplary in their word-setting) suffered the most; indeed they give the impression of having been completed in his sleep. It was not until seven years later that he sat down to repair the damage, composing entirely new recitatives for three numbers and covering over the old incriminating pages.

* * *

One way Bach found to get around the rules and constraints of word-setting was to select an overall idea from the text that sparked the idea of a dominating instrumental sonority in his imagination. He came to know, for example, exactly how best to use the resources of the ceremonial trumpet-led orchestra and choir of his day to convey unbridled joy and majesty without knowing scientifically that the trumpet's upper partials have a stimulating effect on the nervous system of the listener. Clearly he was spurred on by the presence in Leipzig of the municipal Stadtpfeifer, a virtuoso group of trumpeters under their *Capo*, Gottfried Reiche, who were available to him to augment his Thomaner on high days and holidays, and from whom he could have learnt what melodic possibilities these instruments held, both singly and contrapuntally, beyond their basic rhythmic role within a martial band. One has only to think of the high trumpet writing in any of the choruses of the *B minor Mass* to realize what a potent and enthralling power this put at Bach's disposal. From the *Sanctus* we can tell that Bach conceived of a cosmos charged with an invisible presence made of pure spirit, beyond the reach of our normal faculties. As incorporeal beings, angels had their rightful place in the hierarchy of existence: in Psalm 8, humanity is ranked 'a little lower than the angels'. The concept of a heavenly choir of trumpet-blowing angels was implanted in Bach when he was a schoolboy in Eisenach. Even the hymn books and psalters of the day gave graphic emblematic portrayal of this idea. The role of angels, Bach was instructed, was to praise God in song and dance, to act as messengers to human beings, to come to their aid and to fight on God's side in the cosmic battle against evil. The dazzling cluster of cantatas Bach composed to honour the archangel Michael is immense in its sustained bravura.*

Michaelmas must have come as a welcome relief during the Trinity season, with its prevalence of gloomy, sin-related themes. Take the opening of BWV 130, *Herr Gott, dich loben alle wir* – a song of praise and gratitude to God for creating the angelic host. Bach presents us with a tableau of the angels on parade: these are celestial military manoeuvres, some of them even danced, in preparation for combat. In the cantata's centrepiece – a C major bass aria scored exceptionally for three trumpets, drums and continuo – the battle is portrayed not as a past event but as an ever-present danger from 'the ancient dragon [who] burns with envy and keeps contriving new pain' intended to break up Christ's 'poor little flock'. Though there is brilliance aplenty in the steely glint of Michael's sword (including fifty-eight consecutive semiquavers for the principal trumpet to negotiate – twice), this is not an episode in a *Blitzkrieg*. Bach is more concerned to evoke two superpowers squaring up to one another: the one vigilant and poised to protect the *armes Häuflein* (the 'poor little flock') against assault (cue for a *tremulant* throbbing of

* Michael the archangel (the name means 'who is like God') is one of the few figures to appear in the Old and New Testaments, the Apocrypha and the Koran. He appears as protector of the children of Israel (Daniel 12:1), inspiring courage and strength, and was venerated both as the guardian angel of Christ's earthly kingdom and as patron saint of knights in medieval lore. Michael is acknowledged in Christian lore as being responsible for ensuring the safe passage into heaven of souls due to be presented before God. Hence the offertory prayer in the Catholic Requiem Mass *sed signifer sanctus Michael repraesentet eas in lucem sanctam* – 'May the holy standard-bearer Michael bring them into the holy light.' First established under the Roman Empire sometime in the fifth century, Michaelmas (*Michaelisfest*) was an important church feast, as it was one of the traditional quarter-days on which rents were levied and agreed in northern Europe, the start of the new agricultural year for many people and, in Leipzig, the day of one of its three annual trade fairs. When Lucifer, highest of the Seraphim, led a mutiny against God, he became transmogrified into the Devil, appearing either as a serpent or as a ten-headed dragon. Michael, at the head of God's army in the great eschatological battle against the forces of darkness, was the key figure in his rout.

all three trumpets in linked quavers); the other wily and deceitful (perhaps the kettledrums and continuo are intended to be on the dragon's side and not part of Michael's army, as in BWV 19 (see Chapter 3, p. 73)). Probably no composer before or since has written such a profusion of celestial music for mortals to sing and play – and no one could show off a trio of trumpets to such dazzling effect as Bach.

The prospect of joining the angelic choir or concert after death was considered to be a privileged entry-point for German musicians of the time (see p. 553). It is a mirror of Bach's own deep faith as well as his strategies, conscious or not, for bridging in music the gulf between this world and the next, and thereby enriching the listener's experience. Such strategies hinge on his use of certain specific sonorities such as the use of high trumpets or drums in the instances just alluded to, but equally on the evocation of certain states of mind – fragility at the point of death, or how to deal with bereavement. It is in this context that Keats's famous formulation of negative capability has special pertinence – 'when a man is capable of being in uncertainties, mysteries, doubts, without any irritable reaching after fact and reason'. Keats's rationalisation of the subjective allows joy and uncertainties to coexist, and provides an unintended denotation of the effect on the listener of Bach's consoling music. To penetrate to the great riches it offers requires both relaxation and effort, an absence of wilful straining but the most lucid attentiveness. It needs the listener both to let go and to be supremely vigilant. Ted Hughes once said that writing was about facing up to what we were too scared to face – about saying what we would prefer not to say, but desperately needed to share. That is also the cathartic function of Bach's cantatas that deal with the art of dying: their effect is that we are enabled to face the unfaceable.

* * *

It so happens that all four of Bach's cantatas for Trinity + 16 (BWV 161, 27, 8 and 95) give voice to the Lutheran yearning for death and the release of the body from worldly cares, struggles and bitterness. All but one feature the tolling of funerary bells known as *Leichenglocken*, which in Bach's day stood for the passing of the soul and evoked its hourly commemoration. Together they make a deeply impressive quartet of concerted music that is both healing and uplifting. Despite their unity of theme, they are nonetheless full of creative tension, and feature divergent treatments of the convergence of music and words, and of texture, structure and mood. For the earliest of them, BWV 161, *Komm, du süße Todesstunde*, Bach uses a restricted palette of unusually soft-toned instrumentation led by two treble recorders (just as in the *Actus tragicus*) braced mostly in thirds or sixths. They are the leading colouristic element in the extraordinary *scena* that forms the cantata's central movement, in which the believer (in an accompanied recitative for alto), having arrived at the end of his spiritual pilgrimage, stands poised on the verge of death. Each textual image is replicated in the music: the 'gentle sleep' of the soul sinking to rest in Jesus' arms is represented by a descending scale motion by the voice, the continuo and the two recorders, in that order; simple detached chords suggest the 'cool grave' covered with roses; sudden animated semiquaver activity describes the raising from the dead and the closing in of 'the happy day', when the desire for death turns to joy; and the tolling of miniature death-bells marks the 'final hour', punctuated by the sounding of all four of the violin's open strings.

Two of its movements are in triple time, setting a pattern for several of Bach's later cantatas that also deal with the call of death – a device to lull and soothe the grieving heart, as in the magical opening chorus of BWV 27, *Wer weiß, wie nahe mir mein Ende*, an elegiac lament into which Bach has woven the modal tune linked to Neumark's hymn 'Wer nur den lieben Gott lässt walten'. The passage of time is suggested by the slow pendulum strokes in the bass of the orchestra. Against this the downward falling figure in the upper strings and a poignant broken theme in the oboes provide the backcloth for the haunting chorale melody, interlaced with contemplative recitative. Even the harpsichord obbligato and continuo line of the alto aria seem to be imbued with the notion of measured time emphasised by the percussive articulation of the harpsichord keys, a recurrent feature in these death-knell cantatas.

An equally evocative tableau in sound, almost of a passing funeral cortège, is created by purely instrumental means at the start of BWV 8, *Liebster Gott, wenn werd ich sterben*, consisting of an almost continuous semiquaver movement in E major for two oboes d'amore, a muted staccato quaver accompaniment by the upper strings, and a pizzicato bass line punctuating the slow $\frac{12}{8}$ pulse. Soaring above this is the high tintinnabulation of the traversa flute, playing out of its normal range – and so different from the simulated clang of multisized bells he summons to mark the passing of Queen Christiane in the *Trauer-Ode*, BWV 198 (see

Chapter 7, p. 220). An elegiac and iridescent tenderness is established in this movement before even a note has been sung, which gives the impression of someone approaching life's end, witnessing the procession of his own family of mourners. If at times the oboe writing brings to mind the music of Brahms, some of the harmonic progressions anticipate Berlioz's *L'Enfance du Christ*; and Bach gives an almost fairground swing to the entry of the hymn tune sung by the sopranos. The funeral bells return (at least by inference) in the detached quavers of the tenor aria with the words *wenn meine letzte Stunde schlä-ä-ä-ä-ä-ä-gt*, and in the pizzicato continuo.

Bach's imaginative capacity to convey through music and words the final stretch of the Christian pilgrimage reaches a peak in the second part of the opening chorus of BWV 95, *Christus, der ist mein Leben*. Here he depicts the struggle between the forces of life and death before the soul reaches its longed-for destination. It is similar to the climax of John Bunyan's *Pilgrim's Progress*, when Christian 'passed over, and all the trumpets sounded for him on the other side'. Bach uses four successive funeral hymns as the supporting pillars of his structure, giving encouragement to the (tenor) believer as he contemplates his death. The rather muscular syncopated opening exchanges between paired oboes and violins pulsate with vitality and pave the way for the first triple-rhythm chorale. This dissolves at the word *sterben* ('to die'), a voice-by-voice entry building up a diminished seventh chord, coming to a rest and then re-exploding with *ist mein Gewinn* ('is my reward'). This culminates with the line *mit Freud fahr ich dahin* as the connecting link to the next chorale, Luther's paraphrase of the *Nunc dimittis*.

Binding the two chorale statements is an arioso, 'Mit Freuden, ja, mit Herzenslust will ich von hinnen scheiden' ('With gladness, yea, with joyful heart I shall depart from hence'). Bach is highly experimental in the way he breaks up these segments of free rhythm, holding them in check by interjecting fragments of the opening syncopated motif. You gain the impression of a succession of unsanctioned $\frac{7}{4}$ bars (recitatives of the time were always barred in common time). At its climax the tenor sings unaccompanied 'My dying words are on my lips' – silence – 'Ah, could I but this day sing them!' With no break whatsoever the dialogue between *corno* and oboes announces the second chorale, Luther's ebullient 'Mit Fried und Freud'.*

* When I first heard the cantata, in the late 1960s, in a Karl Richter performance, I was struck by Bach's utterly original combination of *corno* and oboes locked together in a

At its conclusion the soprano soloist bursts in with the exclamation 'Now, false world! Now I have nothing further to do with you.' This leads, also without a break, into a captivating arched melody, 'Valet will ich dir geben, Du arge, falsche Welt' ('I would bid you farewell, you evil, false world'). The only true aria in this cantata is one for a high-flying tenor – the mesmerising 'Ach, schlage doch bald, selge Stunde' ('Ah, strike then soon, blessed hour') – in which two oboes d'amore proceed in almost naked fourths, pausing every now and again to alight on a dissonance (the effect is similar to the way the echo of cracked bells hangs in the air) always accompanied by a persistent pizzicato of the *Leichenglocken*.

But what exactly do they represent? Are they simply symbols introduced to resonate in his listeners' minds, non-verbal means to trigger rhythmic patterns and sonorities in the aural imaginations of the bereaved? Following performances we gave of all four of these cantatas in Santiago de Compostela in 2000, there was a big discussion in the hotel bar among the performers as to the meaning and imagery suggested by these *Leichenglocken*. Some felt that the repeated quavers of the flute in BWV 161/iv and in BWV 8/i just stand for the high-pitched funeral bells associated with infant death – that and no more. Others were convinced that the music in that aria from BWV 95/v represents the workings of a clock, the tenor waiting for the chiming of his final hour: the strings imitate the clock's mechanical ticking, while the oboes imitate the wheel mechanism, which on the stroke of twelve grinds to a halt – just as time seems to do when you are impatient. The second oboe's echo nudges the clock around by pulling on the counterweight, thus setting the clock in motion once more.* Such an ingenious (and to me

---

combative tussle. 'Jazz trumpets,' I thought at the time, and there is indeed something of a jam session feel to this passage. We have no idea precisely what instrument Bach intended here by his designation of *corno*. Some scholars take this to mean *cornetto*, but when performed on the archaic cornett it involves the player in elaborate and treacherous cross-fingerings, which inhibits the projection of sound. After we tried this out in London, for our performance in Santiago de Compostela in 2000 Michael Harrison brought along his mid-nineteenth-century German chromatic valve trumpet in C as an alternative, if anachronistic, solution, managing to make it sound credibly cornetto-like in timbre. Ultimately it is not the form, make or date of the instrument that guarantees conviction, but the skill and imagination of the player.

* Peter Wollny has drawn my attention to the existence of a grandfather clock in Weimar installed by Bach's intractable and reclusive employer, Duke Wilhelm Ernst, to measure out the precise duration of every second of his life.

plausible) explanation leads one to reflect on what might have been Bach's preoccupations when composing these pieces. Was it possibly an inner preparation for the likely death of a frail child that inspired in him this succession of cantatas based on faith and trust, so childlike in their simplicity? His eighth child (and his first with Anna Magdalena), Christiana Sophia (b. 1723), was indeed weakly and was to die on 29 June 1726, just a few months before he sat down to compose BWV 27, a cantata imbued with the spirit of simplicity and innocence, and opening with the words 'Who knows how near is my end? Time goes by, death approaches.'*

* * *

In his manual advising a young German Cavalier on etiquette (1728), Julius Bernhard von Rohr devotes thirty-one pages to the subject of death, burial and mourning. As a thoroughly enlightened tutor, von Rohr counsels 'reasonable' conduct as regards preparing for death, setting one's estate in order, proportionate clothing, ceremony and funerary eulogies. He has sharp words for those whom he describes as *Heuchel-Schein und Maul-Christen* ('hypocrites and lip-service Christians'), pastors who allow their burial sermons to develop into *Lügen-Predigt* ('lying sermons'), and he is all for the banning of private nocturnal funerals (*Beisetzung*).[17] Bach might have agreed: the persistent habit of conducting burials at night-time without any music reduced his opportunities for supplementary income in funeral fees. For the same reason, the good health of Leipzig citizens was also of particular concern to Bach; as he complained to his friend Georg Erdmann, 'When a healthy wind blows . . . as last year . . . I lost fees . . . of more than 100 thalers.'[18] On the other hand, the death of a celebrity such as August the Strong, or his old employer Leopold of Cöthen, offered a rare chance for profitable composition and performance – yet it was also followed by a

* Just three years before his death Bach revived this cantata. Since he could no longer justify the services of a professional copyist, he wrote out the parts himself, rather shakily. Such was the labour involved in the downward transposition for this revival (from E to D major) that he must have had compelling artistic reasons for it. It is strange, therefore, to find him going back to the E major version for one last time, incorporating all the changes he had just introduced in the D major version. The *flauto* piccolo now becomes a *traversa* part, with detailed articulation marks inserted by Bach for almost every single note. One seldom comes across this degree of detailed notation in the performing material for any other of the cantatas of the 1720s.

period of mourning and therefore of unprofitable silence. The bald facts of Bach's experiences of death were probably above the norm in eighteenth-century Saxony. (As a reminder, a sister, two brothers and an uncle died during his infancy. Then came the death of both parents before he was ten, the loss of his first wife, Maria Barbara, in 1720, and of their third son, Johann Gottfried Bernhard, in his early twenties, plus four daughters and three sons by his second wife, Anna Magdalena.)

How this cumulative grief was expressed in his private life remains unknown. Instead we have the composer's public expressions of grief and his poignant responses to funerary texts, both in his cantatas and motets. Arnold Toynbee said that in the relationship between the living and the dying, 'There are two parties to the suffering that death inflicts; and, in the apportionment of this suffering, the survivor takes the brunt.'[19] Bach, in good Lutheran fashion, addresses both parties: the deceased falling into a blessed slumber and the bereaved searching for spiritual comfort in the endless harvest of death. His strategies are far more sympathetic than for example Rembrandt's manner of painting the raw truth about death 'in a gust of black mirth'[20] following the attritions of the plague of 1668, which took his only son, Titus, at the age of twenty-seven. Bach avoids that morbid delight in suffering characteristic of some strands of Pietism which bring to mind 'the mysterious eroticism of wounds'[21] and those ugly narratives of violence and revenge that reflect our psychopathology whenever death is portrayed at the centre of religion.

While his library contained copious examples of theologians relishing the opportunities to portray the approach of death and bodily defilement in harrowing terms, Bach's cantatas that deal with the subject offer deep reservoirs of solace to those who mourn. One of the most moving examples of this is the soprano aria 'Letzte Stunde, brich herein, mir die Augen zuzudrücken!' ('Come, O final hour, break forth and close mine eyes') from his Weimar cantata BWV 31, *Der Himmel lacht*, in which he strikes a note of elevated grief but within the rocking motion of a lullaby. The introductory oboe melody with paired quavers and alternations of strong and weak bars, and the way the upper strings wordlessly intone the death-bed chorale 'Wenn mein Stündlein vorhanden ist' ('When my last hour is at hand'), create an unforgettable evocation of the passage from this life to the next and even of 'celestial beings floating above the bed of the departing believer'.[22] Bach's melodies are described in the *Nekrolog* as 'strange, but always varied, rich in invention, and resembling those of no other composer', but this example from 1715 shows him already shedding some of that 'strangeness'. Originality is still present, however, in the length and angularity of certain vocal phrases that could never have been written by a Stölzel, a Graupner or even a Telemann.*

There is no better example of this transformation to melodic ease than the fourth movement of one of his better-known cantatas, BWV 82, *Ich habe genug* – the aria 'Schlummert ein, ihr matten Augen' ('Close in sleep, you weary eyes'), perhaps the paradigm of collusion between music and text in all Bach's vocal works. Composed for the Feast of Purification in 1727, not only does it come as a welcome counterweight to the succession of grief-laden arias that characterise the Epiphany season (such as BWV 123/v and BWV 13/v discussed above and in Chapter 9), but with the gentle lilt of a lullaby it epitomises Luther's description 'Death has become my sleep', an effect reinforced by the dulcet sonority of the oboe da caccia he added for his sixth and last revision of 1748. That is the last line of his hymn 'Mit Fried und Freud', his free rendering of the *Nunc dimittis*. Bach used it for the same feast-day two years earlier as the basis of BWV 125, his cantata of that title, *Mit Fried und Freud ich fahr dahin* – a more public version of the consoling prospect of death than in *Ich habe genug*, yet, in its way, just as intimate and evocative, as the music of the first chorus slides into a quiet sepulchral register at the words *sanft und stille* ('calm and quiet') and again with amazing pathos at the words *der Tod ist mein Schlaf worden* ('death has become my sleep'), which, like BWV 77, seems to catapult the listener 150 years forwards to the world of Brahms.† At this point Bach's librettist inserts lines of his own, words stressing physi-

* There are exceptions. The most distinguished movement in Telemann's funeral cantata *Du, aber, Daniel* (*c.* 1710) is a soprano aria which could have prompted Bach's use of a similar head motif in BWV 63/iii (1714) and still more strikingly in BWV 99/v (1724), a soprano/alto duet depicting the heavy tread to Calvary and the bitter sorrows of the Cross, which in turn is curiously similar in affective impact to the duet Handel composed for the husband and wife fated to meet and separate for the last time (Io t'abbraccio) in his *Rodelinda* (1725).

† Brahms looked forward to the arrival of the tomes of the *Bach-Gesellschaft* complete edition of 1851–7 as others might the instalments of a thriller. This reverence and enthusiasm for Bach are reflected in several of his choral works, notably in his Opus 74 motets – in *O Heiland, reiß die Himmel auf*, which owes much in its structure to BWV 4 in achieving musical unity over a large canvas, and, still more, in *Warum ist das Licht?*, which, like BWV 125, ends with a chorale setting of the *Nunc dimittis* – Luther's 'Mit Fried und Freud'.

cal collapse, so contradicting the serenity and joy expressed in all the other movements: 'Even with weakened eyes, I shall look to thee, my faithful Saviour, though my body's frame falls apart' – a poignant anticipation of Bach's own lot. Bach sets it for alto with flute and oboe d'amore and a basso continuo marked *ligato per tutto è senza accompagn.* Interpreted as cello and organ *tasto solo* (i.e., in unison with no harmonies), it lends a sepulchral tone (indeed an 'empty' one, almost as though the organist himself had just upped and died) to this plaintive and intensely grief-stricken aria, with its persistent heavily dotted French sarabande rhythms woven into a three-voice (sometimes four-voice) texture with richly ornamented, sighing appoggiaturas. For all the nobility and stateliness of gesture with which the frailty of the expiring body and the 'broken' aspect of the eyes' dimming are conveyed, there seems to be a private grieving going on here, detectable in the very fragility of the upper three voices which Bach superimposes over the hollow sounds of the unembellished continuo and its inexorable repeated pairs of quavers. The core of this aria's affecting expression of private grief is sustained even when the text describes solace ('even though my body breaks, my heart and hope shall not fail').

This aria has none of the sensuality or the consoling chemistry of BWV 82, or even of his very first funerary work, the *Actus tragicus*, in which, as we saw in Chapter 5 (p. 147), like Montaigne, Bach sought to deprive death of its powers to terrify. Montaigne was concerned to establish links between physical activities and 'learning to die'. 'Knowing how to die frees us from all subjection and constraint,' he wrote in his essay 'Que philosopher, c'est apprendre à mourir'.[23] 'There is nothing evil in life for the man who has thoroughly grasped the fact that to be deprived of life is not an evil.' It is a 'true and sovereign liberty', enabling us 'to thumb our noses at force and injustice and to laugh at prisons and chains'. Knowing about the shortness and unpredictability of life, and therefore 'always booted and ready to go', Montaigne wants death to find him at work with his daily business but unconcerned with the fruits of his labour: 'I want death to find me planting my cabbages, but careless of death, and still more of my unfinished garden.' Bach could have found recovery from the traumatic shock of losing both parents so young through his deep connection with music. Suddenly needing to face up to his own mortality, music may have been his path to unlocking that part of himself that led him to a very personal perception of the divine, something he shared with other exceptionally creative people and mystics such as Jakob Boehme, who wrote that 'We are all strings in the concert of [God's] joy.'[24] By this interpretation music could have been his means to express his inner turmoil: it is conceivable that he used that pain to unlock a stream of inspirational energy.

Life as both a pilgrimage and a sea voyage is the underlying metaphor of BWV 56, *Ich will den Kreuzstab gerne tragen*, a cantata for solo bass that is the equal of BWV 82 in the way its ingenious structure is so well worked out. What makes it especially appealing is Bach's seemingly Romantic approach to text-setting – a sophisticated instance of collusion. He adjusts his melodic line to accommodate successive changes in mood – moving from a succinct initial upward climb, a harrowing arpeggio to a sharpened seventh (of the sort Hugo Wolf might later use) as a musical pun on the word *Kreuzstab* ('cross-staff'), and thence to six and a half bars of pained descent to signify the ongoing burden of the Cross and the solace that 'comes from God's beloved hand'. Bach reserves the biggest change for the B section, switching to triplet rhythm in the voice part in a kind of arioso as the pilgrim lowers all his grief into his own grave: 'Then shall my Saviour wipe the tears from my eyes.' He fashions an arioso with cello arpeggiation to depict the lapping waves, while the voice line describes how 'the sorrow, affliction and distress engulf me.' Where the first movement was forward-looking, this arioso seems to hark back to the music he learnt as a child, that of his forebears. One can pick up hints of an early reliance on God's protection in the whispered comfort of *Ich bin bei dir* ('I am with you').

As we have seen, with the death of both of his parents when he was only nine years old there was no human substitute on whom he could wholly depend. As the waves die down and the cello comes to rest on a bottom D, the voice of the pilgrim continues in *secco* recitative with the Bunyan-like words, 'So I step from my ship into my own city, which is the kingdom of heaven, where I with all the righteous shall enter out of so great tribulation.' A further metaphor – of the obbligato oboe as guardian angel of the now jubilant pilgrim – is developed in the extended *da capo* aria 'Endlich wird mein Joch' ('At last, my yoke shall fall from me again'). Bach reserves the biggest surprise for the moment when the pilgrim's desire to fly up like an eagle can hold no bounds: 'Let it happen today!' he exclaims, the emphasis shifting from *O!* to *gescheh* to *heute* and finally to *noch*. These are the moments when one senses Bach bridging the gap between living and dying with total clarity and utter fearlessness. Mozart could be speaking for Bach when he wrote, Montaigne-like, to his father in April 1787: 'As death, when we come to consider it closely, is the true goal of our existence, I have formed during the last few years such close relations with this best and truest friend of mankind, that his image is not only no longer terrifying to me, but is indeed very soothing and consoling!'[25]

* * *

We have been attempting to explore the border of contact between music and language. In his church cantatas Bach's music goes to work on the language of his mother tongue, a process that sometimes leads to collusion and at others ends in collision or displacement. Often, as I have tried to show, the results reach right to the heart of the human condition. When it comes to his motets (which date from the whole of his middle years, but of which only a handful have survived), the relationship between music and language is not quite the same, since they entail no collaborative negotiation with a poet or librettist as the cantatas do. Instead they draw on compact and aphoristic biblical passages combined with chorales – selected and arranged by the composer and (as far as we know) no other – allowing him to develop satisfying harmonious unities, which were so much harder to achieve in the church cantatas with their heterogeneous texts and slightly lopsided form. As predominantly funerary pieces, the motets epitomise the Lutheran longing for completion and union with God and that deeply implanted idea of heavenly love which gave justification to the lives of its adherents. They speak to us very directly, because, like several of the cantatas that take the *ars moriendi* as their subject matter, they address something we all share with Bach – our mortality.

This is essentially music for unaccompanied voices, made so gripping by Bach's skill in converting a range of instrumentally conceived figures into vocally expressive phrases through their fusion with words.* This

* Funeral services in the Lutheran church did not normally involve instruments, but an exception was sometimes made with regard to motets. Notwithstanding the likelihood of a basso continuo accompaniment or the (optional) addition of *colla parte* instruments in the double-choir motets, we have Bach's original performing material for only one of these, BWV 226, *Der Geist hilft unser Schwachheit auf*, with strings doubling one choir and woodwinds the other.

makes them hugely challenging to perform, so that it is little wonder that Bach, it seems, insisted that all fifty-four of the boarding Thomaner were in theory available to perform what was called 'the Cantor's music', whether divided up into separate eight-voiced *Kantoreien* (of which there were four, each with two boys per part) or in multiples thereof.[26] Like Mozart after him, with Bach there is no rigid dividing line between his instrumental melodies and sung arias or phrases – so that when some of his best singers were suddenly forced to serve as instrumentalists for a particular service, there was no drastic change of style. Take the middle section of his five-part motet BWV 227, *Jesu, meine Freude*, the subtle vocal fugue 'Ihr aber seid nicht fleischlich, sondern geistlich' ('But ye are not in the flesh, but in the Spirit'): the way that Bach plans the stepwise approach to the word *fleischlich* in the main theme, stretches it languidly over the bar-line and then contrasts it with a long enigmatic melisma on *geistlich* is sufficient proof that even when thinking fugally he could make room for expressive vocal inflection to bring life and particular emphasis to the words he was setting.*

Another matchless example of this fluidity occurs in the long middle section of one of his earliest motets, BWV 228, *Fürchte dich nicht*, this time set as a double fugue in which the three lower voices exchange subjects that are free inversions of each other. If you are told at the outset that the ascending subject derives from the opening motif of the chorale that will soon appear as the soprano *cantus firmus*, it might strike you as just another example of Bach's unlimited cleverness. But when this motif appears for the third time, now sung by the altos in the key of the chorale (D major), the link is made instantly audible (as well

* Despite the attempts by Daniel Melamed (*J. S. Bach and the German Motet* (1995), pp. 85–9) and others to propose a piecemeal assembly of the motet, the fact is that in performance it coheres admirably well – but so, of course, does the *Credo* of the *B minor Mass*, a movement that, as we shall see in the next chapter, was definitely cobbled together from material originating in different times in Bach's life. Bach is so good at erasing tell-tale traces of any grafts and at bringing total assurance to the finished entity that we can never be sure at which particular moment he decided on the final use of any particular work. There are passages which suggest an earlier (Weimar) provenance – particularly the ninth movement, the sublime 'Gute Nacht' duet for sopranos to which the tenors provide a vocal *bassetchen* continuo with the altos threading a line through the middle with the hymn tune. But this in no way detracts from its perfect placement at the heart of the motet. If a movement here or there strikes one as more akin to his keyboard music then it just goes to show that Bach created far fewer stylistic barriers between the various genres in which he cast his music than subsequent commentators would have us believe.

as clever) – not least by the succession of words, the biblical *ich habe dich bei deinem Namen gerufen* ('I have called thee by name') leading climactically to the hymn-line *ich bin dein, weil du dein Leben* [*gegeben*] ('I am thine, for thou hast given thy life'). Bach learnt from his great predecessor Johann Christoph, who also made a motet from a version of these words from Isaiah, how to contrast, overlap and fuse similar words or ideas for expressive, exegetical purposes – and always with musical naturalness and charm. What could be simpler yet more eloquent than the little detached phrase *du bist mein* he interposes as a downward fifth in between the colliding fugal subjects?

At any given point in these motets Bach shows that he is aware of everything that can fruitfully happen to a tune or be extracted from it. With *Jesu, meine Freude* one cannot fail to be impressed by the exceptionally thorough symmetry and cross-referencing that Bach has engineered to provide an unobtrusive scaffolding for his word-setting (see diagram). This allowed him to juxtapose such outwardly ill-matched literary companions – Johann Franck's sugary hymn stanzas and stern verses from the eighth chapter of St Paul's Epistle to the Romans – with apparent ease and, as it turns out, in fruitful dramatic alternation. One does not generally encounter this degree of symmetrical bracing of movements in the church cantatas except in the early BWV 4, *Christ lag in Todesbanden*.

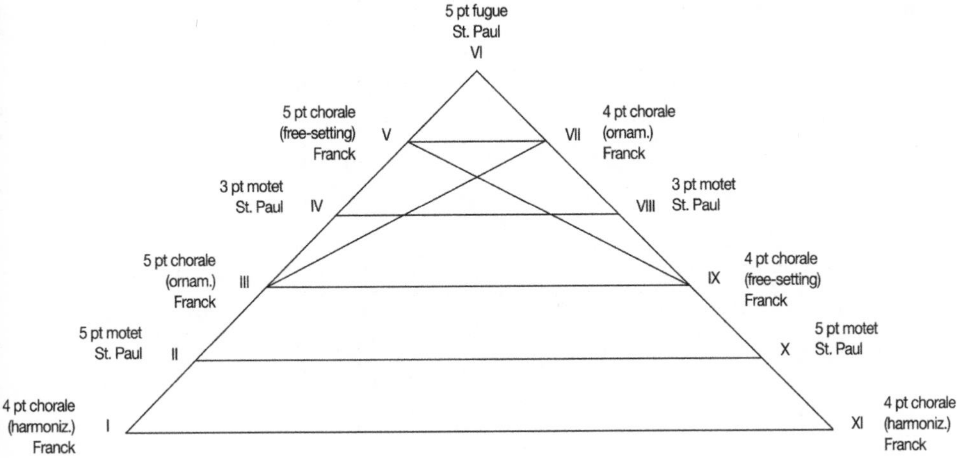

Nor is Bach shy of pinching an actor's cloak from time to time – to seize on the spoken force and rhythm of a single word like *trotz!* and fling it to the four corners of a church. Grammatically the word here is a preposition meaning 'in spite of', but in the context of Franck's hymn and Bach's setting it has resonances of the noun *Trotz*, which denotes defiance and cussedness – a gauntlet thrown down to the 'old dragon' conjured up before our eyes with the graphic vividness of a Cranach or a Grünewald. Then he opposes it with the equally powerful image of a Martin Luther, fearless in his isolated rebellion (*ich steh hier und singe*) and, like the archangel Michael himself, brave and unmovable in his defiance (*in gar sichrer Ruh*), or like Archimedes: 'Give me a place to stand and I will move the earth.' So close is Bach's identification with Luther at this juncture that we sense how he too 'stands here and sings in such certain peace', urging us to do the same with equal vehemence. If one wanted to pick a single example of how Bach harnessed his compositional prowess and capacity for invention as a means of articulating his zeal and faith, this motet would be it.

Equal fervour, but of a less militant, more sensuous kind, is to be found in the most intimate and touching of his double-choir motets, BWV 229, *Komm, Jesu, komm*. Bach's explorations of the dialectical possibilities of eight voices deployed as two antiphonal choirs here, and in his *Matthew Passion* (see Chapter 11, p. 408), goes many steps beyond the manipulation of spatially separate blocks of sound pioneered by the Venetian polychoralists and the rhetorically conceived dialogues of Gabrieli's star pupil, Heinrich Schütz. Having clearly learnt the expressive force of word repetitions and exchanges from Schütz, Bach finds ways of weaving all eight lines into a rich contrapuntal tapestry, with extended cadences and dragging appoggiaturas on the words *müde* ('weary'), *sehne* ('yearn') and *Frieden* ('freedom') that anticipate the world-weariness and nostalgia one finds a century and a half later in the double-choir motets of Brahms.

The opening invocations to Christ – single-word entreaties by both choirs, first alternately and then conjointly – are couched in the expressive and physically explicit language of a love-song. Bach finds a distinctive musical character appropriate to each line of the rhymed metrical text of this funerary hymn. For the melodic outline of *die Kraft verschwindt* ('strength disappears') he inscribes an arc that hints at life's downward journey, beginning energetically in crotchets before the sands of life run out – *je mehr und mehr* ('more and more') – then regaining temporary impetus as one choir interrupts only to augment the expressive eloquence of the other. Again it is the basses who lead the evocation of *der saure Weg* ('life's bitter path') with the anguished falling interval of a diminished seventh given in slow minims and in canon. By the time it has passed through all eight voices and interleaved in a dense contrapuntal web, Bach has achieved an overwhelming depiction of personal and collective distress: 'the shame of motives late revealed, and the awareness of things ill done and done to others' harm'.[27] But Bach is not done yet. With two choirs in play he can give one the fragmented text and have the other interject with just two poignant words, *zu schwer!* ('too heavy') – life's bitter path being too much for anyone to have to bear. Then he rounds off this section with a little more than three bars of D pedal with passing harmonies of ravishing pathos.

Release of some sort is needed at this point, and it comes in the unexpected form of a fresh fugal exposition starting in the altos, *Komm, komm, ich will mich dir ergeben* ('Come, come, I will yield myself to thee'), more madrigal than churchy, to which the second choir provides a syllabic commentary – chirpy and eager in the way that the opening repetitions of *Komm, komm* were languid and pleading. Now he switches metre to $\frac{6}{8}$, passing two-bar segments of a French minuet from one choir to the other for the words *du bist der rechte Weg, die Wahrheit und das Leben.*

Anyone else hitting on the idea of a dance movement at this point might have been happy to let it run its course and move on swiftly to the second stanza of Paul Thymich's hymn. Bach, on the other hand, has barely begun. For the next eighty-eight bars he elaborates one glorious extended sequence after another, first for one choir, then the other, so that the music appears never to stop while conveying the balm and reassurance of Christ's words 'I am the way, the truth and the life' (John 14:6). Lyricism and ecstasy of this degree can be found in several arias in his cantatas but seldom in their choruses. Here in *Komm, Jesu, komm* Bach breaks with the tradition of the Baroque motet as he had inherited it, seizing on the presence of his two four-part choirs to write for them with bold, unprecedented contrapuntal fantasy. The conclusion – two bars of antiphonal exchange, followed by eight more of eight-part imitative counterpoint – is then repeated as an echo, a fitting *envoi*, one that stretches the technical control of his (and every subsequent) choir to the utmost degree. The final stanza is set for the now united four-voiced choir he calls *aria* – but that need not confuse us, as it has past commentators, since clearly this is not a chorale, has no *cantus firmus* and conforms perfectly to Mattheson's definition of a choral aria for voices: 'moving in equal steps with no voice attempting what the other voices cannot to a certain extent equal'.[28] That description, however, does scant justice to Bach's soaring vocal lines as they emerge from an admirably supple arrangement of the words (in $\frac{3}{4}$ bars alternating with others in an implied $\frac{3}{2}$) in a lyrical prayer of submission to Jesus' lead and protection here at life's end.

* * *

'Hardly had the choir sung a few bars when Mozart sat up startled; a few measures more and he called out: "What is this?" And now his whole soul seemed to be in his ears. When the singing was finished he cried out, full of joy: "Now *there* is something one can learn from!"'[29] And why not? BWV 225, *Singet dem Herrn*, is by far the meatiest and most technically demanding of Bach's double-choir motets, but that is not what dazzled Mozart in the Thomaskirche in Leipzig in April 1789, leading him to call for the parts, which he then 'spread all around him – in both hands, on his knees, and on the chairs next to him – and, forgetting everything, did not get up again until he had looked through everything of Sebastian Bach's that was there'. Nothing in Mozart's previous experience of church music had prepared him for this – some of the most exhilarating dance-impregnated vocal music Bach ever wrote. No instruments are actually required beyond the standard continuo (*colla parte* doubling is generally agreed to be permissible but not obligatory here); yet even without his cantata orchestra to draw on, this is the most orchestrally conceived of all Bach's motets, evoking not just the drums and harps called for by the psalmist in praise of God's name, but a myriad of other instruments and percussive effects as well.

At the outset Bach assigns chains of instrumental *figura corta* to one of his choirs, while from the way he sets the single word *Singet!* in Choir 2 he shows that he is out to extract the maximum percussive edge and frisson from the German text, beyond its function of providing the continuo and giving harmonic backing to Choir 1. His method of celebrating, first the community of saints, then Israel 'rejoic[ing] in him that made him', is to exploit the shock waves of strategically placed glottal stops and the syncopated force of plosive and fricative consonants. If the vowels and even the notes were removed, we would still get the exuberant mood of the text just from the collision of these animated consonants.

By the time Bach reaches the final section, 'Lobet dem Herrn in seinen Taten', it feels as though he has dragooned all the Temple instruments of the Old Testament – the harps, psalteries and cymbals – into the service of praising the Lord, like some latter-day *cuadro flamenco* or Big Band leader. King David reputedly had nearly 300 musicians in his employ; Bach in Leipzig had barely thirty, but that was no bar to his inclusion in the hallowed lineage of church musicians appointed to form choirs responsible for songs of thanksgiving since biblical times. Bach wrote in the margin of his personal copy of Abraham Calov's Bible commentary, 'music ... was especially ordered by God's spirit through David.' On another page, in response to the passage (Exodus 15:20) describing how 'all the women went out after [Miriam] with timbrels and dancing', we find Calov speculating on what 'a mighty melody and a tremendous resonance and reverberation there must have been between these two choruses [Moses and the men of Israel, Miriam with the Israelite women]' on the occasion when 'David the king and prophet danced publicly before the ark of the covenant' – to which Bach adds in the margin, 'NB. First prelude, for two choirs to be performed for the glory of God.' And what does Miriam sing? 'Sing ye to the Lord, for he hath triumphed gloriously!'* The 'first prelude' eventually leads to a fugue for the children of Zion to dance to. Only in the *Cum sancto spiritu* from the *B minor Mass* (which it resembles) did Bach ever write a more joyous, fleet-footed fugal subject.

Passages such as these remind us that Bach's is a Baroque version of medieval 'danced religion'. Just as many African languages lack distinct words for music and dance, so these two were once considered inseparable in Christian worship, their pagan, Dionysian fusion legitimised by the early church Fathers. To invoke 'zest and delight of the spirit', according to Clement of Alexandria (150–216), Christians were to 'raise our

* Handel, too, was clearly inspired by the verses from I Chronicles 25 and 28 when he set them to music as the culmination of his double-choir oratorio *Israel in Egypt* (1739).

heads and our hands to heaven and move our feet just at the end of the prayer – *pedes excitamus*'.[30] He also instructed the faithful to 'dance in a ring, together with the angels, around Him who is without beginning or end' – an idea that, despite successive attempts of the church from the fourth to the sixteenth centuries to crack down on religious dancing in church, still held currency for Renaissance painters such as Botticelli and Filippino Lippi – and, I suggest, Bach, too, particularly in his Christmas music. At least Bach could claim the guarded backing of Luther, who, in accepting the legitimacy of 'country customs', said 'so long as it's done decently, I respect the rites and customs of weddings – and *I* dance anyway!'[31] This is not very far from Émile Durkheim's notion of 'collective effervescence' – the ritually induced passion or ecstasy that cements social bonds and which, he proposed, forms the ultimate basis of religion.*[32] Suddenly we have a window on to those regular get-togethers of the Bach family – how their pious chorale-singing at the start of the day slipped into bibulous quodlibets at nightfall. Bach shared with his relatives a hedonistic vision of community based on the conviviality of human intercourse, one that in no sense clashed with his view of the seriousness of his calling as a musician or the funnelling of his creative talents to the greater glory of God. When Bach is in this mood, you sense that, for all its elegance, its dexterity and its complexity, his music has primitive, pagan roots. This is music to celebrate a festival, the turning-point of the year – life itself.

Other qualities Mozart might have admired in *Singet* are its architectural planning, and the way expressive rhetoric is reconciled with long-range continuity. This goes beyond the superficial resemblance of the sequence of its three movements to that of an Italian instrumental concerto (fast – slow – fast): both of the two outer movements are loosely paired on the prelude-and-fugue model. Once the 'First Prelude' has peaked with the 'collective effervescence' of Israel's rejoicing, Bach clears the way for Miriam and her maidens to step forward and lead the fugal dance 'Die Kinder Zion'.

He brilliantly chooses to persist with the *Singet* motto that accompanied the imitative effusion of his initial prelude now as a funky,

* The classic example – from another faith – is of course the Whirling Dervishes. Steven Runciman describes 'their mystic practices, their rhythmic dances that brought them into a state of ecstasy, in communion with God' (*A Traveller's Alphabet* (1991), p. 63). Just as the Christian church tried to expunge holy dancing, so Atatürk's regime tried to suppress the Dervishes.

offbeat commentary to his four-part fugue. This pays high dividends in the build-up of this long movement, as one by one the voices of both choirs re-enter emphatically, this time in reverse order (B-T-A-S), while the rich 'accompaniment' is re-distributed among the fugally unoccupied voices. In his second pairing, the finale of the motet, Bach achieves a different type of transition from prelude to fugue by narrowing the focus: suddenly and without a break, eight voices converge and become four. Out of the hurly-burly the united basses of both choirs step forward in a *passepied* set to the words 'Let everything that hath breath praise the Lord.' This might sound straightforward enough, but in practice it is a challenge to achieve a seamless and fluent transition at this point of liftoff. It needs a readjustment of the singers' 'radar' to pass from a full, dense eight-part polyphony in common time to fusion as a single line, one-in-a-bar, with spatially distanced voices now airborne, insubstantial and still dancing. Several episodes follow in quick succession – exposition, *stretto*, sequence, re-appearance of the subject in the super-tonic, sequence, *stretto* – each with expectations of an imminent conclusion. But Bach's high-wire act still has 113 bars to run, and what promised to be a sprint to the line turns out to be a 1,500-metre race. As the singers move into the final straight, you sense the crowd's excitement. Suddenly it's no longer a flat race – there's a big hurdle ahead, one to take the sopranos up to a top B♭ before they can breast the finishing tape, using up the last *Odem* ('breath') of which they are capable.

If the finale is a middle-distance track event, the central movement is more like an aeronautical display. While Choir 2 glides past in stately homophonic formation with a four-part chorale harmonisation, Choir 1 flies in, inscribing independent yet interlocking flight-paths responsive to thermal currents and the lines of its free poetic text. The antiphony between two parallel texts, one measured and formal as befits a chorale, the other lyrical, even rhapsodical, is unprecedented (Bach's appellation of 'aria' here carrying metaphoric as well as stylistic connotations). His cantatas and Passions are littered with fruitful juxtapositions of personal and collective responses between solo arias and chorales, but this type of choral litany, in which the roles of the two choirs are reversed for the second verse, is another radical departure from contemporary notions of how motets were supposed to function. Bach's motets contain unique bursts of festive and reflective creativity at the very margins of what the Lutheran clergy of his day would have found acceptable.

Their popularity in our time goes a little way towards reversing the process of desocialisation that chased the choral dance first out of church and then from communal recreation of the kind we are told that the Bach family practised.[33] (This was also a feature of my childhood, thanks to my parents' no doubt unconscious re-creation of this pattern – intense sessions of *a cappella* singing, followed by physically liberating sessions of English country dancing based on John Playford's *The English Dancing Master* (1651)). Through their extraordinary compression and complexity, Bach's motets make colossal demands of performers, requiring exceptional virtuosity, stamina, and sensitivity to the abrupt changes of mood and texture as well as to the exact meaning of each word. Towards the end of his more than thirty years as music director of Berlin's Singakademie in 1827, Carl Friedrich Zelter wrote to his friend Goethe, 'Could I let you hear some happy day one of Sebastian Bach's motets, you would feel yourself at the centre of the world, as a man like you ought to be. I hear the works for the many hundredth time, and am not finished with them yet, and never will be.'[34] After knowing them for more than sixty years I feel exactly the same. The glorious freedom that Bach exhibits in his motets, his balletic joy in the praise of his maker and his total certitude in the contemplation of death – this, surely, is the best imaginable response to our mortal entrapment.

* * *

Tying together these threads of Bach's vocal music allows us to appreciate his extraordinary achievement in expressing the essence of Lutheran eschatology – ideas about eternity that can never satisfactorily be put into words. Part of this music's appeal to us today may lie in the affirmation it makes which many of us no longer find in conventional religion or politics (although this may also have been true of earlier responses to Bach, as when Mendelssohn revived the *Matthew Passion* in 1829). In the very special quality of consolation his music conveys, we have a sense of the past and the present being bound together. This is a central tenet of the 'eternal future' envisioned by the seventeenth-century Lutheran theologians represented in Bach's library, such as Heinrich Müller, who saw participation in 'most blessed music' as an evocation of heaven and a powerful incentive for embracing death (see illustration p. 553).[35] This music – playing it, participating in it, listening to it – conveys a strong sense of being in the present and screens out all else. The very act of performing such a Bach piece produces a type of realised eschatology, one which implies that 'end times' are in a sense already here.

We have seen how Bach's music regularly goes beyond a straightforward affirmation of its texts and how on occasion it subverts them in ways he may not have foreseen when he began setting them. The problem for the Leipzig clergy may have been to admit, without feeling antagonised or threatened, that, for all his curmudgeonly behaviour, this cantor was an exceptional asset to the church. He could turn people's heads and even make them listen (though how much, of course, we can only imagine). His motets and cantatas provided an alternative route to Christian edification and contemplation, asserting the bleak truths of their texts as well as providing palliatives that the texts often deny. We today can certainly hear them in this way if we choose. In some respects approaches to his church music have become more straightforward: as in the first two decades of the nineteenth century, when men and women started to look to art and music for the inspiration, hope and consolation they were no longer finding in religion; and as in our own day, when religion is simultaneously in the ascendant in some parts of the world and increasingly absent from many people's lives in others. But at this distance it is easier for us to recognise the potency of his music and its ability simultaneously to reveal, even to insist upon, the unvarnished truth about human weakness – man's thin and easily broken attachment to moral good – and to chart the redemptive way back to decency, compassion and what he called 'good neighbourliness'.

By now we have seen that one of Bach's monumental achievements was to show that music and language together can do things which neither can do separately. But he also proves that music sometimes surpasses language, whether written or spoken, in its capacity to penetrate to the innermost recesses of consciousness and to chip away at people's prejudices and our sometimes toxic patterns of thinking. We can still turn to his cantatas and motets for enlightenment (with a small *e*) about sin, redemption, evil or repentance, with no more difficulty than we can to, say, a widely read nineteenth-century writer like Dostoevsky – someone who 'found in the Christian religion the only solution to the riddle of existence' and who 'uncovered a volcanic crater in every human being'.[36]

Bach in fact makes it a great deal easier for us to focus on the injunction to love one's neighbour than on all the filth and horror of the world. We emerge from performing or listening to a Bach motet chastened, maybe, but more often elated, such is the cleansing power of the music. There is not a whiff here of those 'foul fumes of religious fervour' that Richard Eyre sees today 'spreading sanctimoniousness and intolerance throughout the globe, while those far-from-exclusively Christian virtues – love, mercy, pity, peace – are choked.'[37]

13
The Habit of Perfection

Perfection is achieved, it seems, not when there is nothing left to add, but when there is nothing left to take away.
– after Antoine de Saint-Exupéry, *Terre des Hommes* (1939)

Ky-ri-e . . . Ky-ri-e . . . Ky-ri-e e-le-i-son!

The inscribing of that initial three-fold *Kyrie* in sound at the outset of Bach's *B minor Mass* seems almost a physical act, one in which each of us – as listener or performer – is individually or collectively involved. Those four dense, action-packed bars are presented to us as an imposing succession of imploring gestures – just as graphic in their way as an altar-tableau by a Titian or a Rubens. From the downbeat of that first massive B minor chord and its anguished sequel, our expectations have been alerted. At the conclusion of these bars an immense solemn fugue begins to open out, bearing with it a measured sense of prayer. We soon realise that we have been launched on one of the most epic of all journeys in music, a setting of the Ordinary of the Mass unprecedented in its scale, majesty and sobriety. Once aboard, anchors weighed, we are there for the duration – the next hundred minutes or so – to disembark only when the final chord invoking *pacem* ('peace') has vanished into the ether.

To the unsuspecting listener such a strong sense of inexorable unfolding would imply an uninterrupted, start-to-finish conception and execution in the composer's mind. But the facts and what we can glean of Bach's interrupted steps in constructing his great Mass suggest otherwise. It is only in the last three decades that scholars have generally agreed that Bach completed the Mass in the last two years of his life.

The seeds of its inception, however, lie some forty years earlier, during those exploratory years he spent at the ducal court of Weimar – an early version of one of its movements, the *Crucifixus*, was indeed composed there. He would have been aware that his friend and cousin J. G. Walther had formulated a project to set the *Kyrie* from the Mass as a *de profundis*, a cry from the depths by the embattled sinner, basing it on the chorale *Aus tiefer Not schrei ich zu dir* (Luther's paraphrase of Psalm 130).[1] No trace of Walther's work remains; yet perhaps Bach remembered it when he himself set Luther's *de profundis* chorale in the *Clavier-Übung III*. Significantly he set it in the harsh, anguished key of F♯ minor, which Bach reserved for his most poignant, sin-burdened movements. It resembles both in mood (*Kyrie I*) and key (*Kyrie II*) the urgent entreaties of a beleaguered soul in Bach's *Missa*. A different and shorter *Kyrie* and *Agnus Dei* pairing (BWV 233a) has survived from these Weimar years; then no further Mass settings for another quarter of a century.

It was in his middle years that Bach turned his mind to setting Latin texts. What drew him to the idea of setting the complete Mass, with its immutable Catholic text in Latin, is far from certain: in any case it was an unusual form for an eighteenth-century Lutheran composer to essay. Luther had sanctioned its continued usage in liturgical worship, notwithstanding the sturdy vernacular versions of the Greek and Latin originals he bequeathed to his followers. His main concern was for full, universal comprehensibility – and in this Luther could have misjudged the tenacious attachment by the more conservative members of his congregation to the old Latin. So, the twin movements of the Greek *Kyrie* and its sequel, the Latin *Gloria*, survived to constitute the short *Missa* in Lutheran liturgical parlance alongside their new German-language equivalents. Bach's first attempt in the shorter genre was composed in 1733. It is certainly difficult for us now experiencing those monumental opening bars not to hear them as anything other than the harbingers of his complete Mass. Perhaps that indeed was Bach's plan from the outset, but there is no way for us to be sure. Initially, at least, these bars were but the prelude to the two-movement work he dedicated to the new Elector of Saxony, Friedrich August II. It is entirely plausible that at the time Bach saw this presentation *Missa* as a work *sui generis*, sufficient in itself. Many years would need to pass before it occurred to him to incorporate the Dresden *Missa* as the opening pair of movements of the *Missa tota* with which we are so familiar. Such ambiguity of function and purpose is typical of the piecemeal origins of the *B minor Mass*, which, to the consternation of its nineteenth-century admirers, did not spring complete and fully armed from the imaginative head of its creator. It required years of gestation and assimilation, and for Bach most probably there may never have been the satisfaction of experiencing it directly through performance and so no opportunity to put it to the test as a summation for posterity of his compositional skills.

* * *

Having encountered Bach at his workbench in the Thomasschule, we can picture him leafing through the scores of those 150 or so cantatas on which he had lavished so much creative invention in his early Leipzig years, wondering what would become of them. In black moods he may have feared that they would end up being used as scrap paper or fire-lighters.* Setting the complete Latin Mass, this immutable statement of faith, to music was one way to step aside from the specific and parochial context of his church cantatas, slanted to the weekly homily and geared to illustrating the Sunday sermon, and to uncover fresh compositional challenges. For Bach, as a Christian, the Bible had enormous referential value. It had furnished him with scripts for musical dramas and offered him parables and stories to which everyone of his congregation could relate. In its Latin form, the Ordinary of the Mass allowed him to concentrate on universal themes and in a language weathered by time. At all stages in Christian history it has provided a point of reference and the central means by which individuals can find and redeem themselves. Bach helps us, his interpreters and listeners, towards that end. More than that, through his passionate engagement with the text of the Latin Mass, Bach makes a forward leap, staking out new areas for music to illumine and expound biblical doctrine. His Latin Mass setting is thus both a repository of human doubts and tussles of faith, and a celebration of birth and life. For, compared with other musical approaches to Mass settings of the time, Bach's gave a fresh emphasis to the human

* Only a few years later Caspar Ruetz, the cantor in Lübeck, complained that a huge pile of church music that he had inherited from his predecessors had been reduced by half by these methods: 'who will give anything for it, other than someone who needs scrap paper, for nothing is more useless than old music' (Kerala J. Snyder, *Dieterich Buxtehude: Organist in Lübeck* (2007), p. 318).

story within it. A narrative filament runs all through his Mass, rising to the surface at key moments, such as the appearance of the angels to the shepherds in the *Gloria in excelsis*, and in the three linked movements at the centre of the Nicene Creed, the *Et incarnatus*, the *Crucifixus* and the *Et resurrexit*. But the most poignantly human moment is reserved for that ghostly bridge-passage that links the *Confiteor* to the *Et expecto*. In these extraordinary bars we can detect traces of Bach's own struggles – with tonality, counterpoint and harmony – but perhaps even with belief. The human emphasis here is presented to us as a bulwark against the fear we habitually feel of the terror of the dark. He lets us feel that terror – because he may have felt it, too, and knew how to overcome it.

In 1733 the completion of the Mass lay a long way in the future. The glimmer of an idea of how to improve his situation in Leipzig, or even to escape it altogether, came to him sometime during his forty-ninth year. We have already seen how around this time his professional situation in Leipzig had deteriorated (see Chapter 6). The new burgomaster, Jacob Born (see Plate 11e), having spoken directly to Bach and tried to force him to take his teaching duties more seriously, reported back to the council that 'he shows little inclination to work'[2] and had attempted to have him disqualified from continuing in office.

Despite signs of genuine approbation from his students, in his beleaguered state Bach's willingness to channel all his creative energies into the service of the Thomasschule and the music-hungry liturgy of the town's churches had clearly diminished. Yet there is no reason to conclude that his creative genius was suddenly dormant. It simply needed another outlet. Three years earlier he had told the Leipzig councillors to look to the Dresden Court to see how music can and should be organised. This was not so much a case of sour grapes as a simple acknowledgement that a far higher value was placed on music and its practitioners in the Saxon capital than in Leipzig. There, the glamorous array of musical talent could enable a composer of Bach's professional standing and ambitions to operate and prosper – or so he thought.*

* The Saxon Court is said to have had one of the best-trained orchestras in Europe in the first part of the century, a reputation which drew musicians like magnets to serve under the Elector August the Strong and his son Friedrich August II. When Bach visited in 1717 the Capelle consisted of approximately 33 instrumentalists, not including composers, trumpeters or the Capellmeister. With the accession of Friedrich August II the number increased to around 42, with a regular string strength of 6 to 8 first violins, 6 to 8 second violins, 3 to 4

Everything points to an understandable desire on his part to escape the confines of Leipzig and to become a part of that talent, rather as he had in his Cöthen years. He was already on friendly terms with many of the Dresden musicians and had good reason to see his professional future linked in some substantive way with that of the Electoral Court. Just then, however, a vacancy for organist presented itself at the Sophienkirche, where Bach had previously given acclaimed organ recitals. Ever the shrewd operator of the family network (and, at the outset of his career, as we have seen, very much its beneficiary), Bach set his sights on this prestigious opening – not for himself, but for Wilhelm Friedemann, his eldest son, by then already an accomplished musician. So with the zeal typical of a solicitous father, he wrote Friedemann's two letters of application himself, but under his son's signature. To make absolutely sure that his candidature was cast-iron, Bach even copied his own Prelude and Fugue in G (BWV 541) and, just as a precaution, placed it in Friedemann's music case ready for his audition on 22 June. He need not have worried. Friedemann was offered the position and received warm commendation from within the Dresden Court Capelle.

Bach now had a valid excuse to travel to Dresden to help his son settle in. Scooping up Anna Magdalena and his three eldest children, he set off. Barely a month after leaving Leipzig, he presented a petition to the Elector, Friedrich August II, requesting a court title – 'a *Predicate* . . . in your Hoff-Capelle' – along with a beautifully written set of twenty-one parts of his new *Missa*. This left him a bare month in which to complete the two opening movements of one of his most monumental church compositions. The autograph score – but significantly not the presentation parts – is written out on Leipzig paper of the sort he had been using for the past six months, so that it is possible he had already begun the *Missa*, or at least its opening *Kyrie*, during the Lenten period following the death of August the Strong (1 February 1733). This was a time when concerted music was forbidden in the Leipzig churches, and his duties as Thomascantor (though not his teaching obligations) were less onerous. Two questions arise: was the opening *Kyrie* first performed on

violas, 2 to 4 cellos, 2 double basses and harpsichord, together with whatever other continuo and wind instruments a particular score required (Ortrun Landmann, 'The Dresden Hofkapelle during the Lifetime of Johann Sebastian Bach', *Early Music*, Vol. 17, No. 1 (Feb. 1989), pp. 17–30).

21 April 1733, when the new Prince-Elector visited Leipzig for the Oath of Fealty?[3] And, from the sporadic errors of transposition in his autograph score, can we assume that Bach was copying from an original version in C minor? If so, perhaps it was this version of the eventual *Kyrie I* (but so far without those imposing four bars we referred to at the outset) that was performed in April 1733 in Leipzig. Yet this would hardly have been the most tactful moment for presenting the new Elector with a score or parts, let alone a petition for a court title.

The *Gloria* would certainly have been considered inappropriate during what was still a period of official mourning. Almost all of its nine movements can be shown to have originated in previous compositions, some now lost. So when, at the end of June, he set off for Dresden, Bach may have had the basic outline of the *Missa* already present in his mind and with new ideas as to which of his earlier compositions would be most suitable for inclusion. It would still require phenomenal skill to refit them within the pre-existing structure of the Ordinary before the new *Missa* was ready and parts could be copied. The watermarks of the parts presented to the Elector clearly indicate that the paper originated in Dresden. Some are in his own elegant hand, others in that of the family members accompanying him there – but not written by Thomasschule students in the weekly sweatshop where the cantata parts were normally copied out. On close inspection they are full of the kind of detail that makes sense only in the context of an actual or an imminent performance.

What seems to have happened is this. Bach, as head of the family, having directed his eldest son towards securing the organist post at the Sophienkirche, now saw a clear opening for himself in the professional employ of the Dresden Court. To this end the composition of a new Mass tailored to the talents of the court Capelle and conforming to the idioms of Mass-settings then current seemed an obvious tactic, a tactful adjunct to his request for a court title. Bach doubtless exhorted his family to make a heroic joint effort in support of his scheme. Once having completed both *Kyrie* and *Gloria*, he set them to work copying the parts directly from his autograph score. They had to be flawless, as this was to be a presentation set to be offered to the Elector. For the grand title page, the wrapper and his florid petition he thought it advisable to enlist the help of the official copyist for the council commission in Dresden, Gottfried Rausch. At the back of his mind was the hope that this would clear a way for him to make an honourable exit from the drudgery of

Leipzig, or at the very least to obtain a court title to act as a hedge against further affronts by the Leipzig councilmen.

It is only by making a careful comparison of the parts and the score that we can begin to unlock their secrets. Emanuel, his second son, then a nineteen-year-old law student at Leipzig University (though still living with his parents), was entrusted with copying out the two soprano parts. Admonished to make no error, we can follow his way of discreetly entering marker dots in his father's autograph so as to keep his place every time he starts a new page. Then he makes a slip: midway through the *Christe* he arrives at a bar ending with a tied B♭. Both the next two lines of the autograph begin with a tied B♭, as it happens. Inadvertently he skips a line and is obliged to enter the missing line at the foot of the page. This was an easy mistake to make – unimportant in itself – but it could have arisen only if he were copying directly from the autograph score and not from a pre-existing set of (Leipzig) parts. It confirms therefore (besides other supporting evidence) that the *Missa*, if not conceived there, was carried out *in* Dresden and *for* Dresden.*

The obvious and desirable outcome should have been a performance of this short, two-movement Mass, or *Missa corta* – ideally in the presence of its dedicatee, the Elector. It would have been entirely in character if Bach had prepared the ground for this by enlisting the support of his more influential colleagues and friends within the Dresden Court Capelle. But we cannot be sure that it ever materialised, or, if so, where it took place. It was liturgically appropriate for either the Sophienkirche, where son Friedemann was now ensconced,† or the Catholic Hofkirche, where the court Capelle regularly performed on solemn feast-days, complete

* The organ part is in *Kammerton* – perfectly suited to the organ in Dresden's Sophienkirche, but not to the organs in the Leipzig churches, which were tuned to the higher *Chorton*. However, a prominent feature of Bach's scoring was the use in the *Kyrie* of two oboes d'amore, instruments which, as Janice Stockigt has pointed out, were very much in use in Leipzig in Bach's time, but seem to have become obsolete in Dresden after Heinichen's death in 1729, when they were replaced by the chalumeau (Stockigt, 'Consideration of Bach's *Kyrie e Gloria* BWV 232i within the Context of Dresden Catholic Mass Settings 1729–1733' in University of Belfast International Symposium, *Discussion Book* (2007), Vol. 1, pp. 52–92).

† Christoph Wolff suggests that a performance took place here (the church generally frequented by the Lutheran court officials) on 26 July, the eighth Sunday after Trinity, 'probably as a special afternoon concert comparable to the organ recitals Bach had given there before' with Bach and members of the family participating (*Johann Sebastian Bach: The Learned Musician* (2000), p. 370).

with its troupe of operatic solo singers. There are enough features of Bach's score and the way it resembles the large Neapolitan-style Mass-settings that were just coming into fashion in Dresden to suggest that it had been crafted with this particular ensemble in view – arias for the individual vocal soloists newly recruited from Italy in 1730 and for the several virtuoso instrumentalists within the Capelle. He himself had heard four out of five of the new castrati taking the leads in Johann Adolph Hasse's opera *Cleofide* in 1731, and was thus well placed to adjust his solo music to their capabilities and vocal ranges when composing his *Missa.**

In the same way, his orchestral writing gave plenty of opportunities for displaying the stylistic versatility and the virtuosity that he admired in the court orchestra and singled out for praise in his 'Entwurff' (see Chapter 7, p. 224). Bach would have been made aware by his friends that there had been a major shake-up of the musical Capelle since the time of his first visit in 1717, both in personnel and stylistic orientation. Not only had the entire French comedy and dance company who had served August the Strong been dismissed, but there had been a reduction in the number of instrumentalists, and only six boy choristers remained. The musical side of the liturgy was now in the hands of the court orchestra, the *Musici regii* operating under new regulations. With Capellmeister Hasse abroad, it was directed by Bach's Bohemian friend, Jan Dismas Zelenka. At full strength the Dresden Hofcapelle could muster twenty-six string players to perform both operas and, on solemn occasions, music in church. This was in addition to the multiple woodwind and horns and the separate (and greatly privileged) ensemble of twelve court trumpeters (*Hoftrompeter*) and two timpanists. It could claim to be one of Europe's top-ranking orchestras, but perhaps not at this particular juncture, when its members, jittery because of the recent dismissals, were submitting a flood of petitions relating to back pay and promotions to the Elector's chancellery.†

* Stockigt has analysed the ranges and vocal profiles of the Dresden castrati – Rochetti, Bindi, Annibali and Campioli – from the oratorio and Mass repertoire they undertook in the early 1730s and compared these to the vocal ranges of the two soprano and alto parts in Bach's *Missa*, revealing a close, plausible correspondence (op. cit.).

† It was, however, a flexible body, varying in numbers (see footnote pp. 482–3). On one occasion in 1739 Zelenka directed an ensemble of five singers, four violins, two violas, pairs of flutes and oboes, trumpets and drums, and a continuo section of four players in a work to mark the birth of Prince Clemens Wenceslaus of Saxony, which was celebrated in the small chapel of the Hubertusburg Palace. A striking combination of individual technical skill and panache within the orchestra, and of its discipline under Johann Georg Pisendel's direction,

Tempting as it is to envisage Bach supervising a star-studded premiere of his embryonic *B minor Mass* in the congenial and well-rehearsed company of his Dresden friends, we lack all proof. It is just as likely that he was, at most, a mere spectator, and that if a Dresden performance did in fact take place, it was either Friedemann, encouraged by his father (and naturally keen to show his own credentials so soon after his appointment), who was in sole charge, or Zelenka. This notion is supported by the evidence of the continuo part, which is unusually explicit, not just in terms of figured bass, but also in providing cues for the separate voice entries – valuable, indispensable even, as a mnemonic for a continuo-director to keep a track of the performance, but totally superfluous had Bach as composer been in charge.

Performance or no performance, there was no immediate response from the Elector. Preoccupied with issues of international diplomacy, in 1734 he moved his court to Warsaw for the next two years. Bach would just have to bide his time along with other petitioners such as Zelenka, who in any case might have felt that, having served as the acting head of the church ensemble since the 1720s, he had a prior claim. Bach nevertheless kept up the pressure by producing no fewer than eight secular cantatas in the Elector's honour or that of his family – a none too subtle means of jogging his memory.* It took a further three years, a second letter of application and intercession by the Russian diplomat Count Keyserlingk before Bach finally received his coveted court appointment in Dresden – and even then it brought with it no financial reward sufficient to justify a move from Leipzig. His name finally appeared alongside Zelenka's in the list of composers of church music at the Saxon and Polish courts in the *Hof- und Staats-Calender* of 1738. Meanwhile the combined incomes of Capellmeister Hasse and his diva wife – who for long stretches of time were absent from Dresden – amounted to sixteen times that of Bach's Leipzig salary.

There is an alternative scenario – plausible, too – in which the *Missa*

seems to have been achieved only after a long-drawn-out period of in-fighting between the older French-style musicians favoured by August the Strong and the ardent advocates of Italian music patronised by his son Friedrich August II. This and the fact that each player was allowed and even encouraged to specialise (not like the usual jack-of-all-trades) impressed Bach enough to refer to it in his 'Entwurff' (BD I, No. 22/ NBR, p. 150).

* Actually Bach already had an honorific title, one that bound him for the past four years to the lesser court of Duke Christian of Saxe-Weissenfels, though in Bach's eyes it did not carry anything approaching the prestige or bargaining power of the Dresden title.

did make its mark and on the very musicians with whom Bach so hoped to be associated, those of the Dresden Hofcapelle – Zelenka, Pisendel, Buffardin and others. All except Zelenka (who was then in Vienna) would have remembered Bach's walkover victory in the rather contrived contest with Louis Marchand, the French virtuoso keyboard player, back in 1717. More recently, he had given organ recitals in 1725 and 1731 'in the presence of all the Court musicians and virtuosos in a fashion that compelled the admiration of everyone'.[4] So they already had ample proof of his all-round talents. Regardless of whether they took part in a performance of his Mass or not, in 1733, the manuscript parts would have passed from hand to hand for scrutiny and evaluation. Normally it would have been Hasse as Capellmeister who would have been first to pass judgement on a new score; next in line came Zelenka, for some time past the most active musical director in Dresden during the declining years of Hasse's predecessor, Johann David Heinichen. So far it has not proved possible to unravel the chain of influences in the Zelenka/Bach relationship, but it looks very much as though it were two-way traffic: Zelenka impressing Bach with his performances of large-scale Neapolitan Masses by Sarro and Mancini and of his own works in a similar style; Bach returning the compliment in the way he styled his own *Missa* along Dresden lines; Zelenka then reciprocating with his own tribute, the *Missa Sanctissima Trinitatis* of 1736, which manifestly owed a great deal to Bach's *Kyrie I*.

Even the most sceptical of the Dresden Court musicians could have seen that here in Bach's Mass was a work well attuned to their own house style (and even to the individual talents of their ensemble). Many of the Mass-settings they regularly performed by composers such as Lotti, Caldara, Sarro, Mancini and others, for all their opulence and grandeur, lacked musical substance. Bach's setting extended well beyond these counterparts, and by any objective standards his *Missa* was on a totally different level of invention and complexity. Even in this two-movement form, it already constituted a major work in its own right, testimony to Bach's habit of surpassing all the models he assimilated. This could be the main reason why it does not seem to have formed part of the repertoire of the court chapel.* Probably no one at that stage

* If it had, the performing material would have been housed in the cupboard behind the choir gallery of the Hofkirche and entered into its library catalogue (1765). Instead, it was preserved on the shelves of the Saxon royal library (see Stockigt, op. cit.).

foresaw that it was to be just the starting-point for a *Missa tota*, and one of the most substantial and indeed epic of all Bach's works. That lay some way in the future – and, arguably, the best of it was still to come.

***

The first thing that would have struck the Dresden musicians was the immense seriousness and grandeur of the opening exordium of the *Kyrie*. They would have sensed its emergence as an impassioned *de profundis* – the sinner's cry of help to a forgiving God. Choral writing on this scale was unprecedented, even in Dresden. The principal theme of Bach's opening *Kyrie* begins with a graceful gesture in dotted rhythm and then promptly divides: an ascending, aspiring delineation of prayer, balanced by a responding sigh, more instrumental – like one of his two-part Inventions – than vocal. Ask any singer: it is not easy to keep alive the sense of uplift in the prayer motif while preparing for the appoggiated sigh without chopping the upper line short. The way that the solemn yet lilting fugue stretches out so naturally and coherently in a single panoramic sweep suggests that the momentum needs to be maintained, the pacing deliberate but not comatose, dignified but never plodding. For all its twists and turns of harmonic tension, the fugue subject itself stays constant throughout. Only its tailpiece gets altered, first flattened, then raised. These modifications serve as 'episodes' between the fugal expositions – moments for the listener to step aside and reflect before the procession moves on again. Once re-absorbed within the fugue's development these same intervallic tags are stretched wider and wider. Like a painter allowing the brush in his hand to take temporary charge in shaping a design, one senses Bach, the born improviser, taking momentary control here: the tension is ratcheted upwards – once (bars 92–4), then a second time (99–101) even more emphatically – thrilling in performance. One's attention is drawn to the second soprano line: they seem to be the ones generating all this collective energy. In the process it is easy to miss the fact that it is precisely their fugal entry (in the subdominant) that paves the way for the first sopranos to re-enter (on the tonic) and so to instigate the smoothly effected recapitulation. Bach has whipped up a storm. Yet he has carried all his participants safely through the start of the journey, and at the movement's satisfying conclusion he leaves them chastened but not browbeaten.

Next he enjoins his performers and listeners to follow that epic and polyphonic plea to the Lord with a matching – but far warmer and personal – appeal to the Son. The *Christe eleison* is expressed in the intimate language of a Neapolitan love-duet for two sopranos – home territory to the Dresden Court musicians – in which the singers glide over their parallel thirds and sixths in perfect euphony. No sooner is it over than the appeal to the Lord is resumed, this time with still greater urgency. The stern granite-like outlines of this *Kyrie II* are sculpted in a deliberately archaic style, an impression mitigated by the rhythmic drive and rich harmonic density of a four-part choral fugue. This is not art made to downcast. It exhibits a rare combination of complex musical elaboration and sheer generosity of spirit. Bach's own plea for forgiveness is woven into the fabric of his music, just as Rembrandt's features peer out at us from his *The Stoning of St Stephen*, 'claiming no halo of special piety', as Nigel Spivey observes; 'he is simply there.'[5] So, in this moment, is Bach.

No sooner has the curtain come down on this sombre penitential scene than it is raised again. We might expect the new tableau to depict the heavenly host of angels appearing to the shepherds. This, of course, is the way Handel paints it in *Messiah*: in 'Glory to God' a distant angelic battalion approaches, delivers its message and then retreats into the heavens – naive, theatrical and highly effective. But that is not Bach's way. In his *Christmas Oratorio* his angelic choir will appear to consist entirely of expert contrapuntists. Here, on the contrary, he startles us with his announcement of the *Gloria* as a decidedly earthly dance. There is no upbeat: the music just explodes into action. With its alternation of strong and weak bars in triple time, this is clearly a celebration that is taking place not up in the skies but down here. It is more peasant stomp than dainty celestial waftings, more Bruegel than Botticelli.

Making their first festive appearance in the Mass, the three trumpets and drums galvanise the whole ensemble. It is they who instigate – but do not efface – the exuberant swirling figuration within the rest of the band. Leading off in the 'royal' key of D major with trumpets was standard fare in the Saxon capital, but the writing there seldom reached this degree of sophistication, with the players swapping parts and vying with each other for stratospheric supremacy. The style Bach used to propel the choral voices into action in imitation of the trumpet theme, their ends of phrases cascading like fireworks, had no equivalent in the sort of music customarily heard in the Dresden churches. Bach, as ever, makes not the slightest concession towards vocal, as opposed to instrumental, style. He fully expects the human larynx to be able to function with exactly the same agility as lips pressed to brass tubing or fingers slammed down on wooden fingerboards.* The interjection of an occasional bar's rest is less to give the singers a chance to breathe than for rhetorical effect: to isolate and punctuate their shouts of *Gloria!* A fine web of intricate contrapuntal detail is spun from the eighteen separate vocal and instrumental lines, here compressed into a mere hundred bars of *vivace* triple rhythm. Culminating in the swagger of a collective hemiola – a clear indication of the new unit beat – this great dance flows seamlessly into the proclamation of 'peace on earth'.

There are signs that Bach might once again be having mild fun at the expense of the theologians. First he invites us to celebrate the night Christ was born on *earth* with a festive jamboree (not, like Handel, with the angels *in excelsis*). Then, switching to common time, he introduces the calm prayer for peace as though led by the angels – *et in terra pax*. It has the hallmark of an operatic *scène du sommeil* in Lully's mould: caressing and soothing in its initial syncopated outline, as phrases are exchanged between choir, upper strings and upper woodwind. It also reads beautifully as 'eye' music: in the autograph score the instruments seem to drift upwards away from the fixed bass pedal, like prayers floating heavenwards. We might have guessed that all this is just preparation for a grand vocal fugue, its gentle theme aspiring and its counter-subject made up of the roulades of the earlier *Gloria* dance – now blues-like in the way they seem to vault over the regular bar-lines and the gentle beat-to-beat punctuation of the instruments. The magic of this fugal prayer now begins to take effect. The voices conjoin to proclaim 'good will to all men' (*bonae voluntatis*) and the instruments immediately answer in assent. Even the trumpets are propelled back into action, as though to confirm the imminence of God's gift of peace on earth.

We or the Dresden musicians – it matters not which – have been shown how an essential part of Bach's overall design for his *Gloria* is to vary the texture by exchanging public (choral) with private (solo) utterance. There are no recitatives in the Ordinary of the Mass to break these

* This was, of course, one of Scheibe's criticisms – that Bach demanded 'that singers and instrumentalists should be able to do with their throats and instruments whatever he can play on the clavier' (BD II, No. 400/NBR, p. 338). He had a point – but that is exactly why Bach's works are so challenging (and rewarding) to the performer.

satisfying alternations of movement and scale, and Bach is very particular in the way that he indicates the intended flow and pacing of successive movements by means of pauses, double bars, the absence of both, the merging of one section into the next, or the simple injunction *sequitur*. For the ensuing *Laudamus*, despite its plural pronoun ('*we* praise thee, *we* bless thee', etc.), he narrows the focus here to a single singer, an obbligato violin and the string ensemble in support. The challenge for both performer and listener is not to be flummoxed by all the ornamentation – the plethora of trills he scatters along its path. To know that he could count on the combined technical virtuosity of a violinist like Johann Georg Pisendel, the Dresden Concertmeister, and an accomplished soprano such as Faustina Bordoni (if it was indeed she who first sang the *Laudamus* and not one of the castrati) must have been reassuring for Bach. It was Faustina, according to Charles Burney, who 'in a manner invented a new kind of singing, by running divisions with a neatness and velocity which astonished all who heard her'.[6] Essentially the *Laudamus* is a simple binary folk-melody which he has decorated with garlands of improvisatory ornaments – *fioretti*, or 'little flowers', as his cousin J. G. Walther called them – meat and drink to an Italian opera-trained diva or a castrato. Success in this movement depends on the two solo performers keeping the essential 'bones' of the folk-melody always to the fore, on making adequate provision for breath between the phrases and on gliding effortlessly through Bach's thicket of embellishments. In particular the solo violin needs space and time to hover high above the voice line, like Vaughan Williams's *Lark Ascending*, while supported by the thermal currents – the accompanying figures of the lower strings.

Even before this free spirit has landed, in the ensuing silence a monkish sound of men's voices intoning *Gratias agimus tibi* is heard in a version of the Gregorian chant *Non nobis Domine*, one of the oldest canons in all Western music. Here he is re-working and transcribing the opening chorus of a cantata (BWV 29) for the Leipzig municipal elections of 1731. We can watch him adjusting a German-texted theme, eliminating its strong tonic accents (*wir danken*) by widening the bars into 'breve' units (despite the confusing and corrupt *alla breve* appellation) to make room for the new Latin words (*Gratias agimus tibi*). With the second clause – *propter magnam gloriam* – we are propelled forwards again into the world of Baroque figural music, now firmly locked into diatonic harmony and defined by articulate rhythms.* The whole chronological carpet of diatonic harmony – nearly 200 years of it – is being unrolled before us. The sense of arrival is complete only at that magical moment when the kettledrums thwack out dominant and tonic – always accompanied by their accomplice, the third trumpet – to underpin the bass canonic entry (bars 35–7). Bach's three trumpets seem to be leading off into the thin ozone layer, in the same way that the limbs or gestures of Baroque painters occasionally fly off the canvas as though the frame were too small to contain the full extent of their expression.

* * *

We have now arrived at the apex of Bach's nine-movement *Gloria.* At this point he finds ways of bringing to the surface that partially concealed narrative thread of the Mass Ordinary (which eludes all but a few composers). You sense his delight in juxtaposing a Gregorian-based movement like the majestic *Gratias* with an elegant *galant* duet like the *Domine Deus*, which uses the same rising bass line (three whole tones and a half step) in double diminution and follows it with a similar melismatic figure, proof that with his technical mastery he can encompass any mood or style at will. Next he pairs the *Domine Deus* duet (without its expected *da capo* structure) with the *Qui tollis* chorus. The dramatist in him makes delicious play of the seraphic innocence of the filial relations between Father (tenor) and Son (soprano) in a canonic duet. This he contrasts with the extreme pathos of the *Qui tollis* – the pain caused to the Son-made-man in anticipation of Christ's suffering on the Cross. Everything about the *Domine Deus* is conceived in terms of benediction: the key (G major), the benign mood created by flute over pizzicato bass and answered by muted upper strings, the sense of

* Donald Tovey observes admiringly that now 'the real business begins when no less than thirteen entries of the first subject, all on tonic and dominant, are piled up without intermission, the trumpets providing the 8th and 9th entries in extra parts. This I believe to be Bach's record in such edifices' (*Essays in Musical Analysis* (1937), Vol. 5, p. 31). On the differences between word-setting in German – full of meaning, theological purpose and stress-awareness – and in time-hallowed Latin, I am grateful to David Watkin (admirable continuo and solo cellist and now also a conductor) for his suggestion that one should not try to apply the same interpretative scanning mechanisms to both, Latin being more instrumentally and plainly conceived than vernacular German.

its being a spiritual love-duet – both modern and *galant*. Even the two eldest of Bach's fashion-conscious sons might have approved. But their father is not playing to the gallery. If the task is to find suitable music for such a central doctrinal text, he seems to be saying, then set it with a smile – with euphonious parallel thirds and sixths, syncopated or plain. Musicologists have been oddly perplexed by the clear traces of rhythmic alteration, the back dotting of the paired semiquavers to be found in the Dresden part-books. That Lombard rhythms (back dotting) were fashionable in Dresden in the 1730s, particularly in movements which emphasise Christ's intimate relationship to mankind, does not imply that Bach was currying favour with the Dresdeners; it is merely the gentlest of hints that he was au fait with current trends, one likely to have found favour with the likes of Zelenka and Pisendel.* More to the point, they fit idiomatically with the sentiment of the words and give lilt and charm to the flute theme, with its answer in the strings.

Now, with the words *Domine Deus, Agnus Dei*, a shadow passes across the music as it modulates to E minor, as though in anticipation of the Crucifixion. It is also perhaps an indication to the performer that the back dotting should now cease. If this was Bach's way of indicating to us a B, or a 'middle section', he confounds our expectations by doing away with a *da capo* altogether and merging his duet imperceptibly into the ensuing four-part *Qui tollis*. He then slows the momentum and eases us into the sarabande-like chorus, even adapting the outline of the final phrase of the singers in anticipation of the melodic shape of the new sorrow-laden chorus proclaiming that God in Christ bore the sins of the world on the Cross. This is the central text of the *Gloria* and, by means of this reminder, its most serious moment. As the 'miserable

* It is amazing how the dry, literalist mind-set of successive editors of Bach's great *Mass* can ignore evidence that did not appear to fit with their preconceived notions of how his music ought to sound. Julius Rietz, in preparing the *Bach-Gesamtausgabe* in 1856, found the Lombard rhythms indicated only in the flute's first bar (and not in the parallel violin 1 part). He considered them therefore to be an aberration, so he omitted them. One hundred years later, the Lutheran editor of the NBA, Friedrich Smend, intent on expunging any signs of Catholic orientation by Bach, gave no credence whatsoever to the Dresden parts. So he, too, omitted the adjusted rhythms. Both editors thus succeeded in eliminating one of the few riveting signs of Bach's own performance that have come down to us and in ignoring the type of spontaneous idiomatic adjustment good musicians make as a matter of course: the flute plays the melodic arc with back-dotted rhythms, the violins, automatically and as a matter of etiquette and courtesy, follow suit.

offenders' necessitating Christ's atonement, we are referred back to those desperate cries of help at the outset of the *Kyrie*.*

The prevailing mood of this remarkable fifty-bar movement is one of woebegone heaviness and anguish, generated by the violas, now un-muted. Their paired quavers slice through the texture with sighs of lamentation (just as they did in the opening chorus of the *John Passion*). They are the grieving heart at the centre of the choral and orchestral body. The clarity of the vocal scoring – initially two voices at a time – makes this grief appear to be more personal. A pair of flutes enters high above the dark sonority of voices and strings, a soothing and occasionally disturbing presence. Bach has chosen his Jeremiad cantata (BWV 46), the one predicting the destruction of Jerusalem, as his model (see Chapter 9, pp. 302–3), crucially adjusting its rhythmic inflection – and he makes these adjustments straight on to the score. The measured declamation of *wie mein Schmerz* (two crotchets and a minim stretched over a descending diminished fourth) now becomes the much more urgent *Miserere nobis* (in four consecutive quavers) – a tiny, innocent-looking adjustment, but huge in its new expressive potency. Significantly he also omits the cantata's opening sixteen bars of instrumental prelude, plunging straight into the opening *Qui tollis*.†

There are several ingredients to this remarkable creation. First, there is the background of the familiar Old Testament penitential text, with its reference to the destruction of Jerusalem as predicted by Jesus (Luke 19: 41–8). This is conveyed through the harmonic dissonance and intense expressivity of the vocal lines. Then there is the single emphasis by the bass line at the start of every bar; and the hovering of those flutes – serene at first, but later fluttering like wounded birds. The effect is poignant (still more so in our own times, when the implied references to Jerusalem and the frequent threats to its sites, holy to three religions, are excruciatingly topical). The individual vocal lines begin in imitation. Sometimes they collide, with prolonged bruising dissonances, then part, each apparently

* Stockigt (op. cit., p. 21) points to a feature of Bach's setting that would have clashed with the local Dresden practice of the time – of slowing the tempo down still further, dropping in dynamic and introducing a string *tremulo* in support of the voices.

† This is related to the celebrated penitential text O *vos omnes qui transitis*, set so darkly by the Renaissance composers Victoria and Gesualdo, and much later by Pablo Casals, and in English by Handel in *Messiah* – 'Behold and see if there be any sorrow like unto his sorrow.'

pursuing an independent trajectory. There are momentary pairings (*deprecationem nostram*), and all four voices come together at cadences. This gives to the whole movement a sense of tragic choreography – of slow-motion spirals, of furrows being turned, or of geometric dance patterns loosened and redrawn. Only the highest and lowest voices bind things together: a single harmonic emphasis per bar in the continuo (but pulsated in the cello line like a slow bow vibrato) and the flutes high above the enactment of this pained human ritual. We may be tricked into hearing this amazing polyphony as the result of autonomous melodic movement, whereas all the time it is being controlled by the inexorable harmonic rhythm, the tonal grammar of Bach's bass line. In performance the effect of such a *tableau vivant* etched in sound is spellbinding – provided that every one of its ten strands (four voices, four strings and two flutes) is balanced, combed and always distinct.

Bach has ended on a half-close. In a Passion-setting one might expect a *secco* recitative at this point. In Bach's original (BWV 46) the music now erupts into an energetic fugue. Here, on the other hand, he keeps things moving forward by means of consecutive arias. Once again, as with the *Kyrie* trilogy, we encounter the rubric *Qui sedes sequitur* and *Quoniam tu solus sanctus sequitur*. The music is through-composed, in other words, and no awkward pauses are called for. Doctrinally Bach has moved from Atonement to Mediation. In the first of the two arias, the *Qui sedes* (for alto, oboe d'amore and strings), he portrays Christ's role mediating between God and man, and 'sitting at the right hand of God'. This is symbolic and even ironic; for here the music is anything but sedentary – as an Italianate *giga* it is unequivocally balletic and its ritornello structure is made up of overlapping phrases which erode the stability of its underlying dance pulse.

In the second aria (*Quoniam*) the text refers to Christ's kingly office. It clearly appealed to Bach's particular vein of humour to evoke the 'most high' with the growliest forces available to him: two bassoons, bass soloist and basso continuo. The treacherous *Waldhorn* is the exception here. The bassoon counter-theme, as Tovey rightly insists, 'must always be brought out as a main theme and not treated as an accompaniment',[7] particularly at the point where they chug along above the horn line in *buffo* style (bars 72–4). It seems that he had the sound of a particular ensemble, even of particular individuals, in mind. Five bassoonists were on the payroll of the Dresden Capelle, and two or three of them were on call at any given time (whereas in Leipzig he was lucky to find even a single competent bassoonist). Both Heinichen and Zelenka regularly composed for pairs of solo bassoons, and Hasse had featured the *Waldhorn* in his opera *Cleofide*, which Bach heard in Dresden in 1731. In Bach's hands the overall effect of these instruments in combination is magnificently stilted, bucolic and slightly grotesque. As befits a polonaise, the horn is noble, regal even (but we need to ensure that the singer is never engulfed by the surrounding sonorities), while the continuo line often bumps into – and sometimes rises above – the bassoons.*

The *Quoniam* begins to make sense by its strategic placement, in the way that it follows the pathos of the *Qui tollis* and its dance-like sequel, and heralds the epic razzmatazz of the *Cum sancto spiritu* – the three movements are closely bound together. Bach reminds us that this is the completion of a clause – 'for thou only art holy . . . with the Holy Ghost in the glory of God the Father. Amen.' Towards the end of the aria there is palpable expectancy as the bass-messenger rounds out his proclamation and the instruments pipe him off stage. Immediately the *Cum sancto* takes off with a tremendous jolt, rather like the way a Big Dipper deceptively inches its way along, then suddenly hurtles off. Mention of the Holy Spirit is the key to the changes in both pace and mood of this new music. As in his double-choir motet BWV 226, *Der Geist hilft unser Schwachheit auf*, the invigorating power of the Holy Spirit is the determining factor in the Christian's acknowledgement of Christ's Godhead. This is cue for celebration – in dance as much as in song. The throbbing

* The polonaise was apparently perceived at the time as 'a majestic, processional, ceremonial and chivalric dance . . . [with] its proper, slower tempo, since it was usually danced in tall boots, often with a sabre at the side, at times also with torches' (Szymon Paczkowski, 'On the Role and Meaning of the Polonaise in the *Mass in B minor*' in University of Belfast International Symposium, *Discussion Book* (2007), Vol. 1, pp. 43–51). Dresden composers such as Zelenka, Heinichen, Hasse, Schuster and Naumann habitually turned to music *à la polonaise* for the *Quoniam* and the *Et resurrexit* sections of the Mass, so Bach was following a local tradition here and, according to Paczkowski, achieving a double aim: 'he expressed the sense of the liturgical text in the best possible way and, at the same time, he paid homage to his ruler, to whom the *Missa* was dedicated. Thus the polonaise in the aria *Quoniam tu solus sanctus* should be interpreted in association with the customs of the Polish–Saxon court, as a "royal dance" usable, in both a secular and a religious context, as a symbol of a monarch's power.' Mellers's view is that in Bach's treatment, 'the God of Power seems larger than life and too big for his boots, as did the absolute monarchs who tried to emulate him in mundane terms' (*Bach and the Dance of God* (1980), p. 205).

pulsation of a single note (which was already present in the horn part of the *Quoniam*) passes to the upper strings, and later the trumpets and finally the woodwind, but now with a greater sense of forward propulsion and ebullience. For this is the fourth movement in a row to use triple or compound metre, and in ever-quickening tempo: the *Qui tollis* as a sarabande, the *Qui sedes* as a moderately paced *giga*, the *Quoniam* as a stately but forward-thrusting polonaise, and finally the *Cum sancto*, a free-spirited, corybantic dance.*

The sense of release and of liberation in this fabulous choral dance is contagious. Bach's technique is at first to alternate contrasting groupings of voices and instruments to build structure and generate excitement. The fleet-footed exposition of the fugue then begins in the voices alone (bar 37) and bears a striking affinity with the balletic choral fugue 'Die Kinder Zion' from his motet BWV 225, *Singet dem Herrn* (see Chapter 12, pp. 473–4). Now the instruments re-assert themselves – downward arpeggio cascades in the strings, a jazzy syncopated figure in the winds, and skittish curlicue flourishes which are there purely for high spirits (for they do not advance the thematic argument one jot). The orchestra *wills* the choir to re-join them with their plain, chordal Amens. On their next appearance the vocal lines are doubled by the instruments in a second fugal exposition (which, interestingly, shows slight variants, hinting that a four-voiced original may stand in the background of this movement's creation). The trumpets are finally sucked back into the action, and the music breaks free with the sort of Dionysian abandon one might associate more with Beethoven or Stravinsky than with Bach.

We have seen that the Lutheran year had its feasts no less than its fasts, and again and again in the cantatas Bach delights in the seasonal punctuation of the year and in any of the pagan festivals that Christianity appropriated for its own calendar. Well, here is one – let us say it is for Midsummer's Day – which was *not* included, or as far as we know given official approval. It is celebrated in carnival style – 'almost pre-Christian, if not overtly pagan, in its abandon'.[8]† The contrapuntal

* There is absolutely no way that the absence of a double bar or a metre sign here could indicate that the 'neutral *allegro*' of the *Quoniam* is to be continued in the *Cum sancto* (George B. Stauffer, *Bach: The Mass in B minor* (1997), p. 238). *Vivace* certainly implies liveliness of articulation, but it also inescapably influences the tempo of the movement.

† It is impossible to disagree with Mellers's detecting 'an element of danger in this music's power and glory'. This he contrasts with 'Handel's Augustan assurance' (op. cit., p. 208).

zest that Bach generates in these final bars – and the aural pleasure he gives us – is immense. Part of its magic lies in the several ways he finds of dividing the twelve semiquavers of a bar into different groups, involving cross-rhythmic patterns and syncopations.

What, then, did those Dresden Court musicians make of this 'apotheosis of the dance'? We have seen that there was much that would have been familiar to them in the earlier movements of the *Gloria* – the sectional treatment, the balancing of solos with choral movements, the florid writing for solo voices and obbligato instruments – which displayed Bach's perfect assimilation of modern Neapolitan style exported to the Saxon capital. But a choral movement with this degree of athleticism and secularity was surely something utterly new. The contrapuntal virtuosity was dazzling enough, and the uncompromising exuberance of his writing for voices and instruments – particularly for trumpets – was beyond anything in their repertoire. Perhaps for at least one of them, Zelenka, the spicy rhythmic virility and ornamental daring of the *Cum sancto* put him in mind of his native Bohemia.*

* * *

For the next twelve years we lose all trace of the *Missa* and its potential expansion. Was it dead in the water, as it were, after the big disappointment in Dresden? Did Bach just file it away in the well-stocked recesses of his memory bank, waiting for a new set of circumstances to present him with an opportunity for revival and reappraisal? If so, the single trigger that detonated the creative energy needed to complete the Mass is probably to be found around Christmas-time in 1745. The Second Silesian War had just come to an end, having brought considerable hardship to Leipzig and its citizens. For the first time in his life Bach had first-hand experience of the horrors and suffering of war, as Prussian troops occupied Leipzig in the late autumn of 1745 and devastated its surroundings. Three years later he still remembered it as 'the time we had – alas! – the Prussian invasion'.[9] A special service of thanksgiving to celebrate the Peace of Dresden was held in the Pauliner (University)

* Zelenka's own compositions sometimes contain traces of Czech folk-music. Though generally admired for his skill in counterpoint, it is in his instrumental *capricci* and his seven-part *Hipocondrie* that he shows his originality in matters of experimental tonal colouring, rhythmic groupings and dynamics.

Church on Christmas Day. Sandwiched between the early morning Mass in the Thomaskirche and the afternoon service in the Nikolaikirche, this was one of those occasions when members of Bach's two best church choirs were available to perform together.* Here also was an opportunity to give Leipzig audiences a chance of hearing his unusual five-voiced Latin cantata BWV 191, *Gloria in excelsis Deo* – in which he had hastily re-assembled and condensed three of the Dresden *Gloria* movements (*Gloria*, *Domine Deus*, *Cum sancto spiritu*) into a new triptych. In addition, his six-voiced Christmas *Sanctus*, first heard on Christmas Day in 1724, was almost certainly revived for the same service. So, five of the eventual twenty-seven movements of the *B minor Mass* might have been performed together for the first time. Given the political context and the sense of collective relief at the ending of the war, it is possible that we have here the embryo of a *Friedenmesse*, a 'Mass of peace'.[10] That would have been consistent with the in-built alternation of human woe (*Kyrie*) and its release in God-inspired joy (*Gloria*) latent in the structure of Bach's Dresden *Missa*. Was he struck afresh by the quality of his Latin-texted music? Perhaps he suddenly saw a destiny for it – the potential for incorporating it into a much more ambitious framework,

* In the course of 2012 Michael Maul unearthed new evidence relating to the existence from the seventeenth century to the early nineteenth century of an elite octet of singers (two per part) from among the boarders of the Thomasschule, those who, in the estimation of the cantor, 'outperform all the others' (*Schulordungen*, 1634 and 1723; see H.-J. Schulze, 'Bachs Aufführungsapparat' in Christoph Wolff (ed.), *Die Welt der Bach-Kantaten*, Vol. 3 (1998)). This is the one constant factor in the organisation of the school choir lasting from J. H. Schein's cantorate up to that of J. A. Hiller. This elite octet constituted the cantor's first *Kantorei*, had their own regulations, music lessons and rehearsals, and in comparison with the other boarders were exceptionally well paid (mostly from performing at weddings and other private events), even after the cantor's and other teachers' shares of their earnings had been deducted. Under normal circumstances they would have been the ones to perform the *Haupt-Musik* (the cantata, in other words) at Sunday services, but could be supplemented at the cantor's discretion by other *Alumnen* when extra singers were needed to perform his more elaborate and festive music – a practice well documented for the late seventeenth century, which may well have extended into Kuhnau and Bach's time. These new findings need to be set against all the other fragmentary evidence pointing to the constraints and difficulties both these Thomascantors experienced in fielding an ensemble adequate to meeting the increasing demands of their church music. It goes to show how the realities of performance practice in their time were in a state of continual flux, warning us not to rely exclusively on the same old source material which has proved to be susceptible to widely different interpretations (see Maul, *'Dero berühmbter Chor': Die Leipziger Thomasschule und ihre Kantoren 1212–1804* (2012), and an article in BJb in preparation for 2013).

one which gave him the motivation to create a definitive statement of faith comparable in scale and grandeur to his Passion-settings.

At some stage, then – perhaps immediately after the Christmas peace celebrations, but perhaps not for another two years – came the momentous decision, with the *Missa* of 1733 as its starting-point, to complete his 'Great Catholic Mass'. (This was the title under which it appeared in the estate catalogue of C. P. E. Bach in 1790.) The ramifications were huge. Bach was still in possession of the dedicatory score – but not the parts of the *Missa*. He would have reasoned that any complete Mass-setting would need to match the original *Kyrie* and *Gloria* pairing in terms of scale and structure. It meant that for the *Credo*, for example, he would need to devise a multisectioned movement of comparable weight to the preceding *Gloria*. The risk here was that he would end up with a work on a gargantuan scale, too long, apart from the most exceptional circumstances, to fit into any liturgy, no matter whether it was Catholic or Lutheran. Whereas his *Kyrie/Gloria* pairing was just about within the acceptable liturgical dimensions of the Dresden Mass repertoire, its new portions would be far in excess of what was considered fitting as a setting of the Ordinary of the Mass.* Grouping them in this way for practical use in no way compromised what may have been his twin aspirations in completing the work: to encompass within a single work an encyclopedic survey of all the styles he most cherished in the music of his own and of earlier times, and to achieve perfection in the execution of that work. It shows phenomenal ambition.

His preparations were meticulous, characteristic of the exercises he deliberately undertook every time he committed himself to formulating a definitive statement. Bach was reverting to first principles (in the same way that all good scientists do at some point), wanting to move beyond the limits of what he had done before. If that meant going back almost to square one, that would be a sacrifice worth making: he had decided to carry out a fundamental reappraisal of the very building blocks, mathematical, musical or otherwise, that would enable him to refresh

* Wolfgang Horn (*Die Dresdner Hofkirchenmusik 1720–1745* (1987), p. 192) shows that, at 770 bars, Bach's *Gloria* was in the top 6 or 7 per cent of stand-alone *Gloria* settings in the Dresden repertoire of the time. Interestingly, the ones that are actually longer than his (by Mancini, Zelenka and Sarro) are a great deal longer.

and to bring alive his thoughts and questions about the Mass and its wider implications.

First came considerations of basic structure, logistics and style. The choice of the *Missa* of 1733 as the starting-point for a new *Missa tota* meant that some aspects had already been settled: the five-part vocal scoring and the full-sized orchestra; the division of the text by coherent (though linked) sections fitted into a chiastic structure; the mosaic of solo and choral movements and the intermixture of styles – Italianate *concertato* movements on the one hand, and pronounced contrasts of archaic polyphony on the other. It is conceivable that Bach could have departed from the Dresden-specific style of the *Missa* at this point – but to what end? It had served him well so far and, besides, he had promised to furnish the Elector with further examples of his 'indefatigable diligence in the composition of *Musique* for Church as well as for *Orchestre*'.[11] As things stood, he might have felt that his best chances of obtaining a performance of so ambitious a setting of the complete Mass Ordinary lay in Dresden, not in Leipzig.

Several years before, he had embarked on an intensive period of study of *stile antico* techniques that in his view were indispensable for use in a Mass setting. The first fruits of it are to be found in the organ works of *Clavier-Übung III*, published in 1739: three austere and densely textured organ chorales representing the *Kyrie* and a six-part *de profundis*, *Aus tiefer Not.* In the sharpest of contrasts (reminiscent of his *Missa* of 1733), a *Gloria* was set as a brilliant, nonchalant-sounding Italian trio. Now on his desk lay a selection of settings for these later portions of the Mass. Pride of place was given to Palestrina, whose *Missa sine nomine* he had transcribed and performed in 1742. But there were other models by more recent composers, his immediate predecessors – Caldara, Durante, Lotti, Kerll and at least two by Zelenka.* All these composers had been attracted to Palestrina's polyphony in one way or

* It could have been Zelenka's *Missa votiva* of 1739, with its chant-like melody given out in long notes within his polyphonic setting of the opening *Credo*, which encouraged Bach to use plainchant so prominently in his setting. It could also have been Zelenka's *Missa Circumcisionis* of 1728 which gave Bach the idea of how to approach the *Et in unum*, as well as the chromatic bridge-passage at the end of the *Confiteor*, when the instruments drop out at mention of *mortuorum* ('the dead'). But, as we saw (p. 488), it looks very much as though Zelenka had learnt from Bach's example (*Kyrie I*) when he came to determine the chromatic and rhythmic outline of his *Kyrie II* in the *Missa Sanctissima Trinitatis* of 1736.

another, and had found ways of integrating elements of it into their own style. There was also Pergolesi's exquisite *Stabat Mater*, which, with infinite patience and manifest effort, Bach was to re-work with a German text, BWV 1083, *Tilge, Höchster, meine Sünden*, in 1746–7. These served as his guides and as points of departure for his increasing interest in setting the *Credo* polyphonically. In particular six Mass-settings (encompassing a *Kyrie / Gloria / Credo / Sanctus* sequence) by Giovanni Battista Bassani attracted his attention. He transcribed all of them, and into each of Bassani's *Credo* sections (which begin *Patrem omnipotentem*) Bach inserted the first line, *Credo in unum Deum*, a sign that he may have performed it sometime between 1747 and 1748. Bach composed a new sixteen-bar intonation to the *Credo* of the fifth of Bassani's Masses (BWV 1081) – with an *ostinato* bass line in apparent anticipation of his own opening *Credo*. Closer still there is also an intriguing version – perhaps a dummy run – for his own *Symbolum Nicenum** but a tone lower in G, which survives in the hand of his pupil Johann Friedrich Agricola.

The next stage was to refer back to his earlier compositions, both sacred and secular. It is extraordinary how unerringly Bach's memory store seems to have guided him to the perfect choice from pre-existing movements. It is as though all the possibilities latent in the musical material suddenly flashed on to the screen of his mind, only reaching their full potential through the process of selection. In their effort to trace a stem-like genealogy for the *B minor Mass*, scholars show signs of uneasiness with Bach's way of assembling it.† While they readily accept that his tidy mind favoured cyclical structures, and that from about 1730 onwards there was a gradual shift in his output from German-texted cantatas to Latin works, it was the recycling of perhaps as many as twenty movements in the Mass which bothered them, the way

* Originally *symbolum* meant a token or badge of membership, but by Bach's time it had come to signify an expression of divine meaning contained in Scripture. The Christian 'creeds' were devised to summarise the essential articles of belief. The most controversial of those articles were settled by theologians at Nicaea (hence *Nicenum*).

† Malcolm Boyd, for example, refers to the 'curiously haphazard way of composing a major work'. Yet he concedes that 'at the highest level Bach's process of parody, adaptation and compilation must be accepted as a creative act almost on a par with what we normally think of as "original composition".' He is surely right, too, that the technique works in the case of the *B minor Mass* more successfully because the text has more subdivisions than the short Masses, therefore enabling him 'to match music and words more carefully' (*Bach* (1983), pp. 187–91).

that he resorted so readily – beginning with the *Christmas Oratorio* and culminating now in *this* of all works – to 'parody' technique. But why should not the eclectic, slow-burning origins of the Mass, instead of making it suspect from an academic viewpoint, be precisely one clue to its greatness? After all, Bach was not a compulsive borrower, like Handel, who famously needed the spark of another composer's idea in order to fire up his imagination. Plagiarism may have been widely considered an acceptable literary and musical convention in the eighteenth century, but Bach, unlike Handel, did not need to turn other men's rough pebbles into diamonds.* As we have seen, Bach's was the classic method. First you study your models – transcribe them, add layers of preface or commentary to them, and then assimilate them so fully into your creative processes that, at a stroke, you have a vocabulary with a multiplicity of techniques and styles at your fingertips, all in the cause of being as comprehensive and all-encompassing as you possibly can. The extraordinary stylistic reach and wide range of Bach's sources in no way diminishes his achievement in having synthesised his models into such a unified whole.

* * *

The most striking aspect of the opening of his *Symbolum Nicenum* is its great hieratic force of delivery. In performance from the moment that the tenors launch into the Gregorian intonation we should be pinned back in our seats. Bach has chosen the local Saxon version of the chant (as published by Vopelius in 1682) and articulates it in long notes intoned over an active walking bass: an unequivocal affirmation of faith and a very modern, tonal underpinning to the most ancient formulation of Christian belief available to him.† Bach ends his first section with a dazzling treatment of the chant, whereby he rapidly piles no fewer than seven of them on top of one another, each beginning on a different beat

* This formulation of Handel's method was made by a contemporary, possibly his first biographer, John Mainwaring. It satisfies the criterion of Handel's friend Johann Mattheson when he states that 'borrowing is a permissible thing; but one must return the borrowed with interest, that is, one must arrange the borrowed material in such a fashion that it acquires a better aspect than the setting from which it has been lifted' (*Der vollkommene Capellmeister* (1739)). But I have so far found no evidence in support of Joshua Rifkin's claim that Bach 'lifted' another composer's work when he composed the *Et incarnatus*.

† By this means he is drawing on the musical-rhetorical figure of *anaphora*. J. G. Walther describes this as occurring 'when a phrase or even a single word is frequently repeated in a composition for the sake of greater emphasis' (*Musicalisches Lexicon* (1732), p. 34).

of the bar and all within the time it takes for the vocal bass to deliver a complete statement of the theme.

The formal design of his *Symbolum Nicenum* is still more tautly structured than the preceding *Gloria* that it needs to complement in both scale and content. The two outermost choruses are couched in a hybrid style, half *stile antico*, half Baroque, in the way that they are harmonically conceived and supported by their independent bass line. Two separate but interlocking patterns give it structure. The first scheme, organised on the basis of chiastic symmetry, matches that of the preceding *Gloria* and is underpinned by tonality. In this way the *Crucifixus* stands at the apex of an equilateral triangle which has at its base the twinned choruses: *Credo/Patrem omnipotentem* at the outset, and the *Confiteor/Et expecto* pairing at its conclusion. Christ's Crucifixion, according to Luther's *theologia crucis* ('theology of the Cross'), is the event to which the belief of the true Christian is orientated, the means by which he can perceive God as a result of Christ's sacrifice and suffering. But this is not reflected in Bach's first plan for the *Symbolum*: initially he absorbed the words of the *Et incarnatus* into the soprano/alto duet *Et in unum*. This, in turn, shifted the pivotal emphasis on to the *Et resurrexit* in line with Catholic practice. The autograph score reveals that sometime after completing the *Crucifixus*, Bach changed his mind. To rectify the emphasis on Catholicism in the structural alignment, he was even willing to jettison the expressive word-setting of 'and was made man' and to re-apportion the text to bring it into line with Lutheran orthodoxy. His purpose was to create a balanced and unified work, one with fluent transitions and deliberate contrasts between the arias and add a still greater weight to the choral movements.

But there is an alternative way to interpret the design of the *Symbolum*, one in which it falls into *three* segments, each culminating in a brilliant D major chorus featuring trumpets and drums. These segments coincide with Luther's three articles of belief: that of 'Creation' (the *Credo/Patrem omnipotentem* pairing), that of 'Redemption' (the *Et in unum/Et incarnatus/Crucifixus/Et resurrexit* sequence) and that of 'Sanctification' (the *Et in spiritum* extending as far as the *Et expecto*).[12] The new division overrides, but does not contradict, the chiastic structure. Luther's first article 'becomes flesh' in the second (in other words, in Christ's death and resurrection), and the eschatological events of the second article are re-enacted symbolically through baptism in the third.

This may sound unduly complicated, and of course through Bach's treatment it is characteristically ingenious. But the listener, carried along by the natural flow of Bach's chain of narrative movements – those great successive choruses in triple time (*Et incarnatus*, *Crucifixus* and *Et resurrexit*) – will not necessarily be aware of the huge stylistic shifts that are taking place from one movement to the next, nor of their unusual provenance. For example, the middle movement, the *Crucifixus*, with its extreme anguish, has its origins in the earliest music of Bach's to be absorbed into the Mass – his Weimar cantata BWV 12, *Weinen, Klagen, Sorgen, Zagen*, composed thirty-five years earlier, in 1714. Bach's re-working of this powerful *passacaglia* is outwardly minimal, but extraordinarily apposite: he adds a four-bar instrumental prelude, and two flutes to vary the texture and to give a pendulum swing to the rhythms of the mournful sarabande; strings are reduced from five to four parts; the ground bass is now pulsated by means of bow vibrato (six crotchets per bar, in place of the three minims per bar); and the *passacaglia* cycles are grouped in subtly changed ways, creating tension at different points in the *ostinato* progression.* Whether by substituting and repeating *Crucifixus* for the fourfold *Weinen, Klagen, Sorgen, Zagen* (the opening section of the cantata) he improved the underlay is a matter of taste.† Indisputably compelling, on the other hand, is the conclusion's five modulatory bars (which seem to symbolise the lowering of Christ's body into the tomb) in which the choir is left descending quietly to its lowest tessitura, accompanied only by the continuo. In this, its thirteenth repetition of the *ostinato* pattern, the bass line swerves off unpredictably and with a surge in dramatic intensity.

It has been suggested that the *Et resurrexit* began life as a lost secular ode (BWV Anh. I 9), which originally started with the words *Augustus* [*lebet*] and was performed alfresco in front of the Rathaus in Leipzig to mark the birthday of the Elector Friedrich August I on 12 May 1727.

* These changes are further analysed in René Pérez Torres, 'Bach's *Mass in B minor*: An Analytical Study of Parody Movements and Their Function in the Large-Scale Architectural Design of the Mass', University of North Texas master's thesis (Dec. 2005), pp. 64–5.

† I for one cannot rid from my mind the poignantly stuttered mouthing of *Angst . . . und . . . Not . . . Angst . . . und . . . Not*, where later he substitutes the smoother *passus et sepultus est*. On the other hand the alteration of the melodic intervals to create augmented seconds in the soprano and alto lines in bars 13 and 14 gives an enhanced grief-laden tang to the *Cru-ci-fi-xus*.

This would account for the courtly elegance that marks it out from all the other triple-metre choruses in the Mass – the rising opening motif and the circular triplet figure (associated with the word *Sterne* / 'stars') which stand metaphorically for the rise of August the Strong ('Disperse, you fair stars! The reigning sun is rising before us').[13] From the way the voices immediately proclaim and lead off in this stately polonaise with its throbbing dance pulse, one would not necessarily guess what a prominent role would be given to the orchestra. Bach assigns no fewer than five ritornelli to his orchestra, with witty and delicate exchanges between the instruments. Yet, paradoxically, the most virtuosic and essentially instrumental figuration is reserved for the voices: in the fiery coloratura melismas of *Et resurrexit* and *cujus regni*, and a devilish and acrobatic *Et iterum* for the bass. In performance the presence of conjunct semiquavers strongly suggests *inégale* treatment – that characteristically French way of gracing a line with a rhythmic swing, a feature which would have appealed to August the Strong as a devotee of French Baroque style, though perhaps less to his son, who much preferred Italian music.*

By far the newest and most progressive music here is that for the *Et incarnatus*; yet, remarkably, it was a last-minute addition. In Christoph Wolff's view it could be the final completed musical movement that Bach composed.[14] Nothing, not even the sublime *Qui tollis* that in some ways it resembles, can compare with it for simplicity of design allied to such profundity of expression. The idea for the chain of figuration in the unison violins (a detached quaver followed by two pairs of upward-resolving appoggiaturas) may have come to Bach in 1744–6 while transcribing Pergolesi's *Stabat Mater* (the 'Quis est homo, qui non fleret' section), where it is repeated nine times in seven successive bars of music linked to the theme of self-questioning.† But before meekly ticking the box of an

* This has a bearing on the tempo of the movement, which needs to be a shade slower than that of the *Cum sancto* for example. You know you are 'in the groove' when everyone can swing the adjacent *inégale* semiquavers in a deliciously blues-y lilt without any sense of underlying pressure. Yet at the same time the coloratura melismas need to fizz and sparkle like the 'tongues of fire' in the Whitsun cantata BWV 34, *O ewiges Feuer*.

† This has been pointed out by Christoph Wolff ('Bach und die Folgen', *Offizieller Almanach*, Bachwoche Ansbach (1989), pp. 23–34) and by Reinhard Strohm, who suggests that the recourse to Pergolesi's rhetorical figure 'seems to bring into the Mass the meaning that the incarnation is a "question"' ('Transgression, Transcendence and Metaphor: The "Other Meanings" of the *B-Minor Mass*' in *Understanding Bach*, Bach Network UK (2006), Vol. 1, p. 65).

external prompt (as might be in the case of a Handel) we should remember a similar procedure in the opening chorus of his cantata BWV 101, *Nimm von uns, Herr* (see p. 321), where a persistent three-note 'sighing' figure is tossed between upper strings and oboes in the context of a sombre contemplation of humanity's need for redemption for its 'countless sins'. There appears to be a direct interweaving of the themes of divine incarnation and the paramount need for redemption made explicit in Bach's self-referral, one that exposes the ambiguities of meaning in the art of music itself. For the contemplative stitches that Mary seems to be sewing in her tapestry can also be interpreted as emblems of sorrows to come. Bach might want us to reflect that, in the very act of becoming incarnate, Christ took on 'the grave punishment and grave distress' cited in the text of BWV 101/i. The *Alpha* and *Omega* of his life on earth is here inscribed.

Nothing to do with Pergolesi, however, and entirely Bach's own invention, is the movement's conclusion, in which, after forty-four bars, the hypnotic symmetry of the *Credo* is fractured. For the first time the bass line takes up the 'weeping' violin motif and develops a mini three-part canon with the two violins as they drift downwards. Simultaneously and moving upwards, a second three-part canon is formed among the three highest voices to signal 'and was made man': *et homo fac* . . . (before settling back again on) . . . *tus est.* It is not simply that, as Wilfrid Mellers noticed, the equilibrium between negative and positive tones, in these concluding bars, is wonderfully subtle.[15] Nor is it that the announcement of Christ's Incarnation and his gentle placement on this earth acquires a sudden radiance via the *tierce de Picardie* (in B major). It is that the ensuing silence encapsulates the supreme mystery of Bach's music – pregnant with a sense both of anticipation and of lost innocence, like a childhood faculty miraculously restored. To me it is on a par with the startling midpoint silence in his early *Actus tragicus* (see Chapter 5, p. 149).

The text of the Ordinary of the Mass is not every composer's idea of a perfect libretto, least of all the section following all this vivid narrative drama. Tovey described it as 'the most unmusical part of the Nicene Creed'. As he says, 'after we have been stirred to the depths by those miracles of Christianity which all can recognise though none can pretend to understand, we are now asked to find music for the controversial points that were settled at Nicaea by the theologians.'[16] He goes on wittily to compare composers' different solutions to 'this really appalling problem': setting everything to equally attractive music (Palestrina);

blatantly resorting to the clichés of *opera buffa* (Mozart); or ducking the issue altogether (Beethoven) by introducing enthusiastic shouts of *Credo!*, which almost manage to obliterate the gabbled delivery of the text with all its thorny theological complexities. Bach, on the other hand, seems to be not in the least fazed by Tovey's ('really appalling') problem. When a catalogue of doctrinal beliefs is itemised for congregational assent (and could all too easily degenerate into hectoring theology), he hits on solutions that ensure the momentum never sags. Bach had already exploited the tension between Gregorian chant-derived objectivity and contemporary dance-driven Baroque form in his two opening movements to brilliant effect. Now, faced with the words *Confiteor unum baptisma* ('I acknowledge one baptism'), he sets them in motet-like polyphony, but suddenly cuts into it sharply with a version of the chant given out in long notes and in strict canon by the basses and altos. At its completion the tenors initiate a half-speed version of the same theme, still more stentorian in the way it obtrudes from the texture like an exposed beam or structural girder. Then, without any warning, the forward momentum is halted and the counterpoint dissolves: the throbbing vigour has dropped to a barely perceptible pulse. The vocal lines are collapsed into a slow stretch of probing and unstable bars and a series of murky modulations, pausing on the word *peccatorum*. This is a maze from which there seems to be no egress.

At this point, one feels, the music could go in any direction and seems passive, waiting for a fresh impulse. Even with the help of C. P. E. Bach's annotations in his father's full score it is hard to decipher exactly what Bach intended here. Doubt has suddenly been cast over the very possibility of our sins being remitted. The words change to 'and I hope for the resurrection of the dead', but the music seems anything but optimistic. With the apparent crumbling of the whole doctrinal edifice, we have arrived at a most precarious stage in Bach's Mass. A shadow passes over this illuminated missal, a disintegration and collapse of momentum, a place where expertise in learned counterpoint counts for little. The harmony veers off course, first to B♭ minor before plummeting towards the remote key of E♭ minor (regarded as the key of 'deepest distress, of brooding despair, of blackest depression, of the most gloomy condition of the soul',[17] and rarely used in Bach's day because it clashed horribly with the way keyboard instruments were tuned).

Here is also one of those rare instances when his defences seem to be down and we are privy to his vulnerability and doubts – as to the likelihood of this momentous transformation. Can he look forward to the resurrection of the dead and the life of the world to come, or was the exemplary advocacy of the *ars moriendi* we encountered in the cantatas just a brave front? There is so much at stake here: the horrors of man's transgressions and the need of redemption to lift us out of our fallen state. This could be one of the few times Bach felt Luther's terror of death and found a way, perhaps even a need, to express it in music. How he deals with it will be critical to the success of the work and perhaps to his own future. It is painfully clear from the autograph score that Bach had a gigantic tussle with this pivotal moment. The page is besmirched with emphatic crossings-out and revisions to the inner parts. The bass descends chromatically, but at the last moment swerves away from E♭ minor and comes to a halt on the dominant of D (bar 137). The sopranos inch their way forward to a tentative C♮. This is mysteriously – and enharmonically – transformed into a B♯, an example of that place where in an instant one passes from one realm of existence to another.*

Experience of performing the church cantatas reveals how brilliantly, even on a regular basis, Bach was able to interpret these dark moments, and how resourceful he could be at guiding the listener back to the path of faith and light – never more so than here, the eschatological crossroads of the entire Mass. Struggling to find the most appropriate chordal sequence (which anticipates some of Beethoven's more probing harmonic expressions) Bach seizes this moment to convey, in Wilfrid Mellers's phrase, that 'tremor of fear and dubiety' which any of us, himself included, might be feeling at this point. Those confident affirmations of *Credo* which prefaced nine tenths of the articles of the Nicene Creed have given way to progressively weaker verbs – to *Confiteor* ('I acknowledge') and now to *et expecto* ('and I look for'). Bach may have set *Confiteor* on a par with *Credo* for sureness in affirmation, but not when it comes to *et expecto*. This is the only time in his Mass where he provides two completely opposed settings of the same phrase of the text. First he conveys the shock and horror of realisation: the full extent of

* Observing Bach manipulate and adjust the harmony at this point, we can see how Andreas Werckmeister could define an enharmonic change as 'a mirror and image of our mortality and the incompleteness of this life' (Ruth Tatlow, 'Recapturing the Complexity of Historical Music Theories; or, What Werckmeister's Doctrine and Mattheson's Invective Can Tell Us about Bach's Compositional Motivation', Eastman Theory Colloquium, 28 Sept. 2012).

man's transgressions that have necessitated the Incarnation and the atonement by means of Christ's Crucifixion. Next he evokes the moment of death in sleep (as in *Der Tod ist mein Schlaf* ... that we encountered in cantatas BWV 95 and 125); then the first tentative 'hope in' (by no means yet 'belief in') the resurrection of the dead. This is the stage at which we might discern a parallel with St Paul's mysterious moment when 'we shall all be changed, in a moment, in the twinkling of an eye' (I Corinthians 15:51–2). This then leads to the conviction – *his* conviction – that 'the dead shall be raised incorruptible'. At this point – 'at the last trump' – the dam finally breaks: *et expecto* now becomes *credo resurrectionem mortuorum.*

The new movement, marked *Vivace e Allegro,** propels us forwards, time for only one beat per bar in the basso continuo – but enough for the dead to 'leap from their graves in sprightly almost frisky arpeggios'.† 'Open wide the mind's cage-door!' enjoined Keats[18] – and Bach does just that, leading the way in widening our understanding the mystery of the Resurrection. Coming after that searching enharmonic change, the explosive *vivace* return to life in the *Et expecto* generates colossal energy in the emphatic *re-sur-rec-ti-o-nem* reiterations in four-square rhythms. This is the second jubilant chorus of the *Symbolum Nicenum*, the fourth in the whole Mass till now, each one utterly distinctive and germane to its context.

With any other composer of his generation it might have sounded trite or, at the very least, anti-climactic, but something in his subconscious seems to have flashed a memory of earlier music perfectly suited to the mood – the second line of a chorus, 'Steiget bis zum Himmel nauf' ('Soar right up to heaven'), in the second movement of BWV 120, *Gott, man lobet dich in der Stille*, a cantata for the inauguration of the Leipzig Town Council of 1728 or 1729. This is no straightforward 'parody' but it aptly conveys the revitalisation and resurrection of souls 'at the last

* This is a most unusual marking reserved for movements in which there is only one beat per bar. It simply cannot signal 'a neutral, *tempo-ordinario allegro*' or even 'a return to the brisk *alla breve* tempo of the *Confiteor*' (Stauffer, op. cit., p. 240). The downward scale in the continuo and its arrival on a bottom D is like the starting pistol which fires off a German *galop* of the sort that became so popular in Vienna in the 1820s, starting with Schubert, Lanner, Johann Strauss, and even Rossini (as in the end of his *Guillaume Tell* overture).

† As Mellers aptly comments: 'The introversion of the previous section is replaced by an extraversion as naive as that depicted in the resurrection paintings of Stanley Spencer, or of the medieval painters who were his model' (op. cit., p. 230).

trump'. Bach rifles through the material of this chorus – a four-square *da capo* movement – unsparingly. His task was to find a suitable sequel to the *Confiteor*, one proportionate to those twenty-five mysterious linking bars of *adagio*; but he also needs to balance that other pillar of the *Symbolum* which matches the opening *Credo/Patrem* pairing. So he pares away anything that gets in the way of this inexorable release of energy. Out go the staid formality, the chiastic scaffolding, the closing ritornello; in come eight bars of fresh material (twice), the opening ritornello now shortened and overlaid with voices, a fifth voice not merely appended but extrapolated from the constituent fabric, and 105 bars of irresistible, unrestrainable vigour. Nothing, not even the way that each choral section is enriched by the cumulative addition of instruments, is allowed to get in the way of this jubilant collective sprint to the finishing line.*

* * *

Emanuel Bach at this point comes back into the story. Now principal harpsichordist of the Prussian Court Capelle in Berlin, he had just completed a new *Magnificat* setting (Wq. 215) in Potsdam in August 1749. He appears to have brought it to Leipzig, perhaps to show to his ailing father, and at least one witness claims to have heard it performed in the Thomaskirche during a Marian feast, perhaps on 2 February or 25 March 1750. Was this Emanuel's bid (perhaps with parental prompting) to be considered his father's successor as Thomascantor? Emanuel's *Magnificat* reflects so much of his father's influence, with its striking allusions to the latter's *Gratias* and to the *Et expecto* conclusion of the *Symbolum Nicenum*. The links between his own work and his father's *Symbolum* were so close that years later when he was in Hamburg he performed the two works in the same programme. The benefit concert given in aid of Hamburg's Medical Institute for the Poor in the spring of 1786 contained, besides the works already mentioned, the aria 'I know that my Redeemer liveth' and the 'Hallelujah' chorus from Handel's *Messiah*. While he would have remembered the *Gratias* from the time when he helped copy out the parts in Dresden in 1733, he could

* As John Butt observes, Bach's tendency here to prune away everything that might inhibit his intended momentum contributes 'to the impression of a work which seems to contain twice the amount of music that its duration would normally allow' (*Bach: Mass in B minor* (1991), pp. 56–7).

only have become acquainted with the *Symbolum* much later on and probably just prior to the composition of his own *Magnificat*. This opens up the possibility that he witnessed a performance of the *Symbolum* in Leipzig during his father's last years. Clearly, the date of 25 August 1749 on the autograph score of Emanuel's *Magnificat* provides us with a *terminus ante quem* for at least this portion of his father's Mass. Also, given that he and his elder brother were apparently allowed to perform in both churches during his father's final illness, and knowing the work so well, one cannot rule out the possibility that one of them directed sections of the *B minor Mass* in Leipzig.

This is all highly speculative. Beyond doubt is Emanuel's close connection with his father's Mass at separate stages in its assembly. He was the son who would inherit his father's autograph score and, indeed, his fingerprints are all over it – from the innocent marker dots intended to ease his early task of copying, to the helpful bass figuring in the *Credo* that he added much later in life. Beyond this there are far more radical interventions: the addition of a newly composed 28-bar prelude; and changes of underlay and instrumentation, including the replacement of the (then redundant) oboes d'amore with normal oboes and with violins in the *Et in spiritum*.

Evidently the *Symbolum Nicenum* was the single segment of Bach's *Missa tota* to make the greatest impression on the next generation, not just on Emanuel, but on others within Bach's close circle of pupils, such as J. F. Agricola and J. P. Kirnberger. Emanuel Bach's Hamburg performance in 1786 seems to have led indirectly to copies being made and circulated far and wide. One found its way to England and ended up in the hands of Charles Burney, and from him it somehow passed to Samuel Wesley, whose enthusiasm resulted in an abortive project of publishing it as a demonstration of Bach's skill in vocal composition. Agricola, who had already copied out an early version of the opening movement (see above), referred to the *alla breve* notation of the *Credo* 'from a great Mass by the late J. S. Bach with eight obbligato voices, namely five vocal parts, two violins, and general bass'.[19] Kirnberger (who had been lent the autograph score posted to him by Emanuel Bach in 1769 with permission to copy it before returning it by prepaid post) seems to have been especially drawn to the *Crucifixus* and its *passacaglia* ground bass. He described it as a 'ten-voice example ... from a Mass by J. S. Bach, full of invention, imitation, canon, counterpoint and beautiful melody'.[20] This puts one in mind of Claude Lévi-Strauss's dictum: 'music itself [is] the supreme mystery of the science of man'[21] – a fitting epitaph for Bach's astonishing *Symbolum Nicenum*.

* * *

When it comes to the final part of the Mass, opinions divide. Some scholars have cast aspersions on the way Bach assembled it, and suggest a marked diminution in its creative originality.* But how can this be? True, there are tell-tale signs clearly visible in the autograph of effort and precipitation, of notes doggedly pressed on to the page, and at movements' end of a certain shakiness or indecision as to what movement came next. One could account for this in a number of ways: Bach's unfamiliarity with this closing section of the Catholic liturgy; his failing eyesight; or his determination to complete it, maintaining all the while his high ideals for it as a statement in music of the universal church. But nothing, least of all the recycling process extending to all its component movements, betrays a diminution in quality or intensity, as we shall soon see. Bach was working in a void: there were no Lutheran models for these last segments of the Mass to guide him. From his own library shelves he could have referred to Bassani's Masses, which end with the *Osanna* (as sequel to the *Sanctus*); or to Palestrina's, which did indeed reach the end, completing the Ordinary in unruffled *a cappella* polyphony. In a sense, Bach was a victim of his own success. Having set himself standards of scale, proportion and duration in his original *Missa*, which he then complemented so majestically with the *Symbolum*, he now had the task of sustaining the dramatic momentum and epic proportions, while putting together a final sequence of movements, unified and smoothly interlocked. In this he succeeds triumphantly.

The idea of opening the last part of the Mass with his great *Sanctus* of 1724 – one of the most flamboyant of all his D major choruses – came to him, as suggested above (p. 499) with the peace celebrations at

* Philipp Spitta, critical of Bach's heavy dependence on parody in these last movements, which he felt was due to the fact that the music would have been performed *sub communione* (that is, during the distribution of the bread and wine), suggested that Bach assembled it 'with no great effort'. He found it 'unsatisfactory, not only as regards each of these numbers separately, but as to their connection and their position as finishing the whole mass' (*The Life of Bach*, Clara Bell and J. A. Fuller Maitland (trs.) (1873; 1899 edn), Vol. 3, p. 61). Later Friedrich Smend referred to 'the decline of artistic quality in the last part', finding the music following the *Sanctus* 'distinctly inferior to what comes before' (NBA II/1, KB, pp. 178–87).

Christmas 1745. Judging by the quantity of Bach's own revivals of it over the years, he valued it highly. In its new position, coming hard on the heels of the immense *Symbolum*, there is not the slightest risk of bathos, as every musician and listener can attest. If we might have questioned the function of the individual arpeggiated upward riffs at the conclusion of the *Et expecto*, the way they contrasted with the long-noted imitative exchanges of the vocal lines and then fused in the final section as everyone lunged to burst the finishing tape, the answer is surely to be found in this sequel – the *Sanctus*, with its angelic clanging of church bells in celebration of the final victory over death. Its very scoring entails an augmentation and expansion of forces used hitherto: trinities of trumpets, oboes (a third oboe joining in for the first time) and upper strings are now joined by a *double* trinity of voice lines (despite Bach's new way of grouping them in pairs). Memory of the sixfold wings of the seraphim in Isaiah (6:2–3) may have suggested to him this new sixfold scoring: 'with twain he covered his face, with twain he covered his feet, and with twain he did fly'.*

Whatever the source of his inspiration, Bach provides us with the most monumental music we have heard so far to convey the majesty of God, and he does so with a kind of Byzantine or Venetian splendour. Bach evidently intended his *Sanctus* to be sung and played by angelic forces divided among five different groupings, and, in the case of the vocal basses, iron-lunged heroes capable of imitating a gigantic peal of bells or an organ diapason. With the sequel *Pleni sunt coeli*, however, he brings us back on to terra firma. This is not the same world of peasant round dances of his *Gloria*; instead it is as though a group of tenors have been thrown into the ring to celebrate the glory of God's creation by dancing a vigorous *passepied*. The regular one-in-a-bar swing of the rhythms is varied by hemiolas, and the melismatic runs for the voice lines hint at the possibility of ticklish groupings (of three times three) starting

* Alternatively, according to Mellers, it was the vision of St John Chrysostom which may have inspired him – those 'thousands of Archangels . . . that are six-winged, full of eyes, and soar aloft on their wings, singing, crying, shouting, and saying *Agios! Agios! Agios! Kyrie Sabaoth!* Holy, Holy, Holy, Lord God of Hosts! Heaven and Earth are full of Thy Glory! Hosanna in the Highest!' (op. cit., p. 232). Tovey, on the other hand, sees the *Sanctus* as 'almost drastically Protestant . . . Bach is himself beating time to the angels swinging their censers before the Throne, and has entirely forgotten the awe-struck mortals kneeling in silence before the miracle which gives them immortality' (op. cit., p. 23).

on a syncopation and crossing the bar-line before 'righting' themselves with a huge single arc and flourish.

One has to admit that Bach's division of this final section of his Mass is slightly peculiar. Yet, even in this last phase of his creative life, when he was much concerned with completing cyclical and 'speculative' works, he never conceived of his vocal and texted compositions as standing outside the possibilities of performance, though this may have meant restricting them to shorter coherent units. A glance at his autograph score reveals that he subdivided his Mass into a fourfold physical structure: *Missa* (in other words the *Kyrie/Gloria* pairing), *Credo*, *Sanctus* and *Osanna/Benedictus/Agnus Dei* – one that conforms neither to the Catholic fivefold Ordinary nor to common Lutheran usage. As Robin A. Leaver explains, within the Lutheran liturgy the first three segments could be performed independently, while parts of the fourth could not.[22] The *Agnus Dei* could be performed as an independent movement (and even sung along with the *Sanctus* during the distribution of the sacrament), but the *Osanna* and *Benedictus* were not separable from the *Sanctus*.

Obviously when the Mass is performed in its entirety, Bach's fourfold division disappears automatically. But, in the event that the work is performed sectionally, the *Sanctus*, with its glittering conclusion of *Pleni sunt coeli*, can stand magnificently alone (just as it did originally in 1724 and in some subsequent revivals), while the final five-movement sequence also makes for a satisfactory unit, its *Benedictus* – enclosed in a chamber-like intimacy by the *Osanna* choruses – comprising the centre of a double-choir sandwich. Isolating the *Sanctus* in this way for purely functional purposes did not disassociate it from the final sequence, to which it is artistically and structurally bound and thematically linked. Leaver confirms that the only reason the last two sections of the manuscript score exist in this shape is because of the pre-existence of the separate *Sanctus*, and that conceptually they should be seen as one complete section – *Sanctus/Osanna/Benedictus/Agnus Dei* – forming a symmetrical pattern similar to those of the first two segments:

Sanctus
    Osanna
        Benedictus
    Osanna
Agnus Dei

Lutherans with their respect for the musical traditions of Catholicism could condone the reference in the *Credo* to *unam sanctam catholicam et apostolicam ecclesiam* – so long as, in the words of the theologian Johann Benedikt Carpzov, the '*ecclesiam catholicam* is not to be understood as the Roman-papist church ... but as the universal community of saints [or believers]'.[23]*

Either on its own or, better still, in context, this final sequence is riveting and suitably conclusive. The technique that Bach adopts in all four sections of the Mass – that of contrasting choruses and arias, movements in *stile antico* with others in a more contemporary style, emphasising, indeed polarising, both 'public' and 'private' aspects of the Eucharist celebration – is never more in evidence than here. The very principle of contrast – of sense as much as of style – that has characterised the Mass-setting to this point is now pushed to greater extremes: moving from unbridled joy (*Osanna*), to a wistful quest for serenity (*Benedictus*), and to the heartfelt plea (*Agnus*). The two arias – *Benedictus* and *Agnus* – are still more intimate and chamber-like than their predecessors in the earlier movements, and the flanking choruses if anything still more opulent (the *Osanna*, now for double choir, in eight parts and the orchestra neatly divided into twelve real parts) and uplifting (the final *Dona nobis pacem*).

Each of the final arias is compelling. By showing the pilgrim's endeavour to pursue and complete his life's journey, the *Benedictus* postulates the type of dualism we have encountered before in the cantatas. In the serene (and almost disembodied) voice of the tenor, Bach evokes the 'blessed'-ness of he 'who cometh in the name of the Lord'; and, simultaneously, in the angularities of the flute melody he insists that the path of life is never smooth (one is reminded of *der saure Weg wird mir zu schwer*, which he set so expressively in his motet BWV 229, *Komm, Jesu, komm*). There are of course moments when this is eased and the flute takes on a consoling role: like Virgil guiding and protecting Dante on his journey through Hell and Purgatory in Botticelli's second parchment drawings for the *Divine Comedy*, Bach seems to embrace his travelling

* This implies that the appellation 'Die große catholische Messe' (as catalogued in C. P. E Bach's estate, 1790) denotes 'the universality of the Ordinary of the Mass, shared by both Catholics and Lutherans alike' (Robin A. Leaver, 'How "Catholic" is Bach's "Lutheran" Mass?' in University of Belfast International Symposium, *Discussion Book* (2007), Vol. 1, pp. 177–206).

companion with his melody.* In contrast to the *Benedictus*, the interweaving between voice and unison violins in the *Agnus Dei* is inextricable. Given the trouble it cost him – in one of his very last vocal compositions – to reduce an eight-line-stanza aria-setting to one of merely eight words, Bach must have prized the nostalgic alto aria 'Ach, bleibe doch', from his *Ascension Oratorio* (BWV 11), very highly, although it is likely that both versions go back to a lost original. He discards slightly more than half the cantata material, but adds four new bars for the first vocal entry (in canon with the violins) and eight for the second, ending on a dramatic *fermata*. Here we find him returning to the sighing figure – slurred pairs of conjunct notes – which we first heard in *Kyrie I* and which recurred to enrich the expression of the *Qui tollis*, the *Et incarnatus* and the *Crucifixus*, superimposed over a similar regular, punctuated rhythm in the bass. His mechanism for binding this heart-stopping music into the overall scheme is an extreme, angular re-shaping of the final instrumental ritornello, the violins landing on an open-string bottom G. It provides the perfect link to the ensuing *Dona nobis pacem*, which, in strict liturgical practice, belongs to the text of the aria; but, by detaching it in this way, Bach seems to imply a change in the Godhead being addressed.

Even this, the final *Dona nobis*, has come in for musicological shouts of foul play just because it repeats note for note the earlier *Gratias*. There are no grounds for this. It was a long-standing Lutheran custom to end the main service with 'Verleih uns Frieden gnädiglich', Luther's version of the antiphon *Da pacem, Domine*. In re-using the music of the *Gratias* as the summation of the entire Mass, Bach was connecting with the Leipzig tradition of ending the Eucharist with a collect of thanksgiving – 'Wir danken dir' – taken from Luther's *Deutsche Messe*, published in 1526. A hymn of thanks is thus converted into a universal plea for peace, followed by a prayer of thanksgiving. Bach's decision conformed to precedent in Catholic Dresden as well and justifies its place with convincing naturalness – at least in performance. Whereas in the Mass Ordinary the *Dona nobis* text belongs to the *Agnus Dei* (coming at the end of the

* This is an almost exact reflection of the flute/voice dialectic in Bach's Epiphany cantata (BWV 123), where in the aria 'Lass, o Welt, mich aus Verachtung' the flute acts as a consoling angel or companion to the bass singer, bleak in his isolation, and infects him with new purpose and resolve.

third phrase), it was common in Dresden to set this text to a closing chorus with music derived from either the *Kyrie* or *Gloria*. This served as a recapitulating and unifying device – Dresden Mass composers such as Caldara and Durante, whom Bach had studied, made a practice of repeating the music of an earlier movement in the *Dona nobis*. What also seems to bother the purists is what they regard as slovenly text adaptation: whereas the two clauses of the *Gratias* are perfectly adjusted to Bach's contrasted fugue subjects – (1) *Gratias agimus tibi* ('We give thanks to Thee ...') and (2) *propter magnam gloriam tuam* ('... for Thy great glory') (a perfect transposition from the original cantata composition which served as its model, BWV 29, *Wir danken dir, Gott*) – here there is only a single clause, *Dona nobis pacem*, to be split between the two subjects, an infelicitous grammatical error. Or is it?

Bach cuts the ground from under his critics' feet by creating a new dualism: *Dona nobis pacem*, followed by a re-ordering of the words, *pacem dona nobis*. The appropriateness of this solution is immediately apparent in performance – nothing, simply nothing but the *Gratias* music can follow at this point – provided of course that due adjustment is made to the style and mood of delivery of the second phrase. For where the earlier *propter magnam* was vigorous and assertive, the *pacem dona nobis* is lyrical and gentle, suggesting a dignified restraint in its vocal delivery. As befitting a universal plea for peace, its melismas are equally suited to *dona* ('give') and to *pacem* ('peace'). The solid rock-like steps of the initial fugue subject, which have an inexorable forward momentum in the *Gratias* – a foretaste of the finale to Mozart's 'Jupiter' symphony – are softened and their edges rounded off in the *Dona nobis*. In both versions, Bach holds back the entrance of the trumpets and drums – which represent the final battalion recruited to acknowledge God's glory (*Gratias*) and the most imposing and eloquent petitioners of peace (*Dona nobis*). It is an inspired decision.

* * *

Let us take stock. We have identified several starting-points and perhaps as many as four punctuation points marking the development and composition of the *B minor Mass*. Starting with the Dresden *Missa* of 1733, there is the 'war trauma' hypothesis that brought the *Gloria* and *Sanctus* movements together at Christmas-time in 1745. This is followed by Emanuel's last visits to his father and the (rather remote) possibility of partial performances in Leipzig in 1749–50. None of these wayside markers is in itself definitive proof of the precise moment when Bach decided to complete his Mass. While it is possible that the project took root in his mind very early on and that before completing it he felt he needed to re-educate himself in *stile antico* techniques before committing himself to paper, it is also conceivable that he needed a specific occasion to focus his mind and to move on to the final stage in the process of composition and assimilation.

The final piece in the puzzle takes us back to Dresden. It has been suggested that he may have seen a possible opening for his Mass in the anticipated celebrations for the inauguration of the new Hofkirche in Dresden.[24] The cornerstone had been laid in 1739; and, judging from a landscape view of Dresden by Bernardo Bellotto (known as Canaletto the Younger) painted in 1748, the Hofkirche was nearing completion, its bell tower still encased with scaffolding. Was this the occasion that Bach was looking for? If so, it is supported by the feverish haste evident in the clumsy, effortful handwriting of the last section of the Mass. But if his idea was to present it for performance as part of the dedication celebrations, this was not to be. For, besides his failing eyesight and the two cataract operations carried out by the English oculist Sir John Taylor in March/April 1750, it has been suggested that Bach was suffering from untreated diabetes. Though he rallied for a while, he suffered a stroke on 20 July and eight days later he died.

The Hofkirche meanwhile was not finally completed until the following year. Not without a certain irony, it was his old friend Hasse whose much shorter *Mass in D* was performed at the time of its inauguration. We saw that Bach's *Symbolum* might have owed something to Zelenka's Masses. This is as nothing compared to the close dependence of Hasse on Bach – particularly in the opening of the *Credo* and in the *Et incarnatus* of his *Mass in D*. Forkel tells us that 'Hasse and his wife, the celebrated Faustina . . . also [came] several times to Leipzig and admired [Bach's] great talents.'[25] Perhaps Hasse had after all clapped eyes on the early sections of the *Missa* back in 1733 at the time of its presentation. In his later visits to Bach in Leipzig, Hasse would have been able to examine, or conceivably hear, the later portions of Bach's *B minor Mass*. As an astute professional, Hasse was ideally placed to appreciate that at the moment of its completion Bach had succeeded in formulating a comprehensive survey and a unique synthesis of all that he considered to be the best in his own church music, as well as that of his predecessors and contemporaries; in short, that it was unsurpassed and unsurpassable. At the same time he would have seen Bach's Mass as a practical working score eminently suited to performance. The only thing lacking was a complete set of parts. But it was not Hasse's style to pass over a prestigious opportunity to air music of his own. Were his references to it in his *Mass in D*, and in a subsequent *Requiem Mass* he wrote at the time of the death of his patron Friedrich August II in 1763, conscious gestures of homage and debt to Bach?

* * *

None of this rules out the possibility that had Bach lived long enough to direct or witness a complete performance of his Mass, say in Dresden in 1751, he would have continued to revise and make changes to it. For, unlike a scientist who repeats his experiments to make his work unassailable – and with the aim of getting the exact same results each time – Bach did not get the chance to submit his Mass to equivalent tests. To view it therefore as a static object, a summary and repository for one man's human thoughts and actions, even as an absolute statement of his faith comparable to that in his two Passions, is but one way. Another is to see it as part of a seamless process of self-correction and self-definition that never reached – perhaps never *could* reach – a state of finality. It is only in performance that the essential mobility of meaning contained within its music can be released and savoured. And yet Bach's Mass can and certainly does stand up to repeated 'testing' in performance. He assembled it over time, absorbed into it some of his earliest musical ideas, and then concluded it in such an ineffable way – demonstrating his 'habit of perfection' – that this could have been his way of saying, 'I'm off now from this planet; my work is done. I leave you here with a pure and beautiful idea, and the expression of that idea is my gift to the world, and my ancestors are part of it, too' – a kind of *Nunc dimittis*, in other words.

But we can see from the reactions of his son Emanuel, and of his pupils Agricola and Kirnberger, that their admiration for the master's 'Great Mass' was more technical and theoretical than aesthetic or philosophical. The truth is that the cultural milieu which Bach was leaving behind at his death was not yet ready for the degree of independence of thought and conception that he manifested here. We are his successors and the beneficiaries of his vision. Every time we perform it marks just the latest point in the work's continuing and continuous unfolding.

Performance is a creative physical enactment, one that achieves the provisional completion and realisation of a musical work only as a result of its being 're-composed' or 're-painted' in that particular instant. Part of our role as interpreters is to beckon to the listener, drawing him into a responsive environment so that he becomes privy to the construction and unwrapping of the creative act in which we are engaged. And here it is important to distinguish between the materials of performance – the instruments, be they 'modern', 'conventional' or 'period' – and the people who play them. Of course those of us who have learnt to play or direct period instruments and listened to what they can tell us feel that we stand a rather better chance of re-entering and inhabiting Bach's sound world than was possible when we set out thirty-five or so years ago. An ensemble of period instruments played by expert virtuosi – a whole orchestra, no less, accompanying equally accomplished solo singers stepping out from a choir – carries with it a colossal element of excitement and zing. The performance then becomes a communal rite, one built on complicity and trust; a willingness to adjust and blend on the part of all the participants must be present for it to succeed and for the shared vision to be realised.

The primary role of the conductor is to identify and transmit that vision to all those involved. At every instant he needs to know where the music is headed; and he has to be able to convey to each musician how individual lines fit into the overall pattern. He has to ensure that everyone's antennae are operational and capable of responding to any new impulse at any given moment, while at the same time encouraging the freedom necessary for everyone, but particularly for the solo players and singers, to contribute to the performance. The skill lies in keeping the music's glue, and in making every note urgent and fresh. Achieving the sense of being caught up in a shared experience is crucial to the potency and impact of this re-creative process.

Sometimes this falls short, and a precious opportunity is missed; as musicians we then fail to engage the audience or to draw them in as participants, not just hearing, but 'receiving' and responding. But when we succeed – when technical skill adequate to meet even the stiffest of

Bach's challenges is no longer an issue, when the calibration of vocal and instrumental forces is optimal, when a coordination of style, a matching of timbres and a mutual understanding of everyone's role is achieved – that is the point when interpretation can really begin.

* * *

Bach, in the breadth of his vision, grasped and then revealed to us his conception of the universe as a harmonious whole; yet he was composing at a time when the breakdown of social unity was well advanced and the old structures of religion were fast being eroded by Enlightenment thinkers. Revealing as the work of recent musicologists has proved to be in tracing the varied provenance of the Mass and in uncovering more and more signs of its having been recycled from earlier compositions, it carries a certain danger: it could diminish Bach's music to a bundle of influences, to a collection of parts that are less than the whole; whereas it is precisely his ability to transform material and weld it into new patterns, and his willingness and courage to strike out on his own, regardless of fashion, which is so inspiring about the *B minor Mass*. Without this realisation we run the risk of missing the driving force behind it: Bach's resolve not merely to mime the gestures of belief, nor to interpret doctrine via music of his own invention, but to extend the very range of music's possibilities and through such exploration to make sense of the world in which he lived and whatever lay beyond it.

Even to sceptical and agnostic minds, Bach's *B minor Mass* radiates a recognisable and powerful spirituality, one that does not rely on credal orthodoxy, odd though that might appear. His art celebrates the fundamental sanctity of life, an awareness of the divine and a transcendent dimension as a fact of human existence. Interpreting it is all about the drama of discovering the revelation inscribed in each movement, and is indissolubly fused to his personal style – the inner poet hiding in the recesses of his counterpoint. Above all, as musicians you can never afford to be earthbound – to plod, in other words: it has to dance. Ultimately his style is also vision. Misjudge the style and you miss the vision.

To conduct his Mass is to be filled with a tremendous sense of anticipation: you know as you embark on a journey with and through his music that you are going to be exposed to a heightened sense of consciousness – of the role of music, of its capacity to affect and change people's lives, of its power to reflect and even to mitigate the way people respond to contemporary events. Then, as you approach the final straight of this great adventure and the trumpets soar one last time to announce the homecoming, you realise that Bach's final prayer for peace, *Dona nobis pacem*, is both an invocation and a resounding confirmation of its immanence.

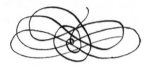

14
'Old Bach'

Since music is a language with some meaning, at least for the immense majority of mankind, although only a tiny minority of people are capable of formulating a meaning in it, and since it is the only language with the contradictory attributes of being at once intelligible and untranslatable, the musical creator is a being comparable to the gods, and music itself the supreme mystery of the science of man, a mystery that all the various disciplines come up against and which holds the key to their progress.

– Claude Lévi-Strauss[1]

Bach, the epitome of a musician who strove all life long and finally acquired the 'Habit of Perfection', was a thoroughly imperfect human being – something we don't usually tolerate in one of our heroes. The hagiolatry that has followed him for the past 200 years reveals a widespread reluctance to come to terms with the complexity and contradictions within the artistic temperament and has been shown to blind people to Bach's true character – his everyday self, the self that lived beside, beneath and within the narrative of his most un-ordinary music-making. It has been a constant throughout this book to suggest ways in which his personality and creative mind interacted and how perfection and imperfection thus coexisted in Bach's life, no matter how much he strove to achieve a matching godliness and virtue as a human being to the harmonic perfection of his music.* We continue to notice

* Given his friendship and close compositional collaboration with his cousin Johann Gottfried Walther, the chances are that Bach would have agreed with him that 'good

signs of the disorder within his professional life and of his conflicted attitude towards authority, but also of his convivial and generous-spirited relationship with his pupils and fellow musicians. Most importantly, we have music that brims over with 'ingenious and unusual ideas' (as the *Nekrolog* tells us) while always staying rooted in given order and true proportion. You come away from hearing or performing it dazzled by how so much self-imposed restraint can be combined with a tingling, edge-of-your-seat vivacity.

This applies as much to the music of his last decade, which saw the completion of the *B minor Mass*, the *Musical Offering* and the near-completion of *The Art of Fugue*, as to his Weimar years (1708–17), which witnessed his seminal encounter with Vivaldi's music and the inception of the *Orgel-Büchlein* project. Yet, looking back when at the end of his life, Bach might have identified the decade 1723–33 – the one framed by his accession to the Thomas cantorate and his submission to the Saxon Elector of his *Missa* – as his most challenging and productive. It saw him making a supreme effort to realise his *Endzweck*, hurling himself at his target of composing complete church cantata cycles for the first three (or at most four) years, then in 1729, bruised and exhausted, retreating to the comfort and independence of the coffee-house. We saw that for him this was much more than just a change of location for making, appreciating and listening to music: it coincided with a significant social change – from the quasi-feudal atmosphere of the Lutheran church, with its hierarchical seating arrangements, to a place where social distinctions played a lesser role and where the city's middle-class intelligentsia could meet and converse with less formality. This was a critical turning-point in the cultural and intellectual life of a central German city like Leipzig.

* * *

When we consider how during the first three years of his cantorate Bach poured all his energies into the service of the Leipzig churches, what makes his achievement so impressive is his utter singleness of purpose.

Harmony will result not only when it is composed after artistic rules, but above all when it is used in virtuous and God-pleasing practices' (*Praecepta der Musicalischen Composition* (1708), Vol. 1, p. 1). Failure to achieve this in practice, and the all too common discrepancy between human ideals and behaviour, is a theme played out in his cantatas (see for example Chapter 12, p. 451).

Despite all the constraints and difficulties that lay in his way, the opposition, the criticism and the public apathy he encountered, nothing was too difficult, no price too high, when it came to realising that ultimate goal. There can be only one conclusion: that the creation of that corpus of church music, unique in the history of music, could have happened only at this time, in this place and under these circumstances. It should hardly surprise us, then, to find that such a striking individual, having reached maturity, saw the possibilities not just in new contrapuntal combinations, but also in the precise historical moment when they were to be delivered, and actively set about their realisation.

Earlier in his career, he clearly did not possess the range, the experience, the structural and stylistic framework, or the opportunity to carry it through to fulfilment. Had he stayed in Cöthen (a Calvinist court) the project would have never got off the ground. Had he taken up the Halle offer in 1713, he might well have suffered the same fate as his eldest son, Wilhelm Friedemann, and become enmeshed in sectarian controversy there. In worldly Hamburg his energies, like those of his second son Emanuel later on, might gradually have been sapped by administrative duties and by the need to spread his music around the city's churches even more thinly than in Leipzig. There, too, he would have become easy prey to the sardonic mockery of Johann Mattheson and other fashion-conscious advocates of the modern *galant* style. In beguiling, Catholic Dresden, with its richly endowed Capelle, he would not have been free to create and perform the succession of Lutheran church cantatas that he carried through in Leipzig. No, it had to be in that provincial and rather mean-spirited city, inordinately proud of its pure Lutheran Orthodoxy, its distinguished succession of cantors and its sporadic moments of cosmopolitan glory. All this was done despite the semi-dysfunctional allocation of powers (imperial, civic and clerical), despite Leipzig's fossilised social stratification – perhaps no worse than elsewhere in Germany but rather better documented – and, as we now know, despite a practically unworkable situation within the power structure of the Thomasschule.[2]

This was also the last possible moment, north of the Alps, for a comprehensive mirroring in church music of the cycle of the seasons, with their still visible reminders of an agrarian year and its festivals, time- and weather-specific activities and pre-Christian rituals. It was the last time Luther could speak – vicariously but authoritatively – to his flock without widespread dissent. It had to be then, in that decade. Any later and the percolation of enlightened thought into middle Germany might have taken the edge off Bach's creative zeal as the doors of fashion began to shut him out.

What is so moving about Bach's realisation of his *Endzweck* in the mid to late 1720s is his capacity to produce works of luminous intelligence, more profound and far more complex than any contract required of him and sometimes at great personal cost. In this he was casting before the citizens of Leipzig music of a quality and consistency that they scarcely deserved. Of course he could have made a very comfortable living had he chosen, like Telemann, to devote himself to opera and to writing agreeable but undemanding *musique de table* and *fugues légères*. Instead, in what Alex Ross describes as a kind of creative rage,[3] Bach experimented with every aspect of the cantata form, creating in his second cycle a benchmark of how music can serve as an eloquent meditation on the day's Gospel reading, and refusing to take the easy option of re-working older pieces, whether his own or those of others. In the music of this decade he was constantly engaged in the task of making explicit his sense of the world and of his fellow humans: it amounted to an extraordinary fusion of scriptural exegesis and social commentary. An immense work of religious music-drama like the *Matthew Passion*, whose beauty may have been considered at the time to be 'darkened by an excess of art',[4] can act as a prism, allowing us to see the entire rainbow of life that Bach makes available to us. Viewed in this way, it seems to say, 'This is how the world might be experienced: now go forth and experience it thus.'

* * *

It is entirely possible that Bach's growing disenchantment with cantatas in the 1730s arose from a sense that the communality of belief that he had once shared with his congregation was breaking down, and that, for whatever reason, he was now failing to make his mark. We saw earlier how he had set a stage for the cantatas of his first three cycles that was both imposing and intimate, the product of an unusual degree of connectedness between form, text and ideals. Whereas we might marvel at the disparity between the parochiality of the liturgical context and music that shows more and more signs of an almost limitless appeal, that was not how his first listeners saw things. Here would be grounds for Bach turning his back on his life's ambition, one that by now – he might have told himself – had run its course and that the edification of one's neighbour was compromised if that neighbour was no longer equipped or inclined to listen to it or grasp what it had to say. The official accusations levelled at him in this decade – that he was in essence 'working to rule' – can be interpreted not so much as a sign of any indifference to his responsibilities, let alone as a personal loss of faith, but as a protest at the shabby way the council, the consistory and the school rector were treating him, and his resignation to the likelihood that things would never change as long as he remained in Leipzig. Manifestly this is a municipal musician who continues to meet (and even exceed) the demands of his office but who at a given point decides to pursue his own evolving artistic agenda. Accepting the leadership of the *collegium musicum* in 1729 was one such step, and a predictable one, as he already had close ties to most of its members. Thereafter, all through the 1730s, Bach oversaw an extensive series of public concerts, and for the first time in Leipzig found himself in the limelight as the genuine Director Musices of the town.

Now Bach the church cantata composer–performer starts to fade out of vision, and for the first time he opens doors to other composers' works. Churchgoers no longer know, and perhaps do not even care, if he performs works by Telemann, Stölzel or his cousin Johann Ludwig Bach, and the text booklets on sale do not tell them what they are listening to. Compare this to the coffee-house concerts, where the public can see who is in charge at close quarters, even if as part of a throng of enthusiastic listeners they are scattered throughout different interconnected rooms. They are free to get up, move around, stand in the doorways, and comment on the music and the musicians in the style of a genteel academy of cognoscenti. Bach's role in the mid and late 1730s embraces an increasingly secular world: urban Leipzig on the threshold of the Enlightenment.

On those occasions when he does return to composing church cantatas Bach displays not just his old skills, but also a new sovereign mastery and fluidity of styles. The manifest ease with which, for example, he transforms in 1738 a bipartite *serenata* (BWV 30a) with a text by Picander into a cantata for the feast-day of St John the Baptist is very telling. Everything about BWV 30, *Freue dich, erlöste Schar*, is fresh and joyous, from its unusual construction of two eight-bar instrumental strophes, both repeated, to its syncopated theme and its boogieing triplets, and it generates colossal energy and fizz in Bach's most brilliant, ceremonial manner. In the pick of its four arias we find an enchanting gavotte for alto, flute and muted violins, with pizzicato lower strings. Even to a congregation well used after fifteen years to his habit of weaving gigues and *bourrées* into his church music, the sheer cheek and cool elegance must have raised eyebrows, and, one hopes, caused his first listeners to smile. It is the perfect riposte to any who might claim that, even for a moment, Bach is heavy or dull.

Throughout the mid to late 1730s he continued to polish his second cycle of cantatas, adding extensive new performance instructions; he also expands his reflections on the life of Christ by composing his (lost) *Mark Passion* (BWV 247) and three oratorios – for Easter, Christmas and Ascension. Around the same time he wrote four short Masses (BWV 233–6) confined to the *Kyrie* and *Gloria* and thus suitable for use in the Lutheran liturgy. In drawing on selected movements from his church cantatas Bach was acknowledging that they had their place there, though the sentiments expressed in them might now constitute a barrier for some listeners. So he recycled them, perhaps hoping that the music could have a wider appeal in this altered form as part of the Eucharist. Conducting the fourth of these Masses (BWV 235 in G minor) reinforced my conviction that the conventional demarcation or separation of genres in Bach's œuvre is misleading. Beyond simply being thrifty in recycling works that would otherwise be forgotten, Bach shows in the *G minor Mass* some of the many ways in which his ideas or musical cells can multiply, having grown out of some kind of anterior conception.

One never tires of Bach in this vein: everything is keen, concentrated and indefatigable. When studying this Mass, I found it helpful to have the cantata model of each movement before my eyes, so as to be sure not to miss a single gesture or inflection. But soon I found that it was a mistake to force a discarded expressive pattern on to a newly formed organism: one sees that the new life form takes on its own shapes and, as ever, the task is to perceive, or 'read', them. In any case Bach rarely transplants in an obvious way or to an obvious purpose. Since towards the end of his life he was increasingly preoccupied by a search for summative formulations, which entailed perpetual self-correction, it is futile to look for a single meaning in individual works: we should try to follow the full spectrum of meanings that they encompass.*

As official encomiums, the texts of the secular cantatas are generally feeble – even weaker than those of the church cantatas. Of the twenty or so individual secular movements that ended up in the *Christmas Oratorio*, none shows the brilliance of Bach's parody technique better than the very first aria, 'Bereite dich, Zion' ('Prepare thyself, Zion, with tender affection'). In the original (a *dramma per musica*, BWV 213/ix) the mood is indignant, as Hercules berates Lust ('I shall neither listen to you, nor acknowledge you, Depraved Lust'), whereas in the oratorio, even though the notes are identical (except for different slurring patterns and the addition of an oboe d'amore), they serve to paint a tender, almost erotic piece exhorting Zion to prepare itself for the arrival of the Messiah. They cry out to be played in a totally different way.

The theorist Gottfried Ephraim Scheibel would have us believe that the effect of music on listeners is the same regardless of its provenance, theatre or in church: 'religious and secular music have no distinctions, as far as the movement of the affections is concerned.'[5] Would that it were so simple. Scheibel's comments refer to emotion rather than to meaning (the two merge, naturally), and there is enough that is distinctive about 'Bereite dich, Zion' – changes of words, articulation and an implied style of playing – for it to have a different effect on the listener. The text of course dictates the musical interpretation; but because of its greater familiarity, we can never wholly shed the associations of the Christmas version and be totally objective when listening to the original. As with programme music, once we know that it is supposed to be about *x* we tend to hear it that way, whereas if we were to hear it

* For example, he raids BWV 187 for three of the middle movements of the *Gloria*, all arias; but where one might have predicted he would use the harvest-festival hymn of thanks for the *Gratias*, no, he uses it for the *Domini Fili* and instead chooses the rather quirky music (appropriately so in its original context for the disciples' vacillation 'What shall we eat, or what shall we drink, or wherewithal shall we be clothed?') for the *Gratias*. But the most impressive transplant or re-working is reserved for the *Cum sancto* concluding chorus. Here he turns to the opening chorus of BWV 187. This colossal canonic (later fugal) movement is shot through with an abundance of invention suited to harvest time (the Gospel text refers to the feeding of the Four Thousand). Motifs which were inspired by the harvest theme – paired oboes in conjunct semiquavers suggesting the waving of corn in the breeze, while the upper strings illustrate the movement of a sickle – seem perfectly at home in their new context of a *laudatio* to the Holy Spirit.

innocently and for the first time there would be nothing extraneous to condition our response.

Bach's word-setting evolved, too, in these later works, in part through his experience of composing Passions. He displays a new reluctance to be tied down to just a single meaning for the words of identically notated formulas; the purpose and mood changed, while remaining technically the same. We have seen how Bach drew on Luther's fertile coupling of words and melody, and habitually adjusted the harmonic ebb and flow of his chorale arrangements, not just to underscore the verbal stresses, but sometimes deliberately to flout them to allow key words to register with the listener, even if it meant blatantly ignoring the rhythm of others.

All through the *Christmas Oratorio* we encounter Bach's fresh ways of handling his chorales. Where his early chorale harmonisations stand out by their strong melodic outline, their steady metric tread and purposeful chord progressions, and later on by a richer harmonic movement and arresting passing dissonances, they now seem to emerge more naturally from the intersection of voices – from voice-leading, in other words – and have an even stronger sense of just proportion and balance. Here, too, one is struck by a greater warmth – as though he had discovered new ways of sculpting four individual lines, each imbued with intrinsic melodic beauty, and of weaving them together to create the most expressive replete harmony. In arriving at the most natural collusion between words, melody and harmony, Bach, one senses, could gladly have endorsed William Byrd's description of his own relationship to sacred texts: 'In these words, as I have learned by trial, there is such a concealed and hidden power that to one thinking upon things divine and diligently and earnestly pondering them, all the fittest numbers occur as if of themselves and freely offer themselves to the mind which is not indolent or inert.'[6]

Bach's *Christmas Oratorio* is a compendium of his evolving styles and approaches during the 1730s and 1740s.* In a sense, too, we can see

* One could say the same of BWV 769, *Canonic Variations on 'Vom Himmel hoch'*, which, in David Yearsley's words, are 'both *galant* and highly complex, enigmatic and yet unambiguously clear in their expressive intentions' (*Bach and the Meanings of Counterpoint* (2002), p. 120). Whereas Bach's habit of adding bars and even whole movements when preparing his collections for publication has been well known to scholars for some time, Ruth Tatlow's research into the construction of the *Christmas Oratorio*, on the other hand,

it as a timely rebuttal of Johann Adolph Scheibe's misleading dichotomies of nature versus art (or art-fulness), and truth versus confusion. Intervening on Bach's behalf in the dispute with Scheibe (see Chapter 7, p. 223), his former pupil Lorenz Mizler argued that, while Bach's music was often more carefully worked out than that of other composers, when so inclined he was perfectly equipped to compose 'in accordance with the latest taste' (*nach dem neuesten Geschmack*) and that Bach knew perfectly well how 'to suit himself to his listeners'.[7] But that was not really the point, Scheibe might have countered. While it could be said that Bach latterly was showing more amenity (*Annehmlichkeit* – the very quality Scheibe accused him of lacking) than in the past, the charge remained – that he was still obscuring the beauty of his music with too much artifice. Was he genuinely able to 'throw off the burden of *res severa* for the sake of *gaudium*' – and do so on a consistent basis?[8] If so (and it would be a rash person who underestimated Bach's ability to adapt) he was not the sort to make a show of it. Something like this must have been behind Forkel's observation that 'He [Bach] believed the artist could form the public, but that the public could not form the artist.'[9]

* * *

During his last decade, Bach withdrew more and more from the squabbles at the Thomasschule that had marred his previous fifteen years, without ever a hint of accommodation with the rector J. A. Ernesti. Both he and Anna Magdalena had bouts of quite serious illness, but he must have been consoled by the knowledge that his two eldest sons were well on the way to success and fame: they were already known as the 'Dresden' Bach (Wilhelm Friedemann) and the 'Berlin' Bach (Carl Philipp Emanuel), whereas by now he had become just 'old Bach'.[10] He had taken enormous pains over all his sons' musical education. Pride and

has produced startling findings. She has shown that in going to the trouble of creating 'inaudible proportional parallelism by adding bars and movements to already excellent music' Bach introduced three large-scale 2:1 proportions within a 3,645-bar structure (see 'Collections, Bars and Numbers: Analytical Coincidence or Bach's Design?' in *Understanding Bach* (2007), Vol. 2, pp. 37–58). The methodological context of her findings and what she sees as 'the significance and motivational morality in the word "Harmony" in Bach's time and location' will be the subject of her forthcoming book. I am grateful to Dr Tatlow for sending me a 'taster'.

joy at the achievements of the two eldest, however, was offset by the shame brought by the third, Johann Gottfried Bernhard, whom Bach referred to as 'my (alas! misguided) son'. As organist in Sangerhausen, Bernhard had got himself severely into debt (repeating the same impropriety that had cost him the job at Mühlhausen after little more than a year) and run away. In his distress Bach wrote to the authorities: 'I must bear my cross in patience, and leave my unruly son to God's Mercy alone, doubting not that He will hear my sorrowful pleading.' Somewhat defensively he adds, 'I am fully confident that you will not impute the evil conduct of my child to me, but accept my assurance that I have done all that a true father, whose children lie very close to his heart, is bound to do to further their welfare.' Nevertheless, he declined to pay his son's debts until they could be proven to him.[11] Unbeknown to both his father and the town council, Bernhard had enrolled as a law student at the University of Jena, fifty miles to the south. He died there of fever on 27 May 1739 at the age of twenty-four.

We get rare glimpses into the domestic situation of the Bach household in its last years from two sources within the family. Carl Philipp Emanuel told Forkel that, while his father had no time for lengthy correspondence, he had instead 'more opportunity to talk personally to good people, since his house was like a dovecot [*Taubenhaus*] and just as full of life. Association with him was pleasant for everyone, and often very edifying. Since he never wrote down anything about his life, the gaps are unavoidable.'[12] With Anna Magdalena, Bach kept an open house: 'no master of music was apt to pass through this place without making my father's acquaintance and letting himself be heard by him.'[13] Guests included several luminaries in contemporary German musical life, among them Jan Dismas Zelenka, Johann Quantz, Franz Benda, Johann Adolph Hasse and his diva wife Faustina Bordoni, and the two Grauns (Johann Gottlieb and Carl Heinrich). Music-making in the home included the returning elder sons: we learn, for example, that in August 1739 Wilhelm Friedemann 'was here for over four weeks, having made himself heard several times at our house, along with the two famous lutenists Mr Weiss and Mr Kropffgans from Dresden'.[14]

The source for this information is Johann Elias Bach (1704–55), grandson of Georg Christoph, Sebastian's father's elder brother, he of the *Concordia* cantata (see p. 64 and Plate 6), a thoroughly decent character who acted as Bach's secretary and live-in tutor to the three youngest boys from 1738 to 1742. It cannot always have been easy for Johann Elias to carry out his employer's instructions, since it might mean chasing recalcitrant debtors or those who had borrowed, but not returned, music. He was even obliged to refuse Johann Wilhelm Koch on 28 January 1741 the loan of a cantata for bass solo: 'my cousin regrets he cannot send it; he has lent the parts to the bass singer Büchner, who has not returned them. He won't allow the score out of his hands, for he has lost several by sending them to other people.'* If he made an exception, Bach was careful to exact the cost of the postage, and requests for printed copies, even from so intimate a relative and friend as Johann Elias himself, were met with a reminder of the published price.[15] On another occasion, Johann Elias wrote, 'I would be glad to have for my honoured cousin a bottle of the brandy made with yeast and a few, *nota bene*, yellow carnations for our honoured aunt [Anna Magdalena], a great connoisseur of gardening. I know for certain that this would give her great delight and ingratiate me all the more with both, wherefore I beg for this again.'[16] Later he acknowledged receipt of 'six most beautiful carnation plants . . . she values this unmerited gift more highly than children do their Christmas presents, and tends them with such care as is usually given to children, lest a single one wither.'[17] Bach was constantly on the lookout for presents for Anna Magdalena, according to Johann Elias. On a visit to Halle in 1740, he tells us, Bach had been impressed by the 'agreeable singing' of a linnet in Cantor Hille's possession, and since Anna Magdalena was 'a particular lover of such birds', Johann Elias was instructed to ask whether he would 'relinquish the singing bird to her for a reasonable sum'.[18]

In the late summer of 1741 Johann Elias's devotion was severely tested when Anna Magdalena fell ill while Bach was away visiting Carl Philipp Emanuel (recently appointed court accompanist to Frederick the Great of Prussia): 'we are sorry to disturb your holiday with this disagreeable news,' he wrote, 'but it would not be right to keep it from you, and we are certain that our dear Herr Papa and cousin will not be

* Six years after Johann Elias's departure, Bach's anger spills over in a letter he wrote himself to the Leipzig innkeeper Johann Georg Martius, who had borrowed one of his harpsichords: 'My patience is now at its end. How long do you think I must wait for the return of my harpsichord? Two months have passed, and nothing has changed. I regret to write this to you, but I cannot do otherwise. You must bring it back in good order, and within five days, else we shall never be friends. Adieu' (BD III, No. 45c/NBR, pp. 233–4).

angry with us.' Bach, in fact, was on the point of leaving Potsdam when he received a second, more urgent letter: 'We are in the deepest anxiety over the growing weakness of our dear Frau Mama. For a fortnight past she has had little more than an hour's rest at night being unable to either lie down or sit up. Last night she was so ill that I was called to her room, and to our deep sorrow we really thought we must lose her. We therefore feel bound to send on the news with the utmost urgency, so that you may hasten your journey and relieve us all by your return.'[19] Fortunately Anna Magdalena rallied and in the following February (1742) she gave birth to their last child, Regina Susanna, who survived into old age.

* * *

Revisiting the Class of '85 in their sixties, we find them in different states of health and creativity. Handel has fruitfully switched from Italian *opera seria* to dramatic oratorios in English, Rameau from musical theorist to becoming France's leading opera composer. Domenico Scarlatti, elegant and debonair as ever, is in a private world of his own and still delighting his listeners with the eccentric brilliance of his musical mind. Mattheson is deaf, but unflagging and still polemical, while Telemann just goes on and on and on. Which of them is still writing operas by the middle of the century? Not surprisingly the first to have given up, back in 1718, is Domenico Scarlatti, desperate to distance himself from the genre that defined the world of his father, Alessandro. Mattheson's last opera dates from 1723, the year in which Bach started as Thomascantor. Telemann (once disparaged by Kuhnau as a mere 'opera musician', but to whom all his Leipzig students flocked) still has one more opera in him (his seventeenth, *Don Quichotte der Löwenritter*, 1761) – although with the Hamburg Opera now closed his musical output has fallen off a little between 1740 and 1755. Aged seventy-four, having given up his hobby of growing geraniums (according to Ulrich Siegele[20]), he returns to paid musical composition, perhaps to keep his second wife suitably attired, and, finding a new spurt of creativity, he begins to write oratorios and cantatas again.* Telemann is reputed to

* This hobby of Telemann's was well known to Handel, who wrote to him on Christmas Day 1750 (so maintaining a lifelong correspondence between the two composers of a kind that is conspicuously lacking in Bach's life): 'If your passion for exotic plants, etc., could prolong your days and sustain the zest for life that is natural to you, I offer with very real pleasure to contribute to it in some sort. Consequently I am sending you as a present a crate

have composed thirty-one cantata cycles (or 1,043 individual cantatas). They were admired at the time by both Scheibe and Mattheson for their expression and harmony. *Deidamia* will be Handel's last opera (his forty-second, composed in 1741). Though his health and his eyes continue to trouble him, he will outlive Bach by nine years. In 1750 he still has two of his greatest dramatic oratorios ahead of him: *Theodora* (1750) and *Jephtha* (1752). The Earl of Shaftesbury writes in February 1750 that he has never seen him 'so cool and well [and] quite easy in his behaviour ... pleasing himself in the purchase of several fine pictures, particularly a large Rembrandt, which is indeed excellent.'[21] A few months later Handel sets off to the Continent for the last time and is injured in a coach accident between The Hague and Haarlem, delaying his arrival in his home town of Halle until a few weeks after Bach's death, and so the two men never meet.*

Rameau, on the other hand, by 1750 is only just past the midpoint in his operatic career: fourteen composing years, two major works (*Les Paladins* and *Les Boréades*) and thirteen individual *actes de ballet* are still to come. Of the Class of '85, only Rameau shows an eagerness comparable to Bach's to assert his independence within accepted conventions. With Rameau this is sometimes considered to be a matter of new wine in old bottles – the spirit of modernity set in the stiff structures of French *tragédie lyrique*, but tempered by fresh tactility of line and extreme suppleness and fluidity of rhythm. The music is light and lithe, brimful of vitality and transparency, and a counterpoise to the sheer density of the musical *étoffe*. That does not begin to account for the startling originality of his musical language, nor for the chasm between the notation and the actual sounds it represents – including *notes inégales* and twiddles galore, things known to baffle even the most accomplished musicians when they encounter them for the first time. Another feature is the psychologically penetrating and acutely observed

---

of flowers, which experts assure me are very choice and of admirable rarity. If they are not telling the truth, you will [at least] have the best plants in all England, and the season of the year is still right for their bearing flowers' (quoted in translation in Donald Burrows, *Handel* (2001 edn), p. 458).

* An anonymous contribution in 1788 in the *Allgemeine Deutsche Bibliothek* (almost certainly by C. P. E. Bach) made a comparison of Bach and Handel, in which its author suggests that Handel 'did not trust himself to challenge comparison with J. S. B.' (BD III, No. 927/NBR, pp. 400–409) – any more than Louis Marchand had in Dresden back in 1717 (see Chapter 6, p. 187).

way Rameau explores human emotion from within the starchy series of operatic conventions. Measure him against Lully or Gluck (one representing the past, the other the future), and he is out of their reach in terms of musical substance and scintillating interest. Remove his music from its stage context (a godsend, some might feel) and it can still come alive, imparting theatrical gesture and movement in the mind of the listener even in a concert hall. This is not dissimilar to the way Bach's Passions can conjure up a multiplicity of theatrical imagery when presented in imaginatively deployed performances in churches or concert halls. They have the capacity to enthral us by the personalisation of the human drama. Ironically it is Bach, still more than Rameau or Handel, who anticipated the ways music-drama could break free of stultifying operatic protocol and so inhabit the same air in which Mozart was soon to breathe.*

* * *

Signs of mental strength and tenacity are to be found everywhere in the music of Bach's last two decades: in the energy he expended in seeing his best keyboard works through to publication, such as the third and fourth volumes of his *Clavier-Übung*, and in the laborious gestation of the work he may have intended as its fifth volume, *The Art of Fugue*. We should not be lulled by any of the late signs of meticulous revision and dismiss them as a kind of musical housekeeping, let alone as a proof of fading creativity. Far from it. The hours of reclusive work spent correcting tiny details of counterpoint (while ensuring that it could all be played by two hands on a keyboard) continued even when engraving was already under way. According to his pupil Johann Philipp Kirnberger, Bach was in the habit of saying 'It ought to be possible to do everything' (*es muss alles möglich zu machen seyn*).[22]

* In conversation Robert Levin used an interesting metaphor for the way individual composers reach their zenith and at some point begin to tail off: they achieve a kind of perfect focus, like the focusing cylinder of a camera (in as much as the lens is within the cylinder, all the focusing needs to be performed by means of the sliding mechanism; and when once the right focus has been found, the cylinder and the camera are firmly locked) and then, having achieved that, they cannot resist giving it a couple or more revolutions, in consequence tipping over into excess or exaggeration of one sort or another. He cites Mozart achieving that perfect focus in *Le nozze di Figaro* and perhaps losing it in parts of *The Magic Flute* and *La clemenza di Tito*. Remarkably, with Bach, as with Rameau and Handel, there seems to be no equivalent diminution in the quality of their final works.

There was to come a time, however, when it became almost impossible for him to do anything. In the spring of 1749, about a year after he had sat for the second Haussmann portrait, we can see signs of deterioration in his handwriting. Suffering from an undiagnosed illness, perhaps a long-standing diabetic condition connected to eye pains, the only hard evidence we have comes in the deterioration of his handwriting around this time. Word soon got out. Whether as a precautionary measure, or as a piece of underhand skulduggery, the Leipzig burgomaster Jacob Born reported Bach's illness to Count von Brühl, the Saxon prime minister, who saw an opportunity to promote – or, more accurately, to be shot of – his Dresden music director, Gottlob Harrer. Following von Brühl's 'recommendation' to the Leipzig Town Council – little short of an order from the Dresden Court – Harrer travelled to Leipzig, was auditioned behind closed doors in the concert room of The Three Swans, applauded and returned to Dresden with the documentation requested by von Brühl, assuring him 'that in the said eventuality [of Bach's death] he will not be passed over'.[23] Even if it was the custom and considered acceptable to sound out successors during the lifetime of an incumbent, Bach must have felt he had been flayed alive. Then, after a while, he rallied. He was robust enough to respond to the slight by performing, on 25 August, BWV 29, *Wir danken dir, Gott*, one of the grandest of his commemorative cantatas for the annual city council elections, perhaps playing the virtuosic organ part in its opening *sinfonia* himself. Not only was he giving thanks for his recovery from his recent illness but publicly proclaiming God's authority above any worldly pretensions. It was a worthy response to the recent snub and a superbly defiant demonstration to the assembled council officials and Dresden Court representatives that he was still in full command of his artistic faculties.

Yet about the same time, when he was still at his most vulnerable, Bach risked sabotaging his own peace of mind by reacting to an unrelated incident in an impulsive way. A less edifying side to his character re-surfaces from that battle within himself, one that we have traced from his childhood onwards: feistiness in defence of his professional standing and a tendency to overreact and to resort to underhand behaviour. Twelve years after his initial public spat with Ernesti (see Chapter 6, pp. 200–201), Bach was still chuntering on (the tension between the two men never really abated) and he now manoeuvred himself into a position of fresh disgruntlement. Late in 1749 he allowed himself to be sucked into a similar dispute fifty miles away in Freiberg – between a former pupil (J. H. Doles, later to be his successor but one as Thomascantor) and J. G. Biedermann (rector of the gymnasium). Biedermann, in the Ernesti role, had gone into print deriding music as a corrupting distraction for youth and an unwelcome interloper in the school syllabus. Tactlessly, he aimed his fire at musicians in general, attacking their moral character and quoting Horace, who classified them with 'bayadères, quacks and beggarly priests'.[24] This caused quite a stir in the German musical world. Mattheson was roused to write no fewer than five essays denouncing Biedermann as 'a wrong-headed teacher, a sad opponent and godless defiler of musical art'.

At this point, his old wounds festering, Bach made an ill-considered intervention from the sidelines. His eyesight no longer up to writing full-length polemical letters, he persuaded a former pupil, C. G. Schröter, to speak out on his behalf, just as Magister Birnbaum had done during the Scheibe dispute in 1738–9. Schröter complied and sent his rebuttal to Bach, leaving him to have it printed. But it seems that Bach connived with the publisher to modify and spice up Schröter's article (to the latter's considerable annoyance) in the hope, as he wrote, that 'the rector's dirty ear [*Dreck-ohr*, punning with *Rec-dor* as spoken in the Saxon dialect] will be cleansed and made more fit to listen to music.'[25] For Mattheson this was going too far: Bach had used 'a base and disgusting expression, unworthy of a *Capellmeister*; a poor allusion to the word *Rector*'.[26] Though the reference was to Rector Biedermann, few in the small world of church music would have missed the implied association with Ernesti. Bach's attack backfired. Did he kick himself when he recalled a passage he had underlined in Calov: 'Why cause yourself irritation? . . . Such people will not hear you and if you fight your way through with ranting you may make it even worse.'[27]

Even now, when his disenchantment with the weekly grind at the Thomasschule was pushing him to the edge, Bach was not giving up – continuing as best he could (despite his failing sight) to explore new worlds of sound and the last reaches of counterpoint. We have so few reliable facts to go on, but it would only take the chance discovery of new documents to dent the provisional image we might have formed in our imaginations of Bach's final years and activities. A recently found letter, dated 27 February 1751, from a former Thomaner, Gottfried

Benjamin Fleckeisen, is an example. Hoping to be nominated cantor of Döbeln, a small town midway between Leipzig and Dresden, Fleckeisen refers to his nine years as an Alumnus of the Thomasschule and four years as a prefect of the *Chorus musicus*. He claims that 'for two whole years' he found himself 'having to perform at services in the two main churches of St Thomas and St Nicholas and obliged to conduct in place of the Capellmeister, and without glory, but always carried out honourably'.[28] Before drawing solid conclusions from this startling claim, we need to establish which two years Fleckeisen is referring to (sometime between 1742 and 1746, but possibly later still?) and, for example, whether he had fallen out with Bach (it is strange that he doesn't mention him by name). If Bach had really handed over the reins to him and been absent for such a period, was it because he was away on his travels, disenchanted or too sick to continue – or a combination of all three? Alternatively, was it Ernesti as rector or perhaps the school inspector, exasperated by Bach's erratic behaviour, who put Fleckeisen in charge? If his claim has any substance, it would show the council's premature decision to audition Harrer for Bach's job in a rather different light.

* * *

The comparison made in the previous chapter between Bach and Rembrandt highlighted an important difference in the way each might be considered to have held up his art as a mirror to his own personality. By portraying himself centrally, as though he were the one about to start the lynching of St Stephen, Rembrandt insists that we notice him – as a rueful participant, maybe, yet manifestly privy to the crime. In those early self-portraits, when he is giving a deceptively positive spin to his social respectability and wealth, Rembrandt is painting *himself* in various guises for all the world to see. Even then he never places himself centre-stage quite as ostentatiously as Dürer did in his third and most daring self-portrait (1500). There the frontal gaze and idealised facial symmetry are both immensely striking and slightly disquieting. The thing that saves it from hubris and blasphemy in its instantly identifiable likeness to Christ is the idea (based on Genesis 1:26) that, since man is made in God's image (*Ebenbildlichkeit*), it is fitting that there should be instantly recognisable similarities between the two. The German-born theologian Nicholas of Cusa (1401–64) had turned the old scholastic teaching about the *imago Deus* on its head by suggesting that the artist, who owes his gift to God, can legitimately attempt to replicate God's work and share in divine creativity, and that the artist's creations are enacted in the image of the prime Maker. God, in turn, acts like a painter in the way He generates living self-portraits in the form of men. This was an idea that gave legitimacy to Dürer's conception of his creative acts as those of a *Deus artifex*, in the tradition of Classical rhetorical imitation. By using the basic materials of pigment on a wooden board, the painter could set himself up as a *secundus Deus*, a second God.[29] The inscription Dürer placed on the front of his picture right next to his eyes stated that he, Albrecht Dürer from Nürnberg, had depicted himself aged twenty-eight, 'with appropriate or imperishable [the Latin expression *propriis coloribus* allows both readings] colours'.* The claim, then, was that these pigments would last – and, since they have already done so for the last 500 years, Dürer's was not an empty boast.

Dürer's self-conscious and innovative concept of artistry found expression two centuries later in the life and works of Bach. He, too, we might say, is constantly asking the question *Quis ut Deus?* ('Who is like God?'). Yet, in his case, the results – the durability, posthumous fame and degree of universality – are if anything still more striking. But when we look for explicit self-portraiture in Bach, this proves harder to discern, initially at least.

Some classical composers, Gustav Mahler for example, manage to inscribe in their music a kind of self-portraiture, which encompasses their personalities in all their vicissitudes; this in turn lodges in the imagination of the listener. Despite Bach's repeated insertion of his name in musical tones in the latter part of his life, this comes over as self-referring, rather than self-revealing. However, on several occasions in the course of this book I have pointed to times when Bach allows the mask to slip and his personality to come through in his music, times when we sense his many moods: his intense grieving, his passionate beliefs, but also his tussles with faith, his bursts of anger, his rebellious

* *Albertus Durerus Noricus / ipsum me propriis sic effin / gebam coloribus aetatis / anno XXVIII*. There is also a dark sign detectable in the left iris – a reflection of light passing through the crossed bars of a windowpane. Dürer is credited with having invented this device, and he employed it in several of his paintings. Beyond the obvious parallel between that image and the idea of the eye as a window to the soul is the remarkable way Dürer inscribes the sign of the Cross into his eyes: thus his gaze out on to the world, even the looks he exchanges with the beholder of his picture, passes through this arch-symbol of the Christian world. I am grateful to Professor Dr Reinhold Baumstark for this observation.

subversive streak, his delight in nature or his unbridled joy in God's creation. Of course we must allow that he was supreme at creating a wide spectrum of *Affekts*, and it is therefore perfectly legitimate to ask whether the mood is merely simulated: is it a true reflection of what he might have been feeling at that moment (or stored up or enduring from an earlier time) when conjuring it up in sound, and is it genuinely a means for us to detect and define his personality? This is harder to determine because of the extraordinarily high degree of clearly audible artifice and the prominent way Bach's music exposes its own brilliance and complexity, rather than being subservient to an external code such as the 'doctrine of the passions' (*Affektenlehre*), which recognised the expression of only one unified and 'rationalised' *Affekt* per movement of a composition.* Because the emotional world of his music is so rich in comparison with, for example, the milk-and-water affectations of Telemann and the absence of purposeful harmonic drive, we have a much stronger sense of Bach's own nature imprinted in the music, with a three-dimensional character which we take to be his own.

These are tantalising areas, arising from a world of subjective feeling and ultimately unprovable. Yet, treated cautiously, they provide us with a bridge – spanning the traces of Bach's personality we think we can detect embedded in his music and such historical truths as we can establish about the nature of his character. Then again, just as any Godlike image that we might superimpose on Bach blinds us to his artistic struggles, so we should also be wary of dismissing out of hand the anecdotal stories about his losing his rag with musicians, ripping off his wig and stamping on it, for these may certainly be things his own sons witnessed in the pressure-cooker of Thomaner rehearsals of the weekly cantatas.

One would not expect such episodes to feature in the version of his early life that Bach handed on to his children – and by them to Forkel, his first biographer – edited to give the most favourable slant to his

* The likelihood is that an across-the-board application of such a doctrine and the related method of musical figures (*Figurenlehre*) was far more irregular in Bach's Germany than was once thought by pioneers such as Arnold Schering ('Die Lehre von den musikalischen Figuren im 17. und 18 Jahrhundert', *Kirchenmusikalisches Jahrbuch*, Vol. 21 (1908)). The enormous increase in recent availability of online source material has meant that rare seventeenth- and eighteenth-century treatises are providing modern scholars with opportunities to reassess the primary materials and for performers to be less reliant on the old nostrums.

character.* Besides, some of his recollections were perhaps too painful to recall, yet they are all of a piece with the irascibility his music – joined with its text – sometimes exposes. Bach lived with indelible memories of his early childhood and surely brooded on the meaning of its events; but it is unlikely he passed much of this on to his children or else we would surely have heard about it. Like Mark Twain, who experienced similar early sufferings – a father dying, a dead sister, two dead brothers and sermons on Sunday 'made up almost exclusively of fire and brimstone' – Bach may have intended to steer clear of probing deep waters in an identifiably personal way.†

Despite the dominance of the family and the clan, the overwhelming impression we get of Bach is of an essentially private person, turned in on himself, pouring his energy, after the death of his parents, first into his schoolwork and then into his music. The persistent presence of death in his life – of parents, siblings, his first wife and then so many of his own children – may have led to an emotional reclusiveness or wariness based on his experience that loving intrinsically carries the risk of losing.

* Karl Sabbagh (*Remembering Our Childhood: How Memory Betrays Us* (2009)) claims that 'all memory, whatever age it is laid down or recalled, is unreliable.' 'It's unnerving to realize that our stories, feelings, memories of the past are reconstructed over time, and that we make up history as we go along.' So what is memory for? It is there, he suggests, to help us to adapt to the conditions around us, in other words, it is designed not to be accurate but to be helpful, so we remember things that are useful to us, and our brains contain an apparatus designed to mould memories into useful stories – to give, for example, a favourable spin to our earthly struggles towards self-improvement or auto-didacticism in Bach's case, even if essentially based on truth and reality (or perhaps not entirely, 'for memory is false and sells to the highest bidder').

† The death of Twain's father – the second of two powerful blows – did not simply hurt; it swept away his confidence and even his hope that life had meaning. Even though Twain's childhood may have developed differently from Bach's, it was the loss, pain and sorrow that made no sense to him: 'It is one of the mysteries of our nature,' he wrote in his autobiography, 'that a man, all unprepared, can receive a thunderstroke like that and live.' Thomas Powers tells us (*London Review of Books*, Vol. 33, No. 9 (28 Apr. 2011)) that Twain was a deeply impressionable boy with indelible memories. 'The pen was in his hand and the memory was too intense to hold back another minute. He thought continually about the people and incidents of his entire life, not just his childhood, and brooded on their significance.' He refers to Twain's nose for the whiff of hypocrisy: 'he went for it immediately, much as a Jack Russell terrier would snap at the neck of a mewling kitten' – a description that could apply just as well to Bach in his cantata jeremiads. In 1889 Twain wrote to a friend that too many subjects had escaped his wrath. 'They burn in me; and they keep multiplying . . . but now they can't ever be said. And besides, they would require a library – and a pen warmed-up in hell.'

On the other hand one could argue that for posterity and even for him, the death of his father, Ambrosius, however shattering at the time, may have been the best thing that ever happened to Bach. It brought him under the wing of his talented eldest brother (who seems to have been a more sophisticated musician than their Stadtpfeifer father), and it paved the way for his far less parochial education in the north of Germany, an opportunity that would have been denied him had he ended up apprenticed to his father in Eisenach.

In acknowledging Bach's humanity we begin to see how similar to us he was. If we forgo attempts to explain his genius (as a divine gift, or the result of genetics or nurture) we gain something richer – a sense of connection as well as a more nuanced, 'grainier' idea of how his music is put together and a clue as to why it should have such a deep emotional affect on us. Perhaps music gave Bach what real life in many respects could not: order and adventure, pleasure and satisfaction, a greater reliability than could be found in his everyday life. It was also there to complete those experiences that otherwise might have existed only in his imagination – part-compensation for those stimulating adventures denied to him but not to Handel, whose travels to Italy provided him with such a fertile source of inspiration. Bach found security in sticking to a regular structure, to proportion and numbers, and to the calendar. It was a trait that took a particular shape, gaining impetus, in his fifties through his almost obsessive absorption with genealogy and family trees.

* * *

How much of all this did Haussmann succeed in conveying when he painted his second, formal, portrait of Bach in 1748? (See Plate 19.) We search for signs of the animation we find in the music: we want Bach to leap out at us, a fiery, seething man whose creative exploits pressed music into new territory while he brushed off or skirted round the trivial obstacles of his employment. I don't recall getting an inkling of that in my childhood: my memory is of the Cantor looking out with a stern, impassive and slightly forbidding gaze. Yet, seeing the portrait again in Princeton after almost sixty years, I was struck by how astutely Haussmann had captured opposed facets of his sitter's character: the serious and the sensual. One is always directed to the eyes to find the most reliable and pertinent information. The moment you divide Bach's face horizontally, say at the bridge of the nose, you notice a high, slightly receding (but smooth) forehead and the look of a man etched with life's travails – beetle-browed, with shallow eye sockets, asymmetrical eyes and slightly droopy eyelids.*

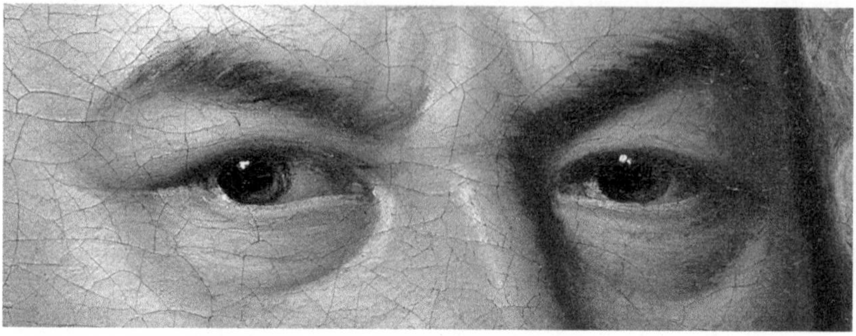

His gaze is intense but far livelier than I remembered it. (Another feature I had never noticed before is that his eyebrows appear to grow or are brushed in the wrong direction – towards the bridge of his nose.) In the lower half of his face one's attention is drawn to the flared right nostril, the distinctive shape of his mouth creased at the corners, the fleshy lips and jowls that suggest a fondness for food and wine, as the records imply.

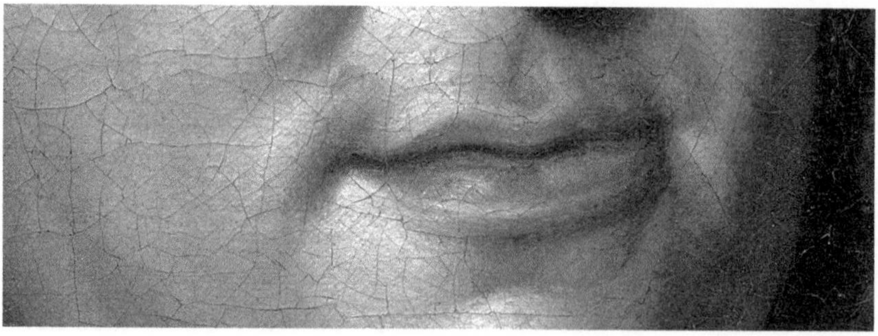

* Their drooping caused perhaps by a hereditary eye disease called blepharochalasis – a sign of the muscular weakness we are alerted to in the *Nekrolog*: 'his naturally somewhat weak eye sight, further weakened by his unheard-of zeal in studying', which could be traced back to the strain of that illicit nocturnal copying in his brother's house.

The overall impression is of someone a lot more complex, nuanced and, above all, *human* than the formal posture of a public figure would seem to allow, and infinitely more approachable than the man in Haussmann's earlier portrait, where his stare is more that of a bland and corpulent politician.* In his right hand Bach holds a page of music – a *Canon triplex à 6 voc.* – one of fourteen he transcribed at the back of his copy of the *Goldberg Variations*.

Apart from its intellectually challenging title, the puzzle lies in the way we read its three lines. As Bach presents it to the viewer, we see it as a straightforward three-part fragment written in alto, tenor and bass clefs – pleasant enough but ever so slightly banal. Surely that cannot have been the reason why Bach had himself painted by Haussmann holding this sheet of manuscript? But then we realise that to Bach himself, looking down on it, it reads quite differently – and for us to see it his way we have to turn the manuscript upside down and read the music back to front: starting from the same place as the 'forward' version, but changing the clefs to tenor, alto and treble, the lines emerge at the fifth

* Dating from 1746 and located in the Stadtmuseum in Leipzig, it has been restored at least four times: after layers of over-painting the canvas is a ruin and the original paint has disappeared in several places (see Plate 18). Controversy still rages over the authenticity of other surviving 'portraits' of Bach. The one with the best chances of being accepted as genuine is the so-called 'Weydenhammer Portrait', owned by successive generations of the same American family and finally coming to light in 2000. Badly damaged and showing signs of having been cut down from a larger bust portrait, it bears a passable likeness of a man in his thirties who might have aged into the corpulent figure we recognise in the Haussmann portrait, but the eyes are utterly different (see Teri Noel Towe, 'The Portrait of Bach that Belonged to Kittel' in *The Tracker: Journal of the Organ Historical Society*, Vol. 46, No. 4 (Oct. 2002), pp. 14–18).

in mirror (upside down, in other words). There is also a double mirror if we reflect the notes along the middle line of each stave. Take the middle voice as an example: we see that the second note written in the tenor clef on the middle line is an A. Put that note in the alto clef, as in 'Bach's' version, and the same note reads as a C.

But if this is a canon in six parts, where are the other three? Bach's expression seems to say 'Look more closely: my music doesn't yield up all its secrets to a single glance.'* The key to solving the puzzle lies in the little signs that appear above bar two, for they show us where the canon must begin. Once all the voices have been realigned, turned upside down, read back to front and played at one bar's distance in the 'right way up' version, suddenly we can see a *canon à 6* unfold. The repeat signs over bars two and three and the absence of a final bar tell us that it is on a never-ending loop – a *canon perpetuus* – so that the music never resolves (as with the last fugue from *The Art of Fugue*). A further clue to the need for transposition can be detected in the outline of an extra clef just visible on the curious triangular sliver of manuscript that seems to have been added to the rectangular folio on its right-hand margin: the midnight-blue of Bach's velvet coat shines through it, suggesting that Haussmann (acting on Bach's instructions) had painted over it as a *pentimento* (see p. 547 and Plate 19).†

Haussmann's portrait shows us the importance of going beyond first

* In *Las Meninas*, Velázquez portrays himself working at a large canvas looking outwards, beyond the pictorial space to where the viewer would be standing. Like Velázquez, Bach seems to be saying 'Don't look at me: look at my music', in the knowledge that, with the upside-down version in front of him, he is hearing so much more than we ever can.

† The walking bass that constitutes the third part of the triplex canon is one of fourteen based on the first eight notes of the bass of the *Goldberg Variations*. The same theme is also reminiscent of the chorale theme of BWV 769, *Canonic Variations on 'Vom Himmel hoch'*. Bach's *tour de force* of canonic counterpoint in his set of variations includes his musical portrait of the notes that spell B-A-C-H at the end. These variations were submitted alongside the triplex canon and the first Haussmann portrait when Bach was admitted to Mizler's

Original clefs, with canon in mirror view
and clef changes that make canons at the 5th
and use the middle line of the stave as
a mirror line.
to us
"Bach's"
to us
"Bach's"
to us
"Bach's"
The same
in C and F clefs

Canon triplex à 6 voci.

appearances. The disparities of character that I suggest it displays are supported by the biographical evidence we have been piecing together, and the multiplicities and contradictions we have encountered. The aim all along has been to keep a hold on the critical connectedness of things – to see Bach in the round and not through the parochialism of small-sampling or the microscopic perspective of single issues that some scholars defend with terrier-like tenacity. It has meant balancing musical analysis with broad historical contexts and establishing how his being in a particular time and place located his achievement in the wider development of European culture and currents of thought. It has meant

Society for Musical Sciences (*Societät der musicalischen Wissenschaften*) as its fourteenth member in June 1747.

piecing together biographical shards, scrutinising the music and looking out for instances when his personality seems to penetrate the fabric of his notation. Our exploration of the *B minor Mass* in the previous chapter furnished us with the paradigm of a quest for a perfection attempted despite the most unpromising, piecemeal process of assimilation. Many people remember that when in 1977 the *Voyager* spacecraft was launched, opinions were canvassed as to what artefacts would be most appropriate to leave in outer space as a signal of man's cultural achievements on earth. The American astronomer Carl Sagan proposed that 'if we are to convey something of what humans are about then music has to be a part of it.' To Sagan's request for suggestions, the eminent biologist and author Lewis Thomas answered, 'I would send the complete works of Johann Sebastian Bach.' After a pause, he added, 'But that would be boasting.'[30]

Another response might have been: here is what many of us consider the most beautiful and profound manifestation that man is capable of in complex harmonious sounds that capture in an inexplicable way the joys and suffering we encounter in our earthly lives, helping us to access the emotional core of human experience. Yet, perhaps because it is easy to be in awe of Bach's achievements, there is still a problem for some people in admitting to his shortcomings. In doing so, we do not have to agree with Edward Said that there is 'something unmistakably demonic and frightening' about Bach's fervour, for, as we have seen, expressions of it in the cantatas are nearly always balanced by others where wit, humanity and compassion are uppermost. Where I am almost persuaded by Said is when he suggests that Bach was trying to control something [that was] 'more exuberant, more hubristic, verging on the blasphemous . . . something within himself, which his music with its contrapuntal wizardry also communicates'.[31] You see it in his obsessive focus on order and structure, and also from that glint in his eye we thought we detected in Haussmann's portrait, which might be hinting at his struggles to keep chaos in his surrounding – and in his inner-life – at bay.

* * *

Although Bach had pulled through in the summer of 1749 after the shock of his sudden illness, the problems with his vision persisted and inconvenienced him to the point when he sought a surgical cure. Carl Philipp Emanuel reported that at this point 'Not only could he no longer use his eyes, but his whole system, which was otherwise thoroughly healthy, was completely overthrown by the cataract operations and by the addition of harmful medicaments and other things.' He tells us that his father was 'almost continuously ill for a full half a year'.[32] It must have taken exceptional bravery to submit to Taylor's two botched cataract operations – a clear sign that he was determined to complete unfinished business. A description of what purports to be his intentions for completing *The Art of Fugue* is included in the *Nekrolog*: it mentions a 'draft for a fugue' that 'was to contain four themes and to have been afterward inverted note for note in all four voices'.[33] This cannot possibly be the same as the unfinished *Fuga a 3 soggetti,* which survives in autograph on paper with a watermark pointing to the very last months of Bach's life. A note on the reverse by his pupil Agricola tells us that it belongs to another 'ground plan', thus suggesting a completely different project, one destined to remain unfulfilled.*[34] After 239 bars this serene and refined fugue breaks off shortly after an episode in which Bach has transcribed his own name. In performance, when the music tails off, it leaves listeners aghast. Of course it could have been a deliberate move by Bach, as though to say *Quaerendo invenietis* (the expression he added to his *Musical Offering*), inviting future generations to search for the solution themselves – literally 'You'll find it if you look for it', or, more poetically (as in the Sermon on the Mount), 'Seek and ye shall find.'

One of the books in Bach's private collection was Heinrich Müller's *Liebes-Kuss* (*Love's Kiss*) (1732), which advised constant preparation

* Generations of scholars, assuming the *Fuga a 3 soggetti* to be the intended conclusion to *The Art of Fugue,* have been puzzled as to why a composer so single-mindedly committed to the cultivation of fugue should have left this climactic exemplar unfinished at the very moment when he was manifestly so close to reaching the finishing line. Bach's almost obsessive need for perfection is evident in the fair-copy scores of works that were not to be published until after his death, such as the second volume of the *Well-Tempered Clavier* (BWV 870–93) and the *Canonic Variations on 'Vom Himmel hoch'* (BWV 769), where he added bars to already completed scores (see note on p. 532). The extraordinary alto aria in BWV 77/v that we encountered in Chapter 12 (p. 451) sums up one of the underlying contradictions we keep finding – of someone devoting his whole life and creative energies to discovering those eternal rules of music that emulate Godlike *Vollkommenheit* ('perfection and completeness') – and yet, as with the flawed trumpeter required to play a series of near-impossible tones, symbolically exhibiting all the marks of human fallibility in the process. This dichotomy goes to the heart of Bach's character: self-awareness, with an acknowledgement of human failings (a theme that runs through so many of the cantata texts), and the knowledge that artistic gifts, like life itself, are bestowed by God's grace.

Fuga a 3 soggetti (BWV 1080/19) *'While working on this fugue, in which the name BACH appears in the countersubject, the author died' (C. P. E. Bach,* c. *1780).*

for death, admitting that the expression of grief was a necessary part of coming to terms with death.[35] Besides the selection of a few well-chosen *Trost-Sprüchlein* ('little words of comfort'), Müller emphasises that 'music offers not only a glimpse of heavenly life, but a tool with which to focus one's thoughts about death',[36] and includes an engraving (see opposite) to illustrate the two realms of earth and heaven 'joined in synchronic concert'. We have seen that in his copy of Calov's Bible commentary, Bach underlined and marked several passages that speak of carrying out the duties of one's 'office' without regard to the reactions of others or what the future will bring, of the need for patience and endurance of all adversities, of the distinction between worldly and spiritual wisdoms. One in particular stands out, a German proverb: 'With one's own thoughts, as with a tautly held cloth, much slides off.' Could this have been Bach's own reaction in his last years? Calov comments: 'Thus stubborn or self-appointed projects seldom turn out well. Also, for me things have never in my life gone according to my plans: I have set a certain plan for myself, but if it had not been God's word and deed which drew me to the project, the greater part was left unaccomplished.'[37]

This second engraving from Heinrich Müller's Himmlischer Liebes-Kuss *(1732) conveys the capability of earthly music to be elevated into angelic song.*

All life-long music, and especially the chorale, provided Bach both with a glimpse of heavenly life and with a weapon with which to combat the terror of death. Like his early mentor Dietrich Buxtehude, Bach may have kept alive a dream of joining the angelic choir (or 'concert') after death, seen by many at the time as the privileged gateway to heaven for musicians. Buxtehude refers to it in the touching *Klag-Lied* he composed on the death of his own father, who, like him, had been an organist: *Er spielt nun die Freuden-Lieder / Auf des Himmels-Lust-Clavier* ('He is now playing songs of joy / on the heavenly keyboard'). Far from trying to evoke the heavenly music his father was now hearing, Buxtehude impregnates his setting with dissonance and a persistent tremulous throb in the strings: it is as though wave after wave of filial love is inspiring him, while inconsolable sorrow buffets him in the act of pinning his music to the page. The effect is far more poignant than that of its companion piece, his setting of Luther's burial hymn, which consists of four movements in strict invertible counterpoint. Music of this degree of learning and 'unfathomability' (*die Unergründlichkeit der Musik*[38]) was considered by a small elite of composers to be a way of purifying their best thoughts as death closed in and a vehicle for their safe passage to heaven. For the music sung by the angelic choir was, in Werckmeister's words, 'nearly beyond the understanding of men'.[39] That never deterred a composer of Bach's imaginative scope from attempting to replicate it, as we have seen, at several moments in his creative life.*

Meanwhile the terrestrial music he composed to commemorate the passing of a beloved member of family or on commission, such as the motets we explored in Chapter 12, still has the power to give extraordinary solace to the bereaved and to anyone susceptible to music's emotive and transformative powers. In the end, no one – absolutely no one – has ever produced such a treasury of consoling music as Bach, and the

* Robert Quinney has suggested to me that the 'heavenly' counterpoint of Buxtehude's *Mit Fried und Freud* settings is *recherché*, emotionally unreachable by mortals – whereas, presumably, Buxtehude's father is tapping his feet to it in heaven. It is only the *Klag-Lied* that we can 'understand'. The miraculous thing about Bach's counterpoint, compared to Buxtehude's, is that it is emotionally reachable: it is not perfection for its own sake, as in the multiple invertible Buxtehude settings of *Mit Fried und Freud*, but music that reaches out to the listener.

amazing thing is how early he acquired that gift – as early as the age of twenty-two, when he composed the *Actus tragicus*.* Intrinsic to this is the sense of certainty we recognise in Bach: his belief that somewhere there exists a path leading to a life of harmonious existence, if not in this world then in the next, one that overrides the endemic stupidity of men and women and all the hypocritical and self-seeking behaviour that blights quotidian social intercourse. Two of Bach's favourite authors, August Pfeiffer and Heinrich Müller, recognised the role of music in transporting believers to that ideal as part of the *ars moriendi*.[40] There are signs of this in what could well have been Bach's very last composition.†

Though C. P. E. Bach was not in Leipzig at the time, he reported that his father's so-called 'Deathbed' chorale, BWV 668a, *Wenn wir in höchsten Nöten sein*, was dictated shortly before his death 'on the spur of the moment' (*aus dem Stegreif*), to an unnamed friend. Taking an ornament-encrusted version of this chorale that he had earlier included in his *Orgel-Büchlein*, Bach stripped it down to a skeletal form. Having purged it of all sensuality, he now re-expanded it with melodic inversion, diminution and *stretto*. The relationship between the two versions is not as extreme as in the two Buxtehude examples referred to above. While it could be said to encapsulate the 'elevated thinking' of a dying man,[41] that, however, is not the uppermost quality to emerge in performance. The moment the funerary text 'Vor deinem Thron' is attached to Bach's intricate contrapuntal lines, the piece acquires a different kind of lucidity and transcendental quality:

I herewith step before Thy throne,
O God, and humbly beg Thee:
Turn not Thy gracious countenance
From me, a poor sinner.

* An example of how adept Bach is at conveying the fragility of life, of how all things 'snap, break and fall' when 'not held by God's own mighty arm', comes in the virtuosic, but unlovely, tenor aria in BWV 92, *Ich hab in Gottes Herz und Sinn*. A later, unforgettable example is to be found in the grand Michaelmas cantata composed in 1726, BWV 19, *Es erhub sich ein Streit im Himmel* (see Chapter 3, p. 73). There a ravishing *siciliano* conjures up the watchfulness of the guardian angels in answer to the tenor's tender plea, 'Stay, ye angels, stay by me!' (*Bleibt, ihr Engel, bleibt bei mir!*).

† But for an alternative possibility, see Chapter 13, p. 507.

* * *

Bach died on 28 July, a little after 8.15 p.m. Three days later this chorale was sung by his Thomaner at his burial in the churchyard of the Johanneskirche, possibly in addition to the arrangement he had recently made with manifest physical effort (as we can see from the handwriting) of a motet by his older cousin Johann Christoph, *Lieber Herr Gott, wecke uns auf* (*Dear Lord God, awaken us*), a prayer with words thought to be by Luther that anticipates life after death. It had been performed at Johann Christoph's funeral in 1703, and it seems it may also have been sung to mark Bach's own passing.* Those closest to him would have seen it as the perfect symbol of his sense of family roots and of his touching desire to re-affirm his loyalty to the one he revered as the most noteworthy composer within the family and his spiritual mentor.

All through this final phase of his life, Bach was searching and penetrating musical *terra incognita*. It has taken generations of composers and performers to explore the equivalent of those blanks on a map cartographers once charmingly described as 'here-be-dragons': to re-trace his routes and come to terms with his findings. Two and a half centuries after his passing, no one could claim that the process is complete. Ignored for a time, then patchily revived, misrepresented, inflated, re-orchestrated, then in a puritanical overreaction scaled down, diminished and minimalised – there seems to be no end to the ways that Bach's music can be manipulated to fit with the prevailing *Zeitgeist* and commercially exploited or used for political ends.†

* Christoph Wolff's assumption is based on several factors: the very late preparation of the material (Bach's shaky handwriting is here even shakier than the last *Art of Fugue* entries); that the original place of the motet (second Sunday in Advent) could not be accommodated in the Leipzig liturgy; and that the text has a broader meaning which applies well to a Christian's faith in the face of death. Finally, as Professor Wolff wrote to me, 'I believe that the cantor didn't want prefect and choir to fall on their faces by trying a more difficult J. S. B. piece. Even the J. C. B. piece gets *colla parte* accompaniment.'

† Bach's first biographer, Forkel, exhorted his fellow Germans in 1802, 'And this man, the greatest musical poet and the greatest musical orator that ever existed, and probably ever will exist, was a German. Let his country be proud of him; let it be proud but, at the same time, worthy of him!' (NBR, p. 479). But, as Christoph Wolff commented in a speech given in the Thomaskirche on 28 July 2000 to mark the 250th anniversary of Bach's death, 'In Germany's name Bach has been many times misused whenever it would serve a political ideology. Unfortunately this has often been the case at Bach festivals in the anniversary years of the past century: in 1900 as a symbol of nationalistic Wilhelmine arrogance; in

All the while his music beckons us to view life through his eyes, the eyes of a consummate artist, as though to imply: this is a way of fully realising the scale and scope of what it is to be human within it. Therefore study and listen to it closely – and not just any performance will do, however well intentioned. In the words of a recent biographer, 'There is no music so demanding to realise in sound, and so quick to reveal a lack of understanding or lack of integrity in approaching it.'[42] For the listener to gain a sense that Bach is exploring all the threads of his music, simultaneously as both composer and performer, his interpreters must strive to do the same. Once again we are drawn to sentiments eloquently conveyed by that great British forerunner of his, William Byrd, who in the preface to his last publication, *Psalmes, Songs and Sonnets* (1611), wrote:

> Only this I desire: that you will be as careful to hear [my songs] well express'd, as I have been both in the composing and the correcting of them. Otherwise the best song that ever was made will seem harsh and unpleasant . . . Besides, a song that is well and artificially made cannot be well perceived nor understood at the first hearing, but the oftener you shall hear it, the better cause of liking you will discover.

Each time we explore Bach's music we feel as if we have travelled great distances to, and through, a remote but entrancing soundscape. Every moment that promises to be an arrival is just another station on the way and the springboard for further journeying – for a new engagement and a new engaging with Bach.

It is tantalising how a generation later Johann Gottfried von Herder (1744–1803) seems at times to be articulating some of the processes in which Bach as both composer and performer was involved, but without referring to them directly. Herder grasped the crucial idea that the creative and spiritual activity of man leads to expressions of an individual's vision of life, to be understood only by sympathetic insight – the ability to 'feel oneself into' (*sich hineinfühlen*) the aspirations and concerns of others. One imagines that he might have understood the supreme value of Bach's vocal works – not primarily as objects or artefacts, but as indi-

---

1935 under the racist banner of the Nazi state; in 1950 and 1985 as a manifestation of the proletarian-socialist aims of the GDR.' Even in 2000 (the 250th anniversary of his death) there were occasional traces of parochial chauvinism.

vidual visions of life and as priceless forms of communication with his fellow man. For this is what is so distinctive when we compare Bach's legacy to that of his forerunners and successors. Monteverdi gives us the full gamut of human passions in music, the first composer to do so; Beethoven tells us what a terrible struggle it is to transcend human frailties and to aspire to the Godhead; and Mozart shows us the kind of music we might hope to hear in heaven. But it is Bach, making music in the Castle of Heaven, who gives us the voice of God – in human form. He is the one who blazes a trail, showing us how to overcome our imperfections through the perfections of his music: to make divine things human and human things divine.

Chronology

EISENACH

1685	21 March	Johann Sebastian Bach is born, seventh and youngest child of Johann Ambrosius Bach and Maria Elisabeth Bach, *née* Lämmerhirt.
	23 March	Baptised on the Monday after Oculi, in the Georgenkirche. Godparents: Sebastian Nagel (town musician at Gotha) and Johann Georg Koch (ducal forester of Eisenach).
1686	3 May	Bach's sister, Johanna Juditha, dies at the age of six.
1691		Death of elder brother, Johann Balthasar, born 1673.
1692		Enters the Lateinschule in Eisenach in the spring.
1693		Enrols in the *quinta* of the Lateinschule in the former Dominican monastery, aged eight. (This implies he was already able to read and write and had probably attended one of the town's German primary schools from the age of five.) He is marked absent 96 times.
1694		Continues in the *quinta*, marked absent 59 times.
	1 May	Death of Elisabeth, his mother, at the age of fifty (buried 3 May).
	27 Nov	Remarriage of his father, Ambrosius, to Barbara Margaretha, the 35-year-old widow of Ambrosius's first cousin, Johann Günther.
1695	20 February	Death of his father at the age of forty-nine (buried 24 February).
		Graduates from the *quarta*, having been marked absent 103 times.

	April	After Easter moves with his thirteen-year-old brother, Johann Jacob, to Ohrdruf to live with their eldest brother, Johann Christoph.

OHRDRUF

1695	July	Enters the *tertia* class at the Lyceum Illustre Gleichense in Ohrdruf.
1696	20 July	Is placed fourth in the *tertia*, and first among the new boys.
1697	19 July	Placed first of twenty-one students in the *tertia* and is promoted to the *secunda.*
1698	18 July	Placed fifth in the *secunda.*
1699	24 July	Placed second of eleven students in the *secunda* and is promoted to the *prima* at the age of fourteen years and four months.
1700	15 March	Placed fourth in the *prima*. Leaves for Lüneburg with Georg Erdmann without finishing the *prima*, officially recorded as *ob defectum hospitorium* (the withdrawal of free board).

LÜNEBURG

1700	April	Choral scholar at the Michaelisschule, initially singing in the Mettenchor, which entitles him to free lodging. 3 April receives *Mettengeld* (salary for singing) for the first time. 'Some time thereafter' (*Nekrolog*) his voice breaks.
	29 May	Receives *Mettengeld* for the last time.
		Becomes a student of Thuringian organist-composer Georg Böhm, at whose house he copies Reincken's chorale prelude *An Wasserflüssen Babylon* in tablature.
1702	April	Graduates from the Michaelisschule.
	9 July	Applies for and is offered the post of organist at the Jacobikirche, Sangerhausen, but another applicant, Johann Augustin Kobelius, is confirmed instead.

WEIMAR I

1703	20 December–June	Employed as musician and 'lacquey' at the Weimar Court.

ARNSTADT

1703		Burial of Johann Christoph Bach, the 'profound composer', in Eisenach.
	13 July	Hired to examine and assess the newly built organ at Arnstadt's Neukirche.
	9 August	Appointed organist of the Neukirche.
1705	August	Bach's dispute with bassoonist Johann Heinrich Geyersbach.
	November	Takes four-week leave of absence to travel to Lübeck to observe Buxtehude at work.
1706	7 February	Returns to Arnstadt after four months unauthorised absence. Disciplinary procedure initiated by the consistory.

MÜHLHAUSEN

1707	24 April	Audition for the post of organist at the Blasiuskirche in Mühlhausen.
	14–15 June	Appointed organist at the Blasiuskirche at a salary of 85 gulden.
	1 July	Starts work at the Blasiuskirche.
	17 October	Marriage to Maria Barbara, aged twenty-three, daughter of Johann Michael Bach of Gehren, at Dornheim near Arnstadt.
1708	4 February	Town council election in Mühlhausen. Performance of BWV 71, *Gott ist mein König*, which is printed and published some weeks later.
	25 June	Released from his post as organist in Mühlhausen following his appointment as organist and chamber musician in Weimar. Formulation of his *Endzweck*.

WEIMAR 2

1708	14 July	Receives gratuity of about 10 gulden for relocation to Weimar, where his salary is 150 florins.
	29 December	Baptism of eldest daughter, Catharina Dorothea.
1709	4 February	Returns to Mühlhausen to perform a cantata (now lost) to mark the town council election.
1710	22 November	Birth of son, Wilhelm Friedemann, baptised on 24 or 25 November.
1711	3 June	Salary increased from 150 to 200 gulden.
1713	February	Journeys to Weissenfels for the birthday of Duke Christian of Sachsen. Performance of BWV 208, the *Hunt Cantata*.
	23 February	Birth of twins, Maria Sophia and Johann Christoph. Johann Christoph dies at birth.
	15 March	Death of remaining twin, Maria Sophia.
	28 November	Invited to apply for position of organist in Halle.
	13 December	Appointed organist at the Marktkirche in Halle, contract dated 14 December.
1714	14 January	Letter from Bach requesting changes in proposed contract in Halle.
	2 March	Promoted to Concertmeister of the Weimar Hofcapelle, with an obligation to compose monthly church cantatas. Salary raised to 250 florins.
	8 March	Birth of son Carl Philipp Emanuel, baptised 10 March. Telemann is one of his godfathers.
	19 March	Letter from Bach, having declined the Halle post in February, refuting accusations of unfair dealings with the Halle authorities.
	25 March	BWV 192 performed on Palm Sunday, the first Weimar church cantata written after his new appointment as Concertmeister.
1715	11 May	Birth of son Johann Gottfried Bernhard, baptised 12 May.
1717	26 March	Performance of a lost Passion in Gotha on Good Friday.
		Journeys to Dresden for an aborted musical competition with Louis Marchand.

	7[5?] August	Accepts post of Hofcapellmeister at the princely court of Cöthen. Request to leave Weimar is refused by Duke Wilhelm Ernst.
	6 November	Arrested in Weimar and detained for four weeks because he 'too stubbornly' forced the issue of his resignation.
	2 December	Dismissed in disgrace from the Weimar Court.

CÖTHEN

1717	10 December	Arrives in Cöthen in time for birthday of Prince Leopold.
1718	May–June	Accompanies Prince Leopold on a journey to Carlsbad in Bohemia, together with another six court musicians.
	15 Nov	Birth of his son Leopold Augustus, baptised 17 November.
	10 December	Birthday of Prince Leopold. Performance of BWV 66a.
1719	June	Unsuccessful attempt to meet Georg Friedrich Handel at Halle.
	28 September	Death of son Leopold Augustus.
1720		Visits Reincken in Hamburg and improvises on the chorale prelude *An Wasserflüssen Babylon.*
	22 January	Starts the *Clavier-Büchlein* for Wilhelm Friedemann Bach.
	May–July	Accompanies Prince Leopold on a second visit to Carlsbad.
	7 July	Death of Maria Barbara Bach, aged thirty-five, while Bach is away.
	November	Journeys to Hamburg to audition for organist post at the Jacobikirche. Summoned back to Cöthen on 23 November and declines Hamburg offer.
1721	22 February	Death of eldest brother Johann Christoph, aged forty-nine.
	24 March	Dedicates the manuscript score of the *Brandenburg Concertos* to Christian Ludwig of Brandenburg-Schwedt.

	3 December	Marries Anna Magdalena Wilke (also known as Wülcken or Wilken), aged twenty.
1722		Starts the *Clavier-Büchlein* for Anna Magdalena. Completes *The Well-Tempered Clavier*, Book 1, BWV 846–69.
	16 April	Death of brother Johann Jacob (born 1682), in Stockholm.
	26 October	Godfather at baptism of Sophia Dorothea Schultze, daughter of Johann Caspar Schultze, cantor at the Agneskirche in Cöthen.
	21 December	Applies for the cantorate of the Thomaskirche in Leipzig.
1723	7 February	Auditions at Leipzig Thomaskirche with performances of BWV 22 and 23.
	Spring	Birth of daughter Sophia Henrietta.
	13 April	Gains letter of dismissal from the Prince of Cöthen.

LEIPZIG

1723	19 April	Signs provisional contract in Leipzig.
	22 April	Leipzig Town Council elects Bach as cantor of Thomaskirche, a post he accepts the following day.
	5 May	Signs final contract.
	8 May	Takes examination of theological competence to confirm his Lutheran creed.
	15 May	First payment from Leipzig.
	22 May	Arrives with his family in Leipzig.
	30 May	Begins first Leipzig cantata cycle with BWV 75, performed at Nikolaikirche.
	14 June	Wilhelm Friedemann and Carl Philipp Emanuel enter the Thomasschule.
	13 November	Publication of the new statutes of the Thomasschule.
	25 December	First performance of the *Magnificat*, BWV 243a (version in E♭ with Christmas *laudes*).
1724	26 February	Birth of his son Gottfried Heinrich, baptised on 27 February.

	7 April	Performance of the *John Passion* in the Nikolaikirche (1st version).
1724	11 June	Begins his second (chorale) cantata cycle with BWV 20.
	18 July	Guest performance with Anna Magdalena in Cöthen.
1725	23 February	Guest performance of BWV 249a in Weissenfels for birthday of Duke Christian.
	30 March	Performance of the *John Passion* at Thomaskirche (2nd version).
	14 April	Baptism of son Christian Gottlieb.
	19–20 September	Guest performances at the Sophienkirche in Dresden.
	December	Guest performance in Cöthen (together with Anna Magdalena).
1726	5 April	Baptism of daughter Elisabeth Juliana Frederica.
	19 April	Performance of an anonymous *Mark Passion* in the Nikolaikirche.
	29 June	Death of his daughter Christiana Sophia Henrietta, aged three.
	1 Nov	Publication of Part I of *Clavier-Übung*, BWV 825–30.
1727	11 April	Performance of *Matthew Passion* at Thomaskirche on Good Friday.
	12 April	Celebration for the birthday of King August II including performance of BWV Anh. 9 (now lost).
	17 October	Memorial service of Electress of Saxony, Queen Christiane Eberhardine, at Leipzig Paulinerkirche, including a performance of the *Trauer-Ode* (BWV 198).
	30 October	Baptism of son Ernestus Andreas (dies on 1 November).
1728	1 January	Guest performance in Cöthen.
	21 September	Death of son Christian Gottlieb aged three (buried on 22 September).
	10 October	Baptism of daughter Regina Johanna.
1729	12 January	Performance of BWV 210a during a visit of Duke Christian of Weissenfels.

	23 February	Guest performance in Weissenfels. Appointed *Capellmeister von Haus aus* to Duchy of Weissenfels.
	Spring	Assumes directorship of Georg Balthasar Schott's *collegium musicum.*
	23/4 March	BWV 244a is performed at funeral service for Prince Leopold in Cöthen.
	15 April	Good Friday performance of the *Matthew Passion* (second time).
	6 June, Whit Monday	As newly appointed head of *collegium musicum*, performs BWV 174, *Ich liebe den Höchsten von ganzem Gemüte.*
	20 October	Performance of BWV 226, *Der Geist hilft unser Schwachheit auf*, at funeral of Johann Heinrich Ernesti, headmaster of Thomasschule.
1730	1 January	Baptism of daughter Christiana Benedicta (dies on 4 January).
	7 April	Performance of an anonymous *Luke Passion* (BWV 246) with some additions by Bach, at the Nikolaikirche.
	2 Aug	Dispute with the Leipzig Town Council about Bach's teaching duties.
	23 Aug	Submits petition to the Leipzig Town Council: 'Entwurff' ('Brief but Highly Necessary Draft of a Well-Appointed Church Music').
1731	18 March	Baptism of daughter Christiana Dorothea.
	Spring	Publication of *Clavier-Übung I* as Opus I.
	23 March	Performance of lost *Mark Passion* (BWV 247) at the Thomaskirche.
	14 September	Organ recital in the Sophienkirche in Dresden, and attends premiere of Hasse's opera *Cleofide* the previous day.
1732	11 April	Perfomance of the *John Passion* (3rd version) at the Nikolaikirche.
	5 June	Performance of BWV Anh. 18, *Froher Tag* (now lost), at dedication of renovated Thomasschule.
	21 June	Birth of son Johann Christoph Friedrich, baptised 23 June.
	31 August	Death of daughter Christiana Dorothea.

	September	Journeys to Kassel (with Anna Magdalena). Examines the renovated organ at the Martinskirche (22 September).
1733		Re-catalogues library, dating his copy of the three-volume Calov Bible.
	21 April	Ceremony at the Nikolaikirche for loyalty to Friedrich Augustus II following death in February of Elector Friedrich Augustus I.
	25 April	Death of daughter Regina Johanna, aged four (buried on 26 April).
	27 July	Journeys to Dresden. Dedicates the *Missa* BWV 232 to the new Elector of Saxony, Friedrich Augustus II.
	5 Nov	Birth and baptism of son Johann August Abraham (dies on 6 November).
	8 December	Performance of BWV 214, *Tönet, ihr Pauken*, a *dramma per musica* for the Queen Maria Josepha.
1734	5 October	Alfresco performance of BWV 215 *Preise dein Glücke* to mark the first anniversary of the Elector Friedrich August II's accession as Augustus III, King of Poland.
	December/ January	Performance of the *Christmas Oratorio*, BWV 248, on 25–7 December, 1–2 January and 6 January.
1735	Spring	Bach turns fifty. He draws up his family tree with annotated genealogy: 'Origin of the Bach Family of Musicians'. Publication of *Clavier-Übung* II.
	19 May	*Ascension Oratorio*, *Lobet Gott in seinen Reichen* (BWV 11), is performed.
	5 September	Birth of son Johann Christian (baptised on 7 September).
1735/6		Performs Gottfried Heinrich Stölzel's cantata cycle *Das Saiten-Spiel des Herzens.*
1736	30 March	Performance of the revised *Matthew Passion* on Good Friday at the Thomaskirche.
	July	Dispute with Johann August Ernesti, rector of the Thomasschule, over the appointment of prefects.
	7 October	Birthday cantata for Friedrich Augustus II, BWV 206, *Schleicht, spielende Wellen.*
	19 November	Granted honorary non-resident post of *Hofcompositeur* (Court Composer) at the Dresden Court by Friedrich Augustus II.

1737	4 March	Temporarily resigns as director of the Leipzig *collegium musicum.*
	May	Journeys to Sangerhausen to visit his son Johann Gottfried Bernhard, appointed organist there in January.
	14 May	Johann Adolph Scheibe publishes a letter attacking Bach without naming him, referring to him disparagingly as a *Musicant* – which sparks off the Scheibe–Birnbaum dispute.
	30 October	Baptism of daughter Johanna Carolina.
1739	17 March	Cancellation of the performance of a Passion due to dispute with town council.
	27 May	Death of son Johann Gottfried Bernhard, aged twenty-four.
	12 September	Godfather at baptism of Johanna Helena Koch, daughter of Johann Wilhelm Koch, cantor in Ronneburg.
	Autumn	Publication of *Clavier-Übung III.*
	October	Resumes position as director of *collegium musicum.*
	November	Journeys to Weissenfels (together with Anna Magdalena) and gives a recital on the Trost organ in Altenburg Castle.
1741	30 May	Withdraws as director of *collegium musicum.*
	Summer	Journeys to Berlin-Potsdam Court of Frederick the Great. Writes Flute Sonata in E (BWV 1035) for King's Chamberlain. Performance of BWV 210, *O holder Tag, erwünschte Zeit.*
	August	Anna Magdalena ill, Bach returns to Leipzig.
	September	Publication of BWV 988, *Goldberg Variations*, Part IV of the *Clavier-Übung*, at time of the Michaelmas Fair.
	17 November	Returns from journey to Berlin with Count Keyserlingk.
1742	22 February	Baptism of daughter Regina Susanna.
	30 August	Performance of BWV 212, *Mer hahn en neue Oberkeet, Peasant Cantata*, for Count Carl Heinrich von Dieskau in Kleinzschocher.
1744		Autograph date in his copy of a 1704 Merian Bible.

	March–May	Five-week journey (reason and destination unknown).
	3 April	Performance of lost *Mark Passion* (BWV 247) at Thomaskirche.
1745	30 November	Birth of first grandchild, Johann Adam (son of C. P. E. Bach).
1747	7 May	Journeys to Potsdam and Berlin. Meets with the Prussian King Frederic II at Sanssouci.
	8 May	Organ recital at Potsdam Heiliggeistkirche.
	June	Becomes fourteenth member of the *Societät der Musicalischen Wissenschaften* (Corresponding Society of the Musical Sciences). *Canonic Variations on 'Vom Himmel hoch'* (BWV 769), including his B-A-C-H musical signature, is his contribution to the Society.
	7 July	Dedicates *The Musical Offering* (BWV 1079) to King Frederick II of Prussia.
1749	4 April	Performance of the *John Passion* (4th version) at the Nikolaikirche.
	May	Sudden illness: eye trouble and cataracts.
	8 June	Gottlob Harrer auditions for Bach's post as Thomascantor in Leipzig.
	6 October	Baptism of grandson Johann Sebastian Altnickol (son of his daughter Catherina Dorothea). Died 21 December.
1750	28–30 March	First eye surgery by the English surgeon Dr John Taylor.
	5–8 April	Second eye surgery by Taylor.
	22 July	Bach has a stroke, and receives last communion.
	28 July	Death at 8.15 in the evening, aged sixty-five.
	31 July	Burial at the Leipzig cemetery of the Johanniskirche.

POSTHUMOUS

1750	11 November	Distribution of his estate.
1752	May	*The Art of Fugue* (BWV1080) is published by C. P. E. Bach.
1754		Mizler publishes the *Nekrolog* (written by C. P. E. Bach and Johann Friedrich Agricola in 1750/51) in his *Musicalische Bibliothek*.

1760	27 December	Anna Magdalena Bach dies in Leipzig.
1788	14 December	C. P. E. Bach dies in Hamburg. His estate contains many of the most significant compositions of his father in autograph sources and the Haussmann portrait (1748).
1802		Johann Nikolaus Forkel publishes the first biography of Johann Sebastian Bach.
1829	11 March	Revival of the *Matthew Passion* (in a shortened and instrumentally adapted version) by Felix Mendelssohn in the *Sing-Akademie zu Berlin.* Robert Schumann, Hegel and others attend.
1841		The major part of Bach's musical estate is given to the Königliche Bibliothek zu Berlin (nowadays Staatsbibliothek zu Berlin – Preußischer Kulturbesitz).
1850		Beginning of the first complete edition of *Johann Sebastian Bach's Werke* (finished in 1899).

Glossary

A-B-A: Ternary form – the three-fold structure of a movement, akin to a sandwich, in which the A section repeats after a contrasting B, or middle section, in a related key.

a cappella (It. 'in the chapel style'): A common term for unaccompanied church music for choir.

accompagnato (It. 'accompanied'): In cantatas (and opera) this is a form of declamatory, speech-like singing with full instrumental accompaniment (usually for strings, occasionally for winds), as opposed to *recitativo secco*, notated with figured bass for basso continuo only.

Affekt (Ger. 'feeling'): Originally derived from Greek and Latin doctrines of rhetoric and oratory, the term came to be used by seventeenth-century theorists to categorise the emotional states expressed in vocal music, which led to the convention of expressing a single 'affection', or unified mood, within a single movement, determined by details of tempo, dynamic, style or *figurae* (q.v.).

Alberti bass: Broken chord or arpeggiated accompaniment, named after Domenico Alberti (*c.*1710–40), in the sequence lowest, highest, middle, highest.

alla breve (It. 'cut time'): Normally indicates two minim beats in a bar of four crotchets and proportionally twice as fast as the preceding section.

appoggiatura (It. 'to lean against'): Literally an ornamental leaning note, one which nevertheless creates a harsh or expressive dissonance with the prevailing harmony and resolves by step (up or down) on the following weak beat.

arioso (It. 'like an aria'): Normally a short melodic section with a regular beat within a recitative of a cantata, though Bach used it also to indicate a short aria or as the equivalent of an *accompagnato* recitative (q.v.).

ars moriendi (Lat. 'the art of dying'): Central to the Lutheran tradition, but originally a mid-fifteenth-century tract (illustrated with woodcuts) expounding the concept of a 'good death' in response to the ravages of plague and warfare. Bach owned several books on this topic.

bariolage (Fr. 'variegated sounds'): The rapid alternation often of the same note between open and stopped strings on a violin, creating a vigorous, frenetic effect.

bassetchen (Ger. 'little bass'): Signals the absence of the normal foundation of the music (an eight-foot organ or cello continuo line) and its migration upwards to the alto line, a texture used by Bach sometimes to suggest an unearthly (literally 'groundless') presence of divine love.

Bierfiedler (Ger. 'beer fiddlers'): Disparaging term used to describe jobbing untrained musicians hired to play mostly at weddings and parties; considered by professional guild musicians to be dishonourable interlopers.

binary form: The two-fold form of a short movement, usually with an equal length to the sections, the second part (B) in a related key to the first (A).

cadenza (It. 'cadence'): A solo passage in improvisatory style, either short when within a movement (as in *Contrapunctus* 2 of *The Art of Fugue*) or, more usually, in extended form at the penultimate cadence of a solo concerto, as in the fifth Brandenburg Concerto.

canon ('rule'): A melody designed to be played or sung as a round in the strictest form of contrapuntal imitation. The leading voice (*dux*) is followed by the second and other voices (*comes*).

cantabile: (It. 'song-like'): An instruction requiring a conspicuously expressive and melodious delivery.

cantata (It. 'sung'): A vocal work, initially secular (and usually for solo voice), later sacred, containing by the eighteenth century a number of movements including arias, duets and choruses. Also referred to as *Musik*, *Concerto*, *Kirchenstück* or just *Stück*.

cantilena (Lat. 'song'): A sustained, smooth-flowing melodic line.

cantor: Refers both to the role of director of a church's music in Lutheran Germany and to that of a schoolteacher (not only of music).

cantus firmus (Lat. 'fixed song'): A melody extrapolated from plainsong or from a chorale used as the basis of a polyphonic composition and often standing out from it in slow, single lines.

Capellmeister: Director of a court *cappella*, responsible for its performances and personnel.

cappella (Lat./It. 'chapel'): An ensemble or group of singers and instrumentalists with, at its head, a Capellmeister (q.v.).

capriccio (It. 'whim'): In Bach's time, a keyboard piece not bound by the usual rules of composition, exemplifying perhaps a comment in the *Nekrolog* that 'when the occasion demanded [he could] adjust himself, especially in playing, to a lighter and more humorous way of thought.'

chaconne/passacaglia: Seventeenth-century instrumental dance forms in triple time, both of Spanish origin (used in guitar music), founded on a ground bass with a slow harmonic rhythm. Whereas a chaconne (*ciaconna* in Italian) entails continuous variations based on a chord sequence, a *passacaglia* implies continuous variations on an *ostinato* (q.v.) that stays usually in the bass, but can migrate to an upper voice.

chiastic (Gk 'arranged crosswise'): Structures – ordered symmetrically, such as A-B-C, C-B-A, A-B-B-A formal patterns, derived from literature and used with underlying theological purpose.

chorale cantata: A form perfected by Bach at Leipzig between 1724 and 1725 in which a chorale is used either as a hymn, developed into an extended melody or used as the basis of a contrapuntal movement.

Chorton (Ger. 'choir pitch'): This was the pitch at which organs in all the Leipzig churches were tuned – a whole tone above the main body of the instrumental ensemble playing in *Kammerton,* and accordingly requiring transposition.

chorus musicus (Lat. 'musical choir'): This term is closely related to the German vernacular *Cantorey / Kantorei*, denoting a church choir.

clarino (It. 'clarion'): The clear and high register of the natural, long-tube trumpet.

Clavier/Klavier (Fr./Ger.): Generic term for a keyboard instrument, harpsichord, organ or clavichord.

colla parte (It. 'with the part'): An indication in a score to direct the player of the accompaniment to follow or double or shadow the main part or voice.

concertante (It. 'like a concerto'): One of the names given to the solo instruments in a *concerto grosso*, as distinct from the *ripieno* instruments, which play the *tutti* sections.

concertato (It. 'concerted'): A style favoured by Italian and German composers of the Baroque to heighten the dramatic interplay of concerted voices and instruments.

Concertisten: (Ger. 'concertist'): The principal ensemble singers of a particular voice type who sing throughout in a concerted piece, or instrumental section leaders as opposed to the *Ripienisten* (q.v.).

concerto grosso (It. 'great concerto'): A work in several movements, related to the suite written for a consort of instruments playing antiphonally, containing a *concertino*, or solo group, alongside a *ripieno* or *tutti* group.

consort: An old English spelling of 'concert' indicating any body of performers, either a whole consort of one family of instruments or a broken consort of mixed instruments.

continuo (It. abbr. for *basso continuo*): Also known as *thoroughbass* or *figured bass*. An accompaniment played from a bass line by a bass instrument and a keyboard, underneath the notation of which figures are placed to indicate chords.

cori spezzati (It. 'broken choirs'): A technique of writing for two or more spatially separated choirs developed by Willaert and the Gabrielis in sixteenth-century Venice and later by Schütz in Germany to exploit dramatic contrasts of timbre and to achieve increased sonority; later adopted by Bach in BWV 50 *Nun ist das Heil* and in the *Matthew Passion.*

Currende/Kurrende (Ger. 'itinerant choir'): Refers to a widely practised tradition whereby boys at Latin and choir schools were required to sing (or 'busk') in town streets several times a week to raise supplementary money for their board and lodging, their takings usually apportioned by strict regulations. The practice sometimes erupted into gang warfare between rival groups over disputed territory or favourite sites within the same town.

da capo (It. abbr. *D.C.* 'from the head'): An instruction at the end of a piece indicating a return to the beginning and to repeat the music until the pause, double bar or *fine* (the 'end') indication.

détaché (Fr. 'detached'): A short, vigorous bow stroke on a stringed instrument applied to notes of equal time value.

diatonic (Gk 'at intervals of a tone'): Music set unambiguously in a major or minor key.

Elector: German Prince-Electors (of whom there were nine at the time of Bach) entitled to elect the Holy Roman Emperor, for example the Margrave of Brandenburg or Augustus, King of Poland.

Endzweck (Ger.): Ultimate purpose or object.

falsettist: Male singer who produces his voice falsetto in a treble range.

figura/figura corta (It. 'a short figure'): Motif or musical cell as catalogued by Bach's cousin and friend J. G. Walther in his *Musicalisches Lexicon* (1732): three fast notes of which the first is as long as the next two taken together.

fioriture (It. 'flowerings'/'flourishes'): Ornamental figures embellishing a plainer melodic line.

fugue (It. 'flight'): A contrapuntal composition in parts or voices using imitation, augmentation, diminution and inversion of the subject, brought to its climax as a form by J. S. Bach in *The 48 Preludes and Fugues*. The overall structure includes exposition, middle and final entries, which are separated by episodes. Fugue was used as an ear-training device for choirboys singing in canon by ear to develop their musicianship.

galant (Fr. 'courtly'): Elegant and light style of music from the eighteenth century, characteristically represented by the minuet.

gigue (Fr. 'gig'): Dance movement – graceful, capricious and jaunty – distinct from the Italian *giga*, which is longer, more stylised and complex.

ground bass: A persistent melody in the bass (q.v. *ostinato*) recurring many times with changing harmonies, accompanied by variations in the upper parts.

Hausmann: Head town piper.

hemiola (Gk 'in the ratio of one and a half to one'): Rhythmic device, often located at cadences, obtained by grouping two bars of triple metre as if they were three bars of duple time.

Hoff Musicus: Court musician.

imitation: Compositional device, whereby a musical figure is repeated after its first statement, either exactly as before or modified at the same or a different pitch.

invertible counterpoint: The art of combining melodies where each line can serve equally as the bass or the melody, whether in two, three or four parts, without grammatical error.

Kammerton*/*Cammer-Ton (Ger. 'chamber pitch'): The term used to describe the pitch at which chamber music and, increasingly, church music was performed in Baroque Germany. It caused problems involving transposition and double notation once instruments tuned at this or at a still lower pitch were required to play with church organs, generally tuned to *Chorton* (Ger. 'choir pitch'), a tone or a minor third higher.

Kammersänger*/*Kammersängerin (Ger. 'chamber singer') (Ger. 'chamber pitch'): Honorific title for distinguished singers bestowed by princes or kings.

Lateinschule (Ger. 'Latin School'): Similar to grammar schools, most were founded in German-speaking areas after the Reformation and were often closely connected to town churches or former monastic foundations.

melisma (Gk 'song'): A group of notes sung to a single syllable.

Mettenchor (Ger. 'Matins Choir'): An elite chamber choir such as the fifteen-voiced ensemble employed at the Michaeliskirche in Lüneburg which Bach joined briefly as a treble.

Nachspiel: Playout or postlude.

Nekrolog: Obituary.

notes inégales (Fr. 'unequal notes'): The practice of performing running quavers unequally with a long-short lilt in some French dance movements and adopted by German composers. Not dissimilar to twentieth-century Blues, it was used to loosen and spice up a regular, even delivery of continuous notes.

obbligato (It. 'indispensable'): When attached to the name of an instrument in a score, the part is regarded as essential to the scoring and must not be omitted, though another instrument can be substituted for it (flute for oboe, violin for organ, etc.).

ostinato (It. 'obstinate'): Persistently repeated figure, generally in the bass (hence 'walking bass'), used to create length and continuity, but can be applied to a recurrent melodic figure, as in the *Crucifixus* of the *B minor Mass*.

ouverture (Fr. 'overture'): An instrumental piece composed as the introduction to an opera, oratorio or suite. Bach adopted the French style of *ouverture*, with its stately, angular and rhythmically dotted character (opening section) followed by a fast, fugato (second section).

parody: A technique involving the replacement of a secular text with a sacred one in a pre-existing vocal work with no pejorative sense of mimicry.

partita (It. 'departure'): A division (for example, a variation) of an instrumental suite or a set of pieces, as in Bach's *Clavier-Übung I*, similar to *ordre* (Fr.).

passepied (Fr. 'pass-foot'): Originally a Breton dance in triple time, a faster version of the minuet, in which the feet move 'as quickly as if greased' (Niedt, 1721).

passing notes: Any unaccented notes which form part of the melodic or polyphonic material, but are not integral parts of the harmony, to which they contribute a passing dissonance.

pasticcio (It. 'little pie'): A composite work, often by several composers, forming a musical entertainment, usually for the stage.

permutation: A contrapuntal technique, particularly in fugues, in which the order of events is carefully formalised to vary the texture, prevent duplication and preserve the character, or *Affekt*, of the composition.

per omnes versus (Lat. 'in all verses'): Use of a chorale melody unaltered in all verses and individual movements, as in Bach's cantata BWV 4, *Christ lag in Todesbanden*.

Pietism: A religious and pastoral practice that grew out of Lutheranism and led to a strong emphasis on individual piety, reaching its greatest strength by the middle of the eighteenth century. The movement was inspired by Philipp Jakob Spener (1635–1705), who founded the University of Halle.

polychoral: Modern term describing Venetian sixteenth-century compositions for divided forces – two or three specific groups of chorus with or without orchestra, often spaced at a distance in performance.

quodlibet (Lat. 'as it pleases'): An ingenious combination of popular tunes, as in the final variation of Bach's *Goldberg Variations*, in which two or more folk-tunes are woven into the harmonic frame of the theme; also a description of the more scatological music that went on in the Bach family get-togethers.

recitativo secco (It. 'dry recitation'): Replacing spoken dialogue, a musical style in which a solo singer accompanied only by continuo (with a figured or unfigured bass line) propels the narrative forwards.

Rector (Ger.): Headmaster of a school, usually an ordained clergyman living on site.

Regalist: Player of a regal – a small portative organ manually pumped by bellows and having a raucous, nasal sound.

ricercar(e) (It. 'to search out'): An instrumental composition, not far removed in style from a motet; a study in counterpoint following the permutations of a melody and one which, from its seventeenth-century origins in the hands of Frescobaldi (1583–1643), led to the development of the fugue. Bach created a six-part ricercar in the *Musical Offering*.

Ripienisten (Ger. 'ripienists'): Singers used by Bach in his cantatas to reinforce, support or act as a foil to the *Concertisten* (q.v.).

ripieno: See ***concerto grosso***.

ritornello (It. 'a little return'): An instrumental refrain in a composition that returns complete or in part more than once, in the same or another key, often between vocal episodes.

rubato (It. 'stolen'): Elasticity of rhythmic performance style in which the pulse is allowed to fluctuate subtly and a sense of freedom prevails.

sarabande: One of four dance movements that made up the instrumental suite (q.v.), it originated in the sixteenth century as a Latin American and Spanish sung dace (*zarabanda*) with lascivious connotations, migrated to the French Court as a triple rhythm dance in slow $\frac{3}{2}$ time with a characteristic pattern of a minim, a dotted minim and a crotchet.

scena (It. 'scene'): A discrete episode in musical drama made up of recitative, arioso and one or more arias, duets and choruses.

serenata (It. from *sera*, 'evening'): A musical greeting, usually instrumental, performed out of doors in the evening.

siciliano: A dance movement of Sicilian origin in a lilting, pastoral style set either in $\frac{6}{8}$ or $\frac{12}{8}$ time, usually presented as a slow movement.

sinfonia (It. 'symphony'): The name usually given to an orchestral piece serving as the introduction to a cantata, a suite or an opera (where it is traditionally called an overture).

Spielmann: A minstrel-fiddler, often itinerant, one rung above *Bierfiedler*.

Spruch/Spruchmotetten (Ger. 'quotation'): A scriptural citation often used as the basis for a motet.

Stadtpfeifer (Ger. 'town piper'): A professionally trained musician employed by a city or town, similar to the English town *wait* (watchman). The Bach family, Thuringian town musicians for generations, held posts as Stadtpfeifer. Leipzig employed both wind and string players in this capacity, and in 1748 Bach auditioned applicants, preferring one who played both oboe and violin 'with greater dexterity', presumably because these instruments were useful in church performance.

stile antico (It. 'old style'): A term describing church music written after 1600, imitating Palestrina, used in the eighteenth century by both Johann Mattheson and Johann Joseph Fux in their theoretical writings on strict counterpoint.

stretto (It. 'narrow' or 'tight'): The introduction of entries in a fugue in close canon.

suite: The stringing together of a number of movements of dance origin (in binary form), of which allemande, courante, sarabande and gigue were obligatory, and to which others could be added; in Bach's usage, interchangeable with partita.

suspension: In harmony, the dissonance caused by holding a note from one chord during the change to the next, which is then resolved usually by falling.

tablature: A shorthand notational system that uses letters, numbers or other signs as an alternative to staff notation. By the mid eighteenth century the system was waning, but Bach used it occasionally in the *Orgel-Büchlein* as a space-saving device and as a compositional aide-mémoire when waiting for the ink to dry before turning the page; also in certain cantatas.

temperament: A term used to designate the tuning of the musical scale in which notes are not 'pure' (that is, not according to the natural harmonics) but are 'tempered' or modified. Bach's term 'Well-Tempered' (as in his *48 Preludes and Fugues*) describes an intermediate stage on the way towards equal temperament which divided the octave into twelve equal semitones, enabling the composer and player to venture into remote keys.

terzetto (Ger. *Terzet*): Vocal composition for three voices without accompaniment as defined by Walther in 1732 and used by Bach in cantata BWV 48.

tessitura (It. 'texture'): The range of a vocal work or, less often, the instrumental compass in which a piece of music is set.

tetrachord (from Gk *tetrachordon*, 'four-string instrument'): Four descending notes contained within a perfect fourth interval, indicating where the semitone can lie.

tierce de Picardie: The raised mediant degree of a tonic chord used for the ending of a movement in a minor mode in order to give it a greater sense of finality.

tonus contrarius/peregrinus (Lat. 'wandering tone'): One of the irregular psalm tones, postdating the traditional eight Gregorian psalm tones sung during Holy Office.

traversa (It.): More usually *traverso*, relating to the German flute, as opposed to the *flauto*, by which composers in Bach's era meant the recorder.

tritone: The interval arising from three whole tones producing an augmented fourth (C–F♯) or diminished fifth (C–G♭) forbidden in medieval theory as the 'Devil in music' (*diabolus in musica*), but tolerated from the Baroque era onwards as the spice in seventh chords.

tromba da tirarsi/tromba spezzata: A natural trumpet fitted with a slide altering the length of the instrument while it is played, so enabling it to fill in the gaps in the natural harmonic scale.

trope (Gk *tropos*, 'turn' or 'turn of phrase'): An introduction to a Gregorian chant or an interpolation within the chant.

turba/turbae (Lat. 'crowd'): Words (and therefore choruses) in Passion oratorios delivered by more than one person, for example, the disciples, the Jews or the Roman soldiers.

Türmer (Ger. 'tower-men'): Musical tower guards working in shifts, equipped with horns or trumpets, fire flags, lanterns and hour glasses, charged with sounding the alarm at the approach of marauding armies; their musical duties, which included 'ringing in' the New Year, varied according to the size of towns.

Vokaleinbau (Ger. 'vocal insertion'): Technique of incorporating the voice part(s) within the reprise of the instrumental introduction.

Notes

PREFACE

1. Words scrawled by Albert Einstein in the margin of a letter from the editor of the *Reclams Universum* (an illustrated monthly) on 24 Mar 1928, reproduced in *The Einstein Scrapbook*, Ze'ev Rosenkranz (ed.) (2002), p. 143.
2. J. N. Forkel, *Ueber Johann Sebastian Bachs Leben, Kunst und Kunstwerke* (1802), p. 82; NBR, p. 459.
3. BD I, No. 23/NBR, p. 152.
4. George Steiner, *Grammars of Creation* (2001), p. 308.
5. Laurence Dreyfus, 'Bach the Subversive', Lufthansa Lecture, 14 May 2011.
6. Robert L. Marshall, 'Toward a Twenty-First-Century Bach Biography', MQ, Vol. 84, No. 3 (Fall 2000), p. 500.
7. Gilles Cantagrel, *Le Moulin et la rivière: air et variations sur Bach* (1998), p. 8.
8. Rebecca Lloyd, *Bach among the Conservatives* (2006), p. 120.
9. Richard Holmes, *Coleridge: Early Visions* (1989), p. xvi.

1 UNDER THE CANTOR'S GAZE

1. Hans Raupach, *Das wahre Bildnis des Johann Sebastian Bach* (1983).
2. Theodor Adorno, 'Bach Defended against His Devotees' (essay) (1951) in *Prisms*, S. and S. Weber (trs.) (1981), p. 139.
3. Milan Kundera, *The Art of the Novel* (1986), p. 25.
4. NBR, p. 161.

2 GERMANY ON THE BRINK OF ENLIGHTENMENT

1. Johann Georg Hamann, *Sämtliche Werke*, Josef Nadler (ed.) (1949–57), Vol. 3, p. 231.
2. Frosch's song from the first draft of Goethe's *Faust* (dating from the early 1770s), quoted by Tim Blanning, *The Pursuit of Glory: Europe 1648–1815* (2007), p. 275.

3. Samuel von Pufendorf, *De statu imperii germanici liber unus* (1667), Vol. 6, p. 9.
4. Joachim Whaley, *Germany and the Holy Roman Empire* (2012), Vol. 1, p. 633.
5. H. J. C. von Grimmelshausen, *The Adventures of a Simpleton*, W. Wallich (trs.) (1962), p. 19.
6. Tim Blanning, *The Pursuit of Glory: Europe 1648–1815* (2007), p. 187.
7. Henry Mayhew, *German Life and Manners as Seen in Saxony at the Present Day* (1864), Vol. 1, p. 178.
8. Hans Carl von Carlowitz, *Sylvicultura oeconomica, oder haußwirthliche Nachricht und Naturmäßige Anweisung zur wilden Baum-Zucht* (1713).
9. Karl Hasel and Ekkehard Schwartz, *Forstgeschichte: Ein Grundriss für Studium und Praxis* (2006), pp. 62, 318–9.
10. Richard Wagner, *Gazette Musicale*, 23 and 30 May 1841.
11. WA, Vol. 12, p. 219.
12. Thomas Kaufmann, *Dreißigjähriger Krieg und westfälischer Friede. Kirchengeschichtliche Studien zur lutherischen Konfessionskultur* (1998), pp. 34–6, 124.
13. *Geistliche Concerten* (1643).
14. Heinrich Schütz, *Gesammelte Briefe und Schriften*, Erich Hermann Müller (ed.) (1976), No. 83, p. 230; and *Letters and Documents of Heinrich Schütz*, Gina Spagnoli (ed.) (1990), Docs. 5, 143 and 145.
15. Claus Oefner, 'Eisenach zur Zeit der jungen Bach', BJb (1985), p. 54; and Christoph Wolff, *Johann Sebastian Bach: The Learned Musician* (2000), p. 16.
16. Eberhard Matthes, *Eisenach zur Zeit von Telemanns dortigem Wirken 1708–1712* (1974), p. 6.
17. George Steiner, *Grammars of Creation* (2001), p. 177.
18. *Missbrauch der freyen Künste, insonderheit der Musik* (1697), pp. 13, 23, quoted by Tanya Kevorkian, *Baroque Piety: Religion, Society, and Music in Leipzig 1650–1750* (2007), p. 137.
19. Stephen Rose in *The Worlds of Johann Sebastian Bach*, Raymond Erickson (ed.) (2009), p. 181, and 'The Bear Growls', *Early Music*, Vol. 33 (Nov. 2005), pp. 700–702.
20. Robin A. Leaver, 'Bach and Pietism: Similarities Today', *Concordia Theological Quarterly*, Vol. 55 (1991), p. 12.
21. Manfred Wilde, *Die Zauberei- und Hexenprozesse in Kursachsen* (2003), pp. 535ff.; and Kevorkian, *Baroque Piety*, pp. 116–17.
22. Robin A. Leaver, *Luther's Liturgical Music: Principles and Implications* (2007), p. 74.
23. Georg Schünemann, *Geschichte der Deutschen Schulmusik* (1928), p. 93.
24. The opening sentence of Daniel Friderici's *Musica figuralis* (1618).
25. WA TR, No. 6248; Jan Chiapusso, *Bach's World* (1968), p. 295, n. 9.
26. Foreword to Johann Reusch's 'Psalms of 1552' (*Zehen deudscher Psalm Davids*) (1553), cited in John Butt, *Music Education* (1994), p. 3.
27. C. Friccius, *Music-Büchlein oder nützlicher Bericht* (1631), p. 90.
28. Jan Chiapusso, *Bach's World*, pp. 3–4.

29. Ibid., p. 4.
30. Johann Buno, *Historisches Bilder, darinnen Idea historiae universalis* (1672).
31. James Ussher, *The Annals of the World* (1658), Vol. 4.
32. *Œuvres de Descartes*, C. Adam and P. Tannery (eds.) (1897–1909), Vol. 6, p. 5.
33. Johann Amos Comenius, *Latinitatis vestibulum sive primi ad Latinam linguam aditus* (1662), cited in Frank Mund, *Lebenskrisen als Raum der Freiheit* (1997), p. 130.
34. Wolff, *Bach: The Learned Musician*, p. 26.
35. '"Ut probus et doctus reddar"', BJb (1985), p. 22, *im wesentlichen Stabilität und Qualität der Schule . . . garantierten.*
36. Rainer Kaiser, 'Neues über Johann Sebastian Bachs Schulzeit in Eisenach von 1693 bis 1695', *Bachfest-Buch* (76, Bachfest der Neuen Bachgesellschaft Eisenach, 2001), pp. 89–98, and 'Johann Sebastian Bach als Schüler einer "deutschen Schule" in Eisenach?', BJb (1994), pp. 177–84.
37. Stadtarchiv Eisenach, Eisenachsche Stadtraths: Akten die ehmaligen deutschen Schulen 1676–1680 betreffend, B. XXVII.1a, pp. 9–10.
38. Eisenacher Archiv, Konsistorialsachen Nr. 929, p. 1.
39. Petzoldt, '"Ut probus et doctus reddar"', p. 22; and Claus Oefner's dissertation 'Das Musiklebe in Eisenach 1650–1750' (Halle), pp. 36, 105.
40. Jonathan Israel, *Radical Enlightenment* (2001), pp. 20, 544–6.
41. Giambattista Vico, *On the Most Ancient Wisdom of the Italians* (1710), L. M. Palmer (trs.) (1988), p. 2–10.
42. Lorenz Mizler, *Musikalische Bibliothek*, Vol. 2, quoting Leibniz. See W. Blankenburg, 'J. S. Bach und die Aufklärung', *Bach Gedenkschrift*, K. Matthaei (ed.) (1950), p. 26.

3 THE BACH GENE

1. Christoph Wolff, *Bach: Essays on His Life and Music* (1991), p. 15.
2. BD I, No. 184/NBR, pp. 283–94.
3. Erfurt town records, *Ratsprotokolle* of 1 Dec. 1716.
4. George Steiner, *Grammars of Creation* (2000), pp. 93–4.
5. NBR, p. 298.
6. Isaiah Berlin, *Roots of Romanticism* (2000), p. 61.
7. BD I, No. 184/NBR, p. 283.
8. Karl Geiringer, *The Bach Family* (1954), p. 10.
9. Ibid., p. 21.
10. M. Praetorius, *Syntagma Musicum* (1618), Vol. 2, p. 89.
11. Geiringer, *The Bach Family*, pp. 66–7.
12. Erfurt town records, *Ratsprotokolle* of 1682.
13. Stadtarchiv Eisenach, B. XXV, C1.
14. Percy M. Young, *The Bachs 1500–1850* (1970), p. 35.

15. Peter Wollny, *Altbachisches Archiv* (CD liner notes).
16. Stadtarchiv Eisenach, 10 – B. XXVI.C.II, Vol. 6, 'Gymnasialmatrikel' (1713).
17. *Nekrolog*, BD III, No. 666 / NBR, p. 299.
18. Ibid., p. 300.
19. Letter by C. P. E. Bach dated 13 Jan. 1775 in answer to questions by Forkel, BD III, No. 803 / NBR, p. 398.
20. Ibid.
21. Wolff, *Bach: Essays on His Life and Music*, p. 15.
22. J. N. Forkel, *Ueber Johann Sebastian Bachs Leben, Kunst und Kunstwerke* (1802), p. 17; and NBR, p. 423.
23. Recorded on SDG 715.
24. Letter from C. P. E. Bach to J. N. Forkel, 20 Sept. 1775, BD III, No. 807.
25. *Nekrolog*, BD III, No. 666/ NBR, p. 298.
26. Abraham Cowley (1618–67) from preface to *Poems* (1656).
27. Forkel, *Ueber Johann Sebastian Bachs Leben, Kunst und Kunstwerke*, pp. 18–19; and NBR, p. 424.
28. Christoph Wolff, *Johann Sebastian Bach: The Learned Musician* (2000), p. 30.
29. Graham Greene, *The Ministry of Fear* (1943), Book 1, Chapter 7.
30. Hans-Joachim Schulze, 'Johann Christoph Bach (1671–1721), "Organist und Schul Collega in Ohrdruf", Johann Sebastian Bachs erster Lehrer', BJb (1985), p. 60.
31. Johann Mattheson, *Der vollkommene Capellmeister* (1739), p. 241.
32. BD II, No. 409/NBR, p. 346.
33. After three years spent combing German archives for new information about Bach, Michael Maul and Peter Wollny of the Bach-Archiv Leipzig found these manuscripts, which had survived the fire by being stored in the vaults of the Duchess Anna Amalia Library.
34. Maul and Wollny, preface to *Weimar Organ Tablatures* (2006).
35. Hans-Joachim Schulze, 'Johann Christoph Bach (1671–1721)', p. 73; Konrad Küster, *Der junge Bach* (1996), pp. 82–109; and Schulze's review in BJb (1997), pp. 203–5.
36. *Expedition Bach*, Bach-Archiv Leipzig (2006), p. 17.
37. Lüneburg Stadtarchiv, Kloster St Michaelis, F 104 Nr. 1, 'Acta betr. Nachrichten den ehemals auf der Abtei befindlichen Schülertisch 1558–1726'.
38. Horst Walter, *Musikgeschichte der Stadt Lüneburg* (1967), pp. 81–2.
39. Küster, *Der junge Bach*, pp. 92–3.
40. Max Seiffert, 'Seb. Bachs Bewerbung um die Organistenstelle an St Jakobi in Hamburg 1720' in *Archiv für Musikwissenschaft*, Vol. 3 (1921), pp. 123–7.
41. *Nekrolog*, NBR, p. 302.
42. Letter from C. P. E. Bach to Forkel, 13 Jan. 1775, BD III, No. 803/NBR, p. 398. The English version omits the key words *geliebt v. studirt*, 'loved and studied'.

43. George B. Stauffer, 'Bach the Organist' in Christoph Wolff (ed.), *The World of the Bach Cantatas* (1997), p. 79.
44. BD III, No. 803/NBR, p. 398.
45. BD II, No. 7/NBR, p. 40.
46. Young, *The Bachs*, p. 35.
47. Wolff, *Johann Sebastian Bach: The Learned Musician*, p. 73.
48. BD III, No. 800/NBR, p. 396.

4 THE CLASS OF '85

1. Foreword to Georg Falek, *Idea boni cantoris* (1688), cited in John Butt, *Music Education and the Art of Performance in the German Baroque* (1994), p. 25.
2. Mattheson, *Grundlage einer Ehren-Pforte* (1740), p. 189.
3. Mattheson, *Der musicalische Patriot*, (1728), p. 178.
4. B. Baselt, 'Handel and His Central German Background' in *Handel: Tercentenary Collection*, S. Sadie and A. Hicks (eds.) (1987), p. 49.
5. Newman Flower, *George Frideric Handel: His Personality and His Times* (1923), p. 40; John Mainwaring, *Memoirs of the Life of the Late George Frederic Handel* (1760), p. 28.
6. Mattheson, *Grundlage*, p. 93.
7. Ibid.
8. NBR, p. 426.
9. Philipp Spitta, *The Life of Bach*, Clara Bell and J. A. Fuller Maitland (trs.) (1899 edn), Vol. 1, p. 200.
10. Christoph Wolff, *Johann Sebastian Bach: The Learned Musician* (2000), p. 65.
11. Spitta, *The Life of Bach*, Vol. 1, p. 468.
12. F. Blume, 'J. S. Bach's Youth', MQ, Vol. 54, No. 1 (Jan. 1968), p. 7.
13. Iain Fenlon, 'Monteverdi's Mantuan *Orfeo*', *Early Music*, Vol. 12, No. 2 (May 1984), p. 170.
14. Anonymous treatise, *Il Corago*, quoted by Lorenzo Bianconi, *Music in the Seventeenth Century*, D. Bryant (trs.)(1987), pp. 170–80, and by Roger Savage and Matteo Sansone, '*Il Corago* and the Staging of Early Opera', *Early Music*, Vol. 17, No. 4 (Nov. 1989), pp. 495–511.
15. G. F. Anerio's dedication to Neri in his *Teatro armonico spirituale* (1619).
16. André Maugars, *Response faite à un curieux* (1639).
17. Le Cerf de la Viéville, *Comparaison de la musique italienne et de la musique française* (1704).
18. H. Wiley Hitchcock, 'The Latin Oratorios of Marc-Antoine Charpentier', MQ, Vol. 41, No. 1 (Jan. 1955), p. 45.
19. Latin preface to Schütz's *Symphoniae sacrae* (1629), Vol. I.
20. Bettina Varwig, 'Seventeenth-Century Music and the Culture of Rhetoric', JRMA (2007).

21. Imogen Holst, *Tune* (1962), p. 97.
22. Ibid., p. 92.
23. Ibid., p. 103.
24. Franklin B. Zimmerman, *Henry Purcell* (1967), p. 213.
25. Ellen Rosand, *Monteverdi's Last Operas* (2007), p. 380.
26. Descartes, *Œuvres: Correspondance* (1969), Vol. 1, p. 204.
27. G. E. Scheibel, *Zufällige Gedancken von der Kirchen-Music, wie sie heutiges Tages beschaffen ist* (1721), Joyce Irwin (trs.) in *Bach's Changing World*, Carol K. Baron (ed.) (2006), p. 221.

5 THE MECHANICS OF FAITH

1. *Bhagavad-Gita*, Chapter 17.
2. Martin Luther, WA TR, No. 2545b.
3. Michael Praetorius, preface to *Polyhymnia caduceatrix et panegyrica* of 1619.
4. Diarmaid MacCulloch, *A History of Christianity: The First Three Thousand Years* (2009), p. 612.
5. M. J. Vogt, *Conclave thesauri magnae artis musicae* (1719).
6. John Butt, *Music Education and the Art of Performance in the German Baroque* (1994), p. 47; and Dietrich Bartel, *Musica poetica* (1997), p. 84.
7. Joachim Burmeister, *Musica poetica* (1606), p. 56.
8. Johannes Susenbrotus, *Epitome troporum ac schematum et grammaticorum et rhetorum* (1566).
9. Henry Peachum the Elder, *The Garden of Eloquence* (1593), p. 143.
10. Joachim Burmeister, *Hypomnematum musicae poeticae* (1599), entry on *pathopoeia.*
11. John Milton, *Paradise Lost*, Book 10, ll. 504–9.
12. Isaiah Berlin, *Three Critics of the Enlightenment* (2000), p. 94.
13. BD I, No. 1/NBR, p. 57.
14. BD II, Nos. 19–20/NBR, pp. 49–50.
15. Georg Thiele, 'Die Familie Bach in Mühlhausen', *Mülhäuser Geschichtsblätter*, Vol. 21 (1920/21), pp. 62–5.
16. *Auff Begehren Tit: Herrn D: Georg Christ: Eilmars in die Music gebracht von Joh. Seb. Bach Org. Molhusino.*
17. Johann Gottfried Olearius, *Biblische Erklärung* (1678–81), Vol. 5, col. 532b; see also M. Petzoldt, 'Liturgical and Theological Aspects' in *The World of the Bach Cantatas*, Vol. 1, Christoph Wolff (ed.) (1997), p. 113.
18. I am grateful to Dr George Steiner for this formulation of the prevalent mood of Luther's psalm translations.
19. See Robert L. Marshall, 'Toward a Twenty-First-Century Bach Biography', MQ, Vol. 84, No. 3 (Fall 2000), p. 504.

20. Martin Luther, 'Second Lecture on Psalm 90 [3 June 1535]', LW, Vol. 13, p. 116.
21. Robin A. Leaver, *Bach's Theological Library* (1983).
22. Montaigne, *Essais* (1580), M. A. Screech (ed.) (1991), Book I, Section 29, p. 96.
23. Martin Luther, 'A Sermon on Preparing to Die', LW, Vol. 42, p. 101.
24. Jacques Gardien, *Jean-Philippe Rameau* (1949), p. 57.
25. Martin Luther, LW, Vol. 13, p. 83.
26. Ibid.
27. See Eric Chafe, *Tonal Allegory in the Vocal Music of J. S. Bach* (1991), p. 52.
28. Quoted in Hannsdieter Wohlfarth, *Johann Sebastian Bach* (1985), p. 96.
29. A. N. Wilson, *God's Funeral* (1999), p. 329.
30. Ibid.
31. György Kurtág, *Three Interviews and Ligeti Homages*, Bálint András Varga (ed.) (2009).
32. BD I, No. 123.
33. Leaver, *Bach's Theological Library*, pp. 22–5. See also his 'Luther's Theology of Music in Later Lutheranism' in *Luther's Liturgical Music* (2007).
34. Ibid., p. 14.
35. John Butt, *Bach's Dialogue with Modernity: Perspectives on the Passions* (2010), p. 53.
36. 'Entwurff ', BD I, No. 22/NBR, p. 149.
37. Rainer Kaiser, 'Johann Ambrosius Bachs letztes Eisenacher Lebensjahr', BJb (1995), pp. 177–82.

6 THE INCORRIGIBLE CANTOR

1. BD II, Nos 280–81/NBR, p. 145.
2. Martin Geck, *J. S. Bach: Life and Work* (2006), p. 175.
3. Arnold Schering, *Musikgeschichte Leipzigs* (1926), Vol. 2, p. 46.
4. Philipp Spitta, *The Life of Bach*, Clara Bell and J. A. Fuller Maitland (trs.) (1899 edn), Vol. 3, pp. 303–5.
5. Andreas Glöckner, BJb (2001), pp. 131–8.
6. BD I, No. 23/NBR, p. 151.
7. NBR, p. 77; Max Seiffert, 'Joh. Seb. Bach 1716 in Halle' in *Sammelbände der Internationalen Musikgesellschaft* (July–Sept. 1905); and C. H. Terry, *Bach: A Biography* (1928), pp. 109–10.
8. George B. Stauffer, 'Leipzig: A Cosmopolitan Trade Centre' in *The Late Baroque Era: From the 1680s to 1740*, George J. Buelow (ed.)(1993), p. 258.
9. NBR, p. 151.
10. BD I, No. 23/ NBR, p. 152.
11. BD II, No. 139.

12. Michael Maul, *'Dero berühmbter Chor': Die Leipziger Thomasschule und ihre Kantoren 1212–1804* (2012).
13. BD I, No. 91/NBR, p. 102.
14. Statutes of the Thomasschule (1634), *Schulordnung*, Para. VII/1, quoted by Michael Maul, *'Dero berühmbter Chor'*, p. 66, and their dilution from 1723 onwards, pp. 784–91.
15. Howard H. Cox, 'Bach's Conception of His Office', JRBI, Vol. 20, No. 1 (1989), pp. 22–30.
16. Howard H. Cox (ed.), *The Calov Bible of Bach* (1985), p. 418.
17. Hans-Joachim Schulze, 'Johann Sebastian Bach – Thomaskantor: Schwierigkeiten mit einem prominenten Amt', *Bach-Tage Berlin* (*Festbuch*) (1991), pp. 103–8.
18. Rainer Kaiser, 'Neues über Johann Sebastian Bachs Schulzeit in Eisenach von 1693 bis 1695', *Bachfest-Buch* (76, Bachfest der Neuen Bachgesellschaft Eisenach, 2001), pp. 89–9.
19. Joel Chandler Harris, *Tales from Uncle Remus* (1895), 'How Mr Rabbit was Too Sharp for Mr Fox', p. 11.
20. J. N. Forkel, *Ueber Johann Sebastian Bachs Leben, Kunst und Kunstwerke* (1802), p. 82.
21. *... eine völlig turbulente und ungeordnete Situation dieser sonst sehr angesehenen Bildungsstätte* in M. Petzoldt, '"Ut probus et doctus reddar"', BJb (1985), p. 24.
22. *Ob turbas, a Domino Cantore Arnoldo excitatas, scholae nostrae valedixerunt*, cited in J. Böttcher, *Die Geschichte Ohrdrufs* (1959), Vol. 3, p. 34.
23. *Ob intolerabilem disciplinam Domini Cantoris Arnoldi in hanc classem translati sunt*, cited in ibid., p. 34.
24. Terry, *Bach: A Biography*, pp. 26–7.
25. Lyceum Matrikel, quoted in F. Thomas, 'Einige Ergebnisse über Johann Sebastian Bachs Ohrdrufer Schulzeit' in *Jahresbericht des Gräflich Gleichenschen Gymnasiums 24 Ohrdruf für das Schuljahr 1899/1900* (1900), p. 9.
26. J. Böttcher, *Die Geschichte Ohrdrufs*, p. 34.
27. *... die Soldatesque darzuzihen und den seinigen schutz verschaffen*, letter of 3 Dec. 1660, in Horst Walter, *Musikgeschichte der Stadt Lüneburg* (1967), p. 79.
28. 'Die Untersuchung und Bestraffung des Schülers Herda', quoted in ibid., p. 81.
29. NBR, p. 43, excerpts from the proceedings of the Arnstadt Consistory for 5 Aug. 1705/BD II, No. 14.
30. BD II, No. 14/NBR, p. 45.
31. Ibid.
32. J. H. Zedler, *Universal-Lexicon* (1732–54), Sächsisches Duell-Mandat.
33. BD II, No. 16/NBR, p. 46.
34. Stephen Rose, *The Musician in Literature in the Age of Bach* (2011), p. 74.

35. BD III, No. 801/NBR, p. 397.
36. Rose, *The Musician in Literature in the Age of Bach*, p. 63.
37. Christoph Wolff, *Johann Sebastian Bach: The Learned Musician* (2000), p. 113.
38. BD I, i./NBR, p. 57.
39. Ibid.
40. Terry's translation, *Bach: A Biography*, p. 83; and NBR, p. 57.
41. NBR, p. 58.
42. Konrad Küster, *Der junge Bach* (1996), p. 186.
43. Georg Mentz, *Weimarische Staats- und Regentengeschichte* (1936), p. 22.
44. Peter Williams, *The Life of Bach* (2004), p. 55.
45. Johann Beer, *Die kurtzweiligen Sommer-Täge* (1683), pp. 418–19, 510.
46. BD II, No. 66.
47. Laurel E. Fay, *Shostakovich* (2000), p. 77.
48. Peter Williams, *J. S. Bach: A Life in Music* (2007), p. 108; and Richard D. P. Jones, *The Creative Development of J. S. Bach* (2007), p. 245.
49. Andreas Glöckner, 'Von seinen moralischen Character' in *Über Leben, Kunst und Kunstwerke: Aspekte musikalischer Biographie*, Christoph Wolff (ed.) (1999), pp. 121–32.
50. BD II, No. 84.
51. Staatsarchiv Weimar, akt.B, 26 436, fol. 126 r+v.
52. Wolff, *The Learned Musician*, pp. 210–110.
53. Ibid., pp. 101–2.
54. BD II, No. 124/NBR, p. 101.
55. BD II, No. 138/NBR, p. 106.
56. Williams, *The Life of Bach*, p. 106.
57. Ulrich Siegele, 'Bachs politisches Profil oder Wo bleibt die Musik?' in *Bach Handbuch*, Konrad Küster (ed.) (1999), pp. 5–30; and 'Bach and the Domestic Politics of Electoral Saxony' in *The Cambridge Companion to Bach*, John Butt (ed.) (1997), pp. 17–34.
58. BD II, No. 145/NBR, p. 104.
59. Otto Kaemmel, *Geschichte der Leipziger Schulwesens* (1909), p. 236.
60. F. W. Marpurg, *Historisch-Kritische Beyträge zur Aufnahme der Musik* (1754); BD I, No. 5.
61. Johannes Riemer, *Der politische Maul-Affe* (1680), quoted in Rose, *The Musician in Literature in the Age of Bach*, p. 91.
62. BD I, No. 23/NBR, p. 152
63. Hector Berlioz, *Selected Letters*, Hugh Macdonald (ed.) (1995).
64. Robin A. Leaver (ed.), *J. S. Bach and Scripture* (1985), pp. 121–2.
65. Carl Ludwig Hilgenfeldt, *Johann Sebastian Bachs Leben, Wirken und Werke* (1850), p. 172.
66. Geck, *J. S. Bach: Life and Work*, p. 175.

67. BD I, No. 34/NBR, p. 175.
68. John Butt, introduction to *Bach* (short biography) by Martin Geck (2003), p. viii.

7 BACH AT HIS WORKBENCH

1. John Butt, *Music Education and the Art of Performance in the German Baroque* (1994), pp. 66, 202; J. E. Sadler, *J. A. Comenius and the Concept of Universal Education* (1966), pp. 196–206.
2. The title page of a volume of keyboard pieces, *Aufrichtige Anleitung* of 1723 (BWV 772–801).
3. BD III, No. 803/NBR, p. 399.
4. Robert L. Marshall, *The Compositional Process of J. S. Bach* (1972), Vol. 2, Sketch No. 50.
5. Letter by C. P. E. Bach comparing Bach and Handel, 27 Feb. 1788, BD III, No. 927/NBR, p. 404.
6. Staatsbibliothek zu Berlin, Preußischer Kulturbesitz, Mus. ms. Bach, p. 13, and reproduced in Alfred Dürr, *The Cantatas of J. S. Bach* (2005), p. 127.
7. Laurence Dreyfus, *Bach and the Patterns of Invention* (1996), p. 22.
8. Ibid., pp. 78–83; also his 'Bach the Subversive', Lufthansa Lecture, 14 May 2011.
9. Christoph Wolff, *Bach: Essays on His Life and Music* (1991), p. 394.
10. Ibid., pp. 391–7; and BD III, No. 87.
11. NBR, pp. 396–400.
12. BD II, No. 499/NBR, pp. 333–4.
13. John H. Roberts, 'Why Did Handel Borrow?' in *Handel Tercentenary Collection*, S. Sadie and A. Hicks (eds.) (1987), pp. 83–92.
14. Bettina Varwig, 'One More Time: Bach and Seventeenth-Century Traditions of Rhetoric', *Eighteenth-Century Music*, Vol. 5, No. 2 (Sept. 2008), pp. 179–208.
15. BD III, No. 801/NBR, p. 396.
16. BD II, No. 441.
17. BD II, No. 409/NBR, p. 345.
18. This was the subject of a paper given by Michael Maul: '*Ob defectum hospitiorum*: Bachs Weggang aus Ohrdruf' in *Symposium: Die Musikerfamilie Bach in der Stadtkultur des 17. und 18. Jahrhunderts* (Belfast, July 2007).
19. BD I, No. 68.
20. BD II, No. 316.
21. BD I, No. 22.
22. BD II, Nos. 420, 336/NBR, pp. 349–50.
23. John Butt, *Playing with History* (2002), p. xii.
24. Albert Schweitzer, *J. S. Bach* (1911), Vol. 2, p. 199.

25. Yoshitake Kobayashi, 'Zur Chronologie der Spätwerke Johann Sebastian Bachs: Kompositions- und Aufführungstätigkeit von 1736 bis 1750', BJb (1988), p. 52.
26. Ludwig Finscher, 'Zum Parodieproblem bei Bach' in *Bach-Interpretationen*, Martin Geck (ed.) (1969), pp. 99ff.
27. *An Essay of Dramatic Poesy* (1668).
28. *Bach Cantata No. 140: Wachet auf, ruft uns die Stimme*, Gerhard Herz (ed.) (1972), pp. 102–5.
29. D. Yearsley, *Bach's Feet* (2012), p. 264.
30. BD II, No. 332; NBR, pp. 328–9; and in shortened form by Charles Burney for his article on J. S. Bach in *Rees's Cyclopaedia* of 1819. See also BD III, No. 943.
31. Johann Christian Kittel, *Der angehende praktische Organist* (1808), Vol. 3, p. 33; and NBR, p. 323.
32. BD III, No. 666/NBR, pp. 305–6.
33. BD II, No. 409/NBR, pp. 344–5.
34. Gesetze der Schule zu S. Thomae (1733), Chapter 6 ('Von der Musik'), Section 3, p. 23.
35. Stadtarchiv Leipzig, Stift. VIII. B. 10: ACTA (1775–1845), 'Die Abstellung derer allzu vielen Feyertage auf der Schule zu St Thomae alhier betr'.
36. BD III, No. 801/NBR, p. 396.
37. Dreyfus, *Bach and the Patterns of Invention*, p. 98.

8 CANTATAS OR COFFEE?

1. W. Goethe, letter to his sister, Dec. 1765.
2. Tanya Kevorkian, *Baroque Piety: Religion, Society, and Music in Leipzig 1650–1750* (2007), p. 24.
3. Julius Bernhard von Rohr, *Einleitung zur Ceremoniel-Wissenschafft der Privat-Personen* (1728), p. 246.
4. Bornemann, *Das wohlangelegt- und kurtz gefasste Haußhaltungs-Magazin* (1730).
5. Joyce Irwin, 'Bach in the Midst of Religious Transition' in *Bach's Changing World*, Carol K. Baron (ed.) (2006), pp. 110–11, 121.
6. Picander, *Ernst-Schertzhaffte und Satyrische Gedichte*, Heft 1 (1727).
7. Quoted by Tim Blanning in 'The Culture of Feeling and the Culture of Reason', *The Pursuit of Glory: Europe 1648–1815* (2007), p. 500.
8. Karl Czok, 'Zur Leipziger Kulturgeschichte des 18. Jahrhunderts' in *J. S. Bach und die Aufklärung*, Reinhard Szeskus (ed.) (1982), p. 26.
9. Martin Geck, *J. S. Bach: Life and Work* (2006), p. 139.
10. BD II, No. 129.
11. BD I, No. 148/NBR, p. 80.

12. Joachim Meyer, *Unvorgreiffliche Gedancken über die neulich eingerissene theatralische Kirchen-Music* (1726).
13. Friedrich Erhard Niedt, *Musicalische Handleitung, oder gründlicher Unterricht* (1700).
14. Reproduced in supplement to NBA (BA 5291) (2011), pp. 2–36.
15. Ibid. and BD II, No. 433; English version by John Butt, *The Cambridge Companion to Bach* (1997), p. 53.
16. Butt, *The Cambridge Companion to Bach*, p. 53.
17. Peter Williams, *The Life of Bach* (2004), p. 152; cf. NBR, p. 305.
18. Heinrich Zernecke, writing of his visit in Leipzig on 17 Sept. 1733.
19. BD II, No. 350/NBR, pp. 163–4.
20. Johann Kuhnau, *Der musicalische Quack-Salber* (1700), Chapter 1.
21. Michael Maul, *Barockoper in Leipzig 1693–1720* (2009), Vol. 1, pp. 475ff., 558–9.
22. Ibid., pp. 211–12.
23. *Das jetzt lebende und jetzt florirende Leipzig* (1736), pp. 58–9.
24. Hans Rudolf Jung, *Musik und Musiker im Reußenland* (reprinted 2007), pp. 122–3.
25. George B. Stauffer, 'Music for "*Cavaliers et Dames*"' in *About Bach*, Gregory G. Butler et al. (eds.) (2008), pp. 135–56.
26. Hans-Joachim Schulze, '"Ey! How sweet the coffee tastes"', JRBI, Vol. 32, No. 2 (2001), p. 3. For the alternative view see Burkhard Schwalbach's review of *The Worlds of J. S. Bach* in *Early Music*, Vol. 38, No. 4 (4 Nov. 2010), p. 600.
27. This is the *Nutzbares, galantes und curiöses Frauenzimmer-Lexicon* of 1715 (p. 285) by Gottlieb Siegmund Corvinus, a Leipzig lawyer and dandy, who, according to Katherine R. Goodman, is likely also to have attended the salon of Christiane Mariane von Ziegler (*Bach's Changing World*), pp. 204, 217.
28. Von Rohr, *Einleitung zur Ceremoniel-Wissenschafft der Privat-Personen*, p. 515.
29. This information, based on a council memorandum to the Elector (*Zucht-Armen- und Waisen-Haus*, 9–10v, 12 Nov. 1701) and *Codex Augusteus, oder Neuvermehrtes Corpus Juris Saxonici*, Johann Christian Lünig (ed.) (1724), Vol. 1, pp. 1,857–60, is reported by Tanya Kevorkian, *Baroque Piety*, p. 212. Criticism of a similar kind came from Johann Kuhnau, Bach's predecessor, in 1709; see Arnold Schering, *Musikgeschichte Leipzigs* (1926), Vol. 2, p. 196.
30. Daniel Duncan, *Von dem Missbrauch heißer und hitziger Speisen und Getränke* (1707).
31. Katherine R. Goodman, 'From Salon to *Kaffeekranz*' in *Bach's Changing World*, pp. 190–218.
32. Georg Witkowski, *Geschichte der literarischen Lebens in Leipzig* (1909), p. 355.
33. BD II, No. 410/NBR, pp. 334–5.
34. David Yearsley, *Bach's Feet* (2012), Chapter 6, pp. 271, 261.

35. E. L. Gerber, *Historisch-biographisches Lexicon der Tonkünstler* (1790), Vol. 1, col. 90.
36. Yearsley, *Bach's Feet*, pp. 265, 276–7.
37. Leipziger Kirchen-Staat, *Das ist, deutlicher Unterricht vom Gottesdienst in Leipzig* (1710).
38. Anton Weiz, *Verbessertes Leipzig; oder die vornehmsten Dinge . . .* (1728), pp. 2–3, quoted in Günther Stiller, *J. S. Bach and Liturgical Life in Leipzig*, Robin A. Leaver (ed.) (1984), p. 44.
39. Kevorkian, *Baroque Piety*, pp. 198–222.
40. Gottsched, No. 9, Feb. 1725, p. 68, quoted in ibid., p. 73.
41. Georg Motz, *Abgenötigte Fortsetzung der vertheidigten Kirchen-Music* (1708), p. 93, quoted by Joseph Herl, *Worship Wars in Early Lutheranism: Choir, Congregation, and Three Centuries of Conflict* (2004), p. 165.
42. St Augustine, *Confessions*, Book 10, quoted by Christian Gerber, *Die unerkanten Sünden der Welt* (1712), Vol. 1, Chapter 81, trs. Herl, *Worship Wars in Early Lutheranism: Choir, Congregation, and Three Centuries of Conflict*, pp. 123, 202.
43. Irwin, 'Bach in the Midst of Religious Transition', pp. 115, 237–8.
44. M. H. Fuhrmann, *Die an der Kirchen Gottes gebaute Satans-Capelle* (1729), pp. 41, 45, quoted in Bettina Varwig, 'Seventeenth-Century Music and the Culture of Rhetoric', *JRMA* (2007), p. 33.
45. Christian Gerber, *Historie der Kirchen-Ceremonien in Sachsen* (1732) pp. 352–3, paraphrased in Kevorkian, *Baroque Piety*, p. 34.
46. Kevorkian, *Baroque Piety*, p. 24.
47. Von Rohr, *Einleitung zur Ceremoniel-Wissenschafft der Privat-Personen*, pp. 258–9, 263.
48. F. G. Leonhardi, *Geschichte und Bescheibung der Kreis- und Handelsstadt Leipzig* (1799), pp. 424–5, quoted in Stiller, *J. S. Bach and Liturgical Life in Leipzig*, p. 63.
49. *Leipziger Kirchen-Andachten*, J. F. Leibniz (ed.) (1694), pp. 91–2, reproduced in ibid., p. 63.
50. BD I, No. 19/NBR, p. 138.
51. WA, Vol. 46, p. 495.
52. WA, Vol. 5, p. 46.
53. Bernd Wannenwetsch, 'Caritas Fide Formata', *Kerygma und Dogma*, Vol. 45 (2000), pp. 205–24.
54. Johann Mattheson, *Critica musica*, Band I (Apr. 1723), p. 347.
55. Winfried Hoffmann, 'Leipzigs Wirkungen auf den Delitzscher Kantor Christoph Gottlieb Fröber', *Beiträge zur Bachforschung* (1982), Vol. 1, pp. 72–3.
56. Johann Christian Edelmann, *Selbstbiographie* (1749–52), facsimile reprinted 1976, p. 41.

57. From a poem by Christian Friedrich Hunold (known as Menantes) on the subject of a *collegium musicum* performance in 1713 (Christian Friedrich Hunold, *Academische Nebenstunden allerhand neuer Gedichte* (1713), pp. 69–72).
58. Peter Gay, *The Naked Heart* (1995), p. 13.
59. Stauffer, 'Music for "*Cavaliers et Dames*"', p. 137.
60. Johann Andreas Cramer, *Der Jüngling*, Achtes Stück (eighth issue) (1747–8), pp. 108–23.
61. John Butt, 'Do Musical Works Contain an Implied Listener?', JRMA, Vol. 135, Special Issue 1 (2010), pp. 5–18.
62. Jacques Rochette de La Morlière, *Angola: Histoire indienne* (1746), Vol. 1, p. 69, quoted in Gay, *The Naked Heart*, p. 15.
63. Ibid., p. 22.
64. Friedrich Blume, 'Outlines of a New Picture of Bach', *Music and Letters*, Vol. 44, No. 3 (1963), pp. 216–18.
65. Ibid., pp. 226–7.
66. Much of this can be found in contributions to the 2008 BJb by Peter Wollny, Tatjana Schabalina and Marc-Roderich Pfau, and by Andreas Glöckner to the 2009 edition.
67. A. Glöckner, 'Na, die hätten Sie aber auch nur hören sollen', *Bach und Leipzig* (2001), p. 388.
68. Kuhnau, 'A Treatise on Liturgical Text Settings' (1710), in *Bach's Changing World*, pp. 219–26.
69. Johann Christoph Gottsched, *Critischer Dichtkunst* (1730) Vol. 2, Chapter 13.

9 CYCLES AND SEASONS

1. Richard Taruskin, *The Oxford History of Western Music* (2005), Vol. 2, pp. 364, 370.
2. Charles Rosen, *Critical Entertainments* (2000), p. 26.
3. Anton Webern, *Der Weg zur Neuen Musik*, 1933/1960.
4. John Butt, *Bach's Dialogue with Modernity* (2010), p. 103.
5. BD I, No. 34/NBR, p. 176.
6. BD II, No. 409/NBR, p. 344.
7. Eric Chafe, *Tonal Allegory in the Vocal Music of J. S. Bach* (1991), p. 248.
8. Isaiah Berlin, *The Proper Study of Mankind* (1998), pp. 346, 354–6, 405, 426–8.
9. Michael Maul, *Barockoper in Leipzig 1693–1720* (2009).
10. Laurence Dreyfus, 'Bach the Subversive', Lufthansa Lecture, 14 May 2011.
11. Heinrich Müller, *Der leidende Jesus / nach den vier Evangelisten erkläret und vorgetragen: die erste Passions-Predigt* (1681).
12. BD II, No. 129/NBR, p. 103.
13. BD II, No. 179/NBR, p. 116.

14. J. A. Westrup, *Bach Cantatas* (BBC Music Guides) (1966), p. 60.
15. LW, Vol. 14, p. 189.
16. Wilfrid Mellers, *Bach and the Dance of God* (1980), p. 232.
17. K. and I. Geiringer, *Johann Sebastian Bach: The Culmination of an Era* (1966), p. 201.
18. Joshua Rifkin, 'The Chronology of Bach's Saint Matthew Passion', MQ, Vol. 61, No. 3 (July 1975), pp. 360–87.
19. Eric Chafe, *J. S. Bach's Johannine Theology: The St John Passion and the Cantatas for Spring 1725* (forthcoming).
20. Kuhnau, quoted in Arnold Schering, *Johann Sebastian Bach und das Musikleben Leipzigs im 18. Jahrhundert* (1941), Vol. 2, p. 18.
21. T. S. Eliot, *Murder in the Cathedral* (1935), Part II.

10 FIRST PASSION

1. Elke Axmacher, *'Aus Liebe will mein Heyland sterben'* (1984), p. 164.
2. Johann Jakob Rambach, *Betrachtungen über das ganze Leiden Christi*, p. 5, the first two parts published in 1722, forming part of Bach's theological library.
3. Philipp Spitta, *The Life of Bach*, Clara Bell and J. A. Fuller Maitland (trs.) (1873; 1899 edn), Vol. 2, p. 528.
4. Quoted in Martin Geck, *Johannes-Passion* (1991), p. 102.
5. John Butt, *Bach's Dialogue with Modernity* (2010), p. 292.
6. Alfred Dürr, *Johann Sebastian Bach's St John Passion: Genesis, Transmission and Meaning* (2000), pp. 3–10.
7. Christian Gerber, *Historie der Kirchlichen Ceremonien in Sachsen* (1732); NBR, p. 324.
8. Telemann, *Briefwechsel* (1972), p. 20.
9. Albrecht Christian Ludwig, foreword to the text of the *Hunold-Keiser Passion* (1719), quoted in Axel Weidenfeld, liner notes to Stözel, *Brockes-Passion* (CPO 999 560–62).
10. G. E. Scheibel, *Zufällige Gedancken von der Kirchen-Music* (1721), p. 30.
11. Axmacher, *'Aus Liebe'*, p. 156.
12. Arnold Schering, *Musikgeschichte Leipzigs* (1926), Vol. 2, pp. 23–6.
13. Johann Mattheson, *Der vollikommene Capellmeister* (1739), quoted in Weidenfeld.
14. Ludwig, quoted in Weidenfeld.
15. Georg Bronner, *Geistliches Oratorium oder der gottliebenden Seelen Wallfahrt zum Kreuz und Grabe Christi* (1710).
16. R. H. Bainton, *Erasmus of Christendom* (1970), p. 285.
17. Raymond Brown, *The Gospel According to John: XIII–XX* (1966); and Eric Chafe, *Tonal Allegory in the Vocal Music of J. S. Bach* (1991), pp. 308–15.

18. Eric Chafe, *J. S. Bach's Johannine Theology: The St John Passion and the Cantatas for Spring 1725* (forthcoming).
19. Martin Dibelius, 'Individualismus und Gemeindebewusstsein in Jh. Seb.Bachs Passionen', *Archiv für Reformations-geschichte*, Vol. 41 (1948), pp. 132–54.
20. *Oeffentliche Reden über die Passions-Historie* (1716 and 1719).
21. Michael Marissen, *Lutheranism, Anti-Judaism, and Bach's St John Passion* (1998), pp. 28–9.
22. Axmacher, *'Aus Liebe'*, p. 160.
23. Laurence Dreyfus, *Bachian Poetics in the 'St John Passion'* (2009).
24. *The Calov Bible of J. S. Bach*, Howard H. Cox (ed.) (1985), pp. 249, 449.
25. Chafe, *J. S. Bach's Johannine Theology: The St John Passion and the Cantatas for Spring 1725*.
26. Johann David Heinichen, *Neu erfundene und Gründliche Anweisung zu vollkommener Erlernung des General-Basses* (1711).
27. Eric Chafe, *The Concept of Ambitus in the John Passion*. I am again grateful to Dr Chafe for kindly showing me chapters of his forthcoming book in draft from which these remarks are taken.
28. John Butt, 'St John Passion (Johannes-Passion)' in *J. S. Bach* (Oxford Composer Companions), Malcolm Boyd (ed.) (1999), p. 427.
29. Chafe, *J. S. Bach's Johannine Theology: The St John Passion and the Cantatas for Spring 1725*.
30. F. Smend, 'Die Johannes-Passion von Bach', BJb (1926), pp. 104–28; and *Bach in Köthen* (1985), pp. 132–4.
31. J. G. Ballard, *Crash* (1973).
32. BD II, No. 180/NBR, pp. 114–15.
33. Günther Stiller, *Johann Sebastian Bach and Liturgical Life in Leipzig*, Herbert J. A. Bouman et al. (trs.), Robin A. Leaver (ed.) (1970; trs. 1984), p. 60.
34. Chafe, *J. S. Bach's Johannine Theology: The St John Passion and the Cantatas for Spring 1725*.
35. Rudolf Bultmann, *Theologie des Neuen Testaments* (1959), p. 406.
36. Luther's preface to the New Testament in John Dillenberger, *Martin Luther: Selections from His Writings* (1961); and LW, Vol. 35, pp. 361–2.
37. Gustaf Aulén, *Christus Victor: An Historical Study of the Three Main Types of the Idea of the Atonement*, A. G. Hebert (trs.) (1931; trs. 1969), pp. 107–8. I am grateful to Eric Chafe for drawing my attention to this important study.
38. Jaroslav Pelikan, *Bach among the Theologians* (1986), pp. 102–15.
39. BD II, Nos. 338–9/NBR, p. 204.
40. BD V, No. 82a.
41. See BJb (1988), pp. 7–72, and Peter Wollny's preface to his editon of Version IV of the *Johannespassion* (2002).
42. Butt, *Bach's Dialogue with Modernity*, p. 35.

43. T. S. Eliot, 'Tradition and the Individual Talent' in *Selected Essays* (1932).
44. J. Gage, *Goethe on Art* (1980), pp. 207–9.

11 HIS 'GREAT PASSION'

1. *Ein starker Stoß mit Passionsmusiken* – second catalogue of C. P. E. Bach's estate (1805).
2. VEB Deutscher Verlag für Musik, Leipzig, 1974 (Lizenznummer 418-515/A 22/74 – LSV 8389).
3. 'Die Noten machen den Text lebendig' from WA TR, Vol. 2, p. 548.
4. From *Der blutige und sterbende Jesus* – an oratorio set to music by Reinhard Keiser in Hamburg, 1706.
5. Elke Axmacher, '*Aus Liebe will mein Heyland sterben*' (1984), p. 156.
6. Adam Bernd, *Eigene Lebens-Beschreibung* (1738), Winkler Verlag edition (1973), p. 302.
7. George Steiner, *The Death of Tragedy* (1961), p. 285.
8. Christoph Wolff, *Bach: The Learned Musician* (2000), pp. 299–303.
9. Albert Schweitzer, *J. S. Bach* (1911), Vol. 2, p. 211.
10. Johann Jacob Bendeler, *Die Historia von dem Leyden und Sterben unsers Herrn . . .* (1693).
11. 'Meditation on Christ's Passion', LW, Vol. 42, pp. 7–14; WA, Vol. 2, pp. 136–42.
12. Ulrich Leisinger, 'Forms and Functions of the Choral Movements in J. S. Bach's St Matthew Passion' in *Bach Studies Z* (1995), p. 76.
13. John Butt, *Bach's Dialogue with Modernity: Perspectives on the Passions* (2010), p. 203.
14. Naomi Cumming, 'The Subjectivities of "Erbarme Dich"', *Musical Analysis*, Vol. 16, No. 1 (Mar. 1997), p. 21.
15. John Butt, liner notes to his recording with the Dunedin Consort & Players of Bach's last performing version of the *Matthew Passion, c.* 1742 (CKD 313).
16. Martin Luther, *A Meditation on Christ's Passion* (1519), pp. 141–2.
17. Steiner, *The Death of Tragedy*, pp. 331–3.
18. Ibid., p. 285.

12 COLLISION AND COLLUSION

1. Mendelssohn, letter to Marc-André Souchay, 15 Oct. 1842, in *Briefe aus den Jahren 1830 bis 1847* (1878), p. 221, translation from Felix Mendelssohn Bartholdy, *Letters*, Gisella Selden-Goth (ed.) (1945), pp. 313–14.
2. BD III, No. 801/ NBR p. 396.
3. Laurence Dreyfus, 'The Triumph of "Instrumental Melody": Aspects of Musical Poetics in Bach's *St John Passion*', *Bach Perspectives*, Vol. 8 (2011), p. 119.
4. Laurence Dreyfus, 'Bach the Subversive', Lufthansa Lecture, 14 May 2011.

5. Raymond Tallis and Julian Spalding, *Art and Freedom: An Essay* (2011).
6. Dreyfus, 'The Triumph of "Instrumental Melody"', p. 109.
7. BD II, Nos. 400, 409/NBR, pp. 338, 344, 348, 346.
8. John Butt, *Bach's Dialogue with Modernity* (2010), pp. 15, 35.
9. Johann Mattheson, *Der vollkommene Capellmeister* (1739); Ernest C. Harriss (trs.) (1981), p. 207.
10. Walter Benjamin, *The Origin of German Tragic Drama* (1928), pp. 174–7.
11. Glenn Gould, 'So You Want to Write a Fugue?', *Glenn Gould Reader*, Tim Page (ed.) (1990), p. 240.
12. Alfred Dürr, *The Cantatas of J. S. Bach* (2005), p. 396.
13. Albert Schweitzer, *J. S. Bach* (1911; 1966 edn), Vol. 2, pp. 46–7.
14. Richard Taruskin, *The Oxford History of Western Music* (2005), Vol. 2, p. 370.
15. Roger Scruton, *The Aesthetics of Music* (1997), p. 452.
16. Gottfried Ephraim Scheibel, *Random Thoughts about Church Music in Our Day* (1721) in *Bach's Changing World*, Carol K. Baron (ed.) (2006), p. 246.
17. Julius Bernhard von Rohr, *Einleitung zur Ceremoniel-Wissenschafft der Privat-Personen* (1728), pp. 660, 666.
18. BD I, No. 23/NBR, p. 152.
19. Arnold Toynbee, *Man's Concern with Death* (1968).
20. Simon Schama, *Rembrandt's Eyes* (1999), p. 676.
21. J. G. Ballard, *Crash* (1973).
22. W. Gillies Whittaker, *The Cantatas of Johann Sebastian Bach* (1959), Vol. 1, p. 124.
23. Montaigne, *Essais: Livre Premier* (1580).
24. *The Confessions of Jacob Boehme*, Evelyn Underhill (intro.) [n.d.], p. 164.
25. *The Letters of Mozart and His Family*, Emily Anderson (trs. and ed.) (1988), Letter 546, p. 907.
26. Michael Maul, *'Dero berühmbter Chor': Die Leipziger Thomasschule und ihre Kantoren 1212–1804* (2012), pp. 88–98.
27. T. S. Eliot, *Little Gidding*, II.
28. Johann Mattheson, *Der vollkommene Capellmeister*, p. 216.
29. Friedrich Rochlitz, *Allgemeine Musikalische Zeitung* (1799), Vol. 1, col. 117; BD III, No. 1,009/NBR, p. 488.
30. E. Louis Backman, *Religious Dances in the Christian Church* (1952), pp. 21–2.
31. David Tripp, 'The Image of the Body in the Formative Phases of the Protestant Reformation' in *Religion and the Body*, Sarah Coakley (ed.) (1997), pp. 131–51.
32. Barbara Ehrenreich, *Dancing in the Streets* (2007), pp. 2–3.
33. Paul Halmos, 'The Decline of the Choral Dance' in *Man Alone: Alienation in Modern Society*, Eric and Mary Josephson (eds.) (1952), pp.172–9; and Wilfrid Mellers, *Bach and the Dance of God* (1980), p. 209.
34. *Briefwechsel zwischen Goethe und Zelter. Vol. 2: 1819–1827*, Ludwig Geiger (ed.), p. 517, quoted in Schweitzer, *J. S. Bach*, Vol. 1, p. 241.

35. David Yearsley, *Bach and the Meanings of Counterpoint* (2002), p. 28.
36. William Leatherbarrow, *Fedor Dostoevsky* (1981), p. 169.
37. Richard Eyre, *Utopia and Other Places* (1993).

13 THE HABIT OF PERFECTION

1. J. G. Walther, *Briefe*, Klaus Beckmann and H. J. Schulze (eds.) (1987), p. 120.
2. BD II, No. 281/NBR, p. 145.
3. Arnold Schering, 'Die höhe Messe in h-moll', BJb (1936), pp. 1–30.
4. BD II, No. 294/NBR, p. 311.
5. Nigel Spivey, *Enduring Creation: Art, Pain and Fortitude* (2001), p. 155.
6. Charles Burney, *A General History of Music* (1776).
7. Donald Francis Tovey, *Essays in Musical Analysis* (1937), Vol. 5, p. 34.
8. Wilfrid Mellers, *Bach and the Dance of God* (1980), p. 211.
9. Letter of 6 Oct. 1748 to Johann Elias Bach, BD I, p. 118/ NBR, p. 234.
10. Gregory G. Butler, 'Johann Sebastian Bachs Gloria in excelsis Deo BWV 191: Musik für ein Leipziger Dankfest', BJb (1992), pp. 65–71.
11. BD I, No. 27.
12. George B. Stauffer, *Bach: The Mass in B minor* (1997), p. 144.
13. Klaus Häfner, 'Über die Herkunft von zwei Sätzen der h-moll-Messe', BJb (1977), pp. 55–74.
14. Christoph Wolff, *Bach: Essays on His Life and Music* (1991), p. 367.
15. Mellers, *Bach and the Dance of God*, p. 220.
16. Tovey, *Essays in Musical Analysis*, p. 42.
17. C. F. D. Schubart, *Ideen zu einer Ästhetik der Tonkunst* (1784), p. 284.
18. Keats, 'Fancy'.
19. *Allgemeine deutsche Bibliothek* (1775), Vol. 25, Part 1, p. 108.
20. Johann Philipp Kirnberger, *Die Kunst des reinen Satzes in der Musik* (1777), Vol. 2, Part 2, p. 172, translated as *The Art of Strict Musical Composition*, D. Beach and J. Thym (trs.) (1982).
21. Quoted by George Steiner, *Errata: An Examined Life* (1997), p. 63.
22. Robin A. Leaver, 'How "Catholic" is Bach's "Lutheran" Mass?' in University of Belfast International Symposium, *Discussion Book* (2007), Vol. 1, pp. 177–206. See also John Butt, 'Bach's Mass in B Minor: Considerations of Its Early Performance and Use'. JAMS, Vol. 9, No. 1 (Winter 1991), pp. 109–2.
23. Johann Benedict Carpzov IV, *Isagoge in libros ecclesiarum Lutheranum symbolicos* (1725), pp. 46, 77–8, 569, quoted in ibid., p. 204.
24. W. Osthoff and R. Wiesend (eds.), *Bach und die italienische Musik* (1987), pp. 109–40.
25. J. N. Forkel, *Ueber Johann Sebastian Bachs Leben, Kunst und Kunstwerke* (1802); NBR, p. 461.

14 'OLD BACH'

1. Claude Lévi-Strauss, *The Raw and the Cooked*, John and Doreen Weightman (trs.) (1969).
2. Michael Maul, *'Dero berühmbter Chor': Die Leipziger Thomasschule und ihre Kantoren 1212–1804* (2012).
3. Alex Ross, 'The Book of Bach', *New Yorker*, 11 Apr. 2011.
4. BD II, No. 400/NBR, p. 338.
5. Gottfried Ephraim Scheibel, *Random Thoughts about Church Music in Our Day* (1721), translated in *Bach's Changing World*, Carol K. Baron (ed.) (2006), p. 238.
6. Preface to the *Gradualia* in O. Strunk, *Source Readings in Music History* (1952), p. 328.
7. BD II, Nos. 920, 336/NBR, p. 350.
8. T. W. Adorno, *Bach Defended against His Devotees* (1951) in *Prisms*, S. and S. Weber (trs.) (1981), p. 141.
9. J. N. Forkel, *Ueber Johann Sebastian Bachs Leben, Kunst und Kunstwerke* (1802), Chapter 11, p. 125; NBR, p. 478.
10. Ibid., Chapter 2, pp. 27–8; NBR, p. 429.
11. BD I, Nos. 42, 43/NBR, pp. 203–4.
12. BD III, No. 803/NBR, p. 400.
13. BD III, No. 779/NBR, p. 366.
14. BD II, No. 448/NBR, p. 204.
15. BD II, No. 455, and BD I, No. 138.
16. BD II, No. 423/NBR, p. 199.
17. Evelin Odrich and Peter Wollny, *Die Briefentwürfe des Johann Elias Bach* (2000), No. 58, p. 148.
18. BD II, No. 477/NBR, p. 209.
19. BD II, No. 490/NBR, p. 213.
20. In conversation with the author, 12 Apr. 2005.
21. Earl of Shaftesbury, letter to James Harris, 13 Feb. 1750, quoted in Donald Burrows, *Handel* (2012), p. 441.
22. NBR, p. 412.
23. NBR, p. 240.
24. Philipp Spitta, *The Life of Bach*, Clara Bell and J. A. Fuller Maitland (trs.) (1873; 1899 edn), Vol. 3, p. 257.
25. BD II, No. 592/NBR, p. 242.
26. BD II, No. 592/NBR, p. 243.
27. *The Calov Bible of J. S. Bach*, Howard H. Cox (ed.) (1985), p. 436.
28. I am grateful to Michael Maul for imparting this information to me by letter ahead of his article in the forthcoming BJb (2013).
29. Norbert Wolf, *Dürer* (2010), p. 127.

30. Carl Sagan et al., *Murmurs of Earth: The 'Voyager' Interstellar Record* (1978).
31. Edward W. Said, *Music at the Limits* (2008), p. 288.
32. BD III, No. 666/NBR, p. 303.
33. BD III, No. 666/NBR, p. 304.
34. Gregory G. Butler, *About Bach* (2008), pp. 116–20.
35. Luther, 'A Sermon on Preparing to Die' in LW, Vol. 42, pp. 95– 115, at p. 101.
36. David Yearsley, *Bach and the Meanings of Counterpoint* (2002), p. 28.
37. *The Calov Bible of J. S. Bach*, p. 448.
38. Johann Philipp Förtsch, *Musicalischer Compositions Tractat*, Staatsbibliothek zu Berlin, Mus.ms.theor.300.
39. Andreas Werckmeister, *Harmonologia musica* (1707), p. 89.
40. Yearsley, *Bach and the Meanings of Counterpoint*, pp. 1–41.
41. Ibid., p. 36.
42. Nicholas Kenyon, *Faber Guide to Bach* (2010), p. 52.

Index

Musical compositions named in the index are generally filed under their composer. Those by J. S. Bach are arranged by genre and name under the heading 'Bach, Johann Sebastian, works', with the exception of the cantatas, the surviving Passions, and the *B Minor Mass*, which all receive major treatment in the book and have their own main headings in the index: 'cantatas of J. S. Bach', '*John Passion*', '*Matthew Passion*' and '*Mass in B minor* by J. S. Bach'. Page references in *italic* indicate illustrations within the text. These are also listed, together with the inset Plates, after the Contents.